The Awakening Giant

Continuity and Change in
Imperial Chemical Industries

The Awakening Giant

Continuity and Change in
Imperial Chemical Industries

ANDREW M. PETTIGREW

Basil Blackwell

The research reported in this book was partly supported by a personal research grant awarded by the Economic and Social Research Council.

First published 1985

Basil Blackwell Ltd
108 Cowley Road, Oxford OX4 1JF, UK

British Library Cataloguing in Publication Data

Pettigrew, Andrew M.
   The awakening giant : continuity and change in ICI.
   1. Imperial Chemical Industries—History
   I. Title
   338.7'66   HD9652.9.15

   ISBN 0–631–13356–9
   ISBN 0–631–13455–7 Pbk

Typeset by Katerprint Co. Ltd., Oxford
Printed in Great Britain by T.J. Press Ltd, Padstow

For Ethna

Contents

Figures

Tables

Acknowledgements

This book is the result of research carried out over the 8-year period from 1975 to 1983. I am extremely grateful to all the people in Imperial Chemical Industries (ICI) who have helped me over that period gather, sort, analyse, and write up this material.

ICI is a very complex set of businesses linked together in the UK in divisional organisations with quite different organisational histories and cultures. However, even with all this cultural diversity ICI has had elements of a common company culture which at various times could be described by adjectives such as technological, stable, conservative, caring, intellectual, and in certain of its spheres of operation – open to the outside world. For all its inevitable hierarchical tendencies ICI can also be described as being made up of a series of loosely linked networks of people who have coalesced around their interests in operating at a certain level in each division, for example, division chairman or works manager, and across the company in functions such as engineering and personnel.

The process of how I gained the quality of access to ICI which was necessary to build up the picture in this book is itself a complex and fascinating story, but without doubt the open and intellectual side of ICI's character helped in gaining access and so did the understanding of its networks of formal and informal association. The mixed role that I have played in the company as a researcher, consultant, and trainer may also have helped me to gain access to people and appreciate situations and dilemmas in a wider fashion than if I had defined my role just as a researcher, or a consultant, or a trainer. Effective, or merely adequate research on any sphere of life has surely to be a mutual process where the need to balance involvement and distance, is a critical part of the process, (Pettigrew, 1983b).

Paul Miles[1], then of Agricultural Division, first suggested that I might consider carrying out a study of the use of organisation development expertise in his division. Prompted by the suggestion that a comparative study across several divisions might be more instructive, Miles, Simon Dow, and Tom James set up the necessary access to Agricultural, Plastics, and Petrochemicals Divisions, and Stewart Dudley opened the gate into Millbank and the organis-

---

[1] Throughout this volume all personal names mentioned are pseudonyms. The only exceptions to this are the ICI company chairmen, who are national figures in the UK context and therefore impossible to disguise.

ation development work which had been going on from the base of the then Central Personnel Department. ICI supplied a research grant for 2 years to carry out this initial work, and Dr Dennis Bumstead joined me at the London Business School in September 1975 as a full-time researcher.

However, the research reported here is more than just an analysis of the differential impact in various organisation contexts of organisation development (OD) activities on organisational change, it also seeks to ask some much broader questions about the patterns of continuity and change in ICI over the period 1960–83; and the role of very senior line managers in creating change. The changes in the character and objectives of this research which occurred after 1977 are a recognition of the useful though always limited role that internal and external specialist OD resources have played in formulating and implementing organisational change in ICI. By the late 1970s there was an open statement of company policy in ICI that line managers were to be the vanguard of the significant changes which occurred from 1979 onwards. I am extremely grateful to the main board directors, division chairmen and directors, senior managers, internal and external consultants, and senior shop stewards who allowed me to interview them and provided documentary evidence of some of the strategic change processes going on in the company over the period 1960–83. Particular thanks are due to Stewart Dudley and Tom James for their consistent help and practical advice throughout the period 1975–83, and to John Harvey-Jones for helping to create the space and climate where this research work could be done.

I gained access to Mond Division relatively late in the day of this study, and just as well because the Mond story of change is a critical one within recent ICI experience. Nicholas Mann, Mark Warwick, Dylan Jones, and Sandy Marshall were a great help in enabling me to appreciate the complexities and significance of the Mond work.

Present members of the Petrochemicals and Plastics Division board, and indeed a number of senior managers and senior shop stewards at Wilton may rightly ask "what's happened to the story of the merging of Petrochemicals and Plastics Divisions and to the analysis of the major changes on the huge manufacturing site at Wilton since 1979?" My answer to that question is that those processes of managing change are too important and interesting to have squeezed them into what is already a long book, and the analysis of the implementation of the Petrochemicals and Plastics Division merger and the Wilton changes since 1979 will appear in subsequent publications. Nevertheless I would like to acknowledge here the support for this research given so far by a number of people in Petrochemicals and Plastics Division.

Although I have carried out the research largely without continuing financial research support and research assistance, a number of individuals and organisations have helped me throughout the period 1975–83. ICI's initial financial support allowed me to recruit Dr Dennis Bumstead to work on the research, and between late 1975 and late 1977 he successfully carried out a lot of the interviewing and analysis for the studies of the impact of OD in Agricultural and Petrochemicals Divisions, and in Central Personnel Department in

Millbank. Some indication of Dennis's skills and effectiveness in this project are evident from the fact that with the end of his research contract he went on to work as an external consultant in organisation development and change for parts of ICI.

Dr Cynthia Hardy, now of McGill University, helped with bibliographic searches for the literature on organisational change and development, and Anne Murray and Dr Lauck Parke were of great assistance in generating and sorting material on the UK and world chemical industries. I am also very grateful to Mike Hyde, the editor of *Chemical Insight*, and Stuart Wamsley of W. Greenwell & Co. for making available their extensive knowledge of the UK, European, and world chemical industries.

The award by the Social Science Research Council of a personal research grant for the calendar year 1981 was of enormous value in releasing me from my responsibilities at the University of Warwick to allow me to collect more data in ICI during the period of great changes in 1981, and to begin the long process of thinking, sorting, and writing the research. The period during 1981 that I spent at the Harvard Business School was of great value in allowing me to share and test my ideas with Professors Chris Argyris, Michael Beer, Paul Lawrence, and Robert Miles, and I hope they will accept my thanks here without taking on any of the responsibilities for the ideas in this book.

Anyone who has spent time at the School of Industrial and Business Studies, University of Warwick will know that the heart of the place is Jeanette Whitmore. Jeanette has spent early mornings, evenings, and weekends – probably many more than she would have liked – typing and retyping drafts of this book. Her conscientiousness and cheerfulness have made the preparation of this book that much easier, and I cannot thank her enough.

My wife Ethna again was merely indispensable. Her unfailing willingness to create space for me to write in amongst all the other pressures of family life, plus her ironic jibes that I would never complete this book, was all I needed in the way of competitive spur to finish it. This book is as much hers as mine, and I dedicate it to her for this and all the other things we've shared together.

Preface

The unfolding of economic events during the 1970s and early 1980s has drawn further attention to the relative decline of the British economy and the continuing loss of competitiveness of large sectors of British industry. In the search for explanations of Britain's declining competitiveness a multiplicity of factors have surfaced. Pollard (1982) has emphasised the short-term focus of British economic policy-making and our failure as a nation to invest in the modernisation of capital equipment. Researchers at the Science Policy Research Unit at Sussex University also dwell on the relationship between technical innovation and British economic performance, pointing to shortcomings in the way certain sectors of British industry develop and improve products and production processes (Pavitt, 1980). Meanwhile economists such as Caves (1980) and Blume (1980) identify the poorer productivity of certain UK industries compared with their US equivalents, and how the UK's financial structures and institutions inhibit our ability to direct savings into appropriate investment channels. The problem of explaining Britain's economic decline has also attracted scholars interested in taking a very long-term view. Wiener (1981) digs into the culture and class system in British society, arguing that there has been a systematic misdirection of talent in Britain into public sector administration, the City, and the universities and away from industry and engineering. Lazonick (1983), on the other hand, argues that the decline in Britain's economy during the twentieth century is due to structural rigidities in its economic institutions that developed in the nineteenth century era of relatively free competition.

But is Britain's declining competitiveness just to be explained by a mixture which includes national economic policies, macro-economic variables, the deep-rooted social and cultural biases of UK society, the peculiarities of our financial institutions and our tax system, and the patterns of trade union activity and industrial relations? I think not. Given the substantial changes in the economic, political, and business environment of large firms over the past two decades, a critical factor affecting the relative competitive position of British firms must be the capacity of firms to adjust and adapt to major changes in their environments and thereby improve their competitive performance. The importance of these adjustment and adaptation processes suggests that the nature of management itself is a crucial input into the competitiveness issue. Part of the management task is to identify and assess changing economic, business, and political conditions, and formulate and implement new strategies to improve the firm's competitive performance. These managerial processes of strategic assessment, choice, and change are not just questions of economic calculation of strategic opportunity carried out by men and women driven by rational imperatives. The process of assessing environmental change and its implications for new strategies, structures, technologies, and cultures in the firm is an immensely human process in which differential perception, quests for efficiency and power, visionary leadership skills, the vicariousness of chance, and subtle processes of additively building up a momentum of support for change and then vigorously implementing change, all play their part.

This volume explores one of the key theoretical and practical problems of the 1980s, how to create strategic and operational changes in large, complex organisations. The theme of managerial processes of creating change is interwoven through a detailed empirical study of one of Britain's largest corporations and its response to the changing environment of the past 20 years. It should be clear this study does not deal with the activities of all ICI's UK divisions, neither is this an officially commissioned history of ICI, although an important feature of the research has been the high level and high quality of research access provided by ICI. The research examines ICI's attempts to change their strategy, structure, technology, organisational culture, and the quality of union management relationships over the period 1960–83. An important and unusual feature of the research strategy has been the collection of comparative and longitudinal data. Interview, documentary, and observational data are available from ICI's four largest divisions – Agricultural, Mond, Petrochemicals, and Plastics – and from the corporate headquarters. These data have been assembled on a continuous real-time basis since 1975, through retrospective analysis of the period 1960–74, and in the case of the divisional chapters by probing into the traditions and culture of each division established long before the last two decades.

The study explores two linked continuous processes. Initially the focus of the research was to examine the birth, evolution, demise, and development of the groups of internal and external organisation development consultants, employed by ICI in order to help initiate and implement organisational change. This analysis of the contributions and limitations of specialist-led attempt to create change, has led to the examination of broader processes of continuity and change in ICI as seen through the eyes and actions of the main board, divisional boards, and senior managers of ICI. The book therefore contributes to knowledge about the part played by very senior executives in corporate-wide strategic changes, the role of divisional boards and directors in making division-wide changes in structure, organisational culture and manpower, and the influence of specialist change resources of the internal and external variety in making changes happen. Throughout the book the emphasis is on describing and analysing *processes* of change in context, illustrating why and how the content of particular changes and the strategies for introducing them are constrained by and enabled by features of the traditions, culture, structure, and business of ICI as a whole and each of its divisions, and by gross changes in the business, economic, and political environment ICI has faced through time.

The findings of this research on ICI reinforce those writers who have discussed the inertial properties of organisations and the enormous difficulties of breaking down the established ways of looking at and behaving towards the world which develop in large organisations. Once a large organisation develops a coherent strategy of how it is going to deal with its external environment, and that strategy is reinforced by the structures, systems, cultures, and political constraints of the organisation, the dominating ideas and assumptions which are implicit and explicit in the strategy it behaves are extraordinarily difficult to break down. Thus when strategic change does occur it tends to occur in radical packages – revolutionary periods interspersed with long periods of absorbing the impact of the radical changes, of further periods of incremental adjustment, and then a period of education, persuasion and conditioning leading up to the next revolutionary break. In the ICI cases reported in this book the periodic eras of high levels of change activity were precipitated by, but not solely explained by, economic and business-related crises. Behind these periodic strategic reorientations in ICI are not just economic and business events, but also processes of managerial perception, choice, and action. The book provides ample illustrations of the role of executive leadership in intervening in the existing concepts of corporate strategy, and using and changing the structures, cultures, and political processes in the firm to draw attention to the need for change, and lead the organisation to sense and create a different pattern of alignment between its internal character, strategy, and structure and the emerging view of its operating environment.

The book has twelve chapters. Chapter 1 presents a detailed and pointed review of the strengths and weaknesses of existing research on organisational change, organisation development, and strategic change, and thus places the book alongside the three bodies of academic literature connectable to the empirical themes of this research on ICI. Chapter 2 builds on one of the central conclusions of the first chapter, the fact that so much of the previous research on change in organisations has been ahistorical, acontextual, and aprocessual, and describes the particular brand of contextualist and processual research favoured in this study. Chapter 2 also describes the political and cultural view of organisational process behind this research, and the methodology and study questions in this piece of work.

Chapter 3, 'ICI in its Changing Business and Economic Context' is a descriptive account of the major trends in the world and UK chemical industry over the past two decades, ICI's broad corporate response to that changing environment, and ICI's business performance over the past 20-plus years compared with its major US and West German competitors.

Chapter 4 begins the process of describing and analysing the use, impact, and fate of organisation development (OD) consultants in ICI. It describes the birth of the central OD resources in the company, and the role those resources played in seeking to justify and implement productivity changes in ICI from the mid-1960s until about 1972. From a company point of view this chapter illustrates the difficulties created when changes fashioned at the company headquarters are thrust upon disinterested and at times recalcitrant divisions.

Chapters 5 and 6 describe and analyse the origins and development of ICI's agricultural chemical interests at Billingham in the north-east of England. The latter part of Chapter 5 describes in some detail the attempt made by George Bridge the personnel director of Billingham Division (as it was known as then) to open up the management culture at Billingham to change, and in so doing to create a new pattern of relationships between management and worker on the Billingham site. Bridge's era of social innovation at Billingham was built on by the OD resources that were created there from 1969 onwards. Their organic bottom-up strategy for creating change in the climate of industrial relations on the site and for improving the processes of commissioning new plant was in stark contrast to Bridge's bow wave of change. Chapter 6 chronicles the organic change strategy of the Agricultural Division OD group and their line manager clients, and takes the story of the use of OD assistance on the Billingham site right up to the quite different business, economic, and political conditions of 1984.

Chapter 7 describes the substantially different business history and management and shop floor culture that developed in Petrochemicals Division, just 10 miles away from the Billingham manufacturing site. Chapter 7 reveals a different context for organisational change and development, and an evolutionary pattern of using OD resources in Petrochemicals Division which was totally different from the Agricultural Division experience. Chapter 7 also illustrates the strengths and limitations of an enforced strategy of change propagated by the Petrochemicals Division Chairman of the early 1970s.

Chapter 8 chronicles the enormously difficult task of using specialist OD change resources in the top management structure and culture that developed in Plastics Division during the 1960s and 1970s. Chapters 9 and 10 offer an important contrast to the absence of change in Plastics Division. The Mond Division chapter chronicles how and why a succession of powerful people on the Mond board, with the assistance of internal and external OD resources, were able to change the process of working on the board, the way the senior managers in the division assessed and dealt with environmental change and industrial relations problems, and eventually build up a coherent view of how the structure, strategy, and manpower of the division should change and did change to meet the harsher business conditions of the post-1979 period.

Chapter 10, 'Strategic Change and Organisation Development at the Centre of Power: 1973–83' is a rare look at the processes of top decision-making and change in a major British firm. The chapter describes the long, additive, conditioning process which was necessary to produce the major ideological, structural, and strategic changes which eventually materialised in ICI from about 1979 onwards.

Chapters 11 and 12 try and draw together some of the threads from this account of continuity and change in ICI. Chapter 11 compares and contrasts the five cases of strategic change reported in the book, and relates the patterns evident in those processes of change to the literature in organisation theory, business strategy, and business history which has discussed the what, why, and how of the evolution of the firm. This chapter also discusses the practical messages about the management of strategic change to be derived from the ICI experience.

Finally Chapter 12 compares and contrasts the natural history of development and impact of the various groups of internal and external OD consultants who worked in the corporate headquarters and Agricultural, Mond, Petrochemicals, and Plastics Divisions. This chapter also reviews the practical management lessons to be derived from ICI's use of internal and external OD consultants.

1 Research on Organisational Change and Development and Strategic Change: Some Limitations

Change is ubiquitous. Or is it? In the micro-events which surround our particular lives and in the daily trumpetings of the media change has an ever-present illusion of reality. Yet observe other men consciously attempting to move large and small systems in different directions, or attempt it yourself, and one sees what a difficult and complicated human process change is. And there is the problem of perspective. Where we sit not only influences where we stand, but also what we see. No observer of life or form begins with his mind a blank, to be gradually filled by evidence. Time itself sets a frame of reference for what changes are seen and how those changes are explained. The more we look at present-day events the easier it is to identify change; the longer we stay with an emergent process and the further back we go to disentangle its origins, the more we can identify continuities. Empirically and theoretically, change and continuity need one another, although as we shall see, many social scientists in their attempts to identify and explain change in organisations in terms of the micro-events of the day have artificially abstracted change out from the structures and contexts which give that change form, meaning, and dynamic. Change and continuity, process and structure, are inextricably linked.

A further conundrum is the choice of metaphors and images which exist in the study of change, each one pregnant with its own world view, model of man, and explanatory language. How are we to choose between growth and development, continuity and flow, life cycle and phase, contradiction, intrusion, and crisis? Are we to go along with the social analysts who would have us believe that cultures grow and perish in the same superb, natural, and aimless fashion as the flowers of the field? Or are we to accept the assumption that human history and social change are about chaps – and nothing else? Gellner's (1973) view is that history is about chaps, but he is quick to point out that it does not follow that its explanations are always in terms of chaps. Societies are what people do, but social scientists are not biographers *en grande série*.

Beware of the myth of the singular theory of social or organisational change. Look for continuity and change, patterns and idiosyncrasies, the actions of individuals and groups, the role of contexts and structures, and processes of structuring. Give history and social processes the chance to reveal their untidiness. Arguments over the true or basic sources of change, while interesting and worthwhile in the sharpening of academic minds and egos, are ultimately pointless. For the analyst interested in the theory and practice of changing the task is to identify the variety and mixture of causes of change and to explore some of the conditions and contexts under which these mixtures occur. That at least is the first stepping stone I offer the reader for joining me on this particular enterprise.

This research on continuity and change in ICI has provided an opportunity to study in a comparative and longitudinal mode the activities and strategies of very senior and middle managers trying to create significant change, and the role of internal and external organisation development (OD) specialists in facilitating change. The study began in 1975 after ICI had been using specialist OD resources at a variety of different levels and divisions in the company, and were pondering particular questions about why and how these specialists seemed to be more effective in some parts of the company than others. From this initial pragmatic question the research began to explore and establish the first theme in this book – the contributions and limitations of specialist-based attempts to create changes in organisational structure and culture. The first process under examination in the research has been the birth, evolution, development, and impact of groups of internal and external OD consultants in four divisions, and the corporate headquarters of ICI. However, as a result of the access and analyses provided by the initial study objectives the opportunity arose to explore a second and more inclusive process, the long-term processes of strategic decision-making and change in ICI in the differing social, economic, and political context of 1960–83. The use of the word strategic linked to change is just a description of magnitude of alteration in, for example product market focus, structure, and organisational culture, recognising the second-order effects, or multiple consequences, of any such changes. This second, broader analysis of continuity and change is seen through the eyes and activities of the main board of ICI, and the boards and senior managers of ICI's four largest divisions – Agricultural, Mond, Petrochemicals, and Plastics.

Given that the completed study incorporates an analysis of senior executive and specialist contributions to the process of formulating and implementing changes of such scope and impact that they can justifiably be described as strategic; and examines the role of line managers and specialists grappling with the introduction of more localised and circumscribed changes; and that OD techniques and ideas were applied to both the strategic and the more limited changes, then it is evident the data in this study are potentially connectable to a number of the various elements of the literature on the management of change. Unfortunately the writing and research on the management of change is a sprawling and none too coherent collection of bodies of literature, some proclaiming pragmatic precepts and transparent values, others coolly analysing and theorising without any commitment to statements of practice, and others being concerned with the lofty analytical formulation of strategic change and disdaining the examination of how such strategies are to be implemented in the political and cultural mosaic of large and medium-sized organisations. Of course, a further and predictable difficulty with a topic like organisational change, is that the study of change has attracted scholars from a number of academic disciplines who identify themselves as being more or less interested in description or prescription; a consequence of this is that these different bodies of literature do not, explicitly at least, talk to one another.

In what follows no attempt is made to find a herculean and grand coherence in the literature on the management of change where none exists. Rather the more limited objective for a review is offered of description, explication, and where appropriate criticism. The aim is to lay out some parts of the writing and research on organisational change and development in the hope that some of the strengths and weaknesses of that literature are clarified, and in the expectation that the identification of such patterns will serendipitously encourage the disparate elements in the literature to talk to one another. This chapter thus begins by briefly defining and reviewing the history of organisation development. Attention is then focused on identifying the strengths and limitations of the theory, research, and practice in the related fields of organisational change and development, and finally a short commentary is provided on the literature on strategic change in organisations. From this review will emerge some points of synthesis which will identify not only the particular and limited forms of theorising about organisational change, but also a recognition of the essentially ahistorical, acontextual, and aprocessual character of much research on organisational change and development. From these themes will appear a statement outlining the theoretical and methodological rationale for this research on the processes of continuity and change in ICI.

ORGANISATIONAL CHANGE AND DEVELOPMENT

The immediate theoretical and empirical context in which the present research places itself is the research and writing in the related fields of organisational change and development. Organisation development (OD) has almost as many definitions as it has practitioners. Thus, Bennis (1969:2) talks of OD as "a response to change, a complex educational strategy intended to change the beliefs, attitudes, values and structure of organisations", while French and Bell (1973:15) emphasise the long-range problem-solving and renewal process objectives that OD denotes to them. Alderfer (1977) meanwhile sees OD both as a professional field of social action and an area of academic study, and emphasises its dual value objective in improving the quality of life for members of human systems and increasing the institutional effectiveness of those systems. Beckhard's (1969:9) definition perhaps best captures the idealized scope that people in the 1960s had for OD.

> Organisation development is an effort (1) planned, (2) organisationwide and (3) managed from the top, to (4) increase organisational effectiveness and health through (5) planned intervention in the organisation's processes using behavioural science knowledge.

This plethora of attempts to find an acceptable definition to use as a focal point for defining a field of practice and study has by no means met with success. Kahn (1974) in an oft-quoted and penetrating article has argued that these different definitions merely reflect a series of preferred approaches in selecting different techniques, targets, and processes for creating planned change. According to Kahn then, OD is what each man wishes to make it, and in consequence the field of OD, while possessing its own house journal, the *Journal of Applied Behavioral Science*, and its networks of associations, lacks a body of ideas and concepts, a theory even, to give it coherence and identity. This, like most pertinent statements, conceals as much as it reveals. Concepts and theories about intervention processes (Argyris, 1970), contingent forms of organisational diagnosis (Lawrence and Lorsch, 1969), theories of change (Alderfer, 1976), and strategies for building and managing consultant groups (Pettigrew, 1975a) have appeared, but these have been faltering and few compared with what the practitioners in the field, given their experience, are capable of writing. Instead, in the late 1960s and early 1970s, there was a torrent of idealised literature, most of it written by external consultants extolling the virtues of OD in general or their particular packaged form of it, (Blake and Mouton, 1968; Reddin, 1970; and Taylor, 1972).

Part of the problem has been the absence of a counterpoint to these espoused theories of change and intervention. Few took up Vaill's (1971) research and proceeded to ask the simple question, what do individuals in organisations who think of themselves as doing OD actually do? Weisbord (1974), who did ask this question, and McLean *et al.* (1982), who followed him, found not surprisingly there were large mismatches between formal descriptions of consultants' roles as portrayed in the OD literature and their actual activities. I am led to conclude, therefore, that merely using what the OD practitioners themselves define and report of their concepts, activities, and techniques is an inadequate basis to use as a starting point for this research. The practice of OD has far outstripped research on and in OD.

ORIGINS, HISTORY, AND DEVELOPMENT OF OD

There have been a number of comprehensive and useful efforts to chronicle the origins of OD (French and Bell, 1973; Greiner, 1977); and to analyse the emergence of certain parts of its technology (Back, 1972); and its values (Tannenbaum and Davis, 1969; Solomon, 1971; Friedlander, 1976). While this is not the place to effect another broadly based survey of the history of OD, given the empirical side of this book closely mirrors a good portion of that history, it is important to examine the ICI experience in the light of the wider development of the field. In addition, exploring its history is a further window to look through in attempting to specify what OD actually is.

The term OD appears to have originated in the United States in the late 1950s possibly by Blake, Shepard and Mouton while they were co-operating on a series of OD experiments at three Esso refineries: Bayonne, Baton Rouge, and Bayway. In 1957, the year before the Esso OD work began, Douglas McGregor, who as we shall see played a brief but important part in the birth of the ICI OD work, started using laboratory training skills at Union Carbide (French and Bell, 1973). It was no accident that both the Esso and Union Carbide work used group methods, for the seeds of OD's emergence were in offshoots of group therapy methods. Laboratory training, unstructured small-group situations in which participants learn from their own interactions and the evolving group dynamics had been institutionalised as a technology by Kurt Lewin, Kenneth Benne, Leland Bradford, and Ronald Lippitt when they created the National Training Laboratories for Group Development at Bethel, Maine, in 1947.

Kurt Lewin had, of course, played an important role not only in research on group dynamics but also in stressing how theoretical and conceptual formulations could be devised from practice. This kind of thinking led to action research work first of all when Lewin founded the Center for Group Dynamics at the Massachusetts Institute of Technology in 1945, and then when the staff of the Center for Group Dynamics moved to join Michigan's Survey Research Center, and created the Institute for Social Research. This happened just after Kurt Lewin died in 1947. The kind of action research usually referred to as survey research and feedback is particularly associated with the University of Michigan at this time and later led to well-known work by Floyd Mann, Rensis Likert, and others.

As French and Bell (1973) point out, although Lewin died only 2 years after the founding of the Center for Group Dynamics and before the first formal session of NTL, he had a profound influence on both organisations and his[1] influence continues today, most notably in the writing of Chris Argyris. Greiner (1977) is careful to pinpoint Carl Rogers' work (1942) as an influence in the group therapy side of OD and also in the theorising about consultant – client relationships which evolved with the training and development of internal and external consultants in the practice of OD. Rogers' work encouraged therapists to reject traditional psychoanalytic techniques and "to advocate methods which focused on 'here and now' behaviour, with special attention to encouraging expressions of affection, trust, and openness as means for healing emotional wounds." Greiner (1977:68). It was not too long before these Rogerian theories and the value emphasis they gave to listening, expressing feelings, trust and openness began to appear in the conduct of T-groups, but this time for "normal" people who possessed the usual assortment of behaviour problems.

If Lewin and Rogers were the intellectual heirs to OD, NTL and the Center for Group Dynamics were its early institutional embodiment, and the T-group and survey research and feedback its initial vehicles, then who translated these ideas into organisational settings? Following on from Douglas McGregor in Union Carbide, and Herbert Shepard, Robert Blake and Jane Mouton at Esso, came Sheldon Davis at the TRW Systems Group in 1961 and then a whole

---

[1] The most detailed account of Kurt Lewin's life and influence is Marrow's book (1969), *Practical Theorist*.

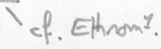

succession of well-known academics and consultants such as Chris Argyris, Warren Bennis, Richard Beckhard, Rensis Likert, Floyd Mann, and Edgar Schein.

During this period in the late 1950s and early 1960s, OD was already taking on board its core values. Solomon (1971) likens these to a philosophy of humanism where man is seen as basically good and is at the centre of all valuational processes. From this humanist dictum that man is the measure of all things, Solomon (1971) goes on to assert that institutions should serve man, and not vice-versa, that individual dignity is supreme and that participatory democracy really only works when individuals have a voice in all decisions that affect them, when present trends toward centralisation and bureaucratisation can be countered, and where there is a place for the non-rational and emotional in the conduct of human decision-making. Alongside these factors humanistic psychology propounded a view of man which saw the self moving toward actualisation, and growthful relationships implying the willingness and ability of partners to be equally vulnerable, honest, and open to change. Solomon (1971) was open enough to note that in his experience there was slippage between ideology and reality as training programmes drawing on these values were implemented. More generally he concluded that the above characteristics of humanism can lead to a fear of control, movement towards a narcissistic autonomy, and anti-intellectualism.

In a beautifully written article Friedlander (1976) outlines another version of the underlying philosophy and perspective of OD. He argues the grandparents of OD can be thought of as three basic value stances: rationalism, pragmatism, and existentialism. The rationalistic side of OD derived from its linkages with psychology and social psychology. These provided logic, consistency, and determinism where the basic purpose was to discover truth through the precise construction of concepts and knowledge. As I indicated earlier, the academic literature on OD hardly suggests that this value has been fulfilled.

Usefulness and effectiveness, the desire to improve practice by acting – doing, were the cornerstones of pragmatism. Existentialism meanwhile provided OD with a phenomenological mode of exploration – everything now was to begin with the actor's own subjective experience in the here and now, and shared feelings and mutuality were to be the hallmarks of good communication.

The elegant part of Friedlander's (1976) use of these three value stances was the way he drew on the uncomfortable mixture which they presented for OD in its "adolescence". Thus, for example, the pragmatist's stance of "if it works, it's good" offends the rationalist's need for precise models and frameworks, and the latter is likely to accuse the pragmatist of becoming a victim of whatever works – whether it be a technique, a fad, or a method. The existentialist meanwhile will feel suspicious that whatever works may turn out to be a manipulation of the person, and both the pragmatist and rationalist will think that the existentialist's mode of feeling and doing will run the risk of pushing experience, intuition, subjectivity, and an idealized humanistic vision beyond the realms of what most people in organisational settings will be prepared to accept.

Greiner's (1977) model of stages of OD evolution is a useful heuristic for revealing when and why some of these value tensions in OD began to reveal themselves in practical project work. He posits five stages:

1. Orthodoxy and Advocacy – the 1950s
2. Packaged Alternatives and Choice – the early 1960s
3. Evaluation and Doubt – the late 1960s
4. Pragmatism and the Eclectic – the early 1970s
5. Reconceptualization and the New Theorists – the late 1970s.

Greiner's (1977) dates refer to the American experience of OD, the ICI experience followed a broadly similar pattern but in a different historical time frame. In discussing the birth of OD, I have already described Greiner's stage 1. The second stage was in some sense a response to questioning of the practical value of T-groups. Blake in particular turned his back on T-groups after the Esso experience, feeling that they did not produce lasting results in the back-home organisation, relied too much on external consultancy help, and excessively stressed human relationships over task performance (French and Bell, 1972; Greiner, 1977). Blake's response was the first and probably most successful of the 1960s packages, the managerial grid (Blake and Mouton, 1964). This was a multi-phase programme focusing on managerial style which integrated people with task accomplishments and which could be run without Blake's presence. Blake and Mouton left their university posts and set up their own company, Scientific Methods Inc. They were reputed to be dollar millionaires by the end of the 1960s. Other packages by Reddin (1967) and Likert and his colleagues (1961) also emerged at this time.

The late 1960s was a period of evaluation and doubt. Managers and academics began to question the utility of many of these person-centred organisational interactions on pragmatic and moral grounds. An academic industry developed at this time critically evaluating not only the T-group's ability to produce behaviour changes (Campbell and Dunnette, 1968; House, 1967), but also the methodological standing and conceptual base of the motivation and job enrichment ideas of Herzberg *et al.*[2] (1959, and Herzberg 1966). Perhaps more to the point, in a survey of OD activities in 149 companies, Rush (1973) noted that the 1969–70 economic recession took its toll on several company OD efforts.

Greiner (1977) describes the early 1970s as a period of pragmatism and eclecticism. Having had their fingers burnt by some of the general packaged solutions of the 1960s, the inability in many specific situations to link, in managers' minds, people with productivity through devices such as job enrichment and team-building, many OD consultants, internal and external, turned to the more pragmatic and less person-centred intellectual approach in structural contingency theory. There was also a feeling that "anything that works" is worth hearing about (Greiner, 1977:72). And so the early and mid-1970s saw a burgeoning of new labels, new technologies, and new settings to

[2] For criticisms of the Herzberg approach, see House and Wigdor (1967).

apply OD values and techniques. The term OD began to be superseded by the likes of human resource management, and even quality of work life. As job enrichment receded, job design and sociotechnical systems surfaced along with team-building, structural interventions, open systems redesign, and career management. The development and content of these OD technologies is well documented in Beer (1976, 1980). The evolution of the concept of sociotechnical systems, and indeed the impact of the Tavistock Institute of Human Relations as a British influence on the emergence of OD, is described in Miller (1977).

The fifth of Greiner's (1977) stages is reconceptualization and new thrusts, and this he dates to the later 1970s. Unfortunately, Greiner (1977) is not able to specify what these reconceptualizations and new thrusts are to be, and the reader is left with a feeling that searching for an identity for OD in a triple concern for "behavioural processes in organisations," helping the longer-term capacity of people in social systems "to cope more effectively with challenges put before them" and "inculcating organisations with humanistic values" are but a return to ideology, and an ideology far out of touch with, for example, the social, economic, and organisational conditions of the United Kingdom in the late 1970s and early 1980s.

RESEARCH ON ORGANISATIONAL CHANGE AND DEVELOPMENT

Having tried to define OD, questioned the value of merely using the espoused theories of OD practitioners as expressed in their writing as a base on which to build this research, and then given some form to our discussion by describing and characterising the origins and development of OD, there remains the task of examining the strengths and weaknesses of existing research on organisational change and development. In what follows I shall spare the reader the pain of completeness for completeness' sake. Instead my objective will be first of all to mention the styles and perspective which some of the review papers in this area demonstrate, then to discuss some of the comparative research which assesses the impact of OD interventions, and then follow this with a critical look at a few of the more solid autobiographical accounts of change which exist. Finally, an exploration of the rare studies which have elements of a longitudinal design, and contextual and process analyses of change, will reveal something of the theoretical and methodological cornerstones behind the design and conduct of this research.

Of the current review papers examining the field and practice of OD, there seem to be three main styles of presenting the literature. There is the descriptive and interpretative approach of Friedlander and Brown (1974) and Alderfer (1977), the evaluative approach of Kahn (1974), Stephenson (1975), and Strauss (1976), and the scientific – rigorous perspective adopted by White and Mitchell (1976), Porras and Berg (1978), and King, Sherwood, and Manning (1978). Not surprisingly, the descriptive approach is the most informative, the scientific the most precise and predictable, and the evaluative the most interesting to read.

Strauss (1976) stores up most of his criticism to the end of his paper, subtly drawing the reader into the invective with an opening gambit that "in the end, OD is likely to be evaluated in terms of gut reactions rather than by dispassionate research" (1976:667). He goes on to discuss OD as a fad, its anti-intellectualism, essentially conservative objectives and methods, and tendencies towards manipulation and violations of individual privacy, but the strongest language is used to decry the hard sell. "For my taste OD has more than its share of evangelical hucksterism. As an academician, I am repelled by the cloying emotionalism and unsubstantiated claims which appear in some of the literature and much of the advertising" Strauss (1976:667).

Stephenson (1975) chastises much of OD for being obsessed with the people variable to the exclusion of structural, environmental, and societal influences, for imposing an exclusive set of humanistic values on people in organisations, for misrepresenting bureaucratic functioning by concentrating only on its negative connotations, and for hypocrisy – appearing to be concerned for people yet at the same time using them as organisational instruments.

Kahn (1974) goes straight for OD's soft underbelly, that part of its literature attempting to theorise about the theory and practice of change. "A few theoretical propositions are repeated without additional data or development: a few bits of homey advice are reiterated without proof or disproof, and a few sturdy empirical generalizations are quoted with reverence but without refinement or explication" (1974:487). Kahn's (1974) eloquence disappears, however, when he moves on to make some prescriptive statements about the kind of research designs which would produce knowledge and theory quite different from what he characterizes in the above quote. In his desire to set up model field experiments to control as many variables as possible, and establish whether or not the OD intervention did produce the predicted changes, he slips into the language of "master" and "slave" groups, albeit in their figurative, mechanical sense. The mind boggles; imagining Orwellian functionaries herding abject organisational citizens into master and slave groups while Dr Strangelove stands aloof waiting to administer the experimental OD treatment. Here at last are the conditions to provide tangible evidence for Kenneth Boulding's aphorism that "knowledge is always gained at the cost of truth" (1972:112)

The Friedlander and Brown (1974) and Alderfer (1977) reviews are a good deal more balanced and comprehensive. It is beyond the scope of this chapter to synthesise the former's 175 references and the latter's 104. Alderfer (1977) is able in part to refute the comments made by Kahn (1974) 3 years earlier about the lack of sophistication of research on OD, especially with the development of the academic interest in evaluation research (Guttentag and Struening, 1975). He is also able to point to a variety of new settings where new OD technologies are being applied although he notes that it is often the relatively successful businesses, often without unions, and stable suburban school systems without urban unrest where OD is being practised. Both reviews end with substantially similar conclusions which are germane to this study; Alderfer (1977) lamenting the lack of theoretical controversies and the relatively primitive form of theorising about organisational change and development, and Friedlander and Brown pointing out the continuing "failure to produce a theory of change which emerges from the change process itself" (1974:336). Shortly we shall argue one of the prime reasons for that failure has been the paucity of research on change which actually allows the change process to reveal itself in any kind of substantially temporal or contextual manner. Research on change continues to this day to focus on change episodes, and more likely *a* change episode, rather than the processual dynamics of changing.

The review papers by White and Mitchell (1976), and Porras and Berg (1978) each examine published research on OD, the former covering the period 1964–74, and Porras and Berg spanning the years 1959–75. Their findings corroborate some of the statements made earlier about the history of OD. Both papers note the heavy emphasis on individuals and groups as the change target in the period up to the early 1970s, and a corresponding lack of emphasis on intergroup relationships and procedural or structural features of the organisation. Porras and Berg (1978) also report that none of the 35 studies they looked at involved work with any groups other than managerial and professional staff. Rush (1973) provides data from a much larger sample of cases also indicating that OD for most companies was an exercise for managers. In a theoretical paper, Kochan and Dyer (1976) argue the reason for the relatively rare use of OD techniques with shop-floor workers is the poor fit, value and conceptwise, between OD models of change and the normal parameters which define relations between union and management.

Probably the most extensive work carried out on assessing the impact of organisational change and development in the late 1960s and up to the mid-1970s was the research at Michigan University. These studies by Bowers (1973), Bowers *et al.* (1975), and Franklin (1976), are important because of the attempts at precise operationalisation of variables, the use of control groups, and the comparative analysis. These studies are also of value because of the effort made to conceptualise the determinants of success and failure in attempts to create change. Franklin's (1976) paper compares 11 organisations with successful OD efforts and 14 organisations with unsuccessful OD efforts around 8 clusters of characteristics ranging from the organisation's environment, the nature of the organisation itself, the process of setting up the project and generating commitment, to the characteristics of the internal and external change agents. His findings are a direct rebuke to those who seek a singular pattern or theory of organisational change. "Thus it appears that a strong case cannot be made for characteristics that are either absolutely necessary or in and of themselves sufficient to determine successful or unsuccessful change in organisations" (Franklin, 1976:487). However, Franklin (1976) was able to report that there were three areas which did seem to differentiate between the successful and unsuccessful organisations. Thus organisations which had already been open to and involved in adjusting to change were more likely to be successful in their OD effort than a more stable and status quo-oriented organisation. Success also appeared to be associated with the existence of an acknowledged specific problem, the ability of the consultant to find these situationally specific problems and their causes, and to aid in the process of finding the appropriate intervention, and to plan it with care.

An undoubted weakness of the Franklin (1973) work which identified the importance of climate setting as a precursor to change was their interpretation of cross-sectional data to imply cause–effect relationships. In one sense, of course, Bowers (1973) did have longitudinal data, but these data were collected exclusively by questionnaires administered in conventional snapshot fashion, before and after the change. Bowers (1973) therefore was unable to disentangle how the cause–effect relationships he was positing unfolded themselves through time. Nevertheless, the factors contributing to success and failure in organisational change identified by the Michigan researchers will be of value in informing this research at least until the present work moves beyond reflecting about the change programme as the unit of analysis.

One of the criticisms made of accounts of OD interventions is that they are often autobiographical (Kahn, 1974). The implication of this criticism is, of course, that self-reports by the consultants and action researchers of change events are bound to be coloured by the investment of their time and egos in the project work, and the written discussions that appear will be selective in the presentation of facts, particular in the asking of questions, and rosy in the interpretation of outcomes. The mere existence of Mirvis and Berg's (1977) set of cases on failures in organisation development and change, and the tone of self-critical writing in some of them is one counterpoint to that argument. Evidence substantiating the dangers of autobiographical accounts is to be found in Blackler and Brown's (1980) book, *Whatever Happened to Shell's New Philosophy of Management?*

The Blackler and Brown (1980) book is a product of a retrospective analysis based on a small sample of interviews of the attempt by Shell UK Refining in the 1960s to introduce a new philosophy of management in their refineries in order to increase employee commitment, efficiency, and productivity. On the basis of a very limited set of interviews, Blackler and Brown (1980) felt confident enough to reject the conclusions of Hill's (1976) autobiographical account of the Shell work, and conclude "from very early on the philosophy exercise achieved but moderate success. There is no doubt about it we believe that the exercise failed, rather spectacularly, to introduce a new philosophy of management to Shell" (1980:5).

The factors Blackler and Brown (1980) list as contributing to the failure include an initial oversell to a limited group in the company, unfavourable antecedents to the change, an overlong analytical and diagnostic phase which led to unrealistic expectations, a failure to get the board of Shell UK to officially adopt the new philosophy, the movement of key people in the change process and their replacement with "nonbelievers"; and a variety of contextual factors, including the competing values locked into the company's reward system, and unforeseen environmental changes which disrupted the emerging pattern of relationships between management and the shop floor. Blackler and Brown (1980) were also highly critical of what they called the naive intellectual base of the Shell work, the belief that profound changes could emanate from better human relations management, and the change strategy adopted by the internal and external consultants, which they caustically dubbed social science as fluoridation. Fundamental also to the change's failure were the divergent interests of the three principal parties involved in the change. These parties were the Shell internal consultancy group, the Tavistock external consultancy team, and the junior and middle managers in Shell who seemed to be the biggest sceptics of the intervention. Ultimately, Blackler and Brown (1980) contend the internal consultancy group became "a character in search of an author", the Tavistock team were "authors in search of a character" and "the play the Tavistock authors wrote was not quite what the actors at Shell had in mind" (1980:61).

To Blackler and Brown's (1980) credit they do allow space in their book for two of the consultants involved to provide a rejoinder to their analysis, but even without these less than impartial retorts there is cause for reflection on such categorical dismissal of the Shell work given the nature and extent of the authors' data, the sketchy analytical use they make of the data, and the overwhelming cynicism of their presentation. Blackler and Brown's (1980) use of their small number of interviews is purely to select out quotes to reveal attitudes. There is little analysis beyond that of either the nature of the developing relationship between the major actors in the change process, or of why in their own admission the Shell programme seemed to take rather more in one refinery than another. For authors, rightly in my view, emphasising the impact of contextual variables on change processes, the differential impact in the Stanlow and Shell Haven refineries offered them a marvellous opportunity to look again at their data and begin the process of developing theoretical ideas which would inform the question, why? Equally well, the factors they usefully developed to help explain the apparent overall lack of success of the Shell work could have been related to other published material such as Walton's (1975. 1978) research on the diffusion of innovations, and the Mirvis and Berg (1977) cases of failures in OD. While Blackler and Brown (1980) have undoubtedly added to the interpretation of the Shell work initially provided by Hill (1976), their criticisms did not dissuade me from examining two other autobiographical accounts of organisational change efforts in the UK published by Klein (1976), and Warmington, Lupton and Gribbin (1977).

The Klein (1976) book is a narrative account of the growth, stabilisation, and demise of Lisl Klein's role as a social sciences adviser to Esso between 1963 and 1970. Klein (1976) admits the book is weakened by its autobiographical origins. Like the Hill (1976) and Blackler and Brown (1980) books, it is also limited by two important requirements of case study work. First, the importance of conceptualisation to place the empirical material in a broader frame of discourse, and secondly the necessity to relate the case studies to similar published materials. Klein's (1976) book offers very few links with other published cases of change, and where attempts are made in part two of the book to develop the more general themes of the politics of social science, and the dynamics of industry and social science relationship, these generalising frames of reference are inadequately connected back to her own case study material.

The book at an implicit level, however, does have a number of important things to say which can aid the present task of drawing out some of the general strengths and weaknesses of the existing research on organisational change and development. In the first place Klein's (1976) narrative account does, through its personal and political realism, provide a counterweight to balance against the normative espoused theory of the OD literature. By stressing the vulnerability of the internal consulting role, its essentially political character, and the continuing problems of territory and competition she had with other related specialist functions such as personnel, and with external consultants, she contributes to those authors (Pettigrew, 1975b) who have questioned the truth, trust, love and collaboration approach to change emphasised by Bennis (1969:77).

The factors Klein (1976) draws out to explain the demise of her role show many similarities with the list prepared in Blackler and Brown's (1980) analysis of the Shell work. These include a permissive rather than enthusiastic senior management, her isolation from the centres of power in the organisation which partly stemmed from her own entrapment inside an employee relations department at the middle of the organisation, and the frequent management development moves of key personnel which created a general and continuing problem between rapid career progression and organisational learning and change. The most significant general message of Klein's (1976) book, and the one that informs the themes and analytical perspective of this research, is the importance she attaches to environmental change as a contributor in the success or otherwise of specialist-led attempts to create change. Although she admits it was a conclusion born of hindsight, she asserts "social science in application involves a continuous interplay between the content of the work being done and its context. Success depends on successfully regulating the relations between the two" (Klein, 1976:9). As we shall see, the specification of the differing levels and forms of contextual impact, and the process of regulating that impact on major changes, will be one of the crucial themes of this research on organisational change in ICI.

The final autobiographical account of organisational change which is of relevance is the work by Warmington, Lupton and Gribbin (1977) in a large UK manufacturing organisation. This study limits itself at this stage to laying out the analytical assumptions and change strategy adopted by the authors and a group of internal consultants to create "open sociotechnical systems change". Regrettably the authors are not able in this publication to include a detailed description and analysis of the actual process of implementing their change programme, in this sense the more important publication from this research is yet to appear. In the theoretical prelude to the cases which they do feel able to describe, and in their concluding practical assessment, they also mention a number of contextual variables which they consider were fateful to explaining the only limited success of the change venture they were part of. Again there are similarities with the accounts of change portrayed by Hill (1976), Blackler and Brown (1980), and Klein (1976).

A central problem of the Warmington *et al.* (1977) interventions derived from the exclusive language and problem-solving rationale built into their open sociotechnical systems approach, and in the other arm of their change strategy which emphasised a cell division concept of diffusing change. They had assumed that a combination of an intellectually powerful mode of problem-solving, plus a strategy of involving participants closely in the diagnosis and initiation of change in a number of separate but relatable cells or projects would, if the process were successful, lead local managers to press for wider changes. What Warmington *et al.* (1977) found was that "the process of implementing departmental improvements using rather unorthodox theories and methods is risky for local managers; its outcome is problematic and there are cases in which the projected improvements never eventualise" (1977:239). When this happened the momentum for the change receded and no amount of logical reasoning or pushing from the combination of internal and external consultants could revive interest either in the mechanism for achieving change, or the wider process of change itself.

Again these authors conclude with a highly contextualist argument which emphasises building into the change process a developed awareness by the consultants and skill in intervening in the political and cultural systems of the organisation in order to build up a nucleus of political support for the changes. In this regard, however, they pinpoint a basic lacuna in the processes of designing a large change programme. "We are in a sense in a vicious circle in that if it is to be effective the design of a change programme can only take place when the culture and power system and modes of behaviour of the wider organisation are fully understood; but these features cannot be properly understood until some processes of change have been introduced and the reactions observed" (Warmington *et al.*, 1977:240).

In this author's view there are at least two broad ways of breaking out of the logic of the above vicious circle and many tactical alternatives within and around those two broad ways. The Warmington *et al.* (1977) change lacuna is predicated on the assumption that change has to be led by a group of change agents with a vested interest in change who somehow represent a better way of organising than those groups who currently are in control of the organisation and define and articulate its culture. In looking at the ICI experience we will be able to examine the alternative strategies of change where the leading edge for change was provided by the chief executives and senior managers of the company. This strategy does, of course, like any other action create its own set of implications and consequences, but not those bounded by the Warmington *et al.* (1977) change conundrum. The other route out of the change conundrum of, you have to act before you can appreciate how to act competently, is to develop more sensitive ways of conceptualising and theorising about change which recognise and help to define the immediate and broader context in which change occurs, and how that context may be mobilised by advocates of change in order to achieve their objectives. In my view the development of such knowledge and theorising about change which recognises both contextual variability, and a continuing process of dipping into the context in order to assess where, when, and how change is possible, requires a quite different strategy for research on change than the approaches dominant today. In this final section reviewing relevant parts of the literature on organisational change and development and strategic change I shall build on other research on change with a longitudinal and contextual character in order to establish some of the theoretical and methodological ground rules for this research.

CONTEXT AND PROCESS IN EXISTING RESEARCH ON ORGANISATIONAL CHANGE

With the exception of Klein (1976) and Warmington *et al.* (1977) most of the studies of change which have been mentioned so far in this review have been ahistorical, acontextual, and aprocessual. This is the tradition in the field and even Klein (1976) and Warmington *et al.* (1977) while contextual in part do not draw on historical materials or provide a processual analysis of change. As with so many other areas in the social sciences the empirical findings and theoretical developments in the field of organisational change are method-bound. For as long as we continue to conduct research on change which is ahistorical, acontextual, and aprocessual, which continues to treat the change programme as the unit of analysis and regard change as an episode divorced from the immediate and more distant context in which it is embedded, then we will continue to develop inadequate descriptive theories of change which are ill-composed guides for action. Indeed as I have implied already there is still a dearth of studies which can make statements about the how and why of change, about the processual dynamics of change, in short which go beyond the analysis of *change* and begin to theorise about *changing*.

These analytical issues, and the way they are represented in the field, are not black and white. There are alternative ways of defining longitudinal research each of which has different implications for whether a processual analysis actually appears from the longitudinal data. An examination of the Bowers (1973) work illustrated how time series data, if collected in a snapshot fashion, would not provide a processual analysis, and how even though Franklin (1976) had data which were amenable to processual analysis he chose to use those data to abstract out cross-sectional categories and factors. Equally well single case study longitudinal work such as Alderfer and Brown (1975) which explicitly uses the term changing as a focal point for the study is actually limited by not being able to relate variability in context to alternative processes of changing. And the important paper by Greiner (1967), which proclaimed the importance of historical analysis and the significance of antecedent conditions in explaining the limitations and possibilities of change, was itself hampered by not being able to relate alternative antecedent conditions to common or variable contexts, and thence to differing resultant change outcomes.

A further area of research which has attempted to provide contextualist propositions about change is the literature on innovation (Zaltman, Duncan and Holbeck, 1973; Kimberly, 1981). This literature, either by defining innovation as a discrete product or programme (Rogers and Shoemaker, 1971), or as a process (Knight, 1967; Shepard, 1967), has attempted to disentangle the variables particular to individuals, to organisational structures or broader orga-nisational contexts which influence rates of initiation, adoption, diffusion and in some more limited cases, implementation of innovations. As Zaltman *et al.* (1973:58) point out most diffusion theorists terminate their analysis at the stage of initiation, where an idea has been accepted by the authority system of an organisation and ignore the rather more intractable implementation stage. Zaltman *et al.* (1973) argue for linking the initiation and implementation phases together in a sequence given impetus in the first place by senior managers' per-ceptions of a performance gap between what the organisation is doing and ought to be doing.

The structural contingency theorists Burns and Stalker (1961), Lawrence and Lorsch (1967), and Duncan (1973) all posit relationships between structural context and innovation potential. Zaltman *et al.* (1973:154) in a useful summary of this literature argue that different configurations of organisational structure are appropriate at the initiation phase of innovation than in the implementation phase. Given the high functional requirement for gathering and processing information at the initiation stage then there is a need for higher degree of complexity of structure, lower formalisation, and lower centralisation. At the implementation phase, however, a higher level of formalisation and centralisation, and a lower level of complexity are required in order to reduce the role conflict and ambiguity which could impair implementations.

There are a number of cardinal and basic faults with this literature on innovation which makes it a poor base to construct realistic theories of change. A central difficulty the innovation literature shares with the writing on planned organisational change is the highly rational and linear theories of process which drive these models. Thus from the planned change theorists we have phases of consultant activity which range from develop need, establish relationship, work toward change, stabilise change and evaluate (Lippitt *et al.*, 1958); to diagnosis, strategy plan, educate, consult and train, to evaluate (Beckhard, 1969). And from the innovation theorists, this time not considering the activities of change agents but a characterisation of the innovation process as evaluation, initiation, implementation and routinisation (Hage and Aiken, 1970); or from Zaltman *et al.* (1973), the more complicated but equally rational and linear; know-ledge–awareness substage, formation of attitudes toward the innovation substage, decision substage, initial implementation substage and continued sustained implementation substage. Zaltman *et al.* (1973:53)) even go on to say that "in the process approach, innovation is viewed as an unfolding process consisting of stages in which characteristic factors not only appear in greater or smaller degree, but *also*[3] in a certain order of occurrence". And even Warmington *et al.* (1977) who elsewhere in their book imply they see change in much more sophisticated processual terms than these argue "the formulation of a strategy for change can be seen as a specific stage in a sequence that includes investigation, analysis of facts, model-building, proposal formulation and implementation of improvements" (1977:181).

[3] My emphasis.

In this research on change in ICI it will be clear that this rational problem-solving approach to planned change and innovation is both an inadequate way of theorising about what actually happens during change processes and an overtly simple guide for action. The field of organisational change badly needs theoretical development along the lines of the literature on organisational decision-making where there are now a variety of process models of choice which include satisficing views of process (March and Simon, 1958); political views of process (Pettigrew, 1973); and garbage can views of process (March and Olsen, 1976).

Moving away for an instant from the process difficulties of the planned change and innovation literature back to other studies of change which draw on contextual variables one can see the promise in this approach. Other writers apart from the structural contingency theorists who have used contextualist explanations of change include Mohrman *et al.* (1977), Lewicki :1977, Elden (1978), Kervasdoue and Kimberly (1979) and Kimberly (1980). Of these authors, the first two define context either exclusively in terms of intraorganisation context or in terms of a combination of that and some notion of organisation environment, while the latter group with varying degrees of specificity draw on intraorganisational, organisation-environmental, and socio-economic contextual variables.

Mohrman *et al.* (1977) report a survey feedback and problem-solving intervention in a school district and ask the question why was the programme almost completely implemented in School B and hardly implemented at all in a high school? Their answer to that question equates very closely with Klein's (1976) observation that success in stimulating change is very much a function of the fit or lack of fit between the content of an intervention and its context. School B was, relative to the high school, small, fairly tightly integrated and with a culture which already supported the kind of group problem-solving activity the change programme was seeking to encourage. It also had a principal who provided both strong general and specific support for the programme and who required attendance at group meetings. The high school on the other hand was much larger, structurally much more differentiated, and had a culture with little history and capacity for working in groups on problem identification and solution generation processes.

Lewicki's (1977) study was an attempt to use team-building techniques among small businessmen in two New England communities. Although similar strategies were used by the consultants in both communities, the intervention in the author's view was a success in "Marysville" but a failure in "Riverside". Lewicki (1977) accounts for the different outcome in specifically contextual terms, "following the research by Shapero (1975) and others, we learned that a community or region like Riverside may not have the environmental qualities that lend themselves to stimulating community development and eventually economic growth" (1977:309). His more detailed explanation for success and failure, however, was a mixture of context and strategy. Thus Riverside was dominated by a single large employer whereas Marysville had a number of units in the business community of reasonably equal power. Riverside's existing sense of geographical identity, interdependence and mutual fate was probably lower than in Marysville, and the businessman who led the change attempt at Riverside was a marginal man in that community, who was too directive in his approach and too poorly tied to the central power structure of the business community to get the correct kinds of changes off the ground in the first place, or to sustain what had managed to start when the economic conditions altered and further threatened the change programme. Meanwhile the businessman who led the change effort in Marysville was well known and liked; had been explicitly selected by the community, had a business that stood to gain from the envisaged changes yet set in motion a process which involved high levels of participation and commitment in choosing salient, initially small-scale, and highly tangible change objectives.

This attempt to link circumstances and behaviour to account for the success and failure of change efforts is also seen in the work by Kimberly and Nielsen (1975), and Kimberly (1980). In the 1975 study Kimberly and Nielsen are able to demonstrate with longitudinal data that crucial to the impact of an OD effort on organisational performance was not only factors particular to the change programme itself, but also more significantly the corporate policies and market conditions of the firm. Kimberly's (1980) study of the birth of a new medical school, his work on French hospitals with Kervasdoue, Kervasdoue and Kimberly (1979), and Elden's writing (1978) all point to an aspect of context virtually ignored in the literature on change and development, the conditioning and enabling influence of the social and economic environment surrounding the organisation.

The Kervasdoue and Kimberly (1979) research is interesting because the authors started by posing their principal research question within the frame of reference of structural contingency theory. They were interested in examining the extent to which variability in rates of adoption of innovations in medical technology in US and French hospitals could be accounted for by variations in their structure. What they concluded was that in order to understand hospital innovation, it is necessary to go beyond the comparative structuralist paradigm and ask questions about sociopolitical, historical, and cultural factors in and around organisations. The reports of the Norwegian Industrial Democracy Programme by Qvale (1976) and Elden (1978) go a stage beyond the Kervasdoue and Kimberly (1979) observations in making normative statements about how the particular political, practical, and professional conditions which have evolved in Norway over the past 15 to 20 years were crucial preconditions for the evolution of the Industrial Democracy Programme. These conceptual and practical acknowledgements of the role that social, economic, political, and historical factors can play in facilitating and constraining change at the organisational level of analysis take us to a brief review of the literature on the formulation and implementation of strategic change, the final body of thinking and writing connectable to the theme of this research.

ELEMENTS OF THE LITERATURE ON STRATEGIC CHOICE AND CHANGE

One of the analytical conclusions of this study is that theoretically sound and practically useful research on strategic change should involve the continuous interplay between ideas about the *context* of change, the *process* of change, and the *content* of change, together with skill in regulating the relations between the three. Formulating the content of a strategic change crucially entails managing its context and process. Without sensitivity to and apposite action on the what, the why, and the how of introducing major change more than likely the change idea will either die shortly after birth or be emasculated at later stages in the processes of formulation and implementation.

But what has the existing literature on strategic change to say about either the content, the context, or the process of managing change? In fact the general literature on business strategy development almost exclusively concerns itself with the content of strategy, while treating context in terms of the crucial but still limiting notion of the competitive environment of the firm (Andrews, 1971; King and Cleland, 1978; Porter, 1980). Even more problematic, however, is the implicit view of problem-solving built into this strategy literature which is as rational as, if not more rational than, the view of choice and change found in parts of the writing on innovation and planned organisational change discussed in the previous section of this chapter. Thus as applied to the development of business strategy the rational approach describes and prescribes techniques for identifying current strategy, analysing environments, resources and gaps, revealing and assessing strategic alternatives, and choosing and implementing carefully analysed and well-thought-through outcomes. This rational picture of business problem-solving has as its concern the content or what of strategy – the outcome which is sought – and has nothing to say at an explicit level of how to achieve that outcome. In other words it has no process theory within it of how and why to create the strategic outcomes so perceptively and logically derived from the analysis of competitive forces.

But what are the potential sources available to try and develop an adequate theory of strategic change which incorporates thinking about the process of managing change? The organisation development literature has rarely been used to inform thinking about strategic change, even though recent writing by, for example, Beckhard and Harris (1977) and Beer (1980) could be used with profit to grapple with some of the practical problems of creating and managing strategic change. Perhaps another route to stimulate process theorising about strategic change is to draw on the work of authors such as Bower (1970), Allison (1971), Pettigrew (1973), Mumford and Pettigrew (1975), March and Olsen (1976), Mintzberg (1978), and Quinn (1980), who at least at the level of observation and description, if not always prescriptively, have sought to rescue research on strategic choice and change from its habitual focus on rational analytical schemas of intentional process and outcome, and to see decision-making and change in a variety of process modes.

We have Simon (1957) and March and Simon (1958) with their concepts of bounded rationality and satisficing to thank for highlighting how the cognitive, learning and search limitations of individuals can curtail maximising models of rational choice. However, March and Simon's (1958) tendency to project individual processes of choice into statements about organisational processes of decision-making means there is a liberal bias to reconstructing the organisation from the perspective of the individual, and not enough on demonstrating how the organisation structures the perspective and interests of the individual. No such theoretical fallacy is evident in Cyert and March (1963). They also conceive of a firm as a goal-directed, economising and learning individual but extend this view by conceiving of decision-making as a political process. In Cyert and March (1963) conflicts of interest are normal features of organisational life, coalitions form, and sub-groups work to generate support for their interests and demands. But although some of the language of political analysis is present in Cyert and March, and there is the prospect that power may cause decision outcomes, the theoretical apparatus to help describe and analyse how political processes cause choices to be made is absent.[4] As Pfeffer (1982:7) has recently argued, implicit in the bounded rationality approach was the normative position that the bounds of bounded rationality could actually be pushed back if new decision technologies or information processing systems could be developed. In this way technology could compensate for the limited cognitive and information processing abilities of man, and more rational action would result.

Another group of scholars also interested in descriptive and prescriptive approaches to choice were the policy analysts (Lindblom, 1959; Braybrooke and Lindblom, 1963). In the complex and unpredictable world of macro-policy-making, how again could boundedly rational decisions be made under time constraints and where search costs were limited? The answer was through methods of successive limited comparisons in which policy-makers would move incrementally from the base line set by practice and precedent. Here again, presumably under the long shadow of the public interest, policy analysts are implicitly trying to be as rational as they can given the difficult contexts in which they operated, and the complex problems they had to solve.

Eventually the process theorists started to take an interest in strategy formulation in business settings where the dominant intellectual paradigm was a combination of a preoccupation with the analytical content of strategy with limited views of context, and an avowedly rational picture of business problem-solving (Ansoff, 1965; Andrews, 1971). Without necessarily over-identifying themselves with any of the particular process theories then emerging, writers such as Bower (1970) and Mintzberg *et al.* (1976, 1978) began to treat strategy not as an output but as a process, and confront the dominant rational/analytical paradigm with the results of their descriptive studies. Bower (1970), like Aharoni (1966), conceived of strategy developing at multiple levels in the organisation through processes characterised as chains of commitment leading

[4] See Pettigrew (1973) for an elaboration of these reflections on the Carnegie decision-making scholars of the 1960s.

to eventual confirmation. Phase metaphors describing the life history of investment proposals from definition to impetus were postulated, and aspects of the impetus phase were described in political terms. Top managers were seen to determine the structural context through which capital proposals would pass and be filtered. Mintzberg (1978), using extended time series data collected retrospectively, rather than through elements of historical and real time data, conceived of strategy as consistency over time in a stream of decisions. This approach allowed him to distinguish between intended and realised strategy, and to pinpoint strategies contributed after the fact, or as he puts it realised despite intentions, (Mintzberg, 1978:934). This was an important if fairly obvious observation, for it drove a stake right through the prevailing orthodoxy that strategies are and should be plans conceived in advance of making specific decisions.

Another of Mintzberg's contributions was to postulate both that strategies appear to have life cycles – periods of incubation, development, and decay; and that distinct periods of change and continuity can be discerned in the overall pattern of strategic development of the firm. This notion that firms may have patterned and periodic shifts in their strategy (Mintzberg and Waters, 1982) has been extended by comparative case study research conducted by Miller and Friesen (1980) using the metaphors of evolution and revolution, and by recent historical work on firms in the pre-nationalised British Steel Industry. In this work on steel firms Boswell (1983) identifies what he calls phases of strategic concentration around values of for a time growth, and then efficiency. This phenomenon of the deep organisational cultural roots of business strategies, and the tendency of strategic changes to occur in packages interspersed with periods of incremental adjustment, will be an issue we shall return to when examining strategic continuity and change in ICI.

In summary, this empirical process research on strategy made a number of descriptive contributions to the understanding of strategic decision-making and change. Strategic processes were now accepted as multi-level activities and not just the province of a few, or even a single general manager. Outcomes of decisions were not just a product of rational or boundedly rational debates, but were also shaped by the interests and commitments of individuals and groups, the forces of bureaucratic momentum, gross changes in the environment, and the manipulation of the structural context around decisions. With the view that strategy development was a continuous process, strategies could now be thought of as reconstructions after the fact, rather than just rationally intended plans. The linear view of process explicit in strategy formulation to strategy implementation was questioned, and with increasing interest in enduring characteristics of structural and strategic context (Bower, 1970; Burgelman, 1983), Chandler's (1962) dictum that structure followed strategy was modified by evidence indicating why and how strategy followed structure (Galbraith and Nathanson, 1978).

However, analytically the Bower and Mintzberg research was weakened by a number of factors. Chief amongst these was the treatment of decision-making just as front stage behaviour, and the lack of concern with non-decision-making, and secondly the lack of development of a specified process theory to explain the descriptions of process and outcome. Quinn's (1980) publication, however, tied itself to a very specific interpretation of process. Drawing on the work of Lindblom and Braybrook, Quinn interpreted his case study data on strategic change as displaying patterns of logical incrementalism. This is described as a jointly analytical and political process in which executives are described as, and are recommended "to proceed flexibly and experimentally from broad concepts to specific commitments, making the latter concrete as late as possible" (Quinn, 1980:56). Strategic change is thus seen as a cautious, step-by-step evolutionary process, where executives muddle through with a purpose.

Quinn's (1980) style of presenting his ideas, moving easily from description to prescription, makes his book extremely attractive as a teaching medium, but the clarity of his belief in the prescriptive value of logical incrementalism means it is not always easy to disentangle what he has discovered empirically from what he would like to see. Certainly Mintzberg's (1978) findings that incremental change takes place in spurts, each followed by a period of continuity, tends to contradict Quinn's (1980) finding or view that strategies emerge in a continuous incremental and thereby additive fashion. Perhaps because Quinn's (1980) work is presented in the language of change rather than decision-making, and he is interested in prescription, he does make the terribly important point that in the management of strategic changes there are process limits to consider as well as just cognitive limits. These process limits, the concern with the timing and sequencing of action and events in order to build awareness, comfort levels, and consensus for strategic change, descriptively we will see was also a crucial part of the strategic change process in ICI.

Although the characterisation and description of process in Quinn's (1980) work is a good deal richer than anything offered by the bounded rationalists, the underlying rationalist perspective that there is an element of "conscious, foresightful action reasonably autonomously constructed to achieve some goal or value" (Pfeffer, 1982:7) is shared by Quinn and the bounded rationalists. No such rationalistic perspective is at the bottom of another process theory developed in the 1970s, the so-called garbage can view of action and choice (Cohen, March, and Olsen, 1972). In this view of organisation, individual and group interests are only partially understood and acted upon, actors walk in and out of decision processes, solutions are generated without reference to problems, and outcomes are not a direct consequence of process. In this anarchic picture of organisational life behaviour can be predicted neither by intention nor environmental constraint, instead decisions appear out of foggy emergent contexts when people, problems, and solutions find themselves sharing the same bed. Fundamentally, "rationality cannot guide action in this view, because rationality, goals, and preferences are viewed as emerging from action rather than guiding action" (Pfeffer, 1982:9).

This is a very attractive view of process precisely because it is such a counterpoint to the rationalists, but one wonders if the view of anarchy has not been overstated – there is greater consistency and continuity of action, clearer beliefs in self and group interest and action derived from those interests, and generally firmer cause–effect attributions in connecting perceptions, information, interests and preferences to action and outcomes than is implied by the garbage can theorists. In addition most of the empirical examples used to support this garbage can approach to choice, are taken from educational organisations (March and Olsen, 1976), where the theory may fit a context widely assumed to contain hapless citizens confused and conflicted about means and ends, confronted by multiple systems and centres of leadership, and unclear about their responsibilities and accountabilities.

The above necessarily synoptic account of the rational, boundedly rational, incremental, and garbage can approaches to choice and sometimes change, will have given a flavour both of the variety of perspectives now available to the student of strategy, some of the strengths and weaknesses and overlaps of each, and a few of the empirical findings that those alternative views of process have encouraged. A task that remains is to sketch out the meaning and utility of a process view of choice and change which combines a political and cultural analysis of organisational life. This task is part of the agenda for Chapter 2.

BEARINGS

The above review of the literature on organisational change and development and strategic change has found that literature wanting in a number of crucial respects. Principal amongst these has been the extent to which the theories and empirical findings in this area have been circumscribed by the limited frames of reference and methodologies and approach used to study change. In the main the research which has been reported has been ahistorical, aprocessual, and acontextual. In this respect the area of organisational change and development is merely reflecting the biases inherent in the social sciences generally, and in the study of organisations in particular. But in other respects the field of organisational change and development has emerged as a rather precious subculture of theory and practice which has not connected itself well either with existing writing or novel theoretical developments going on amongst sociologists and anthropologists interested in social change, (Zald and McCarthy, 1979; Geertz, 1973), or to other advances taking place in organisation theory and behaviour. A consequence is that the field of organisational change and development is characterised by limited attempts at theoretical development, few theoretical debates, highly focused kinds of conceptualisation, and very limited empirical findings. All this adds up to some rather poor descriptive theories of change which beyond a shopping list of prescriptive do's and don'ts, sometimes qualified by contextual riders, could hardly be described as adequate guides to informed action.

A particular limiting problem identified in the literature was the tendency to regard the change project as the unit of analysis, and change itself either as a single event or a set of discrete episodes somehow or other separate from the immediate and more distant context which gave those events form, meaning, and substance. The impression is created in this view of change that each change has a particular beginning and a finite ending apart from the more generalised processes around it. Regrettably this perspective still abounds today both in recent literature examining quality of work life changes (Goodman, 1979), and in that part of the OD literature which condenses organisational change processes down to the minutiae of relationships between consultant and client (Mangham, 1979; McLean *et al.*, 1982). The literature on consultant–client relationships will be discussed in more detail at a later stage of this book as empirical material is being presented about the attitudes and behaviour of the ICI internal and external consultants. The consultancy literature is, however, yet another example of the prescriptive, rather idealised character of the change field (Blake and Mouton, 1976; Steele, 1975), and of a subset of that field focusing in on the change process from a highly limited frame of reference. Even fairly circumscribed attempts to demonstrate how consultant–consultant relationships might influence consultant–client relationships, (Pettigrew, 1975b), and how the strategic management of consultant groups influence change processes, (Pettigrew, 1975a), bring in levels of analysis rarely alluded to in the myopic concern with how consultant relates to client.

Aside from the above problems of limited focus, the above review has also pinpointed the inadequacies of the highly rational and linear process models which drive most planned theories of change and the literature on business strategy development. These planned theories, many of them with highly prescriptive and deterministic phases or stages (Lippitt *et al.*, 1958; French and Bell, 1973), are, as we shall see, divorced from the actual conduct of change projects and processes. For the task of examining how strategic change actually takes place and some of the dynamics behind those change processes we will have to draw upon some alternative models of process (Pettigrew, 1973, 1979; Quinn, 1980) which are able to explain how the possibilities and limitations of change in any organisation are influenced by the history of attitudes and relationships between interest groups in and outside the firm, and by the mobilisation of support for a change within the power structure at any point in time. Such a view of changing does not carry along with it either the ideological baggage of progress identified by Kimberly (1981) in the literature on managerial innovation, or the necessity to see change just as a response of management to improve efficiency, but rather is capable of interpreting change as the legacy of struggles for power emerging through time.

Mindful, however, of my earlier admonition to beware of singular theories of changing, no attempt will be made here to simply substitute planned, rational linear theories with political process theories. The task is to identify the variety and mixture of causes of change, to examine the juxtaposition of the rational and the political, the quest for efficiency and power, the role of exceptional men and of extreme circumstances, the untidiness of chance, forces in the environment, and to explore some of the conditions in which mixtures of these occur.

This leads me to pick up the two final areas where particularly the OD and organisational change literature were found wanting, their use of contextual and processual forms of analysis and explanation. In this author's view the study of organisational change is now at the stage where theory and knowledge is required principally to understand the dynamics of changing in alternative contexts using a framework of analysis which can incorporate different levels of analysis with varying degrees of explanatory immediacy and distance from the change process under examination. In order to do this the field has to move beyond the useful but mechanical statements of contingency theory which emphasise the interconnections between a state of the environment and certain requirements for structure, behaviour or change, and begin to examine how and why changes occur in different organisational cultures and political systems, under different socioeconomic and business conditions, through time.

Such an analysis could properly explore the relationship and interplay between the content of change, the context of change, and the process of managing change. It would require frames of reference and methods of data collection sensitive to alternative antecedent conditions, variety of receiving culture for the change, alternative levels of analysis and explanation, differing change strategies, and alternative change outcomes. Above all, it will require time series, processual data in order to see how and why the above broad analytical factors work themselves through any particular sequence of events and actions.

In the chapter which follows a frame of reference and research design incorporating the above historical, contextual, and processual building blocks will be presented together with the detailed study questions for this research on organisational change and development in ICI.

2 Context, Culture and Politics: The Development of Strategic Change

A central conclusion of the previous chapter was that the theory and practice of change in organisations would continue to remain as circumscribed and ill-developed as it has been for as long as change is studied and thought about as episodes and projects separate from the ongoing processes of continuity and change of which those change projects are a part. The episodic, or project and programme, view of change has treated innovations as if they had a clear beginning and a clear end and divorced change not only from its antecedent conditions, but also from the more immediate and distant context which supplies the enabling conditions for the changes' birth, a framework of opportunity and constraint to guide its development and continuing legitimisation; and possibly still further conditions to bring about the demise of the change. Implicit also within this acontextual treatment of change, has been the failure to ask the kind of how and why questions about the dynamics and processes of innovation from which would emerge empirical patterns and theoretical propositions not just about change, but about the patterns and dynamics of changing. These methodological and analytical omissions and their theoretical and empirical consequences add up to rather more than a discussion of scholarly niceties; they also have had a profound impact on the practice of change. Nord (1974:567) has made this point with some eloquence: "the impotence of the modern human resource management strategies stems, at least in part, from the failure of their adherents to recognize that their own givens are the same forces which produced and continue to sustain the situation they wish to change." A major objective of this research on change in ICI is to use the available depth of contextual data, and extended sequence of longitudinal data, in order to offer a comparative analysis which provides an expanded focus on changing, which gives a central explanatory place to many of the givens in the existing research on change. Chief amongst these will be the role of business and economic factors outside the firm and historical, cultural, and political processes inside the firm, together with the interplay between those two sets of contextual variables, as providers of both the necessary and sufficient conditions for continuity and change.

The central, guiding theoretical influence on this research is the author's continuing work on organisations as systems and subsystems of political action

(Pettigrew, 1972, 1973, 1975a, b, 1977, 1979, 1980). The possibilities and limitations of change in any organisation are influenced by the history of attitudes and relationships between interest groups in and outside the firm, and by the mobilisation of support for a change within the power structure at any point in time. The impact of OD in ICI will be examined as part of an analysis which takes into account not only the beliefs and actions of internal and external OD consultants and their clients, but also the varying organisational cultures and power structures which exist in different parts of ICI, and the capacities of the OD interventions to acquire legitimacy or disfavour from associations with such cultures and political processes. The outcomes of debates about specialist or managerial-led changes in the firm are, therefore, a consequence not just of rational problem-solving processes, or of the weight of technical evidence and analysis, or even just managerial drives for efficiency and effectiveness, though on the surface the custom and practice of persuasion may dictate that initiatives for change are publicly justified in the above ways. Rather changes are also a product of processes which recognise historical and continuing struggles for power and status as motive forces, and consider which interest groups and individuals may gain and lose as proposed changes surface, receive attention, are consolidated and implemented, or fall from grace before they ever get off the ground.

Furthermore, it is important that such intraorganisational processes are not only studied comparatively through time but also with a frame of reference which recognises the enabling and constraining circumstances of changing business, political and economic contexts. Questions are asked in this research not only about how changing economic circumstances in the United Kingdom over the period 1960–83 impacted on different divisions of ICI, but also how different kinds of economic circumstances influenced the quality of relationships and balance of power between management and trade unionists, and the repercussions of changing power balances on the timing and processes of managing change. Connections will also be made between the differing levels of economic performance of the ICI divisions and the birth, evolution, impact, and development of OD groups and their activities, and ultimately on the substance and timing of strategic changes in ICI.

Finally it is recognised that organisations exist in a societal context which is itself undergoing change. The content of OD work, its techniques, language, values, and the systems of justification used to give it legitimacy have changed in ICI over the period 1965–83. Social and political commentators of various persuasions have noted the rise of optimistic, idealistic values about people and progress in Western democracies in the 1960s, and their displacement by tougher more pragmatic rationalities in the 1970s and early 1980s. An attempt will be made in this book to connect over time the processes of legitimisation and delegitimisation which have surrounded OD activities in ICI, both to reports by commentators and academics of changes in UK society, and to the perceptions of the actors in the change processes that they themselves were indeed actors in and users of a wider social and economic context.

Given the unsatisfactory way the existing literature on organisational change and development has been connected both to developments in organisation theory and analysis and to broader thinking in the social sciences this chapter will begin by placing the novel analytical approach in this research within a brief and critical review of the field of organisation theory and behaviour. The implication of connecting this work to more general trends in organisational analysis is that the historical, processual, and contextual character of this research may have something to say not only to some of the premature critics of the field of organisation theory, but also positively contribute to the general development of the field outside this particular topic of strategic organisational change and organisation development. After the necessarily brief attempt to connect this work with some general analytical trends in the field of organisation theory and behaviour, the backbone of this chapter will lay out in detail the frame of reference, levels of analysis, and study questions of the present research.

CRITICISMS OF ORGANISATION THEORY AND BEHAVIOUR

Even a cursory glance at recent academic journals and books in the linked fields of organisation behaviour and theory indicates there is a growing industry of criticism. (Benson, 1977a; Clegg and Dunkerley, 1977; Weinstein, 1979; Salaman, 1979). Some of these critics follow familiar enough paths. Thus Weinstein (1979) asserts that while covering their pronouncements and theories in the sheep's clothing of organisations as purely neutral administrative entities, most organisation theorists adopt the problems and perspectives of management as a predominant bias. Clegg and Dunkerley (1977:3) meantime attack organisation theory for its simple-minded positivism, where organisational life ends up being "analyzed, paralyzed, and reduced to a series of quantifiable variables". Roberts *et al.* (1978:136) take up and extend the positivist theme: "The continued emphasis on narrower and narrower views of responses made by individuals in organisations, concentration on individual differences to the exclusion of environmental effects, or concentration on organisational variables to the exclusion of individual differences or societal variables, will generate more precise knowledge about increasingly trivial matters". Meanwhile Crozier and Friedberg (1980:2) with true French élan criticize the cross-sectional statistical methods of American organisational sociologists, the crude attempts to develop organisational laws, the unduly deterministic nature of structural contingency theorists, and the inappropriateness of American theorising and about organisation, first of all for French conditions, and then for American organisations as well!

Now even the above collection of gratuitous swipes have their value, not just because of the kernel of truth which exists in them all, but because they represent an attempt to begin a critical tradition in organisational analysis where none has existed before. If organisation theory is to emerge from a period of self-questioning of the kind which wonders how much of value do we know about organisations after the last 20 years of research, and a feeling that while much has been written, how much is actually being said, then a period of criticism of existing theories, concepts, and methods seems appropriate and beneficial.

Of the critical approaches in evidence, two seem promising to aid the theoretical refocussing of the field. One, represented by the excellent book by Burrell and Morgan (1979), offers through its paradigmatic metaphors a way of categorising and drawing out the implicit and explicit theories in use in the field, in such a way as to reveal which parts of the range of theories have been used, overused, and abused, and which available theoretical paradigms have hardly been drawn on at all. The other emerging critical tradition is either expressed through Marx's analysis of capitalism, while not being a slave to all the categories and arguments of that analysis (Benson, 1977a, b; Burawoy, 1979), or is self-consciously Marxist in its language and statement of problematic (Salaman, 1979; Esland and Salaman, 1980).

The most succinct summary of the radical structuralist attack upon organisation theory is offered by Burrell and Morgan (1979:366–367). In summary form they list the following points:

> Functionalist theorists in general and organisation theorists in particular, have been accused of being the mere servants of the capitalist system; of being mindlessly empiricist; of neglecting the historical dimensions of their subject; of ignoring the whole body of social thought reflected in the works of Marx; of underplaying the importance of class relationships in contemporary society; of ignoring the importance of the state; and of adopting analytical models which are generally orientated towards the presentation of the status quo, as opposed to accounting for the phenomena of ongoing social change (Burrell and Morgan, 1979:365).

Burrell and Morgan (1979) acknowledge both that some scholars within *their* definition of the functionalist paradigm have criticised their colleagues on some of these grounds (cf. Silverman, 1970; Pettigrew, 1973), and that radical structuralists have not always provided a critique upon all the above grounds. Trying to be a little more specific than Burrell and Morgan (1979) it seems, for example, Burawoy (1979) concentrates his criticisms both of organisation theory and industrial sociology on their lack of historical relativism – for not restoring their timeless generalities to specific historical contexts. While Salaman (1979:7) focusses his critique on the rationalism and goal-directedness explicit in much of organisation theory, and the failure to understand that organisations are not just neutral goal-directed entities but "they also constitute the modern means of exploitation, domination, distraction, and knowledge construction". Organisations are, therefore, seen as structures of control, the mechanisms through which powerful interests pursue sectional objectives. Power within organisations can only be properly understood if related to the distribution of power outside the organisation. The inequalities of organisation reflect the inequalities of the host society.

Now this is an appealing enough statement about the validity of connecting the micro- and the macro-analysis of power – yet it would have more appeal if it could be restated and empirically examined outside the logic of this simple determinism. Salaman (1979) offers no theoretical language or logical argument of why and how societal and intraorganisational power and political processes are interrelated. Where is the discussion of processual and structural mechanisms through which power outside is connected to power inside the organisation?

Yet before using this particular example of the analysis of power relationships as a vehicle for deflating Marxist attempts to bring society back in, we should consider more seriously the role of the societal level of analysis, for it is in highlighting the importance of social and economic determinants that the Marxist theoretical position has the most to say of value for the future development of organisational analysis.

Wassenberg (1977) has argued that in spite of the contribution that the famous three (Durkheim, Marx, and Weber) have made to the analysis of organisations, and in the main through forms of conceptualisation that was sensitive to social and economic forces, organisation theory has gradually lost its analytical capacity and interest in the impact of social and economic forces on organisational functioning. Wassenberg (1977) backs up this broad statement by the pertinent observation that what better example of the isolationism of organisation theory can one find than its inability to comment on how the post-1973 economic depression affected the political and economic context of organisational functioning. A central precept within this concern with social and economic forces is the Marxian concept of totality. Transferred to the study of organisations this implies that organisations can only be understood after the total social formation which provides their *raison d'etre* is conceptualized. For some Marxian influenced scholars this puts in doubt the very existence of the organisation as a unit of analysis, although paradoxically most of the authors who would have us abandon the ontological status of the organisational level of analysis, are quite happy to continue to use the term organisation even in the title of their books (Clegg and Dunkerley, 1977, 1980).

But given the primacy of social and economic forces, what kind of novel questions and topics emerge for examination? For Clegg and Dunkerley (1980) the expressed need is to locate the analysis of organisation process within a general theory of class structure, state power, and world capitalism. For Esland and Salaman (1980:1) the agenda for analysing

> the politics of work in capitalism insists on the relationship between work structures and events, and the structure of interests and power and values in the society at large. It analyses the role of ideology in mystifying and buttressing work hierarchies and irregularities. It seeks to discover the interests that lie behind the claimed rationality and neutrality of much work-based deprivation. Most important of all, it retains and applies a sense of outrage.

So the traditional, and admittedly often bland, treatment of organisation-environment relationships within organisation theory in terms of inputs, outputs, needs, pressures, interdependencies and adaptations, is to be replaced with the vocabulary of class, interests, ideology, and the domination by state power and world capitalism. Through this language it is hoped to offer new perspectives on processes of organisational change and control, the relationships between substructural and superstructural elements of organisation, and new typologies for understanding the role of, for example, multinational corporations within the wider social formation.

This kind of macro-level problematic is both important and manifestly underutilised in thinking about organisations, and in the all-too-rare occasions it is harnessed to ethnographic studies, displays memorable analyses (Beynon, 1975; Burawoy, 1979). The problems of "critical" and "radical" organisation theory are, however, legion and many of these are traceable to the spring from which much of this thinking has emanated, the writing of Marx and his successors, developers, and protagonists. This is not the place to provide a review either of contemporary currents in Marxist theory or its potential applicability to organisational analysis; the former has been attempted recently by Burawoy (1978), and the latter by Burrell and Morgan (1979), and Clegg and Dunkerley (1980). Given, however, the central place that a broad contextual analysis incorporating economic, political, and business forces outside the firm, and conflicts and power relations within the organisation have to play in the theory of change represented in this work, some critical treatment of Marxian attempts to link superstructural and substructural elements of organisation is both relevant and necessary. This is all the more important for as we shall see many of the analytical weaknesses of radical organisation theory's attempts to deal with environment and change are also shared by two of the more recent attempts to conceptualise organisation–environment relationships found in "conventional" organisation theory. I have in mind here, the theoretical writing on organisation–environment relationships and organisation change offered by Pfeffer and Salancik (1978) and Aldrich (1979).

The Marxist theory of history, resting as it does on the derivation of social structures and conditions from the economic relations of production, has always been vulnerable both to accusations of determinism and the harsh but realistic unfolding of events. Isaiah Berlin (1974) in a brilliantly eloquent essay on historical inevitability fires so many intellectual darts into the sagging intellectual ballon of Marxist determinism that I am spoiled with choice for a quotation. Thus, while Marx has been careful to acknowledge that men and women make history, he has also been firm in stating that it is under conditions not of their own choosing. This provides Berlin (1974:169) with his springboard

> when Hegel and after him Marx, describe historical processes, they too assume that human beings and their societies are part and parcel of a wider nature, which Hegel regards as spiritual, and Marx as material, in character. Great social forces are at work of which only the acutest and most gifted individuals are ever aware . . . from time to time the real forces – impersonal and irresistable – which truly govern the world develop to a point where a new historical advance is due.

This notion of history and change behind men's backs is too much for Berlin (1974:164)

> the puppets may be conscious and identify themselves happily with the inevitable process in which they play their parts; but it remains inevitable, and they remain marionettes.[1]

However, as many scholars have noted, Marxism has long overtaken Marx, and there are now a plethora of Marxist alternatives, some of whom – for example Althusser (1969) and Bukharin (1965) – continue to assume that actions and historical events are determined fundamentally by the social formations in which they are located, while others – for example Salaman (1979) – attribute less weight to the ownership of the means of production, acknowledging in the face of empirical reality that variations occur between and within capitalist societies, regions, and even particular industrial plants.

This recognition of the variable expression of capitalist influences in differing contexts has not been picked up and analytically utilised by those scholars who explore two of the other key themes in the Marxist problematic, the role of the world system and the state, in creating hegemony. According to Wallerstein (1974), not only has capitalism pervaded the social and organisational life of Western societies, it has also become a world system, "an expressed totality, in which each nation is subordinated to and devastated by the expansion of capitalism" (Burawoy, 1978:52). The state has appeared as a macro-level variable in Marxian analysis to help to explain, or rather account for, the lack of appearance of the Marxist prognosis of the demise of capitalism and the rise of socialism. Thus when the market begins to fail under monopoly capitalism, the state appears to buttress the capitalist system (O'Connor, 1973). Appealing as the notion of a world system may be, and pertinent as state intervention may appear from observing events in many European countries in the 1960s and 1970s, the problem with such categories in Marxist analysis is the crude way they are defined and the unitary and deterministic fashion in which they are applied in analysis. Thus, the term "world system" is applied in a unitary fashion in such a way as to ignore the uneven development of capitalism, and the role of factors like nationalism in responding to and resisting the development of capitalism. One has some sympathy with Crozier and Friedberg (1980:215) when they criticise "simplistic, mechanistic, overly deterministic and rigid formulas which try to compress a whole economic or social system into a phrase".

Burawoy (1978:58) is equally adroit in pinpointing the unsatisfactory functionalism in most interventionist theories of the state. "A crisis is identified, a functional gap discovered, a contradiction revealed, and the state is invoked as the agency of restoration." Here again an abstract category is mechanically

---

[1] The Nichols and Beynon (1977) ethnographic study of "Chem. Co." has recently been roundly criticized by Willmott (1984) for portraying managers as "pliant and passive agents of capital", and thus for not being able to connect social action theoretically and empirically with a structural analysis.

harnessed to account for change. There is no theoretical discussion of the dynamics or process through which one level of analysis, the state, is linked to another, a particular capitalist class. "How is it that the state does what it is supposed to do? How does it secure and protect its relative autonomy? What are the mechanisms through which it preserves the hegemony of the dominant classes?" (Burawoy, 1978:59).

There are then two principal analytical problems in amongst the promise, afforded by current Marxist attempts to radicalise organisation theory. First of all what we may call the problem of *vertical analysis*, and second, the problem of *horizontal analysis*. The root cause of both the vertical and horizontal difficulties lies in the determinist modes of thought peculiar to both. Thus at the vertical level, the problem of relations between levels of analysis, inert, abstract, unitary categories such as world system, state, modes of economic production, are said to cause phenomena at lower levels of analysis through processes and mechanisms which are neither specified, illustrated, nor explained. Because the levels of analysis are theoretically connectable one has to assume that they have been connected. But they have not. At the horizontal level the problem is often one of a facile retreat to historicism. As Cohen (1980) argues, it cannot be naturally assumed that understanding the present has been logically solved just by an appeal to the past, and especially if the connection between past and present is condensed, as it often is in Marxist thought, into a single and one-directional historical trend. After all, if the present is capable of being seen in terms of crises, complications, conflicts, contradictions, and ambiguities why must the pathways from past to present be analysed in such unitary, linear fashion? Except if in Crozier and Friedman's terms (1980:245) "such theories are ultimately no more than rationalizations useful for giving clear consciences to those who thus commit themselves to blindness".

If Marxist attempts to radicalise or bury organisation theory by positing the ontologically prior status of society in relation to organisation in any theory of social and organisational change can be found wanting on some of the above grounds, what of the recent attempts within conventional organisation theory to posit organisation – environment relationships as part of a more general theory of organisation change? In this regard we must briefly look at the two important books by Pfeffer and Salancik (1978) and Aldrich (1979).

The incorporation of thinking about environments into organisational analysis has moved some way since early attempts by Katz and Kahn (1966) using elementary notions of inputs, throughputs, and outputs to focus attention on the open systems characteristics of organisations. The search for the next line of development after open systems analysis led to a brief and inglorious concern with grafting network analysis onto the study of interorganisational analysis (Evan, 1972; Negandhi, 1975), but the inert, actionless brand of functionalism in open systems theory, and the equally mechanical attempts to codify and measure inter-organisational relationships led nowhere. The Aldrich (1979) and Pfeffer and Salancik (1978) treatment of organisation–environment relationships are analytically very much more profound. Both books are highly contextualist in orientation, arguing that the birth and survival of organisations is highly problematic, and that survival and change can only be understood with reference to environmental characteristics and management.

Resting as it does on a population ecology, or natural selection model, the Aldrich (1979) book shares many of the problems of determinism identified in the Marxist treatment of the environment, although the links between populations of organisations and the organisation as the unit of analysis is treated in far more analytical detail by Aldrich. Although Aldrich (1979) argues for a balanced viewpoint between the importance of environmental constraints and individual choice in explaining organisational change, his treatment of change at the population level is consistently determinist. Change merely evolves from natural external conditions in the environment. This kind of analysis of change may be very powerful, of course, for as long as the analysis is kept at the macro- or population level, and for as long as the time frame of analysis is very long. But as soon as one of these conditions is relaxed, for example, taking the analysis down to the micro-level, it may be possible to trace the historical roots of change to the outcomes of past choices, and behaviours of individuals, interest groups, and organisations (Van de Ven, 1979). Such an analysis has been offered by Miles (1982) in his historical study of the strategic choices made by six major US tobacco companies as they faced the antismoking campaign. Apart from a useful discussion of market characteristics and economic concentration, there is no extended discussion in the Aldrich (1979) book of the impact of economic trends and fluctuations, or societal trends and values, on intra-organisational change processes.

The Pfeffer and Salancik (1978) book is much more avowedly action- and voluntaristic-orientated in its treatment of the relationship between organisations and their environment, and in this sense is much closer to the frame of reference being adopted in this book. Although emphasis is given to constraints in the social context, "management" is seen to have the capacity both to adjust and alter the social context surrounding the organisation and facilitate the organisation's adjustment to its context. Boundaries are placed on this capacity by a view of organisational process which recognizes the coalitional nature of management action, and the perceptual and information-processing limitations of individual actors. Thus once the organisational coalitions sort themselves out, "the organisation responds to what it perceives and believes about the world" (Pfeffer and Salancik, 1978:89).

In spite of the heavy emphasis on the language of social context in relation to environment, the actual definition of environment used in the book either concentrates on behavioural processes, or confines the environment of a local organisation largely to the activities of other organisations. Thus the Marxist critique (Salaman, 1979), that organisation theorists continue to see organisations just in terms of other organisations and not in terms of the wider social and economic context in which they are embedded, is an accusation which still sticks with the Pfeffer and Salancik (1978) treatment of environment. To be fair, though, to Pfeffer and Salancik (1978), although their definitions of environmental boundary (page 32) and levels of environment (page 63) are limited, the logic of their own approach eventually takes them, at least partially, beyond other organisations as the focal point for environmental analysis. In a chapter on the created environment they conclude that when the problems stemming from interdependence are otherwise unmanageable, or when the resources necessary to achieve coordinated action are widely dispersed, organisations will attempt to use the larger power of the political, legal, and social environment (1978:222). Except, however, for a brief but useful discussion of social legitimacy, again there is little treatment of societal trends and social values, or of economic fluctuations, as a core part of the environment of the organisation influencing broad intraorganisational processes and organisational change. Instead, organisational change is seen to be related to some of the limited conditions associated with administrative succession.

ANALYTICAL BEARINGS: LINKING CONTEXT, PROCESS, AND ORGANISATIONAL
CHANGING

The reader may recall the critical review of the literature on organisational change and development in Chapter 1 of this book highlighted that literature's ahistorical, acontextual, and aprocessual treatment of change as its principal shortcoming. Mention was also made of the relative isolation of the organis- ational change literature from developments in conventional organisation theory; although given that organisation theory has itself often been criticized for its timeless and contextless generalities, by for example, Pettigrew (1973, 1979), and Benson (1977a), perhaps the answers to the change literature's difficulties do not lie in a hasty marriage with that particular suitor. Attention was then given to some of the critical perspectives and forms of analysis in radical organisation theory, especially insofar as their treatment of "totality" and the social and economic context of organisational functioning might assist in building upon the recent writings on organisation–environment relationships and organisational change offered by Pfeffer and Salancik (1978) and Aldrich (1979). In spite of being conceived from such disparate world views, the approaches taken to conceptualise and link social and economic context and organisation in the radical literature and in the writings of Pfeffer and Salancik (1978) and Aldrich (1979) show some common problems, and it is to the isolation and attempted resolution of these through a form of contextualist analysis that I turn now.

Central to the analytical building blocks and broader theoretical and methodological contribution of this research is an attempt to specify some of the language and conditions to link the multilevel analysis and processual analysis of organisational phenomena in what may be called a holistic, contextualist analysis. In line with the language used earlier to draw out criticisms of the radical approach to organisation theory, the multilevel will be described as the vertical form of analysis and the processual the horizontal form of analysis. The vertical level refers to the interdependencies between higher or lower levels of analysis upon phenomena to be explained at some further level, for example, the impact of a changing socioeconomic context on features of intra-organisational context and interest group behaviour; while the horizontal level refers to the sequential interconnectedness between phenomena in historical, present, and future time. An approach which offers both multilevel or vertical analysis, and processual or horizontal analysis, is said to be contextualist in character. Any wholly contextualist analysis would require the following prerequisites:

1. A clearly delineated, but theoretically and empirically connectable set of levels of analysis. Within each level of analysis and, of course, depending on the focus of explanation there would be specified a set of categories or variables.
2. A clear description of the process or processes under examination. Basic to the notion of a processual analysis is that an organisation or any other social system may profitably be explored as a continuing system, with a past, a present, and a future. Sound theory must, therefore, take into account the history and future of a system and relate them to the present. The process itself is seen as a continuous, interdependent, sequence of actions and events which is being used to explain the origins, continuance, and outcome of some phenomena. At the level of the actor the language of process is most obviously characterised in terms of the verb forms, interacting, acting, reacting, responding and adapting; while at the system level, the interest is in emerging, elaborating, mobilising, continuing, changing, dissolving, and transforming. The focus is on the language systems of becoming rather than of being; of actors and systems in motion.

   Any processual analysis of this form requires as a preliminary the set of categories identified in point (1) above. Change processes can only be identified and studied against a background of structure of relative constancy. Figure needs ground.
3. The processual analysis requires a motor, or theory, or theories, to drive the process, part of which will require the specification of the model of man underlying the research. Within this research on change, strong emphasis will be given both to man's capacity and desire to adjust social conditions to meet his ends, and the part played by power relationships in the emergence and ongoing development of the processes being examined. As Martins (1974) has pointed out, this view of man contained within the means–end schema of social action theory, avoids the hard determinism identified in some of the radical structuralist perspectives on organisations. Instead of some higher level variable, for example, the world system, or state, determining some lower level phenomena; the relationship between higher and lower is now analysed through a variant of causalism in which actors play parts in bounded social processes.
4. Crucial, however, to this whole approach to contextualist analysis is the way the structural or contextual variables and categories in the vertical analysis are linked to the processes under observation in the horizontal analysis. The view taken here is that it is not sufficient to treat context either just as descriptive background, or as an eclectic list of antecedents which somehow

shape the process. Neither, of course, given the continual reference to the dangers of determinism, should structure or context be seen as just constraining process. Rather this approach recognises that processes are both constrained by structures and shape structures, either in the direction of preserving them or altering them. In the past structural analyses emphasising abstract dimensions and contextual constraints have been regarded as incompatible with processual analyses stressing action and strategic conduct. Here an attempt is being made to combine these two forms of description and analysis. First of all by conceptualising structure and context not just as a barrier to action but as essentially involved in its production (Giddens, 1979; Ransom *et al.*, 1980), and second, by demonstrating how aspects of structure and context are mobilized or activated by actors and groups as they seek to obtain outcomes important to them.

In this analytical approach to understand the origins, development, and implementation of organisational change, the interest, therefore, is in multilevel theory construction. An attempt will be made to formulate models of higher-level factors and processes, lower-level factors and processes, and the manner in which they interact. It is recognised that each level often has its own properties, processes, and relationships – its own momentum, and that while phenomena at one level are not reducible to or cannot be inferred from those at another level, a key to the analysis is tracking the interactions between levels through time. The interest is both in catching reality in flight, and in embeddedness – a return to context as a principle or method. Seeing historical processes of change as a complex dynamic system with a mixture of processes occurring at different levels and at various rates. It is in the dialogue between trends and forces in a multilevel and changing context, and the relationships, actions, and initiatives between groups and individuals seeking to adjust social conditions to meet their ends, that much organisational change – it origins, mechanisms, and forms – can be located and understood.

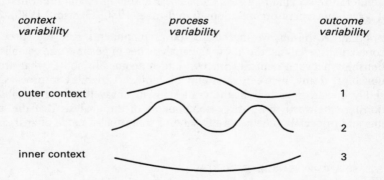

FIGURE 1   Components of analysis: context and process

The above represent some broad principles informing a contextualist analysis of process. But how might those principles be translated into a series of practical components to inform data collection and analysis in any particular study? Figure 1 lays out in highly simplified diagrammatic form a possible series of interlinked components in a contextualist analysis. The figure indicates there are three basic elements to a contextualist analysis; the process component, the context component, and the outcome component of the process under investigation. In terms of the practical research questions of gathering data, and sorting that data into broad categories for analysis, the basic steps may be described as follows:

1. Describe the process or processes under investigation, which, for example, may be processes of conflict, decision-making, or changing.
2. Expose in the above descriptions any variability or constancy between the processes. This variability is, of course, represented in Figure 1 by the different curved lines.
3. Begin the analysis of the above processes by using existing, or developing novel, theories of process.
4. Begin the task of pinpointing the levels of analysis in the context, and some of the categories or variables in those different levels of analysis. Are, for example the levels in the context to be restricted to features of the intra-organisation context through which the processes immediately flow, or is the analysis to include aspects of the outer context such as the social and economic conditions surrounding the organisation at any point in time?
5. Having established the levels of analysis and categories in the context, begin the task of describing and analysing any variability across the contexts through which the processes are unfolding. Seek also to describe and analyse trends and developments in the various contexts through time.
6. Begin to consider the alternative criteria which can be used to judge the outcome of the process under study. This is a difficult practical research problem. Good sources to assist reflection in this problem are contained in the literature seeking to assess the success and failure, and other outcomes of social movement organisations (Goldstone, 1980; Gamson, 1980).

Important as the uncovering of the above components is to the success of the contextualist analysis, the key to the analysis lies in positing and establishing relationships between context, process, and outcome. In short, what are the relationships, if any, between variability in context, variability in process, and variability in outcome? It is in the craft skills in unravelling and establishing relationships between those three components of the analysis that the major benefits and principal problems of this kind of contextualist mode of analysis lie.

DATA BASE AND RESEARCH QUESTIONS

The setting in which any piece of empirical research is conducted, and the chosen research strategy, have a major impact on the empirical patterns which are identifiable, the frame of reference chosen to identify and analyse such empirical threads, and the nature of the theoretical developments and policy implications which follow. This research on organisational change and development has benefited enormously from being conducted in ICI. For a complex set of reasons related to its business, technological, manpower, social, and historical environment, ICI has been a pioneer in the use of OD concepts, values, and techniques in the United Kingdom. Along with a few other large British firms, many influenced initially by North American practitioners, they have helped to diffuse the techniques and precepts of OD to other UK business and public sector organisations. The research access provided in ICI, therefore, represents a unique opportunity to study the processes of initiating and implementing changes in managerial style and productivity, organisation structure and culture, union–management relationships, technological change and business strategy, in a large organisation at the forefront of attempts to make such changes happen.

An important and unusual feature of the research strategy has been the collection of comparative and longitudinal data. Interview and documentary material are available from four divisions and the head office of the company over the period 1960–83. Unique access has been provided to one of Britain's largest companies in order to ask some questions of fundamental and general interest about how corporations of this scale and size are able to build within themselves the capacity for adaptation and change in the increasingly complex and turbulent business, economic, political, and organisational conditions of the 1960s, 1970s, and early 1980s. A particular vehicle ICI has used throughout much of this period in order to stimulate organisational change has been the skills and knowledge of internal and external OD consultants. The experience of using such consultancy assistance in a variety of different organisational settings, on a number of different problems, throughout an extended period of time, will allow this book to explore the alternative strategies which exist for creating innovation in large systems. This research is also interested in the variety of ways of structuring and building innovative groups, and the factors crucial to their legitimacy and credibility through time; as well as how internal consultancy resources can be linked both with external sources of help, and to line managers who may themselves be developing initiatives and skills as managers of change.

Given the expressed interest in exploring the processual dynamics of changing in alternative contexts, attention will also be focused on the ethnography of change. What actually happens in a large organisation during periods of change? Where do ideas for change come from? Who supports the change agents, and why, and who are the opponents and doubters of change, and why? How do those interested in change attempt to get their ideas across, and what are the counter tactics of their detractors, and what impact to different organisational power systems and cultures play in such processes? In short, what are the dynamics of the process which leave one idea for change in the organisational sidings, another completely derailed, and a further one well on its way to implementation?

Looking beyond the fate of particular change episodes; and even the birth, evolution, development, and impact of groups of OD consultants within the various divisions of ICI; this book will also analyse the processes of trying to create strategic change at both the corporate and the divisional level in ICI. Here I will be addressing the most complicated and difficult questions of the study, and with due temerity will draw on not only an extensive data base of information inside and outside the company, but also the contextualist form of explanation outlined in detail earlier in this chapter. Continuity and change will be accounted for through a complex interplay of external and internal factors. Crucial amongst these will be the perceptions and leadership skills of chief executives; the enabling and constraining influences of social, economic and political change; constructed and real organisational crises; the established power structures and cultural systems in various parts of the company; the activities of interest groups inside and outside the firm and, of course, the always limited, but at times pertinent and effective role played by internal and external OD consultants.

Sources of data

Most of the data used to provide answers to the above broad questions are derived either from long semistructured interviews of company documents. The majority of the interviewing was done in late 1975, 1976, and early 1977, the latter parts of 1980 and early 1981, and again in 1982. However, these batches of interviews were also supplemented with intermittent but continuous contact with various parts of ICI from 1975 until early 1982. Some of this contact was of a straightforwardly research character, keeping the evolving story up to date and filling in gaps in the data; other interventions into the company were as a consultant. This continuous real-time data collection was enriched by retrospective interviewing and archival analysis which allowed me to go back to 1965, the date chosen to approximate the beginning of OD work in the company.

This kind of retrospective and real-time analysis of social and organisational processes presents its share of advantages, disadvantages, and threats to reliability and validity. Some of these problems and the craft skills to try and deal with them are discussed in detail in earlier historical work by the author (Pettigrew, 1973, 1979). The process of compiling the semistructured interview schedule and choosing and sequencing the interviews was similar in all the research sites. Relevant theoretical and empirical work, plus long conversations with a small group of people in ICI, were used to build up a very open and flexible set of themes and questions. These themes and questions provided the basis for an early set of individual interviews with a group of internal OD consultants, relevant external consultants, clients of these OD consultants, and people designated as power figures, at times on both the management and trade union side, in each of the five major research locations. From these early open-ended interviews a chronology of events and a further list of key personalities was identified, and a slightly more structured interview schedule prepared.

Further interviews were completed with an additional set of internal and external consultants and past and present clients, together with a group of people identified from the initial interviews as supporters, doubters, and opponents of OD. Care was taken to ensure that these interviews covered people in roles at various hierarchical levels in the company, from main board director and division director, to supervisor, and also to include individuals from different functions and business areas. Where the changes involved management–trade union issues, efforts were made to acquire the perspective of the OD consultants, management representatives, and shop stewards.

Over the period 1975 to 1983 134 people were interviewed from the ICI corporate headquarters and the 4 divisions under study. However, some of these individuals were interviewed on a number of occasions and the total number of interviews for the research amounted to 175. Interestingly, of the 134 people interviewed only one refused to have his interview taperecorded. In total the interviews produced something in the order of 500 hours of tape-recorded information for analysis. The taperecorded interviews were either completely transcribed for analysis or coded directly onto 8 by 5 inch cards around predetermined and emergent categories. Data were also collected in informal conversations on journeys, over a beer, or a meal. Periods of observation in factory and office were also possible.

Various individuals in ICI have been generous in giving me access to archival material. These documents include materials on company strategy and personnel policy, documents relating to the birth and development of the various company OD groups, files documenting the natural history of key organisational changes, and information on the recruitment and training of internal OD consultants, and the use made of external OD consultants. These archival materials have provided valuable information in their own right, as well as cross-validation for statements made in interviews and conversations.

THE POLITICAL AND CULTURAL PERSPECTIVE ON ORGANISATIONAL PROCESS

In Chapter 1 the requirement both to review elements of the literature on strategic choice and change and to begin to alert the reader to the importance of the processual analysis of change, led to a brief description and commentary on the so-called rational, boundedly rational, incremental, and garbage can perspectives on organisational process. Also in the first Chaper, I issued a warning to the reader and myself – beware of the singular theory of choice and change. Behind this warning was the obvious desire to avoid premature theoretical ethnocentrism, expecially as I have shown the analyst of process does actually have a choice of perspective, if not theories, available. Thinking of how conceptual and empirical developments in the study of strategic choice and change could take place there are obviously a number of alternative strategies even within the process type of research favoured here. One approach is to discount ethnocentrism and pursue and refine any particular process theory, if I can be forgiven another metaphor – clip on a single powerful lamp onto the miner's helmet and take that down into the data mine. A second strategy is to be ostensibly a more reasonable man, and go into the mine lights ablaze, looking from many perspectives of process, and hope to see and explain without being blinded by all the distractions and reflections. A third strategy is to keep in mind the different process theories, and work towards making contingent statements of, for example, where and when the different theories of process may be more or less appropriate. This strategy, of course, is already bearing some fruit, with incremental theories perhaps fitting easily alongside programmed or repetitive budgetary decisions (Davis *et al.*, 1966); political process theories seeming to be compatible with the complexity and uncertainty of innovative decisions (Pettigrew, 1973); and garbage can approaches fitting the anarchistic loosely coupled character of educational organisations (March and Olsen, 1976; Weick, 1976). A fourth strategy, and the one favoured here, is to try and develop not only a more unified theoretical analysis, by in this case combining political and cultural views of process, but also by clarifying a methodological approach to process analysis – labelled here as contextualism, which seeks to engage a process analysis of action with features of intra-organisational and social, economic, and political context. This section of the chapter briefly tries to present a unified view of political and cultural analysis as they can be applied to strategic choice and change, and the following section discusses some of the major study questions of this research.

The frame of reference used to inform this research is a continuation and development of the author's previous work on organisations as political systems (Pettigrew, 1972, 1973, 1977), and the politics of organisational change (1975a, 1980). Considering the organisation as a political system directs attention towards the factors which facilitate and hinder change and to the reasons why political energy is often released within the firm at even the prospect, never mind the reality, of change. Political processes within the firm evolve at the group level from the division of work in the organisation, and at the individual level from associated career, reward, and status systems. Interest groups form in organisations around the particular objectives, responsibilities, and intentions of functions or business areas, they also form around differences between groups at varying hierarchical levels, or around collectivities such as newcomers or old timers, or progressives and conservatives. Interest groups may also form around the issues of the day; whether to grow or not to grow; to diversify or not to diversify; to bring in new technology, or to continue to use old methods and procedures. Indeed a key part of the political process of the firm may have to do with which issues become a focus of individual or group interest and attention and move onto the stage of decision-making, and which issues are suppressed or otherwise immobilized and left in the wings, waiting for changes in the power balance of the firm and/or environmental adjustments to redirect the attention of organisational participants.

These interest groups are likely to have different goals, time orientations, values and problem-solving styles. In short, they may have different *rationalities*, which provide the motive forces for their actions and reactions, along with the language and styles of behaviour to express those actions. As the author has argued elsewhere (Pettigrew 1977), strategy formulation and change processes in organisations may be understood in part as the outcome of processes of competition between these rationalities expressed through the language, priorities, and values of technologists; of accounting and finance – the bottom line; or of the rather more diffuse perspectives adopted by specialist groups from planning, operational research, organisational development, or personnel.

Given the present interest in time and social process, and contextual analysis, the clear implication is that such interest group relationships are neither set in concrete, nor is their development bounded just by intra-organisational forces. While at any point in time an organisation may be dominated by a particular rationality – expressed perhaps through the interests and power positions of scientists or technologists, or finance or marketing groups, that dominance is always subject to intra-organisational and environmental changes. The micro-politics of the firm are inextricably linked to the macro-politics of the firm. Nowhere is this more clearly expressed at the moment than in tracing through how the economic policies of the Thatcher and Reagan governments are altering the resource base of many public organisations in the UK and USA and releasing new waves of micro- and macro-organisational politics.

While the concern for organisational resources is likely to be a continuing feature of organisational life, and may be expressed differently in one organisation than another, politics in organisations breed in times of change. The point about organisational changes is that to a greater or lesser degree they are likely to threaten the existing distribution of organisational resources as they are represented in salaries, promotion opportunities, and control of tasks, people, information, and new areas of a business. Additional resources may be created and appear to fall within the jurisdiction of a group or individual who had previously not been a claimant in a particular area. This group or its principal representative may see this as an opportunity to increase his power, status and rewards in the organisation. Others may see their interests threatened by the change, and needs for security or the maintenance of power may provide the impetus for resistance. In all these ways new political energy is released, and ultimately the existing distribution of power endangered.

These processes are likely to receive their more volatile expression not, as is often imagined, at the implementation of changes but during the decision to go ahead with the change (Mumford and Pettigrew, 1975). Constraints are set during the decision stage which can make resistance and manoeuvre at later stages of the change mere ritualistic gestures. The issue, therefore, is less one of where and when is political energy likely to be released than one of to what extent will it be released within the change process. Amongst other factors influencing the extent of political behaviour will be how aware individuals and groups become about resources during early discussions of the change, the actual objective redistributions of resources consequent on the change, the criticalness of the change to any group, and that group's capacity to mobilise power to protect its interests.

There is, of course, a considerable difference between awareness by an interest group of the impact of change on their position and their ability to translate that heightened awareness into effective action. Consciousness of the implications of a change may have to be tied not only to the awareness that the interest group has of its potential power resources, but also to the tactical manner with which those resources are used in negotiating the parameters of, and processes of implementation of, change. It has been suggested elsewhere that the power resources of expertise, control over information, political access and sensitivity, assessed stature and group support may be of considerable importance in making and preventing changes from happening (Pettigrew, 1975b).

More recently (Pettigrew, 1977, 1979) this resource view of power and political process has been complemented with another perspective on organisations which seeks to draw out the synergy between a political and a cultural analysis of organisational life. The acts and processes associated with *politics as the management of meaning* represent conceptually the overlap between a concern with the political and cultural analyses of organisations. A central concept linking political and cultural analysis is legitimacy. The management of meaning refers to a process of symbol construction and value use designed both to create legitimacy for one's actions, ideas and demands, and to delegitimise the demands of one's opponents. Key concepts for analysing these processes of legitimisation and delegitimisation are symbolism, language, belief, and myth.

In the pursuit of our everyday tasks and objectives it is all too easy to forget the less rational and instrumental, the more expressive social tissue around us that gives those tasks meaning. Yet in order for people to function within any given setting, they must have a continuing sense of what that reality is all about in order to be acted upon. Culture is the system of such publicly and collectively accepted meanings operating for a given group at a given time. This system of terms, forms, categories and images interprets a people's own situation to themselves. Indeed what is supposed to be distinctive about man compared with other animals is his capacity to invent and communicate determinants of his own behaviour (White, 1949; Cassirer, 1953). While providing a general sense of orientation, culture treated as a unitary concept in this way lacks analytical bite. A more useful approach is to regard culture as the source of a family of concepts and to explore the role that symbolism, language, belief, and myth play in creating practical effects.

Language provides order and coherence, cause–effect relationship – rationales, in times of confusion and transition. Contextually appropriate words may be used to give legitimacy to faded causes and new ideas, or to breathe life back into established practices which are under threat. In a competitive situation there is clearly a point where ideas for change may become unsupportable, and the issue becomes not one of mobilising power for the pre-existing idea but seeing how the idea can be modified and connected to rising values and environmental priorities, so its power requirements can be assembled. Metaphors and myths help to simplify – to give meaning to complex issues that evoke concern. Myths serve also to legitimate the present in terms of a perhaps glorious past, and to explain away the pressures for change which may exist from the discrepancies between what is happening and what ought to be happening. In these various ways it may be possible for interest groups to justify continuity in the face of change, and change in the face of attempts to preserve continuity.

One of the logical problems that the political and cultural view of process potentially at least shares with other process theories, is the difficulty of demonstrating that the process does in fact produce the observed outcome. In some cases, for example, maximising and satisficing explanations, no process information is actually offered. The reader is merely expected to accept that outcomes have been produced as a result of 'black box' notions such as maximising and satisficing. Political explanations of outcomes can likewise end up as tautologies if, for example, it is merely inferred that the possession of a power resource such as wealth means that some individual or group is powerful. A more satisfactory explanation would in this case have to demonstrate how the possession and tactical use of some resource, for example wealth, was connected to the achievement of some practical outcome. The challenge with the political and cultural view of process is, however, much greater for here what is being proposed is not just a framework to examine front-stage decision-making and power, but also of back-stage decision-making and therefore control. The front-stage view of decision-making and power, closely resembles Lukes' (1974) one-dimensional and two-dimensional views of power, while the interest in deeper processes of control conforms to Lukes' third dimension of power. As Hardy (1983) has succinctly put it, a concern with both power and control as explanations of, in this case, choice and change process, would in effect correspond to two uses of power: power used to defeat competition in a choice or change process and power used to prevent competition in a choice or change process. In both of these processes there would be an explanatory role for unobtrusive systems of power derived from the generation and manipulation of symbols, language, belief and ideology – from culture creation; and from the more public face of power expressed through the possession, control and tactical use of overt sources of power such as position, force, or expertise.

There are two further essential points to derive from the above way of thinking about process. The first is that structures, cultures, and strategies are not just being treated here as neutral, functional constructs connectable to some system need such as efficiency or adaptability, those constructs are viewed as capable of serving to protect the interests of dominant groups. This means that not only can the existing bias of the structures and cultures of an organisation in general terms protect dominant groups by reducing the chances of challenge, but features of intra-organisational context and socioeconomic context can be mobilised by dominant or aspiring groups in order to legitimise existing definitions of the core strategic conerns, to help justify new priorities, and to delegitimise other novel and threatening definitions of the organisations situation. These points, as we shall see, are as pertinent to understanding processes of choice and change as they are to achieving practical outcomes in strategic change. As Normann (1977:161) has so aptly put it, "the only way to bring about lasting change and to foster an ability to deal with new situations is by influencing the conditions that determine the interpretation of situations and the regulation of ideas".

The above political and cultural view of process gives a central place to the processes through which strategies and changes are legitimized and delegitimized. The content of strategy, the other leg of our three-legged stool of content, context, and process, thus is ultimately a product of a legitimisation process shaped by political/cultural considerations, and expressed in rational/analytical terms.

THE LEVELS OF ANALYSIS AND PARTICULAR STUDY QUESTIONS

Having established the important role of political and cultural concepts in this analysis of organisational changing, the remaining task in this chapter is to specify the form of contextual and processual analysis and particular study questions used to explore both the evolution and impact of organisation development groups in ICI and the overall process of continuity and change in ICI. Given the earlier critical comments on the acontextual, ahistorical, and aprocessual character of much research on organisational change, together with the field's tendency to use the change programme or episode as the unit of analysis, this research offers a different approach. The focal point of analysis and explanation here is the birth, evolution, development and impact of five OD groups born into and therefore faced with different antecedent conditions, varying organisational contexts, and living through changing social and economic conditions. Principally I shall be seeking to describe and explain the varying impact each group had in facilitating and inhibiting organisational changes in each of their arenas of action, and the natural history of each group's emergence, development, and fate. Simply stated there is the requirement to explain why by 1983, through different pathways, and after varying life histories and effects, two of these divisional OD groups had ceased to exist, while the head office OD activities and the other divisional OD activities continued in 1983, if not quite in the same size and form as they had emerged in the late 1960s.

The study questions and methodology have been chosen to generate conceptual frameworks and comparative empirical findings rather than to test a *priori* formulations. The research will probe into three levels of analysis and their interconnections. The expectation is that each of these levels will reveal significant data about the birth, growth, decline, consolidation, and demise of OD at various points in time.

The first and focal level of analysis is the *group level*, and here the subject matter is the overlap between two intersecting areas. For the most part at the group level the study is interested in the development and fate of a particular population, the OD groups in the four divisions and head office of ICI. At this group level, however, I am also interested in the activities of OD, for as we shall see in some contexts the population of OD consultants ceased to exist and the continuation of OD was left to other consultants or line managers.

An innovating group such as an OD department more often than not represents the antiroutine aspect of organisation functioning and its members can project and be seen as an insubordinate minority. A group advocating change from a specialist, advisory base is likely to be abnormal rather than normal, extraordinary rather than routine, illegitimate rather than legitimate, marginal rather than central, and powerless rather than powerful. Its activities and resource base have to be justified, its members have to generate credibility in particular and varying contexts, and success, failure, and survival is often a question of the vagaries of the last project or activity. This is the position from which an OD group concerned with change ordinarily begins its struggle for impact.

The study is interested in the antecedent conditions which led to the emergence of the five groups and the form and nature of the birth processes themselves. Why, when, and how did they emerge, and what role did contextual and precipitating factors play in their genesis? What were the backgrounds, aspirations and values of the early group members and what structural form did the innovating group take? Did it take the option of a distinct and separate functional unit on the organisation chart, a temporary task force, a like-minded group of individuals forming a voluntary association, or an adjuct to an existing functional unit, or some combination of these? Who were the early leaders of such groups and how did they tackle what Gusfield (1957) has described as the mobilization and articulation functions of leadership – the concern with building and reaffirming goals, values and commitment inside the group, and linking the group and its tactics to its host environment? Did each group have a strategy and tactics for managing its internal dynamics and external boundaries or did the groups through a combination of unselfconscious and non-reflective action merely adopt a behavioural and ideological *stance* to other interest groups in their environment? How did each group acquire its resources, choose its activities, exercise influence, secure its boundary, and build networks of relationships?

Clearly factors explaining origins do not necessarily explain continuance, indeed early patterns of emergence and development may load the dice in constraining future lines of development. I am interested in describing and analysing in a comparative mode a continuous process. Each of the groups in their different ways persisted through varying time periods in the course of which they mobilized resources, applied them in various forms of activity, through a mixture of tactics, and experienced the consequences and implications of those behaviours in a fully interrelated process that also affected subsequent episodes of action and outcome.

The processual analysis implied in the above questions at the group level of analysis cannot be adequately carried out without reference to the immediate and more distant context within which each OD group had to make its way. The more immediate context, the second level of analysis in the study, is described as the *inner context*. Here the interest ranges from the auspicious or inauspicious antecedent conditions and context each group was born into, to the evolution and selective impact of that context, both in the enabling and constraining senses as each OD group itself developed through time. Particular features of the inner context of each group examined are company and divisional organisational cultures (Pettigrew, 1979), their norms, power distributions and recurring conflicts (Pettigrew, 1973, 1975b), the social control and other attitudes and behaviours directed toward each group by key figures and interest groups in their environment, and the relationship between these factors and the organisational impact and survival of the OD groups.

Given the change objectives of most OD groups and their, at times, consequent insubordinate and deviant stance, the social control activities of their doubters and opponents is an important issue, as of course, is the tolerance and inattentiveness of those doubters and opponents. Social control tactics expressed through subtle processes of characterisation or labelling, and through more tangible practices such as recruitment strategies, withdrawing resources or terminating activities or groups, may determine how far, how fast, and in what form and direction a group or activity develops; the success a group has in generating a network of clients and supporters, and in the tactics and natural history of a group's development. Following the important role attached to politics as the management of meaning in the broad frame of reference for this research a highly action-oriented and interactionist concept of social control processes is intended here. Control agents are not assumed to be representing a highly unified and clear-cut normative system to which others must comply; rather control is seen as a political process of meaning construction and definition in which parties fashion and negotiate how actions and values represent themselves in the identity of relevant others, in order to control, or escape the possibility of control.

The other feature of group context relevant to explaining both the overall pattern of continuity and change in ICI between 1960 and 1983 and the impact and fate of the five OD groups is the *outer context* level of analysis. This is the third level of analysis in the study, the one most novel to the analysis of organisational change and analysis, and the one most difficult empirically and theoretically to handle. The outer context level of analysis refers to the economic performance and competitiveness of ICI as a whole and to each division under study throughout the period 1960–83. In addition, this level refers to corporate and divisional policy in the manpower and personnel spheres over the past two decades. Also included here are the relevance of broad social and economic trends in UK society throughout the 1960s, 1970s, and early 1980s both to the business fortunes and broad personnel policies of ICI, but also to the emergence and changing use made of OD consultants, their techniques, knowledge and skills.

Important as alternative structural forms, leader behaviour and effectiveness, strategies, tactics and cycles of activity and outcome are to group development, this research also emphasises the crucial role that larger social and economic trends play in providing enabling conditions, and sealing the fate of some of our

OD groups and their activities. An important value of these levels of analysis is that each has something of an evolving life of its own which presents constraints and opportunities to the other levels. In line with my earlier strictures about contextualism as a form of analysis, context is neither treated just as descriptive background nor used to drive a simple determinist explanation. Contexts of an auspicious or non-receptive kind to OD activities may derive from environmental change; the accidents and events of intragroup development; or environmental circumstances; they may also be products of the social constructions of men seeking to adjust and label social conditions to meet their ends.

An advisory group interested in creating change must itself create a social context in which it can survive and prosper. A key part of the politics of organisational change reported in this book relates to the legitimisation strategies of the OD groups and the delegitimisation strategies of their doubters and opponents. These legitimisation strategies represent a crucial link between the group level of analysis and the inner and outer context levels of analysis. Here the role of information and perception in political processes are crucial (Pettigrew, 1973). He who understands the political and cultural system of his organisation and the impact of changing economic and social trends on the emergence and dissolution of old issues, values and priorities, and the rise of new rationalities and priorities, is at least beyond the starting gate in formulating, packaging, and influencing the direction of organisational change. Context is then treated as something which must not only be understood, but mobilised to create practical effects. The extent to which the OD groups in ICI understood this part of the politics of creating change, and their skill in using this understanding, is a focal point for this investigation.

Before launching the empirical part of this book with a synopsis of the key points in ICI's historical and business development, and a review of social and economic trends in Britain throughout the past two decades, there is one intractable issue to be mentioned which will follow us throughout the book. I have in mind the question of what constitutes success and failure for an OD group? I take some comfort for the difficulties in handling this issue from the fact that in the literature on social movement organisations where there is also a question of movement outcome and assessing success and failure, after 20 years or more of research the debate continues as hotly as ever (Goldstone, 1980; Gamson, 1980).

Superficially, at least, the problem seems simple enough. The three OD groups that survive in 1983 may be construed as successes, whilst the two that no longer exist can be deemed failures. But under certain conditions, perhaps the inattentiveness of key organisational figures caused either by indifference and/or plentiful resources, a group of OD consultants may survive for long periods without achieving much legitimacy for their activities and goals or much credibility for themselves as individuals. Groups of specialists may also be able to survive, if not flourish, for periods of time by adopting a highly passive interpretation of their role – keeping their heads down, not forcing any controversial issues, becoming relatively inclusive figures in their organisation. Meanwhile a group with a relatively short life might have achieved a great deal of change, either by diagnosing and carrying through the particular change it was set up by power figures to accomplish and then being disbanded – or indeed forcing upopular change through so hard that it sacrificed its legitimacy and credibility in the short run, yet in retrospect achieved change beneficial to the organisation.

Another kind of success may occur when a group either disappears, or is reduced in scale, yet the activities, skills and knowledge which it embodies are perpetuated either by individual internal and external consultants and line managers or by former consultants drafted into more acceptable specialist positions. Indeed the most complete kind of success may exist when a group's skills and knowledge are so institutionalised into the host culture that the consultancy group can either fade away completely or just leave a few super-professionals around to update on developments in the field and continue to transmit the new ideas to line managers as the change agents.

There is, of course, a further problem of what Gamson (1980:1050) labels pseudo-success. A group realises changes only for those changes to appear later empty of meaning; or a group tagging on with another group with similar objectives in order to achieve success. Equally well, a group's environment may change so auspiciously towards its objectives that the group achieves them almost in spite of itself.

Finally, there is the question of whose concept of success and failure does the analyst take, and when does he ask the question? Recognising that the evaluation of any organisational group and activity is as embedded in the political processes of the organisation as the activity is itself, suggests that the analyst has to scrutinise with care the stated attitudes and underlying perspectives of each of the interested parties, and to let the data speak for themselves through as many channels and contexts, and over as long a period of time as possible.

It should be clear that the above way of analysing the birth, evolution, fate, and impact of specialist OD resources on organisational change as a continuous process in context, can also be applied to the exploration of the cases of strategic change in this research. As I argued in Chapter 1 the starting point for this analysis of the how of strategic change is the notion that finding and clarifying the content of any strategic change crucially entails managing its context and process. Given the importance of unravelling the relationship over time between the content of strategic change and its context through a processual analysis, then strategic changes are best analysed not by treating them as discrete episodes or programmes, but by seeing them as continuous processes. The cases of strategic change in this book illustrate the deep-seated organisational cultural and political roots of strategy, and the existence of dominating rationalities or ideologies inside organisations which provide the frame of reference by which individuals and groups attach meaning, make sense of intra-organisational and business and economic trends developing around them. This research points to the enormous difficulties of breaking down such dominating ideologies once a particular marriage of strategic content, context, and process has become established. The breaking down of established patterns of strategic content, context, and process is seen as a long-term conditioning and learning process influenced by the interest and above all persistence of visionary leaders, the changing patterns of competition between individuals and groups representing and projecting different ideologies, the massive enabling opportunities created by business and economic change, changes in the power distribution of the company, and the connecting of what are perceived to be coherent solutions at particular points in time to culturally legitimate problems. The what, the why, and the how of creating strategic change through such long-term conditioning and learning processes constitute the central analytical and practical message of this book about the management of strategic change in large organisations.

3 ICI In Its Changing Business and Economic Context

Any attempt made to examine ICI's efforts to change their strategy, structure, technology, organisational culture, and the quality of union–management relationships over the period 1960–83 has to recognise the significant changes in economic, business, and political context which have taken place over that period.

For large sections of the chemical industry in Western industrialised countries the 1950s and 1960s will probably be looked back on as the great era of capital expansion, sales growth, and dramatic increase in plant size. This growth period, based substantially on product and process discoveries in plastics and fibres, nurtured an ethos of optimism and expansion in the chemical industry. Unfortunately this enthusiasm fostered slow responses to the sudden and continued escalation of the price of oil triggered by the events of 1973; thus by 1980 much of the Western heavy chemicals industry was no longer talking of growth, but of maturity, contraction, and survival. The combination of large increases in energy costs, declining rates of economic growth, persistent inflation, and in the 1970s a large increase in the number of heavy chemical producers in Western Europe, all contributed to the falling away of prices and margins in the petrochemicals and plastics sectors, and eventually for some countries and firms more than others, the response of cutting out excess capacity and manpower.

In the main the UK chemical industry, followed the general pattern of 1950s and 1960s growth, 1970s falling away of growth, and 1980s contraction of the heavy chemicals sector. There is evidence, however, that during the 1950s and 1960s the UK chemical industry grew less substantially than its United States, German and French competitors, experienced a more pronounced decline in growth in the 1970s, and in the 1980s for jointly economic, political, and business reasons has been more active in reducing capacity and manpower than some of its Western European counterparts. The relatively poorer performance of the UK chemical industry compared with its North American and Continental Western European competitors is normally attributed to the weaker performance of the UK economy throughout the 1960s and especially the 1970s. Key UK economic indicators reflecting this poorer record include: lower growth rate of the economy; the relatively high rates of inflation, the accelerating wage demands and settlements made in the UK during the 1970s, the worsening competitive position of the UK chemical industry associated with the high interest rates and strong value of sterling in the period 1979–82, and the deeper recession of the UK economy between

1979 and 1984. These weaknesses in the pattern of demand and inflation in the UK economy from the late 1960s onwards are factors behind one of ICI's major strategic responses of the 1960s and 1970s, the intention to increase the proportion of the company's assets and sales in the faster-growing economic environments of Continental Western Europe and North America.

Given that the context for ICI's strategic and operational responses over the last two decades includes, amongst other elements, trends in the development of the world and UK chemical industries, and macro-economic and political developments in the UK, this chapter seeks to place ICI's own development in the context of those economic, industry, and political trends. Clearly whole books have been written on recent trends in the world and UK chemical industries and political and economic events and trends in the UK, thus the review that follows has to be highly selective in its treatment of such a vast subject-matter. The selectivity which does occur is guided by an attempt to highlight business and economic trends with particular significance for ICI's place in the UK and international chemical industry. The chapter begins with a section outlining general trends and characteristics of the world chemical industry since the 1950s. With the scene broadly set, the next part of the chapter reviews the development of the UK chemical industry over the period from the mid-1950s until 1983. The UK chemical industry is compared and contrasted with the pattern of development of some of its major counterparts in North America and Europe, and the differences which exist are connected to macro-economic developments in the UK over the past 2½ decades. The chapter ends with a necessarily brief answer to the question what is ICI? In addition to a summary description of ICI's business history and development over the last 20 years, including its size, structure, and relative business performance, the final section of the chapter also highlights some of the major corporate business strategies ICI have pursued since the 1960s in the light of changes in their economic, industrial and business environment.

TRENDS AND CHARACTERISTICS OF THE CHEMICAL INDUSTRY

Inevitably definitional questions arise when trying to compile meaningful time series analyses of what has been happening to the chemical industry over a 20- or 30-year period. A particular statistical difficulty is that for most of the 1960s production, sales, and employment statistics were compiled according to the 1958 edition of the Standard Industrial Classification (SIC), and the data for the 1970s and 1980s have been compiled from the revised 1968 edition of the SIC. A similar change in the pattern of compiling trade statistics for the chemical industry has resulted from a revision of the Standard International Trade Classification. Nevertheless, in the main the use of the term chemical industry in this book can be taken to mean the chemicals and allied industries, or the whole of Order V in the 1968 edition of the SIC. Thus the chemical and allied industries sector embraces a wide field of manufacturing activity and products, including paints, petrochemicals, plastics, fertilisers, pharmaceuticals, pesticides, dyestuffs, industrial chemicals, intermediates for synthetic textile fibre production, detergents, soaps, disinfectants, explosives, and polishes, cosmetics, and toiletries.

By way of summary, key trends and characteristics of the chemical industry can be pinpointed under the following headings:

1. Size, pervasiveness, and criticality
2. Rapid growth
3. Capital intensity and scale of production
4. High research and development expenditure
5. International trade and competition
6. Subject to cyclical economic effects
7. Recent hard times in the heavy chemicals sector

Size, pervasiveness, and criticality

The chemical industry has been described as dynamic, innovative, and highly competitive – it is also large. In 1981 the chemical industry represented 7% of world GNP (Sharp and West, 1982:15). The chemical industry in 1980 had a turnover of some $550 billion in the non-communist world compared with $200 billion for steel, $80 billion for telecommunications, and $40 billion for aircraft. In 1976 in terms of value added the chemical industry ranked third among manufacturing industries both in the USA and the UK (Wittcoff and Reuben, 1980:17). International trade in chemicals is sizeable, and significant to national economies. For example, chemicals alone accounted for $138 billion of all OECD exports and $103 billion of OECD imports in 1980 (Nichols and Crawford, 1983).

The chemical industry is also an enabling industry. Davies (1982:41) argues that although the chemical industry in Western countries accounts for no more than 3–4% of GNP and employs under 1% of the work force, it has a strategic impact on perhaps 40% of the economies of those countries. The chemical industry is thus closely interlocked directly and indirectly with other industry sectors such as textiles, cars, health, agriculture, housing, and consumer durables, and if the general economic climate is good, then major sectors of the chemical industry have done and will develop favourably.

Rapid growth

The chemical industry in most developed countries has grown over the last quarter-century at around twice the rate of manufacturing industry as a whole; indeed the chemical industry has grown up to 10% per annum from the Second World War to the mid 1970s (Nichols and Crawford, 1983). Table 1 demonstrates the more rapid growth of the chemical industry compared with manufacturing industry generally in selected countries during the 1960s and 1970s. This great expansion in the chemical industry underscores the major position of the industry as a source of materials and ingredients for industry and commerce generally.

TABLE 1 Chemical industry output growth compared with growth in manufacturing output: UK, USA and West Germany in different time periods, 1963–79

	1963–70			1970–75			1975–79		
	Chemicals production	Manufacturing production	Ratio	Chemicals production	Manufacturing production	Ratio	Chemicals production	Manufacturing production	Ratio
United Kingdom	6.8%	3.2%	2.1:1	3.0%	0.6%	5.0:1	4.0%	3.6%	1.1:1
West Germany	11.2%	6.3%	1.7:1	2.7%	1.0%	2.7:1	6.4%	4.4%	1.4:1
United States	7.3%	2.8%	2.6:1	4.2%	1.7%	2.5:1	9.4%	6.6%	1.4:1

Source: Vivian, Gray & Co. (1980).[1]

[1] Throughout this chapter I draw on, and where possible expand, the excellent analysis of ICI published by Vivian, Gray and Company in 1980.

Although many sectors of the chemical industry grew after the Second World War the dramatic expansion in the 1950s and 1960s is associated with the development of petroleum-based organic chemicals. The USA has been using petroleum and natural gas as raw materials for the chemical industry since the 1920s and 1930s, and the restricted trading conditions from 1939 to 1945 gave a tremendous stimulus to the replacement of many essential raw materials such as rubber, fats, and oils by synthetic organic products. The Western European development of petroleum-based chemicals started during the Second World War but remained small until the consumer boom of the late 1950s, 1960s and early 1970s vastly increased the demand not only for base materials such as olefins and aromatics, but also for new products in the plastics and fibres sectors. As the process technologies in petrochemicals, plastics, and fibres manufacture were developed, and much larger plants afforded greater economies of scale, so the economic advantage of substituting plastics and synthetic fibres for natural materials such as wood, metal, and glass became more pronounced. The cost base of the chemical industry was also favourable at this time because the industry was highly capital- rather than labour-intensive, and crucially because the price of oil (in real terms) dropped steadily between 1950 and 1971. However, the continuing expansion of new production capacity in petrochemicals during the 1970s (due to optimistic growth expectations), and the dramatic increase in the price of hydrocarbon feedstocks in 1973 and 1979 completely altered the economics of the petrochemicals industry and contributed to the falling margins and lack of profitability faced by many producers in the early years of the 1980s.

Capital intensity and scale of production

Parts of the chemical industry have had their periods of using batch production processes, and some sectors still use batch processes, but the modern chemical industry is known for its use of capital-intensive continuous processes. The pattern is to manufacture very large quantities of homogeneous materials, frequently liquids or gases, which can be produced, processed, and shipped most economically on a large scale. Wittcoff and Reuben (1980:246) talk of chemical engineering coming of age after the Second World War, with tremendous increases in the size of plants. For example between 1952 and 1968 the growth of capacity of a single naphtha cracker in the UK was from 70 million lb of ethylene year^{-1} to 1 billion lb year $^{-1}$. Since 1968 crackers have been built with a bigger capacity than 1 billion lb year $^{-1}$, but even before the European petrochemicals industry found itself in 1981 with 32% overcapacity, there was already a levelling-off in the rate of increase in ethylene plant capacity (European Parliament Working Document 1–1108/83).

Corollaries of capital intensity for the chemical industry have, of course, been high capital investment, often relatively low returns on capital, compared with other industries low labour intensity and therefore salaries and wages contribute relatively little to total costs. Since in profit terms, at least in their growth era, the major chemical firms have been able to accommodate to salary and wage movements, labour relations in the chemical industry have been generally good compared with some of their more labour-intensive and less stably profitable industry counterparts (Wittcoff and Reuben, 1980).

High research and development expenditure

Between 1959 and 1970 figures for West Germany and the UK show that cumulated investment in the chemical industry was 19–20% of the total for manufacturing. With this scale of capital spending has come an equivalent scale of spending on research and development (R&D). Data on R&D for the OECD countries show that over 20% of the scientists and engineers working in the manufacturing sector were employed by the chemical industry. In this respect, chemicals were surpassed only by electronics (United Nations, 1981). In the United States in 1976 only the aerospace, electric machinery and communications, and machinery industry groups spent more on research than the chemical industry. Wittcoff and Reuben (1980:2) report that it is quite common for major chemical companies to spend 3–4% of sales on research, with the major pharmaceutical and specialty chemical companies sometimes spending up to 10–15% of sales on research.

The pattern of R&D expenditure in the chemical industry seems to have changed since the early 1970s. The view of chemicals now as a mature industry focuses on the fact that "there have been no major innovations in the industry since the 1950s, only refinements and exploitations of existing compounds" (Duncan, 1982:22). During the 1970s the direction of research has changed, with greater emphasis on improving existing production processes and on applied research at the expense of more basic research. There has also been an added emphasis to more product-oriented research, particularly in pharmaceuticals. For example, in the UK by 1975, pharmaceuticals, along with synthetic rubber, resins, plastics, paints and varnishes, absorbed almost one-half of the chemical industry's R&D expenditures (United Nations, 1981).

The modern chemical industry's requirements for so much capital and research expenditure, and the availability of large numbers of well-qualified scientific, technical, and technician employees is one reason why, until recently, so much of the world's chemical industry has been confined to advanced countries with the necessary social, economic, and intellectual infrastructures. Wittcoff and Reuben (1980:23), reporting on 1976 data on the world's 100 largest chemical companies, note that 55 of these were US companies, and another 42 were divided between Japan (12), West Germany (10), U.K. (5½)[2], France (5), Italy (4), Switzerland (3) and the Netherlands (2½).[2]

International trade and competition

Reporting on conditions at the beginning of the 1970s Reuben and Burstall (1973:121) comment that in the world chemical industry it is the big, highly

[2] Royal Dutch Shell is a joint UK/Holland venture.

TABLE 2   World chemicals production and consumption, 1977

	Percentage world chemicals production	Percentage world chemicals consumption
North America	36	35
Western Europe	42	39
Japan	13	13

Source: Vivian, Gray & Co. (1980).

industrialised countries which count. Countries containing 30% of the world's population produce 90% of the chemicals; six countries (USA, West Germany, UK, France, Italy, Japan) account for 75%. Furthermore, trade in chemicals occurs largely between countries of the developed world. Table 2 show the pattern of world chemicals production and consumption in 1977.

Thus, these three regions accounted for 91% of free world production and 87% of free world consumption of chemicals in 1977. Put another way, Table 2 suggests that consumption of chemicals per capita was extremely low for the 2000 million people in the underdeveloped and less developed countries, and the growth and share of that market for chemicals in less developed countries must be a major strategic issue in the 1980s both for the big Western chemical producers and for the rising new Middle East and Far East producers.

But returning to the history of the competitive structure of the world chemical industry, the break-up in 1945 of the pre-war cartels and agreements was a turning point. No longer could the big American, West German companies, and in the UK largely ICI, divide the world into controlled markets and allocate product. ICI, as we shall see in this book, did encounter substantial managerial difficulties in coping both with the rate of technological change and heightened international competition that they and others faced from about the mid-1950s onwards. Although companies like ICI appear to be, and in certain product areas are, monopolists in their own countries, a combination of the large economies of scale of the chemical industry which make exporting of surplus product an economic necessity, the variety of processes available to produce many chemicals, and the limited effectiveness of patent monopolies have all ensured that trade in chemicals has been, and will continue to be, international, even given the difficulties and dangers of exporting certain bulk chemicals, and the still limited geographical spread of the large and powerful producers.

Subject to cyclical economic effects

There seem to be two major reasons why large sections of the world chemical industry have experienced boom periods and slump periods even in amongst the predominant pattern of output growth over the last 25 years. One important factor explaining these cyclical effects is the enabling and interlocked character of the chemical industry. Grunewald, the chairman of Bayer AG, has recently written "that no other industry, whether it is involved in raw materials, investment goods, or consumer goods, is as closely interlocked with every other industrial sector as is the chemical industry" (1982:91). Thus, if, for example, the car industry is in a buoyant period then the rubber and plastics sectors of chemicals will do well, and if the agricultural industry is in a good period then fertilisers and pesticides are likely to do correspondingly well. Similarly if the construction industry is doing badly and the number of housing starts are down, then home textiles, furniture fabrics and dyestuffs may also have a difficult time.

One way of measuring the cyclical character of the chemical industry is to look at the changing pattern of industrial production in the industry over time. Table 3 sets out the percentage increase in chemical production for the UK, West Germany, and France over the period 1960–80. Apart from showing the stronger rates of growth of the West German and French chemical industries over the UK, Table 3 also clearly indicates across all three countries, but especially in the UK, the falling away of production in 1961, 1966, 1971, 1975, and dramatically in 1980. These dates correspond, of course, to the low points in the general economic cycle over the period 1960–80.

TABLE 3   Percentage increase in chemical production, UK, West Germany, France, 1960–80

	UK	*West Germany*	*France*
1960	11	15	31
1961	1	5	7
1962	5	12	9
1963	7.5	10	9.5
1964	9.9	12.9	9.1
1965	4.5	10.9	9.0
1966	3.7	9.2	9.2
1967	4.7	9.0	7.9
1968	6.9	16.9	9.0
1969	6.6	15.1	19.0
1970	6.0	5.9	10.0
1971	1.9	7.0	9.0
1972	5.6	6.2	12
1973	11.8	15.1	15.9
1974	4.9	2.8	4.6
1975	−9.4	−12.3	−14.7
1976	10.3	14.9	12.6
1977	1.6	0.8	5.1
1978	0	5.2	4.4
1979	0.8	5.1	8.9
1980	−8.9	−4.4	−1.3

Sources: OECD, *The Chemical Industry*, and the *UN Handbook of International Trade and Development Statistics.*

Wittcoff and Reuben (1980:28) describe the other input into the cyclical pattern in the chemical industry as the problem of feast or famine, of the market swinging like a pendulum from glut to shortage and back again. What has tended to happen during the 1960s and for part of the 1970s is a pattern of counter-cyclical investment, with investment peaks occurring in years such as 1962, 1966, and 1970 when the level of output in the industry was at one of its periodic lows. Wittcoff and Reuben (1980) explain that this process has been fuelled by the economies of scale, capital intensity, and relative ease of market entry in the chemical industry if you can afford to buy other people's available technology. What has happened is that economies of scale and expectations of profits lead producers to install more capacity than is needed, and hope that growth in home and export markets will absorb the surplus. But the need to run plants at near to full capacity pushes more product onto the market than the market will stand and prices fall. As prices fall producers with less economic, perhaps older, plant, shut down capacity in the face of falling profitability; as a result the supply of product decreases, purchasers fear shortages and try and build up inventories to meet anticipated supply difficulties, and a true shortage in the market place is created. The price rises, and purchasers, fearing further rises, stockpile more product until their storage capacity is exhausted and the price level deters buyers. Purchasers meantime begin to consume inventory and reduce demand, and the price declines again.

After a while the chemical industry, or that part of it particularly associated with petrochemicals and plastics became used to the feast or famine phenomenon and the 4.5–year business cycle. But what was very much more threatening to price stability and profitability for the heavy chemicals end of the industry was the activities of OPEC, and especially the massive increases in the price of feedstock which occurred in both 1973 and 1979.

Recent hard times in the heavy chemicals sector

A long-term glance back at the development of the chemical industry indicates that, prior to the advent of petrochemicals, producers mainly supplied intermediate products to other industries. While the supplying of inter-mediates is still an important part of trade in the industry the emergence of petrochemicals as a second phase of the industry's development involved the creation of new product lines based on synthetics – tyres, textiles, paint, and clothing intended mainly for the final consumers rather than for industrial customers. As we have already noted, this second phase in the chemical industry's evolution is associated with the growth era of the 1950s to the early 1970s which left, by one estimate, petrochemicals having just below 50% share in the total output of the industry (United Nations, 1981).

Table 4 clearly shows the rapid growth in chemicals output in developed countries over the period 1960–67; with the exception of developing countries, the beginnings of a drop in output growth between 1967 and 1973; and the substantial drop in growth rates in energy-poor Western Europe in the period 1973–79. A glance back at the output data in Table 3 for the UK, West

TABLE 4   Average annual growth rates (percentage) of chemicals output by economic grouping and region, 1960–79

	1960–67	*1967–73*	*1973–79*
Developed market economies	8.8	8.3	3.8
Western Europe	10.0	8.8	2.5
North America	7.7	7.1	5.6
Centrally planned economies	12.9	9.9	7.6
Developing countries	7.6	11.3	5.7

Source: United Nations (1981).

German, and French chemical industries shows that there was negative growth in 1980; what the table does not show is that this negative growth has continued into the 1980s for some parts of the heavy chemicals sector of the industry, and is the clear signal of a new phase in the chemical industry's development into the 1980s.

This falling away of chemicals output in the 1970s and 1980s is normally attributed to a combination of market saturation, rising energy costs, environmental considerations, and technology and policy trends, all of which add up to the labelling of the chemical industry as now mature. What is now foreseen as the next phase in the industry's evolution is a renewed effort by chemical firms in the developed market economies to increase the proportion of their assets and sales in higher added value specialty chemicals at the expense of the lower added value commodity chemicals; moves by chemical firms generally to become more market- or user-orientated and less technology- and output-orientated; and attempts by established chemical firms to create and exploit demand for chemicals in developing countries, whilst coping with the increased tendency of feedstock-rich developing countries to develop their own chemical industries and export their large surpluses to the developed market economies.

TABLE 5   Selected major European companies' trend towards specialty products and chemicals: specialty activities as a percentage of total sales

	1970	*1980*
AKZO	12	28
BASF	20	30
Bayer	32	42
Hoechst	30	40
ICI	17	27
Montedison	15	20
Rhone Poulenc	26	37
Solvay	3	20

Source: Greenwells and GMBATU (1983).

In the section which follows on the UK chemical industry and the UK economy and ICI's place in it, further details will be given on why and how the UK petrochemicals and general commodity chemicals faced such hard times in the late 1970s and 1980s, and how eventually those hard times were perceived and responded to through restructuring and manpower losses. For the time being it is sufficient to note in Table 5 the evidence for a general tendency in the 1970s for major European companies to move from bulk commodity low added value products to specialised low volume but high added products such as those produced in the pharmaceuticals, specialised organic, and agrochemicals sectors.

SOME TRENDS AND CHARACTERISTICS OF THE UK CHEMICAL INDUSTRY
AND ITS ECONOMIC CONTEXT, 1960–83

The UK chemical industry has a significant place in the world industry; it is currently the fourth-largest in the world by turnover, and plays an even more crucial role in the UK economy. Chemicals is the fifth-largest UK manufacturing sector in turnover, accounts for around 20% of all fixed investment and R&D in manufacturing industry, and in the period 1973–79 had an output growth of 13%; only the very much smaller instrument engineering sector achieved a faster growth rate than this in the UK over that period. In addition, in 1980 UK chemicals exports were £6000m and the industry's balance of payments surplus was £2100m, nearly two-thirds of the entire surplus achieved by all of the manufacturing industry. In 1979 of the £1500m balance of payment surplus earned by the chemical industry, about 40% of this was accounted for by the activities of ICI. Both the UK chemical industry and ICI are important figures in UK industry, and in the performance of the UK economy.

A glance at Figure 2 shows how the output of the UK chemical industry has consistently grown at a faster rate over the period 1959–82 than the output of UK manufacturing industry generally. In this series chemicals output peaked in 1979, with a percentage increase from 1959 to 1979 of 187%, whilst manufacturing output peaked in 1973, with a percentage increase of only 60% between 1959 and 1973.

As we have already noted in Table 3 there has been a tendency for the UK chemical industry to mirror the cyclical development in the UK economy. Figure 3 illustrates both the significantly higher growth rate achieved in chemical output than in GDP, the tendency of both GDP and chemicals output growth to decrease in the 1970s as compared with the 1960s, and the peaks and troughs in both GDP and chemicals output. The evident troughs in GDP and chemicals output in 1961, 1966, 1971, 1975, and 1980–82 were also mirrored in ICI's performance at those times, and the conduct of managerial behaviour in ICI around those periods.

Table 6 makes the connection between trends in UK employees in employment and chemicals employment over the period 1959–82. Overall the table demonstrates that employment in the UK chemical industry maintained its

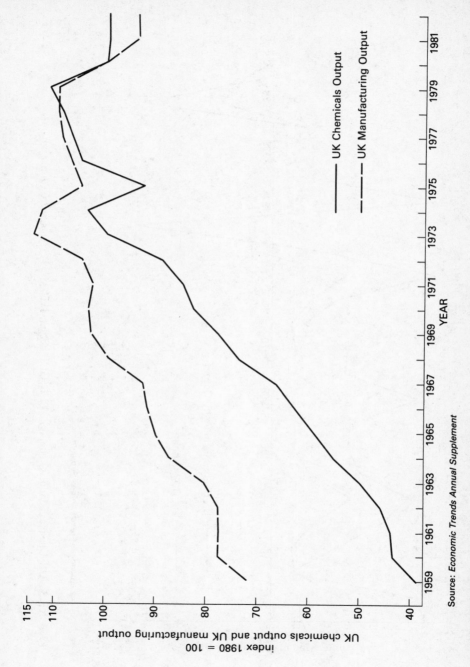

index 1980 = 100

UK chemicals output and UK manufacturing output

——— UK Chemicals Output

— — — UK Manufacturing Output

Source: *Economic Trends Annual Supplement*

FIGURE 2 UK Chemicals output and UK Manufacturing output, 1959–82

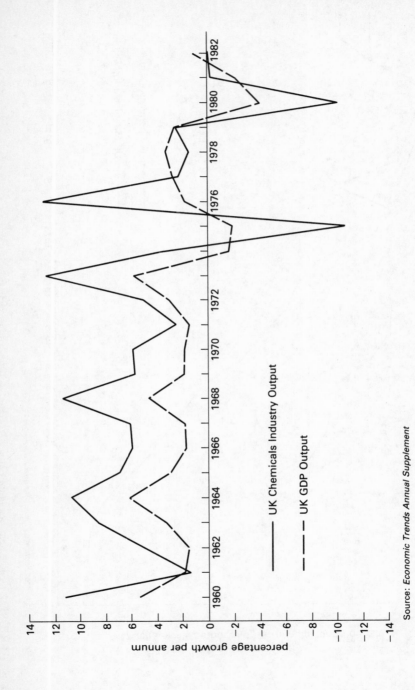

Source: *Economic Trends Annual Supplement*

FIGURE 3 UK Chemicals industry output and UK GDP output, 1960–82. Percentage growth per annum.

levels more consistently against the backcloth of the cycles in the UK economy than did employment in UK generally. Table 6 uses an index where 1975 = 100, but in terms of actual numbers employed the UK chemical industry, with minor fluctuations, had a total manpower complement of around 430,000 between 1959 and the very substantial drop which occurred in 1980. Table 6 shows that there was steady growth in UK employees in employment until the 1966 recession. The shake-out of labour which followed this recession continued slowly until the reflationary economic policies of the Heath Government in 1972/73 gave a boost to employment in general. The dips in employees in employment and chemicals employment associated with the recessions of 1961, 1966, 1971, 1975, and 1979 and 1982 are very evident in Table 6.

Although Figures 2 and 3 and Table 6 demonstrate that, generally speaking, the UK chemical industry has developed more favourably than the UK

TABLE 6   UK employees in employment and UK chemical industry employment, 1959–82 (Index 1975 = 100)

	Employees in employment	*Chemical industry employment*
1959	94.3	99.8
1960	96.4	102.8
1961	97.9	103.3
1962	98.9	102.3
1963	99.1	101.6
1964	100.5	101.4
1965	101.6	103.3
1966	102.4	105.3
1967	100.4	103.7
1968	99.8	98.8
1969	99.6	102.8
1970	99.0	103.0
1971	97.4	101.9
1972	97.4	99.1
1973	99.8	99.3
1974	100.3	101.2
1975	100.0	100.0
1976	99.2	98.6
1977	99.6	100.9
1978	100.2	102.6
1979	101.7	102.8
1980	100.6	100.1
1981	95.5	93.4
1982	93.4	88.7

Source: Economic Trends Annual Supplement

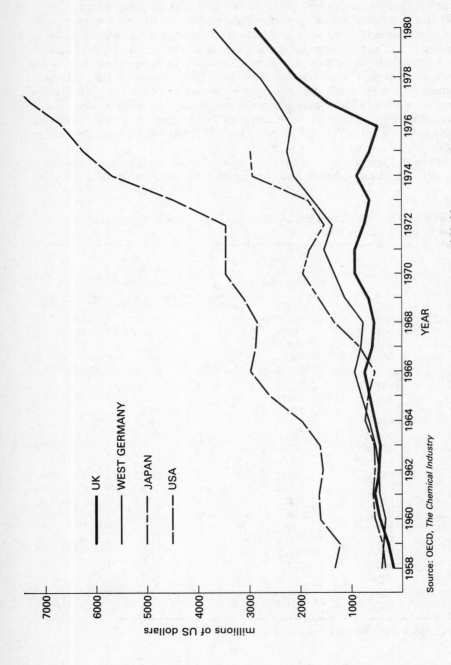

FIGURE 4 Yearly investments in the Chemical Industry; selected countries, 1958–80.

Source: OECD, *The Chemical Industry*

UK
WEST GERMANY
JAPAN
USA

millions of US dollars

7000
6000
5000
4000
3000
2000
1000

1958 1960 1962 1964 1966 1968 1970 1972 1974 1976 1978 1980

YEAR

economy and UK manufacturing industry throughout the 1960s and 1970s, the issue for the UK chemical industry is its international competitive position. Here the pattern of development of the UK chemical industry, and as we shall argue its principal representative firm ICI, compares rather unfavourably with some aspects of international competition. Earlier in this chapter the data on relative chemical industry growth rates in Table 1 indicated that the UK chemical industry performance did not match the rate of output growth achieved by the US and West German chemical industries over the period 1963–79. Figure 4 also demonstrates that notwithstanding currency fluctuations against the US dollar, the UK chemical industry has generally speaking not matched either the USA, West Germany, or Japanese chemical industries in capital investment over the period of the 1960s and 1970s.

It is clear from Figure 4 not only that West Germany and Japan invested at a substantially higher rate than did the UK chemical industry in the 1960s, but also that this discrepancy in rates accelerated in the 1970s. In a 1977 report on the UK chemical industry the General and Municipal Workers' Union, GMWU (1977), indicates that the percentage annual growth rate of capital investment in the Japanese, West German, French, United States, and UK chemical industries over the period 1963–73 were respectively 13.3%, 10.4%, 7.2%, 7.1%, and 5.4%.

Table 7 demonstrates that on top of a lower growth in output and a lower rate of capital investment, the UK chemical industry is less productive. Table 7 describes the value added per employee in US dollars for the chemical industries of the UK, USA, West Germany, and Japan over the period 1961–80, and shows that for the 1960s and early 1970s the value added per employee in US dollars for the UK chemical industry was below their major international competitors. The GMWU (1977) report indicates that the rate of growth of value added per employee in US dollars over the period 1963–73 for the West German, Japanese, and UK chemical industries was respectively 10.5%, 7.9% and 8.9%. By the end of the 1970s value added per employee had risen substantially, and is still rising because of the capital investment peak in the UK around 1978–80, and because of the manpower reductions made between 1979 and 1982, but the UK has a long way to go to catch up with the efficiency of the US and West German chemical industries.

A variety of reasons have been assembled to explain the relatively poorer growth, capital investment, and productivity record of the UK chemical industry. These include the fact that the UK was not in the EEC until the 1970s, an overvalued £ sterling prior to the 1967 devaluation, custom and practice and inertia which had stabilised a pattern of overmanning in British industry which was held in place by a balance of large and small "p" political power which favoured the trade unions, the lower rates of economic growth in the UK during the 1960s and 1970s, and the very much higher rates of price inflation in the UK, particularly in the 1970s. By 1975, when the lower growth of the UK economy was well established into the 1970s, and when the percentage increase of the UK retail price went up 7% from 1974 and the chemical price increase went up a staggering 27.3% from 1974, it seemed that

TABLE 7   Value added per employee in the chemical industries of UK, USA, West Germany, and Japan, 1961–80 (In US dollars)

	UK	USA	West Germany	Japan
1961	5350	17,200	6550	n.a.
1962	5610	18,930	7470	3270
1963	6020	20,160	7770	4430
1964	6690	21,810	8330	5080
1965	6980	22,340	9130	5770
1966	7430	23,810	9700	7860
1967	7700	23,650	10,890	8980
1968	8100	24,760	11,350	9460
1969	8550	27,210	12,020	10,810
1970	8370	23,860	13,270	12,610
1971	9510	n.a.	14,180	13,510
1972	12,190	n.a.	17,390	16,290
1973	13,940	34,870	23,600	n.a.
1974	17,750	42,520	31,450	24,740
1975	18,990	n.a.	32,460	22,720
1976	16,190	60,390	34,600	27,100
1977	18,620	n.a.	38,650	n.a.
1978	19,800	58,820	46,220	33,600
1979	27,190	73,510	58,820	n.a.
1980	31,190	84,150	61,820	n.a.

Source: OECD, *The Chemical Industry.*

faster growth for chemicals would not come from home growth, but could only materialise from export-led growth. Unfortunately, although there was a clear recovery of output and exports in the UK chemical industry after the 1975 recession, by 1979 a combination of overcapacity in the European heavy chemicals industry, continuing high levels of inflation in the UK, and the rapid strengthening of sterling, all put pressure on the international competitiveness of UK industry, and together with the home market slump occasioned by the 1980 recession, all contributed to drastic reduction in demand for the chemicals and products of certain sectors of the UK chemical industry. Figure 2 shows one result of this process, a very substantial drop in UK chemicals output between 1979 and 1980 which was sustained into 1981 and 1982, and Table 6 shows the consequential impact on job losses in the UK chemical industry between 1979 and 1982. Manpower in the UK chemical industry actually dropped by 78,000 (17.6%) from end of year 1979 until September 1983.

The drop in output and employment in UK chemicals in the 1979–82 period had a disproportionate impact on some sectors than others. Between 1979 and 1982 the percentage decline in output of inorganic chemicals was 31%, dyestuffs and pigments 24.3%, plastics and resins 18.6%, and organics 9%

(GMBATU, 1983). Given that inorganics and petrochemicals in 1980 represented nearly 40% by value of all chemicals sold in the UK, and that ICI, the dominating firm in the UK chemical industry, had majored in petrochemicals, plastics, and certain inorganics, it was little wonder that job losses in UK chemicals, and ICI were so high over the period 1979–82.

THE RECENT BUSINESS HISTORY, CULTURE, AND PERFORMANCE OF ICI

The previous two sections of this chapter have emphasised the major changes in business and economic context faced by the world's major chemical firms over the past 25 years. But in the context of those changes what or who are ICI, and how have ICI responded to such changes in their business and economic environment?

From its foundation – by a merger of the four largest British chemical companies in 1926 – ICI has always been a major force in the world chemical industry. Indeed in 1972 ICI was not only Britain's biggest industrial company, it was, according to the prevailing rates of exchange, the biggest chemical company in the world. Throughout most of the 1970s ICI contributed about 25–30% of the sales of the UK chemical industry. By 1981 its sales (in US dollars) made ICI the fifth-largest chemical company in the world after DuPont and the three big German firms Hoechst, Bayer, and BASF. In 1983, in terms of market capitalisation (share price multiplied by the number of shares) ICI was the fifth-largest company in the UK after British Petroleum, General Electric Company, Shell Transport and Trading, and Glaxo Holdings. (*Financial Times* Top 500, 12 November 1983).

Although by the end of the 1970s ICI was active in all major industrial and most non-industrial countries, as the "Imperial" name implies its traditional market focus and production strength had been in Britain, and in the countries of the former British Empire. Crucially, in culture and management ICI was and still is a substantially British-based and managed multinational company. There was a reduction from 52% to 43% in the percentage of total group sales attributed to UK customers between 1963 and 1973, but between 1973 and 1981 that percentage fell only another 4% to 39%. In 1973, 66% of ICI's worldwide employees were working in the UK divisions and notwithstanding interests in North America and Western Europe, the main board of ICI were heavily preoccupied with the UK divisions. ICI in the early 1970s was often referred to in the press as Britain's largest manufacturing company, and today the financial fortunes of ICI are regarded as a barometer for more general upward and downward movements in the stock market. Certainly outside ICI there was the view that ICI was a British institution, and had to behave, and be seen to behave, in an appropriately ethical, regulated, and stable fashion.

ICI is a vast conglomerate that majors in chemicals production ranging from products which are sold in tens of thousands of tons, such as ethylene or caustic soda, to products in the dyes and pharmaceuticals fields which can be sold in units of less than an ounce. "Chemical" covers a vast range of products from basic industrial chemicals through fertilisers and fibres to paints, plastics, herbicides, and explosives. The single most important strength of the company has been in its development of and investment in advanced chemical and engineering technology. A concomitant of this has been the relative lack of emphasis on marketing as compared to companies more heavily involved in consumer goods and with a history of less protected markets. At the same time there exists a long tradition of progressive personnel policies, of relatively stable industrial relations and considerable company loyalty among managers and workers.

The power centre of ICI was, and at the time of writing (Spring 1984) still is Imperial Chemical House, Millbank, London SW1. The main board and executive directors are resident at Millbank and maintain strategic control at the centre over the UK divisions and subsidiaries through two main elements of reserve powers. The main board has final say over the investment decisions that determine ICI's future shape, and also are the final arbiter of personnel policy. In 1983 ICI was divided into eight divisions, largely autonomous and profit accountable, answering to the main board and monitored through a system of planning budget controls.

One highly synoptic way of sketching the broad changes in ICI over the past 20 years or so is to look at ICI along a number of indicators in 1960 compared with 1982. In terms of size ICI has increased its sales in pounds sterling of the day 13-fold (£558m to £7358m) and its total assets 8-fold (£694m to £5379m) also in pounds of the day. However, ICI has reduced its numbers of UK employees from 113,699 in 1960 to 67,300 in 1982, a drop of 41%. Over that same period the number of UK divisions has declined from 13 to 8 (plus Nobel Explosives Ltd). The 8 divisions remaining in 1984 are Agricultural, Fibres, Mond, Organics, Paints, Petrochemicals and Plastics, Pharmaceuticals, and Plant Protection. As has been noted, ICI have managed to change the distribution of their sales, calculated according to territory where the customer is located, over the period of the last 20 years. From 1963 to 1981 the proportion of sales to the continent have increased from 11% to 18%, to North America from 11% to 19%, and to Australasia and the Far East from 9% to 16%. There has been a corresponding decline in the proportion of sales to UK customers from 52% to 39%.

The ICI main board has also changed in size and mode of operation over the past two decades. In 1960 the main board was made up of a Chairman, 3 deputy Chairmen, 14 executive directors, and 6 non-executive directors. In 1983 the much streamlined main board is a Chairman, 7 executive directors, and 6 non-executive directors. There have been 5 Chairmen of ICI since 1960. They and the present Chairman are:

Sir Paul Chambers	January 1960–March 1968	8 years in post
Sir Peter Allen	April 1968–March 1971	3 years in post
Sir Jack Callard	April 1971–March 1975	4 years in post
Sir Rowland Wright	April 1975–March 1978	3 years in post
Sir Maurice Hodgson	April 1978–March 1982	4 years in post
John Harvey-Jones	April 1982–present	

This list indicates a number of features of British culture, and indeed the culture of the ICI main board over the period since 1960. In terms of the British culture the Chairman of ICI is an important post, and this is reflected in the fact that all recent Chairmen have been knighted during their tenure of office. In terms of the recent culture and mode of operation of the main board, the other characteristic to note in the above list is the *planned* short tenure in office of all the Chairmen since Sir Paul Chambers. Prior to the present Chairman's election, for reasons discussed later, that pattern of short tenure has been changed. In addition, John Harvey-Jones, unlike his predecessors, is also the principal executive officer of the company – ICI's rather careful and sanitised way of describing the position of a chief executive officer.

What is not evident from the above list of top leaders of ICI, is the fact that the two Chairmen who have played the most consistently up-front role as innovative leaders in ICI have been the first and the last men on the list. The reasons for this may relate to the characteristics of the men and the needs for change which were recognised in their era in office. It is also of interest to note that neither Sir Paul Chambers nor John Harvey-Jones were lifelong ICI career men. Nor were they chemists or engineers, ICI's traditional source of managerial talent. Sir Paul Chambers joined ICI in 1947 as a main board director, after a successful career in public service mainly in the Inland Revenue. Chambers was then 43 years old, and his educational background had included an economics degree from the London School of Economics. John Harvey-Jones does not have a degree. His background is Dartmouth, and the Royal Navy. He joined ICI in the late 1950s at the age of 31, and worked up through the ranks from being a works study officer in Heavy Organics Division, to being chairman of Petrochemicals Division in 1970, a main board director in 1973, and ICI Chairman in 1982.

ICI's corporate strategy and corporate culture in the 1960s

Before the Second World War ICI "were in every cartel that was going". Immediately after the Second World War, with the cartels and agreements dissolved, and in the 1950s a wide range of new and expanding entrants into the world chemical industry fast building new and larger plant, ICI found themselves in a more international and a more competitive industry. Spurred by the increasing success of the large US chemical companies in European markets, the platform for growth in the Continental Western European industry's fortunes created by the birth of the EEC, pressures from within ICI for innovation from some of the newer divisions and activities such as organics, plastics, synthetic fibres, and pharmaceuticals, and some inauspicious financial results in 1958 and 1961, ICI began the decade of the 1960s in an atmosphere of challenge and change.

At the forefront of ICI's attempts to create strategic change in the early 1960s was Paul Chambers – the first "outsider" ever to become Chairman of ICI. In an article in *The Sunday Times* of 27 September 1964, Michael Shanks describes Chambers as an instinctive reformer, an intellectual, and a rationalist, and someone who seems to make things more difficult for himself by not preparing the ground in advance – as in ICI's abortive attempt in the early 1960s to take over Courtaulds. In that same article Chambers describes his vision for change in ICI:

> We must see . . . that our whole organisation is sensitive to growth and sensitive to change. We have changed from a narrow technical approach to a broad commercial approach.

In fact, like many an instinctive reformer Chambers' optimism for speedy change was ahead of his own or other senior managers' capacity to create it. As a result many of the changes in top management culture sought by Chambers in the early 1960s were still being pushed by John Harvey-Jones and others throughout much of the 1970s. Indeed almost 8 years after the September 1964 analysis of ICI in *The Sunday Times*, there appeared another more critical review of ICI, still not yet very profitable after a decade of unprecedented growth for the world and UK chemical industries. The 16 July 1972 *Sunday Times* article entitled 'The case of the missing catalyst' used the following quote from an ICI senior manager to emphasise that whatever changes had gone on in ICI during the 1960s they were not in 1972 an important part of the company culture:

> We suffer from the problems of size.
> We employ too many highly-paid people to check and cross check other men's figures.
> We are an over-educated company.
> We still have a technical bias. We are not breeding people with an entrepreneurial flair.
> The Chairman has the old belief that the company can only change slowly.
> But I think you could have a dynamic effect with proper leadership.
> Of course one main trouble is that the ICI Board is selfperpetuating.
> Dick Beeching[3] would have changed it entirely – he knew exactly what he wanted to do – but they never let him have a chance.

The journalists who wrote the 16 July 1972 investigative article on ICI concluded that

> if ICI is to snatch and exploit the opportunities of the future, it needs to be flexible and quick reacting, enterprising and risk taking, on a scale beyond anything it has yet reached . . . The catalyst to release ICI's great potential has still to be found.

However, to be fair to ICI, although the style and mode of operation of the main board and the broad corporate culture of ICI were remarkably resistent to change throughout the 1960s and 1970s, major strategic change did begin in the early 1960s. These strategic changes in the spheres of technology, labour productivity, market focus, and management organisation are dealt with in depth later in this book. At this stage it is sufficient to note that in the 1960s ICI made great strides in constructing and eventually commissioning new, larger, and more efficient plant. The capital expenditure programme of the 1960s which was initially driven by needs for modernisation and the productivity gains

---

[3] In late 1967 Beeching, then an ICI deputy chairman, made an unsuccessful bid for Chairman of ICI; both his bid and the change ideas that went with it were rejected.

which would come from larger plants and greater economies of scale, continued with interruptions into the 1970s and was guided by some broad principles for expansion. In particular ICI has concentrated on developing those product areas where it has a strong market position rather than continually attempting to enlarge the product range. In Europe, for example, expansion has been confined largely to low-density polyethylene, polyester fibre, polypropylene, and crop protection chemicals, all products in which ICI developed a dominant UK position in the latter end of the 1960s and early 1970s. ICI also focused strategic concern in the 1960s on labour productivity, and sought to implement their own variant of the fashionable 1960s productivity bargain which was initially called Manpower Utilisation and Payment Structure (MUPS) and later amended to the Weekly Staff Agreement (WSA). In 1960 began the long, and in 1984 still incomplete process of moving their sales and capital away from the old markets and manufacturing sites of the UK and the British Empire towards initially Western Europe, and then belatedly the United States. Paul Chambers also made a start in trying to change the organisation and culture of ICI from its concern with conservatism, rationality, and technology, and towards greater market focus, commercialism, and financial accountability. Chambers encouraged a number of organisation changes which made division chairmen more accountable and led to the dissolution of many of the old functional organisations in the divisions and their replacement with product-business area/functional matrix organisations. In this respect he was aided by the organisation studies of a main board organisation committee, and the services of the McKinsey consultancy firm.

ICI's performance in the period 1960–83

ICI's performance over the past two decades will be examined first of all in an overall sense by cataloguing the pattern of the company's sales and the ratio of trading profit to sales. An analysis of ICI's business performance in those terms also indicates the extent to which ICI's record follows the cyclical patterns in the UK economy, and how after a peak in the company's total UK manpower in 1969, attempts by ICI management to reduce that manpower coincided with low points in the performance of the UK economy generally and in ICI in particular. Attention is then focused on the relative importance of the various business classes to ICI's turnover and trading profit, and the geographical evolution of ICI's sales and profits over the period from 1973 to 1982. This section then ends with a report on the changing pattern of ICI capital expenditure over the period from 1970 to 1983, and reveals the increasing tendency to place new capital in the United States and Continental Western Europe rather than the United Kingdom.

Table 8 shows ICI's sales, trading profit, and ratio of trading profit to sales from the low point of 1958 up to 1983, and the percentage growth per annum of GDP output from 1960 to 1982, and shows how throughout the 1960s the sales and trading profit of ICI showed slow but steady growth against the cyclical background of the UK economy. Vivian, Gray and Co. (1980) report that in the

TABLE 8   ICI group sales, trading profit, and ratio of trading profit to sales percentage, 1958–83 in £m GDP output percentage growth per annum, 1960–82

	Total sales	Trading profit	Trading profit as percentage of sales	GDP output percentage growth per annum
1958	463	51	11.0	n.a.
1959	508	80	15.7	n.a.
1960	558	93	16.6	5.5
1961	550	65	11.8	1.8
1962	579	73	12.6	1.5
1963	624	85	13.6	3.2
1964	720	113	15.7	6.2
1965	816	113	13.8	2.8
1966	885	99	11.2	1.7
1967	979	122	12.5	1.8
1968	1237	175	14.1	4.4
1969	1355	190	14.0	1.9
1970	1462	159	10.9	1.8
1971	1524	130	8.5	1.5
1972	1694	141	10.0	3.1
1973	2166	329	15.2	5.9
1974	2955	461	15.6·	−1.7
1975	3129	325	10.4	−1.9
1976	4135	514	12.4	1.8
1977	4663	545	11.7	2.7
1978	4533	497	11.0	3.2
1979	5368	634	11.8	2.6
1980	5715	332	5.8	−4.0
1981	6581	425	6.4	−2.1
1982	7358	366	5.0	1.1
1983	8256	693	8.4	n.a.

Sources: ICI Annual Reports and Economic Trends Annual Supplement.

11 years from 1960 to 1971 (years of excellent sales growth for the chemical industry) ICI managed to increase real pre-tax profits by only 2.5% per annum compound. The problem was pressure on margins which declined from 11.8% in the 1961 trough to 9.5% in the 1971 trough. Using a measure of after-tax profits as a percentage of capital employed Reuben and Burstall (1973:92) note that ICI only achieved 4.5–7.4% over the period from 1962 to 1971. This performance, they note, was about average for large European chemical forms at that time, but comparable US chemical companies averaged 8–13% after-tax profits as a percentage of capital employed over the period 1962–71.

Table 8 also indicates the high and low points in ICI's business performance since 1958, and the extent to which ICI's record has followed the cyclical development of the UK economy. Thus ICI's troughs have been in 1958, 1961,

1966, 1971, 1975, and 1980–83. A glance at the percentage growth per annum of GDP in the UK economy since 1960 clearly shows ICI's poor years were also years of insignificant or negative growth in GDP output. Exceptions to this trend were the years 1974 and 1979 which were excellent years for the chemical industry and ICI but relatively poor years for GDP output growth.

Profits and margins in ICI soared in 1973 on the back of a demand boom, and rose even more exceptionally in 1974 as in the aftermath of the 1973 oil crisis and the shortages of petroleum-based raw materials, customers were willing to pay high prices to maintain and build stocks. However, the extent of the 1974 stockbuilding feast accentuated even more the expected 1975 recessionary famine. Post-1975 demand picked up again but in 1977 and 1978 overcapacity in fibres and plastics led to price cutting and a squeeze on ICI's margins. Although early 1979 saw a minor stockbuilding boom caused by anxiety over Iranian political and economic difficulties, a combination of a large increase in petroleum feedstock costs after July 1979, the overvalued sterling, high interest rates in the UK, and now massive overcapacity in the European heavy chemicals industry all contributed to ICI's substantial fall from grace in the period 1980–83.

Table 9 describes ICI's total numbers of UK employees from 1965 to 1983, worldwide employees from 1968 to 1983, and UK employees as a % of total

TABLE 9 ICI total employees UK 1965–83, worldwide employees 1968–83, and UK employees as a percentage of total employees, 1968–83

	UK employees	Worldwide employees	UK employees as a percentage of total employees
1965	126,000	n.a.	–
1966	124,000	n.a.	–
1967	128,000	n.a.	–
1968	139,000	187,000	74.3
1969	145,000	197,000	73.6
1970	142,000	194,000	73.2
1971	137,000	190,000	72.1
1972	135,000	199,000	67.8
1973	132,000	199,000	66.3
1974	132,000	201,000	65.7
1975	129,000	195,000	66.1
1976	125,000	192,000	65.1
1977	95,000	154,000	61.7
1978	92,000	151,000	61.0
1979	89,400	148,200	60.3
1980	84,300	143,200	58.9
1981	74,700	132,400	56.4
1982	67,300	123,800	54.4
1983	61,800	117,900	52.4

Source: ICI Annual Reports.

employees over that period. The table reveals that the peak of ICI's UK employment was in 1969, and worldwide employment was in 1974. The large drop in UK employees between 1976 and 1977 was due to their sale of Imperial Metal Industries, and the sizeable increase in worldwide employees between 1971 and 1972 was a result of ICI's acquisition of Atlas, the US chemical company. ICI reduced their UK employees by 83,200 from the peak in 1969 to 57.4% of that in 1983. Since 1968 the percentage of ICI employees working in the UK as a percentage of total ICI employees declined from 74% to 52%. In fact the figures for 1984 will reveal that for the first time ever ICI, once regarded as the flagship of British manufacturing industry, will employ more people overseas than inside the UK. This trend has followed ICI's explicit policy objective of increasing the proportion of their business and assets overseas. Finally, Table 9 also reveals that ICI have tended to be most effective in reducing their numbers of UK employees in the years when they could argue their business performance was not good. Those years have clearly been 1970–72 and 1979–83.

In terms of business areas or classes ICI is one of the most diverse chemical companies in the world. However, capacity to gauge the relative importance and performance of ICI's business classes over time is limited by the fact that ICI has only published figures on the performance of its business classes on a worldwide comparable basis since 1973. Table 10 describes ICI's performance by business classes for 1973–79, and again in 1982 to reveal the impact of the 1979–82 recession on the relative importance of ICI's various business areas to total sales, profits, and margins. Some indication of the internal weighting of ICI's business classes in 1979 is given from the fact that in that year the four major business classes – Petrochemicals, General Chemicals, Agriculture and Plastics – together accounted for 60% of Group sales and 72% of Group trading profits. The dangers of ICI's high dependency on their heavy chemicals businesses became apparent when in the period 1979–82 trading conditions for the heavy chemicals sectors of the industry deteriorated. By 1982 the percentage contribution of ICI's Petrochemicals and Plastics, General Chemicals, and Agriculture business classes to Group sales had declined to 56%, and to Group trading profit to 45%. By 1982 three of ICI's business classes, Petrochemicals and Plastics, Organics, and Fibres, were making losses; Petrochemicals and Plastics alone lost £139m. The company thus became highly dependent on its Agricultural, Pharmaceutical, and oil business which between them contributed 76.2% to trading profit in 1982. Also of significance in Table 10 are the consistently high trading margins in the Pharmaceutical area of ICI's business, a common feature of the drugs industry.

The geographical sources of ICI's sales and trading profits for the period 1973–1982 is summarised in Table 11, which reveals that in spite of a policy objective to the contrary, ICI's UK production accounted for a consistent 55–59% of Group sales in the years 1973, 1976, 1979, and 1982. More significantly, over that same period the proportion of total Group profit accounted for by UK production remained 70% or more up until the difficult UK conditions of the early 1980s. However, the average trading margin by region over

TABLE 10 ICI: contribution of business classes to Group sales, Group Trading profit, and trading margins, 1979, 1982 and 1973–79

Percentage contribution to Group sales		Business class	Percentage contribution to trading profit		Average trading margin	Trading margin percentage	
1979	1982		1979	1982	1973–79	1979	1982
16.7	23.0	Petrochemicals	15.5	(28.7)†	10.4	9.1	(7.3)†
16.1	16.6	General chemicals	22.3	12.4	15.3	13.6	4.3
15.4	16.4	Agriculture	25.1	32.6	17.2	16.0	11.5
11.6	–*	Plastics	8.8	–*	8.6	7.5	–*
8.7	14.0	Oil	12.5	15.1	n.a.	14.1	6.3
8.0	7.8	Organics	1.1	(3.7)†	8.8	1.3	(2.8)†
7.3	5.6	Fibres	(5.2)†	(5.2)†	(1.2)†	(7.0)†	(5.4)†
6.4	6.0	Paints	4.7	4.5	4.9	7.2	4.4
4.9	6.2	Pharmaceuticals	10.4	28.5	22.1	20.8	26.7
3.0	3.4	Explosives	2.8	6.8	11.9	9.2	11.5

* ICI merged their Petrochemicals and Plastics business classes and UK divisions in 1981.
† Figures in parenthesis refer to negative results.

Sources: Vivian Gray & Co., and ICI Annual Reports.

TABLE 11 ICI sales and trading profit by region, 1973, 1976, 1979, and 1982 (percentage)

	1973		1976		1979		1982	
	Sales	Trading profit	Sales	Trading profit	Sales	Trading profit	Sales	Trading profit
UK	59	70	55	70	57	80	55	74
Continental Western Europe	12	6	15	6	15	(1)	12	(1.2)
Americas	13	7	14	7	13	7	15	17
Australasia	10	10	9	10	9	7	13	23
Other	6	6	7	6	6	7	4	5

Source: Vivian, Gray & Co., and ICI Annual Reports.

TABLE 12 ICI capital expenditure and capital authorization, 1970–1982, £m, and capital expenditure by region, 1970–1982, £m

| | Capital expenditure | | | | | Capital authorisation |
	UK	Continental Western Europe	Americas	Other	Total	Total
1970	118	27	12	15	172	192
1971	118	25	22	18	183	111
1972	86	25	14	13	138	99
1973	80	8	17	15	120	180
1974	129	15	35	20	199	369
1975	239	25	46	22	332	390
1976	268	37	102	31	438	516
1977	330	42	82	37	491	804
1978	430	87	107	77	701	788
1979	432	121	120	87	760	552
1980	390	148	117	69	724	324
1981	168	39	118	86	411	327
1982	129	17	79	67	292	246
Total	2527	468	754	488	4237	4898

Sources: Vivian Gray & Co., (1980) and ICI Annual Reports.

the period 1973–79 reveals that trading margins are clearly and consistently best in the UK and Australasia, and weakest in Continental Western Europe and the Americas, the two territories for which ICI had the most ambitious expansion plans. The average trading margins between 1973 and 1979 are 14.1% UK, 2.3% Western Europe, 6.8% Americas, 9.2% Australasia, and 12% other. By 1982, ICI's earlier decision to major in plastics and fibres in its European production programme, plus the unfavourable trading conditions for the general chemicals being produced at ICI's big manufacturing site at Wilhelmshaven, meant that ICI were making losses on their European manufacturing operations.

Finally Table 12 indicates the pattern of ICI's total capital expenditure and capital authorisation over the period 1970–82, and the distribution of that capital expenditure by region for the same period. Apart from the enormous scale of capital expenditure and capital authorisation shown in Table 12, another evident feature of ICI's pattern of capital spending is the fact that it peaked during the 1975 trough, and then rose substantially in authorisation in 1977 and 1978 and in expenditure in 1979. Also noteworthy is the dramatic slowing-down of capital authorisation and spending in the poor years 1981–1982.

Looking at the years 1970–80 by region of capital expenditure, the proportion of total spending in the UK declined from 69% to 54%, while ICI's strategy of increasing the company's manufacturing presence in Western Europe and the USA was reflected in an increase of 16% to 20% of total spending going to Europe over the years 1970–80, and an equivalent increase of 7% to 16% in the Americas. In the bad years of 1980 and 1981 ICI were spending nearly 30% of their total and now diminished capital in the Americas, and around 20% in Australia and the Far East.

ICI COMPARED WITH SOME MAJOR COMPETITORS, 1967–81

There are many difficulties and dangers involved in making comparisons between firms operating in different countries, accounting in different currencies, using different accounting conventions, and with different product mixes, and the brief analysis and interpretation which follows should be regarded as tentative and broadly indicative only.

Using the ratio of trading profit to sales, and the ratio of pre-tax and interest profit to net assets, there is a clear tendency for ICI's performance in the 1970s to lie somewhere between the better average margins of the selected US companies and the lower margins which seem to be characteristic of the performance of the major German chemical companies. On both ratios indicated in Tables 13 and 14 ICI improved its relative performance in the latter part of the 1970s.

Measuring capital expenditure as a percentage of sales usefully removed distortions due to differing inflation rates, thus the data in Table 15 give a good indication of the trends in capital investment between ICI and six of its major competitors over the period 1967–81. Table 15 reveals that ICI's capital

TABLE 13 Trading profit to sales percentage: ICI and selected competitors, 1970–78

	ICI	DuPont	Dow	Monsanto	Bayer	BASF	Hoechst
1970	10.9	14.8	13.6	6.5	8.5	7.8*	9.1
1971	9.5	14.9	13.8	8.5	7.9	8.1	8.4
1972	10.0	16.2	14.9	9.7	9.7	8.7	9.2
1973	15.2	18.6	16.5	15.3	10.2	12.0	10.2
1974	15.6	9.8	23.1	15.7	8.9	10.8	9.6
1975	10.4	7.3	22.0	15.1	6.0	6.5	5.8
1976	12.4	10.9	19.3	15.6	7.5	8.2	6.5
1977	11.7	11.4	16.2	13.3	5.8	6.6	5.5
1978	11.0	13.1	15.2	12.6	5.5	6.4	5.8

* Vivian, Gray & Co. estimate
Source: Vivian, Gray & Co., 1980

TABLE 14 Ratio of pre-tax and interest profit to net assets percentage: ICI and selected competitors, 1970–78

	ICI	DuPont	Dow	Monsanto	Bayer	BASF	Hoechst
1970	9.7	17.3	12.3	7.0	n.a.	n.a.	n.a.
1971	8.2	16.6	12.7	9.8	n.a.	9.4	n.a.
1972	8.8	19.4	14.4	11.4	n.a.	11.0	n.a.
1973	14.5	24.5	17.8	19.4	n.a.	18.2	n.a.
1974	19.3	13.9	32.5	23.0	12.5	20.8	14.4
1975	11.7	10.3	24.9	18.6	7.8	11.2	7.9
1976	14.8	15.9	21.2	19.9	11.2	15.9	9.8
1977	15.2	17.6	17.2	16.6	8.4	12.4	8.4
1978	12.7	21.7	15.5	15.3	8.0	12.0	8.9

Source: Vivian, Gray & Co., 1980.

TABLE 15 Capital expenditure as a percentage of sales: ICI and selected competitors, 1967–81

	ICI	DuPont	Dow	Monsanto	Bayer	BASF	Hoechst
1967	11.6	14.6	13.9	9.8	11.6	17.4	17.4
1968	10.1	9.6	18.5	7.4	8.6	9.2	15.4
1969	11.7	10.7	20.6	11.4	15.2	15.5	14.0
1970	11.7	13.0	18.2	15.2	19.6	15.4	13.6
1971	10.4	10.6	17.7	9.8	15.2	9.1	6.4
1972	8.1	11.7	15.1	7.6	8.9	7.7	11.5
1973	5.5	13.5	13.3	7.7	8.3	8.2	7.2
1974	6.7	14.6	17.6	8.9	9.5	7.1	8.3
1975	10.6	14.7	18.8	14.6	10.7	7.7	9.0
1976	10.6	10.5	21.0	15.2	7.9	7.3	7.1
1977	10.5	8.3	18.6	13.2	8.7	7.8	6.4
1978	15.5	7.4	15.6	9.6	7.6	8.2	6.5
1979	14.2	7.4	13.7	9.1	8.6	6.5	n.a.
1980	5.7	9.9	11.1	11.9	9.2	6.6	6.6
1981	6.8	10.6	9.9	9.6	7.5	6.5	5.7

Source: Chemical Age, 200.

TABLE 16 Sales, investment, and total remuneration per employee: ICI and selected competitors, 1978

	Sales	Ranking	Assets*	Ranking	Remuneration†	Ranking
ICI	67	9	59	5	15.4	9
DuPont	80	4=	80	4	24.0	2
Dow	129	1	150	1	25.7	1
Monsanto	80	4=	82	3	21.0	8
Bayer	74	8	n.a.	–	23.4	4
BASF	108	2	113	2	22.6	5
Hoechst	78	7	n.a.	–	21.9	7

Source: Vivian, Gray & Co. (1980).

* Gross fixed assets.   † Total wages and salaries including benefits.

expenditure lagged its competitors in the late 1960s and early 1970s but approximated the best international levels during ICI's capital spending spree in 1978 and 1979. The German companies invested heavily at the start of the 1970s, but cut back their expenditure in the light of falling growth rates and the growing awareness of European overcapacity. In general the American companies invested more than their European counterparts, and with the possible exception of the big spender Dow, also reduced capital expenditure after the 1975 trough. ICI seem to have cut back on capital expenditure most savagely in 1980 and 1981.

Throughout the 1960s and 1970s ICI has been unfavourably compared with its competitors in the sphere of productivity; indeed our discussion of productivity differences between the UK chemical industry generally and its counterparts showed the UK in a less than favourable light. Table 16 reinforces this notion by comparing sales, investment and total remuneration per employee for ICI and its major competitors. The figures have been converted at the exchange rates ruling at end–1979 and are shown in $000. In interpreting Table 16 Vivian, Gray & Co. (1980) acknowledge that continental chemical companies employ more outside contract labour for maintenance and repairs than ICI, nevertheless ICI's position is at the bottom of each ranking. Vivian, Gray & Co. also remark that it is not possible to deduce from the above figures whether ICI's poor productivity reflects overmanning or underinvestment; however ICI's behaviour between 1979 and 1983 in reducing UK employees by 27,600 (a 30.8% reduction) indicates ICI believe the problem is more one of overmanning than it is of underinvestment. Unfortunately ICI's recent attempts to improve their productivity is being matched by some of their competitors, some of whom such as BASF, Monsanto, and Du Pont are ahead of them anyway, and others who are now behind them in sales per employee – Bayer, Hoechst, and Montedison, are working hard to catch up (*Chemical Insight*, 254, September 1982).

SUMMARY

In the early 1960s the corporate strategy of ICI began to crystallise around four major areas of strategic change. These were the attempt to bring ICI's technology up to the sophistication and scale of international competition at that time; the attempt to improve the manpower productivity of their UK assets; the attempt to change the geographical distribution of ICI's assets and sales away from the UK and the old British Empire towards the faster-growing markets and economies of Continental Western Europe and then the Americas; and finally the attempt to change the company's top management organisation and corporate culture in order to make ICI more adaptable and commercially minded.

The preceding review and commentary on ICI's development from 1960 to the early 1980s has indicated that ICI made significant progress in carrying through and implementing major elements of these strategic changes. As a result of these changes (particularly in technology and market focus) one might argue that at the end of the 1970s ICI had the following competitive advantages. It was firmly placed in the top half-dozen of the world's chemical companies, had strong market positions and shares in the UK, Australia, Canada, and South Africa, and had increased its investments in the USA and Western Europe. Its capital expenditure and R&D expenditure were up to the best international levels and the company operated world-scale plants with, in some cases, its own world leading technologies. Its product spread was wide and its dependence on any one product sector not crucial. ICI had big export businesses and was well placed in cash flow and in self-sufficiency of feedstock from its North Sea oil investments. ICI also had a cheap source of natural gas feedstock in the UK until at least 1984.

However in the late 1970s ICI also found itself with a number of competitive disadvantages. Chief amongst these was the fact that ICI's home market was only 6% of free world consumption and had a history of relatively poor realised and anticipated growth. Yet in 1979 ICI still depended heavily upon its UK production (57% of Group sales) as well as its UK customers (42% of Group sales). In addition the company's UK productivity remained low and no substantial attempt had been made to reduce manpower since the 1971–72 recession. ICI's CCA returns were poor and declining, and the margins realised in Western Europe and the USA were inadequate. Further in 1979 and 1980 ICI suffered from the overvalued pound against the US dollar and the Deutschmark. It also was becoming painfully aware that its earlier concentration of investment and sales in fibres, petrochemicals, plastics, and organics meant that in the worsening market demand for those commodity chemicals, the company was out of balance for the likely market conditions of the 1980s. Finally, as will be demonstrated later, the same criticisms that were being levelled about the constraining effect of ICI's conservative, overmanned, and slow-to-adapt corporate culture were still being made as vociferously in the late 1970s by those eager for change, as they had been made in the early 1960s and early 1970s.

So in sum the period 1960–83 was one of change and continuity inside ICI, with the emphasis for too long perhaps rather more on continuity than change. In what follows we now examine, at both the corporate and divisional levels, some of the forces in and around ICI which either accelerated or dampened changes in technology, productivity, management and organisational culture, whilst ICI grappled to live in a world which refused to stand still.

4 Implementing Corporate Change: A Role For Organisation Development 1965–72

The heart of this book is the description and analysis of ICI's attempts to change its structure, technology, management–union relationships, and organisation culture over the period from the early 1960s until the early 1980s. In examining this 20 years of continuity and change in ICI, a central theme will be the exploration of the possibilities and limitations of specialist attempts to facilitate and implement organisational change. The specialists under examination are individuals, and on some occasions groups of internal and external consultants, using behavioural science and organisation development concepts and methods. Crucial to the analysis of the above theme will be a frame of reference for studying change which recognises the opportunities and constraints for organisational change provided by changing social, economic, business, and political contexts, and how the purposeful actions of specialists and executives are bounded by political processes inside the firm.

The presentation of the empirical data in the book is influenced by the divisional character of ICI's structure, and the existence of the company headquarters in Imperial Chemical House, Millbank, London SW1. Throughout most of ICI's history, and during all of the period of this research, the main board of ICI was resident at Millbank. In October 1982 the announcement was made that the main board was to leave Millbank for a location elsewhere in London, but this change had not been implemented by the end of 1983. Millbank has been the centre of corporate power in ICI, and there will be no surprises in the statement that the framework of policy emanating from Millbank has provided the rationale and motive force for macro-level changes in the company. There is, however, some difference between a group of senior executives and senior staff men sensing environmental change and formulating corporate responses to those changes, and then implementing those substantial changes in dispersed divisions. In fact, one of the core reasons for the creation of internal and external OD consultant resources in ICI towards the end of the 1960s was to assist the centre implement the Millbank-spawned MUPS/WSA productivity bargain which was being resisted in some of the divisions.

This chapter describes elements of the political, social, economic, and business context which produced the MUPS change programme in 1965, and MUPS's relaunch in a different form as WSA in 1969. Since detailed accounts of the genesis, pathway of development, and impact of MUPS/WSA have already been supplied by Cotgrove *et al.* (1971), Roberts and Wedderburn (1973) and Roeber (1975) there is no point in repeating that narrative account here. Instead of focusing on the content and evolution of MUPS/WSA, the focus in this chapter will be to treat MUPS/WSA both as a case of centrally enforced change which ran into problems of implementation at division and works levels, and as the prime vehicle which in turn brought first of all behavioural science, and then organisation development, into Millbank, and then a variety of divisions of the company. Just as no account of chief executive-led change in ICI during the 1960s can ignore MUPS/WSA, so no account of the birth and evolution of OD activities at headquarters or divisional level can ignore the role that MUPS/WSA played as the initial vehicle for OD. Once the OD team had been created in Central Personnel Department (CPD) at Millbank, in turn they assisted with trying to rescue a faltering MUPS, to provide a climate for WSA to be implemented, and then helped to devise and implement a further company-wide change programme, this time for monthly staff, called the Staff Development Programme (SDP). During these activities the central team extended their role to training divisional internal consultants, and thereby helped to create a professional company network of OD resources numbering around 50 people.

The focus of this chapter is then on the origins and development of MUPS/WSA and SDP as central change programmes, and the rise of the CPD specialist OD resources who came with those central change programmes. Subsequent chapters will then examine both the impact of MUPS/WSA and SDP at divisional level, and the varying strategies and impact of OD resources in Agricultural, Petrochemicals, Plastics and Mond Divisions, as those OD resources sought to initiate and facilitate change in the post MUPS/WSA and SDP period. Chapter 10 will then return and pick up the story of the continuing role played by central OD resources in the period up until the early 1980s. Finally Chapter 12 will compare and contrast the different pathways of birth, development, demise, survival, and impact of OD in Millbank, and in Agricultural, Petrochemicals, Plastics, and Mond Divisions.

In order to assist the reader is disentangling some of the similarities and differences in the birth, evolution, and impact of OD in Millbank and the divisions, this chapter and those that follow it will have broadly similar structures, and will be written with an eye to keeping some balance between description and analysis. Given the strong emphasis in the first two chapters on contextualism as a mode of analysis, every effort will be made to present the Millbank and divisional accounts of OD in their historical and present-day business, technical, and organisational contexts. The divisional chapters in particular will carefully set the scene for any analyses of organisational change and development by offering broad analyses of the business history and development of each division, and detailed accounts of the management organisation and culture of each division. With the broad context thus established each chapter will then contain an overview account of the natural history of OD in that part of the company, followed by an analysis of the particular antecedent conditions which led to its birth, and the form and character of the development of OD activities. Each chapter will then review the internal and external evolution of the OD group attempting to stimulate organisational change, and account for the fate of each group and the impact of OD activities initiated by internal and external consultants, and line managers.

In presenting these narrative accounts of the business, economic, and organisational contexts in which OD emerged, developed, and influenced or fell away in its context, there is a need to strike a balance between writing a complex business history of the company and each division, and highlighting only those events with particular significance in relation to OD. Further, there is the risk that a narrative such as this overorganises and oversimplifies the complexities of history, makes it tidier than it is, or was. This is especially a problem with recent history where participants in the story have their own implicit framework and funds of detail. The challenge is to provide an account which captures some of the richness of views which are characteristic of any time, which is clear and is substantiated in detail, and yet in a coherent and additive fashion is able to assist the reader to identify factors to do with context, and individual and group action, which contributed to the success or otherwise of OD and organisational change efforts. In what follows the objective will be to capture a sense of the development of events and personalities so crucial in a processual analysis, and to start the process of teasing out the themes and patterns of cause and effects behind these events and personalities. It will be a prime objective of the more explicitly comparative and analytical Chapter 12, to draw out the similarities and differences between the case studies, and thus to seek to generalise what these ICI experiences tell us about the problems of creating and implementing change from internal and external specialist roles.

This chapter is organised into four sections. The starting point is a brief overview of the birth, development, and use made of OD from the headquarters at Millbank over the period 1964–72. OD, as it had become to be known by around 1970, developed out of a need both to justify and to help implement the weekly staff productivity and change initiative MUPS/WSA, and its monthly staff counterpart SDP. The second section thus moves on to identify some of the key antecedents of MUPS and therefore of OD in ICI, and considers what were the business, economic, social, and organisational pressures which led ICI to produce MUPS in 1965. Section three, "Dealing with resistance to change", chronicles why and how the centrally conceived MUPS was rejected in some of the divisions and works, how it was developed and relaunched in 1969 as WSA, and the role that the Central Personnel Department internal and external OD resources played in shaping, and trying to implement MUPS, WSA, and SDP. The concluding part of the chapter, "The legacy of WSA and SDP" briefly attempts to assess the impact of WSA and SDP on ICI, and considers the fate and future prospects of centrally located OD resources in the aftermath of the widespread relief in ICI that by early 1972 WSA, and SDP had been formally and officially implemented.

THE CENTRAL ORGANISATION DEVELOPMENT RESOURCES 1964–72: AN OVERVIEW

As will become apparent in the chapters which follow this one, on the genesis and development of OD in various divisions of ICI, it is not always easy to be precise where and when an activity such as OD began in a company the size and complexity of ICI. This general problem of identifying points of birth for activities is compounded in this case by the indefinitiveness of the term OD, and by the fact that different people began to use the phrase OD to signify rather different things at different points in time. There is the added problem that by the time the term OD began to have more general use in ICI it had also acquired a variety of negative stereotypes, so that some of its earliest proponents and users had to desist describing their work as OD if indeed they wished to carry on developing the ideas, frames of reference and techniques they would previously have described as OD.

As I pointed out in Chapter 1, the term OD appears to date from work carried out in the United States in the late 1950s. The term organisation development was probably not being used by the specialists who were associated with it in ICI until around 1969 or 1970. But as early as 1963 and 1964 a few personnel people in the company began to hear of ideas about motivation, leadership, and group behaviour at work which were associated with mainly American academics, who variously called themselves, or were labelled, social or behavioural scientists. Some of these American behavioural scientists were already, or went on to become, prominent external OD consultants.

In spite of the fact that not even its proponents would have described their work as OD before 1969, and that behavioural science was the more common term used in ICI throughout the mid and late 1960s, I date the beginnings of OD in the company as 1964 for two main reasons. First of all, in 1964 ICI set up a wages structure panel led by a deputy chairman of Fibres Division, C.I. Rutherford, which in January 1965 produced the Rutherford Report, which started off the chain of events that in 1965 led to the MUPS productivity bargain. MUPS, and then WSA and SDP, provided the main initial vehicle for the behavioural sciences and OD in ICI, and the Central Personnel Department (CPD) in Millbank provided OD with its early home. During the period 1965 to 1971 when first MUPS and then WSA were in negotiation, the always shifting, informal group of people in CPD associated with OD, busied themselves as a subset of the company resources devoted to implementing these productivity bargains. It was, therefore, only after 1971 that central OD had to find an independent role for itself.

The second reason for using 1964 as the starting point for OD in ICI is that 1964 was the year when the first of the well-known American behavioural scientists visited ICI. During 1963 the head of the small research and development section of CPD, accompanied by an assistant works manager from Dyestuffs Division, visited the United States "for the purposes of assessing for the management of ICI the implications of the work of Professor Douglas McGregor and others in schools of industrial management, and the applications of their ideas in some of the larger firms in the United States". One of several recommendations coming out of this visit to the United States was that "Professor McGregor should be retained by ICI as a consultant on the development of management's basic strategy, and on the application of social science findings generally to management problems". Before McGregor arrived in England he was visited by George Bridge of Agricultural Division. Bridge, as we shall see, was a critical figure in the development and implementation of ICI personnel policies and practices over the period 1964–74.

Douglas McGregor managed just one 2-week visit to ICI before his death. In September 1964 he visited Paints, Agricultural, Nobel, and Mond Divisions, and had time for discussions with senior managers of CPD, and the chairman and a number of main board directors. In spite of McGregor's brief contact with ICI, he was able to assist those in ICI pushing for changes in working practices and in managerial style to structure and legitimate their arguments for change, and to give added confidence to those preparing the Rutherford Report.

With the Rutherford Report published in January 1965, and its recommendations accepted by the main board in February 1965, there remained the question of negotiations centrally with the ICI signatory unions. Agreement was reached with the national officials of the trade unions in October 1965 and all those centrally involved hoped for an early start in implementing the productivity bargain at the designated trial sites. In fact by December 1968 only 5% of the ICI work force was covered by MUPS and discussions were still proceeding slowly in 12 works. ICI's central change initiative ran into the well-known problem of resistance to change from individuals and groups on the management and union side who had not been involved in its conception and design.

Throughout 1966 and 1967 MUPS faltered as the craft unions in particular on the big sites such as Billingham and Wilton in the north-east of England refused to co-operate. In late 1967 the first stage of breaking the pattern of MUPS declining fortunes came with the appointment of George Bridge as Manager: Payroll Employees in CPD. Bridge had been sent up to Billingham as Personnel Director in 1962 in order to create social and organisational change there. The period of his social innovations at Agricultural Division is described in the following chapter; but his task at Millbank was to breath life into the faltering MUPS. This he tried to do partly by his zeal, enthusiasm, vision, and political skill in handling his fellow senior managers and the relevant members of the main board, but also by building up in his Labour Department part of CPD, a Development and Applications Group to provide a focus for bringing in behavioural science ideas into the company, to help deal with the MUPS problem of resistance to change.

By 1968 Bridge had brought his right-hand man at Billingham, Tom Evans, into the Development and Applications Group – hereafter the core of what is being called the central OD group. Evans joined a former works manager from Mond Division, Stewart Dudley, who had been doing research and development work in CPD since 1965. Dudley was to become the central and continuing focal point for OD in ICI until his retirement at the end of November 1982.

Two more junior managers with management services backgrounds made up the central OD group. These four had informal contact with the several MUPS liaison officers who worked from Millbank out into the divisions, and with the increasing number of American external consultants who ICI employed. Of these consultants one, Ron Mercer, was to stick. Mercer, who had been introduced to George Bridge by Douglas McGregor, had by this time acted as a consultant to the Agricultural Division Board, and was now invited by Bridge to assist the central OD group get off the ground.

Stewart Dudley seems to have been influential at this time in persuading Bridge that the joint problem-solving approach explicit in the process of operating the MUPS productivity bargain would never work even if the local shop stewards' doubts could be allayed, for as long as the senior management in the works remained reticent and unsupportive in working in the more participative style that was now expected of them. Having clarified the management side of the resistance to change problem in this manner, and after a period of training themselves in the United States in OD techniques and behavioural science concepts, Evans and Dudley threw themselves into helping to design and then run a series of workshops for works managers and assistant managers. Between 1968 and 1970, over the period in fact in which Bridge and others had to abandon MUPS and finally reach agreement with the trade unions on the more acceptable WSA, some 500 managers and assistant managers – "the key climate setters", attended these workshops. The workshops not only focused on problems associated with MUPS/WSA implementation, but tried to emphasise both the part that workshop members played in creating resistance to change, and through a variety of experiential exercises, exposed the works managers to group dynamics and associated behavioural science ideas. A related strategy of trying to influence divisional directors so as to provide support for the works managers does not seem to have been as successful as the work done with climate-setters at the works level.

In parallel with the workshops for works managers, and the attempt to influence divisional directors, a third strategy was used. This was the attempt to develop internal OD consultants within the divisions. This strategy did not have a lot of impact on the relatively short-run problems of implementing WSA – it was a rather late and low-level intervention for that. However, it had a considerable impact on the evolution of OD in the company. The two Eastbourne Events, as they became known, together with subsequent follow-up by members of the central OD group, helped form the ICI "OD network", an informal professional association which provided moral if not always too practical support for many a doubting or beleaguered internal OD consultant in the hard times after WSA and SDP had been formally implemented.

The final major intervention carried out by the central OD group was to design and implement the ill-favoured, and some have said ill-conceived, Staff Development Programme (SDP). One effect of MUPS had been to erode the traditional differentials between staff and labour. Renegotiation into WSA in 1968–69 further reinforced this process, as the pay rates to be negotiated with the unions were significantly increased. SDP was ICI's attempt to deal with this situation. The aim was to provide a MUPS/WSA equivalent for clerical, technical, junior and middle managerial staff, a programme in which they could examine their own jobs and more productive ways of organising them, implement changes, and receive significant pay increments.

SDP was a massive intervention. Some 40,000 people were involved in 1969 and 1970. The central OD group designed the basic format and helped to monitor progress and provide assistance in the form of external consultants as well as by their own involvement. The more detailed accounts of the implementation of SDP in the divisional chapters which follow, reveal that the overall evaluation of SDP is very mixed. Some staff were enthusiastic, but rather more were cynical, believing that SDP was just a short-term device to allow staff to be paid more money. Worse perhaps was the fact that in 1970 and 1971 ICI went into one of their cyclical bad business periods, some monthly staff were made redundant, and some associated SDP's arrival with numbers reductions exercises. There is, however, no doubt that SDP provided a great boost for internal and external OD consultants.

These events, plus the Eastbourne training, helped build experience and commitment among quite a large group (perhaps 100 to 200) OD practitioners and exposed many more potential clients and supporters to behavioural science ideas, group relations training methods, and the use to be made of third-party OD consultants. However, this broad exposure also generated its share of opponents and doubters. The worsening business scene in 1971, the sheer exhaustion amongst many senior managers of finally disgorging WSA, and then the perception amongst some that SDP was a cynical ritual, drew the doubters and opponents of OD out into the open. Some of the questioners of OD and behavioural science felt the methods and style of training were too psychological, long-haired, and dangerous. Others accepted them as a temporary expedient, useful while WSA and SDP were around, but doubted that there was any need for continuing activity of this sort.

By the end of 1971 WSA was "in" – the survival of OD now became problematic. The mother-vehicle's life was over. Could the offspring survive?

In 1972 several things happened. Bridge was promoted to be General Manager of CPD and reorganised the department to get rid of the split between Staff and Labour Sections. MUPS/WSA being over, the MUPS/WSA liaison officers and the two junior members of the Development and Applications Groups were reassigned to other jobs. In addition Tom Evans, a key link in the Bridge, Dudley, Evans development trio left ICI. So within a very short space of time the central OD establishment was reduced from six or seven people to just Dudley. The continuing story of the role of OD in CPD, and indeed at the very centre of power in Millbank, will be the subject of Chapter 10 of this book.

ANTECEDENTS OF MUPS AND WSA

Although from an internal political point of view MUPS appeared to many a surprised manager and trades unionist out in the divisions as an unwelcome white rabbit pulled out of a centrally located top hat, the need for a MUPS, and the particular form in which it appeared and was justified, can be traced back to ICI's long history of progressive personnel policies and practices, and the set of business, political, and social pressures which were closing in on ICI at the beginning of the 1960s. With their newly appointed Chairman Paul Chambers, the first non-wholly ICI career man appointed as chairman, in office in 1960, ICI began a period of for them radical business, technical, organisational, and manpower change, comparable only with the significant changes in organisation and people made around the beginning of the 1980s. It should be clear from the outset that although MUPS and WSA were ahead of their time as pieces of social architecture and organisational change, they and the other innovations coming out of ICI in the early to mid-1960s, appeared because of mounting business and economic pressures. After another period of incremental adjustment in the 1950s, in the face of a broadening set of linked environmental changes, ICI had to innovate in the 1960s in order to survive. As one senior manager crisply put it, in the early 1960s "the real trigger for change in the company was our competitive position".

But what were MUPS and WSA, and in what sense might they contribute to managing some of the environmental pressures facing ICI in the early 1960s? MUPS and WSA are in the first instance most simply considered as examples of productivity bargains so characteristic of the economic and industrial relations history of Britain in the 1960s. McKersie and Hunter (1973:5) suggest a productivity bargain

> involves the parties to the bargaining process in negotiating a package of changes in working method or organisation, agreeing on the precise contents of the package, their worth to the parties and the distribution of the cost savings between the reward to labour and other alternative destinations such as the return to capital and the reduction or stablisation of the product price.

The MUPS bargain required greater flexibility of working practices of both craftsmen and process operators in chemical plants, withdrew restrictions on the supervision of craftsmen by non-craft foremen, aimed to ensure maximum efficiency by getting the right man for the right job and then training him appropriately, and hoped for flexibility of agreement such that working practices would continue to change as other relevant circumstances changed. In return for these organisational benefits, employees would henceforth be known as "weekly paid staff", a new eight-grade payment structure would be introduced for all weekly staff employees based on a management-designed and controlled job assessment scheme, and a weekly paid non-fluctuating, single-element salary calculated on an annual basis replaced the complex miscellaneous part incentive payments which had made up the traditional wage packet. Essentially MUPS hoped to buy out restrictive practices and relax demarcations with a 16% pay rise. In addition improved benefits were stipulated for sickness, supplementary payments for shift and day rotas, overtime and bad working conditions, and trade unions' existing spheres of influence would be respected.

As has been noted the centrally negotiated MUPS agreement ran into trouble at divisional and works level as much because of the manner or process of its design and implementation as the content of its proposals. But focussing for a moment on local objections to its content it seems these were largely from the craft unions, reflecting the greater extent to which they were adversely affected by the proposals. The three problem areas as seen by the craft unions were first of all concern over the flexibility of working practices and the fear that they were "handing over tools" to the general workers. Secondly the salary levels in the agreement were too low compared with comparable agreements in other firms at that time, and thirdly hostility based on fears of redundancy (Roberts and Wedderburn, 1973).

When, by May 1969, WSA had been agreed the differences reflected some of the above craft union concerns. The flexibility issue was clarified so that any fears of major or complete transferability between craft and non-craft were removed. Higher salaries were offered, in fact a further 7% pay rise on top of the 16% offered under MUPS. The job assessment system was also clarified, and more information made available to the unions on the marks awarded to different job factors so that shop stewards could negotiate more effectively.

It was agreed that no enforced redundancy would take place as a direct result of WSA, and ICI conceded the closed shop. Management also reaffirmed, perhaps with greater explicitness in WSA, that job satisfaction was an objective they were committed to as well as greater effectiveness in reconsidering working practices. Finally management emphasised the process benefits which could accrue from WSA, a closer and more mutual process of problem-solving between local management and shop stewards as they sought to use the broad framework of agreement and intent stated in WSA in order to redesign jobs, working practices, and rewards in the workplace.

It should be clear from the above brief accounts of the content of MUPS and WSA that ICI were using MUPS and WSA both to make productivity gains, and to try and change the ongoing character of day-to-day working relationships between their managers and employee representatives. As we have already hinted, these changes in productivity and managerial culture and style were desired by managers because of a complex mixture of business, economic, political, and social changes then facing ICI.

Commercially life has been fairly comfortable for ICI before the Second World War. ICI has been conceived in 1926 as a cluster of monopolies and nurtured under protection. Western Europe was left to IG Farben, DuPont had the United States, in return for ICI controlling the Commonwealth markets. At home ICI had a virtual monopoly in a number of key products from its old business groupings in dyestuffs, explosives, alkali, and nitrogenous fertilisers. Products were more or less allocated; they were certainly not marketed. During the Second World War and throughout the late 1940s and 1950s ICI tried in a fairly unplanned way to diversify into new fields – in plastics, pharmaceuticals, synthetic fibres, and paints. These newer fields appeared to have faster growth rates than the old business areas, tended to be much closer to the consumer, and with all the pre-war cartels now swept away, had to develop in a much more competitive environment than did the likes of alkali, dyestuffs, and Billingham. If increasingly competitive and international markets was a problem all of ICI's post-war business areas had to face, a particular problem that the newer divisions felt they had was reliance on the older divisions for supplies of their raw materials, and dependence on a conservative main board in Millbank largely stocked with men who had made their name at Winnington, Billingham, or in Dyestuffs Division. The 1950s was the period when the epitaph "Millstone House" was most frequently and forcibly used of the main board and the "mandarins" in Millbank. As one senior manager based in Millbank put it to me with casual understatement "what we just about appreciated at the beginning of the 1960s was that something was wrong!".

The problems, however, were not just a function of more competitive and international markets, some of ICI's traditional strengths particularly in dyes and explosives were tied to markets (textiles and coal) which were declining at home and hard to expand abroad. ICI were also beginning to become aware that with the UK economy not growing at the rate of, for example, the USA or Germany, an over-reliance on UK sales would not augur well for the future. As it was, the big US chemical companies were already taking advantage of their much bigger domestic markets to produce larger, and more capital-intensive, plants than ICI. By the end of the 1950s ICI began to find themselves with smaller and less productive plants than their major international competitors.

Although the UK economic growth rates were not on a par during the 1950s with the USA or Germany, the "You've never had it so good" days were times of full employment and therefore of a seller's market for labour. Full employment, a growing and more confident trades union movement, and changing attitudes and expectations of work and authority in a better-educated and more aware labour force, all began to put pressure on ICI's personnel policies and practices.

For much of the 1950s the above trends were masked by the general excess of demand over supply. It was not until the US-led recession of 1958 that this situation was reversed, particularly in organic chemicals where a considerable number of new entrants had helped to swell capacity. Thus, this traditionally cartel-protected industry was, rather suddenly, faced with a typical boom–slump cycle, and the mask was removed from whatever deficiencies had been developing. For ICI 1960 was a good year, with profits before tax and interest of £91m on assets of £694m, a return on capital of 31.2%. The following year profits before tax and interest slumped to £64m on assets of £738m producing a far from satisfactory return on capital of 8.7%. The returns for 1962 and 1963 were not that much better at 9.1% and 10.4% respectively, before a rise to 12% in 1964, and then the all-time low for the 1960s of 8.1% in 1966, when they were at a peak point in capital spending and ran into an embarrassing cash crisis. Not even the normally formal tones of the ICI Annual Report could paper over these sorts of results. The 1961 Annual Report openly talked of reduced profits, substantial falls in world prices, abnormal surpluses in the USA, a fiercely competitive export trade, and lowered profit margins.

The problem was, of course, that ICI did not look good in the difficult commercial times of the early 1960s when compared with their competitors. In 1961, for example, DuPont's net profit as a percentage of sales was 11.3%, and ICI's was just 6.2%.[1] Apart from these differences in financial performance, the other area that began to preoccupy ICI was the comparative advantage of their US competitors with regard to productivity. The leading main board figure in ICI most knowledgeable and vocal about productivity in the 1960s was P. C. (later Sir) Peter Allen, chairman of the company in the crucial period between 1968 and 1971 when WSA was negotiated. Allen had been a President of Canadian Industries Ltd., ICI's associated company in Canada. When he became a main board director, Allan spent a period as Chairman of the overseas policy group dealing with North America.

Although wages in the US chemical industry were twice the rate to be found in the UK chemical industry in the early 1960s, undoubtedly the US companies had taken advantage of much larger domestic markets to make larger investment in fixed capital per employee than ICI, and the US firms tended to place a higher proportion of contract engineering work and catering, and other services out to contract workers; nevertheless by whatever measure of productivity used, ICI came out looking less productive. For example, profit earned per employee in DuPont in 1961 was £2000, for ICI in 1961 the figure was £700. The corresponding figures for each company in 1965 were respectively £2500 and £1000. Allen himself is quoted in an article on US – UK productivity comparisons in *Chemical Age*, 23 July 1966, as saying rather sanguinely "as long as the US employ half as many people and pay them twice as much, it is not a dangerous situation, but obviously we can and should be doing very much better". Later in the same article Allen went on to say efficiency of manpower in the US is about 1½ times better than ICI, allowing for factors like bigger plants, and more contract labour in the US.

Stewart Dudley also mentioned Allen's role in stimulating awareness in ICI of productivity differences with US competitors. Dudley confirmed that the comparative studies tended to find ICI employed 5 people where US firms employed 2. "The areas we were bad at were not process operation, but engineering maintenance, support services, and management. Basically our system demanded very much more work to maintain it than did companies we compared ourselves to. We were very much more bureaucratic. The drive to improve productivity came out of that".

Before ICI moved to try and improve productivity through changes in manning and working practices they took a more established ICI approach to innovation – technical development backed by heavy capital investment. Considering the period from 1955 to 1970, 1959 was the low point of ICI's capital investment, while 1966 was the high point. In 1964 prices ICI invested £39m in new capital, in 1959 this rose to £56m by 1961 dropped again to £45m in 1963 and peaked to £134m in 1966, only to fall dramatically to £73m in 1967, after ICI was forced twice in 1966 to go to the market to borrow expensive capital. Although this investment brought ICI bigger, more sophisti-

---

[1] *Source: Chemical Age*, 2 April 1971, page 19.

cated single-stream plants using at that time more economic feedstocks, these technical revolutions, as our chapters which follow on the divisions show, brought havoc in terms of commissioning problems. A critical consequence was that ICI's return on capital remained relatively modest for much of the 1960s, and downright bad in 1966 and 1967.

Aside from the above capital investments, Paul Chambers also tried, paradoxically enough, to instill in ICI a greater sense of financial and commercial acumen, to temper what had been assumed to be an over-reliance just on technological perspective and strength in the management culture. McKinsey, the American management consultancy firm, were called in and helped to reaffirm both a need for change in commerical orientation and in structure in ICI, and opened the way for an ICI Board Organisation Committee to stimulate both a move to greater accountabilities between the division chairmen and the main board, and organisationally a strengthening of business areas against the previously all-powerful functions. As we shall see these structural changes had only a patchy impact along the lines intended, and by the early 1980s ICI was still searching for organisational ways to sharpen market focus, top-level decision-making, and business responsibilities and accountabilities.

The other, and for the purposes of this book, the focal, point of intervention that ICI chose to improve its competitive position was to try and change the working practices, manning levels, systems of wage payment, and quality of management–union relationship in their plants. The above analysis of business trends has indicated there were strong competitive pressures for ICI to improve productivity. The two obvious questions to ask of ICI's eventual response in the productivity area was why did they choose the productivity bargain, and why did they design the variant of the productivity bargain described by the acronyms MUPS and WSA?

In choosing a productivity bargain as their vehicle to create changes in working practices and management–union relationships ICI were following a pattern of their day initiated by Esso's Fawley Productivity Agreement of 1960. They were also following both a national and an industry concern that unless UK industry improved levels of productivity compared with American and Continental Western European competitors, UK industry would lose out dramatically and permanently. On the national economic scene there was the beginnings of a concern with inflation amongst politicians. Some politicians could see that in conditions of full employment there was a seller's market for labour, which had a tendency to facilitate wage increases and stimulate cost-push inflation. In a buoyant domestic market for goods and services cost increases due to rising wages and salaries were merely absorbed into price increases. Further wage increases could then be secured on comparability and cost of living changes. These cycles of increasing costs created further problems for UK firms in international markets and adversely affected both the balance of payments and the value of sterling.

When the Labour Government took office in 1964 they looked to incomes policy as a way of curbing the above inflationary cycles. In 1965 the National

Board for Prices and Incomes (NBPI) began their work. Now wage rises had to be formally justified through the NBPI. Wage rises could only be justified now by productivity increases, and not just as a result of cost of living changes and comparability. The worsening economic scene in 1966 eventually led to the imposition of a prices and incomes standstill. This more strictly administered prices and incomes policy meant that the productivity bargain became a much-used vehicle to relate increases in pay to improvements in productivity arising from increased effort and more adaptability on the part of the workforce. McKersie and Hunter (1973) note that prior to 1963, the Fawley productivity agreement practically stood on its own as an example of this kind of agreement. Between 1963 and 1966, however, 73 agreements were made, and after the 1966 prices and incomes standstill and up until 1970 there was a veritable explosion of agreements – 4091 in all.

The reason why ICI chose a productivity bargain is then fairly clear to see; they were caught up in a national and an industry concern with productivity, and national economic policies which tied wage rises to productivity improvement. The reason why ICI chose MUPS and then WSA as their particular variant of a productivity bargain is a more complicated story. Critical factors in this story were undoubtedly the competitive pressures ICI were facing at the time, the way that the new process technologies and plants introduced at the beginning of the 1960s were requiring a new level of skill of process workers and putting pressure on an old job assessment system, and a generalised concern amongst the company and the unions that the company's payment structure was over-complex in terms of grades, and over-dependent on work study-based incentive schemes and bonuses.

It would be wrong to suggest, however, that to some people in ICI MUPS "was just" a productivity bargain. The notion that it had aims and a social philosophical base broader than an instrumental need for more productivity was of course captured in the title of Joe Roeber's book on MUPS/WSA, *Social Change at Work*. Roeber (1975) has adequately chronicled the progressive employee practices ICI has implemented since the days of Brunner Mond. He has also noted the gap that was beginning to emerge by the end of the 1950s between ICI's paternalism in the personnel field and its manifestation in certain kinds of managerial style, and the better-educated, more demanding, more affluent, and less compliant work force that ICI was dealing with by then.

ICI had always seemed to have progressive thinkers, from a managerial viewpoint, in personnel matters. Mond in the 1920s was certainly way ahead of his generation in terms of his attitudes and behaviour to the people who worked for him. Mond's successor in personnel policy-making was undoubtedly Alexander Fleck, later to become ICI's chairman, and to retire in 1960. Fleck had written the oft-referred-to memorandum of 1942 suggesting that the division used in the UK between the two classes of "workers", "staff" and "workmen" was arbitrary and should and could be eliminated in order "to improve the mental attitude of work people". Someone who Roeber (1975) makes much less of than Fleck, however, and yet who was critical in terms of maintaining and institutionalising Mond's strain of thinking in ICI was R. Lloyd Roberts.

Lloyd Roberts had been brought into Millbank from the old Brunner Mond company to head a Central Labour Department, a job he did right up until the early 1950s. Roberts' ideas on reducing a worker's identification with "class", and substituting this with first a greater sense of individual self-worth and ambition, and then identification with his firm, are contained in a paper circulated in ICI, 'A Labour Policy for a Large Undertaking', 24 May 1949. The essence of this paper is a recommendation that the practice of joint consultation in ICI be more fully developed so that the idea of consultation between and within all levels of management, supervisors, and workers be absorbed into day-to-day practice. The Roberts paper also suggested that the hourly basis of payment of manual workers be gradually discontinued in favour of an annual salary. This meant the application to the manual workers of the principles governing the remuneration and conditions of junior staff. Roberts then went on to justify in more detail the appropriateness of such "a reform" at that time. His own words are important here so I quote him at length:

> The adoption of any such plan as this involves an "act of faith" by any Board, but its boldness is its justification. Conceptions of the proper treatment of manual workers have become so stereotyped with the growth of trades unions and employers organisations that only a complete break with tradition as suggested will effectively secure the necessary new alignment of the worker's interests. The worker will learn that his own personal fortunes are linked primarily with those of his own firm and only secondarily with those of other workers elsewhere, and with the full development of joint consultation there will follow naturally a closer association and co-operation with his own management.

The ICI board were not ready to accept this "act of faith" in 1949, and neither did they wish to put all employees progressively on to staff conditions as recommended in the Report on Terms and Conditions of Employment (the Inglis Report, 1955). Some changes were made in the direction of offering staff status for all, including the bureaucratic device of merging in 1964 the old Staff and Labour Departments and calling them the Central Personnel Department; but there were still some ICI managers who kept up pressure in the system for staff status for all ICI employees in spite of the reticence of the main board for radical reform. By 1964, however, the right mixture of people, circumstance, rational justification, bureaucratic mechanism, and political will had assembled themselves, and there now at least seemed the possibility of combining the economic and instrumental need for productivity improvement with the more libertarian desire to create one class of employees in ICI, and a character and quality of satisfaction at work, combined with a more mutual process of problem-solving between management and employee representatives which would bring human relations in ICI into the 1960s, and prepare them for the uncertain future of what the 1970s would bring. The Rutherford Panel of 1964 was the bureaucratic mechanism which brought these various strands together, produced the offspring MUPS, and led to the birth of organisation development beliefs, activities, and techniques in ICI.

Having established the antecedents of MUPS, we now return to discuss in more detail its birth and fate, and thus the genesis of OD in the company.

DEALING WITH RESISTANCE TO CHANGE: THE BIRTH AND EARLY LIFE OF CENTRAL ORGANISATION DEVELOPMENT

The purpose of this section is to provide a chronological view and some limited analysis of the major activities and events in the birth and development of the central OD group. For this purpose conceptual elaboration is kept to a minimum, but a distinction is made between the "internal evolution" of the group and its "external evolution". The internal aspect refers to the evolution of the group's membership, values, distinctiveness, commitment, conflict, and leadership, and to the intra-group and environmental factors that influenced these. The external aspect refers to the group's strategies of boundary management, its external sponsorship and opposition, the focus and nature of the group's work, and the evolution of the group's legitimacy in its context. The importance of this set of internal and external factors in influencing the impact and survival of internal consultancy groups was suggested in Pettigrew (1975a, b), and has been further confirmed in subsequent research carried out in parallel with this research (Pettigrew and Reason, 1979; Pettigrew *et al.*, 1982). However, even with these concepts the major objective is still to tell the story of the birth and early life of the central OD group.

As has already been explained, the company productivity bargain MUPS/ WSA provided the crucial vehicle for the entry and development of behavioural science and OD in ICI. It could also be said that OD's association with MUPS/WSA also provided the seeds, if not the kernel, of OD's eventual demise in large parts of the company. But in the beginning at least MUPS needed behavioural science, and behavioural science in ICI needed MUPS, and when eventually WSA appeared, WSA certainly needed OD as a contributing source of ideas and techniques to aid its implementation. Behavioural science and OD thereby provided initially two functions in ICI. In the first place McGregor and then Herzberg provided novel ideas on leadership, managerial style, and motivation to help express and thereby legitimate in slightly more formal language the social and organisational objectives of MUPS. Secondly the developing set of ideas and techniques on the management of change in the field of OD helped ICI find and fashion decentralised processes of problem-solving to cope with the continuing problems of resistance to change to the centrally created company productivity bargain and participative styles of management now expected in the divisions and works.

Legitimating MUPS: a role for behavioural science

The previous section of this chapter on antecedents of MUPS clearly made the point that the need for *a* MUPS, and indeed many of the ideas and principles within it, had been around in ICI for some time before the broad outlines of the productivity bargain were acknowledged as a necessity by the main board in February 1965, and agreed by the trade union national officials in October 1965. The need for a MUPS was a product of competitive pressures, techno-logical change, an outmoded and troublesome payment system, and doubts amongst a small subset of senior managers and directors in ICI that paternalistic personnel policies and practices, and in many cases authoritarian works management, could carry ICI through a period of social and economic change which appeared to be altering workers' attitudes to authority and expectations of employment.

However, as any student of the development and implementation of strategic change will know, there is a world of difference between the development of a need for change in an organisation, people's differential awareness of such a need, their capacity to pull together an appropriate vehicle or mechanism to satisfy that need, and express it in a way and in forums where it becomes politically acceptable, and then to find the political will, climate of co-operation, systems, structures, and human capabilities to ensure that strategic change is successfully implemented. In the case of MUPS the gestation period that there was a need for change on the grounds of competitive pressures, started with the bad results of 1958, were helped by the appearance of a new chairman Paul Chambers in 1960 determined to give greater emphasis to financial and competitive factors, and consolidated by the bad results of 1961. Meanwhile the productivity thread had been given political visibility in ICI by Peter Allen's presence on the main board after a period of time in North America where he had been persuaded of the differences between US and UK working practices and manning levels. With a MUPS forerunner, the Esso Fawley Agreement, in place, an emerging national economic and political climate indicating that productivity agreements were an answer to contain inflation, the need for change and the outline character of the device to create that productivity change had come together around the period 1963. Politically and practically speaking ICI still had to find a productivity bargain appropriate for their organisation, systems, and people and the right arguments, political sponsorship, and language to get their formulae accepted first by the main board, and then, because of the centralised bargaining, by the national officers of the signatory trade unions, and then by managers and other employees out in the divisions.

The fashioning of the particular response of MUPS came partly from staff work conducted in the small research and development section of CPD, and then principally from the activities of a number of senior manager-composed wage structure committees, culminating in the 1964 wages structure panel called the Rutherford Panel.

The Rutherford Panel in total comprised six personnel and production people from Millbank and the divisions. A critical part of the Rutherford Panel's findings, again in terms of the politics of justifying this kind of change, related to the results of the so-called ideal manning studies. Teams of local managers were given the job of working out theoretical manning patterns for five ICI works of varying sizes, ages, technologies, and geographical locations.

They were told to "assume there are no constraints and you are starting from a green field". As Roeber (1975:58) reports "these studies were influential with the Panel – and later with the main board – and provided the solid base for their recommendations". Apart from offering a carrot of cost savings at the end of a programme of change, they demonstrated in vivid form the high cost of the current patterns of manning ... "an early estimate of savings from the new proposals, assuming a 15% saving in manpower, put the money saving for ICI at an immediate £1.75m per year, rising to £7.28m per year in 10 years time." What this meant in terms of the politics of formulating strategic change was that the emerging consensus that change was needed was solidified by the prospect of manifest and tangible outcomes, if only some concrete change project could be got off the ground.

Backtracking for a moment on the productivity theme, the climate which had allowed the Rutherford Panel to be set up and produce their carrot of manpower savings had really been established as a result of the manpower studies of 1962 and 1963 sponsored by one of the Company's deputy chairmen, Peter Allen. Again as part of the process of creating awareness of a need for change, Allen had encouraged teams of ICI managers to go off to North America and examine working practices and manning levels there. Critical in terms of impact in ICI had been a detailed study of the practices of the Union Carbide Corporation of New York.

Independently of these manpower studies, but again in 1963, the manager of the research and development section in CPD had gone to the United States with an assistant works manager as part of his own searching process to develop thinking about personnel policy in the company. This duo met a number of leading American behavioural scientists, including Argyris, Likert, and McGregor, and visited some of their clients such as DuPont, Union Carbide, Sears Roebuck, and Imperial Tobacco Company of Canada. They were followed to the United States in April and May 1964 by George Bridge. These two visits were critical in terms both of helping to clarify the broader management and social philosophy component of the MUPS change, and, of course, thereby to connect the behavioural sciences with MUPS, and bring McGregor and others into ICI.

There were a number of things that made McGregor and his ideas connect with the few people in ICI in 1963 actively trying to create a new management philosophy in the company. Principal amongst his attractions was his personal style and the interpretative and low-key way he presented his ideas. The research manager in CPD commented:

> The thing that made me wish to invite him into ICI was the person of Doug McGregor. He was so basically sound and wise that I had no doubts that he would go down with ICI management as a credible person; and that he would be listened to.

But, of course, there was also the attraction of the content of McGregor's approach in *The Human Side of Enterprise*, his focus on the virtues of individual responsibility and self-motivation, and participative styles of management; at a time when, as one person put it, there "were worries among your university educated, liberal, middle class ICI manager about the inequalities inherent in the officers and the men". Basically also McGregor provided a language that fitted some of the predispositions of the people in ICI pushing for change. The "McGregor philosophy" provided a framework, a set of principles to point a way forward that people felt was culturally appropriate for ICI in the UK, and yet couldn't express clearly enough on their own.

The ICI documents preparing the ground for MUPS are full of implicit and explicit reference to McGregor. One report described the essential task of management as a "process of involving employees in setting their own goals in their work within managements' objectives for the business, providing conditions for the exercise of initiative and self control in achieving these goals with a minimum of interference from above, creating opportunities for individuals to take on greater responsibilities and scope, encouraging growth and development of individuals," and so on.

One person close to ICI at that time commented that when the above kind of ideas came along around 1963, "they provided a kind of seed crystal around which the worries of some liberal ICI managers could coalesce. They also provided people with a rationalisation for proceeding forward to forms of organisation that were very threatening to traditional ways of doing things."

Certainly George Bridge, who was not a traditionalist in ICI, found it a strain to convince some of his colleagues on the Rutherford Panel, and later he was to have even bigger problems with managers and shop stewards out in the divisions:

> That was terrible, that Rutherford Committee, because you didn't have all the facts to argue against, all the logic of ICI over all the years – all you had was a belief that what was going on now couldn't go on forever; and that there had to be change, and that of all the options open this sort of way forward – and it was only a very general, thinking way forward – of co-operation with the unions, problem solving. That was really the key. Somewhere, somehow we had to start talking to the unions.

As it turned out, and again using Bridge's words, the Rutherford Panel "came out with quite a forward looking proposal . . . and it got through the main board to our absolute astonishment". What the main board were voting for, however, was a productivity bargain to save fixed costs, not a revolution in the management philosophy and style of ICI.

After the main board agreed to go ahead with negotiating a productivity bargain, Bridge and the other supporters of MUPS still had the industrial relations experts in CPD to deal with, for neither the head of CPD or his chief negotiator had been on the Rutherford Panel. Bridge remarked:

> After the Board agreement a central committee was set up to take the Rutherford recommendations further. That was pretty balls-aching too because nobody in Central Personnel wanted it. I remember meeting the head of department and he said "oh, you're not still wasting your time with that MUPS stuff".

These differences in the management view about MUPS, even between those who wanted to proceed with some variant of a productivity bargain, if not a new management philosophy in ICI, surfaced and further complicated the negotiations with the national officers of the trade unions. Bridge's recollections of those negotiations confirmed the caution of the trade unionists, and indicated what won through was the reservoir of goodwill ICI had built up with the national officers:

> My memory of the meetings with the unions over MUPS was that they were difficult because the members of the management had different objectives. Some of us were reaching out for the stars, others saw it as a little move forward . . . It was difficult also because you were talking to some pretty old trades union leaders. You couldn't really talk these OD concepts. But they did have a pretty big residue of trust in ICI.

Trust the national officers may have had, but neither the national officers nor the central management negotiating team had the support of shop stewards or managers in the divisions. Crucially perhaps the managers neither expected, were trained in, nor felt confident in behaving in the more co-operative problem-solving mode that was now necessary.

> What the company did was to say to the unions "let us sit down together in a problem solving orientation". This was completely new. Nobody had ever thought of asking the unions to co-operate before. But throughout the whole period between 1965 and 1968 the management didn't really understand co-operation. They were amazed when the shop stewards in the trials works said no.

Having taken so long to gain acceptance of a need for change, having delegated the design of the vehicle for change to a small group, and now having assembled the political will to act in the productivity area, ICI now found themselves with a beached whale, a strategy they could not implement.

Rescuing MUPS: OD finds a clear role

For reasons summarised earlier in this chapter, and chronicled in detail in Roeber (1975), between 1965 and 1967 MUPS seriously faltered. At this stage Millbank was faced with what was tantamount to a rejection of the agreement by the shop floor and, except for a very few, by managers as well. Bewildered by the continuing strength of resistance, the decision was taken to try to stage a revival. The man chosen to lead the revival was George Bridge, who believed in using behavioural scientists, and who himself was a powerful, charismatic, driving figure. One subset of people under him in his role as assistant general manager – payroll employees, was the development and applications section of CPD, henceforth described as the core of the central OD group. Over the period late 1967 until 1972, coincidental to his main task of getting MUPS/WSA in, Bridge provided crucial sponsorship for the central OD group. He created openings (sometimes difficulties as well) for them and he took the bulk of the "political flack" that was generated. Behind Bridge's bow-wave, the OD group of Tom Evans, Stewart Dudley, and the two more junior, ex-management services men, pursued a quieter but continuing task, which had two central elements: first that the primary blockages to change in general and specifically in MUPS/WSA were in the attitudes of managers, and second, that the key to changing these attitudes lay in OD concepts and techniques.

So the period of central OD between 1967 and 1972 had three key elements: the attachment to the MUPS/WSA and then the SDP central change programmes, the attachment to a powerful sponsor, and the growing adoption of behavioural science and OD. As we shall see in this and subsequent chapters, this period was characterised by initial rapid growth of the scope and influence of OD out into the divisions, followed by rather serious reversals and loss of key figures at the centre which almost eclipsed the central OD activity.

The birth and internal evolution of central OD

The central OD group core activities centred around running increasingly behavioural workshops for divisional managers involved with developing local responses to MUPS/WSA, then on the training of internal consultants for the divisions, and the sponsorship and management of an increasing number of mainly American external consultants, and finally implementing and co-ordinating the monthly staff equivalent of WSA, the SDP. These activities will be described and analysed more fully shortly; first, however, there is the question of the birth and development of the internal character of the central OD group. In exploring the internal evolution of each of the ICI OD groups, enough descriptive material will be presented to clarify the origins and membership of each group, its leadership, core values and other distinctive features, and the extent of cohesion and commitment in each of the groups.

The birth of central OD was straightforward enough, it was part of the company strategy to provide works management in the divisions with a further rationale, together with confidence and skill in participative modes of problem-solving, to aid the rescue of MUPS. In 1966 and 1967 ICI realised they had a strategy without the capability to implement it, and their vehicle for creating the necessary skills and knowledge was the central OD group.

In terms of the internal evolution of central OD, what seems to have happened is that Evans and Dudley established themselves as central OD enthusiasts and gurus, and became a sort of left wing or behavioural wing of those involved from the centre. They identified quite strongly with the values, language, and styles of OD as well as with OD activity. This came from their American OD training and their continuing association with American OD consultants. Somewhat less enthusiastic and committed to OD, to their "right" were their own subordinates, and the MUPS liaison officers, most of whom had also had some exposure to American OD but had not taken to it to the same extent. Further to the "right" still were other members of CPD engaged in more traditional staff and labour personnel activities.

There was then the basis for a certain amount of conflict and schism in the

OD group, and this was overlaid with their love–hate relationship, anxieties about, and dependency upon, their powerful visionary leader George Bridge. Bridge was the messianic figure at Millbank driving MUPS/WSA "for his own and the company's ends", seeking "to revolutionalize the relationships between the workers and the management through MUPS", and prepared to use OD as a means to that end. But even Bridge with all his pushing for change amongst directors through the medium of "T groups" saw the behavioural activities as sometimes going too far. The OD converts meanwhile saw some of his "political behaviours" as violating basic tenets of their new faith concerned with trust, openness, and non-manipulation.

There are three important points about these intra-group conflicts over values and style. They occurred to greater or lesser degrees in all the ICI OD groups, and have appeared in other specialist groups and organisations concerned with change (Pettigrew, 1975a; Freeman, 1975; Zald and McCarthy, 1979). The other side of the conflict coin is the establishment through testing and modification of a commitment to a set of values which are new to the culture where change is being attempted, and which provide a basis for the distinctive contribution which the group may make in the medium and longer term. Of course, the development of such exclusive values and their public proclamation through idiosyncratic language, behaviours, and activities may also create the kind of dynamics which lead to the stereotyping, isolation, and eventual demise of change-oriented groups.

As we shall see, in the main, the conflicts in the central OD were relatively contained, at least as long as the group were associated with the clear and legitimate task of introducing MUPS/WSA. When that task was over and the group moved over to the always less legitimate activity of implementing SDP, the intra-group and inter-group conflicts surfaced more, and played a part in the partial break-up of the group in 1971–72.

When in 1967 George Bridge left his appointment as personnel director of Agricultural Division to come down to Millbank to try and rescue MUPS, one of the first things he did was to arrange for Tom Evans to join him. Shortly after this Bridge recruited the two ex-management services men for the OD group, and made one or two new appointments as MUPS liaison officers. It was part of Bridge's management strategy to recruit his own men and to demand high measures of commitment and loyalty from his subordinates, so he could feel relaxed that the detail would get accomplished, while he did the necessary projecting of MUPS vertically to the main board, the Millbank general managers, and the various division boards.

Like many energetic and purposeful people who entered Millbank at a fairly senior level Bridge felt the usual sense of being lost, almost being powerless in amongst this highly divisive and power-conscious world:

> Actually working in that big office [Millbank] it's a pretty miserable exercise. There's no sense of team. If you are in Billingham you can feel a team, and an objective, and a way. If you are in London, the whole thing is politics and

problems – no sense of being part of anything. You feel you are continually up against everybody, that you are continually politicking yourself to try to get enough elbow room to bring your WSA through the Board.

Bridge, however, in choosing his own team could relax a little on that score. Tom Evans had helped to translate some of the elements of Bridges' imprecise vision into operational reality at Billingham; perhaps he could play the fixer to the moral entrepreneur, now on a company-wide scale. Evans was very conscious that Bridge "saw MUPS as both a vehicle for his own ambition and a vehicle for ICI, and a model of what large-scale organisation ought to try to do". Evans could also see that, so far at least, Bridges' rise to fame meant being pulled up with him, and that as I suggest above, their skills were complementary.

He took me up through Personnel at Billingham. He took me down to London. For most of that time we had a very constructive relationship. His vision, he did have a vision, his charisma, and his political skills created space to go forward, and my role was complementary in terms of making things happen.

Bridge and Dudley, however, ran straight into open conflict. To this day Dudley still describes with great feeling his surviving those conflicts as being one of the big successes of his career and life. Part of the reason for the conflict was undoubtedly differences in views about what was necessary to rescue MUPS, part was due to Dudley's requirement to move from being a solo operator to being a member of a loosely constituted team, and part the fact that Bridge and Dudley had at least one developed personality characteristic in common; they were both strong individualists. Bridge had the advantage in the early skirmishes, after all he was the more senior and much better politically connected than Dudley. Dudley was convinced he would be fired within 2 weeks of Bridge's arrival in Millbank. As it happened Bridge merely arranged for Dudley and Evans to go off to the United States to be trained in OD at the National Training Laboratories (NTL) at Bethel, Maine. Interestingly when Bridge was interviewed he unsolicitatedly mentioned Dudley's 2-week deadline for being fired:

Stewart Dudley – his view was that I would sack him within 2 weeks of coming down. The reason I suppose at that time I thought he'd got himself very muddled up between being a works manager and the new stuff (OD). In fact I decided and said "well you can go to the States and go and try to learn what the hell it is you're talking about, and then we'll see where we go from there". And he went to the States and he came back and he played the part of behavioural science proper.

Dudley meanwhile maintains that whereas Evans and the others were recruited into OD by Bridge, "I chose myself". Not only did he choose himself, it was clear to him from his work during 1965–67 with shop stewards and managers that rather than, as Bridge believed, the problem of rescuing MUPS being a union problem, it was largely in Dudley's view a problem of convincing an unwilling set of works managers. Dudley takes up the story:

> For Bridge it was "it's all the unions – we've got to get them doing it". In the end I just started working the other way, so there was a split. I was trying to do more things like the job enrichment studies, but do them from a management angle. I slowly won Bridge over to beginning to allow some managerial things to happen in the form, first of all, of getting Mercer (the American consultant) in to work alongside us in central OD.

Eventually Bridge and Dudley's relationship stabilised, and after Evans and Dudley had returned from their American training, Dudley and Evans "made a very strong pairing and worked very well together". Although Evans was the more senior of the four in the development and applications section he acknowledged that "it wasn't led. We came to the conclusion that we were a pair of senior partners and a pair of junior partners. Apart from training type things we didn't do much work together".

During late 1968 and well into 1969 Bridge was tied up politically trying to get WSA through the main board, then reach agreement with the unions, and eventually help tackle the hard nut to crack of Wilton resistance. In this period Evans and Dudley had more and more contact with OD ideas and American OD consultants as they all sought to get the workshops for ICI management off the ground. By this time it was becoming clearer which of the development and applications group, and which of the MUPS liaison officers, were prepared to take on board, and proclaim their values as being OD men.

George Bridge continued his socialisation strategy of sending all the central OD group over to the States for 2 months' training. He commented that there "were huge difference in their reaction to it. For example, Smith came back, he'd learned a tremendous lot but being very clear about the things he thought were absolute balls. Whereas Tom [Evans] tended to go bingo, right over."

Evans when interviewed was prepared to acknowledge that in ICI in the late 1960s it was a time "when we felt that we had better and different values than others, but I don't think they were . . . I know some people found some of my values difficult. I am basically optimistic and in favour of the individual and I'm basically off organisation. I'm in favour of the underdog not the boss". Dudley recognised that there was "never a group proclamation of values, but there were lots of individual proclamations" – including his own. Dudley said:

> Yes the values were distinctive. Things around the dignity of the human being. We saw organisations and roles as debasing human dignity . . . We would have very, very simplistic and ill-defined visions of the future. We would have values about openness of communication. We had values about job satisfaction particularly at lower levels in the organisation.

On top of these distinctive values Evans and Dudley also admitted using "the same shorthand, we got it from the same NTL Training programme, and reading the same things, this was difficult for others". They also tried to set norms on their own training programmes at Warren House of "tee shirts and old sweaters . . . we were deliberately different in our behaviour – to try and work participatively in workshops where we knew the managers would expect us to be authoritarian, and we deliberately used that as a learning point".

George Bridge remembered Evans and Dudley's distinctive language, dress, and behaviour in more graphic terms:

> Evans and Dudley turned up at meetings with the most outrageous clothes on . . . Tom himself became a bit difficult to fit in because you'd have a meeting and Tom would suddenly get up and rather ostentatiously lie full length with his hands behind him. Well I suppose in California this was great, but in ICI it was a little beyond what people could accept . . . Also from Evans and Dudley there was a huge input of jargon against which others in the Labour Department (of CPD) rather stood up and formed ranks.

There were then differences of language, values, and even styles of behaviour between in particular Evans and Dudley, and the more traditional members of CPD, but relationships in CPD were already complex because of the "two ends of the corridor thing – between the labour Department and the staff department", and because of the "fraught" relationship between Bridge and his boss the general manager of Personnel.

In terms of cohesion and commitment the OD group certainly held together well during 1968, 1969, and 1970. "There was a lot of backing each other up between George, Tom, and Stewart. A lot of covering for each other, supporting each other, and explaining each other to other people when they got mad." But the relationship between Evans and the two more junior members of the OD group was "more like a boss – subordinate relationship", and between them and Dudley, in the latter's words "it never really worked". But things ticked over amicably inside the group as long as they all continued to be active on training programmes and other activities associated with WSA and SDP. As soon as the inevitable vacuum appeared with the two central change programmes out of the way, a rather different set of dynamics came into play which caused the central OD group to all but disappear.

The central OD group engages with its environment

In exploring each of the ICI OD groups' relations with their respective environments a number of broad categories of analysis will inform the presentation of the data. These will include the form and extent of political sponsorship each group was able to generate and maintain, the broad strategy they used for managing their boundaries, the range of activities they concerned themselves with, and who and where their networks of contact were.

To a very large extent the legitimacy of the central OD group was predicated on their association with MUPS/WSA, and their political sponsorship wrapped up in the energy, vision, political skills and contacts of George Bridge. As Tom Evans remarked, "Bridge was the knight on a charger. He was the man with the cause leading."

Politically Bridge handled the two major interfaces, links with the main board and the divisional chairmen, and with the unions. As Evans commented, Bridge "was heavily connected at the top, first with Peter Allen (chairman 1968–71) and later with Jack Callard (chairman 1971–75), both of whom supported MUPS/WSA. He'd also worked for both Rowland Wright (Personnel Director in late 1960s and Stan Lyon (Main Board Director late 1960s, early 1970s at Billingham." Being politically well connected was a necessary but not a sufficient condition for influence at Millbank, Bridge still had to drive and push against all the forces of inertia in ICI. Life at Millbank was "all politics and problems". Bridges' zeal was a measure of ICI's inertia at first, but in the long term his forcefulness and desire for change created enemies. Bridge takes up the story:

> I had a strong feeling inside me, and a sort of stubbornness-zeal. Unless you really feel something like this at some point there's got to be one man – not entirely alone, but I think I certainly was the centre. I was able to convince Peter Allen and Rowland Wright. I certainly wasn't able to carry all division chairmen but I was able to carry a lot of them . . . Unless there's somebody there who will drive and drive and drive, it will not happen – someone who cannot and will not take no for an answer . . . It does tend to drag (in ICI). Things are always tending in a large organisation to get into a routine. People like to be comfortable and this is a very, very uncomfortable procedure. There's got to be tension and crises otherwise everything is slipping back again.

Bridge's energy, risk taking, and intuitive political skills generated respect not just from his old colleague Evans, but also the much more sceptical and wary figure of Dudley. Evans commented that Bridge "saw things in a massive scale and in brilliantly instinctive ways, saw what was necessary to make them happen. It wasn't infallible but it didn't desert him in any of the major crises." Dudley's admiration for Bridge, for personal reasons, was more grudging and controlled:

> In the early MUPS/WSA times Bridge was a great help. Once that is we were through the initial problems of him trying to throw me out . . . But he did lots of very good things. He produced a focus, he produced charismatic speeches and talks; he'd take ridiculous bloody risks, he'd got no sense of potential failure. So yes he was great at times.

With Bridge's lines of support into the main board established if not always secure, his main problems in 1968 were "the resistance of the AUEW, particularly the new leader, Len Edmundson who had not been involved in the building of MUPS, and the resistance of sites, particularly Wilton". The huge manufacturing site at Wilton was a thorn in ICI's side in the late 1960s not only because Wilton was the focal point of union resistance against MUPS and WSA, but also because the management there were so obviously not managing the site – they were too preoccupied with their own works and division. A fuller story of the Wilton site's problems and how they were tackled will be presented in Chapter 7 of this book. For the moment it is important to note that Bridge was instrumental in persuading first Jack Callard, who in turn persuaded Peter

Allen, to set up the review of management activities on the site, known as the Callard Committee, and that Bridge and the then chairman of Heavy Organic Chemicals Division (the "landlord" of the Wilton site) fought hard over the form and character of MUPS. Bridge commented on the Wilton problems in these terms:

> Why I'd got so excited was that the chairman of HOC decided that MUPS was not going to work and he produced what he called "mini MUPS". And just before I went down to London, he'd got this through Central Personnel. I fought it tooth and nail. I said "you're not going to have mini MUPS. You're going to have one personnel policy in ICI and that's it". So we were absolutely toe to toe over it.

Bridge won that battle with the chairman of HOC, but was on the losing side when they clashed again in 1974.

Bridge by early 1969 was of the opinion that no more life could be breathed into MUPS and if his vision of new working relationships between management and unions in ICI were to be reality he had to find another vehicle. This, of course, was WSA. The differences in content between the MUPS and WSA agreements were described on page 92. Bridge considered "there was no fundamental difference in principle between MUPS and WSA", the essential difference this time was to be in the process of formulating and reaching agreement on the character of the change. Thus Bridge said:

> The major difference were things like it had to come from the bottom up. We couldn't impose it from the top. The words had to be written in a very different way. And the consultation had to come now.

But the other great piece of learning that had come out of the MUPS failure was the lack of management preparedness. One of Dudley's contributions of this period had been to persuade Bridge of this fact. Bridge again comments:

> One of the great sadnesses was: The original MUPS agreement had a covering note which was really driving at management, that the whole of management must be concentrating on the philosophy behind it, and how they might move when the time came. And nobody did a bloody thing about it. That was our failure. It seemed to me that the management had a long time and they never prepared themselves. So when WSA came on they had a hell of a lot to catch up.

One of the contributions of the central OD group from mid-1968 onwards was to help facilitate the process of management catching up. Their prime vehicles for doing this were the Warren House workshops for senior works managers. The first of these was in June 1968. By the time WSA was agreed in May 1969, the management were better prepared to handle WSA than they had been MUPS. Again Bridge's sponsorship left Evans and Dudley with a clear run to get up and carry through the influencing of the "key climate setters" as they were called from the works. Evans had this to say in summary about Bridge's broad success in creating the political climate for them to get on with the operational OD activities:

But with having Bridge around, with MUPS and WSA, their visibility, his access to the main board, and their support, you didn't need many other hidden sponsors. You know they said to Bridge – "if you want all the works managers in ICI through the course at Warren House, have'em". The effort as a whole didn't need more sponsors.

At least the OD effort didn't need any more sponsors for as long as the main board needed Bridge to drive through MUPS/WSA, and SDP. After the implementation of those programmes, the OD groups' singular reliance on the activities of MUPS/WSA and SDP for legitimacy, and the main board – Bridge connection for political sponsorship proved to be near fatal. But the years 1968, 1969, and 1970 found the OD unit preoccupied with the short-term and compelling activities of the Warren House workshops, the Eastbourne development activities for internal OD consultants, and the afterthought of SDP.

Internal and external OD consultant activities

Although the preceding section has emphasised the extent to which the group I am characterising as the central OD group were dependent on the legitimacy provided by MUPS/WSA, and the political sponsorship of George Bridge, in Dudley's words the "central OD group was never given an organisational position. It has always maintained a roving commission." By that he meant both that it did not exist formally as a designated unit on the organisation chart with a formal remit, and that its membership of the development and applications section of CPD, some of the MUPS/WSA liaison officers, and the increasing band of American consultants, was to a large extent self-selected. The other thing to be clear about was that Evans, Dudley, and the others' networks of contact and relationships were largely outside Millbank. As Dudley said "I used to spend 75% of my time out in divisions or on workshops."

The workshops Dudley was referring to were the Warren House workshops; these were the core of the OD group's activities in the period 1968–70. Faced with management and union resistance to MUPS, Dudley and Evans approached some well-known American consultants for their help and assistance. They worked with a small group of people in ICI to help them diagnose what lay behind this resistance to change. After much discussion a new-style training workshop was mounted to help managers diagnose why change was being resisted (including their own part in this resistance) and to supply them with information and help them generate plans for overcoming the resistance. (Eventually between 500 and 600 managers participated in these week-long workshops.) For many of these managers these training events were the first occasions they had been on a workshop as distinct from a course, where instead of being "taught" or "lectured to" they found their own and others' behaviour and feelings in the workshop and back at work, part of the material for learning. For many of them it was also the first occasion they had been introduced to the OD jargon and message that the social process of doing something was as crucial, if not as crucial, as the content of what was being done. Writ large in front of their very eyes, the frustrations, failures, and to some the irrelevancies of MUPS, was the everyday example of an organisation being preoccupied with the content of outcomes to the exclusion of knowledge and skill in the process of achieving those outcomes.

These workshops were generally viewed as helpful and successful. They brought out into the open managers' insecurities and anxieties about managing people and organisational change, about their fears of losing control if they got into open-ended problem-solving relationships with the shop floor, and concerns about their own skills in motivating and working co-operatively with their shop stewards and local employees. Thus these workshops not only served the manifest function of helping to introduce WSA, they also served the latent function of exposing a large group of important and respected managers to behavioural science in the service of practical ends – in other words to OD as it was now beginning to be known. In fact Evans and Dudley were rather taken aback by the requests that came from these workshops for consultancy services back in the divisions. The managers already looking for ways of creating change could see there might be a role for third-party helpers or consultants, as they became known, to support them with team-building and inter-group work with subsets of managers and shop stewards in their own factories. Some of this early OD work in the divisions will be described in Chapters 5 and 6.

Here again the central OD group had to learn and react from their experience. One of their responses was to encourage more American consultants to seek clients in the company; a further response was to work with a group of those external consultants to develop a cadre or network of internal OD consultants in the divisions.

The ICI OD network really has its roots in the two workshops run to develop internal consultancy skills for divisional staff. The workshops were run in 1970 at Eastbourne, with about 40 people at each, although the first one also included employees from Procter and Gamble, Europe; Shell; and British Oxygen. Both workshops were modelled on a design used to train internal consultants by NTL, and were staffed largely by Americans. The personal, almost psychiatric emphasis of the first course got a little out of hand at times and participants now tend to remember the workshops with the mixture of pain, awe, and bravado that one associates with initiation rituals.

The idea was to attract to the workshops people from the divisions already predisposed to OD, and perhaps already involved in helping implement WSA and SDP, plus a cross-section of people from personnel, training, management services, and line management roles who might be capable of going back and acting as change agents and third-party helpers in order to keep any change momentum started by WSA and SDP an ongoing and continuous process.

Tension between two groups of consultants with different institutional affiliations didn't help Eastbourne, neither did the great variability in background, skill, and experience of the participants. Interestingly, both workshops produced a split between a heavies' group of participants who were for rules, order, and structuring of the learning experience, and a "thunderground" group wanting to experiment more and more with unstructured groupy learning exercises. For some participants this just added to the confusion and anxiety of the workshops. Some participants found the programmes an extreme experience, some of these were "paralysed" for quite some time after the event. Others were "turned on"; it changed their attitudes to work and authority, and led to questioning of their life styles, and in some cases tension in their family life, when wives and children felt left out, not possessors of this new elixir of life. There are probably more myths about the Eastbourne events than any other single activity in the ICI OD history. The divisional chapters will reveal more of what some of the participants felt of the experience and the impact it had on their job effectiveness. For the time being Bridges' evaluation was "I don't think it was terribly successful. I don't think they chose the best resources from the divisions. I think they tried to be too much like NTL."

Certainly there was no attempt on a company-wide basis to train another cadre of OD resources on anything like the scale or format of the Eastbourne events until the early 1980s, and OD was a very different beast in 1980 than it had been in 1970.

The last major activity that the central OD group concerned themselves with in the period 1968–70 was the development and co-ordination of the junior and middle managerial monthly staff equivalent of WSA, SDP. The reasons for SDP's creation at that time, the broad outlines of what it entailed, together with the very mixed reaction it received as a change process as distinct from a device to allow staff salary differentials to be retained, were dealt with briefly at the beginning of this chapter. The more detailed aspects of its implementation, and the views it generated about OD and central personnel policy will become apparent in the chapters reviewing divisional OD work which follow this one. Two further points about SDP will suffice at this stage. Firstly, although the central OD group was based in Bridge's labour section of CPD, and SDP would normally have been run by the staff section, the central OD group managed to take control of SDP as a natural continuation of all the developments they had made in MUPS/WSA. Secondly the sheer scale of the SDP intervention, involving as it did 40,000 ICI employees, involved still more work for the ICI internal OD network and their American external consultants. The diffusion of OD concepts, techniques, and consultants into ICI took a still more extended form, and with that extension surfaced more people prepared to take an attitude to OD, whether it be of doubt, support, or hostility.

One of the questions often asked about the ICI OD experience of the late 1960s and early 1970s was why they relied almost exclusively on external consultancy help in the behavioural sciences and OD from American academics? Why was a predominantly American approach adopted by a very British company? In broad terms the answer is supplied by the long history of ICI's American connections, by the technological culture of the company which meant there was some history and predisposition to be looking outward to universities and other firms for signs of innovation-led technological and commerical advantage. Not, of course, that OD was seen to offer any particular commerical advantage, at least not in the short term, but it was connectable to the image of ICI as a progressive and forward-thinking company on matters of personnel policy, practice, and organisation.

But why particularly was American help sought? One reason was that much of the early behavioural science literature was North American-based, and certainly attempts to develop and apply that work in industry under the flexible umbrella of OD were almost exclusively in the United States. ICI's pre-war cartel arrangements with DuPont and frequent and continuing interchange of information on manpower and other matters, as well as ICI's own interests in Canada through Canadian Industries Ltd, had all made it quite natural for ICI to visit and talk to academics and businessmen in North America. The visits by the CPD research and development manager to the United States in 1963, and by Bridge and his colleague from Billingham in 1964, had established the link into the major academic centres of behavioural science in North America. McGregor's acceptability had reinforced Bridge's early confidence in using Americans. Before McGregor died he had introduced colleagues from MIT to ICI. Bridge, aided by Evans and Dudley, who could by this time see where the demand for external help could most profitably be used, brought in others. Ron Mercer, the constant American in the ICI OD story himself also sponsored other Americans into the company. Bridge and Evans before they left Billingham also arranged for the company's first full-time internal OD consultant, a young American Noel Ripley, to work in their division. Ripley's activities in Agricultural Division form a central part of Chapters 5 and 6 of this book. Through all these various contacts a number of the ICI internal OD consultants received training in the United States, and eventually a number of ICI directors began to go to T-groups in the United States.

The number of American accents around the company, as we shall see, inevitably led to cries from line managers of "well, all that stuff's American and of no use". Even some of the consultants became cynical about ICI's apparent willingness to offer work to anyone who was recommended by one of their American colleagues. One American consultant remarked that in the late 1960s ICI became well known in American behavioural science consultancy circles as "a pigeon for American consultants". Another American consultant commented that:

> If you were around at the time of MUPS/WSA and you had something that sounded like expertise and a way of helping people to become more participative, if you couldn't get work with ICI you didn't deserve to be in the business. I don't know anybody who is anybody in the general field of OD who didn't work with ICI at that time . . . SDP also produced a lot of work – but for internal people. As there was increased sophistication, there was less use of outsiders. That was a major change.

ICI tried to use some British academic consultants in the late 1960s but rarely with anything that they would describe as success. According to Mercer and Dudley the problem with British academic consultants was that they were too academic, too theoretical, too concerned with their discipline's problems and not prepared to openly commit themselves to helping to solve ICI's problems. Mercer's view was that:

The English looked to America for help and felt there was no comparable intellectual help, or rather it was over intellectual, classical business school type resource ... They are seen as theorists, more interested in theories than improving profits. Not really collaborating. No commitment to really help run the organisation better. A kind of professional removal: "I don't want to get in bed with you. I am a consultant and I must maintain my Doctor or Professor role." That's the perception that's caused the problem.

Dudley said ICI had tried to use a well-known British Social Science Institute, and indeed British university-based academics, but he and Evans "got disillusioned. Every time we tried our own very flimsy credibility was going down the drain too." The individuals Dudley mentioned were either seen as "thinking too much in national change terms", "researchers and theorists", "too confrontatory and outspoken", "standing 10 steps in front of management rather than 3", or not having "enough intelligence and personal strength". The British, it seems, were a complete wash-out.

By 1971, and with WSA and SDP "in", the central OD group, in the absence of a collective perpetuation strategy, had a survival problem. In so far as the group had had a strategy that was wrapped up in the success of WSA and SDP, which of course had involved influencing the key climate-setting group in ICI of the works management, and spreading OD skills and knowledge through the ICI OD network. With a cast of OD characters, internal and external consultants, and the vicariously placed senior manager or director supporters of OD, in place, an after-the-fact intervention strategy for the company began to emerge out of the partial behaving of that strategy in different parts of the company. Evans described the intervention model thus:

> The model we had was we wanted some of the internal consultants with a Noel Ripley, a visiting external like Mercer who did things at the top of the division, and a visiting Evans or Dudley from the central OD group. That was the model and I don't think it exists anywhere ... because you can't get all the people there.

By the end of 1972 Evans had left the company, Bridge had been promoted to be General Manager Personnel, and Dudley was left as the sole survivor of the central OD group. How Dudley survived, along, of course, with Mercer, to fight another day, is itself an interesting story, and one bound up with the way they both managed their way through the emerging attitudes towards WSA, SDP, and OD which existed in ICI in the early 1970s. Those attitudes and ICI's responses to them are the subject of the final part of this chapter.

THE LEGACY OF WSA AND SDP

The scale, objectives, and visibility of the MUPS/WSA change programme attracted a considerable amount of short-term newspaper comment at the time the negotiations were in process;[2] since then a number of books and articles

[2] For example, 'ICI aims to change attitudes', *The Financial Times*, 18 March, 1970 and 'Some spanners in the works', *The Times*, 9 September, 1970.

have reviewed different aspects of MUPS/WSA. In the main the Roeber (1975) book was neutral to positive in its evaluation of MUPS/WSA, while the TUC-sponsored Roberts and Wedderburn (1973) paper was neutral to negative in its tone. The Paul and Robertson (1971) account of the ICI job enrichments studies was overwhelmingly positive in its analysis of those studies, and the Horner (1974) account of the job enrichment work in ICI was overwhelmingly negative. From my perspective, Cotgrove *et al.* (1971) presented a very balanced analysis of the implementation of MUPS at ICI's Gloucester Works.

The fact, however that MUPS/WSA has attracted what might be perceived to be partisan writing is not the reason why I draw back at this stage from attempting an evaluation of the economic, political, or social strengths and weaknesses of those programmes. The reader may feel himself or herself better able to evaluate MUPS/WSA after reading the considered views of managers and shop stewards to be reported in the divisional chapters which follow this one.

In so far as this chapter is concluding with a partial review of MUPS/WSA and SDP it is because the attitudes to MUPS/WSA and SDP in 1971 provided a critical part of the operating context in which OD as an activity would or would not survive and flourish in ICI. The fact that by 1971 and 1972 OD, as a means of creating change, was in doubt, indicates that one of the more idealistic notions associated with WSA and SDP, that processes of change could be set in motion and survive on a continuous basis, was itself therefore seriously questionable. The fact also, as Roeber (1975:273) reports, that one of the major pieces of learning to be extracted from the MUPS failure was that management were unprepared with skills in managing organisational change, and yet OD had the questionable reputation it did in the post-WSA/SDP era, suggests how little claim the OD consultants inside ICI had to be considered as credible experts or helpers in organisational change. It is possible, of course, that the aversion that many ICI managers had to organisational change in the post-1972 period was not so much just an aversion to OD and change agents, but also an aversion to centrally pushed change they little understood or cared for. Maybe the ICI system just needed to stabilise itself again after the upheavals of WSA and SDP. Certainly it wasn't for another 10 years, until 1980–81, that the whole ICI system mobilised itself for a scale and intensity of people and organisational change which made the discomforts of MUPS/WSA and SDP look like something rather inconsequential in comparison.

But while I am sure part of the inertia that surfaced in ICI in the post-1972 period was a product both of a desire for a return to stability, now legitimated, of course from 1973 onwards by good financial results, the other reason why this was a bad time for OD was because of negative feelings towards MUPS//WSA, SDP, and OD itself.

Senior personnel people in ICI, while now recognising that "WSA may have been appropriate for the 1970s", even that "its principles are inherently endearing", can also admit doubts that "the spirit of WSA, as seen by the management and the unions has ever been fully applied". Another personnel man remarked "if WSA was about transferring loyalty from the unions to the company then the events of the 1970s showed that didn't happen". A further senior personnel man, also unconnected with the OD effort, remarked that the premise behind WSA was that if everybody co-operated in a growth situation then more money could be generated which could then be spread out amongst everybody.

> Well first of all we stopped growing, so we produced it when it was no longer in keeping with the socioeconomic conditions of the time. And then people couldn't relate an annual salary increase to what they were being asked to do next Monday on the plant, so we failed to crack the motivation thing.

But the above criticisms, all with the benefit of hindsight, came from personnel professionals, the managers out in the divisions had stronger feelings many of which were directed at CPD.

> One of the consequences of WSA was management in the divisions said never again, we're not having that centrally imposed sort of thing put on us again, it just produces exhaustion.

The negative views about WSA presented above need to be balanced by the views of those line managers, often from smaller cohesive works who, as one manager put it to me, felt that WSA "had set a tremendous example of what could be achieved by people working together in a fairly open environment . . . I think the company got a lot out of it, and so did the individuals."

With SDP, however, the data from this research go quite against Roeber's (1975:184) view that "SDP was a success and that the success was achieved at a low level of energy". Very few people interviewed in this study had anything positive to say about SDP, its impact on ICI as a change programme, and its contribution to the development of OD in the company. SDP was widely described as a cynical exercise to pay monthly staff another 15%, as being reactive, ill-prepared, badly timed, coinciding as it did with monthly staff number reductions in 1971, and as something that was done with the acquiescence of senior monthly staff to middle and junior monthly staff by "head shrinkers", "trick cyclists", and various other epitaphs used at that time to describe the internal and external OD consultants. One external consultant compared WSA and SDP in these terms:

> WSA was a positive initiative to deal with some problems before they became problems. But SDP was a reaction. It was not part of the original plan. It was not thought through . . . and it was predicted by at least some organisational specialists, including myself, that it would be a disaster.

Bridge commented on the reactive nature of SDP:

> In fact it was a bit of a scramble after WSA came in and the rates [of pay] were seen, and the staff got a bit jumpy as they were bound to. So then we rushed around and produced SDP.

Dudley remarked on how significant the union–management agreement side of MUPS/WSA had been to the fact that eventually things did happen in problem-solving terms at local level. Of course there was no equivalent agreement with SDP.

> Therefore there was nothing to make it [SDP] go . . . Therefore when you had a manager who was a moral entrepreneur it went well. Other managers just went through the bloody drill to grab the money and get it off their backs. So it was really a pretty desperate sort of thing.

The strong feelings about WSA and SDP naturally enough were easily linked to OD. One external consultant put it in a nutshell:

> WSA was *the* major stimulus for the development of OD in the early years. And the failure of WSA and SDP to produce the expected results was the major reason for the anti – OD backlash.

Strategy and tactics of using OD: some lessons of the MUPS/WSA and SDP period

The centrally driven change programmes provided OD with its first chance in ICI. The will "to make WSA happen was a political will by the main board and put into the hands of this powerful figure George Bridge". OD then "became part of the means". But when ICI managers became weary of WSA and SDP they became weary of OD; it was guilt by association. WSA and SDP "provided both OD opportunity and some backlash". In strategic terms one of the lessons the ICI power system drew from the WSA and SDP was not to force centrally concocted strategic change on the divisions. For 10 years after WSA no major across-the-company strategic changes in the organisation sphere were attempted by ICI. The company went back into one of its periods of incremental adjustment, of evolutionary change. This pattern of adjustment continued until around 1980 when calamitous financial results in several key business areas of the company again shook the slumbering giant, and another, this time even more fundamental period of revolutionary strategic change, was driven from Millbank.

The people involved with OD also drew some lessons from the WSA and SDP period. They naturally reflected on the guilty by association phenomenon, and across-the-board change efforts and packaged training solutions went into sharp decline as a feature of the OD armament. But not all the anti OD backlash came after the implementation of WSA and SDP; there were doubters and opponents during the process of implementation itself. As Dudley remarked, "quite a range of middle managers were doubters in that some of the McGregor theory Y assumptions about people sounded unlikely to them." There were other senior people, division and main board directors "who were genuinely not in touch and were out and out doubters". There were also, of course, strong opponents of MUPS/WSA – particularly "the Wilton Lobby" as it became known as. Others opposed "because of the protagonists of WSA and OD –

some people found Bridge very hard to deal with. There were some who thought it all an unnecessary distraction".

A lot of the senior management questioning and opposition to OD was, of course, based on the assumption that WSA and SDP as behavioural change programmes was something that they did to others, that others needed, but not themselves. Elements of this view were present in all the divisions studied in this research, but "OK for them, but not for me" was strongest in Plastics Division. Attempts by internal OD resources to deal with this problem were easily brushed aside, and pressure from Bridge to open up the divisional boards by sending directors on American-based and run T-groups, while having the occasional success, also provided the senior doubters and opponents of OD with a focal point for their opposition. A division chairman at the time of SDP had this to say about the directors for T-groups intervention:

> The enthusiasm with which T-groups were espoused was viewed as being weird almost to the point of madness. It was quite usual to be rung up by George Bridge and told: "I think it's about time you sent so and so on a T-group". "Well amongst the things you don't do is to *send* people on T-groups (i.e. give them no choice) . . . but even now I can barely believe what went on – great big, beefy American chief executives rolling on the floor and crying . . . I mean really, to an Englishman far too way out for the sort of people we are or were.

But the T-group problem was just one element of learning about how to create change using OD resources and techniques. Strategically it can be argued that OD in the late 1960s and early 1970s was presented as, or was capable of being perceived to be, rather too exclusive in character. It was too exclusively associated with WSA and SDP, too easily associated with George Bridge and the CPD, too easily associated with internal specialist resources and American consultants and not as something to be used by line managers, and of course too over-identified with behavioural and psychological frames of reference and solutions, together with values which appeared to cherish individual growth and development to the detriment of organisational or sectional interests. Elements of these characteristics of exclusiveness were present in all the divisional OD groups and as we shall see in Chapter 12 which compares and contrasts the pathways of development of the various ICI OD groups, the balance between exclusivity and inclusivity represents one of the core dilemmas for the strategic management of specialist activity.

Returning to the fate of the central OD group, we have already noted that by 1972, Dudley was the sole survivor. Evans later described the group's demise in these terms:

> We had a survival problem. That group was on a loser from the beginning. We couldn't require anybody to take any combination of us. It had no potential for survival except on this notion of collective credits for good work done by individuals.

Evans had been in a difficult situation to generate credibility without the vehicle of WSA. As he put it "if I worked *up* in ICI the issue of what I was going to tell

Bridge – the power thing – became very important and made things very difficult." But if he tried to operate as a third-party consultant down into the ICI system his association with the central personnel system and Bridge didn't help either. As he put it "I didn't have many clients which lasted much . . . I did have useful discussions but more between me and another OD person than with clients." Evans' long-standing relationship with Bridge became tense and eventually "I saw myself less and less central. From being an adjutant or favourite nephew of George Bridge to being very peripheral, and I didn't like the idea of not having an interesting life . . . so I left ICI".

Dudley of course had the advantage of being able to project himself as an ex-works manager; this together with his carefully guarded independence from Bridge, meant that he was able to escape the label of being either an exclusively personnel or Bridge man. Undoubtedly the fact of Dudley's skills in maintaining clients out in the divisions, and the implicit recognition by the ICI power system that there had to be *a* central OD resource helped Dudley's survival in 1972. He explained his own survival in these terms:

> I was an ex-works manager that they knew, and that was my base. I think I was able to establish that I was not just doing George Bridge's work . . . I was very much more effective at keeping clients out in the divisions than Tom Evans because he was seen as a personnel man and more as George's man too . . . I also avoided the management role of central OD – kept all that in with Tom, which allowed me freedom to operate and initiate, and maybe look to have that bit more independence in the system.

Dudley survived to be the focal point for central OD for another decade. George Bridge was promoted to General Manager, Personnel, and remained in ICI until 1974. Bridge's successor had these shrewd words to say about the use made of OD resources in ICI over the period 1964–74:

> I now accept that the efficiency of ICI's expenditure on OD had to be low . . . because of the learning process that the organisation was and is in has to be slow . . . you are concerned with helping and persuading people to change.

5 The Heavy Hand of History: Business Development and Social Innovation in Agricultural Division

The purpose of this chapter and the four chapters which follow is to reveal the birth, evolution, and impact of organisation development activities in Agricultural, Petrochemicals, Plastics, and Mond Divisions of ICI. Each of these chapters will present a process description of the use and fate of OD resources set in the context of the historical and present-day business, technical, and organisational evolution of each division. These chapters provide unique processual data on line manager and specialist attempts both to implement corporate changes emanating from Millbank, and to initiate significant changes in the business strategy and structure, technical base, quality of union–management relationships, and organisational culture in each division.

Given the analytical objective of this research, to locate process description and analysis in trends in a changing business, economic, and organisational context, each chapter uses a number of broad conceptual categories and themes to reveal the business history and development of the division. Chief amongst these broad conceptual categories are each division's business conditions, strategy and competitive position, its products, technology, sales and profits, the composition and size of its manpower, the character of industrial relations in the division, and its managerial culture. Focus will also be given to the division's organisation structure, the relative power of various functions, areas, and units, and some of the recurrent problems and conflicts faced by the division. Throughout, the emphasis is on changes evident in each of these areas.

As the title of this chapter on Agricultural Division suggests, a combination of the long history, and stable location of ICI's UK interests in agricultural chemicals and products at Billingham in the north-east of England, together with a history of independent executive tradition in Billingham/Agricultural Division, and, of course, the relative geographical isolation of that division from corporate pressures in London, all contributed to a strong sense of business and divisional loyalty and a particular management and worker culture at Billingham which was eventually challenged by business, technical, and social changes in the 1960s. Given the importance of the traditions laid down at Billingham in the first 30 years or so of its existence in setting the tone for the content and processes of change which developed during the 1960s and the

1970s the first part of this chapter chronicles key elements of the business history, organisation, and management and shop floor culture at Billingham over the period 1920–57. The second section of the chapter then reviews the business history and development of Billingham/Agricultural Division over the period 1958–84. With the business and organisational context thus well established, the middle part of the chapter provides an overview of the use of OD resources in the division in the period from the mid-1960s until 1984. The chapter then concludes with a major section providing a chronological view and some analysis of the major activities and events in the period of social innovation in Agricultural Division during George Bridge's tenure as divisional personnel director from 1962 to 1967. Bridge's era as a social architect at Billingham is an important feature of the division's history in its own right, but that period of social innovation is also of significance as a crucial antecedent for the birth, evolution, and impact of OD in Agricultural Division from the late 1960s onwards. The story of the Agricultural Division OD resources role in organisational change and development from 1969 to 1984 is picked and fully developed in Chapter 6.

BILLINGHAM DIVISION: BUSINESS HISTORY, ORGANISATION AND CULTURE, 1920–57

ICI does not publish financial data about the performance of its divisions in the United Kingdom. It does, however, group its financial results on a worldwide basis by class of business, and publishes statistics for the agriculture group. This agriculture group largely comprises the activities of Agricultural Division and Plant Protection Division, with the bulk of sales and trading profit emanating from Agricultural Division. In 1980, admittedly a bad year for ICI as a worldwide group, the agricultural part of the company turned in profits of £151m on sales of £1071m. This £151m represented 45% of the total profit for the ICI group for the year ended 31 December 1980. Since 1975 the agricultural interests of ICI have been turning in trading profits of between £114m and £182m, with trading margins of between 11% and 20%. Over the period 1974–83 ICI's agricultural interests have consistently provided the highest contribution of all the company's business areas to group profits; although as we shall see energy cost factors and increasingly competitive conditions were by 1980 beginning to significantly pressurise Agricultural Division's commodity businesses.

Agricultural Division in 1980 was one of the largest producers of ammonia and methanol in the world. It controlled 60% of the UK markets in straight nitrogen fertilisers and about 40% in compound fertilisers, and had significant market shares in Canada, Australasia, South Africa, India and Malaysia. Its successful development of the steam reforming and low-pressure ammonia and methanol processes meant that it was a world technology leader in its field, and it had built up a tidy business selling catalysts to licensees of these technologies throughout the world. With a favourable gas contract from the British Gas

Corporation ensuring a relatively cheap and plentiful supply of its major feedstock, natural gas, it was in a very strong position as a business, although the continuing upward negotiation of gas prices is changing the competitive position of the division's methanol business.

The agricultural interests of ICI have not always enjoyed this favourable business and technological position. Agricultural Division would probably have been bankrupt in 1969 or 1970 had it not been part of the large ICI group. Ten years before that, when it was known as Billingham Division, it was in equally dire financial straits, and between 1926 and 1930 the first big capital investment in ICI's history – at Billingham Works – collapsed when the world prices for fertiliser dropped and left 50% of the new production capacity at Billingham idle; and sent around 6000 new recruits to Billingham Works back onto the unemployment queues of Teesside, in northern England.

The public announcement of the creation of Agricultural Division was made in two short sentences in the ICI annual report of 1963. Between 1944 and 1963 it had been known as Billingham Division and before that the Fertilizers and Synthetic Products Group.[1] However, the history of chemical manufacturing at Billingham on the north bank of the River Tees goes back to 1920, six years before the creation of Imperial Chemical Industries Ltd.

Billingham was born out of some of the pressures created by the German submarine blockade of Britain during the First World War. Finding it increasingly difficult to obtain the supplies of Chilean nitrate needed to manufacture explosives, the government appointed a committee in 1917 to assess the possibility of starting manufacture of ammonia and from it nitric acid and nitrates. Billingham was chosen early in 1918, and the government purchased several hundred acres of flat farmland close to the Newcastle Electric Supply Company's new power station, and with readily available supplies of coal, water, salt, and anhydrite, good communication by rail, road, and water, and a supply of skilled labour with a tradition of shift working.

With the ending of the war, the government's plans were abandoned and in 1920 the site was sold, along with certain contracts, information and patents, the buyer to undertake to make ammonia and nitric acid. The purchaser was Synthetic Ammonia and Nitrates Ltd., which had been established by the chemical manufacturing firm of Brunner, Mond and Co., Ltd, to develop Billingham as a fertiliser factory using the same synthetic nitrogen fixation process as the government had planned to operate. Before the formation of ICI in 1926 a small-scale experimental plant had been built and tested at Runcorn in Cheshire and plants No. 2 and 3 were built and brought into production at Billingham. Research was also started at Teesside on urea and methanol, and on a process for manufacturing oil from coal.

The key event and launching pad for Billingham, however, was the joining together in 1926 of Brunner, Mond and Co Ltd, the United Alkali Co Ltd, Nobel Industries Ltd, and the British Dyestuffs Corporation Ltd, to form ICI. A major argument for the merger was to develop an organisation capable of competing with the German giant – IG Farbenindustrie AG. A feature of this

[1] This was from 1931.

competition was to develop the size and hence the industrial muscle through a range of products, market dominance and share, financial strength and security of future, to be able to negotiate from a position of reasonable power balance with other companies on such matters as prices, and spheres of market influence throughout the world. Sir Alfred Mond, the man instrumental in purchasing the Billingham site in 1920, and the first chairman of ICI, together with Colonel G. P. Pollitt, who had been chairman of the Billingham directors in the period 1920–26 and was now one of the eight first board members of ICI, persuaded Sir Harry McGowan, ICI's first president, that expansion of ammonia fertiliser production to be sold to the farmers of Britain and the British Empire was a key to the development of ICI's market power.

In 1927 the fateful decision was taken by the ICI board to sanction capital expenditure at Billingham works which eventually involved spending £20 million.[2] This was a decision driven by Mond's imperial dream and Pollitt's technical leadership – the marketing problems of selling all the new fertiliser capacity were not grasped. By 1929 there was 50% overcapacity at Billingham works and the return on capital employed had dropped below 5%. Reader (1975) has estimated that between 1929 and 1932 the total number of ICI employees in Britain dropped by 20,000, and a high side of a one-third of these were at Billingham. Disaster on such a scale could not be hidden and the ICI ordinary shares fell dramatically. People began to talk about the fertiliser factory being closed altogether, and for good. The total value of property and plant not in production at Billingham in 1931 was £11m. Billingham, far from carrying ICI as had been intended, was a burden for the rest of ICI to carry.

Billingham did not recover from this blow to its business and its pride until 1937 when preparations for the Second World War were dragging British industry out of the Depression. Even in this difficult period between 1929 and 1937 Billingham's scientists and engineers continued to make developments which led to new plant. Methanol was being produced by 1928, Nitro Chalk in granular form by 1931, Concentrated Complete Fertilizer (CCF) by 1930, with government assistant, a plant producing petrol from coal and creosote in 1935, and the plastic "Perspex" in 1936. Meanwhile an anhydrite mine had been opened in 1928, which served the Billingham complex until 1970 and which supplied an essential ingredient for the manufacture of sulphuric acid. By the end of 1931 the factory payroll strength was down to 5,700 and the technical and other grades employed on the staff was 1,200. In 1939 the total factory payroll and staff had risen to 12,500. At its peak around 1960 the Billingham Division employed 17,000 people. The Agricultural Division in 1984 now employs 6,800 people. But I anticipate another thread in the story to be picked up later.

One of the people interviewed in this research described the period 1926–40 as the era of the civil and mechanical engineer at Billingham when new buildings and plant were constructed. He called 1944–55 the era of the chemist

---

[2] Much of the detail in this historical review is based on *Imperial Chemical Industries: A History Vol. II 1927–1952* by W.J. Reader (1975)

when new products were developed, and 1955 and beyond the era of the chemical engineer. Blench (1958) has emphasised the key role that engineers and scientists played in Billingham's development – it has always been much more than just a large production complex. During the Second World War the number of senior men occupied on research increased from 90 to 130 and expenditure on research increased 2½ times over those six years. Billingham technical people played an important part in the design work for the "tube alloys" project, the atomic bomb, and Billingham scientists carried design work to an advanced stage for a process for the large-scale production of heavy water.

Before discussing some of the key events in Billingham's post-war expansion, it is important to pick up two further threads from the pre-1939 and 1939–45 period. Fearful of Billingham's exposure on the north-east coast of England to German bombers, the government encouraged the building of external factories to produce ammonia and aviation fuel in such places as Clitheroe, Dowlais and Heysham. Clitheroe and Heysham are still in production today with more modern technology. During the 1960s the external factories under Billingham control which still remained were added to by new production facilities at Severnside near Bristol and Immingham near Hull. These plants used Billingham Division's steam naphtha reforming process for ammonia manufacture – but more of the troubles associated with that new technology later.

The other important theme to pick up from the pre-war and wartime periods is the more general pattern of ICI development taking place not only north of the Tees at Billingham, but also south of the Tees at Wilton. Mention has been made of the factory producing "Perspex" on the Billingham site. When the ICI Plastics group, a forerunner of the Plastics Division, was created in 1936, this plant was placed under their control. Previous to this a caustic soda and chlorine plant had been hived off the General Chemicals Division – now Mond Division. In 1948 Dyestuffs Division – now Organics Division – started a new plant to produce nylon polymer. All three of the above plants relied to some degree or other on Billingham Division-produced services and materials. But in 1943 ICI started to plan for a new kind of factory site – a factory which would provide space and facilities to any ICI division planning large-scale developments for the post-war years, and provide the integration of materials and services so crucial to the effective running of a large chemical site. The final choice of a site south of the Tees at Wilton led directly to two further decisions of great significance to Billingham: first the decision to locate the division's post-war oil operations at Wilton; and second to link this major development by a group of pipelines under the Tees to the existing plant at Billingham. Eventually the oil-based, heavy chemicals on the Wilton site grew to the point where on 1 January 1958, ICI Heavy Organic Chemicals Division was formed. This in time became Petrochemicals Division, the subject of Chapter 7 of this book. Today the Billingham and Wilton sites of ICI constitute one of the largest chemical complexes in the world.

The post-war development of Billingham is a story of almost continuous growth of sales and employment up to around 1960. The relevant markets for fertilisers, ammonia, methanol, sulphuric acid, "Drikold" and cement expanded steadily, providing safe outlets – administered by a tellingly named "sales control" department – for the prowess of the graduate chemists and mechanical and chemical engineers who managed the division. But the ground was beginning to move beneath the feet of the 17,000 employees of Billingham Division by the late 1950s. ICI was not the only large chemical enterprise to expand after the Second World War and increasingly ICI's markets were becoming worldwide and subject to fierce international competition as production capacity increased in North America and Western Europe, and as the comfortable cartels and monopolies of the 1930s and 1940s were dissolved. In this situation a number of the older established divisions of ICI found themselves in an exposed situation with falling world prices and increased world capacity, and with a rising cost base derived from increasingly obsolete technology, and relatively poor manpower productivity. As we shall see, Billingham, of all places, which had prided itself on scientific and technical innovation, woke up in 1958 to find itself behind in the technology of ammonia and methanol production. The responses it made to that discovery were to lead to some startling technical, organisational and manpower changes of the 1960s and early 1970s which produced, among other things, the birth of organisation development activities. But before I sketch out these technical changes and their repercussions, it is important to pick up a crucial theme so far missing in the evolution of Billingham – the social system, and managerial culture and organisation, which had developed at Billingham since Brunner, Mond arrived on the site in 1920.

Manpower, managerial culture and organisation at Billingham, 1920–57

Up until some of the changes in the late 1950s and early 1960s, it is possible to identify a number of key influences which stamped their mark on the broad social system of Billingham. Chief among these include the impact of the Brunner, Mond tradition of employee relationships, which through Mond's influence, carried themselves into ICI personnel policy; the technocratic managerial culture and organisation that built up on the site because of the employment of so many able scientists and engineers; the relative isolation of Billingham from the ICI seat of power at Millbank; the tradition of employment on Teesside and throughout the north-east of England in the declining heavy industries of coal, steel and shipbuilding; and of course, the eventual company town character of Billingham itself, as Billingham Division grew and took up a formidable amount of unemployed men and women who were the involuntary victims of the 1930s Depression.

Mond, like his father and the first Lord Leverhulme, had an outlook on labour relations which was that of the late Victorian paternalist employer. His belief in copartnership did not, of course, extend to matters of policy in running the firm – that would remain with the management. The core of copartnership, for Mond, lay in profit sharing. "The best answer to socialism", he wrote in

1927, "is to make every man a capitalist."[3] Mond's own family firm, Brunner, Mond, had introduced the eight-hour day, holidays with pay, share ownership schemes, housing, schools and recreation clubs, and in general an enlightened, if paternalist, labour policy based, in Mond's words, on "foreseeing reasonable demands and . . . granting them even before they were asked" (Reader, 1975:60).

Mond quickly imported the Brunner, Mond labour policy into ICI. His chief labour officer, Richard Lloyd Roberts, was appointed to a similar post in ICI and Roberts set up the ICI Central Labour Department. Henceforth all labour and staff, and then personnel policy, was a central activity controlled from the new ICI headquarters at Millbank, from its completion in 1928. Before long works councils were set up along with sick benefit, staff grade, share ownership, and bonus schemes. The trade union movement, losing members and otherwise weakened by the aftermath of the General Strike of 1926, unwillingly acquiesced to these policies which were seen at the time by key union leaders such as Ernest Bevin as divisive of working-class solidarity and union power. Lloyd Roberts and Mond knew what they were doing, to ensure ICI employees made their attachments to the firm and not to their union. By and large the ICI labour policies up to and including the 1939–45 war worked well both across the company and at Billingham. During the war, for example, only about 80,000 man-hours were lost in strikes and nearly 95% of those man-hours were lost in the metals and explosives parts of ICI. I have only been able to find evidence of one major strike at Billingham in the period 1945–57; and this only involved one union, the AUEW.

In spite of the setbacks, of 1929–31 when around 6,000 people were laid off, most individuals I have spoken to on the managerial and union side looked back on "the ICI" of the 1920s to 1940s at Billingham with affection. Managers were "hard but fair" and there is a strong feeling that "the ICI" of those days saved Teesside. After all, in 1922 Billingham was just a village green with about 40 houses, one pub, and one church. By the mid-1950s the population had risen to 30,000 and by the present day it is nearer 75,000. A long-serving member of the management recalled the drift south of Durham coal miners into "the ICI".

> There was a lot of very good labour in the Durham coal fields which flocked down to Teesside . . . They were a very good work force . . . We didn't have any union trouble . . . They were thankful they'd got a job on the surface with fairly reasonable conditions.

In time, of course, they were also glad there were jobs for their sons in the post-war expansion both at Billingham and Wilton. Between the wars ICI built 2,330 houses at Billingham, but since 1945 it has been the company's policy to leave this task to the local authorities. An indication of the concentration of people around the Billingham site in 1955 is given from data provided in *Teesside at Mid-Century*, by House and Fullerton (1960). At that time 30% of the factory

---

[3] I am grateful for this and other detail in this section on Mond to the research and writing of Reader (1975)

TABLE 17 Labour turnover – males (comparative percentage figures)

Year	Billingham site	Wilton site	Chemical industry	All industries
1949	15.3%	—	22.6%	27.4%
1950	17.2	19.3%	24.3	30.3
1951	16.8	23.5	25.2	31.3
1952	13.0	21.0	23.5	27.9
1953	13.9	22.8	21.6	27.0
1954	12.0	15.8	23.2	27.7
1955	10.7	22.1	21.8	29.0
1956	10.7	26.3	22.7	26.6

payroll lived in Billingham itself and nearly 100% of the remainder lived in towns and villages such as Stockton, Norton, Middlesbrough, Thornaby and West Hartlepool, which are all within a few miles of the Billingham factories.

Some indication of the relative attachment of the Billingham labour force to their jobs, if not always to ICI, is given from Table 17, taken from House and Fullerton (1960:169 and 183). Table 17 illustrates that total turnover at Billingham compares very favourably with figures obtained from the then *Ministry of Labour Gazette* for the chemical industry and "All industries" in the United Kingdom. Although the Wilton turnover is slightly lower than the average for the UK chemical industry over the majority of the seven years in the table, it is appreciably higher than that of Billingham. A possible explanation of this difference between the Billingham and Wilton sites was that at that time Wilton was expanding rapidly and a large proportion of the payroll was engaged on construction work where the turnover was generally greater than on production. I shall return to some of the similarities and differences between the Billingham and Wilton sites when the Petrochemicals Division case is discussed in Chapter 7. For the time being, the point to note is the apparent relative stability of the male labour force at Billingham.

And then, of course, there was the Billingham Synthonia Recreation Club and the international standard running track nicely juxtaposed so that errant apprentices could run off a few pints of "Camerons" after a visit to the Synthonia, what a *Times* special correspondent described as "the largest public house in Britain" (*The Times*, 30 May 1961). Those days are long since over. I was often reminded of this:

> In the old days, if you were a blue-collar worker, you lived as near the factory as you could throw a stone because you had no means of transport except a bicycle or a bus. "The bosses" tended to live further away. More recently, a lot of people irrespective of their collar live some miles from the factory . . . This has affected the club [the Synthonia]. Twenty years ago it was thriving with something like 25 sections . . . All the local authorities are now producing their own sports facilities. Because there are things like theatres and night clubs about, people don't want to come back to where they work.

Mind you, ICI's presence was pouring wealth into the local community. The gross amount of wages and salaries in 1959 at Billingham was nearly £15m. Employees there in the same year were allocated over £1m in profit-sharing bonuses. Moreover, in the year ended 31 March 1960, the Billingham factory supplied £400,000, more than half of Billingham urban district council's income from rates. The county council precepts 72% of the rates from Billingham council and they represent a significant element in Durham's revenue (*The Times*, 30 May 1961). *The Miracle of Billingham*, a glossy brochure prepared in the early 1960s by the district council, notes the fact that industry occupies twice as much space as housing, is "a distinction which had worked in every way to Billingham's advantage". But living next door to a Leviathan can be a mixed blessing, especially if the Leviathan becomes sickly and unpredictable, but that was not the case at Billingham until after 1957.

Managerial culture and organisation

As Brunner, Mond had a hand in influencing labour and welfare matters at Billingham, so, too, did that piece of the early ICI jigsaw influence some of the tradition which later evolved into the Billingham managerial culture. Across in the north-west of England, in Cheshire, the Alkali Group, a forerunner of Mond Division, was the reincarnation of Brunner, Mond. And here in the Alkali Group was Winnington Hall Club, a unique amenity in British business for the management first of Brunner, Mond, and then ICI. Reader (1975:71) presents a colourful description of pre-Second World War life at Winnington Hall. Membership was by election. Within the hall, in its bars and on its lawns, the "fellows" moved in an agreeable, masculine atmosphere, very English in tone, of cordial informality ... The whole setting was reminiscent of an officer's mess or an Oxford College, which was not surprising, since by the time ICI was founded Oxford was the university which many of Alkali Group's technical establishment came from.

Billingham, as a Brunner, Mond colony, inherited something of the Winnington tradition, though considerably modified. In the first place the demands of high-pressure technology made Billingham a better place for engineers. Second, there was rather less devotion to Oxbridge, possibly because both of Billingham's founding fathers had been educated at Manchester University. Nevertheless, Billingham had its management club, Norton Hall, perhaps always with less of a college atmosphere than at Winnington, yet another side of traditional English life – field sports – was cultivated by Pollitt and Slade. Later on the Billingham Rugby Club, and to a lesser extent the Billingham Cricket Club, and of course, the annual review, the *Norton Hall Smoker* were to become in their differing ways important parts of the Billingham managerial scene.

One of the people interviewed with knowledge of Billingham's pioneering days recalled:

In 1924 we bought Norton Hall and refurbished it. Early in 1926 we put a man called Humphries in there to live – rent free. He was the bossman who was developing the site. He was a civil engineer. He lived there with all his servants around him. The pair-and-trap picked him up and took him into work and back again in the evening. In 1926 the total salary for Billingham staff was £78,000, and Master Humphries got £5,000. Can you imagine – and he lived free. He retired in 1928.

Another manager, talking of Billingham around 1947, drew out some nice comparisons with Alkali Division and Winnington Hall:

> There was a very mechanistic style from top to bottom at Billingham. Everyone in his place and knew his place . . . At Alkali Division it was very much a division where there were gentlemen and others. At Billingham things were less stuffy but still authoritarian. In fact, my boss in London at the time had a letter from the director I was going to see at Winnington saying, "is he the sort of person that we would want to accommodate in the Winnington Hall Club?" And the reply went back saying, "Yes, he's the sort of chap who won't slop his soup and what not!" So I stayed at Winnington Hall Club – it is a very splendid place.

By 1957 Billingham Division had settled into a fairly differentiated functional organisation structure run in an authoritative fashion by talented, and in some cases eminent, technocrats. The Research Department housed Billingham's scientists. The first permanent buildings erected on the site in 1922 were laboratories and from the beginning research had played a vital role in Billingham's development. Some of these scientists had been Fellows of the Royal Society, and others were to become so as a result of work completed in the 1960s and early 1970s. One scientist recalled the concern with hierarchy and double-checking in the Research Department:

> There was a status pyramid we used to have in Research Department. I remember there was this framed letter we had which, depending on who was about, we might hang on the wall. In those days, if a research chemist wanted to write a letter outside, he got the letter written; he initialled it, and any other technical officer involved, then his group manager, and then the boss man signed it. The one we framed has 14 initials on it! This was the way the place was run. It was all status. You didn't step over your status boundary . . . It was comfortable. The outside world was something out there, which you didn't bother with.

Loosely linked to the Research Department was a Development Department, a Technical Department, the Chief Engineer's Department and the Engineering Works. And then there were the five operating works, known as Gas and Power, Ammonia, Products, Oil, and Casebourne. Each of the works had a works manager responsible to a works general manager, who was responsible for the Engineering and Commerical Works for the whole site, the Olefine Works at Wilton, and the five external factories.

On the commercial side there was a supply department, a distribution department, a sales control department and the commerical works responsible for the reception, storage, and issue of all incoming stores, the storage, packing and dispatch of the factory's products, and the operation of the site internal transport system. In addition to these functional units there were Billingham's personnel departments – labour, staff, medical, education, work study, and office administration. And on top of all this lot a divisional board with a chairman, three deputy chairmen and several directors with mainly functional responsibilities. Truly an organisation structure acting as a monument to the past.

How did this structure work before it started to change in 1958?

> When I joined the company at Billingham we had an awful situation in engineering . . . They had the technical department doing the outline design. The chief engineer's department then designed in detail . . . A part of engineering works would look after construction, and then they handed it to the works to run it . . . Four camps, each blaming the other for everything that went wrong.

A manager with experience on the commercial side recalled similar interfunctional problems between the Products Works and the Commercial Works. His illustration also gives a flavour of how changes were handled in the late 1950s.

> There was a very tight interface between the Products Works and the Commercial Works, with endless arguments going on about whether the raw material had been there or not and what product movement had occurred . . . The works manager of Products Works, who had a reputation among the men for being "hard but fair" was the architect of the demise of Commercial Works . . . I was startled to hear the Commercial Works manager stand up at a works council meeting and say, "I'm telling you what's going to happen and I've not been consulted." . . . In fact, he may well have been privy to what was going on, but not for it.

Aside from these interfunctional rivalries between managers, other kinds of recurrent conflicts in the culture were beginning to emerge both because of a new sense of power and confidence from a new generation of shop stewards, but also because of increasing mutual frustration with the we/they culture of management–union relationships that had emerged in the late 1950s. One present-day senior line manager described the christian-name basis relationship between managers and some key shop stewards in the early 1950s, which allowed for "backstairs" deals to minimise conflict. Another close participant in, and observer of, the Billingham scene throughout the last 30 years, who was never on the ICI payroll, said:

> Up to the early 1960s this site was dominated by a group of works managers and convenors who'd all been in office for very long periods – all old school, all guys who knew the 1930s. They all went in about a five- or six-year period. And there was a great vacuum left behind.

Ever since the early 1950s ICI had been a pioneer in the use of work study techniques – indeed, their use had allowed ICI to appreciably reduce their manpower around 1952–53. But by the end of the 1950s pressures of a continuous and irritating kind were starting to break out at the shop floor level. One manager recalled:

> In those days the shop stewards were getting increasingly aggressive. We had work study in the division and in most areas there were bonus systems working. As you know, it's easier to measure process work than engineering work, and the process workers felt the engineering workers were being paid a bonus on the fiddle and they themselves were being ground into the dust by ruthless work study officers. There were endless, endless disputes. Ninety-five per cent of the disputes I was involved in were about work study values that were being challenged . . . I was so utterly sick of this that I was very happy to see this massive change towards WSA.

This same manager went on to describe an incident illustrating how the we/they attitudes between management and union were sustained by provocation and counter-provocation – and how this influenced the development of his own managerial style:

> There was an incident in my third or fourth meeting of the works council involving a shop steward from my department, who had been aggressive with me and Dr Stone. Dr Stone had made a statement and my shop steward hardly allowed him to finish before he was in with, "That's a lie, a downright lie, and it's not the first lie you've told this council." I sat back in horror thinking "It's alright when the cat squeaks, but who's going to get kicked." But, Dr Stone switched off his hearing aid, a public gesture for everyone to see. The steward went on and on, and when he'd finished, Dr Stone said "let's calm down and start again" . . . that illustrated to me a way of dealing with the aggressive shop steward. I found it paid off.

Aside from asking about the nature of recurrent conflicts and how they were handled, another way into disentangling the Billingham management culture was to ask – What was the concept of a good manager? This produced some highly consistent answers for the 1950s and early 1960s, and some equally consistent changes by the late 1960s and 1970s. The picture has changed yet again now in the early 1980s, but that's anticipating some later developments in this story.

The following quotes, all from managers at Billingham in the late 1950s and early 1960s, convey the flavour of managerial behaviour at that time:

> The division always was, and probably still is, a "technocracy" . . . You weren't credible if you didn't have a technical background . . . particularly in ammonia technology.

* * *

ICI has always been very kind to its employees, but the individual works managers were very autocratic when I came to Billingham in 1957 . . . No one could stop them except the works manager who lived next door.

* * *

Well in 1958 the chief engineer was the best engineer. He wasn't particularly skilled in man management or in the techniques of organisation – he was the best engineer, which usually meant a mechanical engineer, because 80% of them were.

* * *

In those days if you were bloody good technically that was alright. The labour department, the staff department would look after your problems from the human side of the enterprise. That's no longer so.

* * *

Going back a long way to the mid-1950s when I joined the division you really felt that unless you'd been to Cambridge, got a first-class honours degree, ideally you were a Scot, and a member of the rugby club – then you were severely hampered . . . I don't think it's a bit like that any more.

Finally, two senior shop stewards recall their view of managerial behaviour in the late 1950s and 1960s and its impact on the nature of management–union relationships:

There were a lot of long-service managers and supervisors. The respect afforded management was incredible. If you had to see someone above assistant foreman level, you assumed you were in real bother. You had to get your best togs on to see the plant manager in his office over here. There was a feeling at that time to break this sort of thing down and to give shop stewards and weekly staff more voice and access, to bring a manager down to our level in the mess room.

* * *

Over the years there's been an evolution in ICI, a lot of the managers now aren't the same type – like there are more from working class backgrounds. Previously most were from middle- or upper-class backgrounds, you know, daddy owned the business and all they knew about industrial relations was what they read in a book.

It must be remembered that these views of managers and shop stewards is a retrospective one filtered through some 20 years of societal change, as well as change in ICI. Nonetheless, the above quotes and illustrations capture something of the beliefs and behaviours of a managerial culture which was to come under increasing pressure to change from forces within and without itself.

BUSINESS HISTORY AND DEVELOPMENT, 1958–83

The reader may recall from the review of the whole ICI group's commercial and economic fortunes in Chapter 3 that the years 1958 and 1961, 1970 and

1971, and 1980 and 1981 were bad years. These years were also precursors to, or directly involved, major organisational and people changes. Thus major changes in divisional labelling, responsibilities, and boundaries, and manpower reductions, took place in 1958, 1962 and 1963, 1971 and 1980.

Billingham Division in the late 1950s and then under its present title of Agricultural Division from 1963, followed the ICI trend for part of that period. As I have already noted, ICI in the late 1950s was experiencing heightened levels of competitive pressure in home, but especially in world, markets, and was facing price reductions in many of its chemicals. This was also happening at a time when the basic technologies in some of its divisions were getting behind international competitors. One has a feeling that ICI suddenly awakened in the late 1950s and early 1960s, and a steady flow of changes emerged in technology, commerical and market orientation, organisation structure, manpower and industrial relations, productivity and social and political awareness, all designed to ensure the company's survival and prosperity, not just in the traditional markets of the United Kingdom and the ever-disappearing Empire, but also worldwide.

Billingham Division found itself in 1958 with an outmoded technology, being priced out of world markets by a combination of the relatively high price of the feedstock for its technology coal-coke, with 17,000 employees organised in a basic functional structure inappropriate for handling market and technological innovations, and with increasing problems in the industrial relations sphere. What it did have was a host of talented scientists and engineers, but how were they to be redirected in order to tackle some of these problems?

What happened was a series of major technological changes in ammonia production to rid the division of its dependence on coal-coke and to move to oil as a feedstock. This happened in the period 1962–65. This was followed by the construction of large new single-stream ammonia plants and a further change in feedstock from oil to natural gas in the period 1966–71. By 1970 a new long-lasting catalyst had been developed at Billingham which enabled a highly efficient, low-pressure methanol plant to go into production. This was followed by a fourth large, single-stream ammonia plant in 1977, new plants manufacturing urea, "Drikold", "Nitram" and the most recent technological innovation the manufacture of a single cell protein called "Pruteen" from methanol in 1980. The above technological changes, especially in the 1960s, were true innovations, and have placed the Agricultural Division as a world leader in ammonia and methanol production. Those innovations and the outcomes they have produced were achieved through, at times, a highly painful business, technical, and human process. This was most notably so in the period 1966–70 when the division could first of all not get the new single-stream ammonia plants to work and then could not get them to work to predicted levels of efficiency. But more of that in a moment. How did these technological changes start? What associated changes in organisation went along with them and what wider repercussions did they have on the division?

A technical manager at that time recalled:

Yes, we were nearly bankrupt in 1960. If we'd been Agricultural Division Ltd, we'd have gone out of business twice in my opinion, once in 1960, and again in 1969. We were technically arrogant. We didn't think there were any better ways of making fertilizers and gasses. We slept for five or six years – then woke up, almost too late and produced the famous steam-reforming process which saved our necks. We started researching this in 1958, and all the breaks went our way, and by 1962 we had a complete process buttoned up and patented. My God, we were lucky. That saved us then ... And then, not having learned that lesson, we just went on overstaffing. And our selling people never really sold, they just allocated. So we were lulled into a false sense of security twice inside 10 years. Then we suddenly went full circle on this technological side and developed this new ammonia system (the single-stream plants of the late 1960s) which as far as chemistry was concerned, was years ahead of its time. The engineering hadn't kept up with us, and the very first ammonia plants we built, we had hell's trouble with materials and construction equipment.

The change from coal to oil (naphtha) as the feedstock had a big impact on manning levels. Between 1957 and 1965 the total number of employees in the division declined from 17,000 to 13,800. The great monuments of engineering of the past, coke ovens, hydrogen plants, water-gas plants were pulled down. But the changes weren't just physical or manpower,[4] new ways of thinking about and controlling these processes were required:

If for years you've lived with a technology of coke making, and then suddenly you're confronted with a steam-reforming process in which you're shoving naphtha up a tube and attacking it with steam, then you're moving out of a dirty, heavy, solid thing into a rather small-scale, fluid process in which a great deal of rethinking has to take place. You whole process control system changes. If one coke oven unit went out of action, you still went on making 90% of the coke. But if one steam-reform unit goes down, then you stop making 30%-plus of the total product.

The change from multi-stream ammonia plants to single-stream plants and from naphtha to natural gas as a feedstock in the period 1966–72 brought another large reduction in manpower. Uneconomic plants and products were discarded, and the anhydrite mine was closed down. From 13,173 in year end 1969, the total employees of the division had dropped to 10,376 by the end of 1972. More automation meant fewer numbers but also "the demands that it put on people were of a different order". Single-stream plants, instead of multi-stream units, put on greater pressure to keep the new plants running – this as we shall see put stress not only on the quality of maintenance engineering, but also on the quality of industrial relations on the site.

The financial situation of the division in 1969 was indeed disastrous, more money was "being made out of royalties licensing the new technologies than out of a production". Another director has commented that the patience of the ICI main board was running out:

[4] Some of these manpower reductions were also due to the hiving off of part of the division in 1958.

At the turn of the decade the business was pretty well flat on its back ... ICI's enthusiasm for fertilisers and ammonia was diminishing. In fact, there was a main board minute of that era – so I'm told – saying never again will we invest in ammonia or fertiliser.

Nearly as bad as the financial problems, the closure of plants, and the manpower reductions was the blow to the self-esteem of the technical managers who ran the division. A director closely involved in the technical scene at the time said:

> There was a tremendous gash to people's pride because it was a technically proud place and there were these bloody plants which didn't work ... The division board would go euphoric when all three plants were working and then go deep into depression when they broke.

It was in this situation, in 1969, that formally, at least, OD in the division was born.

Throughout this period of business and technical adversity in the division some changes in organisation structure were made but not of the substantial kind characteristic of Petrochemicals Division. Perhaps the most significant changes were made in the period at the end of the 1950s. On 1 January 1958, ICI (Heavy Organic Chemicals) Ltd was formed and this new division took over the organic chemicals side of the business from Billingham Division and became responsible for the expansion of the petrochemicals business area at Wilton throughout the 1960s and 1970s. Billingham lost about one-third of its staff strength to the new division and the total production of two Works, Oil Works at Billingham and Olefine Works, south of the Tees at Wilton.

Some inroads were also made around 1958 into clearing up the more obvious conflicts between functional units and departments by getting rid of Commercial Works as an entity and the central services unit in the Chief Engineer's Department. The Technical Department was wound up, and the long-term aspects of its work went into a Planning and Co-ordination Department, and the rest into a newly constituted Projects and Engineering Department. The Research and the Development Departments became a single Research and Development Department. The old Chief Engineer's Department was renamed and put under a new Production, Projects and Engineering Director. These organisational changes, just be reducing the number of functional departments, did not really deal with the attitudinal and behavioural problems that were occurring between the units. There was some coming together at the board level but major problems of integration persisted at the head of department and middle management levels, particularly on new project-development activities, and in the commissioning and operation of new plants. These problems surfaced all too clearly in the new plants brought fitfully on stream in the period 1966–69. This pattern was not to be broken, for reasons we shall explore in detail later, until Methanol 2 was commissioned in 1972.

The other structural changes of note to occur were in 1963. At that point the division changed its name from Billingham to Agricultural Division, and took

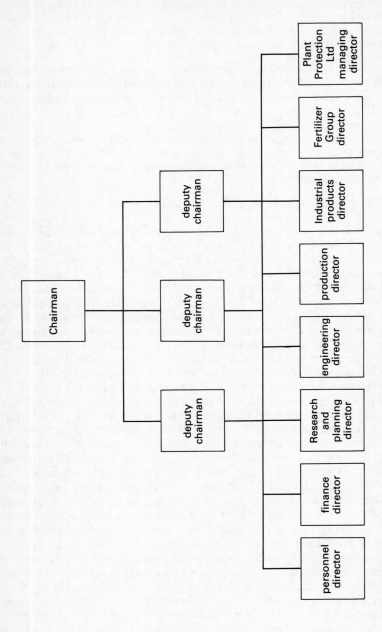

FIGURE 5 Agricultural Division: top organisation chart – 1969

on board responsibility for Plant Protection Ltd. In 1963, ICI's own organisation study and a McKinsey report on company organisation brought forward the necessity to strengthen the marketing activities of the company, and Agricultural Division thus moved from a pure functional organisation to a mixed or matrix structure. Figure 5 illustrates the structure as it was in 1969 with five functional areas and two product groups or business areas, plus Plant Protection Ltd. With relatively minor changes (including latterly the loss of deputy chairman as a distinct level in the structure and a new business area), this structure prevailed from 1965 to 1983, and this represented a source of stability amidst the many other changes in the business of the division during this period.

If the 1960s were for Agricultural Division a period of economic and technical adversity, then the 1970s can only be characterised, after 1971, as a period of recovery and resurgence. The division had a relatively cheap source of natural gas contracted on extremely favourable terms for the period 1968–84, successfully commissioned very large new methanol, ammonia, and nitram plants with the most up-to-date and efficient technology, and happily poured product into growing markets. Everything was set fair. However, continuing questions about the economic viability and growth in their new "Pruteen" business area, doubts about the division's relative competitive position in ammonia, methanol, and bulk fertilisers because of increasing competitive pressures and rising energy costs, plus a downturn in the prices in their traditional markets, were all creating an atmosphere of concern by the early 1980s, even in amongst profits of £100m a year plus.

Table 18 offers yearly statistics on Agricultural Division manpower from year end 1964 until January 1984. The table shows that the division has reduced its manpower by 49% from 1964 to 1984. Apart from showing the largish drop in numbers between 1969 and 1972 already referred to, it also indicates an appreciable sudden drop in monthly staff numbers from year end 1973 to year end 1974, a consequence of the creation of a separate Plant Protection Division, and then a long period from 1974 to 1979 when the division's monthly and weekly staff numbers were fairly stable. The 22% drop in manpower from year end 1979 until year end 1982 was a product of divisional managerial action to reduce numbers plus a number of corporate changes such as the creation of regional engineering and regional purchasing and supply functions which further denuded the division's monthly staff. The increase in numbers during 1983 was a result of the transfer of Cassel Works on the Billingham site from Mond Division to Agricultural Division's manpower numbers.

Table 19 indicates the sales, trading profit, and trading margins for ICI Agricultural Group world wide over the period 1968 to 1983. As I indicated earlier in this chapter some care has to be taken in interpreting these numbers. ICI group the sales and profit figures for their agricultural and agrochemical business classes. Table 19 thus refers to the worldwide activities of Agricultural Division and Plant Protection Division. Estimates by Vivian, Gray & Co. (1980) of the Plant Protection Division record for the 1970s period would suggest that

TABLE 18 Agricultural Division weekly and monthly staff employees 1964–84

Year End	Weekly staff	Monthly staff	Total
28.12.1964	9107	4333	13,440
27.12.1965	8900	4878	13,778
2. 1.1967	8292	4698	12,990
1. 1.1968	7900	4346	12,246
30.12.1968	7905	4321	12,226
29.12.1969	7927	5246	13,173
28.12.1970	7610	5399	13,009
3. 1.1972	6122	4866	10,988
1. 1.1973	5843	4533	10,376
31.12.1973	5683	3171	10,216
30.12.1974	5757	3177	8934
29.12.1975	5769	3244	9013
27.12.1976	5540	3041	8581
26.12.1977	5407	2959	8366
1. 1.1979	5492	2973	8465
31.12.1979	5460	2977	8437
29.12.1980	5148	2871	8019
4. 1.1982	4610	2885	7495
3. 1.1983	4332	2275	6607
1. 1.1984	4483	2350	6833

TABLE 19 Agricultural Group: worldwide sales, trading profit, and trading margins, 1968–83 in £m.

Year	Sales	Trading profit	Trading margins
1968	147	15	10.2
1969	145	8	5.5
1970	157	10	6.4
1971	158	18	11.4
1972	166	26	15.7
1973	313	43	13.7
1974	464	89	19.2
1975	554	114	20.1
1976	645	103	16.0
1977	848	139	17.2
1978	873	150	17.2
1979	995	159	16.0
1980	1071	151	14.1
1981	1245	182	14.6
1982	1369	158	11.5
1983	1507	174	11.5

removing 10% of the above sales and profits for the period 1975–80, and more like 20–25% for 1973–74, would give a truer reflection of the progress of ICI's agricultural business class. Nevertheless what is unambiguously reflected in Table 19 is the dramatic improvement of the business fortunes of Agricultural Division from 1972 onwards, although the heightened competitive pressures of the 1980s are evident in the drop in trading margins since 1980, and £100m-plus profit in 1983 pounds sterling is a drop in real terms from the profit levels of 1977.

Having established the business history and development of Billingham over the period 1920–57, the impact of that history on the Billingham manpower, labour relations and managerial culture; and then traced through the dramatic changes in technology and business fortunes in the period 1958–81, a number of questions remain for this chapter. Chief among these are to examine how and why these changes in manpower, organisation, in technology, and in business occurred. To catalogue the impact the changes had on the quality of industrial relations and in managerial attitudes and behaviours on the site, and to discuss the role that the social innovations of the 1960s played in those processes of changing. Therein lies the next challenge.

AGRICULTURAL DIVISION ORGANISATION DEVELOPMENT: AN OVERVIEW

Trying to ascertain when an activity or process begins in a large, complex organisation is never a particularly easy thing to establish – though if the activity turned out in retrospect to be significant, important, or otherwise successful, there are usually no shortage of claimants crying out – "it was from my loins it came". In the case of organisation development there is the additional difficulty of the very indefiniteness of the term itself. As I pointed out in Chapter 1, the term organisation development appears to date from work carried out in the United States in the late 1950s. There is no doubt that George Bridge, the personnel director who came to Billingham Division in 1962, started off a process of change which could later be labelled as OD. Indeed, just before he left the division in September 1967, he wrote a policy statement for the division board called "A Policy for Organisation Development", which was meant to establish a link between the change processes he had helped to start, and his hopes for their continuance after his departure. An examination of other archival material shows that the personnel officers in the division were debating their role in "organisation and management development" activities in 1966, and some of the trainers in the division had been involved in management and supervisory development courses, and group work with various individuals and groups from Products Works during 1966 and 1967. There was also the contact with a number of well-known American behavioural science consultants, sensitivity training (T-groups), and the job enrichment work of 1967 and 1968. It was not, however, until February 1969 and the arrival from the United States of Noel Ripley as a full-time internal OD resource that the OD group was constituted and began to sketch out its mission, style, activities and impact.

The informal group that Ripley drew together were primarily from personnel and training. Shortly thereafter some of them became the responsibility of a personnel manager, Paul Miles. It is important to note that most members of the OD group always retained other formal jobs throughout. The OD group at Agricultural Division was always more of an informal association that the OD unit at Petrochemicals Division.

In its early years, the period which may be characterised as *birth and pioneering*, the OD group informally concerned itself with clarifying its values, activities, sense of distinctiveness, commitment and leadership, and externally sought to establish sponsors, and a network of potential clients. Initially the group continued existing training work, much of which was novel and drew from T-group activities. In addition there was some on-the-job consulting, particularly in projects and engineering, and to a lesser extent in research. A watershed for the group was provided by their heavy involvement with the Methanol 2 project, the first big piece of capital investment sanctioned at Billingham after the struggles with the three new ammonia plants in the late 1960s. It was critical to the division that this major plant construction project was very successful, and OD was seen as having made an important contribution.

Methanol 2 was commissioned in August 1972. The period from late 1972 until summer 1976 can be characterised as the time of *diffusion and doubt* for OD in Agricultural Division. In fact, as we shall see, it was also a difficult period for OD throughout most of ICI – one of the OD groups, the OD unit in Petrochemicals Division, disappeared altogether in 1973. Within Agricultural Division the OD group continued to build up quite a dense network of clients and supporters among production managers. This network did not extend far outside production, nor did the group become much involved with the division board, or its individual members. The soundest evidence in the period from 1972 to 1976 for the diffusion of OD ideas and technologies into the division was the work done on joint problem-solving among managers, and between managers, supervisors, and shop stewards in Ammonia Works and Engineering Works. This work was important because it was OD being owned and led by senior line managers, but using specialist help, and not always necessarily the informal OD group, where, and as necessary. As a result of this line manager led work, further mini-networks of OD practitioners and sponsors came into being.

The OD group over the period 1972–76 lost some of its cohesiveness and direction. This was happening at the same time as doubts were being raised about the group's impact by managers, and those personnel managers and personnel officers who had never been accepted into its fold. Noel Ripley moved his office and attentions away from the production area to try and work with the division board and senior managers in other functions, and business areas. This proved to be stony ground, and with his important contribution as a thinker and catalyst over, he returned to the United States in March 1974. Meanwhile the OD group was sponsoring into the division three external consultants, two of whom still work regularly with the division in 1983. One of these two consultants, Ken Larsen, was to carry on the group's contribution in the construction and commissioning of new plants manufacturing ammonia and "Pruteen". The other members of the group worked with varying degrees of involvement in the joint problem-solving work on Ammonia Works and assisted more generally on industrial relations development matters on the Billingham site. In addition, most members of the group were involved in the social policy work that ICI discreetly carried out in the Teesside community. These activities tended to be with schools, social services and local government, and the churches.

Nevertheless, when in March 1976 Paul Miles, the personnel manager who had been formally responsible for the still informal collection of OD resources left the division, the OD group in Agricultural Division was drifting, and the development work led by line managers in Ammonia and Engineering Works had either faded away or was beginning to run out of steam. In 1976 responsibility for OD in the division passed from the personnel manager level to the assistant personnel manager level. Peter Moores, the new assistant personnel manager, who had been a founder member of the OD group, fashioned a role attempting to link career-personnel, organisation development and training matters. This turned out to be a shrewd move. When by 1980, ICI as a whole was encountering severe business and commercial problems, and pressure was being exerted from Millbank for even the relatively successful divisions such as the Agricultural Division to reduce their cost base, Peter Moores had laid the ground for another contribution for OD in the division; though by this time not even the specialist OD resources in the division used the phrase organisation development to describe the process and activities they were hoping to get off the ground. The period from 1976 to 1983 can therefore be characterised as one of *opportunism and refocusing* for organisation development.

In what follows I will return to describe and account for the antecedents and origins of OD in the Agricultural Division. In Chapter 6 I will then present a thematic narrative which organises and explains the evolution of OD around the three characterisations mentioned above – birth and pioneering; diffusion and doubt; and opportunism and refocusing. Again it is appropriate to acknowledge that processes of the above kind, played out as they were over nearly a 20-year period, are so complex that one despairs of capturing the subtleties and rendering them on paper. It is only possible to do one's best and suggest them.

ANTECEDENTS OF ORGANISATION DEVELOPMENT

One of the natural tensions evident in divisionalised firms is that between headquarters and division. ICI has tended to try and ameliorate these potential conflicts in a number of ways which will become apparent later in this book. Throughout its history, as Reader (1975) has demonstrated, these centre–circumference tensions have often focused around Millbank's central control over the financing of capital investment and personnel policy, and the additional pressures created by the ebb and flow in the business fortunes of the company as a whole, or of individual divisions. Obviously divisions that are not doing well attract additional interest and scrutiny from the centre, and divisions that are doing well become themselves interested in the centre, often for more resources or additional freedom, and in consequence stimulate rivalries with other less well-placed divisions. In the way of things, this is all quite normal behaviour.

As I have already indicated, in the late 1950s Billingham Division was beginning to experience commerical difficulties. In fact, probably the first substantial business difficulties since the much worse traumas of the early and mid-1930s. Interestingly, Millbank responded in not dissimilar ways to both situations. Reader (1975:158–159) has described what happened over the period 1934–36 at Billingham. In 1934 George Pollitt, virtually the creator of Billingham, ceased to be an executive director of ICI (he remained on the board) and took to farming. Also in 1934 the Billingham managing director, R. E. Slade, went temporarily to London to report to McGowan on research, and stayed on as research controller. There were other changes, on the board and below, in 1935 and 1936; and finally, in 1937, the chairman, W. A. Akers, who had been in office since 1931, was succeeded by Alexander Fleck. The top management was remodelled.

In the meantime in 1935 a main board director, J. G. Nicholson, accompanied by A. R. Young of the treasurer's department, carried out a visitation. One outcome of this was the decision by ICI to write off huge chunks of the idle capital at Billingham, but not before the newly emerging management had asserted their independence. While the old chairman Akers was still there in 1935, and as his board was changing around him, Young complained "where we expected spontaneous interest, co-operation and active assistance, we were faced with an apparent self-sufficiency which completely frustrated any attempts to enter into any agreed line of investigation."[5] As Reader (1975:159) crisply puts it, "to dispose in this way, as Akers succeeded in doing, of the formidable Nicholson was a notable victory, for the circumference over the centre".

Some of these events were to repeat themselves at Billingham in the late 1950s and early 1960s. A succession of new directors and senior managers arrived in the division to replace key managers and shop stewards, many of whom were retiring after service on Teesside, going back to the 1930s, and before. Simultaneously, Billingham was trying to put its own house in order – at least in the area where its core identity lay – technological innovation. The famous ICI steam-naphtha process was born of economic necessity at Billingham between 1958 and 1962. But Billingham's difficulties were more than just technological and it took one of these new directors, George Bridge, to grasp the nettle and begin the process of social innovation which he and other farsighted men in ICI at that time could see, was an essential complement to technological change and business success.

[5] Quoted in Reader (1975:159).

SOCIAL INNOVATION IN AGRICULTURAL DIVISION, 1962–69

The changes in the division during this period paralleled and, to some extent, led changes in the company as a whole. The MUPS/WSA productivity bargain was in process between 1965 and 1972, and, of course, towards the end of the 1960s and early 1970s, ICI introduced their staff development programme (SDP). The division led the company in the sense that it became involved very early on in focusing attention on the need to change managerial attitudes and behaviours as much, or more than, those of the work force.

As in later initiatives in Heavy Organic Chemicals Division (later named Petrochemicals Division), there was a central figure at Agricultural Division. This was George Bridge, who was the division's personnel director from 1962 to 1967. His was a pivotal role in MUPS/WSA both in the division, and in the company's central personnel department, to which he moved in September 1967. Bridge created a bow wave on Teesside which dented the rather tight and insular managerial culture on the site. His impact illustrates the role that powerful, charismatic individuals can play in social and organisational change, even in a company the size of ICI.

George Bridge's observations as a newcomer of the Billingham managerial culture, and of its impact on union–management relations, and business effectivenesss, closely mirror the statements collected together earlier in this chapter. I chronicle them here because of their powerful evocative character, and as a reaffirmation and summary of the point of departure for social innovation at Agricultural Division.

Entry – I was told I was to go to Billingham as personnel director, which was pretty traumatic because Billingham was then really the toughest place in the country. Nobody could imagine why I'd been sent . . . except as the most revolutionary, impossible person, who was always suggesting dreadful things to central personnel.

Isolation and Identity – Billingham . . . they seemed to be completely out of touch with what was going on in the world . . . There was this vast site, 17,000 people, the whole place was so solid in its cultural norms . . . there was Norton Hall, and the grouse moor where the staff lived, and the other place where all the others lived . . . I found I was responsible for 4,000 houses and a vast estates department administering them.

The Board: Concern for Production – Most of the board, their background was Oxford and Cambridge and the south (of England). Science, innovation and research had been the great Billingham thing, that was where your reputation was made . . . I do not believe that a board ought to be sitting on top of a business. I can remember you'd be sitting around the lunch table and you'd hear a bang and the whole board left the table and swept to the window. Their whole mind was on the Works.

The Managers: Concern for Technology – So many of the managers got tremendous pleasure out of the technology, out of keeping those huge plants running. They would say to me, "Look if that plant breaks down, the amount of money that I will lose in a week will pay for 50 chaps for a whole year – so don't talk to me about numbers (reductions). Numbers are irrelevant. The real thing is that the plant's got to keep running." And my answer was "That plant's got to keep running *and* there have to be 50 less people" . . . but their life was science and technology.

Where the Power was and How it was Used – They [works managers] were the king pin in their works. They were technically very good. They were paternalistically very good – good managers in the old sense. I'm not knocking that in its own way. I merely thought it was getting a bit out of date . . . It wasn't a business, it was a vast, vast technical works with brilliant people running it . . . The sales boys had to get rid of the stuff – the "bloody commercials" they were known as.

Dealing with the Unions – The managers were still able to manage the unions – that meant keeping them in their place, but keeping them chatted up. They drove the plant. They made technical innovations. They encouraged the young graduates.

Bringing in the New Graduates – So they would come from university into the research department until they were 30 or 35 .. and then they were sent down the yard [the production area]. They'd never met a shop steward in their lives, they were terrified of them.

The Role of Personnel– You had a labour department in the middle that was meant "to get on with the chaps". You had to have a pint in the [Synthonia Workers] Club twice a week. It was incredibly we-and-they to the *n*th degree. And the personnel function behaving in that way just did not close that gap. It's a management–man gap . . . the management didn't really *feel* what the men were feeling.

Bridge's Imprecise Vision – I didn't go there with any clear ideas . . . I had changed very clearly in my view of unions and had been preaching for a number of years that management had to come to terms with a new kind of unionism . . . Co-operation with the unions and consultation were my aims at that time . . . I thought there must be a way of problem solving before negotiation.

Bridge's Entry Point for Change – I thought if you could get the culture to change, then we might come through . . . You go in and feel something and feel a way forward and either get absorbed by them or start to change them and its damned hard with 17,000 like that, to retain your beliefs . . . I did carry around early on six points, in a cigarette case for all the time I was there – broad objectives for change . . . I had to hang onto my beliefs to stop myself from being absorbed into their very comfortable and happy system.

The content of what Bridge actually did, and the how and why he did it, is clearly stamped on the minds of the people who helped, opposed, and doubted him; it is also well-documented in a mass of archival material. Looking back at this attempt at managerial-led change, a striking and important thing about it was how poorly it conformed to the planned theories of change which were beginning to emerge from the writings of behavioural scientists of that time, Bennis, Benne and Chin (1961). Here was a process which was far from the planned, rational, diagnostic intervention. Rather one sees a complex, untidy, at times faltering, and political process being driven hard by a powerful man who knew only imprecisely where he was going and how to get there, tried several things along the way, learned from some of his mistakes, was not easily diverted once momentum had been created, and took others along with him behind his bow wave. Here was a social architect, and organisational changing in practice.

What Bridge did was to look carefully around him for the appropriate point to begin the change; try and build up his personal credibility with his fellow directors by doing conventional personnel activities well; wait until powerful opponents left, or could be neutralised by counter pressures, and used whatever support or mechanisms inside and outside the organisation he could find to galvanise others into action. Thus before long he and some of his fellow board members went off on T-groups in the United States, new kinds of training began for managers, supervisors, and shop stewards; the personnel and training activities in the division were decentralised, and the personnel officers were encouraged to spearhead development activities; and a stream of well-known American behavioural scientists came into the division – one to work with the division board and to examine human problems between manufacturing and engineering, another to spread group process knowledge and skills in the division, and a third to begin job enrichment projects in research and engineering areas. Some people were enthused by these people and ideas, and went on to learn more and try and apply the ideas themselves, others couldn't understand what was going on and took no part, and a few individuals among the management groups and shop stewards were overwhelmed by the pressures in some of these novel happenings and the implications they created for them back on the job.

George Bridge takes up the story:

> You have to do two things. You have to do your day-to-day job. If you have to go to the board with something very mundane like graduate selection, it has to be absolutely first class. In order to be able to achieve that which you want to achieve, your department and your ordinary routine business have got to be absolutely first class.

But Bridge had to wait, first of all for the outgoing chairman to go, and also for the respected and likeable senior manager in the labour department to retire before he could act.

> The chairman was against me, very much. That was the most difficult thing of all.

Politically, however, the die had been cast by Millbank. Billingham had to change.

> That was the first time that outside directors had come in to Billingham. That was done as a quite clear policy by ICI to break up the hierarchy at Billingham.

At least four other new board members arrived, including a new chairman. They began pushing in the production and engineering areas.

So don't let me give you the impression that I was the saviour of Billingham

Although Bridge felt from a very early stage his task ought to be try and change the Billingham management culture, he was not easily able to find the appropriate words, or the appropriate vehicle to do so. The trigger was supplied by the late Douglas McGregor. In April and May 1964, and following contacts and advice supplied by the head of the small personnel research group at Millbank, Bridge and a young Billingham labour officer, Tom Lawson, departed for the United States to look for themselves at the behavioural sciences. Lawson later recalled:

> I'd barely even heard of the term behavioural science, and certainly didn't know what it meant ... The purpose of the visit was to go to the academic establishments and to test that out with the firms who'd experimented with this stuff ... The impact that Douglas McGregor made was enormous. He really stood out head and shoulders over anyone else we saw. He came across as not only being a highly talented academic, but also with an immense feeling for people, and perhaps above all, the quality of wisdom. He was at great pains to emphasise the tentativeness of what they were doing. That visit really catalysed in George [Bridge] some views about what the division should be doing about organisation change.

Bridge confirms the above statements:

> McGregor, it was with him that one started to see a light to change the culture. He gave me a method of dealing with the culture – instead of it just being personnel, or "this is the way that you manage", which was easily rejected ... So partly it was a great help to me in trying to get my own thoughts straight, and partly it was a great help in getting other people enthused and coming on board.

Bridge didn't waste any time in inviting McGregor to England.

> He turned down the offer to be a central consultant [at Millbank]. But he spent a week at Billingham and accepted the offer here. Then, of course, he died. He was an extraordinary person. His theories were just good common sense ... In the week at Billingham, he met group after group. At the end, I took him to see the chairman and he shook John absolutely rigid. That had a big effect that week ... As a result, we started to look at getting at our business objectives through the internal organisation.

Bridge's next move also turned out to be fateful for the long-term development and character of OD in ICI. Bridge takes up the story:

> When I lost McGregor I spent a great deal of time trying to find somebody else that would fit ICI. I met Mercer and he came up to Billingham ... Ron is a funny, tough little operator. He's very acceptable to people. He's very down to earth. He's not much good if people want a shoulder to cry on. But he works.

Mercer "worked" all right. His part in the evolution of organisational change and development in ICI was a crucial one. From around the mid-1960s right up into the 1980s he has worked at various times with different parts of ICI – usually with the most senior managers, but also notably with the main board, and with individual main board directors. He has also assisted with the development of ICI's internal OD resources in ways which will become apparent in later chapters. But as we shall continuously see, the fortunes of individual consultants, and the momentum of change processes, is intimately tied in with the idiosyncrasies of personality and the chemistry of relationships, and when Agricultural Division acquired a new chairman in 1968, Mercer's work in the division was wound down.

Mercer's view of George Bridge's style and methods in the Agricultural Division are instructive. Mercer, working as he usually did with the top layers of management, could see the importance of working the power system and assembling a critical mass for a change process:

> You need a critical mass. Bridge was an aggressive guy and a very smart political person, who knew how to work the power system. He was very abrasive and always a troublesome person in the company. But he was the social architect, really . . . Bridge was strongly influenced by McGregor and felt there was a need for some other relationship between management and worker which involved trust – somebody taking the first step to set up a contract for improved productivity. He was also a missionary and was trying to introduce a different kind of climate into the division of which he was director . . . He wanted to create a theory "Y" climate . . . but he started with the environment of the work force and the things in his own division . . .

As can be seen from Bridge's shrewd use of external consultants, he knew that although changes require a champion and that a champion needs powerful acquiescence, if not always open support; for new ideas to penetrate a system and start to influence behaviour, there has to be activity and involvement in as many levels and functions in the organisation as possible. Bridge recruited an able lieutenant, Tom Evans, with a similar philosophy and managerial style, and the pair of them introduced the behavioural sciences into the division on a "seeding basis". "It was broadly educative rather than technique of package orientated."

There was the much recalled visit by Herzberg:

> Bridge just summoned a whole raft of managers and marched them off to the rugby pavilion which had a meeting room and Fred did his song and dance act . . . it was a very inspiring thing.

A senior production present said:

> There were about 50 managers who hadn't heard what a social scientist was and I think they were quite amazed . . . We sat there with open mouths . . . I was quite impressed.

This visit led on to the job-enrichment studies in engineering and research later published in Paul and Robertson (1971). These job-enrichment experiments at Billingham (and elsewhere in ICI) were part of the productivity objectives of the MUPS/WSA personnel strategy. The way the studies were carried out is still a controversial subject, and certainly no studies of this type using experimental groups and control groups have been repeated in the company. Two of the Billingham people involved in this work have subsequently argued that the impact of the job-enrichment studies in research was not entirely negative.

> But I still say that the people who took part in that project not only enjoyed it, but they got a lot of extra responsibility they'd never had before. By and large we eliminated an area of management.
> We got people to maximize their talents, to pursue projects, to think out innovations instead of just carrying out technical officer's experiments. The changes seem so small and yet I think they brought in a new culture . . . It directly led on to the SDP programme . . . Research SDP groups tended to be a lot more natural than in other areas because they'd done this work.

This phenomenon of the additive effect of one change on another, though I doubt planned, was an important piece of learning from this era. People began to see that where things went well they provided other kinds of opportunities for innovation. The linking that went on between the management and supervisory training that started in 1965; the Sandsend Teesside community group events involving managers and shop stewards from various north-east organisations, and people from the Teesside Industrial Mission; and the shop steward training – much of it within Billingham – flamed again by preparation for MUPS, led to the opening up of new possibilities for the emerging development resources in the division. A trainer at that time recalls:

> I was drafted in to set up a management training programme . . . It was a kind of crash reorientation programme to oil the wheels for the productivity deal [MUPS] . . . One of the consequences was that we began to get involved in the sort of problems which managers try to deal with in their normal workplace. With hindsight, it was on a sort of consultancy basis, although we didn't describe it in those terms . . .   . . . It also grew out of having to talk with managers and trade unionists in rather unfamiliar – collaborative ways.

In the period around 1967, of course, the MUPS programme had become thoroughly stalled across the whole of the ICI Teesside complex. The trade unions would have nothing to do with it (Roeber, 1975). Management was beginning to look to the behavioural sciences not just to help with the redesign of work and improving productivity, but also with how to deal with the problems of resistance to change. Here the work on organisation change and group process became relevant. Another American consultant appeared in the division and began to run workshops on group process skills.

The Mills workshop was really the start of it for me. I can't explain adequately the shock I got being invited to something that didn't have a programme – just gaps between meals. The only equipment you needed was a real problem you were working on . . . It sent me back determined to adopt some of that to the work I was doing.

Some of the management and shop stewards became more daring, and especially in different corners of Products Works where a combination of a supportive line manager, a couple of trainers, and a MUPS co-ordinator managed to get off the ground a series of "barrier meetings" exploring links between process and maintenance, and then the first management–union workshop, in 1968.

This Products Works one-week workshop, where the average working day was 18 hours, was a modified T-group attended by 36 people from fitters to the deputy works manager. Some of the shop stewards who agreed to come on it had been to shop steward training events and the Sandsend community group events, so had the Products Works trainer who spent a year with a management–union working party trying to get the workshop off the ground. Again MUPS provided part of the enabling mechanism to allow this extremely novel kind of activity to take place. But there was still the local politics. The trainer recalls:

The works manager said he was backing us and recognized that it was a risk, he had an awful lot to lose but he gave the sanction . . . There were some trade unionists who thought it was terrible and tried to stop it . . . but failed . . . They were the most stressful training experiences I've ever been involved in, and the most exhilarating . . . The vast majority of managers and unionists who attended always came back saying it was worthwhile . . . not that some didn't say, "never again" . . . From that we grew another two workshops on Products Works and then it began to branch out to other works.

It is difficult perhaps at this distance from the late 1960s to appreciate the extent to which this kind of unstructured group process event, involving various levels of management, supervision, weekly staff, and shop stewards cut across the normal pattern of workplace relationships at the time. It was totally counter-cultural both within ICI and British industry generally. Again this breakthrough, small as it was, and quickly overshadowed as it was by the technological and business traumas Agricultural Division was just about to face, provided some experience and climate setting for the joint problem-solving work between management and unionists which was spawned in Ammonia Works and Engineering Works in the mid-1970s.

Before this Products Works management–union workshop got off the ground, and indeed right up until 1970, some directors and senior managers of Agricultural Division atttended T-groups. Often these took place in the United States and there is a fair bit of correspondence in the files from returnees reporting on their experiences. The following extracts reveal something of the colour of these events as seen by a manager of the day:

The group work was certainly not like an English group. The people who attended were, in the American term, "switched on" before they go through the gate. As soon as the group starts they are rearing to go. For example, a man who felt slightly inferior to his bosses and covered it by a "cool image" was held down by a few strong men while one or two others reviled him to break his coolness. A man who had a devil in him had it exorcised by describing its physical appearance – and then talking to it until it came out and sat in a chair opposite where he argued with it. During this session the man in question went berserk and rushed round the room seizing the women in the group and throwing them out of the door. The T-group trainer eventually collared him and two or three people sat on him till he cooled down. As the man stood about 6'3" and was heavily built, this was a quite alarming experience.

The author of the above report concludes with the superb understatement that the culture of the above event was so different from England that it would not be understood. No recommendations were made for others in ICI to attend this particular T-group.

Much later George Bridge was to say:

I think I get my fingers burned more over T-groups than anything else. I went on one myself and found it an amazing experience. We got most of the [Agricultural Division] board to go on them and that was a great opener. But there was the appalling business where somebody saw this as the second coming . . . I think the average Englishman regards this sort of thing as the nearest thing to seances . . . I think the most acceptable thing was running good courses. You keep on working at it and eventually it takes. They swore they'd close down Norton Hardwick [the training centre] as soon as Bridge left, and its still going.[6]

The one major structural change that Bridge engineered as an enabling mechanism to bring about the attitudinal and behavioural changes he was looking for was to break up the old central labour, staff, and education department at Billingham and to decentralise personnel and training activities into the works and other departments. Tied to this structural change was a change in how personnel policy was to be formulated, and a change in role for the personnel officers. This happened in 1965, and predates many of the activities described above. Bridge recalls:

I put in a line manager as production personnel manager and under him I put younger men in who were totally responsible to a works, and the works manager. What I wanted to do was to break down the isolation of personnel department which worked in its own way and bring the management into personnel and make them responsible for decisions. I weakened the function and strengthened the line.

Now the personnel officers were to be responsible for everything on a particular patch from straight negotiations to behavioural change. The

---

[6] Norton Hardwick was eventually closed down in 1983, 16 years after Bridge left the division.

interchanges in the records between the personnel officers and the personnel managers, and then Bridge, indicate the kinds of pressures this change had created in 1966, one year after implementation. A personnel manager characterised the change thus; in a note to G. Bridge in June 1966:

> The principal difference between the new and old concept of the personnel function in the management team is the increased emphasis on *positive* means of getting people working more effectively and enthusiastically, rather than the more negative but by no means easy task of avoiding disruption of effort by disaffection.

The personnel manager then went on to query the personnel officer's ability to act towards managers either as experts on human behaviour, as an organisation expert, or a developer of managers. He complained the personnel officers were in danger of riding one fashionable hobby-horse after another and that they remained the manipulators of the (personnel) machinery and as such "had little effect on the basic thinking of managers in the works". The above note was quickly circulated to all the personnel officers and a lively correspondence ensued. Most of the personnel officers felt extremely uncomfortable with their new development responsibilities, complained that they were not professionally trained in the behavioural sciences, or organisation matters, and suggested their new-found change activities be delegated to an expert, or experts. A more perceptive member of the group could see that they were not necessarily being asked to become instant behavioural science experts, but rather were being encouraged to ask managers about the balance appropriate between technical and man-management aspects of their jobs. The personnel officer was also there to "encourage managers to experiment with new ideas in man-management and when appropriate to assist in the development of the ideas". Having said that was the way forward he doubted whether much progress had been made in the first 12 months, and called for a review of the training of front-line personnel officers.

Later in 1966 the above personnel officer wrote to George Bridge stating there was a gap between his high-level formulation of personnel policy and the practical application of that policy at the lower levels. The gap he felt would only be narrowed by allowing each personnel officer in a "piecemeal approach", to gauge the different situations they were in and their "different interests and backgrounds", and act in consort with local management. The piecemeal approach for creating change recommended by the personnel officer was acknowledged as sensible by Bridge in his reply – but he was still pushing for the broad objective, and the grand design. Bridge concluded his letter to the personnel officer in this way:

> You say start from the other end and obviously from the way you lay out your objectives – i.e. involvement with managers and getting a toehold in the process – you are right on target. While this seems a sound practical approach . . . unless we start grappling together with the concept of what is management et alia . . . to have a standard in our mind to put performance against, we are no better equipped

than managers to answer daily problems or to form objectives. In short, I accept your approach but I believe mine has got to be achieved – but my methods must be improved!

The above interchange and correspondence which preceded it on the tensions implicit in the new personnel officer role, between the personnel systems and the developmental aspect of the job, illustrate some general issues about creating change which will recur time and again in this book. Can organisational changes be led from people in specialist roles, and if so how? Is it possible for individuals with an administrative and political component to their role, such as personnel officers, to act as developers of people and organisations? Can change be created by the broad sweep of a social architect such as Bridge, or must we rely on the more circumscribed and piecemeal approach recommended by the personnel officer? Indeed can both of those approaches be combined in the same organisation at the same time, or are the dynamics they create basically opposed to one another?

Social innovation in Agricultural Division, 1962–69: a review

Drawing together some of the threads from the period of social innovation in Agricultural Division in the 1960s and making an assessment of its impact on attitudes and behaviour in the Billingham manpower scene and management culture is a difficult task. The comments I have been able to extract from the voluminous archival material available indicate naturally enough that for those in the middle of those changes it was a time of confusion, stress, exhilaration, pain, and learning. For some people, and especially the individuals who later went on to become specialist OD resources in the 1970s, or the managers excited by the 1960s work who led some of the important development work in the next decade at Billingham, the social innovations of the 1960s were a founding experience. It affected the concept of themselves as human beings, the way they treated their peers, superiors, and subordinates, how they behaved at home, and how they attempted to make future changes at work.

I have no hesitation in arguing for the case that George Bridge, and Tom Evans, the general manager of personnel who worked closely with and for him, opened up Billingham in the 1960s. But their impact and the contribution made by the people they enthused and left behind, has to be set beside the repercussions on the site made by the business and technological traumas at Billingham of the early and late 1960s. Equally well, one has to take into account the impact on managerial attitudes and behaviour of the conduct of industrial relations, and changes in the educational system and in social values going on contemporaneously with life at Billingham. One cannot talk comfortably here about linear causal relationships, in a world more realistically characterised as a complicated mosaic of cause and effect.

In what follows I leave it largely to the views of those specialists, managers, and shop stewards involved in the social processes of innovation to make their own assessment. I think it proper to wait and draw together my own reflections later in this book. The reader will see that running through the views of those who were at Billingham in the 1960s is the stamp of change, a feeling of continuty and opportunity into the 1970s and a clear notion of an aversion or backlash against some of the methods and processes used to create change. The 1960s was a period of experiment and of learning at Billingham – and regrettably perhaps, it is in extreme situations that individuals and organisations acquire their most fundamental learning.

In an earlier section of this chapter George Bridge expressed his later reservations about using T-groups within the British culture. Here I draw only on his comments on what he felt he left behind at Billingham, and his reflections on his personal style, and its impact on others:

> By the time I left there was a fairly strong converted lot within the management and certainly in personnel . . . I felt there was enough critical mass that it wouldn't go back . . .
> I have never seen myself as a power person but when you are pushing things through, you're bound to get some opposition. And the chap who comes after you does inevitably have a difficult time . . . The chap who came in, on my advice entirely, was Ray Williams . . . He got up against the board. At that level it was desperately difficult. On the other hand, he really built up the behavioural side, encouraged Noel Ripley, and Williams drove through WSA . . .
> Don't forget that technically they were having one hell of a time with all the plants. A lot of the management saw themselves, very fairly, as having to put up with two revolutions, a technical revolution and a social revolution. And they said that's too bloody much.

It is instructive to follow through the comments of the four personnel directors who followed George Bridge. All of them point to the successes of the Bridge era, the opportunities it created for future development work but also, in some cases, the deeply held resentments. None of these personnel directors supported and pushed development activities in the open, driving manner Bridge had done, but all of them, to varying degrees, provided a loose political umbrella for OD work, as it then became known as, to continue.

> I knew Bridge and Evans very well, both were very forceful people. Bridge had been experimenting like mad at Billingham. I don't think it would have happened without him . . . What he left behind at Billingham was a seedbed, ultimately worked out as very good. But at the time there was a lot of confusion and misunderstanding as to what all this OD was all about.
> While Bridge was there people who found it illegitimate kept a low profile, so it was afterwards, when I got there that there was considerable deeply held objections . . . They'd have talked about pieces of behaviour – apparent free thinking behaviour where somebody they'd seen before as a clear, firm, controlling, big machismo guy was turning into some sort of obscure, arcane, unforecastable person. It didn't happen too often but where it did, it was influential.

* * *

> The concepts had penetrated very widely down the organisation, partly as a result of the Teesside Industrial Mission and the Sandsend events. That did lead to the beginnings of a very different attitude to relationships at work . . .

There was quite a network at the lower levels and no consciousness in the board at all . . . Bridge and Williams had really overdone it and turned the board off.

* * *

I quickly got all sorts of powerful impressions that the behavioural science initiatives of the 1960s had been very definitely a mixed blessing. The business went through very dramatic adverse circumstances after that work and left the feeling "if we'd not been messing about with all that stuff we might have seen problems sooner and more clearly – a resentful feeling . . .". This convinced me one clear way not to succeed was to launch a divisionwide campaign of some kind. It's not that kind of culture.

Naturally enough, those individuals who, from personnel, training, or line management roles, were able to use the new ideas and people brought in by Bridge and Evans to create meaningful changes, and to develop their own knowledge and skills, regarded Bridge's arrival as a breath of fresh air.

Bridge was a tremendous pioneer, trying to do things that were very different from the things around him. For me he really opened up new possibilities. They did create opportunities because it was the first time that somebody at board level was saying perhaps we should be moving along these paths.

* * *

Bridge and Evans were very much the engine and motor behind all this in the 1960s. One important early decision was not to go for a total, across the board change programme such as a "Managerial Grid". Bridge and Evans opted for an eclectic . . . Home grown – developmental was the word used – programme. That threw up opportunities left, right, and centre. Any problem you came across was fair game.

* * *

Working on the management and supervisory development programme led various managers to come and ask for more tailored work along these lines – this created a network of activity at lower levels, and a group of sponsors for us in the 1970s.

Shop stewards were cautious of getting involved in development activities spawned by Agricultural Division in the 1960s; this is understandable enough given the organised resistance to the company-led MUPS/WSA programme on Teesside. Nevertheless, shop steward training started in the mid-1960s, first of all on the neutral ground of a local technical college and then inside the Billingham site. As I have already noted, the first management–union workshop was held in 1968.

There is a risk for shop stewards in involvement in development work. When the OD started there was a word that came out – behavioural science. An emotive word, you can put all sorts of interpretations on it – you can think of Chinese brainwashing!

Job enrichment – most people tend to be highly suspicious of that sort of things, wary of it. The company was trying to get as much as it possibly could get for a given amount of money.

*   *   *

Many union people in ICI are very suspicious of OD. People think of it as a lot of undercover, underhand stuff. Training is a more acceptable term. I got involved in the first Sandsend course in the 1960s where two or three shop stewards were among 50 managers, clergy, etc. I had some trepidation because I thought the managers were all very clever people, but I found I could hold my own and in many cases help other people. That sort of stuck with me.

The caution, suspicion, and learning described above did not stop a much larger number of shop stewards, including the ones quoted above, from attending a wider range of management–union joint problem-solving activities in the 1970s. The reasons why will become apparent later.

The final quotation I would like to use catches very clearly the resentment that a number of managers at Billingham felt about the way behavioural science ideas were introduced into the division, about the feeling of personal threat those ideas and experiences created, and the positive impact it did have on management thinking and behaviour there.

I disliked it intensely and dislike it even more now. Not as a science or an input but I have no patience for a philosophy which says, here is the answer. Everyone will go through it, and end up a better manager . . . I saw behavioural science coming in a very simple form . . . a number of people began to look at themselves and say "hell, I'm in this category and I'm not very good – they don't like me, that's not acceptable today". I didn't want the information and I didn't know what to do with it when I'd got it. There was some success, it introduced a new vocabulary, it introduced a way of looking at management style that was rather less haphazard. The whole movement, the whole idea did get a lot of people looking at management style, putting much more emphasis on problem-solving and analysis, more ordered in where they were going and in reviewing whether they had got there. Before it was by intuition and seat of the pants.

Agricultural Division had been opened up, at least partially as a social, technical, and managerial system – but who was to capitalize on this development, and how? The next chapter on the OD work in Agricultural Division over the next 15 years has that as one of its starting points.

6   The Organic Strategy for Creating Change: Agricultural Division

The narrative presentations in Chapters 4 and 5 indicate the extent to which the 1960s were a period of business, technological, and industrial relations change for all parts of ICI. The form in which these changes manifested themselves in each of the various divisions of the company was a product both of the particular technical and commercial circumstances of each division and the way, for example, each division responded to MUPS/WSA, the centrally driven companywide productivity initiative.

In Agricultural Division the 1960s had been a period of technological revolution, and by the end of the decade, near business failure; there was also the difficulty in implementing MUPS/WSA. At a formal negotiating level MUPS/WSA appeared to have almost as much difficulty at Billingham as south of the Tees at Wilton. The craft unions refused to become formally involved very early on, and it was only accepted after some six years which included a major revision of the programme (as WSA in 1969). However, outside the formal negotiating arena, there were significant differences between Billingham and Wilton. Informal talks continued at Billingham almost throughout the period, and the bitter divisiveness of Wilton was avoided, despite the fact that Agricultural Division was engaged in a fairly steady reduction of its work force from some 13,000 employed in 1967 to under 10,500 by year end 1972.

George Bridge's personal involvement with, and commitment to, MUPS/WSA undoubtedly influenced this. The influence came partly from his own rather undefined, but strongly expressed, belief that there was a need for new forms of social relationships at work. It came partly from the periodic visits of the American consultants who presented confident views based on combining theory with practical experience of applying behavioural science ideas in American organisations. And it came partly from the restructured personnel and training staff who helped to introduce off-site shop steward training and a range of management–union activities and workshops which were radical innovations in terms of British industrial relations of that time.

Thus, in the second half of the 1960s, there was considerable emphasis on change in Agricultural Division. The division continued to draw on its established innovation sources in research and engineering. At the same time a parallel set of initiatives into social and organisational areas was beginning to make itself felt in various ways across the division. As I indicated in a review of the social innovations at Billingham in the previous chapter, the content of those innovations, and crucially the way they were introduced, was not well received at the time, or subsequently; although those innovations may have provided the enabling conditions for further attempts at social change in the 1970s.

For some managers and personnel officers the "behavioural sixties" was a time when "a hell of a lot was going on, with very little to show for it". The resentment implied in that statement is understandable given the tough business and technical problems faced by managers at the time, their desire to find quick answers to their problems, and a residual feeling that all T-groups and unstructured group process training did was to create further uncertainties and slow the process of managing down. The fact that there was no strategic plan behind the above innovations, only Bridge's imprecise vision, also left a feeling that no constructive outcome appeared in the form of *a* clearly identifiable change. The fact that first Bridge, in 1967, and then his key colleague, Evans, in 1968, departed for Millbank to pick up the stranded MUPS initiative, meant that their guiding hand and the force of their personalities and authority was lost to the division's process of social innovation. Meanwhile the front-line change agents in Bridge's concept of the future pattern of social relations at work, the personnel officers, were floundering because of an unavoidable lack of experience and skill in internal consultancy work, and were being driven more and more into a personnel administration and industrial relations fire-fighting role by the pressures of MUPS/WSA and their local line managers' overriding concern to cure the huge new ammonia plants of their technical difficulties. It was in this context that in February 1969, Noel Ripley, a 30-year-old American engineer with a Ph.D. in organisation development, and three or four years of consultancy experience in OD, arrived at Billingham to give new shape to OD in the division.

The purpose of this chapter is to provide a chronological view and some limited analysis of the major activities and events in the birth and development of the Agricultural Division OD group. Paralleling the treatment of this subject in Chapter 4, the material here on the Agricultural Division OD group is presented so as to unravel the internal evolution of this group through an examination of the group's membership, values, distinctiveness, commitment and leadership; and also to expose its external evolution – the group's boundary management activities; its external sponsorship and opposition, and the changing pattern of its legitimacy in its divisional context. However, even with these broad conceptual categories, the major objective here is still to tell the story of the OD group, and to tell it within the three characterisations mentioned in the previous chapter. The reader may recall these were birth and pioneering, diffusion and doubt, and opportunism and refocussing.

As will become apparent, the strategy for using OD resources to help create change in Agricultural Division was distinctively different at Billingham compared with the other divisional cases reported in this book. At Billingham during the 1970s there was no sustained top-down attempt to create large-scale cultural and structural change of the kind eventually achieved in Mond Division, or an attempt at the kind of top executive-led structural change stimulated by John Harvey-Jones whilst he was chairman of Petrochemicals

Division, rather the OD resources in Agricultural Division after George Bridge's era of social innovation were assembled around a bottom-up strategy of trying to create change organically. At Billingham OD was harnessed to the two key business problems of the day: how to develop and improve the culture of industrial relations in various works across the division, and how to dramatically improve the division's Achilles' heels, the commissioning of new production facilities. The organic strategy was essentially Noel Ripley's strategy. To him it meant an evolutionary and experimental approach to change. Starting with real problems recognised and owned by managers, long-term in its intentions, but pragmatic and additive in its approach.

BIRTH AND PIONEERING, 1969–72

In July 1969, four months after Noel Ripley's appointment as Agricultural Division's first full-time OD resource, a simplified version of the organisation chart of the personnel function looked like Figure 6. This chart shows that the general manager–personnel post held by Tom Evans had now disappeared on Evans' departure for Millbank, although there were still four personnel managers. By 1977 this had been reduced to two: a personnel manager responsible for all personnel matters across the division, including negotiations with monthly staff unions (virtually nonexistent in 1969), and a personnel manager responsible for weekly staff union negotiations across the whole Billingham factory site. The latter post had become necessary as a belated response to the fact that the weekly staff had organised themselves both at Billingham and at Wilton on an across-the-site basis. What the chart cannot convey is the fact that each of the personnel and training officers reported, and had their offices close to, the line managers whose departments they worked for. They had only dotted-line relationships with the four functional personnel managers.

On his appointment, Ripley reported at first to the production personnel manager, Clive Oldham. By July 1969, Figure 6 shows that he appears on the organisation chart as the only person beside the label organisation development and now reporting to Paul Miles, the other new arrival in the personnel function who held the title personnel manager–commercial and development. Figure 6 also shows that Ripley was granted status equal to the personnel officers and the manager responsible for management (and supervisory) training. The division records indicate Ripley's terms of reference were as follows:

> Dr. Ripley will have a broad role in the division in helping personnel managers and officers and line managers to apply some of the more modern techniques and thinking arising from the behavioural science researches which have been going on in the world in recent years. Dr. Ripley's appointment will last for about two years . . . one of the early parts of his job will be to establish the right priorities.

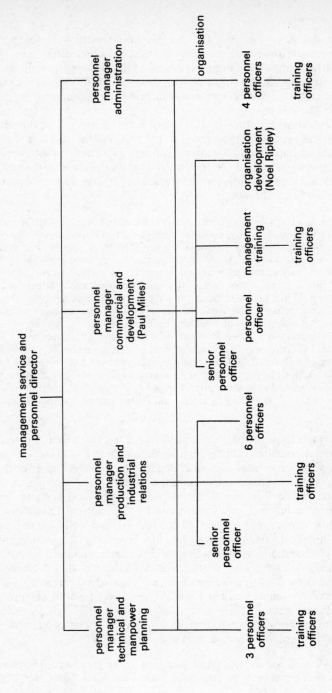

FIGURE 6 Agricultural Division personnel function – July 1969

Although it was generally expected that he would work with the personnel officers, in practice Ripley focussed his efforts in two other directions. The first was towards building up an informal group of like-minded people who were involved in training and related work; the second direction was towards engaging managers – initially from research, and projects and engineering; and then production – as clients.

All the data from this study of ICI indicate that how each of the divisional OD efforts was initially born and set up was fateful to their long-term development and impact, and for this reason it is important to dwell on Ripley's early perceptions and actions. Naturally, he found the receiving culture for his brand of OD work greatly influenced by residual feelings about the personality and style of Bridge and Evans:

> The impression I had of Bridge was that he had some vision of what he wanted but he was pretty rough . . . Evans was also rough – a real rugby player – they were too rough for some managers. Bridge wanted Theory Y and he put a lot of pressure on people to move. His enthusiasm and energy were infectious but his impatience and lack of tolerance created a tension which didn't help . . . OD was not in very good shape. There had been a lot of tree shaking . . . which left very little cohesion. When I arrived there was a great vacuum in personnel – the new personnel director had just arrived and there was no general manager to replace Evans. So I had a hell of a lot of freedom. . . . There was also tension in personnel between those that were heavily involved in OD and others that were not. . . . But the personnel function was decentralised, that is very important, so there was no establishing of a (central) OD unit. . . . But there was a lot of receptivity to the general OD approach, particularly to an *organic* approach. They didn't want a "Grid". They wanted something more low key . . . I think my personal make-up suited that culture. I'm a quieter person. I don't tend to rush. Nothing happened quickly.

In fact two months into his job Ripley sent a memo to all the personnel managers and personnel officers in the division, and a group of trainers, outlining his views on central personnel departments' report on job-enrichment studies in ICI. He used his comments on the strengths and weaknesses of these "experimental studies" to reveal his own philosophy and style for creating change, a style he felt was now appropriate for Agricultural Division.

First of all, change efforts had to be mutual and collaborative and not unilaterally imposed. Because some of his objectives for change were to increase "collaboration, self-direction and initiative taking", then change processes had to have those characteristics built into them. Second, and crucially, changing an organisation was not just about creating particular change objectives – more enriched jobs. Therefore, it would be unwise and result in a lot of wasted effort to try and crank up the division on a crash programme in job enrichment. Rather, future change efforts need to be cast "in terms of a long-term, continuous, and organic process".

> Our future efforts will be organic as they grow at the pace needed to produce significant and permanent results. Crash efforts do not produce this kind of

product. "Organic" means to step off from the base one has established and in so doing expand to a larger base for a next step off, and so on.

As far as who was to be involved in creating these organic processes of change, Ripley, drawing on the support of a personnel officer from the research department, suggested "our conclusion was we have to define a pool of resources outside of personnel – otherwise we could never meet the growing demand we expect". There then followed broad reference to managers from research, and projects and engineering, who could form a base for creating change which might lead to a situation where line managers could serve as consultants to other line colleagues.

If Noel Ripley's note of April 1969 was his opening shot at defining something of the character of OD in the division, then his paper of February 1970, when he was one year into his task, represents something of a full broadside. This paper contains sections on his definition of OD at that time, the values and end states he was using in his work, a review of the implications of the Bridge era of social innovation, a statement of today's needs for development activities, his approach to realising a more effective organisation, and the role of "third parties" in creating innovation. My own view of this document is that it was way ahead of much of the academic literature on planned change and consultancy at that time, and it is a pity its length precludes its publication in this book. Nevertheless, it is important to record some of the highlights of this paper in so far as this example of Ripley's thinking influenced the practice of OD in Agricultural Division.

Ripley's definition of OD indicates he was not tied to an arbitrary fixed concept – it had to be situation-specific, subject to change, and above all a statement of what is needed in order to help the organisation effectively deal with its tasks and also allow the individuals in Agricultural Division to have exciting and rewarding experiences in their jobs, and as he specified "this doesn't mean being happy all the time". The end states for OD carried a very heavy concern for individual, interpersonal, and group issues. Thus his concept of appropriate problem-solving behaviours was to minimise defensiveness, closedness, and the impact of position, level, status, and age; and to encourage true collaboration through direct confrontation, learning from critiquing, and through creating a climate where feelings were dealt with openly and directly. Individuals were to be allowed to grow and to be held responsible for their own behaviour in a world where class structure is seen as something to be minimised, and where differences between people are only made when it comes to solving problems; and are in terms of expertise, knowledge, or information held. So organisation effectiveness was to come from providing opportunities for individuals to increase their own effectiveness. This as a view of the starting point for the content of changing has subsequently been roundly and understandibly criticised for its naivety about the structural and political impediments to change, and it is perhaps in Ripley's view of a process for creating change that a more enduring message in his approach lies. But before I further clarify Ripley's change strategy and the role of third parties in those processes, it is important to briefly chronicle his diagnosis of some of the key problems of Agricultural Division in 1970, here at least one sees a match between his target for change, individual behaviour change, and a diagnosis that focusses on interpersonal and group relations.

Ripley characterised interpersonal and group relations in the division as being "the crunch problem" in 1970:

> It doesn't make sense that people deal with each other out of defensiveness, that the basis of their interaction be primarily protective and, therefore, leading either to aggressive or withdrawn behaviour. This kind of behaviour spills over into lowering the quality of group problem solving by creating cycles of defensiveness, where initial threat leads to withholding information, blaming others for difficulties, erecting walls and moats between groups and departments – and still further defensiveness.

It is significant that although Ripley may have witnessed such behaviour while managers were wrestling with the overriding business and commercial problems they were facing in 1970, no mention is made in Ripley's paper of those business and technical problems, or the manpower reductions they necessitated. Ripley was clear at that time that the cycles of interpersonal and group defensiveness had to be broken, and the mechanism he had in mind for doing that was to use third parties

> The special person – who is less or uninvolved, and who is to some extent outside the circle, is needed to help those on the inside gain perspective on themselves, and bring out the hidden issues which produce the defensiveness.

Third parties were not there to produce jumps or discontinuities, to "tell and sell change" as Bridge and Evans had done, but started from the premise that authentic development of an organisation is the consequence of a natural evolutionary process, wherein the members of the organisation (who wish to do so) define for themselves the problems they want to tackle and the timing and steps for doing it. The third party role is to facilitate the above process but not to take sides; as soon as the third party takes sides, then he becomes part of the problem.

Finally, Ripley recognised that the division required a "third-party organis-ation", not in the sense of an instant department or unit of consultants, but a loosely constituted voluntary association of people who would build their own ethos, so as to not become a "living contradiction", and would evolve slowly from their initial base. There was to be "no crash effort. To try would produce at best a house of cards". Rather, the focus of the third parties' work was to be the job family (the group that is a group because the individuals have a job relationship with each other). They were to work where there is interest and receptivity, and on the problems the "customer" is prepared to tackle.

The "third-party organisation" that Ripley was after had in fact met for the first time in July 1969, seven months before Ripley's paper on OD in Agricultural Division. As with most papers outlining and justifying strategy, it was written after part of the strategy had been acted out. The way in which the informal group of third parties – which became the OD group – developed in its early stages is as important for subsequent development as the receiving culture Ripley faced and his outline strategy. Ripley's own description of the birth and internal evolution of the OD group gives some feeling for this:

> I was looking for resources – who can I work with, who do I feel mutually in tune with? . . . So I started identifying people. We had to spend time together, just to share what we were individually trying to get together. The composition of the group didn't make sense in terms of an organisation chart, but emotionally we were a good combination. After the second meeting, I suggested we go off to a hotel[1] for a couple of days. We never asked anyone for permission. It's a principle of mine that if you ask to do unconventional things, you'll be told – don't. So the thing is to just do them – but don't do the ones that are so far out that you can't handle the consequences.
>
> We met that way for a couple of years and the group grew naturally. . . . We always had an agenda of what we'd been doing and what we might do. We would talk about what was coming up in the company that we might be able to influence. We also did some relaxing. It was at that time (1969) that I purchased the Clive Oldham record player and the Oldham Memorial Record Library. I like music, so I bought a record player and sent the bill to Clive Oldham. I didn't hear anything about that for a couple of years and then one day at a meeting Clive just started coming on. He said, "I'm sitting at my desk and going through a pile of things and there's a bill for £150 – what the hell is going on?"
>
> We also worked on our own personal things, about us or things about our working relationship. It always came back to the trust thing about sharing information, instead of holding it back. We could have emotional flare-ups and there was time to think it through.

The above quote indicates the group was used partly for agenda or strategy formulation in relation to the external life of the group. I will return to that aspect shortly, but the quotation is also revealing about important aspects of the internal life of the group. By creating time and space away from work, the group gave itself room for experimentation and learning, for the development of cohesion and commitment. This was enhanced by what amounted to practising the skills of OD and group dynamics amongst themselves; working on issues that were personally important to them. The fact that it was done "unconventionally" without "permission", and that the group did not "make sense in terms of an organisation chart", helped to set precedents for moving across organisational boundaries and taking risks in terms of unconventional approaches to traditional problems.

Asked much later about the values, styles of operating, sense of commitment and cohesion, and distinctiveness of the "Swallow group"[1], two of the original three personnel officers and the sole trainer had these kinds of things to say:

---

[1] In those early days the group acquired a name – "the Swallow group" – which was taken from the name of the hotel where they held their meetings.

In the early days the flavour of OD had a quasi-religious taint to it . . .

* * *

Noel was anti-establishment. He felt there were no barriers in the lowest of the low talking to the chairman.

* * *

There was an exclusiveness, like a London club. People who wanted to join were not necessarily allowed in.

* * *

It was very cohesive – it was like being a member of an ongoing T-group.

These feelings were confirmed by other individuals, some external consultants, and some trainers who joined the group in 1970:

> In the first phase of the group a certain amount of cohesiveness and momentum was generated. I know of no better way to build up a group than by personal, charismatic magnetism, of getting close to you bright people who you like, and working with them round their own personal development . . . then gradually convince them that's the right set of values to be working on, and then they will start themselves on the task.

* * *

> I think the individuals always had a sense of purpose. Their values were the thing that kept it together because their values were closer to each other than they were to the rest of the organisation . . . That purpose centred around the dignity and value of the individual before the value of the group.

* * *

> It was a very highly committed group, but not to the extent of being missionaries – there was a realisation that the missionary zealot would turn off as many people as he turned on.

The above quotations clearly indicate the sense of commitment and cohesiveness created by the "Swallow group" meetings. But it is important to remember that the commitment was to each other and to certain values, the group was not a highly task-centred group committed "to walking out the door with an agreed agenda". The kind of values and beliefs which the group engendered were strong and distinctive: they seemed to centre around "concern for people, with a strict resistance to organisational values", as one group member described it. Another went further – "It was almost anarchistic – certainly different values from the [divisional] norm." The notion that the group was distinctive is reinforced by the fact that myths (for example, about nudity in Ripley's early T-groups, and near physical combat in early union–management workshops) are alive in the division several years after those "early days".

There was the danger that this high group commitment and distinctiveness would lead to total exclusiveness and separation from the rest of the organisation. Several factors limited these tendencies. One was the fact that the OD group members had other, indeed primary, organisation roles as personnel officers or trainers attached to various works and departments in the division. Another factor was Ripley's strategy of trying to attach their activities to work problems perceived by line managers. As Ripley put it:

> I felt a lot of OD is forced. It wouldn't help to talk about Theory Y, or participation. We had to work on the managers' concrete problems and, through that vehicle, the culture, the climate and the way the organisation operates would change.

A further, and very important factor in connecting the group into the divisional context was the arrival, in July 1969, of Paul Miles, the personnel manager who gradually took responsibility for the emerging OD group, and retained that responsibility until he moved to another part of ICI in 1976. A career ICI personnel man, Miles was older, and more senior than the "Swallow group" members. Miles later recalled the emerging suspicion and sometimes downright hostility that existed towards the fledgling OD group amongst more conventional personnel managers and personnel officers, and some line managers. Ripley's nonconformity "in talking to people without getting his boss's permission", "talking to union representatives outside the formal negotiating and communication processes"; all this emphasised and reinforced that he wasn't one of management. People began to ask the normal bureaucratic questions – trying to place this young American and the group he was building around him. "Who's he really working for? Who's his boss? What's his remit?" To which my answers were "Well no one really" or "I suppose it's me" – all those things were totally against the culture. . . . And what is etched into my memory is people coming into my office and opening up with – "When are you going to sack Noel Ripley?" Miles' reaction to this situation was "to step straight into a protective, an umbrella, role" – and to concentrate on the strategic and political issues of the group's survival. Almost inevitably, this shared leadership of the group between Ripley and Miles produced conflict.

Ripley had collected the group together – he was their guru, the informal leader with a vision of a less hierarchical, more open organisation, and with the interpersonal skills both to build the group and take a lead in initiating internal consulting activities; as Miles put it, "They got landed with a boss, and they put me on trial, and invited me to the Swallow group – which is an indication of the way the hierarchy works in this business [OD]." Miles' attempts at light-reined management, trying, as one group member put it, to introduce some "formality and structure", were not entirely successful in the eyes of the group, who saw him as "unable to flow with the group . . . trying to nail things down", in terms of task and schedules. Ripley's own recollections of this period in the group's development mirror those of other group members:

> I remember a couple of Swallow meetings when Paul (Miles) was there and they were different. The reason Paul was there – very important point – was because of his position. Everyone else was there because of who they were. In effect, that finished it. . . . Paul was impatient with our behaviour and process. His influence was to move us towards the productive activities of planning and scheduling and

the other group-building activities he was uncomfortable with – and that was half the reason we were there. As a result, those total "Swallow group" meetings sort of ended.

Paradoxically, the jolt given to the "Swallow group" by Miles' arrival and the less inward and exclusive character of the group's internal workings throughout 1970 and 1971, may have been an important factor contributing to the OD group's survival. Ripley had come into the division and provided real task and process expertise to a set of individuals in personnel and training (and, as we shall see, in management) who could only be characterised as enthusiastic amateurs.[2] He had brought them together, built a group where people could learn in safety and receive interpersonal support, and most importantly, had articulated an organic approach to organisation changing which offered some continuity, but also a change of direction from the social innovations of the 1960s, and real focus and a practical pathway for change in the 1970s. The base was there, and now the OD group had to spend more time managing its boundaries and demonstrating some success with "the early adopters" in the management system who could see there was help to be had from the OD group. It is hard to imagine that the OD group could have developed from the base provided by Ripley and the "Swallow group" without Miles' political umbrella. As Ripley put it, "it was a tough job to represent us and Miles carried that into meetings". As time proceeded, conflict over leadership became less of an issue. Ripley's expertise was no longer unique, and group members were busily involved with clients and less with each other. It is to these change activities, the attitudes and role of management in OD, in effect to the group's external evolution, that I now turn.

The OD group in its context

While the Swallow group was coming together the group members, sometimes individually, sometimes in pairs, and sometimes in small teams, were following Ripley's organic strategy and seeking to find clients with problems and the personal predisposition to work with "third-party helpers". What happened was that Ripley attracted into the OD group the personnel officers from the two departments – research, and projects and engineering – where the social developments of the 1960s had taken most hold. There were managers in those departments facing problems of reorganisation and team development who had been attracted by some of the broad messages of the "behavioural sixties" and were looking around for more specific help on problem-solving in their departments. As important as this initial seeding in projects and engineering was, it was really the export of those early adopters of OD into the production works and elsewhere that created a modest network of OD activities in the

[2] The emerging OD group received their first formal training in OD at the two Eastbourne training events in 1970. As I have already noted these training events helped to build some of the mythology and group identity across the now broader ICI OD network. They may also have contributed to individual skill development.

division. This group of managers carried with them something of a commit-ment to doing things differently, together with an interest in developing appropriate methods for whatever it was they as a manager set themselves to do. This is precisely what Ripley had hoped for – managers setting the pace, focussing on problems of meaning to them, and using the OD group as facilitators and process helpers and trainers, and not heavy-handed professional experts.

One of the issues of general importance from this study of OD in ICI is the question of who, and why, do certain people take on responsibility for change more readily than others? In all the divisions studied there is evidence of some individuals taking a lead in change efforts, being early adopters rather than laggards in the use of new techniques and ideas. I do not wish to pre-empt a later and fuller discussion of the early-adopter phenomenon, but it is important here in chronicling the external life of the Agricultural Division OD group to mention the spectrum of interest and disinterest in the OD group, and some of the motives behind using OD resources.

More than one manager indicated there were three kinds of responses to OD. "There's the group [of managers] who actually believe there is something in this OD." Another manager, who was not claiming to be one himself, said that the "believers" were often people who had already logged high perform-ance as managers . . . and who absorbed OD and its risks on "the basis of confidence". A second group was "taking OD on board because they couldn't see any other way to go – essentially they had problems, and couldn't see any other way to go". And finally, "there's the group who feel that it's just a useless sidetrack".

Two of the early-adopter managers were clear that the key to their absorbing OD ideas and using the OD group were commonalities around values and style of working between themselves and the OD group:

Miles' people were in no way influencing the direction of what we were doing . . . We saw them as people who had the same set of values and who were highly supportive when we came to them for help.

* * *

I don't see OD as just a problem-solving tool . . . a lot of the early OD helped me with standards . . . with how I saw other people, being more tolerant and more positive about people.

Other managers talked about Noel Ripley "switching me on" and of Noel "making legitimate what I was already doing in a closed cell". For others "OD really was a very appropriate tool at a very appropriate moment".

Whatever the motives, and the above comments indicate they were various, the OD group began to pick up a series of clients at the middle and senior management level, mostly in the projects and engineering and production environments of the division. With these sponsors they began to work on some of the key problems of the division around "getting the existing plant right", helping with industrial relations developments, and then, crucially, assisting in the commissioning of a big new plant producing methanol.

Methanol 2

There is not space in this book to describe all the work carried out by the OD group in the pioneering phase of its development. Later in this section I will return to look at the impact of T-group training, and in the next section I will cover in more detail work begun in 1970–72 on joint management–union problem-solving which flowered more obviously in the next period of the group's development – the period characterised as diffusion and doubt. I have chosen to focus in on the commissioning of the Methanol 2 plant because, as a project, it was a technical and commercial watershed for the division, and also because in giving confidence and increased legitimacy to some members of the OD group, it was also a watershed in the evolution of OD in the division.

The design, construction, and commissioning of Methanol 2 was a success by any of the standards used to evaluate such projects. The plant was commissioned on time, reached its predicted flowsheet within four days, and has run smoothly ever since. This was achieved by a small underspending on the capital sanctioned. On 10 August 1972, six days after commissioning, a deputy chairman wrote to the senior manager responsible for the project "congratulating everyone associated with the project for an outstanding achievement. I have never seen a plant which looked better built or smoother in flowsheet operation within the first week of its life." This letter was passed on by the manager to one of the internal OD group members, expressing his appreciation to him "and all other OD chaps for your help". The manager also said he would write personally to the two external OD consultants who had played their part in the success of Methanol 2.

Millbank sanctioned the capital for Methanol 2 in May 1970, when Agricultural Division had just about ironed out the technical difficulties it had been having with its new ammonia plants, but before the division had cured its business difficulties. Let there be no doubt, Methanol 2 had to be a success. Future investment in the division depended on managers re-establishing their technical and managerial competence. The managers on the project team knew their security and promotion depended on a favourable outcome – and some "saw this as an opportunity to remove the guilt associated with other project outcomes".

Two divisional reports were prepared describing and evaluating Methanol 2: one written in 1973 by a member of the OD team on the project and another written in 1979 by two managers. The latter report compared the differing use made of OD resources on Methanol 2 and the next big plant commissioned – Ammonia 4. I shall draw on these documents plus interviews with the managers and OD team members on the project.

Both reports emphasise that no unique solution to the problems of new plants was achieved in these plant commissionings. Instead, effective methods and processes were discovered to link the people, the organisation, and the technology on the project. "Here, perhaps for the first time in the company, there was a clear notion that the people and the organisation were just as important as the technology." A "People Plan" was used to bring people on to the project in advance of the tasks they were required to do, but only after the technology had been largely defined, and after the concept of a commissioning management team had been agreed, a project group manager appointed, and extensive team-building amongst this team had established a pattern of harmonious working in this top group.

The OD complement on the project in retrospect seems weighty. It comprised two external consultants and four to six internal consultants – all were part-time on the project. Their role was to work on role and task clarification, organisation and team-building, process consulting and training with nearly all the horizontal and vertical interfaces between the various groups on the projects right from design, through procurement, to commissioning.

The project group manager was asked why he involved OD resources.

> No one said to me you ought to be using OD – I was told that my organisational relationships were for me to work out. . . . Just about that time I attended a British Institute of Management seminar and heard a consultant (who later played a key role on Methanol 2) talking about using behavioural science on a major commissioning project. . . . As a result of that seminar, it occurred to me we should do some team building and that's how the OD work started on Methanol 2.

There was scepticism about using OD resources at the beginning from some of the senior managers – but this evaporated and was replaced "when we got down to the next layer – because there were some plant managers and engineers who never ever accepted all this OD". One of these sceptics later recalled "shocking some of the people on these team-building events by saying, 'I don't actually need to get into bed with someone to work with him'". Others complained at the time that the use of OD techniques took some of the interest and excitement out of their work. There weren't the normal interpersonal tensions, the heights and depths of involvement. Some people "felt cheated out of an experience which they thought they ought to have had". But as the author of one of the in-company reports said, "was the objective to give excitement to people, or make methanol?"

Politically, of course, what mattered as far as the development of OD was concerned was that the senior managers of the division were prepared to acknowledge that OD help had made a difference to the success of Methanol 2. That much is clear both from documentary sources and interviews. Two of the senior managers of the division always sceptical and sometimes hostile to OD were prepared to say:

> On Methanol 2, I think OD helped in sorting out the frictions, but you might also say that OD was a success because Methanol 2 was a success. But I think it almost certainly contributed.

* * *

You never know, scientifically, whether OD is good or bad, but the feeling about Methanol 2 was that it was a good activity . . . OD is most appropriate in "start-up" situations.

Although OD resources were used in a considerably lower key way on the next two big plant start-ups, they were used; a clear indication of a successful evaluation involving actions and words. But I should really leave it to one of the senior managers on Methanol 2 to indicate why OD help on that project was perceived to have made a difference:

The conclusion I drew was if you had personality problems, or power and authority problems, or responsibility problems, it was often beneficial to take time off to talk about them off the job in the presence of somebody who was skilled in OD technology.

Methanol 2 was commissioned in August 1972. In the period since Ripley arrived in the division in February 1969 some considerable progress had been made in following his organic strategy of seeking out, and focussing on, managers' problems. This provided access to clients, or built on links which members of the group already had. As a result, there evolved a series of consultant–client relationships, mostly in the production areas, and mostly at the level of works manager and below. The OD group's posture with respect to evaluation was a logical extension of their strategy of attempting to marry new and non-legitimate methods with existing business problems. They argued that they should not be evaluated in terms of some vague criteria about the group as a whole, but rather in terms of specific clients' views of their contributions to particular works or projects. In addition, since the managers and union leaders who were their clients tended to stay in the organisation, satisfied clients provided repeat business.

Crucial to the OD group's success at this time was that they worked on problems in the production and industrial relations spheres which were defined neither by themselves nor by board remit, but by their clients. They were also associated with the demonstrable success of the Methanol 2 project. The fact that some members of the group acquired credibility with individual clients, and that evidence of repeat business and managers beginning to use some of the language and techniques of OD, may be construed that as a "set of values" and a "problem-solving approach", OD was acquiring some modicum of legitimacy, certainly did not mean that the whole organisation, nor indeed that the division board, accepted OD.

Two of the board members in the period commented that until the business and technical problems of the division had been solved in 1971, "OD activities were really not relevant to the crucial issues". "So that the attention you'd get to OD from your average division director was minimal." Some senior people who "were directive by nature, strong rugby backgrounds, thought this OD thing was lowering the moral fibre of the whole place at a time when there was a crying need to order, structure, and plan the mending of the technology, and indeed the repair of certain markets." For people one step or more removed from involvement in actual OD activities, the OD group also represented "folk devils". One of the group's protectors on the board had this to say:

> One of the overt accusations of the OD system was that they were revolutionary. Some of these lads were making ideological statements ... sounding very revolutionary. That I never did respect very much. ... Some were trying to put a coherent political philosophy behind it ... talking about destroying the system. There wasn't a lot of it about but enough to give some ammunition to opponents.

Of course the managers favourably disposed to OD, and therefore already close enough to individual group members to interpret some of the proclaimed values of the OD group in different ways, were able to tone down language which to others sounded like "overthrowing the system" to mean "they were very interested in trying to change the culture so that more risk taking was accepted, that there was a general loosening up of the structure, that people became more open and frank". The politics of managing the OD group's external image was a continual problem – one that wouldn't go away, and indeed one that couldn't go away for as long as they were an insubordinate minority helping others with more muscle than themselves to change the system they were all part of.

In addition to their vulnerabilities around the value questions, of being perceived to be "antisystem", "revolutionary", and "caring more for individuals than the organisation", the OD group also ran into opposition when they put on culture change training events which were more universalistic in their aims, and not therefore tied to particular, clearly perceived management problems; and when they encroached too obviously on the territory and power base of the more traditional members of the personnel function. An example of a culture change training event that ran into difficulties was Ripley's first broad intervention into the middle to senior levels of the management system. Ripley ran two 1-week training events in January and May 1970 for around 40 managers in the division. These were called "laboratories for individual development and organisational effectiveness", though undoubtedly they were of the T-group genre. This kind of training was useful for building the confidence and skills of those members of the emerging OD group and some of their early clients – but a third similar event was cancelled and something of a backlash ensued which put further pressure on the legitimacy of this kind of OD activity. One of the senior managers who attended one of these training events commented:

> Noel was trying to unlock tensions between people. I don't think he was very successful. They were personal relationship things. So I would not blame Noel Ripley for that.

Another manager had no doubts that "sending[3] people on T-groups to try and change them wasn't on. These were autocrats, and were promoted for being so."

[3] It is important to note that none of these managers was "sent". Noel Ripley invited them and some declined the invitation.

172 The Awakening Giant

One of the consequences of the mixed messages from these laboratories was it led to an increased scrutiny of the OD group's activities throughout the latter part of 1970, much of 1971, and then into 1972. The evidence of a desire to scrutinise and reshape the organically emerging OD activities and group is crystal-clear from the archival material covering the period August 1970 until December 1972. As early as August 1970, Ripley was responding to a memorandum from a director asking him to prepare an "inventory, review and projection" of OD activities in an effort to get OD "onto more of a business footing". Ripley's response to this was to say "I am optimistic the process of doing this will clarify the positions of key people, and help screen out activities not directly related to critical operating problems." What Ripley was more concerned about in the note was that he, and not just two of the divisional personnel managers, should carry out the review.

By early 1971, when an "overheads panel" had been established in the division to review all overheads units and areas with a view to reducing costs,[4] two of the division board who were protecting the OD activities were sending messages to the group that they should "be less organic" in their approach in order to get the OD efforts "more directly matched with potential financial pay off" and the OD group should "support the development and maintenance of the divisions 'mechanical personnel systems' and procedures as the structural framework from which the division has to operate". This was a reference to the integration of the OD work with existing activities, mechanisms and roles – particularly on the works in the industrial relations area. The trigger for that message was increasing alarm at the "informal" work going on amongst some individuals in the OD group with the shop stewards and conveners outside the formal negotiating processes, at a time when it looked as if the local unions would finally accept the company WSA package, and as development work was going on to bind local management into a more cohesive site management system to cope with the now established and effective union sitewide political organisation.

By June 1971 when it was apparent that in November of that year a formal review would be made by the division chairman of OD activities, Paul Miles sent a note to all members of the OD group[5] entitled, "Management of Organisation Development." Miles amongst other things mentioned "at board and general management level there is little support for OD work and no more resources would at present be authorised". While, said Miles, "present changes are effected by committed line managers, almost exclusively in their own areas, assisted on a full- or part-time basis by members of the OD group" – there is a need to deal with two of the "prices" of our "organic and flexible approach". He was referring to instances of confusion and inefficiency resulting from individuals in and outside the OD group "not knowing what was going on"; and

[4] 1969 and 1970 were very bad business years for ICI's Agriculture Group interests. See Table 19, Chapter 5.
[5] The group by this time comprised Miles, Ripley, two full-time OD consultants recruited from inside with trainer backgrounds, a personnel officer, and two external consultants.

personnel officers feeling excluded from "a privileged activity" because of the development of an OD club mystique.

Ripley's response to these statements was to reaffirm that in his view the OD group's progress so far had been due to their posture of working, on a voluntary basis, "where we can work", and of preserving their "neutrality". As soon as the OD group was seen as being "owned, directed, or controlled by any segment of the division", they would lose their capacity to work between groups, and especially "along union/management interfaces". Ripley concluded this memorandum to the division chairman, at the time of the latter's review of OD work, by summarizing the principal characteristics of OD in the division:

> An *organic process;*[6] *evolving* and *experimental*
> *Task-based* (upon real, day-to-day problems).
> *Personalised* by those doing, and the conditions that make up the division.
> *Division-owned* as against a top-down management team.
> *Long-term* and not a quickie panacea.

The OD group survived the overheads panel and the chairman's meeting for reasons which can now only be conjecture. No detailed account remains of the chairman's meeting to review OD, only a brief note prepared by Paul Miles outlining some of the comments made by the chairman about OD. One of these comments referred to his perception of the content of OD work and contained a worry that the "organisation was being swamped by consideration of individual needs". Significantly, the chairman acknowledged the "worthwhileness of our OD approach" because of the work of the industrial chaplain[7] and Noel Ripley. He saw them "as people without a long-term interest in the organisation, having no particular axe to grind and therefore to be trusted". But surely OD survived the threats of 1971 and 1972 also because by this time OD activities were now things that some recognisably competent managers and not just the OD group did. Ripley's organic approach had diffused the knowledge and skills of OD beyond a small professional circle, and Miles, and successive personnel directors, had put a political umbrella over those specialist resources and toned down some of the excesses of their exclusiveness. In a thin and faltering way OD was now in the division's bloodstream – and everyone had a much-needed success on Methanol 2.

DIFFUSION AND DOUBT, 1972–76

As I have already noted, the arrival of Paul Miles in the division in 1969, the increasing interest and scrutiny of OD activities by the board, the personnel function, and in some cases by senior managers – some of which was meant to protect it rather than kill it, all meant pressure to put OD on a more "businesslike footing". The organic approach of Ripley had created space and

[6] These are all words emphasised by Ripley in the original.
[7] The Rev. Hinton, of whom more will be heard later in this chapter.

freedom for successful marriages to take place between managers with real problems, who were prepared to accept the risks of attempting to deal with those problems by means of the novel methods quietly flagged by the emerging group of OD resources in the division. But a combination of the exclusive character of the Swallow group; the willingness of some members of the division to portray the Swallow group's interest in the individual before the organisation as "antisystem, and revolutionary", the Swallow group's continuing belief in keeping all doors open with as many groups as possible by casting themselves in a neutral third-party role – and the unorthodox boundary-crossing activities this led to – produced a desire to contain the group.

By mid-1972 the process of winding down the group building activities associated with the Swallow period of 1969 and 1970 was all but complete. The OD group were now spending their time with their various clients. Some group members regretted the loss of their psychologically supportive "home" and some blamed the loss on Miles' now public attempts to manage the OD group. In February 1972 Miles sent a note to the now nine members of the OD group based on his discussions with the personnel director and site general manager. This note, entitled "Future OD Effort", explicitly referred to the project method of working used on Methanol 2 as an analogue for future OD work. Certain activities were clearly listed as priority areas – the areas in fact to be described in the diffusion work of 1972–76 – group members were allocated roles in these areas. Miles continued:

> If we effect these changes it means diminishing the visible centre OD group or unit. The alignment with specific projects will necessitate a look at the roles that people have and the remits where they exist. We will have to face the basic question of how proactive the OD man should be as he becomes more like a local manager of OD resources and more involved in the political system rather than a resource and a facilitator.

This shift in emphasis from the internal group-building and loose organic pattern of client development and working of the Swallow period to the more structured approach recommended – but not always wholeheartedly carried out – in the note by Miles, seems to have been highly functional for the further successful evolution of the group; at least for a time. The network of contacts of the OD group widened. In particular, as will be described in a moment, very extensive OD work went on in two major works – Engineering and Ammonia – where senior management moved from being clients to being advocates and even practitioners of OD, and where there grew up mini-OD networks around the managers and personnel and training officers in those two works.

The above personnel and training officers became members of a collectivity that Miles started to label in correspondence as "the extended OD group". Meanwhile the "core OD group" continued to be asked to work on the critical areas of industrial relations and increased their credibility with trade unionists. They continued to work on the organisational problems of plant construction – Ammonia 4 – though the OD work was not on the same massive scale as it had been on Methanol 2.

It must be remembered that there were continuous strains and tensions in the lives of the OD group members. They had little formal security or recognition for their work. Where it was associated with success, much of the credit went to the manager clients and, of course, it was always difficult to clearly evaluate the OD contribution. There was continuing scepticism and opposition from some managers which received some added impetus by the mid-1970s by the host of new technical graduates coming into the division who saw the division as a marvellous arena to practise their new-found technocratic skills. This group had, of course, missed out on the management skills message powerfully hammered home in the "behavioural sixties".

The pattern of limited support and sponsorship of OD from the division board continued throughout the early and mid-1970s. Seeing the way works managers and heads of departments were given great freedom, at least on matters of management style to "run their patch as they wished", one personnel director commented that "OD developments could only flourish if I encourage cells to go on and do their own thing." In the period since 1967 when Bridge brought in the American consultant, Mercer, to work with the division board and Mercer had been ejected by a new division chairman in 1969, no consultant, internal or external, had got near the division board. This changed for a brief period in late 1972 and 1973 when Noel Ripley left his office in the "yard" and moved away from the production people and production problems to concentrate his efforts from a new office in the division headquarters on OD work "amongst senior managers in the division".

In fact, Ripley began to explore some of the most politically charged "interfaces" in the division. How the board worked as a group, the relationship between the chairman and his board, and the relationships between the board and the group of senior managers just below them. He also invested time in doing process consulting on some of the sitewide committees that were attempting to build coherence on policy matters across all the divisions represented on the Billingham site. Finally, he tried to open up some of the headquarters commercial departments to OD work. They had been, and continued to be, barren territory while the OD resources of the division were concentrated on production, engineering and industrial relations matters. This was all too little and too late, and Ripley had only faltering success in work with the division chairman, and had little impact on board working, or the other interface problems he thought worthy of attention. People's minds were elsewhere. Agricultural Division by 1974 and 1975 was producing its best trading margins of the 1970s, ICI as a whole was cash-rich and in the middle of a capital investment boom, and managers at Billingham were understandably enjoying their success and fighting for their share of all this new capital being sanctioned by Millbank.

In March 1974, just before Ripley left the division to return to the United States, he prepared a prophetic missive which he was happy to circulate and describe modestly as a "situation paper". This paper contains a brief diagnosis and some earthy statements – friendly ones, mind you – about how he saw the division "from my particular vantage point". He concentrated his remarks on "the management" and prophesied correctly that "the problem of numbers and levels is the keystone problem for the effectiveness and health of the division". He contended that the six levels of management between division chairman to plant or section manager was having "a massive effect on performance and job satisfaction; it breeds frustration, confusion and dissatisfaction . . . my very subjective feel for the division tells me that the amount of work available calls for four". Ripley further argued that although "the attention given over the past 5–8 years to costs, plant performance, markets and numbers [of people] had produced a slimmer and financially healthier division . . . the development needs of staff had received little direct attention". By development needs of staff he was referring to having "an interesting and hopefully stretching job to do, *and* being able to work constructively with one's interdependencies". But these messages of Ripley fell on stony ground – this was intellectually correct but contained the wrong language, the inappropriate symbols for the comparatively financially rich and technologically booming times of the mid-1970s. Six years later in 1980 there was a near-perfect match between Ripley's diagnosis and the economic and business circumstances of the day – and Ripley's prophetic concerns became everyone's concerns – and another discontinuity took place in the division's development; which provided another role for OD. But more of that later.

Ripley, in his own words had "come for two years and stayed for five". With the demise of the Swallow meetings, the increasing skills of other OD group members, and the growing network of clients, his role as a pioneering informal leader was less essential. In any case this role was being increasingly filled by Ripley's American friend, Ron Larsen. Larsen also had a Ph.D in OD and had been working as an external consultant in Europe since 1970. This had included some small amount of time in Agricultural Division and from 1974 onward he began to work an average of two days per week there. But what activities were Larsen and the other members of the OD group concerned with in late 1972, and how did these activities and the attitudes they stimulated justify the characterisation "diffusion and doubt" for OD in Agricultural Division in the period 1972–76?

OD and management–trade union problems, 1970–76

In the memorandum "Future OD Effort" of February 1972 from Paul Miles to the extended OD group,[8] Miles set out priority areas of work agreed between himself, the personnel director, the site general manager, and the extended group. The priorities were defined as "site management, supervisors, inter-union and management–union activities and the problem of maintenance effectiveness". The latter was a reference to management's continuing concern about what they believed to be overmanning amongst craftsmen on the

[8] The reader may recall this comprised the full-time internal and external OD resources of the Swallow period *and* a training manager, a personnel manager, a personnel officer and a productivity services officer.

Billingham site. These definitions of priority areas caused no great difficulty for the OD group members, for as we shall see they were already working with some effect, particularly on interunion and management–union problems. What caused a reaction back to Miles, which he signalled to the personnel director, the site general manager, and Ron Larsen in a memorandum called "Growth of OD Activities" dated March 1972, was the senior managers' perceptions on *how* this OD work involving union–management problems was to continue in the future. In a nutshell the issue was that although senior management could see the benefits of individual OD resources working on union–management concerns in an "organic fashion" and "where they were personally welcome", this way of working was difficult to live with managerially – it couldn't be planned and controlled in the usual sense. The third party consultants became ambiguous characters who didn't fit like everyone else into the political fabric of the organisation. What a conundrum in creating change – management could see the benefits, wanted them to continue, but couldn't cope with the methods and the people who were helping to produce the results.

Management's alternative suggestion for using the third party consultants would mean bringing them into some of the institutions on the site such as the Billingham Site Management Committee and the Billingham Site Personnel Department[9] which were being rapidly strengthened at that time because of management's continuing difficulties in dealing with union organisation which had a history of sitewide institutions and organisations. Management felt that this would bring the third party OD resources "organisationally closer to the problems". The OD group thought the management suggestion to bring them into "their institutions" would dissolve their only power base – their neutrality as an agent between union and union and in some cases management and union, and even management and management; and kill them and their work stone dead. Interestingly, both the management and the OD resources turned out to be partially right and partially wrong.

But Miles in his March 1972 memorandum put the dilemma with some eloquence and in words meaningful to all the parties in that context, and at that time:

> The full timers [the OD group] have some common features in their origins and motivations. In crude terms they are counter dependent on formal organisations and they have moved into this kind of work because they do not like what organisations do to people. They therefore limit the extent to which they join organisations in order to effect changes from inside them . . . This results in an unwillingness or inability to tackle political systems . . . We need to be much clearer about the expectation we have of people in the OD business. I now suspect that some of these may be quite impossible to live up to, and that there is some element of scapegoating in our views about them. The union-management area provides excellent examples of this. We regard as significant and praiseworthy the work that has been done in this area by third parties who are seen by the union hierarchy as being independent of the management. We want this to continue. At

[9] This was the focal point for weekly staff industrial relations on the site.

the same time we want people to be much more involved with the formal aspects of the organisation where policies in relation to unions are developed. Increasingly this will become impossible, and we will have to live with the reality whereby people who do get involved with the formal system get cut out from some of the most important third party work. Thus, Noel Ripley is no longer acceptable to the conveners because he is associated with the management through the Billingham Site Management Committee. Jack Brown still is credible but we must resign ourselves to the likelihood that the more he gets involved with the Site Personnel Department, the less chance there is of his sustaining his relationship with the unions.

As well as stating some of the dilemmas in using OD resources as third parties in union–management problems, the above quote also indicates something of the nature of Miles' role in attempting to manage the OD resources in the division. He was himself acting as something of a third party, a catalyst and a communication filter and amplifier between the OD group and senior managers. He was never able to manage the OD group in the strict and conventional sense of the term – as he said himself:

> Yes, it's management of the unmanageable really because all the variations and the independencies and the problems and the doubts really represent the strength of the (OD) activity, and immediately you tidy those up you're dead . . . It's just a nonmanageable, nonmanagerial grouping.

But the above correspondence and the attitudes and dilemmas which it reveals were going on in 1972, and by this time a variety of joint problem-solving work, as it became known as, had started and faltered in Products Works, had got under way across the site with a tough occupational group called the "riggers", was beginning in Ammonia Works, and was about to start in Engineering Works. The above work, involving as it did shop stewards and conveners, management, full-time OD resources and personnel and training officers using OD methods, is nearly unique in the story of ICI OD throughout the 1970s, and extremely novel in the context of the grass-roots handling of British industrial relations not only at that time, but also subsequently. The space that can be allocated in this book describing this joint problem-solving work amongst "the riggers", and in Ammonia and Engineering Works does not do justice to the learning that can be derived from its implications, successes and failures.

Again it is important to address the questions from what context and structure did this work emerge; what confluence of circumstances and individual action made it happen, and influenced the process of its development; what were the motives of the parties for tackling these established problems in such novel ways; and what impact did this work have on the personal objectives of the individuals involved, and the causes they represented? But these are big questions, and they are at the heart of whatever theoretical and practical learning comes from this research. Any answers offered will be suggestions rather than hard-and-fast explanations – and especially at this stage of my pulling together the elements of one case, even though it does contain several examples to explore.

Looking at the context, a number of threads present themselves. MUPS/ WSA had offered a productivity bargain, had encouraged grass-roots dialogue between the management and union representatives around job grading and wages, it was seeking to establish a consultative style of handling and breaking the "them and us" divide between management and union, and one of the vehicles it sought to do this was to establish and develop the role of shop stewards in such processes. The Rev. Hinton, a key figure in the Teesside Industrial Mission, who after three years in theological college had spent a number of years as a labourer, machinist and shop steward, and who was to play a long-term and vital role as a neutral third party in this joint problem-solving work, commented:

> The MUPS programme was important [in the mid-1960s] because it released shop stewards in hordes for full-time activity. I'd never seen in my life before, shop stewards doing nothing in terms of physical work.

Not immediately, but over a period of time, some of the power was decentralised in the union hierarchy from the conveners to the senior stewards and stewards operating at the work group level. As one powerful convener commented, "Before everything came through me. Nobody would move unless they got the O.K. . . . This was a whole process of getting the shop stewards to stand on their feet." But this put great pressure on the shop stewards and many of the old stewards "couldn't cope, the older guys who had been used to either thumping the table or working most of the time, and just occasionally doing a bit of negotiating – they were replaced by younger men". As one senior shop steward said, "it causes problems this way of working, the sheer amount of time and energy you have to put in to it. I'm lucky if I spend 15 minutes a day in my office. There's more incidents of shop stewards having heart attacks and ulcers than management. I go home sometimes, I don't know what day it is." One of the management's responses to new pressures created on the full-time stewards was to offer training – at first this was refused, but eventually training started in the neutral ground of a local technical college and eventually it came "on site".

While the pattern of union activity was being opened up in the above way, George Bridge and his compatriots and successors were working to introduce management to more participative ways of managing, and in particular to help create changes at the work group level through the use of behavioural science ideas and group process skills. The strength and weaknesses and impact of this work was described in the previous chapter in the section on "Social Innovation at Billingham". Out of these parallel and complementary processes appeared individuals on the union and management side, "the early-adopters" who, when they came into positions of power in their respective hierarchies in the early 1970s, were able to take the necessary personal risks to attempt to solve their problems in a more mutual, and where possible more continuous, fashion. Henry McGill, the works manager who jointly led the Engineering Works OD work in the 1970s had in the late 1960s been manager of a small, new, plant with a relatively low degree of unionisation. This had been the first Agricultural Division plant to accept WSA, and the experience and confidence acquired in this had "been a tremendous example to me of what could be achieved by people working together in a fairly open environment". He later applied change processes with similar values but different methods in the much tougher and more conflict-ridden environment of Engineering Works. Similarly, Philip Marsh, the personnel man in Engineering Works who also played an important leadership role in this 1970s work, had been an engineer in Products Works at the time of their joint management–union workshops in the late 1960s.

But the following characterisations of union–management relationships by shop stewards from the Transport and General Workers Unions (T&GWU) and the Amalgamated Union of Engineering Workers (AUEW), both of whom were at that time vigorously resisting the MUPS/WSA change, indicate that in the late 1970s the general pattern of union–management relationships was far from mutual:

> In the 1960s there wasn't the dialogue there is now. It was a cut-and-thrust situation where you had to negotiate on the spot. We'd stop the job until we got the money ... Works managers were faceless people – they were out of touch. (AUEW)

* * *

> Weekly staff were very suspicious of all monthly staff. There was a great deal of mistrust. It was a hire-and-fire situation, people floundered in and out according to overtime requirements but the monthly staff were very static. Power was on the management side – you got the odd bit of rebellion – but it tempered out. (T&GWU)

As far as the unions were concerned there were one or two other factors in the context that influenced their attitudes to innovation in workplace relationships. One was the continuing dependence on Teesside on a few large firms in heavy industries for employment. This meant few jobs to pick from and understandable feelings of "getting a bit frightened about changes affecting our jobs". And there were significant plant closures in 1970 and 1971 which meant, as one convener said, that "co-operation had to be there between management and the unions so that people weren't going out the gate". On the more positive side, a senior steward acknowledged that around the late 1960s "we got a lot of managers who were very enlightened ... and things started to develop from there, although it [OD] didn't get off the ground straight away". And there was the added local complication of interunion conflicts on the Billingham site usually featuring the process and ancillary workers in the T&GWU and the craftsmen in the AUEW and EETU/PTU (the electrical and plumbers union).

Finally, from a union point of view they were organised into a district system of organisation with district committees pulling together the senior union representatives from both the Billingham and Wilton sites. These were powerful groups seeking to co-ordinate strategy and tactics across both sites "to defend" against management moves such as MUPS/WSA, and to formulate more proactive measures. Although these district committees could become arenas for solidarity, they also represented situations where the differences in union interest and workplace culture between Billingham and Wilton sites were played out. As one shop steward said, "there's usually a big difference between what the two sets of stewards (Billingham and Wilton) want on the district committee. It's a fact that someone will dictate or determine what you end up doing, people want to handle their own little piece of the action."

In the chapter which follows, I will explore in more detail the similarities and differences between Agricultural Division and Petrochemicals Division, and by implication the Billingham and Wilton sites; as part of the process of asking and answering the question why did one kind of change take place here but not there? Let me only say here that the OD group in Petrochemicals Division were never allowed near management–union relationship problems, and no management or union initiatives of the joint problem character got off the ground at Wilton. The perspective of stewards with experience of working on both sites gives an indication of the differences between them:

> I've worked at Wilton and keep in touch. I believe the industrial relations developments at Wilton are nil. It's chalk and cheese compared with Billingham. I wouldn't go back to Wilton. The industrial relations is of the oldfashioned type of conflict, you win one, you lose one. Relationships here are better even at the worst of times.

* * *

> Billingham is regarded as the right winger in the Teesside district. I was one of the biggest accusers of this until I came here and realised it was a much pleasanter way to work.

These attitudes are, of course, a product of some of the development work on Billingham in the period 1970–76, the management attitudes and behaviour of 1980–83 may be starting to dent and dull some of those more positive feelings. But this does not detract from the basic point being made about the differences in management–union culture on the two sites. One final, pointed, rather whimsical quote from a shop steward captures well the rather unstable, fast-moving, self-interested culture at Wilton and the more densely interconnected, stable, factory town atmosphere at Billingham:

> The Wilton site is cosmopolitan . . . a newer site . . . people were brought in . . . and an attitude prevailed that it was every man for himself . . . At Wilton people were all talking about the new car, the fitted carpet, the mortgage and the fact that they may go out one night for a "half" with the gentry. When you came to Billingham they said – how many pints did you have last night, and whose wife are you sleeping with?!

Looking at industrial relations from the management point of view the research interviews indicate it was one of the most often mentioned sources of conflict – an area clearly to be managed, and worthy of development time. Although it is important to keep in mind, as more than one manager mentioned – we are talking about a process industry "and therefore we are able to be a lot more relaxed about our labour relations than we would be if we had a production line to run. The only time when we get really critical is when we get a plant shutdown and we want to start it up again." A focal point for considerable tension on the site therefore was allocating maintenance resources when the large shutdown of plant occurred. These required massive resources and there was the issue of what happened the rest of the time when those resources were under-employed. This issue which, of course, mainly affected the craft unions but also non-trade groups involved in shutdowns such as "the riggers", was tied to the ever-present concern of ICI to increase productivity, not just through technological change but through "getting the numbers down". Although ICI followed a policy of no involuntary redundancy, spasmodic attempts were made to operate a natural wastage and no replacement way of keeping labour costs down. This was resisted by the unions. Other areas of conflict centred around "both sides wanting to control overtime", irritations around job assessments, and as one manager put it, the "inter-union volcano", craft versus general union. Undoubtedly some kind of management commitment to joint problem-solving was a necessary prerequisite to build and maintain the right climate for gradual change in some of the above potential and actual recurring sources of conflict.

But the question was how were such climate-building activities to take place? There was no grand design for this – no great attempt at planned organisational change – there couldn't be, even if it had been desirable, and Ripley knew it wasn't – especially when one looks at how the Billingham site operated from the management point of view.

In 1972, five ICI divisions were represented on the Billingham site, of which Agricultural Division was the largest single representative. It had rather more than half the employees but rather less than half the total capital. The site was also characterised by diversity of product range and technology. For example, two works Ammonia and North Tees, contained low-labour, high-capital single-stream plants. These plants had infrequent major shutdowns and the organisation of the site needed to respond accordingly in terms of resources. The remaining works did not need this service, but were expected to contribute some of their resources for the benefit of the other two. At times this conflicted with the best interests of individual works, who as we have seen were often run by powerful works managers who traditionally were given considerable freedom in choosing the appropriate means of achieving whatever ends were deemed by the board to be important. Relatively speaking two works were more critical to the site than the others: Ammonia Works because it supplied the ammonia essential to other "downstream" works, and Engineering Works because it offered the expertise and labour for some part of the commissioning of new plant, and the major shutdowns. In 1972 these were also the two largest works, Engineering having 1,800 weekly and a monthly staff, and Ammonia having 1,050. These two works composed 21% and 12% respectively of the total employees on the site.

On top of the above sources of diversity by division, works, product range, technology, plant size, and power, the diversity on the Billingham site also extended to trade union representatives. In 1972 10 unions were represented on the site, but 84% of the weekly staff belonged to only two unions, the T&GWU and the AUEW. The T&GWU had approximately 4470 members (63% of site total), and the AUEW 1,500 members (around 21% of site total). Through different methods, and with different controls, the union members elected their shop stewards. The shop stewards in turn had their own hierarchy of shop steward, senior shop steward and convener, and were organised on a plant, works, site and district basis.

In terms of the present interest in organisational change on the Billingham site, and the role of OD resources in such changes, two important implications derive from the above contextual and structural complexity on the site. In the first place, a need to cope with additional industrial relations pressures and to optimise ICI's resources in plant and service areas meant that the pre-1970 Billingham site pattern of a series of works physically close but organisationally loosely connected had to be replaced by the organisation of management activities on a site rather than just a divisional basis. Hence the Billingham Site Managers Committee (BSMC) was created, and a Billingham Site Personnel Unit and manager, and co-ordinative and policy committees for engineering matters. It was these important policy-making and political groupings, and their associated systems and procedures so necessary to management's operation and control of the site, that the management were keen to connect the third party OD resources to, and to which those OD resources for a time felt they should avoid if their neutral position between management and union was to be sustained. But in terms of a practical process of changing, it seems the tremendous diversity and complexity of the site precluded any sitewide initiatives on joint union–management problem-solving. While developments of a structural kind such as BSMC could occur, the underlying structural diversity of the site, and perhaps more crucially the cultural patterns of wishing to act relatively autonomously, on both the management and union sides, meant that Ripley's organic approach of starting with individual managers in particular works, or individual stewards in particular occupational groupings or plants, and letting them lead the way, define the problems and steps, was the most practical way of creating movement to influence the pattern of union–management problem-solving and relationships on the site.

This piecemeal approach to change had, of course, started before Ripley's arrival in the division – most notably in Products Works – but changes in management personnel in key positions and substantial reductions in the numbers of weekly staff in 1970 and 1971 had choked off that particular spring of change. It was work amongst the "riggers" and in Ammonia and Engineering Works that became the focal point for joint management–union problem-solving from the early to the mid-1970s, and it is to the brief description, analysis, and assessment of this OD work that I now turn.

The riggers

The story of the riggers' joint development work with management in the early 1970s illustrates well how a combination of existing work in an organisation loosely interested in climate setting to encourage new ways of working together, the availability of a mutually respected third party OD resource (Jack Brown), powerful individuals on the management and union side with strong feelings of dissatisfaction with traditional patterns of working, and a willingness to take the risks to break that traditional pattern – and with a loose umbrella of political support from relevant groups from the local environment – can get a process of change going, at least for a time, which achieved some measures of progress for all the parties concerned. Here were some of the ingredients for success in organic processes of changing; the confluence between favourable antecedents, a set of individuals with some measure of skill, knowledge and risk-taking ability, triggered by a joint problem, assembling political support to begin a process of changing together where there was no idealised and premature notion of an end point. This was the antithesis of an "intervention", of the traditional view of planned organisational change.

Some descriptions by the parties involved in the change process will give form and colour to the above stark conclusions. First of all, who were the riggers? They were a non-craft or trade group who played an important part in the maintenance work on the site assembling scaffolding and generally working in dangerous circumstances providing the physical structures for other groups to gain access to, to maintain, or otherwise disassemble, or construct, the plant. Any kind of maintenance activity involved rigging – so they were a powerful group. Unionwise the riggers were general workers, but "workwise and psychologically they are craftspeople and didn't like being part of the T&GWU". In 1972 there were 700 riggers on the Billingham site. They had a very strong group loyalty and sense of distinctiveness, perhaps because of feelings that their skills were not recognised by other union groups and management. They had a powerful set of shop stewards who tended to act independently of other union groups. Their normal reaction to having a problem was to take some sort of industrial action. This conflict mode of response both with other union groups and management did not always lead to their problems being solved in a way that they liked. A member of the management commented:

> The riggers were the most difficult group to handle on the site – even their stewards were expressing dissatisfaction with their image. They walked around the place like a bunch of cowboys. Many of them are big blokes – physically big, strong – they have to be. The other concern was the ineffectiveness of their tactics. It really was like High Noon, a powerful way of getting some kind of esteem, with kind of Mafia norms about looking after "our" people.

The senior member of the rigger steward group who led them into the joint problem-solving work said, "Our success had been based on strength, pure and simple – but this would also create sheer frustration. We were getting further and further away from what we wanted. It was sort of desperation." Two individuals provided a route for the riggers out of the deadlock they were in; a new manager and Jack Brown, the OD man. The rigger's convener takes up the story:

> The new manager came around 1970. He sort of flummoxed me. He had a different style. He was interested in a different way of working – working without conflict. He was not the usual off-the-conveyor-belt type of management. He had some ideas of really giving us some say in what we were doing . . . having decided I was going to test the water, you have to have people who are at least seen to be acceptable. And then I was very fortunate in meeting up with Jack Brown . . . And the third step is – how are you going to protect yourself, because there's always going to be problems . . .
> One of the dangers in doing this work is that the trust is implicit, if that isn't there you haven't got a cat in hell's chance, but once you start trusting people then you are really putting your head on the block. If that trust isn't reciprocal or if management, through some other influence, can't do it, then that shatters you. And we've lost stewards through this, who couldn't face that reality and felt they'd been let down . . . But I started off from a very strong power base (with the riggers) and ordinarily if it went wrong, I could go back. I kept a life line – but if you got involved with management and they let you down, that could be the end of it for me. So I think you need a person strong enough to take a risk.

Jack Brown as the neutral third party was able to see the risks being taken by all the parties, the reasons for some of the doubts and opposition on both sides, and how the whole exercise was dependent on a few "individuals". Some management said "you are crazy to do this – what will happen if it goes wrong – there was a totally legitimate concern that it was going to screw up a lot of other things". On the riggers' side "there was always a knife-edged balance between those who were prepared to collaborate and those who said we are throwing away all our trump cards". And overall, "the big problem was that the thing was highly dependent on a few individuals, particularly the rigger convener and the manager responsible for working with them".

What happened was that 10 managers, 12 rigger shop stewards, Jack Brown, another internal OD resource, and the irrepressible Rev. Hinton went to a hotel for a week "and bashed through some of the issues – how much can we trust each other – and came out with a series of action plans". This contact became institutionalised in the formation of the Rigger Working Party composed of six stewards and an equal number of management from the different works. In the rigger convener's words, "that was a new concept of understanding. We used it for ideas on training . . . new methods of working . . . pay. That became a pretty powerful group. Since then it has become directly attached to the Works Engineers. So it reports back to the structure there." In order to create space for developing their own ideas the riggers stewards asked for time away from the site by *themselves*. "This really threw the managers. We wrote it down . . . they chewed it about for a month and we were lucky in that our managers put the case for us to the directors." Another example of what was done was the development of an extensive two-year training programme for riggers. The management had wanted to stick to the existing six-month programme and ironically this led the riggers to use the Rigger Working Party to obtain the commitment of the managers. The convener commented, "the only way you could do it was through the working party – because you get the management committed!"

Jack Brown described the outcome in these terms:

> The riggers stuck very rigidly to the action plans. One of the results was that they agreed that any problems which had site implications would be fed into a joint working party which they set up . . . They committed themselves to trying a collaborative stance for 12 months – before walking off the job they'd bring that problem up . . . They did stick to it. In fact, ever since then we haven't had a walk out or anything like it.[10]

The convener corroborated Brown's statement, "And we've had no significant industrial problems or stoppages for well over two or three years now. That's a terrific change from five or six years ago." But perhaps the most significant part of the riggers story was that the parties recognised that a change process could be mutually set-up and managed, could be continuously reviewed, and that the goals and aims of the process could themselves be altered without throwing away the process of change itself.

Ammonia Works, 1971–75

The OD work carried out in Ammonia Works in the first half of the 1970s represents the earliest case of extensive adoption of OD methods by line managers and training staff in a works. Again antecendents are crucial in explaining how the work got off the ground. The impetus for the work, which ranged from joint workshops in the T-group tradition for managers and shop stewards, joint industrial relations training events for managers, supervisors and shop stewards, and a reorganisation of the works "to reduce the number of technocrats and put in good foremen as managers", came from the seeding of interest in OD created by the "behavioural sixties", and the early third party work of the Swallow OD group. With the pressure off a little by 1971 – Ammonia Works had been the scene of the division's great technical difficulties of the late 1960s – new managers were appointed who chose to spend time and resources developing the human and organisational capital of the works.

The Ammonia Works case illustrates not only line managers taking a lead in using OD, but also a training manager interpreting and using his role in a neutral fashion to help get off the ground highly novel development experiences in the sensitive industrial relations area. Although these training events were generally one step removed from the action-oriented joint problem-solving of the riggers case, there is evidence they did influence the attitudes and behaviour

[10] He was talking about the period 1972–76.

of some managers, supervisors and shop stewards, at least until the 1975 craft union strike swept away some of the working arrangements between management and union that had evolved out of this work.

If Ammonia Works was the first clear and extensive diffusion of OD into the division, it was also the first strong evidence of retreat from too singular a pursuit of the practice of participative management which had been so forcibly articulated in the 1960s by Bridge. One of the key managers who started the Ammonia Works development activities had this to say as his entry position for beginning the work:

> I came to the conclusion that I wanted to adopt a participate style because my predecessor hadn't. Because I was new in the job, I needed a great deal of help from my work group. Another manager was also keen on this he'd just been on some OD course. We thought it was the right way of developing things with the unions. So we did it.

When, by 1976, the development work in Ammonia Works had run out of steam, the same manager had developed a more considered view of adopting a "participative approach", had begun to appreciate the risks of being an innovator, and at the same time had a more balanced view of the place of OD specialist resources in the general scene of things.

> I've moved more and more in the authoritarian direction over the last five years. I think that's right too for business reasons and because I need less help in making decisions . . . Maybe I got too far out of line for my own good . . . I would have said that there is probably a negative correlation between the leaders in this field (OD) and advancement in the company . . . Six years ago I might have seen OD as a crusade converting the heathen. I don't feel like that anymore. It's just a technique I can use, drawing on my resources as necessary . . . I feel quite happy about having the OD group as a resource, just like we need computer applications people . . .

But the OD group were not the leaders of the Ammonia Works development work, they were more exactly helpers, to be called in as required. A look at the aims of the union–management workshops (four were carried out between November 1971 and May 1974) will give a clue as to why they had only a limited impact on culture change in the works but did help in setting the context for the more practical and job-related industrial relations training which followed these workshops. The aims of the workshops were to "provide an opportunity for trades union and management personnel to jointly explore their working relationships . . . to become more aware of how relationships develop between individuals and groups . . . and to broaden each participant's understanding of the process of communications and of himself as a communicator". In an evaluation of the impact of these workshops, by an external consultant, in relationship to the above aims, he concluded that "although people changed their view of themselves and others at the workshop", there was little evidence of behaviour change back in the work situation. Both managers and shop stewards three months after the workshops "felt more confident, more skilful, more relaxed" in meetings, but "managers tended to believe a meeting was better if the *processes* had improved. Shop stewards on the other hand were more concerned with *outcomes*." But the major limiting problem of such workshops was that they represented cultural islands of learning, and people returned to the plant to face the social expectations, interests, procedures, and policies which had been shaping behaviour all the time.

Unlike the riggers' work, the power figures from the shop steward group kept their distance from these workshops, at least for a time. The training manager described the shop steward response to the management–union workshops in these terms:

> The experimentalists [amongst the stewards] went to the first workshop, the confused ones felt they were missing something and went to the second one, and the power figure stewards went to the third one.

One of the most powerful of the steward group described the process of setting up the joint workshops in these terms:

> The Rev. Hinton came in and talked to some of the stewards and they organised the first one. I was one of the stewards who was very, very suspicious of this event about getting to know people – deep down. But the other stewards went ahead. When they came back, they told us weird and wonderful things . . . we thought it was the ramblings of a lot of people who had been brainwashed. There was a second event . . . and there was a quite dramatic meeting called, where some of the stewards wanted the senior stewards to go . . . so eventually we did go.

This senior steward's view of that workshop just afterwards was "never again", it took him "perhaps a year to start realising the benefits". In the meantime he and the other powerful stewards put a lot of more energy into the IR Steering Group which had been formed earlier in the process by the "experimentalist" stewards and the management. The Steering Group "worked extremely well in sorting out problems in the works . . . and in getting industrial relations training going . . . everything in the garden was rosy, but we didn't look to how solid the foundation was". In 1975 the craft unions went on strike to redress the "differentials and relativities which had been eroded by WSA between us and the noncraft unions". This three-week strike was the first one for 19 years. It led to "a blowing out of the IR Steering Group . . . We did that because we had no confidence in management. But when we got back the management put it around I couldn't be trusted any more. In one period it was how constructive you were, how helpful, how they needed you. Then you turn the other page over and the management say, 'after all he was unconstructive' . . . The management reacted out of all proportion, with hurt like I've never seen before . . . because they felt they had something really good on the works."[11]

---

[11] This strike was not just confined to Ammonia Works, it involved the craft unions on the Billingham site and the craft unions and T&GWU on the Wilton site.

The stewards later regretted "blowing out" the IR Steering Group and formed a Shop Stewards Training Committee to keep some of the earlier work going. It was ironically enough at this point that the stewards began to appreciate some of the learning from the joint workshops. They made sure that commitment to the above training committee "was spread out across all the stewards . . . so it ain't just a couple of people who are involved". There was also a renewed appreciation that "we've got to work together, develop industrial relations but we've got to accept that at times there will be conflict".

Engineering Works, 1972–77

The OD work jointly led by Henry McGill, the works manager of Engineering Works and his personnel officer Philip Marsh, probably represents the high point in the diffusion of OD into Agricultural Division. In the five years of their tenure as works manager and personnel officer McGill and Marsh set in motion a process of change, based on the idea of joint problem-solving, which touched all levels of management and supervision, and in turn influenced the shop stewards and the men on the shop floor. By the end of 1977 McGill could claim that the structure and process of change he had helped to create had reduced the number of formal disputes per year from their high point of 26 in 1972 to 2 in 1974, and to a trickle thereafter; had taken £1.5 million off the costs of running the works in 1976 and 1977, had reduced the numbers of employees in the works by around 20% over the five-year period, and through the works consultancy skills programme, had left behind sufficient residue of skill and confidence for the managers, supervisors and shop stewards to cope with the difficult events of 1980 and 1981. By the time the different economic circumstances of 1980–81 came around, while the management objectives of getting fixed costs down through numbers reductions were still there, the *process* of achieving those objectives was quite different from the McGill era.

But the Engineering Works change process didn't start in 1972 with numbers reductions as its prime objective. One of the senior managers described the state of the works in 1972 as "desperate". "The works was in a hell of a state as a result of reductions in numbers of workers, changes in management, the supervisors being alienated – a whole lot of things which really made it a desperately unhappy place." McGill mentioned the level of conflict with the unions, fragmentations between all levels and tremendous distrust between the managers and the shop floor. "I realised I had to change this, but I also realised I couldn't make the works tick if it continued to operate as an autocratic organisation . . . My view was that I had to foster a process in which development was taking place at all levels, I was lucky in that I was able to select a new management team, and I was able to select people who had values similar to mine. The one value I imposed was that I was not going to impose the 'what' of solutions – the task was to get a process going where people at all levels would identify their own problems and solutions."

The vehicle McGill used first of all to unite his management group and then to extend this to other levels in the system was the open system ideas and process training developed by Clark, Krone and McWhinney, a trio of American consultants. As one observer of the competition between the works on the Billingham site noted "although Ammonia and Engineering Works were picking up development activities at around the same time, they would clearly not follow in one another's footsteps, if one did one thing one way, the other went a different route. Ammonia went down the problem-solving sausage machine route, Engineering went down the open systems route."

If one group in Engineering Works didn't wish to take part in the open systems works and consultancy skills programme which followed it, "we didn't impose". But gradually groups of managers, supervisors and shop stewards "began to pick up problems . . . and simply where there was an initiative I supported it . . . which made those who were sitting back feel slightly uncomfortable. It was management by embarrassment . . . So we now have so many groups beavering away, tackling problems which management could never have introduced."

The above account, largely taken from interviews with McGill, is broadly supported by other managers and by the personnel officer Philip Marsh who played an important role in the process of change. One manager noted, as McGill had done, that there was only rather distant and variable support from the board for this development work. "He [a director] started off by questioning very critically what we were doing – 'you spend money like drunken men, if you want to keep your jobs you're going to have to prove that OD pays us something. You don't have disputes any more, but when are you going to get your numbers down'." This director regrettably was a little less colourful in the research interview:

> I see their work [OD group] as sorting out the relationships within fairly autonomous groups like the works . . . I don't think it's up to me to tell people to use them. Henry McGill uses them and I don't actively discourage him . . . I think OD is one of a number of tools that can be used to change people's activities in relation to improving the way the business is run.

If one basis of scepticism on the management side was "produce results more than an improvement in working relationships" – there was also concern "about the amount of time people spend doing these OD things", a "feeling that we've lost some of the technical things", and the view that "around planning, decision-making areas we tend to be much less crisp".

The managers were asked what was in it for the shop stewards, why did they participate in the change process which started with objectives to reduce and improve relationships within and across levels in the works, and led onto more tangible objectives such as reducing fixed costs?

> They were as fed up as we were. When you get into that degree of conflict life isn't fun any more. The image of the British shop steward of knocking the table and whistling the lads out the gate, there isn't that much satisfaction in it, and they

weren't being treated as people. What they got out of it was: they were being treated as individuals, they were being given far more information than they had been given in the past. Fundamentally they were able to influence decisions before they took place. They had had two decades of management announcing on Monday morning, "the following is going to happen", and then having their members say – "nonsense, stop it, block it". We had by then a formal Joint Consultative System but that talked about meals, cost of milk and cigarettes. We were offering them a system to informally get involved in things around work – changes in working practices, the crucial things . . . What was in it for the shop floor was very much more difficult to judge. In a sense what was in it for them was not being called out on strike – when ultimately they are in the main losers financially.

The interviews with the shop stewards from Engineering Works revealed a broad spectrum of views towards the joint development activities in the works. At one extreme there were statements such as, "I think it was a con", or "I didn't get involved. I realised it was the management taking advantage of the shop stewards – it didn't help the shift workers one bit." For those who did get involved, there were the normal problems of the gap between the open and relaxed atmosphere on the off-site events, and the return to the short-term pressures and social expectations back on the plant. "People quickly got back down to what they saw as trade union business." The design of the process had, of course, allowed for some of these difficulties of transfer of learning back to the plant, and maintaining the process of change in the working environment. Work groups formed on the off-site events were asked to reflect on plant problems. On returning to the plant they were then expected to produce action plans and implement them on a continuous basis in the plant. Sometimes these groups gelled and the momentum was continued; in other cases they faded away. The early practice of having shop floor employees and shop stewards on the off-site events had the effect of bringing shop floor workers into the management–union information stream and increasing the pressures on both parties. One shop steward said, "The men were suddenly in a situation where they knew everything and they had me in a corner." A number of shop stewards were voted out of their representatives roles by the men "for getting a bit too familiar with management". Quite a bit of management time was discreetly put into protecting the power bases of shop stewards.

But even the stewards with the above sceptical views, and the added one that too much of their time became absorbed in joint development activities, were prepared to acknowledge that the increased information and voice they had, and the added confidence and skill they acquired from closer contact with management and supervision on the off-site events, and from the consultancy skills course, allowed them to play a role in the development of Engineering Works they had been denied in the past.

It was also clear that the general circumstances of the division in the period 1972–76, when large profits were being made, gave added freedom to individual managers and their board supporters to release resources for climate building and change process activities which had a relatively slow return in the short term but had the potential for medium-term pay off. As one of the managers commented, "the risks are that the results may not come in the first two years and I had neither the support or understanding of the board as a whole. So it was a very high personal risk . . . what we were trying to do was to foster an attitude change, and slowly we have built up a problem-solving relationship."

The stewards were in the same position of risk, and those that could not justify to their members results from involvement with management in "a problem-solving relationship" sometimes found themselves voted out. Looking at the stewards who did not benefit from the development work this can often be explained not just in terms of their individual propensity to take risks and a skill in protecting their power base, but also the strategic position of the group represented by the steward in the pattern of work activities on the site. One steward commented:

> The management needed us therefore we were having some success because of our circumstances, but other groups weren't in our situation. The fact that business picked up and shutdowns were important again, and obviously had to be done in as little time as possible meant we did little deals with management. Other stewards were not in that position. . . . It's put money in the men's pocket (development work). If I relied on my brothers for my well being, I'd be out of a job; so I've got to make sure I protect my own position. Therefore, I build up those relationships with management which are built on trust.

And so just as eventually Henry McGill had to justify to his new director boss appointed in 1976 that not only had disputes declined and the general climate of relationships with unions improved, but also that he could use the process of change to get the works costs base down, so also did the shop stewards involved in the joint development work have to justify to their members that it could "put money in their pockets", and/or create the conditions for their particular group's survival. This is the reality of the politics of creating change in organisations.

The above case illustrations and other less visible OD work amongst supervisors, in research engineering, and a host of individual counselling relationships that were established with managers and trade unionists, illustrate the extent of diffusion and indeed institutionalisation of OD in the production areas of Agricultural Division over the period 1971–76. With all its successes, failures, and doubters something had been learnt about an approach to creating change which fitted to some degree the diversities and complexities of the Billingham site. As one senior manager put it, "It was not prescribed. It was not packaged. It was not total. It was organic, stimulating, encouraging, variegated. It was tolerant of a whole lot of different approaches aimed at helping people work out their own future." But if some considerable success had been achieved at lower and middle reaches of the division in stimulating participative ways of working which led to some consequential changes in fairly autonomous units and works, by and large the bulk of the division was still virgin territory as far as OD was concerned. Noel Ripley, before he left, had flagged all kinds of issues in commercial parts of the division, and across some of the major horizontal and vertical structural boundaries, but these were not picked up, in fact, could not be picked up by the OD group or its supporters around the mid-1970s.

Even in the production areas some of the managers and personnel people who would argue they had broadly supported OD, or who had consistently used them were talking in terms of OD having lost its cutting edge or of "the old business of familiarity and contempt – the longer you go on using someone in one of these roles, the more you tend to feel that he isn't treating it as vital as you think it should be". With institutionalisation had come a feeling of ordinariness, the value position of OD of the earlier period of championing individual worth and free choice had become buried as the OD group members became themselves buried in the works. One manager said, "I think initially they [OD group] had distinctive values and possibly they still have but it doesn't show so much". OD was becoming just another management tool. With this kind of acceptance, which was not in any sense universal, came requests by some senior managers for other managers to use one of the OD group. "He's been told [a manager] would you like to use [an OD group member]. The way he's been told it's like the Queen would be pleased if you would. He's not even sure who the Queen is!" Some of the managers had also by this time acquired a good deal of experience in using OD consultants and had their own working theories of what the ingredients for success were. The wise "clients" were using their "consultants" with greater care.

> I found there were three things needed to ensure OD success. First, there had to be basic agreement about objectives [between the parties] . . . if you get cases where people disagree fundamentally then it wasn't helpful. Second, it needed preparation – like people writing down what they thought the problem was a week before. Third, you'd got to have a problem, a conflict, people had to feel a need for it, for it to succeed.

The OD group by the end of 1975 and beginning of 1976 existed in name only. Ripley had gone in 1974, and only Ron Larsen of the three regular external consultants still worked for the division. Larsen's contribution as an individual became more and more important throughout the 1970s and he was the crucial professional link from the mid-1970s into the new OD work begun in 1980. But Larsen never played, possibly could not have played, the informal, social and professional leader role that Ripley had played. The list of OD core group members in May 1975 contained 9 names. Four of these were personnel officers, one was the training co-ordinator for the division, another the secretary of the Billingham Site Management Committee, Ron Larsen, Jack Brown and Paul Miles. Of these, only Jack Brown was still described as a full-time internal OD consultant. Miles periodically attempted to get the group together, but there was little energy there for such meetings, and quite often meetings were cancelled at the last minute.

Miles said in an interview late in 1976 "our biggest single problem now is that we have got respectable". Other group members also echoed the problems of limited acceptance and institutionalisation. "In 1969, OD was seen as something different, alien and threatening . . . now, those that want to can work in these ways." Some individuals talked of being relieved at having a legitimate personnel or training role to play, that way entry to client problems was more natural and politically easier, and there wasn't "the millstone round the neck" of the OD tag. Another talked of dedication to his value stance as the only thing that kept him going. And, "if there's a common thing amongst us it's more a way of life than just a job . . . But it's not a collective commitment, more a personal thing."

One of the most reflective members of the group summed up clearly the other side of institutionalisation – boredom, loss of a sense of what they were trying to achieve in the way of future change – and just plain tiredness.

> Where OD is successful it makes life terribly boring . . . it's like when you get managers who are better OD guys than you are, you ought to be very pleased about it, but the tendency is to feel terribly redundant . . . The situation is that we've got more work than we can do . . . We've become very much institutional-ised. Not many scandalous things happen around OD any more. It's become very ordinary – in some ways duller . . . Maybe I've just been in the job too long.
>
> There is also the danger that you end up managing things – not behaving as a consultant, but saying, "you guys ought to be doing this". I've caught myself doing that often enough. I'm really very doubtful as to whether we ought to be doing that. There is the risk of OD becoming just another way of managing.

So the period 1972–76 in Agricultural Division can be reliably characterized as one of partial diffusion and institutionalisation of OD into the division. There is indisputable evidence that a number of managers and trade unionists, with varying motives, problems, and objectives took a lead in setting processes of change in motion which drew on the precepts, values, and technology of OD, and the day-to-day assistance of the, by this time, loosely composed group of OD resources in the division. But there were also the opponents and doubters. The personnel officers who felt they had been excluded from the original Swallow group created by Noel Ripley, the more senior personnel staff who knew it "wasn't practical to acquire a strong, overt OD label, but nevertheless wanted to be involved, trying to relate OD to the ongoing personnel and industrial relations work". The large group of middle managers in the division who, as one who knew then well said, "They would look on this OD stuff as just one more fad that they've got to go through. After work study, manage-ment by objectives, now it's OD. They say, 'We'll sit this one out and we'll play along'." And the attitudes at the top of the division which, after the disappearance of George Bridge and Tom Evans, were always a mixture of quiet scepticism, disinterest, and at times from a few board members, relatively passive but strategically important support. Even the OD group members themselves by 1976 were expressing doubts that with institutionalisation came a sense of distancing from the values which had drawn them into OD work, and a feeling that perhaps OD was becoming just another management tool.

Paul Miles, the personnel manager who from mid-1969 acted as "the manager of the unmanageable", as he put it, but whose more enduring contribution to OD had been to draw it away from some of the more exclusive posturing of the Swallow group era to a more politically viable stance in relationship to the division, departed for a new post in ICI, in March 1976. To the day he left he carried on his belief in the viability of the division's organic approach to developing OD. Miles commented:

> I never felt that OD was seriously threatened. My comment on that has been over the years that the degree to which the work is grounded in day-to-day activities and not special projects and events means that you could actually sweep away the OD group tomorrow, and the thing would go on.

Miles was correct in his belief that the organic approach had helped to create both the conditions for some of the particular successes the group had had, and also that it had produced some degree of institutionalisation of OD skills and knowledge in the division. But, as we have seen, the organic approach worked in that context at that time partly because it fitted in with some of the diversity and complexity of the Billingham site; partly because it had a clear and consistent exponent in Ripley – and the organic approach fitted his confronting yet low-key personal style; partly because the culture of the site encouraged managers to choose their own means, if not the ends in management; and partly because of some of the advantages and disadvantages of the high visibility, across the division, top-down change approach adopted by George Bridge. The organic approach, and its success, was crucially affected by its antecedents. The antagonisms created by Bridge's bow wave provided a backcloth of contrast for the organic approach; for those who were interested in change but were searching for another way forward. And crucially, Bridge opened up the division and enthused many of the early adopters, who subsequently did the work in the 1971–76 period of diffusion and institutionalisation.

The broad message for learning in this is that Bridge's bow wave, social architectural approach to change, and the organic approach pioneered by Ripley, and modified in the Miles era, needed one another. There isn't one correct approach to creating change independent of circumstances, antecedents, problem areas, and people. The available evidence indicates[12] that by 1975 and 1976 the organic approach in Agricultural Division was running out of energy, and so were some of the individuals who had produced its successes. The change process in the division was in need of self-renewal. This was recognised by one senior manager who commented:

[12] Quoted earlier on in this section on the problems created by institutionalisation; see pages 193–194

I think if you are going to have a cultural change in the organisation, it can't be totally organic. There has got to be some sort of visible leadership, and I think we've lost that since Bridge and Ripley . . . One needs new ingredients to continue to make progress.

But where were these new ingredients to come from, and out of what combination of circumstance and individual or group action were they to be fashioned? In the next era in the development of change processes in Agricultural Division we will see further evidence for that old aphorism that politics is the art of taking adroit advantage of circumstances.

OPPORTUNISM AND REFOCUSSING, 1976–83

In ICI's annual report for 1975 there was a bigger than usual commentary on the economic background to the company's results. 1975 was described as the deepest economic recession since the Second World War. World industrial production had fallen 9% from 1974, and from a peak in the third quarter of 1974, world chemical output for 1975 as a whole was down 9% from 1974. Even though ICI's worldwide operations had experienced higher than average increases in selling prices, a marked reduction in sales volume and increased costs had resulted in a 23% drop in trading profit from 1974. Part of the increased costs were a function of the roll-on effect of oil price increases, part was due to the record inflation rate of 27% experienced in Britain by the summer of 1975. Politically 1974 had seen the authority of the Heath Conservative government being dissolved amid industrial chaos, power cuts, food shortages and the "Three-Day Week". With the return of Harold Wilson's new Labour government in the spring of 1974, wage demands and government spending increased dramatically. ICI's wage and salary settlements for 1975 were in the order of 26%. It was no wonder that 1975 also saw a level of expenditure on new capital by a considerable margin, the highest in the ICI group's history, and that increasing proportions of this new capital were going abroad, principally to the United States and West Germany. This high level of capital expenditure was to continue until 1979, when a combination of excess capacity in the world chemical industry, falling prices, and ICI's declining profitability and inadequate cash flow after inflation adjustment, made them pull back on investment at previous levels. By the second quarter of 1980 ICI was making the first financial losses since its formation in 1926.

The fortunes of Agricultural Division did not follow the broad pattern of difficulty outlined above for the whole ICI group. Table 19 on page 138 of Chapter 5 shows that 1975 was a peak year in terms of trading margins, and trading profits advanced right up until 1979, and fell back only modestly in 1980. New capital was successfully brought on stream at Billingham between 1976 and 1980, and these efficient plants poured product into growing markets. Agricultural Division was the "cash cow" for the ICI Group. With this new capital the division had dramatically increased its productivity, had reduced its numbers over the late 1960s and early 1970s, only doubts about ICI's ability to place new capital at Billingham to protect its world position in ammonia and methanol; uncertainties about the commercial viability of the new "Pruteen" plant and business area; and the impact on the division's cost base of negotiating the new natural gas contract were clouds on the horizon. Additionally, there was an undoubted increase in competition and some pressure on prices in traditional markets, but to nowhere near the same extent as in other business groupings and divisions of ICI. But in spite of the relatively speaking favourable business position of Agricultural Division, the combination of doubts about its competitive position in the 1980s and the worsening fortunes of the whole ICI group led to a heightened management interest in increasing productivity of monthly and weekly staff, through whatever mechanisms were available. The increased business orientation throughout the whole ICI Group which was at the back of this drive for productivity improvement led to more meaningful and sustained pressure from the main board on even the successful divisions, and ultimately culminated in, for ICI, the quite massive structural and manpower changes of 1980, 1981 and 1982. It is in these business circumstances that one has to see the further evolution of thinking and action about organisation development and change in Agricultural Division over the period 1976–83.

Managerial culture and management concerns, 1976–83

In Chapter 5 a picture was painted of the managerial culture of Agricultural Division, of the 1950s and early 1960s as seen by its managers, specialists, and shop stewards, which emphasised a group of highly capable technocrats managing, in a firm but fair fashion, a fairly autonomous set of production facilities on a large multidivision site, in a relatively insular manner. How were many of these same people characterising the culture of the division when they were being interviewed in 1976 and 1977, and again in the early 1980s?

One theme evident from the mid-1970s interviews, and especially obvious from the few managers interviewed with experience of other ICI divisions, was the continuation of the insularity, but now an insularity laced with confidence, even arrogance – for the technological failures of the late 1960s had now been superseded by business and technical success.

> It's very confident, arrogant place that has come back from the dead. It has very powerful technology and a mass of ability. It's highly competitive, pretty supportive to subordinates, but not so good in peer relations – it's not terribly open-minded . . . The rugby club aspect of it has gone, but I'm very conscious in social chat at lunch that there is a group there that were the rugger and cricket players of years ago who have got all the history and camaraderie of who did what, of which I'm no part, and never will be.

> * * *

> We are a very in-bred organisation. We are seen as not open to new or outside ideas. You need to have been raised here, "man and boy", to have any real credibility.

Along with the persistence of insularity in the culture there was still the tremendous pull of the technology as a determinant of attitudes, behaviour and distribution of power:

> We are a technically oriented management locked into a system which fosters this. This tends to militate against profit cost consciousness and optimisation of human resources. There are few *real* businessmen around.

*   *   *

> This is a very old site with a lot of custom and practice. It's very capital intensive. The profit on each ton of ammonia is very small. The essential part of the business is to keep the plants running. This means designing plants that will last for a long time and require very little maintenance. Production people must have a final say in everything. It means paying a great deal of attention to industrial relations – the shop stewards must be placated.

If the heart of Agricultural Division was still its technology, one thing that had changed was the number of increased pressures on management. These pressures originated from the increasing internationalism of the business, the pressure of social trends toward increased participation and sharing of information, increased union power and more government legislation influencing the conduct of business. All these factors were contributing to a situation where "no authority without personal effectiveness and acceptance", and "no effectiveness without presence and contact", were the order of the day. For managers on the Billingham site in 1975–76, the balance of power had changed dramatically. Non-negotiable areas had all but disappeared; all actions were open to challenge; all results had to be striven for. The most basic requirements of work planning, allocation and communication required much more management effort than ten years ago, in 1965, and were much less certain of achieving the desired outcome. Works management, therefore, had to deliberately invest a significant part of its resources in providing a *climate* in which there could be achievements for all concerned. All these increased pressures had sharply changed the balance in most production managers' jobs from the predominant technical orientation of the mid-1960s to a situation where in the mid-1970s the technical had itself become more complex but had been superseded in complexity by the people-management aspects of their job. Since both the technical and the people had become more difficult, their integration in the management role was that much bigger a task.

ICI's corporate responses to the above pressures were, of course, MUPS/WSA, SDP, the joint consultative arrangements introduced in 1972, the divisional and company business investment committees introduced in 1975, and in Agricultural Division the joint problem-solving work already described in Products Works, Ammonia Works, and Engineering Works. At Billingham this meant, as a senior industrial relations manager commented, that "the way managers think about industrial relations is really quite radically different from the way they thought in the early 1960s. It's a subtle, slow but very real change. Just to take a mundane example you can now talk to managers about the process . . . it's engrained in the culture. There has also been a quite substantial change in the degree of management involvement and ownership of the business of formulating and operating personnel policy." But if the development work at a policy level by the Billingham site industrial relations team and the BSMC, and the grass roots development work in the works, had produced "a fairly participative management style at the lower area, certainly in the relationship between the management and the unions – at the top end of the division it's fairly autocratic, and right at the top it's still very autocratic."

If OD resources had been used to help assist participative relationships between management and unions and build climates for incremental change, those OD resources, as Ripley stated in his final situation paper, had never been allowed to influence the conduct of events at the most senior level. As several managers put it, there were now "strains given that some autocratic management is appropriate at the top". Senior management – the board included – were seen in 1975 to be exerting more rather than less control. Again, part of the explanation seems to be technological.

> There is more restriction on people now than there has ever been. To some extent this has been because of the technology. Twenty years ago there were large numbers of small plants here – more difficult to control and less disastrous if one goes wrong. Whereas now with large single stream units, the people on top feel they have to control things more.

The scale of the technology was now producing a situation where although "management of the total scene and people skills are seen as totally legitimate and a credible alternative to technical skills", overlayed on top of people and technical skills in the concept of a good manager was also a need for reliability and conservatism. One senior manager described well the requirement of "don't rock the boat management".

> I think the reward and punishment systems are all geared to giving you bad marks for mistakes and there's a lot of suspicion if you do something out of line and it works. If you play it down the middle and don't make any mistakes, you're the chap we want . . . The general feeling is – and it may well be right – that the percentage for getting it right is maybe 1% on profits, but if it doesn't come off, the losses are so dreadful that they can't be contemplated.

Agricultural Division had got its technology and business right by the mid-1970s – nobody wanted to endanger this success. The climate for OD work became more difficult. Two of the OD group well connected into the works environment had this to say:

> OD isn't very adventurous or high risk now . . . the fact this division is now making a profit means that the prevailing climate is not to rock the boat. It doesn't pay to take risks – what we need is steady production runs. This is very much the climate amongst the works managers.

* * *

I believe people feel if they do something innovative, they will not be supported by their manager. Instead they run the risk of being criticised in such a psychologically deprivating way that it isn't worth the pain.

But on top of this risk aversion factor in the culture there were other developments, some inside and some outside the division, which were adjusting the context for OD work, and for organisational change. By the end of 1975 the ICI main board, in consultation with division chairmen, was pushing for more initiatives in the productivity area in order "to reduce its numbers and not just invest until the present numbers are absorbed". Each of the divisions were asked to enter into a "productivity contract by consent" with the main board reflecting target reductions in manpower over the period 1975–80. Such activities were to proceed and "a higher risk of industrial conflict will probably have to be accepted". Such productivity improvements had to be made in the context of the Employment Protection Act and ICI's oft-stated public policy of no involuntary redundancy.

Agricultural Division had a particular problem in responding to such productivity drives. They had an excellent profit performance which was likely to remain good, were in an area of relatively high unemployment and little alternative employment growth, and there was no prospect of major technical rationalisations providing similar opportunities for productivity gains to those which occurred in the late 1960s and early 1970s. However, pressure was exerted from the main board to the division board, and from the Agricultural board to works managers. One manifestation of this pressure already referred to was the decision by Engineering Works to launch in 1975 a productivity initiative designed to install "business operating imperatives" into their development programme. The reader may recall the Engineering Works management were told it was not enough to reduce industrial relations conflict, they had to get their numbers down. Earlier on in 1975 there had also been the three-week craft union strike at Billingham which had "shattered" some of the management and shop stewards who believed in the value of joint development work. The pressures for management to make productivity gains, the 1975 strike, and the beginnings of a feeling which was to slowly build up during ICI's worsening business performance in the late 1970s that participative management had led to "a loss of confidence", "a loss of leadership", "management by committee", all produced first a drift, and then a clamouring for tougher management. One of the people centrally involved in the Engineering Works OD work in 1976 had this to say about OD, culture change, and management concerns at the time:

With the resurgence of the hawkish side, particularly after the 1975 strike and getting back to strong management, whatever that means . . . actually trying to shift the [total] culture is an impossibility. You can only do bits of it. We've used OD because we reckoned it was the only way to stay in business. We've been tolerated . . . but we've actually had an instruction from a director not to allow our OD resources to work in other areas without those works managers' agreement.

If the seeds of a more confident, businesslike, and directive management were evident to some of the more acute observers of the Billingham scene in 1976, those seeds were not to be harvested across the spectrum of British management until late 1979 and 1980. As we have seen in Chapter 4, in the General Election of May 1979, the Conservative Party returned to power, this time under Margaret Thatcher's leadership. In the worldwide recession of 1980, inflation in the UK was already high, interest rates increased and unemployment increased even more dramatically. Mrs Thatcher daily told the British people as a nation we had become soft, economically stagnant and overreliant on the state. The message was get production going again and produce more wealth. There will be more private incentives and less public subsidies, above all, there must be an insistence on financial rectitude. In the context of this daily trumpeting of economic values, and of trade union power severely circumscribed by high unemployment and the prospect of further unemployment, the pendulum swung mightily towards tough management across much of British industry.

Like many large and small British firms, ICI used the economic and political context of 1980, 1981 and 1982 to carry through substantial changes which had been slowly maturing as ideas in the wings, waiting for the assembly of the right context and set of actors on the stage. Petrochemicals and Plastics Divisions were merged, and major changes were made in setting up and strengthening central research and engineering functions. Uneconomic factories in poor business areas were closed. Great attention was given to reducing inessential activities, and in reducing numbers of both monthly and weekly staff. Throughout all this ICI carried through with its policy of no involuntary redundancy. Employees were given very substantial financial inducements to leave.

Agricultural Division as a relatively successful business operation was not affected as much, as for example, Petrochemical and Plastics Divisions, by the 1980–81 changes, but the climate of the day was reflected in the attitudes and behaviour of managers and shop stewards. One senior manager had this to say about the management culture at Billingham in 1981:

> There are two cultures in this division at the moment. One bullish and using the opportunity of the recession to feel and behave powerfully, and I object to that. The other culture that has always been here is one of wanting to manage, caring for people that are managed, consulting, making a decision and implementing it . . . The organic bit of the culture, letting things develop informally through association has been the behaviour, but I don't see that as being appropriate for the future. That kind of behaviour is not caring, it's just letting things happen, it's not direction, being led from the top. The nature of caring has changed, faced as we are with fierce competition, we must improve productivity not just once but continuously. The caring is to keep the business profitable and secure jobs for the future. I see that happening not by organic development but through clear exposure of facts and honest management, and leadership from a senior level . . . Market competition has changed the culture in the sense that pound notes are

seen to be more important and maybe production at all costs is no longer the message. Maximum production at the right cost, rather than maximum production at all costs is the message . . . Previously the philosophy had been don't rock the boat . . . give into the unions, work the overtime, don't lose production, back away from that issue – let it all happen around you. My view is rock the boat as much as possible, but it would be unforgiveable to sink it.

This view of the 1981 management culture was also shared by another important figure in the Billingham scene. He talked of it being much more "clear that change was the order of the day", there was "less playing around with the greater industrial relations vision", being "much clearer what are the flows of funds across boundaries each manager is responsible for understanding and making decisions about" – "it's more cost effective". "We are changing towards a lean, hungry, highly competitive, businesslike outfit, from a huge club with chemical innovators and operators." But there were discontinuities in this picture that both of the above men acknowledged. The first manager had distinguished between the bullish culture of managers who were taking advantage of the recession "to feel and behave powerfully", but did not have a strong enough business orientation or the appropriate change management skills to act in a way that projected change as a continuous activity. The latter person saw the divide in the management system as being between the maintainers and the developers. The developers were "dealing with the business issues", the maintainers "were trying to transmit the [old] culture all the time".

The shop stewards naturally saw little "caring" for people coming either from the bullish managers or the others. One commented:

> ICI managers are taking advantage of the economic circumstances and the general attitudes to trade unions. They have overreacted. The situation is very gloomy. It has built up tension, people are saying we won't half kick you in the backside when the pendulum swings and we get the opportunity.

Other shop stewards talked about the insecurity amongst the men, people in the 35–45 age group hoping to hold on until the storm had passed, some of the older workers taking the generous severance terms with a sense of relief, a distancing from the management, and a breakdown of the unofficial understandings at "the coal face" with management; of trying to fight back tactically with overtime bans, and applying other restrictions to make it difficult for management to implement all the changes they deemed necessary. One shop steward who had seen more than one swing to and fro of the pendulum could still be philosophical, with even a tinge of optimism, in amongst the more general attitudes of insecurity and despair. Wait, and the continuities will re-emerge even after such an apparent discontinuity.

> In the short term it's going to be extremely difficult. It will rely on a few people on the management and shop steward side who are going to agree to ride out the storm. As things start to improve and we get back to the situation where people become attractive again, the company needs them, then things will improve. Like

a sort of chemical reaction, take things out and put them back in and they will settle down again ... The pendulum will swing back, I'm certain about that. Eventually it's got to come back so people have some influence again. That indication will come when management starts to release the purse strings, when that happens people will be more prepared to talk – then there will be more co-operation.

By 1981 the OD resources of Agricultural Division were nowhere to be seen down "the yard". What changes were going on in the works environment were being managed firmly, but also from a process point of view, in the main skilfully, by line managers. Some of these managers are willing to say that their own skills of managing change had developed from association with OD specialists and their technologies, but that was a rather distant image compared with the pressures of the day. In 1981 the term organisation development was rarely mentioned by either its practitioners, doubters, or opponents; but change and development activities were still going on involving members of the OD group – this time away from the works environment, and with a sense of purpose not experienced for some time. Was this refocussing to be another example of "the old hands" linking some of the familiar skills and new knowledge and change mechanisms to take advantage of circumstances, or was it to be a false dawn? In this penultimate section of this chapter we may find some clues to answer the question.

Refocussing of OD, 1976–81

The period of doubt, and in some cases indifference, to OD around 1975 and 1976 which coincided with some of the changes in context toward less risk taking, and the beginnings of a tougher, more businesslike view of management behaviour, also coincided with Paul Miles' departure from Agricultural Division. By that time the OD group in the division had largely drifted apart, although as individuals they could still find themselves busy working, as one OD member put it, "with client friends". The development work led by line managers in Ammonia and Engineering Works had either faded away altogether or was beginning to run out of steam. Some members of the OD group were literally physically and psychologically worn out after several years of coping with the stresses at work and home of living in a marginal role, and being part of an activity which many people in the division regarded with indifference or hostility. The continuing friction with some members of the personnel function had been particularly psychologically draining. An attempt had been made in 1975 and 1976 to integrate a Ph.D. anthropologist into the personnel function to work a good part of his time on OD activities, but this individual was soon tempted away by an attractive offer from outside ICI.

In the summer of 1976, with Paul Miles gone, responsibility for OD in the division passed from the personnel manager level to the assistant personnel manager level. Peter Moores, the new assistant personnel manager, was an engineer who had moved into the personnel function in the late 1960s, and had been closely associated with the OD work in projects and engineering department which predated Noel Ripley's arrival in the division. He had then in turn been an active member of the Swallow group, and had been the internal leader of the OD team on the successful Methanol 2 project. Towards the end of 1972 he had left the personnel function and day-to-day contact with the OD group and its activities in order to become secretary of one of the key political groupings of senior managers on the site, the Billingham Site Management Committee. This job brought him into regular contact with all kinds of managers on the site and gave him an added appreciation of managers' concerns and the politics of how the division operated.

What happened slowly over the period 1976–81 was that Moores fashioned a role linking together the career and manpower planning aspects of personnel work with organisation development and training matters. In the prevailing ICI climate of the time of additional responsibilities being allocated to individuals when other persons left existing posts, this was encouraged. But the way Moores built up his role was not just cultural expediency, it was also related to the emerging viewpoint of the base that he and others felt OD activities should increasingly be working from. Some of the criticisms of the way OD and training were organised and operating around 1976 will give a context for Moores' views about how it should be refocussed. The following quotes were taken from interviews with managers and internal and external OD resources:

> OD – I've heard the phrase being used, it has something to do with consultants – the offering of a resource. I don't find it very helpful or effective. It has little to do with implementation or achievement in my mind . . . I don't see any direction – it's passive. It has a hell of a role to play but isn't playing that role anywhere I'm aware of. They wait to be called, I don't like that.

> * * *

> The OD group – oh, there are all the usual personal agendas being worked, nothing concrete on the table, and no action steps, just philosophising.

> * * *

> OD has an image of those guys doing what they like, when they like – no pressures. If they don't like the client, they clear off to where there's a friend.

> * * *

> Well, I think that the way OD had been organised and run before was largely ineffective. I know there were some successes here and there, but I think first of all the contact with the variety of managers was not as great as it ought to be, and the opportunity for discussion and presentation of ideas was longer than it ought to be – the strike rate was too low . . . OD people flitted around the outside of the division looking at problems and then trying to persuade the owners of those problems to let them in to help them. They weren't actually in there with the problem.

Moores' view of the continuing evolution of OD in the division is that it should work from the inside out, rather than from the outside in. He hoped to better connect OD resources in the division to management and organisational problems by using the legitimate entry points provided by his personnel role in training, career management and succession, and manpower planning. The combination of the access and information that his role provided, plus the external consultant Larsen's acceptance at board and senior manager level, would provide the necessary contact with the Billingham political system – but what problems would they work on, and through what vehicles or mechanisms, was not clear in 1976 and 1977. What was clear by then was that the needs for OD help in the works area in the emerging climate of bullish management was not there, and that if some activities were to arise to give some meaning and substance to this strategy of engagement with the political system, then those activities would either have to come from contact with commercial managers and departments, or across-the-divisionwide problems.

Although I have already used the word strategy more than once to describe what in 1976 and 1977 could only be properly described as hopes and aspirations for OD work, there was throughout the late 1970s a loose stance taken that OD work would have to be more inclusively linked to both personnel work and management and organisational problems. The more politically astute members of the OD group knew that in the messy process of creating change, "We are not in the grand strategy business, because it is both inappropriate, and has been demonstrated widely to be vulnerable to shifts in organisation power. Old strategies have the habit of being discarded by victors in power struggles, or movement of high-level supporters." In the process of trying to decide what to do, there were attempts to draw on past learning. One OD group member commented on how the companywide MUPS/WSA programme crucially "had provided a context – something to latch onto that provided a rationale for managers to accept the need for training". He went on to say that "for the future I believe we need to set another context – rather than set something up in vacuo". Of course, in a broad sense the OD group couldn't "set another context", what they could do was monitor carefully the present and emerging context, professionally re-equip themselves, get alongside key people in the business where that was possible, and wait until these different pieces in the jigsaw gelled, and then launch themselves into a favourable context.

By the middle of 1980, just as the context was about to move in a direction that provided them with a new role, but in a sense a return to an old method of working, a short statement was prepared for internal distribution within the OD group which labelled their then stance as "opportunistic working". The document began:

> The crispest adjective to describe our method of working is "opportunistic". This does not mean the rootless seeking of benefit, but in our context is an expression of a growth process with firm foundations. These foundations are values and beliefs about individuals and organisations, and provide a position against which present and future organisations and behaviour can be evaluated ... Given this position, the practical expression of "opportunistic" is to be capable and alert to change opportunities so that managers and staff can make changes and examine any alternatives for change available to them. Our part in this is to facilitate that process from a position which is identifiable and clear.

By January 1981 the OD group had found their opportunity and could even claim they had helped to create both some of the intellectual justifications, and elements of the vehicle, for tackling the problem. The opportunity was a manpower productivity exercise formally launched by the board as a part of a clear statement of business strategy and objectives over the next several years. The productivity exercise "provides the first real opportunity to set a pattern of management behaviour which recognises the possibility that the human resources of the division can be managed with a greater purpose and precision opposite the needs of the business and the individual than has been the case hitherto".

The return to an old pattern of working was reflected in a project team of working which the OD group had not used since the Methanol 2 project of the early 1970s. Peter Moores became the project manager responsible for "managing and establishing values and consistent action for the total operation". Roles were allocated to a manager responsible for resettlement and job finding for individuals wishing to leave the organisation; the training manager was given a clear remit to deploy training and development resources to match the needs for career development, retraining and restructuring; and a new member of the OD group was asked to help with the development of appropriate computer systems to supply information relevant to job finding, career development and manpower resource planning. Larsen, the external OD consultant who had provided a good deal of the value stance for connecting into the manpower productivity exercise, and a great deal of the energy "to go formal, to go public, and to go accountable", had also provided a crucial training vehicle – for the times the appropriately enough named life business planning workshop.

The first of these workshops was run for managers in the division in early 1980. By early 1981 the third one had been conducted. The idea was to use business accountancy methods and language to encourage individuals to look at themselves as a business, and to examine where they were going, and what they needed in the way of resources to get there. With his employment business area hat on the individual's first job on the workshop was to prepare a set of budgeted accounts. The purpose of this exercise was to determine whether or not with his current skills (production capacity) his most likely job situation (sales contacts in hand), and the energy he was currently expending (production, marketing, sales and distribution costs), he was likely to be able to reach his desired level of increased satisfaction. It if appeared that the individual was able to reach his satisfaction objectives within current job, skill and energy constraints the individual had no business planning problem. But the situation of ICI in 1981 was that many managers did have a life business planning problem, and it was in the tension between individual needs and goals and organisational needs and goals, that the OD team's work of the early 1980s were centred.

In the quiet period between Moores' taking over responsibility for managing the division's OD resources in 1976 and the economic recession and ICI's first financial losses in 1980, the OD group had been working at the problem they initially labelled "the motivation of mid-career staff". Central to their definition of this problem was a view that the "unwritten contract" between the employee and the company was "failing". The unwritten contract which had held for many years was that "the employee delivers hard work, loyalty, ICI centredness, and the priority of ICI life over private life, in exchange for a satisfying career, promotion, social status, security and good remuneration". Even in 1978 ICI could no longer deliver its side of the contract, and the structural changes and manpower reductions of 1980 and 1981 certainly demonstrated they couldn't. Some employees were also showing increasing reluctance to value contracts of this sort even before ICI acted in 1980 and 1981. The issue for the OD resources in Agricultural Division was to do something positive in the way of offering the systems and mechanisms needed to implement a new "unwritten contract". There were many obstacles in the way of doing this, not the least of which were the way the existing career and personnel systems, and the attitudes and behaviour of the managers inhibited treating the mutual relationship between individual and organisation more openly. The business pressures of 1980, the prospects for further increased business pressures in the 1980s and the divisional requirement for a manpower productivity exercise, were enough to break through and destabilise any forces of inertia and inhibition. The OD project team were in business again in 1981 – but this time in a more visible, and from a value point of view, more fraught, role than ever before.

Here then were the beginnings of a change process, where insofar as is possible within the complexities of large organisations, the content and even language and symbolism of the change fitted the context. The economic and business realities of the day provided the overriding justification to break the forces of organisational inertia. The need was to reduce the cost base of the business by reducing the number of employees, and yet to "export not cadavers, but live bodies" while retaining lively, committed people who could find and help to develop a new unwritten contract with the organisation. All this was meant to be not a change event, not a short-term interruption to "normal" life, but rather an expression of "normal" life itself – a continuous process of changing rather than a change project. One of the prime vehicles for energising this process – the life business planning workshops, together with the activity in day-to-day superior–subordinate relationships which it was hoped would develop from and sustain this process – was itself using the language of accountancy and business, which was driving the change at a macrolevel. And the decision to go public, to publish their mission, and the very organisation of the OD team with their leader, their roles, their bar chart and their accountabilities; all mirroring the urgency and task-centredness of the day. Symbol for symbol, the content matched the context.

But nothing in organisational life is that tidy. Were there any discrepancies between the OD group's values which emphasised the dignity and value of the individual, before the value of the group or organisation, and the business imperatives driving this manpower productivity exercise? One response was:

This exercise will make the division a more productive place to work in but I fear in practice this will mean ignoring people, it will be all numbers and organisational change.

A more emphatic statement of the tension between the old OD values and the new OD work was:

> I think the situation is being exploited to the detriment of the people. The hard men are in the ascendency and some of the OD men are going along with them. They are reluctant to stand up and say "Hold it!" . . . There's much more a value now of the organisation has got to come out on top and its harder on the people . . . Sometimes the sort of stuff that people like me used to preach about – trust and openness, I realise that was far too idealistic, but I think unless we get some of the words we talked about into action now – like participation; I'm afraid when the thing does swing the other way then people are going to say "That's for the birds that stuff, it was just a bloody big con." It's being said now, and with some justification.

The other side of the picture was that "there are values about personal choice and personal development built into it . . . There is a value about caring, as well as the organisation point of view built into it. But there's also a kind of new value which is to do with the needs of the business, people in the organisation have to recognize that there is a corporate group which has in itself a requirement for particular things to happen." Even more persuasively perhaps was the view that said:

> I see no conflict between my own values as a change agent, and paring down this organisation. One of the harmful things about this organisation is its largeness, its fatness, so few people are ever at their boundaries . . . There's so much buffer, so much float, so much excess. People aren't alive. Efforts to make them alive while all the people stay here are very difficult to being about . . . I see the good for people leaving, as well as for those staying but only if there's an investment for people leaving . . . I invite people to think about their lives in a different way . . . for some it will be a chance to see that the loyalty contract I've signed onto the ICI ship for the rest of my life, isn't the only way in the future. Another option is, I'm going to take control. I'm going to manage my life. ICI is a possible market, it's not the end of the world. I'll look at other markets. I may stay, but I'll be choiceful about it.

If one danger for the OD team in 1981 was a discrepancy that could be found, or in the future created, between their old values and their current behaviour, and a wedge driven along the axis of what they said and what they did – a further problem could lie in their very inclusiveness. The OD team was now actively seeking to play down the use of the organisation development label and any claims to be associated with a special, and exclusive, body of expertise. One OD man said:

> This division doesn't talk about OD any more – the term doesn't mean anything any more. We're personalities now more than OD practitioners.

Another said:

> No, not at all – I never use the OD label – it's an unfortunate term which has got a
> bad press. I contact the issue at the level at which it is presented. I have a very
> fundamental way of dealing with it. One is not to say as some are inclined to, there
> is a great body of technical expertise which is called OD, and can be summoned
> up theoretically to any problem. I think that turns people here off actually. What I
> do is to try to just deal with the problem as it arises, and to make suggestions about
> possible ways of dealing with it in practical ways.

But if the OD team were seeking to project a low profile as specialist experts,
they were now projecting a high profile in association with a management-led
manpower productivity drive. As one OD man commented, "The thing that will
keep us alive is that our purpose is coincidental with the board." Therein lies
perhaps the greatest threat to the OD team's longer-term survival and future
cutting edge as facilitators of processes of change. The greater their perceived
success on the manpower productivity exercise, the greater will be the threat to
their continued existence and their impact in change. As one of the more
successful members of the OD team put it, prior to his public involvement in
the manpower productivity exercise:

> I've been included [in senior management meetings] but don't ask me to say or
> do anything . . . They've deified me. Symbolically what I represent is good –
> humanity – conscience, those aspects of ourselves not being met in everyday life . .
> . If we'd created big changes we wouldn't be here now.

Now there's a conundrum in specialist attempts to create change, and one we
shall see is still alive in Agricultural Division in 1984.

POSTSCRIPT: BUSINESS SURVIVAL AND REGENERATION:
A ROLE FOR ORGANISATION DEVELOPMENT FOR THE 1980s

ICI Agricultural Division continues to make annual profits in excess of £100m
in the year ended December 1982, but as we noted in Table 19 in Chapter 5
the profit margins for ICI's agriculture business sector have been declining
since 1979 The business competitive difficulties faced by Agricultural Division
since 1981 may seem less than pressing whilst profits of £100m and more are
being made, but looked at in the medium and long term those difficulties are
fundamental. The relative competitive advantage of the division's methanol
business in the 1970s was based on technological superiority and advantageous
feedstock prices due to a cheap gas contract arrangement with the British Gas
Corporation. Both of those advantages are now disappearing as competitors
acquire the latest plant and as energy cost factors increasingly swing against
European producers of methanol and towards the manufacture of methanol in
parts of the Middle East and Far East where natural gas is considerably
cheaper.

On the fertiliser side of Agricultural Division there have also been changes since 1981. Norsk Hydro have purchased the UK fertiliser business of Fisons and promise to be a very much stronger competitor than Fisons. Given that UK fertiliser prices are higher than those in Continental Western Europe there is a natural incentive for fertiliser producers in West Germany and France and Eastern Europe to invade the UK market. The actual rise in fertiliser imports between 1980 and 1983 has affected the price structure of the UK market and the market share held by Agricultural Division, Norsk Hydro and UK Fertilisers. Part of ICI's response to this pressure has been to try and strengthen their position in the UK during 1983 by acquiring the 50% of Hargreaves Fertilisers Ltd not already owned by ICI and by purchasing the UK fertiliser and agro-chemicals business of Albright and Wilson Ltd.

A further strategic response to the above competitive pressures which has been the subject of speculation in the financial press is for ICI to change the point of manufacture of methanol to countries such as the United Arab Emirates where natural gas it relatively cheap. This is a clear alternative for ICI over a period of time rather than allowing UK energy costs to eventually force the division out of the methanol business.

But if trying to manufacture against a background of cheaper feedstock is at the moment just the subject of press speculation, what is obvious as a survival strategy for Agricultural Division since 1981 is the continuing drive to reduce manufacturing and other costs. In 1984 production managers at Billingham are predictably being exhorted to keep plants running in a climate of good human relations where fixed and variable costs are reduced, product quality is high, production goals are met, productivity-based capital investments are made and where managers train and retrain their staff so they are capable of doing bigger things in the future. Table 18 in Chapter 5 also demonstrated that Agricultural Division dropped its manpower numbers by around 20% between 1980 and 1983 without making any substantial changes in its own structure, believing that numbers reductions may eventually suggest structural changes but that structural changes can create noise in the system to affect the pace of manpower reductions.

All of the above business strategies naturally reflect a concern with business survival, but the final plank of the division's business strategy into the 1980s recognises that the division has the twin dilemma to wrestle with of cultivating the business and organisational conditions to foster both survival and regeneration. The "Pruteen" development was, of course, seen in the 1970s as a key part of the division's strategy for regeneration into the 1980s which might conceivably have led to the creation of an entirely new division, but so far the price advantages of soya beans and fish meal seem to have defeated the commercial success of ICI's single cell protein. "Pruteen" may have to be seen as part of the downpayment to get into a new market. It may also be that the "Pruteen" plant experience can create other biotechnological spin-offs and be a major source of learning for the division as it seeks to develop further new ventures during the 1980s.

But to return to the evolution of OD resources in Agricultural Division, how are those resources engaging with the above business pressures and priorities? Is the strategy still one of opportunism and refocussing? What vehicles are the OD resources using to engage with business problems and how are their resources being assembled to develop and implement any new tasks?

In 1984 Peter Moores is still providing leadership for the division's developmental resource from his role as an assistant personnel manager. Larsen the American consultant still travels over from the United States one week in four to engage with the Agricultural Division board and to act as a creative stimulant for Moores and the small number of individuals who report to him, and the strategy of pragmatic opportunism is still at the core of what the OD people are doing, although the rationale for their work is now more broadly based and involves the use of additional vehicles than the Life Business Planning training workshop.

The highly pragmatic and political stance of OD in Agricultural Division in 1984 is reflected well in these remarks:

> Opportunism means you can't relax on context at any time ... priorities will change and priorities have to relate to what is really hurting in the division. There's no use in standing back and pulling beads and beards as we used to ... you have to be very close to the centre of power and thereby to be able to sense what is happening and how and why things are shifting and moving so you don't get caught out applying help that isn't needed.

But what are the new priorities suggested by the business, political, and cultural context of Agricultural Division in the mid 1980s?

> In the 1970s OD energy went into dealing with specific and major problems in sectors of the business, like how to build new projects to time and cost, or how to minimise the adverse effects of trade unionism, or to put it more positively how to improve the industrial relations climate. But after five years of Mrs Thatcher the trade unions are pretty quiet and since we're not building much new plant that need's gone ... Where we are now, we're in a much more complex area, a broader area in that the issues we are into affect the whole business and all the people in it ... how can a business be made effective in developing, training, and deploying its human resources into areas important for the business, and how at the same time can individuals aspirations, hopes, and concerns about life and career in the organisation be discussed and accommodated. Using human resources effectively whilst limiting numbers, that involves every aspect of what we do – it's more pervasively important than the sectoral issues and needs of the past.

The above mind of definition of need is leading the development resources in Agricultural Division (OD as a collective term has long since been discarded at Billingham) to ask questions such as:

1. What way is the business strategy going to develop and what impact will that have on the division's human resources?

2. How should career management procedures change to take into account reduced career opportunities?
3. How can the division's management and professional staff be encouraged to take on more responsibility for their own working lives, be clearer about their own choices in the context of a realistic view of their own performance and the opportunities now open to them in Agricultural Division?
4. How should the structure and culture of Agricultural Division change to provide a context which will keep to satisfy the division's business needs of survival and regeneration?

The need for development resources is for all of those questions to be worked on together as the "front end" of what they are doing whilst still satisfying the division's everyday requirements for management and supervisory training, computer-based training for process operators, selecting staff, running Youth Training Schemes and managing the division's "prospects advisory group", the information and counselling service available for those seeking to leave the division.

A key strategic question suggested by the above highly pragmatic and business-focussed view of positioning developmental work, is can a group so obviously tuned to the business, political, and cultural needs of the day still retain the sharpness of cutting edge so often necessary to be a source of innovation? It is a paradox which will run through all the accounts of using internal specialist resources in this book, of how to be inclusive and exclusive at the same time. It seems that in order to achieve change the initiator of change must understand the forces of continuity in his local system. But to get such an understanding of business needs and their political and cultural expression, the initiator of change has to have some level of acceptance in the system he is seeking to change, both to understand what changes are supportable and how support can be mobilised for those changes. But if the development resource is that close to the operation of the business, and few developmental resources in this study have been, is there the scope for distancing, questioning, and even insubordination necessary to face the division with uncomfortable messages about the need for change? One of the current development resources at Billingham acknowledged the position:

> Yes maybe we are, we do in some respects represent the system, that's why we know it so well . . . I've thought about this many times and often wonder if all we do is a variation of, a modification of what the organisation wants anyway. All we're really doing is varying things which are approved of . . . But I dont think that's entirely true, if the career work we've been doing had gone wrong, if key people had left for Fisons or Norsk Hydro, we'd be in dead trouble . . . But I'm pretty clear if you belong to an organisation like this one and in the end if you have to choose between what is good for the business and what is good for the individual, I'd choose the business; and I don't make any secret of where my ultimate loyalties lie.

The unequivocal clarity of that statement of value made in 1984 seems a long way from Noel Ripley's value position of 1969, but then again the business, political, and social context for OD is vastly different in 1984 from what it was in Agricultural Division in the late 1960s, and for the pragmatist who recognises that continuing survival and impact means being aware that priorities change and "you can't relax on context", then one has to acknowledge the viability of the strategy.

But talking of differences in context, we must move on now to consider the quite different context and natural history of development of OD resources, a few miles away from Agricultural Division, south of the River Tees, at Petrochemicals Division.

7 The Enforced Strategy for Creating Change: Petrochemicals Division

Early in 1971 ICI announced one of their periodic reorganisations involving a reshuffling of business areas and redrawing and relabelling of divisional boundaries. Nobel's Explosives Company Ltd was formed to take over and operate the explose assets of Nobel Division. ICI Fibres Ltd was reconstituted as a division. Dyestuffs Division combined with parts of Nobel Division to become Organics Division, and Heavy Organic Chemicals Division acquired parts of the old fibres and dyestuffs operations and was renamed Petrochemicals Division. To many of the managers who had left the old Billingham Division in 1958 to form Heavy Organic Chemicals Division (HOC), who were part of the tremendous technological and market growth of ICI's chemicals from petroleum interests in the 1950s and 1960s, the naming of Petrochemicals Division (PCD) symbolised that period of individual and business sector success.

Almost exactly ten years later, in March 1981, PCD no longer existed as a separate division of ICI. As a senior manager of ICI put it, in April 1980, PCD "fell off a cliff". On the way down they met Plastics Division and in April 1981 those two divisions were merged to form Petrochemicals and Plastics Division. In 1979 the ICI worldwide petrochemicals business had made a profit of £98m. The extent of the fall off the cliff can be gauged by looking at the corresponding figures for the year ending December 1980. By then ICI's petrochemicals business was making a loss of £44m on sales of £976m and the plastics business a loss of £35m on sales of £738m. Because of these losses, and similar difficulties in their Fibres and Organics Divisions, ICI as a group made losses of £10m and £6m in the third and fourth quarters of 1980. These were the first losses in the group's history and were widely used as a barometer of the extent of difficulties in the UK economy in late 1980 and early 1981. How ICI, as a group, changed during and as a consequence of the business traumas of 1980 and 1981 will form an important part of the concluding section of this book. The objective of this chapter is to return to an earlier period in the business and organisational history of ICI's petroleum chemical interests in order to explore first the context in which organisation development activities emerged in Petrochemicals Division, and then to chronicle and broadly analyse the birth, functioning, and demise of the OD unit in Petrochemicals Division. The above analysis will reveal a quite different pattern of birth, evolution, and development of OD activities, and a different kind of impact for OD resources in PCD than that which occured in Agricultural Division, even though by the early 1970s we will be discussing divisions of the same company, of comparable size, both based on large multidivision manufacturing sites, and with their headquarters initially only a quarter of a mile from one another.

HEAVY ORGANIC CHEMICALS/PETROCHEMICALS DIVISION: BUSINESS HISTORY, ORGANISATION, AND CULTURE: 1958–81

In order to adequately explain the creation of HOC Division in 1958, its growth and development into PCD in 1971, and to understand some of the antecedents and evolution of OD in PCD, it is important to know something of the origins of the large chemical manufacturing site south of the River Tees at Wilton. Even though from 1958 until 1974 the headquarters of HOC/PCD was north of the Tees at Billingham, and indeed some of PCD manufacturing capacity is on the Agricultural Division-managed Billingham site, the rise of the HOC/PCD businesses and their associated manpower and managerial cultures is very much also the story of the Wilton site.

The idea of basing a good deal of ICI's post-war expansion plans on a large, integrated manufacturing site dates from deliberations of the ICI Development Executive Committee of 1943 (Reader, 1975:392). By the end of 1945 the 3,500 acre Wilton Estate, complete with nineteenth-century mansion, Wilton Castle, had been purchased for a sum of £190,000. In 1947 the main board of ICI sanctioned £25m of investment for various divisions at Wilton. By 1957 £114m had been sanctioned for Wilton, by 1965 £330m had been invested there (in 1972 pounds) and by 1972 the figure was £560m, representing a quarter of the company's assets (Roeber, 1975:120). In 1981 the investment on Wilton in 1981 prices was around £2,000m. Driving past the Wilton complex in the evening, the site appears the apotheosis of technological glamour and industrial power.

There are various reasons why the Wilton Estate was chosen as the focal point for ICI's postwar development. The Tees offered access to the sea for the import of materials and the shipping of chemicals and finished goods. The Tees also provided water for cooling and the tidal river or sea an outlet for effluent. Coal and salt were close at hand in Durham, and as a "development area" there would be financial and other encouragement from the Government and local authorities. Wilton also had one other big advantage – proximity to ICI's existing large chemical works at Billingham on the opposite bank of the Tees. This made possible the interconnection of Billingham and Wilton by means of a 10-mile-long pipelink soon to be built by ICI for this purpose. Eventually the advantages of scale and integration were to be reinforced by the construction of a further tunnel under the Tees through which raw materials, products and services could flow in both directions. The Teesside ICI complex is also linked by pipelines to other related chemical plants and processes in the north-west of England, and central Scotland.

ICI had been researching in petroleum chemical processes since 1929. At Billingham knowledge had been built up by operating the high-pressure hydrogenation process to produce petrol from coal or coal tar middle oil. The experience gained in operating this hydrogenation process, the techniques developed in working up its by-products, and the vast amount of research work carried out, provided the basis on which to develop petroleum chemical activities. In 1933 ICI scientists at Billingham discovered polythene. By the late 1960s this was the world's largest tonnage plastic. Yet for 12 years after 1939, when the first commercial polythene plant began operating, all of ICI's requirements of ethylene for polythene were derived from ethyl alcohol obtained from the fermentation of molasses. When, therefore, in 1951 ICI started up its first naphtha crackers at Wilton with a capacity of 30,000 tons a year, it did so essentially in support of polythene and other near consumer products such as "Perspex", in order to achieve an economic raw material base. What these "crackers" do is to break down their raw materials – naphtha or natural gas liquids – and produce chemicals called olefines. These olefines in turn become the raw materials required for the plastics industry.

In the course of the next 15 years, three large olefine plants were built upon the Wilton site with a combined cracking capacity of 600,000 tons of naphtha per annum. By the late 1960s, Olefines 4 and 5 had a combined capacity of 650,000 tons of ethylene per annum. Around these olefine plants grew up fifteen other plants producing intermediate and finished petroleum chemical products for the plastics industry and an aromatics complex which provided raw materials for "Terylene" and nylon manufacture.

This picture of expansion of petroleum-based chemicals to be sent down-stream to ICI's own plastics or artificial fibres businesses, or to be exported to facilitate the growth of those industries in Western Europe, was influenced by worldwide economic recessions, and the cycles of boom and slump within the chemical industry. In the period 1951 to 1957 ICI poured capital into Wilton. All the other large chemical companies and some of the cash-rich oil companies did the same thing at the same time in order to keep up with the competition and growing world demand. As Roeber (1975) has argued, the economies of such heavy investment were compelling. "The more completely ICI could make use of its proliferating streams of products and by-products, the more efficient and profitable would the operation become. Allied to it is the logic of scale: in continuous process industries there are almost unlimited benefits to be gained from building bigger plants" Roeber (1975:120). As we shall see, however, the singular pursuit of these economic and technological logics eventually produced severe strains in the emerging workforce and managerial cultures which developed on the Wilton site.

The 1950s expansion of the world petrochemicals industry eventually produced its harvest of worldwide over-capacity and, with the 1958 US recession, dumping of chemicals in Europe followed by the price wars of the 1958–62 period. Faced with these developing business pressures in the late 1950s, ICI made one of its periodic reorganisations. On 1 January, 1958, ICI (Heavy Organic Chemicals) Ltd was formed and this new division took over the organic chemicals side of the business from Billingham Division. This involved the transfer of roughly one-third of the staff strength from the old division and the total production of two works. The new division, which employed 2,300 staff and payroll workers, was made entirely responsible for its own research and technical work and had an extensive engineering organisation. In the period 1958–63 this engineering organisation had a relatively quiet time. ICI's investment in Wilton virtually stopped in those years. In the period 1951–56 new expenditure on the site as a percentage of last year's total had been running between 33% and 21%. In the period 1959–63 expenditure on the site as a percentage of the previous year's total had declined to between 9% and 5%. But the chemical cycle picked up again and 1965 and 1966 were years of large capital expenditure on the Wilton site only to fall back once more in the period 1968–72, and pick up with massive new investments in the years 1974–79 when ICI was cash-rich.

The boom investment years of 1965 and 1966 were associated with unheralded expansion in the downstream plastics and fibres businesses. In 1964, for example, demand for plastics in the UK was expanding at 15% per annum. 1964 also saw the creation of ICI Fibres Ltd out of British Nylon Spinners and the "Terylene" and "Ulstron" interests of the old Fibres Division. ICI also in 1964 bought into English Sewing Cotton Ltd, Viyella International Ltd, and three other smaller textile companies. But these were volatile years for the textile industry, 1965–67 saw nylon sales and prices down, and after a brief upsurge in 1968 the textile interests of ICI had bad years from 1969 to 1971. This led to the reorganisations of the fibres, explosives and dyestuffs business areas which produced in 1971 an expanded Heavy Organic Chemicals Division which was renamed Petrochemicals Division.

The ICI Annual Reports have shown the performance of its business classes (worldwide) only since 1973. This makes it relatively easy to follow the worldwide profits and sales of Petrochemicals Division from 1973 until 1980 but virtually impossible to analyse the profitability of HOC Division from public sources through the period of its creation in 1958 until its reconstitution as PCD in 1971. Judging from evidence of the world economic and chemical recession of 1958–61, ICI cost-cutting and reorganising around that period, and the big drop in capital sanctioned and spent at Wilton then, one can reliably assume both that those were bad financial years for HOC, and that HOC benefited from the upturn in 1964–67. By 1969, however, interviews from authoritative sources in HOC at that time indicate "the most appalling financial results ... with something like £200m invested ... we didn't turn a bloody cent". Internal sources indicate PCD made a profit of around £1m in 1971 and perhaps £5m in 1972. By 1973, PCD worldwide was turning a trading profit of £22m on sales of £272m. These fairly unspectacular financial results of HOC in the 1960s, and PCD in its first two years, do not justify the confident managerial culture that built up in HOC/PCD in the 1960s and early 1970s. But if the profits were not growing in the 1960s, the capital invested at Wilton continued to grow and that was the more likely spring from which the confidence of the division's managers developed.

PCD's 1973 profits increased on the back of a demand boom. Table 20 shows that PCD prospered in the wake of the oil crisis of 1973–74. With shortages of petroleum-based raw materials customers were willing to pay high

TABLE 20 Petrochemicals Group worldwide: sales, trading profit and trading margins in £m

Year	Sales	Trading profit	Trading margin
1973	272	22	8.1
1974	503	73	14.5
1975	493	49	9.9
1976	669	82	12.3
1977	699	61	8.7
1978	673	54	8.0
1979	1076	98	9.1
1980	976	(44)	(4.5)

prices to maintain and even build their stock levels. Profits dropped again in the economic recession of 1975 but discipline among producers not to chase market share at the expense of prices, even in the overcapacity situation in plastics and fibres, meant that profits were healthy though volatile right up until the end of the 1970s.

Back in the mid-1960s two events had strengthened long-term petroleum chemical activities on Teesside. One was the decision made in 1964 to complete the vertical integration of ICI's petroleum activities at Wilton by taking a 50% stake in a new oil refinery to be built and operated jointly with Phillips Petroleum Company. This refinery was placed alongside North Tees Works and began to supply part of the naphtha requirements of ICI's plants at Billingham and Wilton. Crucially, however, 1964 also saw the setting up by ICI and Burmah Oil of an oil consortium to begin oil exploration in the North Sea. By the time Olefines 6 was commissioned in 1979 – a joint venture between ICI and British Petroleum – ICI had created ICI Petroleum Ltd and made them responsible for ICI's interests in exploration and development of oil and gas in the North Sea and refining of crude oil. ICI now had its own supply of an increasingly expensive raw material from the Ninian Field of the North Sea. By 1980 ICI was a partner in oil and gas interests in the North Sea, the Gulf of Mexico, offshore California, and in Alberta, Canada. After provision for petroleum revenue tax, the worldwide oil interests of ICI made a trading profit in 1980 of £97m on sales of £770m. But although Petrochemicals Division was benefiting directly in 1980 from ICI's oil and gas interests in the North Sea, those £97m trading profits were firmly under the oil, and not petrochemicals, business area.

1980 witnessed disastrous trading conditions for Petrochemicals Division. There was a worldwide recession and after record petrochemical sales in the first quarter of 1980 weakening demand for many products was exacerbated by heavy destocking by customers. For the year as a whole, crude oil prices were more than 50% higher than in 1979. The gap between United States and West European crude oil and petrochemical feedstock prices widened and this, coupled with the recession in the US demand, meant increased supplies of low-

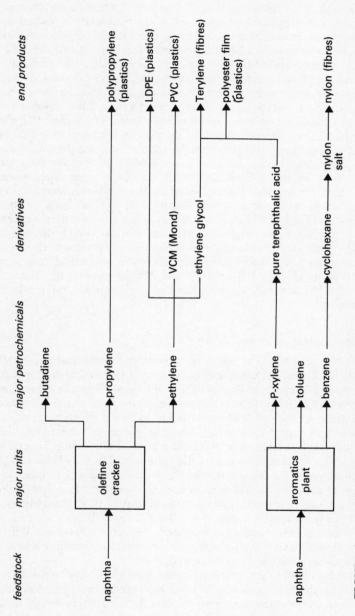

FIGURE 7 Simplified flow chart for Petrochemicals in ICI

priced petrochemicals products from the USA. The ICI fibres business, a largish customer for PCD intermediate chemicals, was still further depressed by the dumping of US synthetic fibre in Europe. The resulting overcapacity in the European petrochemical, plastics, and fibres businesses provoked intense price competition and a severe squeeze on margins. In addition, realisations from all markets were reduced by the strength of sterling against the dollar and the Deutschemark, and were insufficiently compensated by exchange rate benefits on oil and gas feedstock costs. With costs on the feedstock (input) side escalating, a dramatic falling away of demand in a situation of worldwide overcapacity, prices collapsed, and PCD fell off a cliff. This was much worse than the 1958 collapse and one of its many implications within ICI was the merging of PCD and Plastics Divisions. If costs on the input side couldn't be controlled, and neither could prices on the output side, one thing that was still actionable upon was the middle-fixed costs. Reorganisation was the result.

Nevertheless, by the end of the 1970s the large, composite, integrated chemical site ICI conceived of at the end of the Second World War was in place at Wilton, along with the new headquarters of the landlord of the site, Petrochemicals Division. Figure 7, in a highly abbreviated form, presents a flow chart for petrochemicals operations on the site and lists which division of ICI used PCD chemicals and chemical derivatives to make products. By the end of the 1970s, in the UK, Petrochemicals Division still was selling around nearly 50% of its output to other ICI units. As one PCD senior manager put it, "The big pool is still ICI demand, we are in fact a power station for ICI, producing all her feedstocks."

The Wilton site organisation and culture

The context in which OD activities in Agricultural Division developed had a crucial role in shaping the evolution and impact of OD in that part of ICI. The relatively short life, task, and impact of the OD unit in Petrochemicals Division was also moulded by the manner in which it was born and the history and setting in which it emerged. Although the history of the Billingham site and the Billingham/Agricultural Division is, from an operating production point of view, 25 years or so longer than Wilton and HOC/PCD – and this exerted an important effect on creating some of the cultural differences between the two sites and divisions – the shorter Wilton/PCD story is a more complicated story to tell. One reason why the Billingham story is a simpler one is that the history of Billingham is so much more singularly the history of Billingham/Agricultural Division than was the case south of the River Tees at Wilton. Indeed, as the opening section of this chapter has indicated, the whole point of the Wilton site was that it should develop into a composite manufacturing setting where many of the ICI divisions would be represented.

Compared with the centrifugal role that Billingham/Agricultural Division played at Billingham, it was not until 1968, ten years after its creation, and four years after it was formally required to, that HOC actively began to take a managerial and political role in trying to pull together and co-ordinate what at that time was beginning to appear as an uncontrolled Wilton site. As we shall shortly see in more detail, the control problems on the site were not only in the management–trade union arena, but also in the conduct of relationships between manager and manager. In fact, the control problems in both those areas nourished one another. But in considering the developing organisation and culture of the Wilton site as part of the backcloth of OD in the HOC/PCD Division, it is important to remember the degree to which it is, in fact, separated out from the work of the OD unit. There is a separation of time in that the development work initiated to try and deal with some of the Wilton site's control problems began in 1968, some two years before the OD unit was created. There is a separation of focus in that the Wilton development work centred on the management of production, management–management relationships across the site, and the management of weekly staff, while the OD unit's work focussed entirely on the management of HOC/PCD divisional structure and monthly staff. There is a separation of personnel in that few of the members of the OD unit or their associates were much involved with the Wilton work. Finally there was also a geographical separation in that the OD unit and most of its clients were located in the HOC/PCD divisional headquarters building on the Billingham site. Nonetheless, the Wilton work did introduce organisation development activities on a wide scale for the first time, and the chief sponsor of these activities at Wilton, John Harvey-Jones, subsequently became chairman of the HOC/PCD Division and a major sponsor and user of the OD unit.

The differences in culture which emerged on the Billingham and Wilton sites are widely recognised and freely talked about by managers and trade unionists on both sites. But the differences acquire part of their fascination because we are talking about industrial sites with some crucial things in common. Crucially, one would think, we are talking of chemical sites employing people from the same company, located only 13 miles apart in the same industrial community, of broadly similar size, and part of the same broad industrial grouping. Billingham, of course, was built up around fertiliser products and Wilton around petrochemicals – but they are members of the same technological family in design principle terms and offer similar working conditions and rewards for the people who work on the sites. In the mid-1960s both sites comprised several works, each a self-contained factory, employing from 1,000 to 4,000 people. Also in the mid-1960s each site employed some 10,000 payroll and 4,000 monthly staff. By 1973, although both sites still had plants from five ICI divisions on them, and the type of labour on each site was still comparable, the plant closures on Billingham in the late 1960s and early 1970s had reduced their labour force to around 6,400. Table 21 provides a detailed picture of the ICI direct labour employed by both sites, by type of labour in 1973.

As Roeber (1975:87) has argued, probably the most crucial similarity between the two sites lay in employing people from the same part of the country. Teesside is one of Britain's oldest industrial communities. Coal mining, iron-ore mining, iron and steel manufacture, shipbuilding, heavy

TABLE 21   ICI direct labour on Billingham and Wilton sites, 1973

Type of labour	Wilton site	Billingham site	ICI numbers on Teesside
Fitters	1081	791	1872
Electricians	313	278	591
Instrument artificers	380	248	628
Plumbers	200	164	364
Platers	116	100	216
Welders	86	59	145
Riggers	142	256	398
General workers	5735	4133	9868
Miscellaneous	288	372	660
	8341	6401	14742

engineering, and railway engineering had been dominant employers in the area for a century or more. But with the decline in those industries, employment prospects in the area were deteriorating and there had been the manifest suffering amongst working people in the area during the 1920s and 1930s.

But in spite of these important similarities, the differences in the histories of the two sites, the places they occupied in the local communities, and what seemed for a time differences in the commercial future of the two sites all contributed to the emergence of contrasting cultures on the sites. These contrasting cultures were to manifest themselves most obviously in the different reactions coming from the sites in response to the variety of social innovations coming out of Millbank in the period 1965–72.

Billingham was a much older site – its history went back to the 1920s. In the context of the decline in the older industries on Teesside, and the high unemployment of the 1920s and 1930s, the arrival at that time of the newer chemical industry offering better working conditions, fringe benefits, and prospects than local competitive employers was one of the few optimistic events in a very bleak Teesside. First fathers and then sons went to work at "the ICI". Under "hard but fair" management, amongst a management group which was itself relatively stable and secure, an aura of paternalistic working relationships developed on Billingham where in spite of the normal frictions there were deep-rooted relationships where "dad knew best and handled change in a fair, sensible fashion". Billingham was also very much a factory town, the *Teesside at Mid-Century* report by House and Fullerton (1960) showed that by 1955, 30% of the factory payroll lived in Billingham itself in houses built by ICI before the Second World War.

In contrast to this Wilton had grown rapidly in the conditions of full employment of the 1950s when the trade unions were growing in size and confidence, and in social conditions where managerial prerogatives and practices were increasingly under question. Because there was little housing within a five-mile radius of the Wilton site, and by the 1950s, ICI had discontinued the practice of house-builder and landlord for its employees, Wilton employees had to come further afield to get to Wilton, and the communities they returned to after work were not so exclusively ICI as Billingham was. By the 1950s other chemical firms were investing in plants south of the Tees, and the steel industry was going through a period of local expansion. Wilton never became a company town in the way Billingham had been. A Wilton senior shop steward of many years standing had this to say about the emergence of the Wilton site:

When I first came here in 1952 this site had a nucleus of Billingham people here, but ICI was recruiting from shipbuilding and other industries as far away as Newcastle. People who came here had no paternalistic feeling about the situation. They were coming to do a job. There were a hell of a lot of Geordies, hell of a lot of Scotsmen. Knowing the background where they lived and the type of industrial relations they were used to – they were fairly militant. With regard to how they saw their jobs, the demarcations were fairly finely drawn, and everyone stood up for what he believed was his right . . . Billingham was a mature site even during the War. Although they recruited a lot of ex-coal mining people from the prewar era – they were quite happy, their allegiance to the company became paternalistic. The company looked after them. But on this site they came from all over, and they all had their own idiosyncracies in protecting their own spheres of influence.

Several Wilton shop stewards, some of whom had been floating "pool men" for a time and had thus worked at both Billingham and Wilton, described the lower management at Billingham in the early 1960s as being "much more friendly and helpful". There was clearly a difference in the concern for people on the two sites. Here a Wilton manager captures some of the social system differences between the sites north and south of the Tees:

A friend of mine from Dyestuffs Division in Manchester had regular contact with both Nylon Works Billingham and Nylon Works Wilton. He said they were quite different. When you came into Billingham you came into something approaching a family concern, a human organisation with a social organisation attached to it. Going to Wilton – it's clinically clean. But it's just like going into a hospital. There's nothing wrong. Everything is right, but it certainly ain't a social organisation. That was probably 1960s, but I suspect that's still true today [in 1976].

An experienced industrial relations manager at Wilton had this to say of the origins and implications of the differences between Billingham and Wilton:

Billingham is ICI, the place is ICI. Wilton isn't ICI. Wilton is a farming village, and we draw our labour from the centre of Middlesbrough and East Cleveland, and there is nothing like an ICI identity at Wilton in the way there is at Billingham. Wilton is ICI, but not with the same local, family associations as at Billingham. At Wilton we have a more business-oriented relationship. Like we come to work and we go home, and it's not the same at Billingham. That shows in a number of ways. Relationships between site managers and shop stewards here are very different from Billingham. They are much closer, they have more docile shop stewards who are not as politically motivated (with a small "p") as our shop stewards. Our shop stewards have a history of political aspirations within their union and within the district trade union organisations. Consequently, they have a very privileged position in terms of knowledge. Our shop stewards see themselves in an advantageous position because they sit on district committees, and in some cases national trade union and governmental bodies. They present themselves in a different way and this alters their relations with management. Managers feel vulnerable in that situation and that builds up resentment from managers . . . The shop stewards here at Wilton haven't the time and don't like to be huddled together in a hotel boozing with management. I've not perceived a management desire to do this here either. The stewards want to be negotiating all the time. They like to be sat at the other side of a table negotiating, tackling management, and management has done exactly the same now . . . unconsciously we must have colluded together to create this culture.

Wilton had grown very rapidly in the 1950s, there was also the constant change as plant after plant was built and commissioned, and the composition of the labour force on the site was in continual flux as waves of ICI and non-ICI construction workers swept in and off the site. Table 22 shows the rapid increase of ICI payroll and monthly staff employed on the site between 1946 and 1957. Table 22 also indicates both the large number of non-ICI contractors' men on the site and the fluctuations in their numbers associated with ICI's capital expenditure activities. These contractors brought onto the site a different tradition of industrial relations from that developing in the chemical industry and in ICI, and added their contribution to the rather unstable, brittle, and self-interested culture at Wilton. As a shop steward with trade union

TABLE 22   Employment growth on the Wilton site, 1946–1957*

Year	ICI payroll: production and construction workers	Non-ICI contractors	Total labour strength	Monthly staff
1946	86	745	831	250
1947	149	847	996	354
1948	474	914	1388	378
1949	959	1466	2425	411
1950	1861	1913	3774	436
1951	2358	1321	3679	727
1952	2672	1169	3841	837
1853	3390	1798	5188	985
1954	4404	1268	5672	1270
1955	5654	2065	7719	1554
1956	6086	3747	9833	1849
1957	7015	1887	8902	2284

* Abstracted from House and Fullerton (1960).

experience on both sides of the Tees put it, the attitude which prevailed at Wilton was "every man for himself". Shortly we shall see there were elements of that kind of attitudes and behaviour amongst the managers in HOC division who grew up at Wilton.

Managerial organisation and culture: the Wilton site and Heavy Organic Chemicals Division

From a management point of view the problems of lack of control and integration on the Wilton site got so bad in 1968 that Wilton attracted the interest and scrutiny of a main board committee headed by a future chairman of the company, Sir Jack Callard (Roeber, 1975:169). The trigger for the setting up of the Callard Committee had been companywide trade union resistance to MUPS, ICI's productivity bargaining exercise. Nowhere was the resistance to MUPS better organised or more vociferous than on Wilton. Before long, changes in structure and top management behaviour became evident on the Wilton site and in HOC Division. The reasons for these changes have important historical roots, not only in the developing workplace culture on the Wilton site, but also the pattern of managerial organisation and culture that existed at Wilton generally and also in HOC Division.

Crucial to the development of both the workplace and management culture on the Wilton site was the decision made at Wilton's birth to allow each of the divisions who came on the site to be responsible for its own works. Each division retained complete technical and commercial control of its plants. The Wilton Council was set up to direct the site. This council was accorded the same status as a division board and was composed of the chairman of the boards of the divisions establishing plants there and senior officials of the council's central organisation at Wilton, i.e., the chairman, the managing director, engineering director, technical director, works and personnel director, and the chief accountant. The main functions of the central organisation under the Wilton Council were to plan the layout and development of the site, to provide all common power, maintenance, and transport services, with the co-operation of the divisions to help all employees and provide eating and other facilities, and to co-ordinate the company's labour policy throughout the site.

The Wilton Council functioned as *the* integrative device until 1962, and apart from its overriding service-providing and technology-building role, managed to generate "a strong sense of belonging". But the business difficulties of 1961 meant that "the company was hunting overhead, as it does periodically, and gave to a reluctant HOC division board the responsibility for running the Wilton site instead of the Wilton Council". This takeover is important to the rest of the story; first, because it throws some light on the culture and style of the new HOC division; and second, because the site later became a major source of industrial relations problems, and dealing with these problems helped to develop some aspects of OD in the division. One manager who was part of the Wilton Council's central organisation described the takeover in this way:

Really it was a model of how not to do it . . . It was done in a brutal and insensitive way. The whole of the Wilton Council board disappeared. The most notable of them was retired prematurely when that was tantamount to being caught raping your secretary or with your finger in the till . . . The HOC people moved in instantly and the head of almost every Wilton department was demoted or generally removed.

The same manager continued by contrasting the style and orientations of the old and new managements:

The Wilton organisation, as it was, had been very highly people oriented. We didn't have any operating responsibility so we knew our board. HOC was apparently highly achievement oriented but in the most ludicrously bullshit way. You got marks if you rushed in, rolled around, bit the carpet, tore your hair, and cried generally about the terribleness of the problems you were facing, and then rolled back minutes later and said: "Oh! by the way, I managed to sort those out." Enthusiasm and efficiency were equated with long hours and apparent dedication to the cause.

This description is more colourful than most, but it complements the descriptions given by other managers of a young, aggressive, highly technical, managerial culture. Asked in broad terms what adjectives he would use to describe the HOC/PCD managerial culture, one manager said:

I joined HOC in 1960 – it has consistently through all the 1960s and for much of the 1970s seen itself and been seen by others as young, aggressive, Americanised in many ways. There has been an American approach to a lot of things, technology, marketing, aggressive, rash, go go – all these types of adjectives and I think that lasted right through until the mid-1970s.

The managers and consultants asked to describe what the concept of a good manager was in HOC were highly consistent in mentioning, "technical competence and applied intelligence"; "highly task oriented and hierarchically conscious with a strong loading of a tough use of authority"; "very sharp, aggressive, fairly authoritarian, the ability to answer every question". One manager rounded these kinds of statements out a bit by describing the kinds of criteria which made you promotable in HOC:

I think the general feeling would be that people are promoted on a fairly short-term basis. If they are successful in completing a job, like starting up a new plant, then that counts for more than the longer-term thinking . . . So probably the image is that professional success in your job, ability to keep your people under control, and to have the answers when required, goes a long way.

This picture of hierarchically conscious, rather cocky, growing, optimistic, and technologically aware division, is highly congruent with the evolution of the division's business throughout the 1960s which involved continuous expansion and building of highly capital-intensive plant. In this period Wilton became the largest concentration of investment in ICI, the glamorous power station for the downstream fibres and plastics businesses. Psychologically, as Roeber (1975:119) has argued, Wilton and HOC division represented a large part of ICI's claim to a place in the modern chemical world and for much of the 1960s it was all go go, and quick promotion for the high flyers in HOC.

All this must have appeared in stark contrast to the managers of Billingham Division who were just about to go through first a technological, and then a period of social, innovation on the Billingham site. Perhaps because some of the managers of the new HOC Division had come from Billingham Division, perhaps also because of the differences in the two divisions' business fortunes at that time, and maybe also because throughout the 1960s and up until 1974 the headquarters of HOC/PCD Division was at Billingham, only a quarter of a mile from the Billingham Division headquarters, there was an active, almost conscious attempt by the HOC managers to be different from "the hidebound, gentlemanly, paternalistic" Billingham management scene. Two HOC managers had this to say about the differences between HOC and Billingham:

> Certainly in the late 1960s there were many senior people in the division who were the young guys when the division was born. Then it was small and they knew each other. They were the pioneers and they were going to show that they were different from bloody Billingham. That's part of the reason for this technological efficiency culture.

* * *

> HOC, when set up, drew on the younger, more intolerant members of the old Billingham Division. We were much more intolerant of red tape. We were prepared to change things and discuss things . . . Since those days, HOC has gone through more organisational [structure] change than Agriculture . . . in this division we are operating in much more rapidly moving business environment. It's used to change. I see Agricultural Division as being more rigid in its attitude to structural change, less willing to undertake it.

The above characterisation is in part correct. Certainly the organisation structure at Billingham did not change radically throughout the 1960s and 1970s, but maybe they had enough to cope with in the way of technical and social change. In HOC it became one of the core beliefs and practices that the best way to make change in the organisation was by redesign, reappointment, and regrouping. These responses were already built into the HOC Division, itself, of course, a product of being structurally hived off from Billingham, well before the OD unit was born at HOC and acquired its initial organisational structure change task.

Throughout the 1960s HOC Division was structurally organised on a functional basis. Figure 8 shows the top of the division's organisation chart in 1969. Within this structure "the real power lay with the deputy chairmen", and without contradiction, in the mid-sixties managers commented that in a very capital-intensive and capital-growing division, "it was those parts of the division

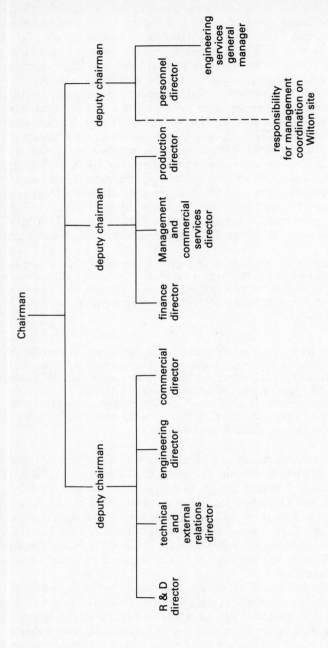

FIGURE 8 HOC Division: top organisation chart 1969

concerned with capital spending and development that were always seen as important". This meant that Technical Department was very powerful functionally, to be followed by marketing and production. Marketing (commercial) increased in power relative to technical areas in the late 1960s and 1970s as the amount of HOC/PCD product sold within ICI declined from 85% to around 60% or less with a vastly expanded business. Personnel for much of the 1960s was seen "as a service department outside the real business", but they increased in influence as the industrial relations and other people-related problems were given more attention at ICI main board level, and as industrial relations conflict broke out into the open on the Wilton site at the end of the 1960s.

Although production was strong at HOC Division, it never acquired the singular and pre-eminent position it did at Billingham Division. The focus of HOC production strength was at the works manager rather than at the director level, and although the works managers had prestige and a clearly defined position, the real prestige lay in the headquarters departments where the technical and marketing people were. Although engineering was influential at times at HOC, it and R&D were much less important in the history and development of HOC than they had been at Billingham Division and were regarded by the managers interviewed at HOC as being on a distinct plane lower in power than were the triumvirate of technical, marketing, and production.

The recurring conflicts mentioned in HOC Division in the 1960s were primarily interdepartmental ones. Most often referred to were conflicts over the allocation of resources between functions, and issues about which department controlled a piece of new capital investment as it proceeded through its various phases. These conflicts were seen to be persistent right up until the organisational changes of 1972 strengthened the business areas. As one OD unit member put it, "it was co-ordination without authority". These issues have been partially resolved but re-emerge to some extent between the business areas. When pressed, managers did indicate that there were recurring industrial relations problems but, in their view, these were not the major source of problems. In fact, by 1965 when MUPS was presented to Olefines Works on the Wilton site and ran into the strongest trade union resistance, it became very clear that there was an enormous power vacuum on the site which the trade union organisation filled. HOC had not been discharging their responsibilities as managers of the Wilton site. In a situation where managers were conflicted in their loyalty to the site or their parent division, "that could only be decided in favour of the divisions – which controlled the managerial reward systems . . . the dynamics of the site management were now completely wrong: there was no individual with an interest in running the site as a unit, nor with the power and authority. On the contrary, there was a confusing and conflicting web of responsibility and power in which none of the interrelated systems matched" (Roeber, 1975:122). The Wilton site had to put its house in order, doing that also required complementary organisational and people changes in HOC Division. Out of both of those requirements permeated the first use of OD technologies and ideas at Wilton, and in HOC Division.

MUPS/WSA and the Wilton site, 1965–72

MUPS/WSA, the companywide productivity bargain, has been extensively explored by Roeber (1975) and we have considered it and its intertwining with the evolution of OD in Chapters 4, 5, and 6.

MUPS (Manpower Utilization and Payment Structure) emerged in the company in 1965 as an agreement between the company and its Trades Union Advisory Committee to work towards greater manpower flexibility in keeping with the changing competitive, technical, and social developments which the company faced. Crucially, the attempt was to go beyond a straight productivity bargain of the type which became common in the UK in the late 1960s, to develop more joint problem-solving between company and unions, and to reduce the rigidities of bargaining itself. As such, it was recognised that there would be much bargaining about bargaining, that much time would be required, and that "trials" would need to be conducted at various sites to hammer out the agreement in practice. In the event it took about seven years and an extensive revision of the original guidelines (MUPS became WSA – the Weekly Staff Agreement – in 1969) before the agreement was in place across the company.

One works at Wilton (Olefines Works) was chosen for one of the first trials, partly because the company expected Wilton to be a difficult case. It more than lived up to that expectation.

As we have mentioned, the overall responsibility for the management of the Wilton site had been given, in 1962, to the HOC Division. Despite the fact that most of its own expanding production plant was located on this site, the divisional headquarters remained at Billingham, north of the river and the divisional management showed no great enthusiasm for site management. Thus by the mid-1960s the only effective sitewide "managing" bodies at Wilton were shop steward committees.

The shop stewards were naturally suspicious of MUPS on the basis that it was handed down to them initially by the company and by their national officials. And the craft unions were particularly suspicious of the "flexibility" aims which they saw as an obvious basis for the erosion of the hard-won skills and prerogatives which defended their membership. In addition, one must not lose sight of the issue of money; it was not clear that the proposed levels of payment under MUPS were sufficiently attractive. Some craftsmen had built up quite high levels of earnings in the existing, complex payment scheme with its estimated incentive bonus and with overtime.

In any case one group of stewards at Wilton (the AEUW stewards) refused to take part in even the initial talks about the first trial of MUPS at Wilton. They were soon joined by their other craft colleagues. It is important to remember that at Wilton and on other ICI sites there are essentially two separate, but interlinked, sides to production. The plant is operated to maintain a series of chemical processes which transform oil into intermediate chemicals. The managers of this side of the business are largely graduate chemists and the operators are general workers – mainly members of the T&GWU. An important aspect of MUPS was to recognise reward and maximise the flexibility in these jobs which became increasingly important with the development of giant and highly interdependent plant. This plant, however, requires construction and maintenance and this, engineering, side of production is managed largely by engineers and manned by members of craft unions. In the middle 1960s some 2000 men worked in these areas at Wilton and they essentially blocked any significant progress on MUPS for several years, despite the fact that slow progress was being made elsewhere in the company.

By 1968 the setting up of the Callard Committee to focus main board attention on the problems within MUPS was also a signal that the Wilton site and HOC management constituted something of a negative landmark in the company. In particular a running battle was developing between the company's central personnel department, which was the architect and prime mover behind MUPS, and senior HOC managers who were arguing for more local authority and the development of "mini-MUPS", more adapted to local conditions. This was never granted, but the overall package was redesigned centrally and emerged as WSA in 1969.

There are many colourful and in the main consistent descriptions from managers of the Wilton site problems of the period 1965–68. In the search for causes of the lack of control on the site most managers talked of their HOC colleagues at that time as "not wanting the people problems of the site", or of "only being interested in the Olefines plants and couldn't care less about the rest". The site works managers "went their own way. They didn't meet."[1] There "was a tendency of some works managers to run their works as private feifdoms answerable only to some distant prince" back in their division. "The disintegration that started was very obvious . . . the unions picked this up and very rapidly started playing off one works management against another . . . it was near to cracking up. Productivity was appalling. Labour relations were terrible. Nobody at any level was co-operating – except the unions." By this time the senior shop stewards on the site had organised themselves into an unofficial site committee complete with an off-site office and newsheet. As Roeber (1975:122) has argued, "the only body with a structure appropriate for operation on a sitewide basis, the power and will to do so was the unofficial committee of senior shop stewards".

ICI publicly acted to take a grip on Wilton in October 1968. HOC appointed its then personnel director, John Harvey-Jones, as a divisional deputy chairman with responsibility for the Wilton site. Harvey-Jones takes up the story:

> We had a site, in terms of its leverage on ICI which was absolutely key . . . There was a very strong shop stewards organisation, they faced a totally disparate and weak management who took their instructions from seven different divisions, each of whom couldn't give a —— about the totality . . . The problem became how to get a grip of the management without the use of hierarchical power – because I couldn't get that. I tried but it was just too much for the main board to swallow.

[1] This was not literally true. The works managers did physically at least meet at a Works Managers Committee every Monday, but this was not at that time an effective site-wide policy or co-ordinating body.

Harvey-Jones later described his objectives in these terms:

> I tried to do three things. The first was to try and get management to have some mutuality of respect and some identity of interest. So I had to get a grip on them and remove some of the disintegrative interventions from the divisions and from the centre (Millbank). The second thing was to try to rebalance the power between management and shop stewards. We solved it really by taking and winning a number of quite small strikes, culminating by firing the leader of the shop stewards committee. The third thing was to try to introduce a totally different style of management on a more collaborative, problem-solving basis.

While the above objectives were being pursued, Harvey-Jones and the chairman of HOC Division adopted a deliberate public relations strategy towards Millbank to try to improve the perceptions of the site and to give themselves room to make the changes which were needed. There were then three related elements in the site development strategy which emerged in the period 1968–72. These concerned:

1. Site management committees
2. The Coverdale programme for management development
3. Continuing negotiations with the trade unions on WSA

As regards the first of these, a number of co-ordinating committees were introduced or strengthened. The most senior of these was the Wilton co-ordinating committee which was made up of a deputy chairman from each of the five divisions with works on the site. It was chaired by John Harvey-Jones and served the important function of symbolising a high-level commitment as well as providing a forum for policy initiatives.

The most important committee in all this was probably the works managers committee which already existed, but which Harvey-Jones used as a central focus for his efforts towards "siteliness", as it was called. The works managers were the senior, landed representatives of the various divisions and had, in effect, become barons on the site. Besides spending a lot of time with this group, Harvey-Jones sent them on a Coverdale course, and got agreement from their divisions to include his assessment of them in their annual appraisals.

In addition a number of other cross-site committees were set up at lower levels – for example for engineering management. All of these things served to provide a statement of purpose and a framework for co-ordination and exchange of ideas, not least in regard to the continuing issues of WSA.

The second major strand of the change strategy was an attempt to put some flesh on the bones of this framework in the form of a common managerial language and set of procedures as developed in the site Coverdale programme. The basic building blocks of this programme were one-week courses. These courses aim at developing a common "systematic approach to problem-solving" by giving small groups of managers (who do not normally work together) a series of problems to solve. The emphasis was on the recurrent *processes* of group problem-solving, such as information-gathering, planning, acting and reviewing, and on the need to avoid losing sight of consciously managing these under the weight of detailed tasks.

The courses were run by a combination of Coverdale staff and Wilton managers who were seconded to do this training and to co-ordinate the programme. The first, abbreviated, courses were run for works managers in January 1969 and by the end of 1970 more than 1000 managers and supervisors had been through the courses. The programme continued on a diminishing scale through 1971. The total cost of the programme was estimated at about £300,000. Assessment of its value varied among those involved. To an extent the programme was itself hampered by the balkanisation problems which it was to help solve, because some works and their top management were more enthusiastic than others, and it was generally hard to get commitment to cross-works follow-up projects. In addition, it should be noted that the management of the engineering activity (ESW – Engineering Services, Wilton) opted out of Coverdale and developed their own PERA-based programme for supervisors. Nevertheless, the programme contributed considerably to the development of a common language and to the sharing of common problems across the site, particularly at middle managerial levels.

The third major strand of Wilton's development during this period was the continuation of attempts to get the MUPS/WSA negotiations under way. In the winter of 1969–70 a senior craft shop steward was fired and, after arbitration, the dismissal stood and a few months later a brief strike by general workers petered out with no gain to the strikers. A number of managers remember these events as morale-boosting demonstrations, for the first time in years demonstrating that the Wilton management could stand up for itself. But the deadlock on negotiations remained, and it was now well into its fifth year.

The deadlock was really only broken in the autumn of 1970 when the company, from the centre, made a major policy shift to allow individual unions to "go on" to WSA rather than sticking to the insistence that sites "go on" as a whole. What this meant at Wilton was that the general workers accepted WSA and the disparity in the pay rates forced the craft unions to follow in 1971. As Roeber (1975:133) has expressed it, "The management got their agreement, or a form of it; the craft unions got their pay increases. Neither side got much else. There was little change in the direction of more flexible working."

This is, perhaps, an overharsh judgement made in the light of the original ambitious aims of MUPS/WSA and of the greater successes achieved at other sites. After all the resistance, even a limited agreement made without the incidence of a major strike must be regarded as an achievement. In addition, the Coverdale training and the development of site management committees were beginning to show results. In 1970 the chief sponsor of these activities, John Harvey-Jones, was promoted to the chairmanship of the HOC Division. The problems of HOC's stewardship of the large, multi-divisional site, with its expanding and complex technology were by no means solved, but a start had been made and the exhausting evolution of MUPS/WSA was over.

HEAVY ORGANIC CHEMICALS/PETROCHEMICALS DIVISION ORGANISATION
DEVELOPMENT UNIT: AN OVERVIEW

The life histories of organisation development activities in Agricultural
Division and Petrochemicals Division could not be more different. One
difference subsequently crucial to the fate and impact of OD in both divisions
was how OD was born in each division. A further difference was in how each
activity was structured once in existence, and there were still further differences
in the kind of organisation changes attempted by each group, and the strategies
each group used to build networks of contact and otherwise influence their
respective environments. It should also be apparent by now that both OD
groups were born into quite different organisational contexts, although they
were created within a year of one another, in different divisions of the same
company. Their fate was also quite different. OD in Agricultural Division,
albeit in a form quite unlike its birth, can still be said to be alive in 1983;
whereas the OD unit in Petrochemicals Division (PCD) was born in May 1970
and had ceased to exist both as a structured unit and virtually as an activity by
November 1973. As a former member of the PCD OD unit later crisply put it:

> "OD [in PCD] *was* the OD unit – however much we as individuals within it tried
> to explain it to others. The need for the OD unit being over, there was no further
> need for "OD".

The OD unit was born in 1970 as HOC Division was experiencing
temporary but difficult business conditions. At the bottom of a trading cycle the
division was barely profitable and senior managers were looking with discom-
fort at data from studies of the division's international competitors which
suggested that high relative manning levels and low manpower productivity
were potential problems threatening the long-term profitability of the division.
In, for HOC, a quiet period in terms of capital sanctioning and expenditure,
some members of the HOC board were also questioning the extent to which the
still largely functional organisation in the division provided the business focus
and orientation necessary to flourish in an increasingly crowded and competitive market for petrochemicals. There was also the more limited problem of
what to do with a 90-strong Management Services Department which had
grown steadily throughout the 1960s on the back first of all of traditional work
study and work measurement skills and then more recently in association with
the company Staff Development Programme (SDP) and new knowledge and
skills in management training and the behavioural sciences.

Without anticipating too much of the forthcoming story, it became clear that
this Management Services Department was vulnerable in a number of counts.
Its sheer size as an overhead unit in a division experiencing financial problems
meant that senior managers began to scrutinise its role and impact. Its core
technology, work study and work measurement was now obsolete given that ICI
had with its WSA agreement abandoned incentive systems of payment, and yet

the management services operation was continuing to compete against the newer problem-solving technology of operations research/systems analysis being housed in the rival Central Investigation Department.

In short, what happened was that the Management Services Department was sacrificed and its personnel scattered to various parts of the division. Tom James, the manager of the now defunct Management Services Department, was asked to join a senior technical manager, Bill Heath, and an experienced production manager to form a task force "to study the organisation of the division". This group of three shortly after acquired one of the old sections in the Management Services Department which had been called Organisation Development Projects. The leader of this section, Ken Ward and four others, joined the task force as a resource group. Within a short space of time the task force and resource group were formally designated the HOC Organisation Development Unit. The senior of the three managers in the task force, Bill Heath, was appointed manager of the OD unit.

The primary remit of the OD unit was set out in a memorandum to the HOC board dated 15 May 1970. It was "to study the organisation of the division as a total system and to recommend changes designed to increase efficiency of operation and simplification of management". Other parts of the OD unit's remit included studying interface problems between departments in the division and where appropriate, recommending changes in organisation. Other suggested work areas were "to select, in conjunction with heads of departments the next steps in changing management style", and "to revise and develop the training programme for the division".

From the OD unit's beginning there was an uneasy split between the organisation structural aspects of their work, and their more behavioural process work. This split almost exacly corresponded to the board level organisation study given to the task force component of the unit, and the extension and continuation of SDP work by the more junior members of the OD unit who had been the rump of the Organisation Development Projects section from the old Management Services Department. This business-behavioural split in the group was never the object of group interest or energy. In contrast to the early days in Agricultural Division, the leadership of the OD unit was resistant to behavioural group development of the unit itself. This may be related to the visibility and high status of the original task force trio and the pressures on that trio to produce.

This the task force did. They prepared a report recommending organisation changes which would have strengthened the product and business areas vis-à-vis the functional managers. Their report was noted but shelved because in 1971 an enlarged HOC Division became Petrochemicals Division and the division became fully involved in coping with the consequences of merging with parts of the old fibres and dyestuffs operations. But the trio's division organisation study had given the OD unit visibility and broad-but-shallow top-level involvement and set precedents for unit activity. The production manager member of the original trio left the OD unit in 1971 to help with the amalgamation of parts of the old fibres division.

The behavioural work of the OD unit was mainly led by Ken Ward. Most of this work related to SDP and in the main was located with middle managers in non-dominant areas of the division, i.e. primarily research and development and engineering. With the exception of a few section managers, this team-building and group-process work was treated with reserve and scepticism. By 1971 there was much cynicism about effort spent on SDP and alarm even amongst some senior managers about the humanistic values propounded by some of the members in the behavioural wing of the OD unit. The board level network of the more senior members of the OD unit generated suspicion and wariness among senior managers rather than trusting relations based on client requests for help. Cynicism amongst middle managers about SDP and the OD unit's association with it, and wariness amongst senior managers were all intensified by the sizeable drop in monthly staff numbers in PCD from 4890 in 1971 to 4276 in 1972.

Early 1972 was a watershed in the fortunes of the OD unit. With the production manager of the original task force trio already gone, early in 1972 the OD unit lost its manager Bill Heath. The old rival of the Management Services Department, the Central Investigation Department had been wound up and a new advisory group – the Central Resource Group – created. Bill Heath was appointed manager of this Central Resource Group. Neither of the two senior members of the OD unit were replaced, nor were two junior members who left. What remained was a small team of ex-Management Services Department people. Tom James was appointed manager of an OD unit that now contained himself, Ken Ward, and three others.

Throughout the middle of 1972 and into 1973 the major focus of the OD unit's efforts was another study of the division's structure and organisation. James took the lead and co-ordinating role in this study and worked with the American external consultant Ron Mercer in supplying information to the board. Mercer also worked as a process consultant to the board. This time no external events were there to crowd out the impact of the OD unit's work, and structure changes were thought through, adopted, and implemented in the division.

With the departure of Heath and the production manager, the OD unit in 1972 had a more cohesive and consistent behavioural orientation. But Tom James himself was heavily committed in working on the division reorganisation, and, for the most part, he left the other members to work on with the few clients they still had at the middle management levels of the research and development and engineering functions. James did not push to restore the OD unit's dwindling strength and other members, somewhat resentful of this, looked for positions elsewhere in ICI and outside it. By the end of 1973 with the divisional restructuring over and Harvey-Jones the division chairman and the OD unit's chief board sponsor on his way to the ICI main board, the end of the unit was in sight. In November 1973 Tom James was appointed to a companywide internal consultancy role and left PCD. Shortly thereafter the OD unit was would up. "Its task considered completed and its original sponsors having moved on."

ANTECEDENTS OF THE ORGANISATION DEVELOPMENT UNIT

The description and partial analysis of the birth and evolution of OD activities in Agricultural Division in the previous chapter emphasised the extent to which both the immediate business, technical, and organisational context, the long-term history of business development and culture in the division, and some features of the immediate pre-history of OD, shaped and moulded the career of organisation development activities in that division. New organisational activities do not spring into life unencumbered by the historical and present-day context. In most aspects of organisational functioning the past weighs a heavy hand; and not just in the sense of imposing constraints but also in providing enabling conditions and opportunities. On balance the argument can be made that in Agricultural Division efforts to use the specialist OD resources to help stimulate various kinds of organisational changes were facilitated more by historical and more immediate antecedent conditions than they were hindered by them. Equally crucially perhaps in Agricultural Division a case can also be made that the OD consultants there understand enough about the context in which they attempted to make their interventions to be able to adjust the content and locus of those interventions to at times match the context. This ability to understand the historical and emerging present-day context and to *mobilise the context* to help justify the content and process of particular changes is a crucial general aspect of the politics of creating change in organisations.

I shall return to take a more detailed and considered look at the relationship between the broad historical and present-day context surrounding specialist-led attempts to create change and the efficacy of the strategies for change pursued by those specialist groups in Chapter 12 of this book. For the time being, one aspect of the context which influenced the birth, evolution, and subsequent impact of OD in PCD were some features of the immediate pre-history of the OD unit. It is to these antecedent conditions and their role in shaping how and why the OD unit came into existence that I now turn.

There are three aspects of the immediate prehistory of organisational development in PCD which influenced the character of OD in the division, and the tasks and fate of the OD unit. One of these, MUPS/WSA, the centrally enforced companywide productivity bargain, harshly exposed both the shortcomings of the pattern of management–union relationships on the Wilton site, and one of the root causes of those shortcomings – Wilton management's failure both to communicate with one another through any systems of coherent organisation, and indeed their capacity and interest in identifying with the site. The way Harvey-Jones, the then deputy chairman of HOC Division, put together a development strategy composed of reactivating some old site management committees and creating some new ones, together with his launching of the Coverdale programme for management development – all to increase managers' capacity to identify with and control the site – has already been described. These efforts were the first explicit attempt to introduce organisation development activities on the site. It is important to say in passing here that OD was being used as a management tool not so much in a positive sense to assist a locally generated change which was working, but almost in an atmosphere of crisis and retribution, to assist an externally imposed change process which was clearly not working. Apart from the massive coverage amongst managers and supervisors of the Coverdale programme, and some brief team-building work stimulated by a member of the Wilton site office, that was the extent of specialist OD involvement on the Wilton site.

At the time of the creation of the OD unit in May 1970 a Wilton site organisation development co-ordinator was appointed with a role "to act as a focal point between the Wilton management, the HOC board, and the OD unit". An upshot of the appointment of this OD co-ordinator was that nothing further of an identifiable OD character occurred on the Wilton site and the new OD unit was given clear instructions "to keep off the Wilton site". With the culture of management–union relationships as they were on the site, and with the WSA package still a focal point for conflict, this was not the context, or probably the time, to initiate the kind of OD-led joint problem-solving work which was getting off the ground across the river at Billingham. Whatever other directions for developing OD activities were to present themselves on the Wilton site and in HOC Division, it was already fairly clear before the OD unit was created that one avenue that was firmly closed was the organisation and functioning of the Wilton site, and the pattern of relationships between management and union.

If MUPS/WSA at Wilton could hardly be characterised as a catalyst or facilitator for OD activities, what role did the other two antecedents to the creation of the OD unit have? I have in mind here the activities and image of the Management Services Department (MDS), the department where the majority of the OD unit members came from, and SDP, the particular vehicle they were using to project themselves and OD technologies prior to the creation of the OD unit.

When in 1966 Tom James arrived at Wilton from Millbank to become manager of the MSD at HOC Division, the management services activity was a strange mixture of method study 15%, work measurement 25%, apprentice training school 50%, and management training 10%. Shortly after he arrived, James appointed Ken Ward as head of a small section in MSD. This section was initially called Organisation and Management Projects Section and busied itself trying to introduce management by objectives into the division. By 1968 Ken Ward's section was being called Organisation Development Projects, and then in 1970 on the creation of the OD unit Ward and two of his four-man group became the rump of the "behavioural" wing of the OD unit. In terms of activities the continuing thread from the Organisation Development Projects section of the MSD to the OD unit was Ken Ward's group's involvement in helping to implement the companywide staff development programme. The SDP work began in 1969.

In a situation where half of his department was the apprentice training school, and a fair proportion of the remainder was based on the fading technologies of work study and work measurement, James was probably under-stating the point in contending "we didn't have very high credibility. We weren't seen as a driving force and we weren't." The more up-to-date management problem-solving technologies of operations research and systems analysis were at that time housed in the chillingly named Central Investigation Department. If James's MSD was to have a growth area, the two most promising contenders in 1966 were management training and the new section doing MBO work being built up by the forceful and energetic Ken Ward.

Ward and his most regular co-worker Brown, partly through the novelty of their techniques and message, partly from their obvious energy and commit-ment, and helped also by their own background and experience as scientists, were able to stimulate interest in their work in some of the sections and units in the engineering and research and development (R&D) functions. Pushing out from their base of MBO work, they sought to involve themselves in team-building, role clarification, and other intra- and inter-group problem-solving work in whatever parts of the HOC management system they could. Early attempts to use MBO in production environments had been rebuffed, "some works managers wanted to use MBO to screw people down rather than as a development thing". Ward and his team seemed to have more success getting work either "to revitalize" a unit such as Technical Services and Market Development which had "lost prestige and potency", or where they were charged by a director to assist a department such as R&D which was seen to be "ineffective". Some of the middle managers in those departments at that time later acknowledged that Ward and Brown's work had been "helpful" and "useful" but Ward and his section got little political capital from this work. In the case of the Technical Services and Market Development section, it was because "that unit folded because of divisional economic problems" shortly after the Ward intervention, and in the case of the R&D function because consultant–client relationships were always strained there. As Brown said, "We were put into that department."

While Ward and Brown were trying to get their behavioural work off the ground, James was asked in 1967 by the division chairman to launch an operations improvement programme (OIP). As James later said, "some senior company personnel people had been to the United States and seen this at Union Carbide. The chairman agreed to try it, along with two other divisions. I was put in charge of doing it." The principle of the exercise was that all monthly staff should submit ideas for improving anything, and each staff member would be involved in processing the ideas. Departmental OIP co-ordinators were set up and "for a time suggestions poured in ranging from the trivial to the useful". But ten months after its launch, James went back to the chairman and said, "This has outlived its usefulness ... We stopped it and in effect it died completely." Another member of the division cited the OIP as an example of the HOC Chairman's superficial adventurousness. He took "adventurous acts but didn't have a fundamentally adventurous philosophy".[2] Triggered by the

[2] Unlike George Bridge, who in 1967 was still personnel director of Billingham Division.

Callard Committee, a more cohesive and consistent set of acts were just about to be carried out by the flamboyant HOC deputy chairman, Harvey-Jones. Way down in the organisation hierarchy in Ward's section of the MSD, "1968 was a worrying time. We were searching out and selling possibilities [for change]. Our ability to operate was dependent on our own credibility." In March 1969 with the launching of yet another central initiative, the company SDP, Ward's section was given a temporary but forceful push forward. Brown later said, "It was the SDP programme which was the company policy which created a legitimate framework for doing more OD work. It was a crucial thing for getting OD forward in ICI." A more jaundiced view of SDP might be that in the short term SDP represented "a great leap forward" for OD, but in the middle and long term it more accurately became a great step backwards for those internal OD consultants closely associated with it.

If WSA became son of MUPS, then SDP may be construed as cousin of MUPS. In exchange for demonstrable short-term increases in productivity and improvements in working practices, MUPS had brought ICI weekly staff wage increases which had substantially reduced the differentials between weekly staff and the junior reaches of monthly staff. At the end of 1968, it looked as if further increases to weekly staff under the shortly to be negotiated WSA, would reduce those differentials even further. Staff discontent was becoming apparent on some of the MUPS sites and there was always the fear that "if the company was not prepared to look after the interests of junior staff, there were staff unions only too prepared to do so instead" (Roeber, 1975:183). Politically, there was also the requirement at this time that all pay awards had to be referred to the National Board for Prices and Incomes and justified in terms of productivity improvements.

SDP was launched in March 1969 by the ICI Central Personnel Department with objectives and procedural arrangements similar to MUPS. In each division a board-level SDP review panel was created, a divisional co-ordinator, departmental co-ordinators and a divisional SDP resource group which sometimes drew on the services of external constulants. Salary increases were to be awarded to staff when the divisional SDP review panel agreed that objectives had been agreed and set for each work group and department, and working practices at the individual and group level had been reviewed and increases in effectiveness made. Such reviews had to involve all members of staff. Aside from "an exceptional and demonstrable improvement in organisational effectiveness in the short term", the other objective of SDP was "in the longer term, an environment in which major improvements occur naturally and continually without being enforced or imposed".

With the experience in goal setting and group process work from MBO and its derivatives under his belt, Ken Ward saw SDP as "a spring-board for developing a divisionwide initiative". Ward proposed a structure for handling the SDP training which involved taking groups of staff off together in their back-home work groups on three-day workshops. The workshops were to use group exercises on process and problem-solving in order to stimulate diagnostic and action planning work on back-home departmental role interface, group interface, and team-building problems. The scale of the task – SDP was meant to cover all the monthly staff[3] of HOC Division – required focussing the three-day workshops on training people to do the work themselves. Ward's proposal was accepted by the HOC board and he and his team threw themselves into it with gusto. Here was a clear task, and apparently some measure of board support and legitimacy for Ward and his organisation development projects section to do it. Ward was later to say:

Really we filled a vacuum. We took it [SDP] over. That was a massive intervention. We trained about 50% of the division . . . here was a resource (us) to do something which had a lot of visibility and importance in the eyes of the board . . . We really did indoctrinate the whole division – though it didn't really stick everywhere.

There were two primary sources to evaluate the impact of SDP in HOC Division. One is a research report based on interviewing a sample of managers who had attended SDP workshops, together with the researcher's own observations from attending one such workshop (Summerfield, 1969). The other data were collected as part of this research some seven years later, in 1976. Both sets of data produce highly consistent patterns and conclusions. Summerfield (1969:3) began his report with the epitaph "until SDP becomes important to the people involved, it will not be successful". He went on to identify seven problems "attaching to and built into the programme which are hindering its acceptance and progress". These included a fear that SDP was a redundancy exercise; a suspicion that the HOC board was merely going through the motions to implement a change exercise spawned and imposed from Millbank; a lack of clarity what SDP was, and hoped to achieve; a belief that in the light of WSA, SDP was merely a sop to the staff with just a cost of living type of salary increase at the end of the exercise – and fundamentally that SDP was yet another "management gimmick" being peddled by the Management Services Department. In 1976 the managers and consultants we interviewed had these rather emphatic statements about SDP to offer:

My own personal feelings which you can have recorded are that it (SDP) was basically a waste of time, and everybody thought so. Behavioural science techniques were used to try to get people to think about their jobs when they should have been doing it anyway. (Senior Manager)

* * *

It was an imposed programme which created strains with senior managers, therefore managers did what was minimally required. (Internal Consultant) ·

* * *

The companywide numbers cutting exercise in 1971 made rather a nonsense of all the bold and hopeful SDP statements. People felt rather conned. (Internal Consultant)

---

[3] Approximately 3400 people in 1969

I think there was a general positive reaction in my group. I suppose that was not maintained because of the fact that it didn't achieve the expectations . . . But we had an oscillation, great – hell – well, better. (Manager)

* * *

It was a company initiative based on embarrassment at the effects of MUPS/WSA on differentials, so the reasons for doing it were all wrong – it didn't stick everywhere, once the money was paid, some groups abandoned the approach. (Internal Consultant)

Although attitudes to the concept and implementation of SDP were largely critical there were pockets of HOC Division, most often specialist units in R&D and Engineering, where managers felt that working relationships had been improved by the behavioural concepts and skills introduced by SDP. Some of these managers used the resources of the soon to be created OD unit. But SDP was no more than a pinprick for the still essentially technical and market-driven HOC/PCD management culture. If anything, SDP created a negative aftermath for any subsequent structured OD interventions that might possibly have come from within the HOC/PCD Division.

Here was something imposed substantially from the company centre with a commitment, forced, I think . . . It eventually boiled down to a control operation, concern with increases in salary. That to my mind has created a reaction. It has really inhibited any possibility of a programme that might be internally generated within the division with the same sort of objective. Because people will lift a lip and say that's just like SDP – and SDP is black . . . I think the market for interpersonal and intergroup stuff went when SDP went.

If SDP's real downfall was a function of its external origins and imposed implementation, and the poor fit between its essentially behavioural content, process, and message, in a technology- and marketing-dominated context; then the manner in which it was introduced by Ward and his team and their association with other "management gimmicks" from the Management Services Department didn't help either.

Ward and his section members recall their group in 1968 and 1969 as being highly task-oriented with that part of the group with strong interests in the behavioural sciences, as being "enthused" and "highly committed". There was also the use of a distinctive language – "I suppose we tended to use jargon at that time because we thought we were the bee's knees. (Laughs.) Other people would comment not to use jargon, so we must have been using words that were not part of the division's culture." Ward's section also recall having somewhat distinctive values about "openness", "data rather than opinion", "boundaries not being sacrosanct – something to be pushed against and not accepted"; and of emphasizing the importance of "people values and growth potential" at work. This kind of subcultural distinctiveness earned them the labels "headshrinkers and trick cyclists" and a feeling that "we weren't very identified with the business". The fact that when Ward and Brown met OD people outside their division and company, "we were seen as way over towards the business orientation rather than to the behavioural side . . . so we saw ourselves as being very business oriented" perhaps emphasises rather than de-emphasises how far apart culturally the OD projects section in the Management Services Department was from the dominant concerns and values of HOC/PCD in 1968 and 1969.

But Ward's sections' high profile on the SDP activity also brought out into the open jealousy and resentment from other individuals and groups in HOC Division who may have laid down some specialist claim to be in the management training and OD business. "I have to be honest and say I really found them a bit unbearable, like I thought they were trying to teach me to suck eggs . . . and I really did believe that they had gone overboard on participation and team building, and neglected some of the values problems, and the functional aspects of organisations." Even Tom James acknowledged, "We were perceived to be going a bit far out in all this OD stuff – particularly in the training area . . . there was doubt and uncertainty among the senior management."

A long-term operator and survivor in the HOC/PCD management culture pinpointed the real affrontery about Ward's section was that they were beginning to offend the core of the HOC culture – its concern with hierarchy, structural clarity, and management control.

> Ward and Brown were doing their thing with SDP – they were working very hard on the autonomy self-direction axis. All of a sudden this became for real. Ward and his men had tapped some energy, some real dissatisfaction with what was a very mechanistic bureaucratic organisation. A lot of fears were expressed to me about loss of control in what was really a bottom-up situation with no commitment or understanding from almost any of the senior group . . . the director responsible was a systems man by training and didn't like this because it was kind of a "thousand flowers grow" thing – and that's a phrase we used. He was saying, "I don't like what's happening. I feel we're losing control." . . . You know we were starting by then early in 1970 to feel the first breath of the whirlwind on real economic stringency. Anyway, one day, out of the blue, the director says management services is to be disbanded. Bang! Caput! . . . the signs of the coming economic problems were already there to the senior people, so what a better way to get a name for yourself then by doing away with a department!

This director recalled his part in the downfall of management services in slightly different terms:

> When I got on the board there was an enormous Tom James' department (MSD) and there was the Central Investigation Department, and there was Tom James' fear that I was going to be unfair and support my old department against him. There was an almost universal whisper that Tom James had far too many people, and they farted about and wasted too much time. I dithered about and I consulted the deputy chairman . . . in the end I decided that good management required a touch of steel and in that I was backed by the deputy chairman and we did it . . . We wound up Tom James' department and, I think the OD unit was one of the valuable pieces of fallout from that.

And so the OD unit was born out of the ashes of the Management Services Department, not an auspicious beginning. James was told his old department was to be dismembered just after he returned from an OD course.

> It was a most astonishing bit of work. I had just been to Eastbourne learning about change, I was now being put into a role which was expected to make organisational change and I had just been obliged to force on my department a change which broke every rule in the OD book. I felt hurt for myself. But I felt worse for them . . . I couldn't get across to [the director responsible] the personnel problems he was giving me.

Ward later recalled the break-up of MSD "was really done in a most brutal way. There was a tremendous sense of hurt." Brown commented that part of the problem was that James was taken straight out of his old role and put onto the organisation structure task force:

> James was hardly able to manage the dissolution of the department, people felt very sore about that. People felt . . . we felt he'd deserted us. I felt that to some degree . . . but later it seemed to me that he was prevented from carrying out his job by the organisation.

With this kind of immediate prehistory, and with the nature of the task and leadership it was given, there seemed every likelihood that the OD unit at HOC/PCD would never be anything more than a tool, and possibly a temporary one at that, of the senior management of the division.

THE BIRTH: FROM TASK FORCE TO ORGANISATION DEVELOPMENT UNIT, 1970–72

Compared with the rather slower and arguably deeper process of evolution of OD resources in Agricultural Division, the birth of the OD unit in HOC/PCD was an instantaneous event. With board approval the three-man task force to study the division's organisation was in place in May 1970. Tom James had come from the now defunct Management Services Department. John Parker came into the trio as an experienced production man, and Bill Heath with his status as ex-manager of the powerful Technical Department was the leader of the task force. Shortly after the task force began their work, they acquired Ken Ward and most of the Organisation Development Projects section of the dismembered Management Services Department. Ward and his group of four were to be the resource group for the task force. Under pressure from the resource group, who "felt second-class citizens", the task force of three shortly agreed that all eight should go under the banner of the OD unit. Bill Heath was appointed manager of that unit.

Although the OD unit made an instantaneous appearance as an identifiable structured department, the departmental origins of its personnel, and in particular the mixed attitudes which already existed to Ward's section and the "zealous and forceful" manner they were introducing SDP, meant that the OD unit by no means started off attitudinally with a clean sheet. The OD unit also had the opportunity and the problem of being openly sponsored by the new chairman of the division, John Harvey-Jones, though formally they reported to the organisation and training director. Harvey-Jones had by this time gone some considerable way to successfully tackling the change problems of the Wilton site, and was now turning his not inconsiderable skills as a flamboyant leader and articulator of the need for change, to HOC Division. A paper Harvey-Jones wrote for the HOC board called "Very Long-Term Organisational Aims", about six months before the formal creation of the OD unit, contains some of the rationalisation which eventually appeared as the remit for the OD unit. In this paper Harvey-Jones talked of pressures to change our organisation from a realisation that "we cannot obtain sufficiently high productivity or efficient use of our people from the existing structure". There was also a recognition "that our present organisational structure is not meeting the changes in technological advance and human needs which are occurring both outside and inside the company". Harvey-Jones was also prepared to reinforce what he saw as "experiments towards a form of participative management", and to argue that increasingly he thought younger managers would be seeking clarity of objectives, within more flexible structures where there would be "complete frustration with rigid and authoritarian systems, and contempt for power derived from a hierarchical position".

Even coming from Harvey-Jones this must have been a pretty heady message for many senior managers in HOC Division to take, for as one manager said of the HOC/PCD management culture, "underneath the christian name bit we're a pretty bloody stuffy hierarchical organisation". Harvey-Jones later acknowledged that his predecessor had started the process of changing HOC Division, but that when he became chairman he saw OD resources as a tool to carry this process forward:

> I do not believe that running OD through Personnel or through Training gives it the best chance of success. Certainly my attempt was to try to get the thing linked through to some direct line management power . . . I saw a growing need to have OD consultants because my hope when I took over as chairman was to introduce a much more open management style. That was the first of the three objectives I set out when I became chairman. The others were slimming numbers and a fairly conventional profit objective . . . Heath, James and Parker, that was mine. I set it up as a task force. They were used by me, but were available to anybody else to help the process of change in the division that I saw as necessary . . . I used to drop in on that team of three about once a week. I used them as a sounding board and for specific tasks . . . eventually they wanted to become an OD unit rather than a task force.

Although Harvey-Jones created the original task force and then used it in a fairly direct and close fashion, there were early suspicions from his board about the task force, and Harvey-Jones had to deal with the wishes of some of the traditionalists in the division by appointing Heath and Parker to the original group. Harvey-Jones takes up the story:

When I became chairman my two deputy chairmen were both old, miles older than me . . . I had a major problem keeping one of them on board . . . The sort of way I wanted to run the division and the sort of division Chris wanted were just about at the opposite ends of the pole . . . When I set up that group [task force] Chris and the other deputy chairman were both petrified that I was going to have in it a bunch of long haired spooks who were going to upset everything . . . So when I set up that unit I did it with considerable debate with Chris and the other deputy . . . Bill [Heath] had tremendously high credibility particularly with Chris . . . and John Parker was one of the hardest nosed managers around the patch.

Harvey-Jones's recollections of the reasons for setting up the task force, and the areas it might work in, are confirmed by James, Heath, and Parker. Harvey-Jones had some fairly definite ideas about OD. He saw the need to expand the division's business, contract its manpower, and relax it in terms of its attitudes and behavioural processes. He saw the need "for more openness, frank talking". Judging from the comments made later both by the initial task force and members of the HOC board, some of the seeds of the OD unit's eventual destruction were there right at its birth. It is clear both that not all the members of his board accepted Harvey-Jones's vision of the future character of HOC Division, or of a role of OD in influencing that future character. There were quite different implicit assumptions in the board about the role of the OD unit. Some saw it – perhaps a very small minority – as a primarily behavioural way of improving existing processes. Others saw it as diagnosing needed structural change, and others saw it as largely contributing information to deal with the numbers/costs problem. Only Harvey-Jones saw these as linked. For example, Parker later commented that one of the deputy chairmen "saw us simply as a group of people who might help him in certain specific and numerate exercises – counting heads, etc. He was very competent – but not particularly oriented to people problems."

Another deputy chairman who was interested in organisation problems because he believed that "most of the division's problems would be solved by filter-free, accurate communication", was also seen to be "very strongly opposed to all this long-haired behavioural science stuff". A member of the board at that time acknowledged the differences on the board; the difficulties the OD unit would run into; but recognised there was some advantage in Harvey-Jones's approach to try and change HOC Division:

It sounded to me at the time to be a bit artificial. And that was the view of a lot of people in the division. It was a creation of John Harvey-Jones. I didn't really see how that particular group of people, Heath and Parker, although very able, would be able to bring much to bear on the organisation thing. I thought Tom James on his own would have made more sense . . . but the advantage of doing it that way was to hit the donkey [HOC] Division between the eyes with a brick. That's not a bad way of tackling the thing if you've got the power, the personality power.

But if the donkey was to be hit between the eyes with a brick, a further difficulty the task force and the OD unit had was that at birth the senior managers expected that the task force would only be given one, perhaps two, occasions to throw the brick. Both Heath and Parker recognised this was literally a short-term assignment to a task force. James also commented on the particular and temporary nature of their initial assignment:

> They created a task force that I think was perceived to be a one shot thing. The job was to work out what the division's organisation should be in ten years time. I think it was perceived that we'd do that, help begin implementing it and, in two years time go and do something else. Because of my OD training at Eastbourne I didn't agree. I thought we needed an on-going change unit, not endless, but not one shot.

The nature of the task force's rather singular and personal sponsorship, the mixed assumptions about its role, and the manner and form of its creation did not augur well for its impact or longevity, but in June 1970, Heath, Parker and James began their study of the HOC Division organisation. Initially the task force trio "were closeted a lot together, and we interviewed a lot of senior (not board) managers" about their views of the functioning of the present – largely functional HOC organisation structure. Even though the trio were themselves fairly senior managers who already had established relationships with the division senior manager group, and some measure of personal credibility from their previous functional roles, they ran into difficulties. One of the trio commented that they had credibility problems working as consultants – "we had to try to learn the skill of making an intervention fairly quickly". But their more basic difficulties derived from three other components of the change process they were part of.

In the first place they encountered problems with one of the core tenets of the functional, and hierarchical organisation they were seeking to analyse and change – the belief strongly held by many managers that "they should own and solve their own problems". This led to "a basic difficulty in getting over questions about what exactly was our role . . . what are these self-styled experts going to do? . . . particularly when each one of us was well known for what we are. In other words I was known as an experienced production man, so what am I going to talk to marketing about, or technical department?" Second, the trio had to live with the mixed images that came from being associated with the board. "We had a lot of relationships with senior members of the board. Some people saw this as a threat. Other people saw that we really didn't have all that much backing – so why bother? It could get you both ways." Finally, as one of the trio said "the process around the study was all wrong". The idea of the study had been largely Harvey-Jones's idea and few of the board members had been drawn into the data collection and analysis phases of the study.

Early in 1971 the trio produced a yellow paper – a paper meant for discussion rather than decision. This paper introduced the idea of a matrix organisation to the HOC board and senior managers, and recommended a strengthening of the product area managers against the functions. The yellow paper at that moment turned out to be a "lead balloon". One of the trio remarked:

The time constraint was always there. The listening constraint was always there. When we produced your yellow paper one of the deputy chairmen (broadly supportive of the trio's work) said "Your big problem, of course, is communicating with the board. You'll be lucky if some of them read it."

Those board members who did read it did not long concern themselves about local organisational changes for bigger structural changes were already under way, which only one or two members of the HOC board were aware of. Since early in 1970 a three-man working party of the ICI main board had been looking at company organisation in the light of "declining profitability in some business areas". The upshot of this main board working party was the reorganisation announcement made in early 1971 involving Nobel, Dyestuffs and Heavy Organic Chemicals Divisions and ICI Fibres Ltd. Out of this company reorganisation HOC Division became Petrochemicals Division and amongst other things acquired ICI's unprofitable nylon operations. Harvey-Jones as the HOC chairman had of course been consulted in this arrangement, but there was a widespread recognition amongst HOC senior managers "that the change was imposed by the main board with virtually no consultation with the division".

The impact of all this on the task group and their yellow paper was instantaneous. The yellow paper went out of sight and out of mind. With memories of previous amalgamations involving HOC, Harvey-Jones was determined there was to be no crude takeover by the old HOC Division of the former Dyestuffs and Fibres operations. "I instructed that none of the functional departments or the OD unit were to go tramping around saying you've got to do it this way, but that the Nylon people could come and ask for help." As it turned out, Parker was transferred out of the three-man task group and asked to discreetly assist with the merging of the new production facilities into the division. The OD unit's first attempt to influence structural change had been overtaken by events.

While Heath, Parker, and James had been working on their organisation study and writing the yellow paper, the other part of the OD unit, Ward's section from the disbanded Management Services Department, were in something of a state of limbo. By the middle of 1970 they found themselves a victim of the break-up of the Management Services Department, as a resource group to a task force which largely kept to itself, and in a situation where the former intensity of their work on SDP was fast declining as more and more of the division's managers passed through the programme and qualified for their salary increments. Faced with these uncertainties Ward, Brown and the others tried to focus some of the OD unit's energy on its role, purpose, and internal life.

Internal life of the OD unit, 1970–72

By the time Ward and the others appeared the task force trio had a clear task and had developed a very easy working relationship. "Heath was notionally the head but we operated as a triumvirate." But "we [the trio] were closeted a lot and this generated some suspicion ... which Ward and Brown raised. So Heath instituted an informal Monday morning meeting. Here we discussed pressures and priorities." These meetings were kept fairly task-oriented and businesslike. Heath resisted any off-site team building events of the kind practised by the Agricultural Division Swallow group, although occasionally the OD unit did use external consultants for discussions about "role, objective and strategy". But basically the two parts of the OD unit never gelled into a cohesive whole. The trio had a clear task and a powerful sponsor, the other members of the unit had to find their task and negotiate their sponsorship wherever they could. Given their association with the now discredited MBO, and the fast-becoming-discredited SDP, this was not easy. They were widely seen as "behavioural types". Heath was later to say "my view is that behavioural OD was, and still is an infertile field with this particular set of people" (the PCD managers).

From the creation of the OD unit there "was a difference of approach in the group which we were aware of, and referred to as a 'left–right' difference. The left were the behavioural types, and the right the structurally oriented, and we pulled each other's leg about it." Heath in particular was seen as "right wing", as being "miscast as the head of the OD unit", of being "suspicious of some of this behavioural stuff", and of finding "OD a bit embarassing to live with". Intellectually Heath was a firm believer that changes in managerial attitudes would only follow changes in organisation structure. There were also basic differences in the unit about values, and the way to create change. One member of the unit commented:

> The schism was Heath versus the rest, leaving Parker aside. In the early days Heath had no idea what the values of OD were. Before he left he had some idea but he didn't change his values ... For the rest there was a belief in change through ownership; that change is a learning process; values around the dignity of the individual.

A member of the behavioural wing said: "we valued openness, data not opinions, and confronting. None of these were shared by Bill Heath. He would be more political, more into power and power relationships. He was probably more of a realist than we were." But Heath's realism was later seen to be not at the service of the group but as a control strategy by the directors who recommended his appointment. "Certainly at the start of OD, and I'd like to emphasize this point, there was a distinct element of control as well as credibility. Bill Heath to my mind was there, part as a manager, part as a watchdog to see that these wild and woolly men didn't go clean off the rails." Another factor which divided the "right" and "left" wings was their commitment to OD as a vehicle for helping people. The left wing saw the right wing as treating their work just as "another job". The right wing saw the left wing as being overcommitted. "For some of them it almost amounted to dedication to the need to help people. In my opinion this at times led to over-confidence in their ability to help people."

No doubt partially influenced by their observations of work going on in Agricultural Division, the behavioural wing of the OD unit at PCD had visions of working with the Wilton shop stewards. But "the OD unit was not, and specifically agreed not to be concerned with payroll, because the Personnel Department have the problems of dealing with the payroll". Another member of the right wing agreed with Heath's clear intention of preventing the behavioural wing from getting involved with union matters. "Heath and I were dead against it. We felt we were not ready and certainly the people who were talking about it weren't ready." So unlike their opposite numbers in Agricultural Division the PCD OD unit "stood very clear and very separate from the personnel function". The one OD resource on the Wilton site who John Harvey-Jones had encouraged was located in the personnel function but he was described by members of the OD unit "as a colleague at a distance". The personnel function was described by the OD unit left wing members as "a great stopper rather than a great initiator". During the assimilation of part of the fibres business into PCD, one of the OD unit accompanied members of the engineering function to discuss their personnel concerns. "As a measure of how OD was seen by personnel, I was accused of being a shop steward."

By the summer of 1971 the lack of cohesion and direction in the nine-man OD unit was exacerbated by personnel changes. Parker left to work on the merging of new production facilities into PCD, and eventually resumed a successful career in the division as a works manager. With the end of the formal side of the SDP activity one of the OD unit was made redundant, and another individual was transferred to the personnel function. Of these three only Parker was replaced – by a production man more junior than himself. Heath meanwhile "was gradually losing interest, and focussed himself on the directors". With the yellow paper shelved Heath concentrated more and more on working with the directors on division business planning.

Towards the end of 1971, the director who had been instrumental in breaking up the Management Services Department partially, it was felt, because the MSD continued to compete with his "up-and-coming operations research/systems-based Central Investigation Department, himself left the division. With the CID's sponsor and protector gone, in characteristic fashion there was a further structural realignment. The CID was disbanded and a Central Resource Group created. This Central Resource Group became a new and fairly prestigious source of help on "one-off jobs the board saw as necessary in the economic forecasting, computer, production scheduling and planning, and strategic thinking" areas. Bill Heath was transferred from the OD unit to become its first manager.

With Heath gone, James was made manager of the OD unit. Up until this point James had uneasily straddled the right and left wing split in the group. His prior training and experience in work study and his association with the 1970–71 organisation study and yellow paper had given him a clear right wing image and role, but his encouragement of Ward's OD projects section in his former role as MSD manager, together with his exposure to OD technologies and values at the Eastbourne training event, had left him predisposed to behavioural process issues. How he was to interpret his role as OD unit manager was largely decided for him by the renewed interest of Harvey-Jones and one of his deputy chairmen in structural change along the lines of the 1971 yellow paper. In his own words, the activation of the second board organisation study meant that for the last 18 months of the OD unit's history James was to become "more of a doer than a manager. I reported direct to a deputy chairman . . ."

DEMISE OF THE ORGANISATION DEVELOPMENT UNIT: 1972–73

1970 and 1971 were bad years financially for HOC/PCD. The problems of running the division were further complicated in 1971 by the acquisition of the ailing nylon operations from the ICI group, and the new capital projects and production facilities of parts of two other divisions. PCD also had to make its contribution to reducing the ICI group's employees at that time. With some of the initial problems of the merger over, Harvey-Jones returned to one of his original three objectives of bringing about some structural change in PCD to strengthen the business orientation of the division. The main focus for the OD unit's external links throughout 1972 was the second organisation study. By the end of 1972 the PCD board had accepted the need for, and had implemented a significant structural change away from, a largely functional organisation toward a stronger matrix organisation than had been recommended in the yellow paper. The changes mainly affected the board and senior management group. There was to be no more "top box" composed of the three deputy chairmen and to which directors would report. Directors would now report directly to the board with deputy chairmen acting as "resources not bosses – uncles not dads". Further business focus was given to the division by greatly strengthening the business area concept and putting each business area under a director's wing.

The process by which this change was achieved was quite different from the abortive first organisation study. The first study involved a longish period of fairly isolated data collection, thinking, and analysis by the task force trio, with some contact with senior managers, but little contact with individual directors, and certainly no collective board work on the ideas produced in the yellow paper prior to its appearance. The second study was also vulnerable because initially it was still only being sponsored by Harvey-Jones and one of his deputy chairman. "There were board suspicions about the chairman's motives and the deputy chairman's motives – a fear of a fait accompli . . . Some directors felt a bit personally threatened . . . There was not as much commitment in the board as Harvey-Jones thought."

James was the leader and co-ordinator of the study and in the absence of Parker and Heath the other members of the OD unit played a bigger, more public role in the work. Data were collected by the OD unit in three areas. "The first was factual, facts and figures about the existing structure. The second was feelings about the existing structure, and the third was theoretical – we drew heavily on Lawrence and Lorsch" (1967). One device used to engage the initially "very antagonistic board" in the study was to take them to other parts of ICI, and other firms to discuss alternative structures and their operation. "And it was amazing to see the change in attitude of these people. They suddenly became much more interested. There were different ways to run a business. We got much more commitment from the board."

James was the major internal link man with the board and had role problems with them. "One of the big issues for me was to get the board on board. I had a personal problem with some of them to understand how an insider can stand aside and behave like an outsider. I asked Harvey-Jones to allow me to meet with the whole board once a month . . . I told Harvey-Jones I needed some consulting help from Mercer and that was agreed."

> The process we worked was definitely OD but the focus was structure . . . if the focus had been norms or culture that would have been much less acceptable. Harvey-Jones would never have set up a study which had the avowed aim of changing the culture . . . Generally the legitimization [for OD in PCD] was roles, structures, tasks and so on.

But in fact as James was to acknowledge as far as the board's attitude and behaviour was concerned, "we were building on some foundations which Mercer had helped lay". Here again is another illustration of the general point that successful change often requires longer-term process preparation and climate building; and yet another particular example of Mercer's impact in ICI. Explaining the how and why of Mercer's impact in this situation is worth a short diversion.

Before the appointment of Harvey-Jones as division chairman, and indeed for a while after his appointment, the PCD board had not operated well as a team. A director commented that "when I got onto the PCD board I found them all worth knowing, expert, full of ideas but a group that was unable to use its total talent. The tradition was you put up a note and if there was any criticism of it everybody (from your function) lost marks." Harvey-Jones was encouraged by George Bridge, then in central personnel department, to invite Mercer to do some process work with the board. The HOC board, unused to thinking in process terms, were sceptical before and after Mercer's first encounter with them. A director had this to say about Mercer's early contact with the HOC board:

> Well, when Harvey-Jones first introduced him I think a number of members of the board were very, very sceptical, and when after his first day at the [Wilton] castle, Mercer in his normal way hadn't really done anything, they thought "well bugger that, what's he getting his fat fee for?" But latterly the board found it to be valuable, but there's no enthusiasm.

Another director felt that Mercer "had loosened the process up . . . I think by the time I left the PCD board it was a very coherent team – very supportive . . . a lot of that was due to OD . . . I think they've lost it under Harvey-Jones's successor." Harvey-Jones was clearest about some of the keys to Mercer's impact:

> Ron has supremely good skills at operating at board level – less as you go down. He is a very, very sensitive and acute process intervenor and he also has enough mechanisms – in a sort of gimmicky way – the ease the problems. So the two things reinforce each other ... The "right wing" grasp the usefulness of the mechanisms without even seeing the process interventions.

Mercer had had time to influence the PCD board before the second organisation study began. This process work, plus Mercer's involvement at the time of the study, and James' own view that "at the end of the process of his meeting with the board for 14 hours over a two and a half month period – the level of openness, honesty and maybe even trust had increased", all contributed to acceptance of the change. By the end of 1972 the board had agreed to the detail of who was to have which business areas; and the rest of the division had been informed. In 1976 James did another survey of board attitudes to the structure created in 1972 "and the board saw no need for fundamental restructuring – as they had done in 1971".

Behavioural work in R&D and Engineering

Throughout the history of OD and related activities in HOC/PCD the powerful production, technical, and marketing functions were a closed book as far as the OD unit was concerned. If any behavioural type work was to go on this left only the relatively lower prestige R&D and engineering functions. There were occasions when Ward, mainly in R&D, and Brown, mainly in engineering, were able to find receptive clients for their ideas. Some of these clients came from earlier associations made at the time of the MBO and SDP work, some of the work came at the request of directors responsible for those functions. Most often the context for the intervention was either just before or after redundancies in those functions, or to help with the merging, realignment, or reshaping of sections in those two functions. An example of morale and redundancy-related problems was the work done in R&D and Engineering in 1970 and 1971 as a consequence of the collapse of the division's capital programme between 1969 and 1971. In 1972, the left wing of the OD unit were also involved in helping to merge different parts of the R&D function. Some of this work was successful, to the point where a few middle-level managers in those two functions carried on using OD technologies long after the OD unit had been disbanded. But Ward and the others had often to push pretty hard to break in, and where they didn't have to push hard, they were often landed with some messy human problems.

Heath commented:

> Certainly Ward, Brown and Castle were respected, felt to be useful, but they had to go and look for jobs, they didn't have people bumping on their doors. And usually they were turned to by a manager when he had a nasty difficult problem to deal with – like having to get rid of some people.

One of the managers who became a periodic user of the OD unit confirmed they had to, and did push for work:

> I don't think they employed the dripping on the stone technique. They came in with a bang, and therefore you had to have a receptive customer . . . I had some problems and saw them as helpful . . . They were prodding, proactive, saying there must be scope for improvement. Ward certainly talked in that vein. He came and provided some alternatives . . . If you went to Personnel and said I'm having a problem, the answer usually was "bloody well solve it", the OD people were just not part of the management structure – they were seen as a team of advisors and they insisted that what we said and did was confidential.

But the OD unit found it much more difficult to project and sustain an image of not being part of the management structure than their equivalent OD colleagues at Billingham. The PCD group were too close in many people's eyes to a select group of the board, and to the board's obvious interest in 1970 and 1971, in slimming numbers. As one of the OD unit put it:

> I've a general belief that numbers reduction never helps OD. OD may help numbers reduction.

One of the managers who later used the OD unit acknowledged that "it started out with a bit of a gestapo image. I never thought it, but I heard it around: they're going to come and tell us how to run with so many less people. Around the SDP time or a little after." The OD unit members were aware of their image as the tool of the board:

> I feel we gradually built up a lot of credibility with the board and with the departmental managers – the people we'd been working with. But below that level there was still a bit of fear, particularly when the numbers started dropping – the OD unit were seen as the hatchetmen doing the dirty work for the board . . . The number of people we were directly dealing with was quite limited, about 50 or 60. These were the only people in a position to really judge what we were doing.

Sometimes the OD unit were able to influence individual directors to use OD methods to create change. Ward said that a director "was all for carving up R&D as he had done management services. I persuaded him to let me work with them and make these changes themselves over 18 months." Where this happened, the OD unit were better able to control their impact and image and win friends who returned more than once for help. A manager in R&D who had used MBO in 1967, worked with the OD unit in 1972 and 1973, and then in effect became his own consultant. He commented:

> Yes . . . OD has become a way of life to me, and I think a lot of this is spinning off into members of my section . . . I have used OD at times because I've found myself in trouble, because of the way people in my section have responded to a change in the environment. For example, company policy in response to its economic situation has lowered morale (via manpower cuts).

The team-building, objective-setting, and role-clarification work did often have its successes, particularly where they were working with a relatively self-contained section. Where, however, they got into interdepartmental problems, for example between Research, Development, Engineering, and Technical Departments, a lot of this more politically charged work "was totally abortive". An exception to this was team-building work in some of the fairly important product areas (before the structural change to business areas), and getting R&D integrated on a business area basis.

But the penetration of the OD unit into PCD was always very limited. They had their legitimate channel to the board – the organisation studies. They had one or two active supporters on the board who at times sponsored them on work into their departments, and they had their middle manager friends and clients in R&D and Engineering built up during the MBO and SDP days. Many of the division managers had so little contact with the OD unit, they were not in a position to say what the OD unit did:

> I asked the managers what they thought the OD unit does? It wasn't a question of them saying, "Oh my God. They're way out." Wasn't that at all. Either they didn't know, or somebody had done a study on transport drivers for them, or somebody had sat in, as a process resource. Or nothing had happened, and they didn't have the faintest idea or interest in the OD unit.

The great majority of the managers in PCD were "doubters – people we hadn't worked with". There were few "active opponents, people putting the knife in". Of course, in the powerful functional departments – the marketing and technical areas – they found some of the cornerstones of the divisions management culture. The concern for hierarchy and status, the technical arrogance which combined to produce attitudes where "apart from person to person relationships, a guy that is not as senior as you can't offer anything of value". This led to a stated view towards the OD unit, "I know how to run my outfit. We don't need you cowboys!"

In this climate of ambivalence and rejection, some of the OD unit added to their problems by overmarketing their services – pushing too hard:

> We've had a succession of things – MBO, Blakes Grid, OIP, SDP and OD itself. These have been introduced by the enthusiasts . . . There are fashions which are promoted by good marketing. And I think this has done a great disservice to OD. If you call it SDP or OD, it will tend to be rejected by a lot of managers as a gimmick, when all it is really is just a sensible approach to your job.

Some of their board level supporters were fairly fickle and unpredictable friends. In one case this was because of the personality make up of the director, "He had an intuitive understanding of OD . . . He would listen to them but he was never really in sympathy with them. He distrusted feeling components because he was a very shy, private man." On other occasions there were intellectual doubts, "OD hadn't been thought through sufficiently. There was a conflict between OD being a kind of group psychotherapy and it being an actual change programme . . . What was missing was proper systems studies . . . so that the hard systems stuff was thought through and then the soft systems, the team building, goes in." And, of course, there was the normal businessman's impatience with the speed of change using OD people and methods:

> I find OD people terribly good at creating an environment conducive to change, and hellish bad at organising the change programme . . . So you get swirling activity consuming immense amounts of time – all very heady – but not making enough actual change progress.

But as with the powerful functions, so also with the board, there was a basic question mark about the legitimacy of internal consultancy help in the people and organisation area:

> They were seen by many members of the board as rather amateur shock troops pretending to have skills with people when maybe skills with people were diffused throughout the organisation and couldn't be concentrated in a special unit. So there was a lot of antagonism among my colleagues on the board and they had to be protected.

By the beginning of 1973, with the second organisation study completed and the structural change implemented, protecting the OD unit was beginning to become a thankless and impossible task.

ORGANISATION DEVELOPMENT: THE END

> They (PCD managers) weren't in the business of innovation . . . Their notion was minimum disturbance and maximum production. That was heavily ingrained, and where you were having fun on new investment that was a deeply technical matter . . . straight down the line was the PCD culture. After WSA and SDP, they simply blew off the froth – organisation development, and got on with the straight drinking!

The recommendation to disband the OD unit was made in a November 1973 memorandum from a deputy chairman to the PCD board. By then, Ward had left the company, and Brown was about to join him. John Harvey-Jones had arrived on the ICI main board, and Tom James, with Harvey-Jones's sponsorship, had been appointed as a companywide internal consultant on organisation matters. James returned to PCD in 1976 at the then chairman's request to review the operation of the structure implemented in 1972. No changes followed James's 1976 work. In 1981 James returned again to play a part in the structural and people problems associated with the merging of PCD and Plastics Division.

On the death of the OD unit only one of its members still remained in the division. He was transferred to a Management Training Section which was then renamed management and organisation development section. This unit did some respected work in the training design and community relations area, some of which was picked up by other divisions. The sole transferee from the OD unit also did work at the divisional and company level using OD techniques, and a handful of managers in R&D and Engineering carried on using skills and techniques learnt from Ward and Brown, but essentially OD died in PCD when the OD unit withered away.

OD had been seen as a lever to cause changes desired by its initial sponsor John Harvey-Jones. "It had assisted many powerful people but likewise was resented by others who felt they were disadvantaged or hurt by its activities." The antecedents and origins of the OD unit were very important both in setting it on a path which focussed primarily on a particular task, and in creating a feeling of ambivalence and disinterest to the behavioural work in the unit. By the time the task was complete nothing had happened to change the top management's initial view that this was a task force. Even the task force idea was forced by Harvey-Jones onto a board full of doubters. A director commented, "Harvey-Jones had to push to get that through. And the rats were really at it from the beginning . . . I think the board, by and large, supported the analysis of their own activity but once that was over, there wasn't much feeling for continuing. It was: O.K., forget about it . . . so it really came and went with John Harvey-Jones . . . With the coming of Harvey-Jones's successor you had a switch right over from a fairly extrovert guy who was interested in the OD scene, to a man who was authoritarian, and who had been brought up in the old school – a much older man too."

John Harvey-Jones as the initiator of OD in PCD perhaps deserves the final word in this discussion of its demise. His words acknowledged he also had some learning from the PCD story:

> I think PCD organisation development is a sad case, because I really believed that I had started an irreversible force. I knew there would be attempts to halt it, but I really believed it wouldn't be easy to halt it. I was dead wrong – well 80% . . . The concept that I had was to start at the top and work down.

8 The Change Strategy Without Political Support: Plastics Division

The story of ICI's interests in plastics dates from the 1930s although ICI Plastics Division was not formed until 1945. The division grew rapidly in the 1950s and 1960s on a host of new products for the construction, motor car, engineering, and packaged food industries and then in the 1970s ran into increasing competition, large rises in raw materials costs, and difficulties with maturing products. Unlike many ICI divisions, Plastics is close to the consumer and much influenced by a 4.3 year cycle of boom and slump. In the 1970s the bad years for the division were 1971 and 1975 and it was expected that the economic recession of 1980 would produce some inauspicious financial results. In fact, from worldwide sales of £748m in 1979 and a profit of £56m Plastics Division made a loss in 1980 of £35m on sales of £738m. Plastics Division, like its upstream chemical neighbour Petrochemicals Division, had also "fallen off a cliff", and produced not just inauspicious financial results but "intolerable losses". The merger of Petrochemicals and Plastics Divisions which followed on 6 April 1981 was described in *Plastics News*, the division's newspaper, as "part of the fight for the survival of both businesses". The fortunes of Plastics Division had changed dramatically from the heady and optimistic days of research-led growth in the 1950s and early 1960s.

The banner used by the new chairman and chief executive of Petrochemicals and Plastics Division to launch the new division was "innovation through integration". The merger, it was hoped, would bring a single direction on matters of business strategy, raw materials utilisation, and product development by combining ICI's upstream activities in oil and petrochemicals with its downstream activities in polymers. Undoubtedly the merger would also allow significant reductions to be made in management costs as service activities duplicated in the divisions were pruned back and, of course, only one board of directors was necessary and not two. The integration of their petrochemicals and polymers businesses will be a challenge for ICI into the mid-1980s. Looking back into the late 1960s and 1970s it is already clear with the benefit of hindsight that Plastics Division's response to an increasingly threatening business environment was found wanting. Some of the reasons for their diffi- culties will be unravelled in this chapter – not all of those reasons can be explained by the harsh changes in their environment; there are also legitimate questions to ask about the managerial behaviour and organisation of the division.

Although the OD resources in Plastics Division often asked the appropriate questions about the division's organisation and behaviour, and throughout the

1970s came up with sharp diagnoses, neither the OD resources nor their message were perceived to be credible or legitimate enough to have an impact in the centre of power in the division. Unlike Agricultural Division, where OD had had the tacit support of the board, and at times the active and sustained support of a number of key line managers, and in Petrochemicals Division where OD had been part of the change strategy of the division chairman; in Plastics no such political support was ever afforded OD. The story of OD in Plastics Division is, therefore, not so much a chronicle of missed opportunities, though undoubtedly some opportunities were missed, but rather a story of opportunities that were never made available. However, within the restrictions of their environment and the ways they chose to relate to that environment, the OD resources did attempt to influence the managerial style and culture of the division, though some of their more effective interventions probably had a greater impact outside the boundaries of ICI Plastics Division than they did inside the division.

In seeking an answer to the more limited question why the limited impact of OD in Plastics Division, and to the much broader question of why did the division experience problems of adaptation to its changing environment in the 1970s, one has to examine the culture of the division and how that culture emerged out of the history and business development of ICI's interests in plastics. The purpose of this chapter is to present a narrative account and some basic analysis of the business history and development, and managerial organisation and culture of Plastics Division over the period from its creation in 1945 up until its merger with Petrochemicals Division in 1981. Having established some of the key events and trends in the development of the division's business and managerial culture, this contextual backcloth will then be interwoven into an account of the process of development and impact of OD resources in Plastics Division.

PLASTICS DIVISION: BUSINESS HISTORY, ORGANISATION AND CULTURE, 1945–81

W. J. Reader's (1975) account of the emergence of ICI's interests in plastics during the 1930s is replete with illustrations of the difficulties of championing a new business area in the solidifying structures of interest which had formed in ICI only ten years after its birth. In the late 1920s plastics was seen merely as an adjunct to the more established heavy chemicals businesses; its role was to serve as a market for the products of other business groupings rather than as a promising field for development in its own right. Spasmodic developments in plastics were allowed to emerge in the Dyestuffs, Billingham, General Chemicals, and Explosives business groupings but there was the fundamental weakness that the plastics efforts were "dispersed among the groups with no central authority" (Reader 1975:344).

One potential avenue open to break this pattern was to purchase one of the still small but leading firms in the British plastics industry. In the summer of 1932 Bakelite Ltd., probably the biggest UK plastics firm, turned down ICI's purchase offer, but in January 1933 the number two firm, Croydon Mouldrite Ltd, agreed to sell 51% of their capital to ICI. ICI now had goodwill and an immediate footing in the market. With this belated toe-hold into plastics ICI now started to tentatively grapple with the problems of organisation and co-ordination of their plastics interest. The realities of power at that time were that none of the chairmen of established groups were willing to give up their embryonic plastics interests and no-one at the centre was prepared to insist that they did so. In 1933 ICI responded to these political realities by setting up a co-ordinating body with neither executive authority nor financial resources, which they called Plastics Division.

If one source of inertia in the development of ICI's plastics business was the political interests of its existing businesses, another was what seemed the rather undisciplined way the small businesses in the UK plastics industry behaved towards one another. There was little scope for "harmonious working", that is, price-fixing, so characteristic of much of the rest of the international chemical business scene at that time. (Reader 1975:347) quotes Hodgkin, one of the senior ICI executives leading their plastics developments in 1935, as saying of the rest of the UK plastics industry "there is no organisation or community of interest whatever . . . competition is keen, and at times unscrupulous . . . Prices are cut as and when individual firms feel inclined to do so". A key way of handling these instabilities was to invest in research and develop new products which, for a time, could earn monopoly profits. Although by 1935 the ICI Dyestuffs Group had come forward with the major plastics invention "Perspex", and in December 1935 the Alkali Group had discovered polythene the amount of research money going into Croydon Mouldrite was still very small.

Progress towards central control of plastics in ICI was made in 1936 when ICI purchased the remaining capital in Mouldrite Ltd and was further accelerated by the creation of a Plastics Group in March 1938. But "the vested interests of the established groups were not speedily overridden, and demarcation disputes, conducted with careful courtesy reached considerable heights of refinement and subtlety" (Reader, 1975:349). Having discovered polythene, "the gentlemen with a taste for chemistry" at the Alkali Group took a grip on the commercial and technical development of polythene which was not fully relinquished until 1958. In the meantime, however, the Second World Ward led to greatly increased demands from the electrical and aircraft industries for "Perspex" and "Welvic" and by 1945 ICI Plastics Division had been recreated, this time as a true commercial division of the company in anticipation of the great growth in the world plastics industry which followed post-Second World War recovery. The headquarters of the new division were located at Welwyn Garden City in Hertfordshire.

The period of business growth, 1945–67

The creation of Plastics Division in 1945 was associated with a change and expansion of the management group running the division. Grafted on to the staff of Mouldrite Ltd, and the ICI scientists and managers who had come into the Plastics Group during the late 1930s and early 1940s, there now came a strong infusion of talented chemists from the Alkali Group at Winnington. As we shall see, this combination of Mouldrite entrepreneurs and "gentlemen chemists" was to have a profound impact on the development of the managerial culture in the division along lines which inhibited the division's adaptability in the quite different social, economic, and business conditions of the 1970s.

The post-war growth of Plastics Division was based on a number of inter-related factors. One of these was the availability of a more economic way of producing ethylene than the old process which had derived ethyl alcohol from the fermentation of molasses. This upstream problem of large-scale economic raw materials availability was largely solved in the 1950s and 1960s with the production of ethylene from the increasingly large olefine crackers on the Wilton site. The previous chapter on Petrochemicals Division has described how ICI achieved further vertical integration in the 1960s by going directly into the oil business to secure their feedstock supplies. But if Plastics Division's raw materials problems were solved by the development of Wilton their real growth could only lie in their success in the market-place. Crucial to success in the market-place was skill in developing new products and manufacturing pro-cesses which could be patented and earn high prices and monopoly profits. All this was dependent on high growth rates in the Western economies stimulating the expansion of consumer goods, electrical, engineering, and construction industries and plastics products maintaining price, utility, or fashion edge over the materials such as glass, wood, and metal for which plastics were substitutes.

Plastics Division built up largish and politically powerful research and technical service and development departments which concerned themselves with the discovery of new products and processes and the modification of existing lines. By 1950 Plastics Division employed around 1600 staff and 2400 workers scattered around 6 works at Billingham and Wilton in the north-east of England, Hillhouse and Darwen in the north-west of England, at Wandsworth in London, and Welwyn Garden City. The division made a wide range of materials for the plastics industry, including moulding and extrusion composi-tions, resins, sheet, tube and monofilament. Its major products in the early 1950s were "Perspex" sheet, rod and tube, "Diakon" moulding powder, dental and optical products and materials, and vinyl chloride polymers and co-polymers. By this time Plastics had been given responsibility for the technical service and selling of "Alkathene" (the ICI brand of polythene), but polythene was still manufactured by the Alkali Division.

All this was, of course, still pretty small stuff in comparison with the scale of operations in the other groupings of ICI. In 1952 for example Plastics Division's employment of capital in manufacturing activities was only 3% of the total employed, as against 32% in Heavy Chemicals, 24% in Fertilizers, and 17% in Dyestuffs. But plastics was seen as a product for the future, and although the capital employed in plastics in 1952 was still small, they had 84 technical officers engaged in research and development while the much bigger operations in Fertilizers and in Alkali and General Chemicals combined, only had 135 and 138 technical officers respectively. (Reader, 1975:446 and 450).

The substantial growth in Plastics Division occurred in the late 1950s and up to the mid-1960s. By 1965 the new plastics, polypropylene and polyester film, had been added to the product range and the division acquired new products through the acquisition of British Visqueen Ltd and Marrick Manufacturing Company Ltd. Plastics Division, along with Fibres Division, also led in the early 1960s ICI's first move into Western Europe. Plants were built first of all at Rozenburg in the Netherlands and then much later production facilities were developed in France and Belgium. In the meantime newer and much bigger plants were commissioned at Dumfries, Hillhouse, and Wilton and older ineffi- cient plants were closed down. Among the plants to go was the one at Welwyn Garden City and in consequence Plastics Division found itself with a geographically highly dispersed set of production facilities many miles from the Welwyn headquarters.

But questions of unity of purpose and integration of effort were not to the forefront of people's minds in Plastics Division in the early 1960s. In 1963 the largest single field of research in ICI continued to be in organic polymeric materials such as plastics, fibres, and films. Even in 1961, cyclically a bad year for ICI in general, and Plastics Division in particular, half the total value of ICI's exports came from the Fibres, Dyestuffs, and Plastics Divisions. The company Annual Report for 1964 noted that the demand for plastics materials was expanding by 15% per annum in the UK. Figures are not available to assess Plastics Division's levels of profitability in the late 1950s and early 1960s but interview reports indicate that profits were made, though made in an atmosphere where the excitement of new product development and of growth in sales volume were more significant than profitability as such. Two Plastics directors of the late 1960s and 1970s era had this to say about the business orientation of the division in the 1950s and 1960s.

> In the 1950s and 1960s we (in the commercial areas) were a bunch of gifted amateurs. We did our own thing, we were very much functionally organised. Conditions were so much in our favour we found at the end of six months we were making quite good profits, but we were not profit oriented. We could have made much bigger profits had we been more professional.

* * *

> When I joined the division (in the 1960s) there was a very strong emphasis on looking for either entirely new products or new applications for the existing products. The emphasis was on entirely new products or novel methods of fabrication. Now (in 1976) there is rather more emphasis on the geographical diversification of our products, making types of products suitable for particular markets, and a very considerable emphasis on reducing the cost of making our existing range of products, and that is very often synonymous with a greater manpower and capital productivity.

The 1950s and 1960s were halcyon days for Plastics Division. A senior director quoted sales growth figures in 1975 £'s from £14m in 1945, to £45m in 1955 and to £150m in 1965. The division became accustomed to growth rates of 20% per annum in some of its products.

Commercially we had a strong position in practically every product we made. We could sell our products, we had good products to make, we had pioneered some of them, and it was only later on that the pinch began to hurt. I suppose it was starting to hurt by about the mid-1960s, and then it gained momentum.

Throughout the 1950s and for much of the 1960s "it was always assumed the business was doing all right". Growth and effortless success, but without very large profits, became the pattern of stability. Not many major new products were introduced by Plastics Division after 1965. The last really important product to be introduced was polypropolene over the period 1962–65. Even the process technologies remained substantially the same after the late 1950s and early 1960s breakthroughs. A technical director commented:

I can't think of any of our products now being made by an entirely different process. The processes have been modified to improve efficiencies, to reduce costs and so on and nearly always to produce larger volumes of output per unit of either manpower or capital. I cannot think of a single case where we have gone over to an entirely different process.

The above pattern of business growth with product and technical stability was, as we shall also see, complemented by stability in senior management personalities, organisation structure, and management culture. Before the 1981 merger with Petrochemicals Division practically the only change in organisation Plastics Division had to manage was the 1964 move from a functional to a product structure. Plastics Division was substantially untouched by the periodic adjustments in business area and divisional boundaries that ICI made from 1958 to 1980. Even the swings up and down of the trade cycle were expected every 4.3 years.

The earliest signs that "growth forever, profits forever" might not last came in the rather severer downturns of 1967 and 1971, but it would be way into the 1970s before those early signals and the ones that followed them were interpreted and then acted upon as indications of a basic structural or irreversible change in the fortunes of Plastics Division.

Maturing products and tougher competition, 1967–81

The story of Plastics Division's business fortunes from the late 1960s until its merger with Petrochemicals Division in 1981 is one of sustained environmental pressure and inadequate company response. Plastics Division, for a variety of reasons which will be explored later in this chapter, did not adapt to and manage the speed and complexities of the changes in their business environment as comprehensively as they might have done. But in searching for explanations for Plastics Division's difficulties the analyst has to go beyond the division's capacities and capabilities to manage change and examine some features of the business systems and organisation, and management culture of ICI as a whole enterprise. This will be attempted in Chapter 10 of this book.

However, what can be said descriptively first of all about the evolution of Plastics Division from 1967 to 1981? The ICI Annual Reports have shown the performance of its business classes (Worldwide) only since 1973. Table 23 indicates the pattern of Plastics Division sales and profits from 1973 to 1980. The Table shows that the bumper year for Plastics during the 1970s was the post-oil-crisis 1974. Although many industries were immediately adversely affected by the oil crisis of 1973 the worldwide chemical industry was not; with shortages of petroleum-based raw materials immediately after the oil crisis many firms were willing to pay high prices to build up their stocks of chemicals, but the stockbuilding of 1974 produced for Plastics Division very bad financial results in the downturn in the trading cycle in 1975. Thereafter Plastics Division showed an unexceptionable and volatile profit position until the losses of £35m in 1980. These losses continued during 1981, and were still continuing at substantial levels in 1982, eighteen months after the Petrochemicals–Plastics divisional merger.

TABLE 23   Plastics Group worldwide: sales, trading profit and trading margins (£m)

Year	Sales	Trading profit	Trading margin
1973	265	32	12.1
1974	399	70	17.5
1975	357	2	0.6
1976	538	42	7.8
1977	602	50	8.3
1978	625	39	6.2
1979	748	56	7.5
1980	738	(35)	(4.7)

A number of environmental and business changes have helped to produce the above worsening financial position for Plastics. Chief amongst these have been real reductions in the growth rate for bulk plastics during the 1970s, and an increasing number of new manufacturers in Western Europe leading to overcapacity and depressed margins. Apparently the problems of overcapacity in bulk plastics has been exacerbated by undisciplined marketing. Vivian, Gray Investment Research (1980) have argued that in 1978 overcapacities in Western Europe in the manufacture of low-density polyethylene (LDPE) meant plant utilisation averaging 75–80%. "Such loadings would not in themselves have been disastrous if the producers had ordered their marketing and refused to chase volume at the expense of price. However, with 23 major European producers this was easier said than done, and the result was an estimated loss of £200m on LDPE by these 23 producers in 1978 alone (nearly £60 for each tonne sold) with ICI itself losing £11m" (Vivian, Gray & Co. 1980:64).

The chemical industry in the 1970s failed in large measure to appreciate the onset of maturity. In bulk plastics the 15–20% growth rates of the 1950s and

1960s were largely a consequence of high rates of substitution for traditional materials in the construction, engineering, motor car, and packaging industries. By the 1970s economic growth in the markets was beginning to take over from substitution as a growth factor, but increasingly throughout the 1970s the contribution of economic growth as a stimulant to the plastics industry was itself being undermined by the slowing down of the growth rates of major West European economies. With a maturing plastics industry, and certainly in the bulk polymers area, mature products, capital investment being poured into new plant by a combination of established producers updating their technology, and new entrants from cash-rich oil companies, and state-run enterprises more interested in employment than profitability, it only needed the severe world recession of the mid and late 1970s to expose the problems of the plastics industry.

TABLE 24 Plastics sector of ICI: geographical split of sales and production, 1978 (percentages)

	Sales	*Production*
United Kingdom	42	59
Continental Western Europe	23	15
Rest of world	35	27

By 1978 Plastics Division was a major world producer of three major bulk plastics in a maturing industry with great overcapacity. In terms of sales and production Plastics was also largely a UK and Continental Western European operation. Table 24 shows the geographical split of sales and production in the Plastics sector of ICI in 1978. But by 1978 more worrying than the geographical concentration in the United Kingdom and Western Europe was ICI's still heavy commitment to bulk plastics products with their mature technologies, slowing growth, and over-capacity situation. In the late 1970s ICI was a leading world producer of three of the five bulk thermoplastics. The three ICI chose to concentrate in were low-density polyethylene (LDPE), polypropylene (PP), and polyvinyl chloride (PVC). Again focussing on 1978, the above three bulk plastics products made a contribution of 52% to sales, with another 20% coming from plastic films, and a further 28% from specialty plastics. But in terms of contribution to profits the situation was very different. Vivian, Gray Investment Research (1980:62) have suggested that over the period 1975–78 the bulk plastics products of ICI "have at best been at break-even . . . virtually all the profits in the plastics sector, certainly as far as Europe and the Americas are concerned, have been earned in films and specialty plastics". The conclusions in the Vivian, Gray research paper are corroborated in ICI's Annual Reports of 1977, 1978, 1979, and 1980. Referring to the bulk plastics products in 1977 the Annual Report notes that "selling prices were generally affected by over-capacity and were much below the levels required to justify investment". The 1979 Annual Report said prices for bulk plastics "were below those needed to earn profits". While these statements were being made new plants to manufacture PVC were being sanctioned at Wilhelmshaven in West Germany, and Hillhouse, Lancashire, and a new polypropylene film plant was sanctioned for Dumfries in Scotland. These plants had all but been completed when Plastics Division "fell off a cliff" in May 1980. The loss of demand and overcapacity in bulk plastics which had been building up throughout the 1970s was now accompanied by a deep recession, high UK inflation of costs, and a strong pound. ICI's plastics interests have been making losses since May 1980.

The story of ICI's response throughout the 1970s to the declining fortunes of their plastics interests is a complicated and fascinating one which illustrates many of the difficulties large organisations have in seeing and then adjusting to environmental changes when the weight of existing structures, people, and company and divisional cultures and ethoses are propelling them along predetermined lines. The contribution of Millbank to the evolution of Plastics Division in the 1970s, and the ICI main board's decision to merge Petrochemicals and Plastics Divisions will be dealt with more fully in Chapter 10 of this book. For the moment I shall concentrate on outlining the views of some Plastics Division directors and managers on the division's response to the changing business environment of the 1970s. These views on managerial response offer some insight into the management concerns and culture of the division, and therefore provide a prelude to the section which follows on divisional organisation and culture. These views also set a further part of the context in place for disentangling the what, why, and how of organisation development activities in the period 1969 to 1981.

Interviews conducted in 1976 with Plastics Division directors and managers suggest that the earliest signs that the heady days of business growth were being checked came in the increasingly severe impact of the low points in the trading cycle from 1967 to 1971 and then to 1975. A manager commented:

> In the 1950s this division was on the crest of a wave with major technological innovations and profitability despite falling prices. I suppose 1967 was the first realization that things might be on the change, with 1971 very much more so.

One consequence of the 1967 trading difficulties was that Plastics Division started the process of consolidating their product range and more carefully scrutinizing new technical and product developments. Further impetus was given to this consolidation process by the even more difficult trading conditions of 1971.

> One thing has certainly changed a great deal in the last five years [1971–76] we have begun to drop products. Where products are failing we have stopped making them. That is an incredible turnup for the book. I can't tell you what a revolutionary idea that is. It has forced managers to become more profit conscious. My boss here has bridged this whole period in this product and when he started his remit was virtually consuming as much propylene as you can from Wilton to make "Propathene" out of because that is a good thing. Now his remit is all about our performance.

But 1971 and 1972 produced a much bigger shock for Plastics Division, the trauma of enforced redundancy.

> It was a time when the Axeman Cometh. What happened over about two years was a 20% monthly staff cut which was unprecedented and traumatic for a division with growth built in to it since 1945.

The man who had to carry through these redundancies commented:

> It was a very considerable reduction in the numbers in the division done with a great deal of compassion for people but nevertheless a great deal of firmness, and we shed very large numbers of people quite quickly. At that time that was my job to be the hatchet man, it happened at a time when the former Chairman was very ill, dying in fact, and just before our present Chairman came in. I and the other Deputy Chairman were left to implement the policy over a period of about a year. It was a very painful year that very much had an effect on the division culture.

A senior director who came into the division in 1973 recalled the mood in the division in 1973 and traced it back to the business difficulties and 1971 redundancies:

> This division suffered a terrible shock in 1971–72 because for the first time in their history they were finding business wasn't running their way. They had to accept a tremendous cut in staff and there was a period of major reductions and redundancies, forced redundancy. They had never had that experience, it had been one of all growth. When I came here in 1973 they were smarting under it and really the morale was low right across the patch. Everyone was in their little burrows with the ramparts up defending what they had.

These numbers reductions in Plastics Division were, of course, part of the beginning of a wider concern with manning levels and productivity throughout ICI in the 1970s. Several other divisions lost numbers in the 1971 recession but with the possible exception of Fibres and Organics, the two divisions with the most visible and continuing business difficulties, for the rest of the 1970s there was rather more talk than action about manning levels in ICI, at least until the worsening business situation of 1979 and 1980 forced ICI's hand. Plastics Division certainly stepped back from further redundancies until the very big reductions of 1980 and 1981.

Part of the problem in Plastics Division after 1971 seemed to be the management's definition of what the business problem was. While there was an undoubted recognition that the unbridled days "of growth forever, profits forever" were over, in amongst "a fairly difficult problem of profitability against a trade cycle which hits us quite hard", there was still a strong belief in the growth ethic as the driving force for the business. A survey by ICI of future plastics prospects described in detail in *European Chemical News*, 6 September 1974, noted that longer-term growth prospects for LDPE, PP, and PVC are if anything improved as a result of increased oil prices. ICI forecasts of LDPE and PVC annual growth rates in the UK were still of the order of 7%. ICI described its own findings as "confident and reassuring". The authors of the *European Chemical News* article noted that "the unqualified optimism of the ICI survey is unlikely to go unchallenged". *European Chemical News*, 6 September 1974, page 23.

However, only two months later in the profile interview in *Chemical Age*, 1 November 1974, and under the banner headline "Plastics Growth will slacken but Future is Still Bright", the Chairman of Plastics Division offered even more optimistic figures about the growth prospects for the plastics industry and ICI Plastics Division. "We see a large and expanding future for all the plastics", he said, and while more selective investments would be necessary any over-capacities would be more likely to be periodic than continuous. Tellingly the Chairman concluded by saying "the division won't alter vastly in the next 10 years . . . It's a vast ship already. New products will broaden the base, but major products will stay a large component of business for a long while". *Chemical Age*, 1 November 1974, Page 24.

Further evidence that the above growth possibilities were not to be realised came in the 1975 downturn. A senior director commenting in 1976 on the previous years results said:

> Until the last down-turn, the 1975 down-turn, we had always shown growth in every year, even at the bottom of the trade cycle. In 1975 really because it was an ordinary trade cycle with the oil price thing superimposed on top, and oil prices go straight through to our raw materials, there was for the very first time ever an actual drop in the production of plastics in this country as a whole, and in Europe as a whole, and certainly in this division. Our sales in 1975 realised less than sales in 1974.

And yet in spite of the 1975 figures and the realisation that median profitability (allowing for cycles) had been declining since the late 1960s, the director who made the above point went on to say in the same 1976 interview that although "the 20% per annum growth for products like polyethylene and PVC is very much a thing of the past, we are settling down to a 6–8% per annum growth". Why was there a continuing belief, against a good deal of contrary evidence, in the persistence of optimism about growth prospects for bulk plastics products in Plastics Division throughout much of the 1970s?

One director argued that critical to the persistence of the growth ethic was the sheer momentum of the investment strategies associated with the belief in growth, and then the desperate fight to hold on to market share or increase prices once the new investment came on stream. Speaking in 1981 this director said:

> In the late 1960s and early 1970s people became adjusted to a high growth rate and started to plan new production capacity. We landed up therefore with over capacity that caused 70–80% occupacities in plants. This caused producers in Western Europe to go for keeping their volume or market share, or if they had newer plants to invade others' market share. Eventually by the end of 1980 all the Western European producers were operating at a loss. It has taken a long time for investment strategy to catch up with the realities of the market.

A further problem was that within Plastics Division there was this belief in the trading cycle with its good years and bad years. This belief tended to act to obscure the basic irreversible structural change in the industry and market underlying the movements of the trading cycle. A director admitted:

> In retrospect the growth rate stopped in 1975, but started to hit us in 1978–79–80. You are trying to disentangle peaks and troughs that take place from an underlying structural change. The 4½-year cycle is there still but what you don't know is the amplitude; in 1980 it was horrific.

Another director recalled the significance of the trading cycle pattern in division management thinking, the continuing optimism in the division, and the increasing doubts at Millbank after 1975 about Plastic Division's business performance:

> In its own terms the division had had a successful year in 1974, and then it came down. And then in 1979 it did a lot better. The division had locked itself into a belief that there was a sort of cyclical pattern of years. What was also true, but perhaps less well perceived below board level, was Millbank's view that Plastics Division had never really delivered anything. It was always "jam tomorrow", it was always a bow wave of investment, there was always a bow wave of potential sales volume, there was always a bow wave of good profits coming, and therefore there was a disillusionment, growing disillusionment with the division at Millbank.

The growing scepticism at Millbank of Plastics Division's performance may have accentuated what a manager described as the wishful thinking planning processes of the division throughout much of the 1970s.

> When you make a plan there's an awful temptation to make up a plan that looks good – optimistic, in the hope that something will turn up and you'll get it right anyway. Psychologically there's still an awful fear of being found out. It puts enormous pressure on people, plans will be sent back if they aren't showing enough profit. There's extraordinary pressure to produce the £35m or whatever is acceptable at Millbank ... There was this enormous temptation to make things look better than they are.

These problems of perspective and business planning were undoubtedly compounded in Plastics Division by "a lack of divisional institutions" to sew the division together and carry through board decisions into effective action. As I shall demonstrate shortly in detailing critical aspects of the management culture of the division, the Plastics board did not operate as a team, and there were at times rather distant relationships between the board and the group of senior managers immediately below them.

> The division was broken down very strongly into product groups which were very separate and the directors on the whole behaved at board level more like spokesmen of their product or function than people controlling the division as an entity. Hence it was extremely difficult to get things done on a divisional basis.

So the optimistic beliefs were located in a division where there were difficulties in stimulating a divisional perspective on problems and of carrying through actions which had divisional as distinct from just product or functional implications. These forces of inertia no doubt inhibited attempts to move out of the slower-growth bulk plastics into the higher added value specialty plastics, and to produce manning levels and a structure in the division which was less geared to the capital expansion era of the late 1960s and early 1970s and more to the mature products, overcapacities, and highly selective developmental opportunities of the late 1970s and early 1980s.

Basically, however, in Plastics Division, as in Petrochemicals Division, until the irrefutable reality of the 1980 business crisis, people who had grown up in good times, and had optimistically wished throughout the 1970s for those good times to continue, just did not wish to hear bad news. This is one aspect of the human reality of big business which influenced so many large UK organisations, public and private, in the latter half of the 1970s. One Plastics Division manager put it, in specific terms:

> It's something about not wanting to be a Cassandra, not wanting to be a carrier of bad news. It's easier to manage when you assume growth.

Another manager commented that people did know the growth "wasn't there but failed to make the connection between what was happening and the effect it would have on our business". Another manager argued that it takes the unambiguity of crisis to produce real learning, the desire to listen, and the willingness to act:

> It seems as if you've got to have a very stark, unambiguous situation about which there can be no argument before the whole family says Christ! . . . It ought to be possible to learn things by intellect, you have knowledge, you can see trends . . . But you've got to be in a position to hear, and secondly to be interested enough to listen, and thirdly to have enough understanding and awareness to actually understand what's being transmitted – and then to act.

A fuller picture of how ICI as a company acted in Plastics Division during and after the past 1980 crisis will be a feature of Chapter 10 of this book.

Managerial organisation and culture, 1945–63

It should be clear from the accounts of the business history and evolution of OD in Agricultural and Petrochemicals Division that crucial to explaining the kinds of business, technical, and organisational actions in those division was the managerial organisation and culture from which those responses emanated. Although, as we shall see, the organisation and management culture of Plastics Division was different in important respects from the two north-east Divisions, the same analytical connections can be made between the birth, evolution, and fate of OD in Plastics Division and the particular culture that evolved in Plastics. Part of the reason for what has been described as the inadequate

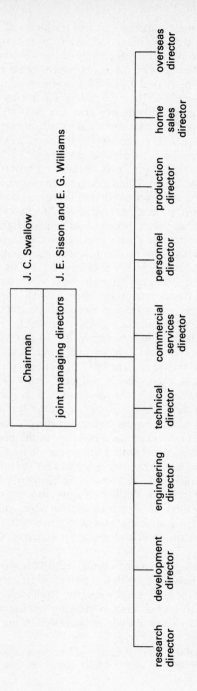

FIGURE 9 Plastics Division: top organisation chart 1962

Chairman — J. C. Swallow

joint managing directors — J. E. Sisson and E. G. Williams

research director

development director

engineering director

technical director

commercial services director

personnel director

production director

home sales director

overseas director

management response to the escalating business problems of the late 1960s and 1970s, and the relatively shallow impact of OD resources in Plastics Division was the management culture and organisation of that division.

In describing the development of the management organisation and culture of Plastics Division over the period 1945–82 a useful dividing line to break up this sequence is the year 1964. In 1964 following the recommendations of McKinsey's, the management consultancy firm, the division's formal structure changed from purely functional to a matrix structure incorporating functions and product groups. Figure 9 shows the top of the division's organisation chart in 1962 before the incorporation of product groups.

Each of the nine functional directors listed in Figure 9 had their own functional department headed by a departmental manager and in many cases several assistant managers. It is noticeable that there was both a research and a development director, and an engineering and a technical director, but no marketing director. The home sales director had beneath him again the tellingly named sales control department. Plastics was a division, structurally at least, with a modest market focus. The two largest and most powerful functions in Plastics Division throughout the 1950s and into the 1960s were the research and technical service and development departments which were headed respectively by the research and development directors. The 1950s was the pioneering decade in plastics as far as scientific discovery and product development was concerned; this led to the pre-eminence given to research "and the feeling that the division was run by Oxford physical chemists". In fact, the division was not only controlled by its scientists but at a personal level by a very small group of individuals who came into the division in 1945 from the Winnington Laboratory of the Alkali Group. These men, "the gentlemen with a taste for chemistry", had been closely connected with the discovery of polythene, ICI's major discovery in the plastics field. P. C. Allen had come into the newly created Plastics Division in 1945 as its first managing director, so had J. C. Swallow as research director, and E. G. Williams as a member of the research department. By 1960 P. C. Allen had been promoted out of the division but J. C. Swallow was now chairman, and he was to be succeeded in 1963 by another long-serving member of Plastics Division, J. E. Sisson. This pattern of continuity of leadership was sustained by E. G. Williams's appointment as division chairman in 1965, and only broken by his death in post in 1972. One of the cornerstones of the Plastics Division management culture was this historical pre-eminence of the research function and the great stability of its top leadership group.

A number of important patterns of attitude and behaviour had established themselves in Plastics Division by 1963. The rapid growth of the division to about 11,000 weekly and monthly employees, the employment of large numbers of scientists, and easy business success in growing markets with new products led to an almost free and easy academic atmosphere in the division.

In the mid 1960s the division was expanding and had been expanding for 20 years at a fairly steady rate. The style of the whole place was that there was money available to spend on any reasonable activity for which some sort of case could be made, that it was not difficult to get extra staff for any projects, and that promotion opportunities for staff with any degree of potential at all were really quite good.

This academic atmosphere was presided over by the triumvirate of the division chairman and his joint managing directors. Although "the culture at board level was very much a club, a kind of old-boy network" the club atmosphere was more obviously seen at Digswell Lodge, the divisions director's guest house, than it was in the board room of the division. One director recalled that it wasn't until the arrival of a new division chairman in 1973 that "a formal monthly board meeting was established". A manager pointed out how even in the late 1970s Digswell Lodge was still run on "fairly snobbish lines". If you're not a director you cannot get a drink – you've got to be invited by a director. It shows up some of the worst, non-democratic things." The absence of formal board meetings in the 1960s encouraged a pattern of control by the chairman and his two managing directors, and created a habit of special pleading and other interest group behaviour by the functional directors. The exclusive use by directors of Digswell Lodge symbolised the status and authority gap between the directors and the rest of the division's management. These managers recalled how 'hierarchical' and 'authoritarian' the division was for much of the 1960s.

In spite of the division's concern with growth and innovation, the aloof and rather autocratic behaviour of the top management created an atmosphere of conventionality and low risk-taking. A manager in the 1960s who was later to be a director commented:

In the 1960s it was a non-risk-taking place. The division has always been cautious. If you took too much of a risk and it didn't pay off you'd be more criticised than if you did nothing.

Two internal OD consultants recalled:

There was a conventionality – and there still is. Very few people admit error or ignorance, or ask for help. Mostly, I think, the senior people see that as not virile.

* * *

Don't take risks, don't do things which are likely to rock the boat or cause trouble where you are not sure what the outcome is going to be.

Asked what the concept of a good manager was in the early 1960s there was a consistent theme in the answers of technical ability, rational thinking, high energy, and compliance and conformity.

It's a very intellectual division so the force of rational argument is a very powerful influence.

* * *

Somebody who is a quick, logical thinker, who is energetic and prepared to take decisions having thought things through.

You don't argue in public with your boss. You are seen to be supportive of the line, you know seniority in public.

* * *

He had to be deferential, intelligent, neatly dressed ... shortish hair, and competent technically ... Conservative, that is, not full of ideas for changing things and loyal ... And low key, not emotional or excited or dynamic even ... not *too* anything. The taboos were don't be emotional, don't feel strongly about anything, and don't just throw up ideas – you argued logically.

The above characterisation of Plastics Division management culture with its themes of scientific and technical dominance, rational and logical thinking, autocracy, hierarchy, social stability in amongst technical development and business growth, and low risk-taking and conventionality is, of course, very much the atmosphere at the division headquarters at Welwyn Garden City. Unlike Agricultural Division and Petrochemical Division whose headquarters were located very close to much of the manufacturing capacity of their divisions, the Plastics Division headquarters was just a centre of white-collar and professional employment. There once had been a small plastics works at Welwyn, but by the early 1960s this had long since closed. The absence of production people at Welwyn Garden City, and of any predominant trade union and works culture of the kind obvious at Billingham and Wilton meant that another potential source of influence to dilute the Welwyn management culture was missing. Plastics Division thus had its manufacturing facilities in the UK spread geographically well away from Welwyn in sites in north-west and north-east England and in Scotland. Not only did this mean that the production function was not culturally influential at the headquarters site, but it also meant that different sub-cultures built up at each of the works sites and contributed a further source of complexity to the management of the division.

Managerial organisation and culture, 1964–80

The above account has highlighted that from its origins the division's management culture was dominated by the research chemists who were essential to the new product developments of the first twenty years. However, by the early 1960s the confluence of a number of factors, some external to the division and others intended responses to those environmental changes, led to the beginnings of a weakening of control of the researchers on Plastics Division. From a business viewpoint the early 1960s brought much stiffer international competition for Plastics Division products and with this came a realisation that marketing and financial interests ought to play a larger part than they had previously taken in division thinking and action. A key mechanism used to try and change the power system and values of the division was the McKinsey recommendation to move the structure of the division from a functional to a matrix structure. This decision was implemented in 1964 and the matrix structure with its focus on product groups put more emphasis on commercial and marketing aspects of the business. This structure remained with only minor

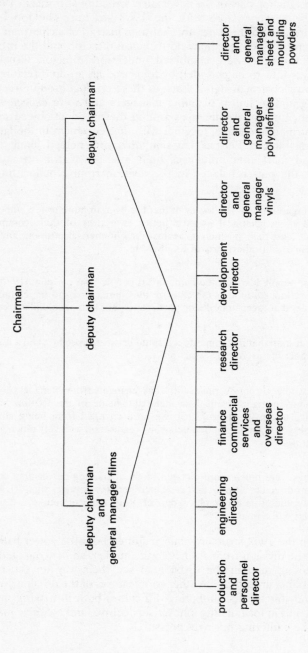

FIGURE 10 Plastics Division: top organisation chart 1967

alterations until Petrochemicals and Plastics Divisions were merged in 1981. Figure 10 shows the top part of the new matrix structure as it was in 1967. The figure indicates that compared with the 1962 structure the top box now included a chairman and three deputy chairmen instead of a chairman and two managing directors. There was now no technical director, and the production and personnel functions were combined under one director. Crucially the market focus was now to be provided by four product group directors, one of whom had deputy chairman status. Each of these product group directors had their marketing and technical planning managers and were expected to pull together relevant functional influences around their product objectives.

The above structural change, together with the retirement in the late 1960s of some old-established Plastics Division directors, helped along the new commercial and marketing influences built into the matrix structure, and helped change the power balance in the division from function to product group.

> The 1964 reorganisation – the legacy of that has been to more or less impose on research and other technical areas a better awareness of their commercial position, or at least their position as against the commercial position, and their interdependence with other parts of the division.

> *   *   *

> The technical people lost and the commercial people won . . . now [1970s] the people who are looked upon as the elite are the commercial and the commercial support people, that means marketing particularly, but also people like accounts.

> *   *   *

> There's no question that if it comes to a dispute between a product and a function – I would expect the product to win.

> *   *   *

> I think the whole corporate philosophy has changed from being a centre of excellence in producing innovatory raw material to being an organisation that says we must make a consistent profit. So we have changed from being almost a university research organisation into being an organisation with very much a profit orientated attitude.

> *   *   *

> By 1970 things were much more dictated by the marketing department and the product group directors. Production remained perhaps stronger than McKinsey intended, by virtue of its geographical spread. Remember of course that the top box is also very influential.

But although the 1964 structure change shifted both the power balance and core values of the division from science to the market, and encouraged the up-and-coming young men in the division to see their way up the hierarchy through the product groups, some other core features of the division culture did not change, and this led to continuing difficulties both in making the matrix structure work and in formulating innovative, decisive, and cohesive managerial responses to the gathering business pressures.

Key features of the pre-1964 management culture which persisted for the remainder of the 1960s and way into the 1970s were the authoritarian, distant, and reactive style of management by the chairman and one or two of his senior directors, the apparent lack of cohesive working amongst the board itself, and the at times competitive and distant relationship between the board and the senior manager group below them, and indeed between the product groups, and the product groups and functions. Plastics Division continued to have problems as a human system which intruded on its capacity to act as a purposive and coherent business and technical system.

The chairman's management style in the period 1965–72 was crisply described by a senior director who lived through that period of the division's history:

> The culture of an organisation like this depends very much on the chairman. When I joined he had his own style of management. It was a curious mixture of autocracy and laissez-faire. Decisions tended to be made very rapidly by him if he picked it up as something in which he was interested in, or alternatively he would say to one of his deputies you look after that, tell me what you have done. You got what was really a rather curious culture in a sense, this curious mixture of rapid decisions made in a very autocratic and non-participative manner with a good deal of delegation.

It will be recalled that it wasn't until 1973 with the appointment of a new division chairman that the Plastics Division board formally instituted a set of monthly board meetings and executive committees to help formulate policy and make decisions on a regular group basis.

Managers below the board talked of the board being "a difficult culture to penetrate". "A lot of things are played very close to the chest." "They're a bit closed. I personally see it as a weakness because, they haven't resolved their own internal differences."

A director acknowledged that there were continuing tendencies for the division to fragment:

> There was a power game – the division was trying to fragment itself all the time. Product groups would love to be XYZ incorporated, nothing to do with this organisation. They kept saying the board didn't delegate enough ... it's particularly the mature products; if he was on his own he wouldn't have to supply money for this bugger over here – he could use it for himself. He kicks against the planning and justifying he has to do.

Another director admitted the division had never made the McKinsey change work:

> One of the things which has worried me about our post-McKinsey organisation is that to some extent we operate almost as if we were 4 or 5 separate little divisions. We do not always find it easy to manage a situation when for example product A has to be cut back in sales, we really ought to easily be able to move people working on that product. Our structure is such that it is not too easy to manage that. When it was a wholly functional organisation then it was much easier.

Other directors and managers talked of the division being "role bound", "there was very little cross-fertilisation", and of board relations being "a bit water-tight, I've been clipped a number of times for interfering in function A or function B."

Although the scientific and technical functions in the division had lost power the scientists and engineers were still formidably cohesive groups, and in the case of the research function were adroit at practising defensive styles of leadership.

> The research director was absolutely superb at producing barriers of intellect that stopped people encroaching on what research did ... He and his managers conspired to protect themselves against personnel or board policies ... There were some world-famous scientists there, but a prima donna sort of culture which because it's strongly differentiated, had the utmost contempt for other cultures.

The engineers at Welwyn also "formed a very clear sentient group – I guess because they were surrounded by Oxford physical chemists . . . They tended to do things differently, for instance they had their own staff assessment scheme for a while. This almost became a bit of a joke, they took it to extremes, it seemed to me."

But on top of the above signs of differentiation amongst the board, between the product groups, and between the product groups and functions, there were often clear indications of differentiation on hierarchical lines between various levels of management. A middle manager of the late 1960s era remarked:

> Around the late 1960s there was a lot of talk about the cultural gap between the younger people, particularly the young graduates and the more senior managers and it certainly was an enormous gulf really. It was very difficult to find a common language at all for the people sandwiched in the middle like myself. Curiously it was the young people who were talking about profit all the time. I think what was being talked about by senior managers at that time was growth, and scale, and full capacity, and research-based industry. What the younger men were talking about was: wouldn't it be better to stop doing this because you might make more profit? Why don't you just drop polythene, you never make any money on it? They were quite willing to say heretical things.

Of course the conclusion should not be drawn from these statements about differentiation in Plastics Division that the culture was rent with continuing and open conflict; the management processes were a good deal more subtle than that. If anything the management culture was characterised by the absence of confrontation. As we have seen decision-making at the top was autocratic and direct where the chairman was interested and intervened, and there was a kind of laissez-faire attitude leading to delegation where the chairman was not interested. But the chairman was taking direct action and delegating into a policy and planning vacuum, and into an organisation structure where "there were few co-ordinating mechanisms":

We had a chairman who was I suppose pragmatic. He didn't believe in plans because the one thing you knew about plans was that they'd be wrong. He much resented the time accounts department spent on budgets for next year. There were quite a lot of people who took their cue from this, we were reactive.

The absence of mature policy-making and planning processes, and the group and interpersonal skills to make them work had they been encouraged, meant that reaction was the order of the day. Many of the core business issues relating to heightening international competition, what to do with maturing products, and how to create space to develop new products were not faced up to. Some attempts were made in the late 1960s to implement a forward integration business strategy, buying smaller firms who used plastics and were closer to the consumer. But "we had limited expertise in buying and handling these smaller companies, and we swamped them with overheads". Having failed in this the division "became very introspective and retrenched". Not even the tremendous shock of the 1971–72 redundancies, and in 1972 the death of their chairman in post, could break the pattern of caution, reactivity, and independent working which by then had been firmly established in Plastics Division management culture.

Mention has already been made of the reasons for the 20% redundancies amongst monthly staff between December 1970 and December 1972, and how those redundancies were handled by a combination of voluntary and enforced means. Here I shall concentrate only on assessing the impact, if any, the redundancies had on the division management culture. Table 25 details the

TABLE 25   Plastics Division UK employees, 1965–81

Year	Monthly staff	Weekly staff	Total
1965	5052	6743	11,795
1966	5066	6768	11,834
1967	4946	7250	12,196
1968	5037	7597	12,634
1969	5230	7638	12,868
1970	5497	7637	13,134
1971	5048	7276	12,324
1972	4435	6808	11,243
1973	4248	6671	10,919
1974	4210	6666	10,876
1975	4092	6231	10,323
1976	3969	6192	10,161
1977	3817	6064	9881
1978	3818	6049	9867
1979	3713	6070	9783
1980	3460	5587	9047
1981	2958	5004	7962

monthly and weekly staff manpower numbers over the period from December 1965 until December 1981. The table shows that the peak year in the division's manpower numbers was 1970. Thereafter the numbers declined and by 1981 were only 60.6% of the 1970 figures. The figures over the period 1970–81 reveal not consistent active erosion year by year but two periods of two years when nearly all that erosion took place. On the monthly staff side numbers decreased by 19.3% from 1970 to 1972 and fell even more sharply, by 20.3% from December 1979 until December 1981. The equivalent percentages at those two time points for weekly staff were 10.8% and 17.6%.

Some of the managers and specialists interviewed in 1976 were still talking of the shock and pain of the 1971–72 monthly staff numbers cuts.

> That was quite a trauma . . . there wasn't a manager anywhere who didn't have to face up to saying I'm sorry. And remember, ICI, it was thought, offered security of employment.

Views on the impact of the 1971–72 manpower cuts varied from the optimistic, "that changed a lot of people in their attitudes and brought them up with a jolt and stopped them being fat and happy about the way everything was", to the hopeful "they felt there were a number of problems that had been buried for too long, and that they ought to be trying to deal with them". The senior director who led the manpower reduction exercise felt that paternalism disappeared and a new sense of discipline appeared in the division around fixed costs:

> This led to rather different relationships between staff, particularly the more junior staff and the management and the board and the main board. Paternalism disappeared rather rapidly and people started viewing their relationship with the company in rather a different light. Had it not been for the 1971 reductions I don't think the trade unions would have been so successful in their recent [1976] recruitment. I think the background was a realisation that if one looked at other companies doing similar things abroad, we were lavish with our manning. This was very much a top dominated feeling, not a feeling people down the line had. It was really quite a time before managers, instead of saying "I need more people", began to say "I cannot afford these costs. I must see if I can do things more efficiently." That has been a change in culture if you like which has taken place over the period 1972–77.

But if the 1971–72 manpower cuts helped to focus people's attentions on internal efficiencies these new concerns with reducing fixed costs did not produce regular weighty numbers reductions in the period 1973–78. In that period of 6 years total manpower numbers were only reduced by an average of 1.6% per annum when the target norm was 4% per annum. In Plastics Division the core values of caution, stability, hierarchical control, and continuity persisted throughout much of the 1970s. Of course, the simpler forms of authoritarianism of the 1950s and 1960s were largely gone; "now the style is different, one is consulted up to a point, but people at my sort of level, middle management don't have enough influence". And undoubtedly the "leaders", "jolly good chaps", "enthusiastic amateurs" who had dominated the marketing and commercial areas in the 1950s and 1960s had by the 1970s been replaced by a "much more professional group – more numerate, more articulate – including a higher degree of professionalism in man-management." But as one manager put it "there have been some cultural changes but the thing that surprises me is the lack of cultural change . . . in this organisation". For explanations of persistence in the Plastics Division management culture one has to return again to the attitudes and behaviour of the Plastics Division board and the great influence those attitudes and behaviours had in setting the tone of the division as the business problems got deeper and deeper.

Reference was made earlier in this chapter to the leadership style of the Plastics Division chairman who died in post in 1972. One of his senior directors argued that this style was a combination of autocracy and laissez-faire; autocracy where the chairman was interested in an issue, and laissez-faire where he was not. This same director bridged the period 1972 to 1978 when the next chairman held office. He compared the old and the new chairmen's leadership styles in this way:

> The present chairman's style is entirely different. He is a great consultor . . . when I came here we never had division board meetings even, whereas the present chairman when he came immediately instituted a formal monthly board meeting and a system of executive committees. The executive committee is a decision making body on which the chairman sits with his deputies. These executive committee meetings are places where the directors and managers are consulted on key decisions. The division board is for policy making. We have this fairly formalised board now and some of the managers may have commented on this. Also I know that many of the managers feel a greater, and perhaps unnecessarily great concern about the level of detail required by the executive committee.

But although the board now met regularly the lack of team working evident in the 1960s continued. One director commented the board was "10 individuals doing their own thing" and another said "they [the board] still can't handle conflict. You speak from your expertise and are only accepted from your expertise. We're not using the talent on the board." And in more detail a director tellingly said:

> It was a very closed group, run by the chairman and his deputies [the top box]. As such the responsibilities were far from clear, the board certainly didn't have a role as a group. Information was fed into the top box and then there would be agonising as to what to do. It was just a series of guys who appeared and occasionally sat around the table, and then went off and did their own thing. That actually was bloody frustrating – there wasn't any collective thing, so the board became reactive and tactical . . . Insufficient time was spent in standing back and considering where we would like to be . . . and trying to push the external environment to that end. Too much time was spent feeding data to the centre [Millbank] and reacting to situations.

Another director put it openly and succinctly:

> We are details men – so we'll never be caught out by Millbank.

This continuing problem of lack of strategic perspective and team working on the board also influenced another persistent theme in the management culture, the poor integration between products and functions, and between management levels. In examining the question of management levels as one specialist reminded me, one has to remember that an ICI division board is only just over half way up the management hierarchy:

> Decision making is very compartmentalised, nobody is looking at decisions in their broadest sense. Finance is decided up in the stratosphere at Millbank, technology by the division technical planning people, marketing strategy by the product group directors, and marketing tactics by the marketing managers . . . As far as I could see going on in those groups would be a lot of buck-passing. "We could get the marketing sorted out if only we could get the money."

Floating in and around the division and between the division and Millbank were a series of inconsistent objectives. A director said:

> On the one hand there was this tremendous drive for expansion, for growth, and there was some tremendous capital programmes going on, and therefore the marketing managers really saw volume as their key. At the other end of the scale the board were struggling to reduce costs and trying to get a grip of the price situation in an over-capacity market. And yet the fundamental equation of if you go for volume you can't actually go for price as well seemed a bit lost. But volume was the key reward. Now, if you're going for volume and high production levels then concentrating your mind on manpower reductions becomes a very difficult task.

A consequence of these inconsistencies was, as we have seen, "we weren't doing anything about numbers reductions [in manpower], we were just vaguely talking about it". Furthermore, as another director commented, "pushing up prices and hoping the market would follow us eventually led in some products to reduced market share and a price level that was disastrous".

In 1978 and 1979 four new directors and a new division chairman came into Plastics Division. Attempts were set in train fairly quickly to improve team working on the board. One director commented that:

> We acquired a cabinet system whereby opinions were asked for, there are meaningful debates, freedom to say what one thinks, but at the end of the argument the chairman decides, agreement or not.

This approach to board working was, of course, greatly assisted by the worsening business situation and then the business crisis of the second quarter of 1980.

It became a board welded together, and started to tackle for the first time the cost base problem as a result of that savage swing in profitability.

Action initially taken alone by the Plastics board, and then the redundancies following the 1981 merger, led to an 18.6% drop in monthly and weekly staff employees between December 1979 and December 1981.

There was now irrefutable evidence that the wishful thinking of much of the 1970s was going to be no preparation to survive in business in the medium term in the 1980s. The days of 10–15% growth were now officially over. As one manager put it:

> Before, when we were in a recession, it was a pause in the growth graph, this one has been a colossal, observable crash.

In describing the management culture in 1981 words like "shocked", "worried", "the emergence of business performance as an overriding setter of the climate" were used. The concept of a good manager in 1981 was now someone who could:

> Run a tight department, keep control of costs, do tough things with his people and get away with it – be an instrument of torture and a feather bedder. Be a good salesman, put across to his people the division policies so they made sense.

Whether this singular concern with cost-cutting will contribute to business performance is a theme I shall return to when I examine on a more general level the course and impact of the major changes in organisation made in ICI over the period 1980–82.

Having established the business history and development of Plastics Division over the period 1945–81, and key features of the division management organisation and culture over that same period, it should now be apparent that the process of development and impact of OD resources took place in a very particular and clearly unreceptive context. One of the remaining tasks of this chapter will be to chronicle the story of the attempts to use OD resources in Plastics Division to influence organisational change. In exposing the limited impact of those OD resources explanations will be sought both in features of the context and in the actions of those concerned with trying to use OD concepts, values, and technologies. But before getting into the detail of description and analysis I shall follow the pattern of the chapters on Agricultural and Petrochemicals Division and present an overview of the birth and development of OD in Plastics Division.

PLASTICS DIVISION'S USE OF SPECIALIST ORGANISATION DEVELOPMENT
RESOURCES: AN OVERVIEW

The point has already been made that the life histories of organisation development activities in Agricultural Division and Petrochemicals Division could not have been more different. The Plastics Division OD story is quite different again from either of the two north-east England divisions. The differences between Plastics Division OD and the other two divisions are at all levels – the antecedents and origins of OD, its location in the organisation structure, the leadership and internal life of the Plastics OD resources, the nature and extent of their sponsorship in their divisional context, and ultimately their impact on the division's business, organisation, and culture. Ironically it could be argued that of the three divisions it was Plastics division that needed the skills of a change resource group the most, and yet of the three divisions Plastics was the one which was least able to use the change resources they had.

The origins of the Plastics Division interest in OD go back, as it did in the other two divisions to the late 1960s. But whereas in other divisions of ICI at that time there was quite high level interest in American behavioural scientists, it was an assistant personnel manager, Paul Miles, and the division education officer, Simon Dow, who took the lead interest in Plastics Division. Because of their location at the Welwyn headquarters neither Miles nor Dow had a great deal of contact with production or weekly staff matters and they had little involvement with WSA and its introduction into Plastics Division. The character and focus of OD in Plastics Division was, therefore, very much set towards monthly staff and the Welwyn headquarters, although notable development activities led by works managers did take place in three of the production units. Dow also later acknowledged that Plastics OD work began "very much in an educational sense – not for consulting and diagnosis", although there were developments in the consultancy area later.

Just as Miles and Dow were beginning to develop some understanding of what the behavioural sciences and OD were, and what they might offer the division, Paul Miles was promoted out of the division in 1969 and took up an appointment in Agricultural Division. We have already discussed the significant role he played there over the period 1969–76. Before Miles left, however, he did initiate the process of recruiting a "behavioural scientist" – a 25-year-old British-trained Ph.D. social scientist with no industrial experience – David Cowan. With Miles off to Billingham the behavioural mantle, such as it was, and the new recruit, Cowan, passed to Simon Dow.

At this point Dow, with two or three graduates and the apprentice and secretarial school staff responding to him, had the name of his department changed from education department to training and personnel development department. Dow had joined ICI Plastics Division in 1951 with a D.Phil. in chemistry, had worked as a research scientist for 7 years, and then spent 3 years in Millbank as personal assistant first to the ICI chairman, Lord Fleck, and then Paul Chambers. He returned to Welwyn in 1960 somewhat broadened by these experiences but worked again in Plastics on technical development work. His move in 1966 into the role of division education officer was a reflection of personal interest in the development of people, and a realisation by others in Plastics Division that Dow was one of the few active thinkers and writers in the division who was looking out of the division and trying to examine how changes in the social and economic environment of the firm would require increasingly novel responses in the human and organisational area. Having his department's name changed to training and personnel development department was one novel response which, while appearing to set his flag in a particular direction, also caused confusion: Dow takes up the story:

> This was [the new name] interpreted by me and my boss as OD but people misconstrued this and it caused great confusion and still does with personnel department. I was responsible to the personnel director, and at board level it was he who had OD responsibility. But that came more from Millbank than being formally understood and agreed on the division board. Really he looked to me to take the initiatives.

Interestingly the initial objectives for the Training and Personnel Development department (T&PD) were couched in highly businesslike terms. The 1969 statement of department objectives was as follows:

> To provide a service to the division which, through the media of education, training, and consultancy, assist the division board, the product groups, and other departments to obtain in both the short and the long term, more productive effort and positive net cash flow from the division's human and other resources sooner than could be obtained from their own efforts alone.

This businesslike but also rather vague statement of objectives was probably a genuine reflection of the real feelings of lack of clarity about ends and certainly about means that Dow must have experienced at that time. He as yet, of course, had had little formal training in the behavioural sciences or organisation development, and there was no-one of Noel Ripley's calibre or experience to assist him in framing a mission and the ways of realising any particular objectives he had.

Whatever the statement of objectives, T&PD began "very much as a department devoted to apprentice training". Over the period 1969–72 the department expanded its role, doubled in size, and came to include three people who were primarily involved with OD. In 1970 Tom Hunt temporarily gave up a career in sales and marketing and joined Dow and Cowan to make up the OD trio in T&PD. Hunt and Cowan had the titles training and development adviser. The other professionals in T&PD included an assistant manager, and five training officers each with training responsibilities in a particular functional area. From the beginning there was a conflict between the OD trio in T&PD who were quickly dubbed the "in-group" and the "out-group" of the assistant departmental manager and the training officers. This conflict between the in-group and the out-group survived the exit of the assistant manager in 1972, and changes in the individuals in both groups as well as Dow's change of post in 1975. The conflict weakened the department throughout its history and was still around when T&PD was wound up as a separate department in 1979 and became just the training section of the personnel department.

In terms of activities the key T&PD event of 1969 was a letter from Dow to his personnel director boss heavily criticising Plastics Division's low commitment to training, and particularly behavioural training for senior managers. Dow's letter sent in the context, of course, of both MUPS and the recently launched companywide SDP, led to the creation of a board subcommittee in 1970 and to a series of senior people sampling various management training packages. Faced with "a primarily reactive, non-planning divisional culture", Dow took the view that "our chief strategy should be to change the culture – it obviously needed change at the top more than anywhere else – so we went for the top with all the methods we could". Dow later said "it was like driving horses to water that didn't want to drink". But between 1970 and 1972 senior managers and directors did attend external courses on Action-Centred Leadership, Coverdale, Blake's Grid, Reddin's 3-D, and one or two T-groups. In addition a series of potential senior-level external consultants came into the division, but they were deemed as unsuitable as some of the training packages.

These reversals were accompanied in 1970 and 1971 by some distinct successes which might have translated into more solid gains but for the dampening and anxiety-producing effect of the bad financial results of 1971, and the 20% redundancies amongst monthly staff in late 1971 and 1972. The successes included Dow's participation in the companywide and month-long workshop in organisation development at Eastbourne, his first sustained training and skill development experience in OD. In terms of project work 1970 and 1971 witnessed structural and team-building work in one of the marketing groups, Hunt's opportunity to do similar work in a production environment, and T&PD's first real impact across the division in the training sphere, their creation of a problem-solving and human relations course for middle managers called the Group Achievement Course.

The successes that T&PD were able to conjure up in 1970 and 1971 have to be set against a background of continuing scepticism of the value of management training, and relatively low legitimacy for the much more explicitly behavioural objectives of T&PD. In 1971 the T&PD department objectives were:

> Continuously and systematically to improve individuals' skills, the effectiveness of individuals' work in groups and the way in which corporate objectives are achieved by the groups.

But three years into its existence T&PD was faced politically with no active senior sponsor, considerable senior opposition, and in spite of the seeding provided by the group achievement course no broad client base at the middle levels of the division. In addition the development activities or aspirations of the OD in-group part of T&PD were in some conflict with both the personnel and the management services department, and T&PD had no sustained external consultant support to the group itself. The department's standing in the division was not helped either by the public disagreements between the in-group and the out-group, and by Dow's not always successful attempts "to walk the talk" and manage his department along the participative lines his group were advocating on training events.

In this situation of tentative success with a few activities, continuing high-level opposition, and lack of internal cohesion and group commitment T&PD had to face the redundancy threats of 1972. Initially Dow was told to reduce T&PD from 24 staff to 4, but in the negotiations which ensued the actual reduction was held to 12. Dow tried to manage these events by a process that was "open" in the sense of facing his people with the problem of redundancy and the fact that he (and the personnel director) felt it was important to retain the OD component of T&PD. This is an extremely difficult process to manage. Given the stage of limited cohesion and self-confidence in T&PD there was great stress and some tendency for all involved to interpret the experience as showing that "you can't manage openly" or, indeed that "OD doesn't work".

As it turned out, although Cowan and Hunt, the two full-time OD members of T&PD, were not made redundant in 1972, both of them actually left the department during the following year. All of this left a much-reduced department with reduced OD capability operating in a context which had become, if anything, less receptive.

The period from 1973 to 1975 was a time for limited rebuilding helped briefly by an improvement in the division's profitability, the appearance of a new deputy chairman and a couple of directors who at first seemed to be willing to push for organisational and behavioural change from the top; and perhaps a lessening of the in-group – out-group split in the T&PD department. One internal OD consultant was recruited to replace the two who left in 1973, and he joined the training officer responsible for the engineering function – who had had works OD experience – and that pair became the behavioural or OD focus in T&PD.

In terms of activities T&PD continued their middle management division training work through the group achievement course and a new course on leadership. Works-based OD activities which had got off the ground during MUPS carried on at Stockton, Wilton, and Hillhouse but only Dow of T&PD at Hillhouse Works, was involved with this work. On occasions the OD pair in T&PD were able to carry out project-based OD work with individual clients in headquarters departments, but repeat work was rare, and there was never any sense that OD work was systematically taken up by any of the Welwyn departments.

Perhaps the most important work in the 1973–75 period was Dow's attempt to get back to his original objective of changing the management culture on the Welwyn site. Before the Ph.D. social scientist Cowan left the division he completed two pieces of interview-based diagnostic work and wrote penetrating reports on "Organisation Problems. of Plastics Division" and the "effects of financial control systems on management behaviour". For reasons we shall explore later this work fell on stony ground, so Dow tried again – this time for the first time successfully opening the door for a well known British Social Science academic to work as a consultant to the Plastics board. Again the available archival material reveals both the accuracy and incisiveness of the consultant's diagnosis and the promise in some of his suggestions for dealing with Plastics Division's top-level problems of management organisation and behaviour, but this consultant and his message, together with another external consultant who followed him, were also deemed inappropriate or otherwise unsuitable. Looking for tangible success from this board level work, the only sign that Dow could point to was the board decision in 1975 to formulate and publish the division's objectives.

In November 1975 Simon Dow left his post as manager of T&PD to take up a role as division staff resources adviser. In the six months or so before Dow took up this new role, he put energy into trying to bring developmental activities in the division closer together by forming a tripartite meeting of a sympathetic personnel manager, and a newly appointed divisional management services manager, and himself. The new management services manager, Michael Reilly was an experienced production man who had been an OD activist and thinker at Wilton. Eventually Reilly was given the dubious responsibility for providing a focus for OD in the division, and he, Dow, and the personnel manager continued to meet to see if they jointly could make an impact on the Plastics Division management culture. Two streams of activity emerged from this trio. One was a highly innovative joint management and weekly staff educational package called "Minding Our Own Business" (MOOB). This package of videotaped material, overhead projector slides, and syndicate work, was designed amongst other things to aid division employees to understand the business information they received, and to further their ability to appreciate "better the disciplines and controls that are necessary to the company's survival and growth". Before long the package had been sold to four other ICI divisions, was being actively sponsored by leading members of the CBI, and was being taken up and modified by other large UK employers. The trio who created it in Plastics Division, however, had to shield it from board scrutiny whilst it was being put together and then were roundly criticised by more than one division director for "wasting division resources". MOOB was eventually licensed to a training films organisation for wider marketing.

The other activity of a culture change character which Reilly and Dow got off the ground in 1976 and 1977 returned more explicitly to the theme of the board culture and the relations between the board and the 60 or 70 senior managers just below them. Three conferences were held for the senior managers and chaired by three different directors in order to provide an input for the senior managers into discussions about division objectives, organisation, and productivity. Undoubtedly these were cathartic experiences for a group of senior managers still smarting under a hierarchical, controlled, and detail-conscious board, but although the deputy chairman who originally sponsored the conferences described them as a major breakthrough in terms of board and senior manager understanding, many of the senior managers became disillusioned when "overnight the board didn't suddenly change its style of behaviour". Worse still for OD resources in the division, some of the board members felt threatened by these assemblies of senior managers below them, and this confirmed their suspicions that the individuals leading OD activities were championing illicit causes through irregular means.

In 1977 Dow was promoted out of the division and the mantle for internal change through OD techniques fell singularly upon Reilly. He tried in a worsening business climate both to bring in external consultants and to encourage group building amongst the set of OD resources still identifiable in T&PD, and his own management services department. But the arrival of a new chairman in 1979, a tough new personnel director who assumed responsibility for driving some organisation change matters, and an increasing climate to hunt overheads meant that OD and training resources in the division became increasingly vulnerable. As we have already noted, between December 1979 and December 1981 monthly staff numbers in Plastics Division were reduced from 3713 to 2958. Included in that group of 755 monthly staff who left ICI were all the individuals who would have described themselves as offering an OD service, together with nearly all the trainers from the old T&PD department who had earlier been relocated as the training section of the personnel department. Plastics Division had now merged with Petrochemicals Division and the numerically Plastics-dominated component of the new division board were tackling the business, organisation, and manpower problems of this new entity with a purpose and vigour appropriate to their troubled business circumstances. Senior line managers were now firmly in the seat driving organisation changes and at Welwyn there was no place for the division's indigenous OD resources in helping along those changes. The indigenous OD resources were clearly seen as part of the division's problems, and more clearly than ever as not part of the process of solving those problems. Having for so long tried to awaken Plastics Division, now that the new giant had stirred, the OD resources were one of its first victims.

ANTECEDENTS

In what follows I will return to describe and account for the antecedents and origins of OD in Plastics Division. Following the pattern of presentation of the chapters on Agricultural and Petrochemicals Division conceptual elaboration will be kept to a minimum, although focus is provided on the antecedents of OD and a distinction is made between the "internal evolution" of the Plastics OD resource group and that group's "external evolution". The internal aspect refers to the evolution of the group's membership, values, distinctiveness, commitment, conflict, and leadership, and to the intragroup and environmental factors that influenced these. The external evolution of the group refers to the group's strategies of boundary management, its external sponsorship and opposition, the focus and nature of the group's work, and the evolution of the group's legitimacy in its divisional context. These broad analytical categories will be located in a largely chronological presentation which focusses first on antecedents, and then is organised around the three characterisations of creation and early life of Training and Personnel Development Department 1969–71, redundancy and the false dawn 1972–77, and demise 1977–81.

Of the three ICI divisions examined in this book undoubtedly Plastics Division was the most unreceptive, some would say hostile, to the goals and methods of OD. Crucial in explaining the unreceptive context in Plastics Division must be some of the factors highlighted in our earlier discussion of the management organisation and culture of Plastics Division. The reader may recall that some of the core features of the Plastics Division management culture were business growth and ease of profitability throughout the 1950s and into the 1960s, great stability and continuity in the top management of the division right up until 1972, the relative isolation of Plastics from many of the structural and business area changes of ICI, the geographical separation of the Plastics headquarters from their production sites, and the attitudes and behaviour characteristic of the management culture with its emphasis on hierarchy, deference, scientific rationality, and non-risk-taking. Added together the above features make up a context which was unreceptive to organisational and behavioural change, whether the pressure was from an OD resource group, or as we shall see in the 1970s from individual directors or groups of senior managers below the board level.

Aside from the heavy hand of constraint provided by a stable context, a further antecedent condition which made the early life of OD in Plastics Division difficult was the absence of a period of social innovation at Welwyn, or indeed of powerful social architects of the calibre of George Bridge or John Harvey-Jones. Compared with the two north-east England divisions the late 1960s antecedents of OD at Plastics Division were low-level and low-key. Behavioural science ideas were being picked up by an Assistant Personnel Manager, Paul Miles, and with the assistance of the Division Education Officer, Simon Dow, being communicated as best they could throughout the division. Dow takes up the story:

> During the period 1967–68 Paul Miles carried the OD flag [but unofficially] with me as an outside admirer and provider of forums for him to preach from on courses. We had a very good relationship. I listened and got an interest in behavioural science . . . But much of this was presented in the educational sense – not for consulting or diagnosis – and it was quite often rejected, but Paul pressed on . . . He had a list of allies which he passed on to me – people who were beginning to be out of their cradles on this, but it was not nearly as much as Paul or I would have liked.

There were, of course, towards the end of the 1960s, other attempts to introduce changes in attitude and behaviour in Plastics Division but these were located in production environments. Hillhouse Works in Lancashire had been one of the trial sites for WSA, and Darwen Works also in north-west England had been one of the earliest sites to try and introduce management by objectives (MBO).

> MBO in the division went the way of MBO almost everywhere else. It was a complete failure, so people thought, in terms of people adopting it. But it wasn't a failure in all senses. I personally think it was a success in seeding the idea of objectives into a primarily reactive, non-planning divisional culture.

But sitting as they were down at Welwyn, and without production experience themselves, both Miles and Dow were not part of these early experiments in the works. Dow later said of WSA:

> At the time, I simply didn't understand the significance of it. It was something that happened up at the works. I was a headquarters man.

So when in 1969 Paul Miles was promoted to a personnel manager position in Agricultural Division all that had been possible to achieve in the way of preparation for OD at Plastics Division was to attract and gain Dow's enthusiasm, to set in motion the recruitment of the young British Ph.D. social scientist David Cowan, and to use educational experiences and internal documents such as *Management, People and Change: Notes on Behavioural Science*, to begin the process of drawing to people's attention the potential role of the behavioural sciences to create organisational change. OD, as it was starting to be called by the few in the know, now passed to a forward-looking training manager Dow, leading a training and education department with no history as a force for innovation or change, and including a new recruit Cowan with no previous industrial experience. Neither Dow nor Cowan had at this stage any formal training or professional experience in using OD concepts and techniques, and because of his headquarters location Dow had missed the opportunity of establishing himself through the WSA change programme. There had been no George Bridge or John Harvey-Jones to push a bow wave of pressure for change through Welwyn, and Millbank was more preoccupied with the problems of the massive investments at Wilton than the still less obvious organisational and business problems at Welwyn. In these inauspicious circumstances Simon Dow launched OD on to the prickly and inhospitable rocks of the Welwyn management culture.

CREATION AND EARLY LIFE OF TRAINING AND PERSONNEL DEVELOPMENT DEPARTMENT (T&PD)

Explicit in the above discussion of antecedents of OD in Plastics Division was the lack of preparation and climate setting for the OD resource that began to emerge in the division in 1969. Looking back to the division in the late 1960s it would not be an unreasonable question to ask that given such an unreceptive context why and how was it possible that an OD resource group ever got off the ground there at all? The answer to that question probably lies in two areas. Firstly the pressure coming out of Central Personnel Department at Millbank to build up divisional change resources to ensure the implementation of the centrally created change programmes of WSA and SDP, and secondly the circumstantial availability of individuals such as Miles and Dow who were interested enough to see the possibilities of developing their own role and function by using new ideas from the behavioural sciences and OD, and aware enough of local problems of organisation and behaviour to recognise that such new ideas may have been of some assistance in tackling those problems. Given a certain amount of Millbank pressure on the Plastics personnel director, and the willingness of Dow to follow Miles' lead, politically what was required in the hierarchical and differentiated culture at Welwyn was for Dow to recruit the support of his functional director boss and begin the process of getting OD on its feet. The personnel director and Dow thus agreed that the old division education department was to be renamed,[1] and that this new department was to be the home for any internal specialist OD resources in the division. As we have already noted this arrangement between Dow and his boss "was not formally understood and agreed on by the division board". Using the legitimate and possibly only channel of his functional boss, Dow therefore set up T&PD with the barest kind of divisional understanding and legitimacy. T&PD were never fully to recover from this probably necessarily illegitimate birth; indeed some of their actions over the next two years were to endanger their fragile legitimacy even more.

No doubt using the pressure and support for more management training coming out of Millbank, and the more favourable environment for trainers created by pressure on management from the new industrial training boards, Dow was able to expand a department which in the past had been largely devoted to apprentice training. By the end of 1970 T&PD came to include three people primarily involved with OD (Dow, Cowan, and Hunt) and an assistant manager Walsh, who assumed responsibility for a group of mainly graduate training officers each of whom took up responsibilities for training in various of the key functions of the business. The relic from the past, the apprentice training part of T&PD, seemed an odd bedfellow with the above OD resources (called in fact training advisers), and the training officers. Hunt recalled:

> I don't think the apprentice trainers ever began to understand what my job was because it never impinged on them, or anyone they knew, and they really had no conception of what I did, although I sat and had endless cups of tea with them. They ran their section at that time – the apprentices as part of their daily routine used to wash out the toilets – they ran it as if it was a ship, they were all ex-naval, and that was how it was run.

But if the link between the apprentice trainers and the rest of T&PD was at times a source of bewilderment the link bettween the OD trio and the training officers was a good deal more troublesome, and throughout the period 1969–72, and beyond, a further drain on T&PD's attempts to acquire some legitimacy in a largely indifferent or even hostile environment.

---

[1] Dow later acknowledged that "it was fortuitous that T&PD was the chosen name – my boss was sick at that time and the division secretary dreamed it up".

External evolution of T&PD, 1969–72

One indicator of how tentative OD was in Plastics Division in 1969 can be gauged from Cowan's account of how he was recruited:

> Curious, they advertised for a behavioural scientist. They clearly had little idea what they wanted beyond sombody who could inform our discussions with research evidence. I got put into training rather than personnel purely because Paul Miles initiated it and Simon [Dow] was the only other person who understood what it was about . . . I don't think I was recruited initially to do OD. It gradually changed, partly because I got interested by going on lots of courses, more in OD than research.

Dow and Hunt also acquired their training whilst they were seeking to define their activities, identify their potential clients, and formulate a strategy to influence their environment. Hunt also emphasised the boot-strap character of their beginnings:

> Oh yes, Simon took a very wide view of his role . . . he certainly saw OD as a terribly logical extension of the training activity. I don't think either of us really understood how it was going to be done . . . neither of us had terribly clear ideas of which way to run and so we just took a number of actions like going on a few training courses, meeting a few other people who were doing that sort of job and actually pitching in and trying to do a few things with anybody who was willing to listen.

Both Dow and Cowan acknowledged that in its earliest days the OD resource group in T&PD had no strategy, although there were attempts to develop one. Cowan remarked:

> There certainly wasn't a strategy of OD that I was recruited into [in 1969]. There wasn't by the time I left [in 1973]; mainly we responded to any opportunities that came up. We also publicised what we could do with a brochure . . . a training booklet, and by going round to senior managers to talk about the training for their staff . . . The idea of this talking was that if organisational – non training – things came up then Tom, Simon or I would get drawn into that. It didn't happen much.

Dow agreed with this:

> I remember many meetings when we were saying what the hell is the strategy? This was a response to the fact that there was not a nice, neat defined strategy. It was a much more opportunistic approach which also reflected the culture of the division. As professional OD people we always felt guilty about this. That's not to say we haven't tried . . . but the plans didn't always work . . . the degree of acceptance we've had has always been low.

What Dow was clear about, however, even in 1969, was that "there was a need for an OD thrust serving the total system, and for training officers suited to the particular sub-cultures" (functional departments). He was also clear "that the major objective of OD was changing the division culture". But how were he and the others to attempt that? The route that Dow initially chose was behavioural training for the board and for senior managers immediately below; "we tried to get board members doing what Mond and Agricultural Divisions had done – to experience the kind of thing that would enable them to see what SDP and OD were all about".

Frustrated already by the lack of senior management interest in training, Dow sat down during the Easter holiday period 1969 and wrote to his boss what in the context of the Welwyn culture must have been a blistering and highly risky letter. Dow talked already of being "despondent", of the "cynical and complacent" reception given by Plastics Division managers to the recently launched SDP, of the training initiatives being taken by other divisions showing Plastics in an unfavourable light, and crucially "the fact that this division appears to be spending only about half as much per capita on management training as is ICI as a whole".

Before going on to make specific recommendations Dow indicated "it is also clear that I must proceed beyond the point at which the present management culture in the division would suggest I ought to stop, otherwise we shall only be tinkering with the problem". His recommendations included:

1. A clear initiative from the division board in implementing SDP.
2. Training at board level by an external consultant to facilitate attitude change.
3. Reorganisation at board level to permit co-ordination of management effectiveness improvement.
4. Personal involvement by general managers and functional directors in training their work groups.
5. A decision by the board on which type of management training is to be implemented across the division.

Stung by these accusations of board indifference and reticence in matters of organisational effectiveness and human resource training, the personnel director "felt it was a serious situation and he persuaded the chairman to set up a committee in 1970 consisting of two deputy chairmen, the personnel director and myself to consider what management training was required at senior levels". Having forced the issue, however, Dow realised that "none of the other board members believed that anything needed to be done – so we began with a very low commitment". The result was that over the period 1970–72 "the board found all sorts of excuses – only about half the board experienced some form of training for change", and the reactions of those who agreed to go varied from "saying his time had been wasted, to coming back quite enthralled, and I felt it was necessary to restrain him because he was evangelising, to damning it with faint praise saying it might be useful to section managers". Crucially perhaps an already sick chairman "himself went on a T-group, not long after, had a serious illness, a stroke, and died. There were those who attributed this to the experience of the T-group."

One of the deputy chairmen around the period of the early 1970s who successfully resisted any encouragement to sample these management training experiences focussed his doubts on T-groups.

A number of our directors and possibly some senior managers went on T-groups and this is where I am declaring prejudice. It isn't prejudice, I have very strong views about T-groups, I think they are wholly wrong and almost evil actually. Somebody who had been on a T-group, a man who went onto the main board of the company, summed it up by saying T-groups turn a strong man into a real bastard, they don't touch a normal man, and they destroy a weak man, and that is entirely the wrong direction, any course should do the reverse. Anything that leads to people bursting into tears, weeping, and in the case of one man I know, I definitely attribute his need for early retirement to the fact that he went on a T-group. I would not dream of going on one myself . . . Of the other courses people have been on Blake, Reddin etc, the effect has not been particularly strong but anything I have observed has been favourable. Whether it in fact matches the cost, I have no way of judging.

The downright opposition or reticence of board members eventually culminated in February 1972 with a board minute that "although it would be advantageous if all its members attended a Reddin seminar, the time was not ripe to make the board the focal point for extension of the training". Instead the board recommended that a controlled experiment be conducted in one of the product groups, further information collected and a "go/no go" decision made on whether Reddin training would be applied across the division. As one of the managers in this product group put it, "one day a board member came in and said we're going to do this – just like that. There was a combination of interest from previous exposure to Reddin, and resentment." Dow himself commented that it wasn't entirely successful because the director left, so the ownership was unclear. The new director allowed it to continue but without commitment and the most senior manager had never agreed with it in the first place, so he was lukewarm. Eventually, of course, the "go/no go" decision was not taken and the assault on the Plastics Division management culture through the mechanism of director and senior management behavioural and attitudinal training drained into the sand.

While Dow was making his first attempt to change the division culture through management training events, there were three other events going on in the division all with actual or potential organisation development significance and which barely involved T&PD. Two of these events could probably be regarded as successes – indeed were so by many managers involved with them – but paradoxically because they were successes, and they took place in works environments (Hillhouse Works SDP and Plastics Works at Wilton, Coverdale training) their successes did not spread to Welwyn, and may even have weakened T&PD's attempts to do similar things at the headquarters. A senior manager in the plastics factory at Wilton commented on the gap that developed between his works and his headquarters after Coverdale training:

> Plastics Division didn't accept Coverdale. So we as members of Plastics at Wilton, were very conscious of being different. I mean flip charts were unknown at Welwyn, indeed positively frowned upon. They were regarded as a Wilton gimmick.

A senior director from Welwyn echoed the above manager's perceptions of the exclusive character of Coverdale's impact up at Wilton, noted the success up there and his own resentment at not being part of the Plastics works sub-culture, but of course did not encourage Coverdale as a culture change vehicle to spread down to Welwyn:

> Coverdale was a very different matter from Blake, Reddin, and the other training courses because it was taken up by parts of this division with enormous enthusiasm, particularly our Wilton works. There was a time when it was divisive that people who had been on Coverdale courses were able to talk to each other very well but they could not talk to the rest of us because they built up a new language. Five years ago [in 1971], when I used to hold meetings with Wilton people, I couldn't tell what they were talking about because they used English words with entirely different meanings, and I used to get irritated by this but they were so convinced in their local environment. The works manager was absolutely convinced that he was getting much better results from his staff because they had all been on Coverdale – the overall effect of Coverdale on those bits of the division which picked it up was very favourable but I just felt slightly jealous at not being allowed into the club, as it were.

Dow also noted the success of Coverdale at Hillhouse Works – it had "a big effect on the culture, you got a tremendously positive and supportive climate there". But there was no diffusion of the learning from Coverdale from Hillhouse Works either. Dow commented:

> However, they did nothing to spread their leadership position in change to Welwyn . . . that was one of the things I tried to get them to do.

Presumably the Hillhouse management saw the bad feeling that emerged at Welwyn as a result of the Coverdale subculture that developed at Plastics Works, Wilton; maybe they also realised that it would have been politically suicidal to push for change from a subordinate position and a production base in a division which was so hierarchy and status conscious, and so influenced by the research and marketing people at Welwyn.

With the lack of success of Dow's attempts to change the Welwyn culture, and little scope for diffusing ideas and methods successfully implanted at Hillhouse and the Wilton Plastics Works, there was only the centrally driven SDP change mechanism left to try and influence the Plastics Division culture. The SDP was not only a rank failure at Welwyn, but because by 1971 T&PD had publicly changed their departmental objectives to closely correspond with SDP's objectives of "improving individual skills in groups, and the way corporate objectives are achieved by groups", T&PD's reputation was sullied through association with SDP. This was all the more tragic because none of the T&PD staff were formally responsible for co-ordinating the implementation of SDP in Plastics Division.

Dow in the letter to his personnel director boss of April 1969 had already pointed out that even at the launch of SDP in Plastics there was evidence of managerial "cynicism and complacency" about SDP. When, however, SDP began to be introduced in a "terribly mechanistic" fashion into the division, and with the wrong aspects emphasised – "how can we reduce the numbers", the person co-ordinating 'its implementation' didn't like the job and was soon moved". Dow then found that he became, "not officially, but people and the division newspaper referred to me as: 'Keeper of the division's conscience on SDP.' That meant I was the butt of complaints from staff that the division was not keeping faith on this." Dow thus became guilty by association. On top of this, however, the redundancies of 1971 became associated in managers' minds with SDP, and this sealed SDP's fate as a change vehicle, and further weakened the use of OD based attempts to change Plastics Division. The following comments reveal characteristic attitudes to SDP and some of its consequences:

Divisions differ and I think SDP was regarded as a bit of a charade here. (Senior Manager)

* * *

I think SDP really fell on its face because it was brought in immediately after WSA but without anything like the consultation . . . the difficulty I found was that a lot of the managers were not behind it. In general the staff were, but it does not take them very long to find out that the managers are cynical about it. (Training Officer)

* * *

You see it came at a very unfortunate time because we immediately started running into financial troubles in 1970/71. There was a most extraordinary reaction from the majority of managers. They did not see it as anything new at all, what they did was to turn round and say – look we do this already, all good managers do this, now let's forget it and get on with our work. (Training Officer)

* * *

SDP has hindered quite a number of times when I have suggested some OD to the managers. People said "oh you mean another SDP?" and the implication was that would be a bloody waste of time. SDP was not a real exercise. I think it was basically sold to the management as being: look, we've given away on pay to the unions with WSA, we have got to do something for the staff as well, and here is something we have dreamt up, it will not be too much trouble, it will keep them quiet. (Training Adviser)

Neither Dow's own initiatives to change the division culture through management training nor indeed the Millbank-driven SDP had any great impact at Welwyn. The question was, would any other opportunities present themselves to create culture change through other mechanisms? A chance meeting in mid-1971 at the Welwyn staff club bar between David Cowan and the division chairman provided Cowan with an assignment to do a study of the division's problems. In the worsening business situation of 1971 and in the context of still greater competition developing at the prospect of Britain entering the EEC the division chairman had written in the *Plastics News*, 24 September 1971, that:

> We shall have to find ways and means of achieving the expansion of our business by means of greatly increased productivity without expansion in our overall personnel numbers. This is bound to involve a readiness to accept change at all levels and innovation in our organisational methods can be just as important as technical innovation . . .

Was the chairman's statement of the importance of organisational innovation and the opening provided for Cowan likely to provide the catalyst for cultural change? Cowan interviewed 15 managers with experience in all the major functions in the division and in seniority terms covering the range from junior manager to division chairman. He then fed back the patterns in the interviews to the 15 managers, received confirmation and additional interpretation of the data, and then in December 1971 prepared a report titled "The Organisation Problems of Plastics Division". Regrettably perhaps in terms of its political impact the report contained only an incisive diagnosis – no solutions were offered for the problems identified. Cowan picked up five key problem areas in his 1971 report which were to reappear time and time again from other diagnostic work throughout the 1970s. The problems were stated in these terms:

1. There are too many management levels for the amount of management the division's business requires.
2. As a division we do not do enough strategic planning, nor do we have sufficiently clear objectives.
3. Too much decision-making power is concentrated at the top of the division.
4. Individuals and departments work too often in isolation, and collaborative work is impeded by both the formal and informal reward structure.
5. The division's culture is too cautious and deferential – people seek to avoid mistakes rather than to grasp opportunities.

Dow takes up the story of the burying of Cowan's report:

> He produced an excellent report which lots of people said hit the nail on the head. It surfaced in December 1971; by this time the chairman had been on his T-group. He wasn't well himself. He'd forgotten the report and he got it only within a fortnight of having his stroke. It was passed onto the deputy chairmen who knew nothing about it and had more worrying business problems. They were horrified by what they read – some of it ought never to have been written, they said. So the whole thing got buried until the new chairman came along in 1972. The personnel director gave the new chairman a copy but I've no idea how he reacted.

Against this picture of apparent failure T&PD did have their successes. Two of the successes involved OD project work in a Welwyn marketing group and in one of the distant production units. In both cases the stimulus for the work had been heads of department with real problems of creating change in people and organisation who had been sensitised to OD methods, and had enough confidence to use novel methods of tackling their problems without a great deal of public support from their line manager peers. The works manager who successfully used Hunt as an OD consultant in his works on objective setting, team building, and training assignments later said:

> I think we made great steps. We shut down a quarter of the plant with no IR problems because everybody knew that was the objective, and replaced it with other plant. But we had to keep it [the OD activities] very quiet from headquarters because the product director had said we will not spend any money on training . . . I really had to put a veil around it.

T&PD's most significant success at this time, however, was in getting a division-wide management training event off the ground which subsequently provided them with one of their few continuous activities throughout the 1970s. This training course, known as the Group Achievement Course, got division support partly because it was a joint venture with interested people from the Management Services Department, and partly because the behavioural elements on the course were played down and the problem-solving component of the course emphasised. T&PD were now beginning to recognise that political processes could be used to create as well as inhibit changes. Hunt takes up the story:

> Walsh and I started to develop the Group Achievement Course and we very quickly realised that we could not progress without the full co-operation of the Management Services Department. Luckily for us Howard Dudley was enthusiastic and joined in. They had a number of training courses that taught problem-solving. We saw that if we based the whole thing on the concept of problem solving that was very suitable to the culture, that would go down well . . . the personal element was worked in insidiously.

Dow also recalled that the course "was strongly OD oriented but the people who went through it wouldn't necessarily experience that because it was almost de-jargonised". But undoubtedly another reason for the group achievement courses' continuing viability was that its target audience was the middle reaches of management. As Dow said, "it's really become the prestige course of the division. It's supported by the chairman and it hasn't got many detractors . . . but again it didn't come up above the middle management group."

Internal evolution of T&PD, 1969–72

As we have already seen, soon after its creation in 1969 T&PD was made up of the apprentice and secretarial training schools components, Cowan and Hunt as the OD specialists, Walsh the assistant manager, and five training officers, each with responsibility for a particular functional area. Dow as the manager certainly concentrated on the OD and behavioural side of the department's work, while Walsh, formally second-in-command of the department, was largely kept on the conventional training side. In terms of group building and socialisation the group began in 1969 with almost no significant personal experience of behavioural work. So learning their own business was something of a boot-strap operation. Dow, Cowan, and Hunt sampled a variety of OD and human relations training packages. The training officers were exposed to similar training opportunities but to nowhere near the same extent. At the beginning there was nothing that would be recognised as team building in the OD sense, and certainly no group activities of the intensity, of Ripley's Swallow Group at Billingham. By 1970, however, a number of attempts were made to engage in team building activities using off-site events, and on some occasions external consultants. But given the group's inexperience, plus the sceptical predispositions of some individuals in the department, these attempts at group building were difficult, halting, and groping sessions.

Even before these 1970 attempts at team building were attempted T&PD had already firmly split itself into the in-group of OD specialists Dow, Cowan, and Hunt, and the out-group of Walsh and the training officers. This in-group – out-group split in T&PD persisted throughout the department's history and was a continuing source of further weakness as T&PD sought to increase its legitimacy in an always resisting and sceptical environment. Dow described the source of the split in his department in these terms:

> The groups were formed as much as anything by the structure of the department . . . certain people were designated as doing OD . . . OD had a glamour at the time – it seemed to be a key to the corridors of power; this meant the outs resented those who were in . . . The differentiation made my life difficult because I felt there was a need for an OD thrust serving the total system and for training officers suited to the particular sub-cultures . . . I still don't really know [in 1976] how to solve it.

The strength of feeling of the outs to the ins can be gauged from these comments from out group members.

> Whether they feel superiority they certainly acted as though they were. There was definitely them and us, and I found that most uncomfortable. The culture of the in-group was: oh well until you have worked a long time in this area we dare not let you loose on the world at large, you just keep to the training thing and do not get too involved in these behavioural science things. You really need a hell of a lot more development before you can do them. To join the in-group one had to gain credibility in the world at large but it was difficult to know how to start. It certainly produced all sorts of nasty tensions in the department; and it was obvious to the outside world. I would have thought it got near to being disastrous for the department as a whole because the credibility of the department was going down because they were looked upon as being too long-haired anyway, being too theoretical, too behaviourally oriented.

There were a lot of personal contests and largely people went their own way. I don't think they were ever resolved. Individuals who did not like the behavioural sciences thought it was a load of crap and thought they would go on with more structured training.

* * *

There was a terrific gap. There were Dow, Cowan, and Hunt in that group and the rest of them in this group, and this group would very much stick to themselves in the office together and go to lunch together. There were two distinct groups altogether.

As some of the above comments reveal the consequences of the in-group–out-group split were real enough in terms of its pattern of internal working and external image. Internally there was interpersonal conflict and at times resentment, the in-group screened their "glamour OD work" from the out-group, and the out-group jealously held on to whatever contacts, work, and credibility they acquired in their functional parish. The lack of cohesion in T&PD, and the resulting discrepant messages which this communicated to their potential clients at Welwyn, provided further data for the sceptics who were looking for ammunition to say no to many of the OD and behavioural science initiatives attempted by the department. Only in the running of the group achievement course did T&PD pull together as a department and work well as a team in an activity widely supported in the division.

A factor related to the internal evolution of T&PD between 1969 and 1972 was the evolution of Dow's own managerial style. Dow himself recognises that his own development from a conventional, highly conceptual physical scientist to behavioural scientist/manager was not particularly smooth either for himself or for his department. Dow recalled "at the time OD came in there was a clear value for participation and I deliberately moved in that direction . . . in the early days, 1969–71, we went through a tremendously open and high risk-taking period when I really broke taboos and gave (to particularly the OD in-group) a tremendous amount of information". However Dow's strong value for participation, which he genuinely tried to implement, allied as it was with a desire to release sensitive information just to the in-group, sometimes created confusion and indecisiveness amongst a group which was already lacking in cohesion. Three members of T&PD commented on Dow's leadership style and its consequences in these terms:

Well it was kind of authoritarian/participative. Dow wanted desperately to be participative. Our meetings would oscillate wildly from our being told, to Simon [Dow] sitting back and taking no lead at all and our wandering around in small circles, enlivened occasionally by rather personal and obviously very deeply felt rows and altercations between Simon and Peter Walsh.

* * *

Simon called meetings fairly often, he shared out a lot of information which many managers would not have shared out, he went to great lengths to pass on information. But even so I still found him rather selective about it.

Simon would think it was participative, I would call it laissez-faire where you did your own thing in your own way. It slowly changed though. Simon became more aware of what the division wanted and I think he also became more aware of the politics of the division and then he would direct us rather gently into fields where we should be working.

In summary what emerged from this pattern of internal development during 1969, 1970, and 1971, was a rather uneasy agreement for people to work their own patches. Individuals were committed to what they were doing but not to any common set of priorities or purposes, and certainly not through agreed means. But ground had been broken, beginnings made in a hostile context, and with very little external aid. What happened next might easily have flattened a lesser enterprise, and it did in fact cause no small amount of pain.

The 1972 trauma of the first enforced redundancies in Plastics Division affected T&PD more than most Welwyn departments. Initially Dow had been told to cut T&PD from 24 to 4, but he managed to hold his department to a 50% cut when the average across the division was around 20%. Dow's own account of how the process of handling the redundancies in T&PD were managed was the real learning experience which moved him away from his attempt to lead through openness and participation.

> From 24 we in T&PD came down to 12 with pressure to come further. The one bit of success was that my director said you retain the OD people because we'll need them when we're through this. So it was a question of getting rid of the apprentice and secretarial trainers . . . My strategy with the department had been an open and participative one and I saw this as putting that to the test . . . so I was pretty open and said this was what was required. In retrospect I think it was a mistake. People couldn't take it and got worried. My assistant manager was affected more than anyone else and he left. It exacerbated the in-group–out-group conflict . . . It should really have been handled by more traditional methods. I was too open . . . I still maintained a fair degree of openness but I retracted a bit after that.

Image of T&PD by 1972

A useful means of providing a summary of the positioning of T&PD in its context in 1972 is to examine data on the image T&PD had acquired after three years of its existence. In addition to interview data collected explicitly for this research and archival material reporting on particular activities, one other significant source of data on T&PD's effectiveness and image is a report prepared by a Plastics Division manager dated July 1971. Dow had suggested to the manager that as a training project before taking up a new post the manager might complete a data-based study on the effectiveness or otherwise of T&PD and make any appropriate recommendations for improvement.

On the positive side the report describes favourable attitudes to the traditional training activities of T&PD and acknowledges that since Dow took over the education and training function there had been an "immeasurable improvement". This view was also echoed in the research interviews. The deepest questioning of T&PD's activities was in their behavioural science related work as it was described in 1971. No mention was made in the manager's report of the term OD; thus a proportion of the respondents in the managers sample – perhaps 40–50% – held the view of the whole of T&PD, and of Dow, as being more interested in behavioural science than in training. T&PD were seen "predominantly as odd, off-beat people with no hair, long hair, funny waistcoats or unusual approaches, although there were one or two 'sane', normal characters about". But while the data in the report revealed this scepticism and antagonism towards T&PD as a group – and certainly to their behavioural science work – there were also attitudes of interest, sympathy, and curiosity shown by some managers towards the behavioural sciences. A feeling that "behavioural sciences had a contribution to make, but they were not sure where".

Dow in his own comments on the manager's report thought that his own department had been "stereotyped". It is interesting, he wrote, "that individually people showed sympathy towards behavioural sciences; collectively they seem to be more antagonistic". Probing beneath these statements about the reasons for T&PD being ladled with these negative stereotypes, it is likely that T&PD's own responses to the unreceptive context where they worked helped the development of the negative views. Faced with a management culture that emphasised hierarchy, deference, autonomous action from individuals with strong positional power, and strong values of technical rationality and control, perhaps some members of T&PD pushed too hard with their own rather exclusive values and language system. Certainly when the OD in-group were interviewed in 1976 they all agreed that their approach in the period 1969–72 had been too exclusive, too particular and not pragmatic or political enough for the harsh environment they were working in. Dow commented that in 1969 "we tried, or were seen to try to peddle values, humanistic psychology and the like. This wasn't altogether successful." Hunt remarked that around 1970 and 1971 "Theory Y, and being honest and open were regarded generally like motherhood as being a good thing; there was a kind of do-gooders syndrome of saying yes, participation, co-operation and delegation and all these things were absolutely marvellous." Hunt went on to say that "by the time I had done enough jobs I began to see how successfully some parts of even our operation here work on the basis that most people would describe as Theory X. I think maybe it is much more a matter of doing what is necessary in a situation." Cowan was even more sure, as he put it, that they had only got hold of one piece of the jigsaw:

There was a mini-culture in T&PD that there were lots of things wrong with the way the division worked and the way ICI worked, and we knew what should be going on and if only people would listen to us things would change dramatically for the better. In retrospect that wasn't true. It was because we'd got hold of one bit of the jigsaw that actually very few other people were bothered about. Had we ever been able to put that bit [OD] together with everything else we might have had some effect. We were swamped by much more powerful considerations like major wage bargains, like the technology, and the competitive pressures.

For a time some of the training officers in the out-group sought to protect T&PD's overall standing by playing down behavioural science language and values. One member of the out-group put it this way:

> I was very anxious to get outside managers on my side and on the side of the department. I felt we could do a tremendous amount for other departments and groups if only they would come along with us and I felt I was prepared to sacrifice principles of OD and behavioural science for the sake of getting alongside people.

But in the period when the in-group were acquiring their own OD professional language and technologies of analysis this kind of out-group pragmatism was not acceptable and by the time members of the in-group had adjusted their own influence strategies most of the out-group had distanced themselves emotionally and personally from the in-group's "glamour" work and were "doing their own thing in their own way in their own patches". This was their recipe for influence and survival during the high period of anxiety of the 1972 redundancies.

In fact Dow managed to protect the rump of the OD in-group, and the out-group of management and supervisory trainers during 1972, although in 1973 Cowan left ICI and Hunt left T&PD for a line management position in another part of Welwyn.

The period 1969 to 1972 had been a very difficult one for all members of T&PD and although there had been some successes these must have seemed minor compared with the problems of trying to gain acceptance to tackle problems of people and organisation through methods which were still alien to most managers at Welwyn. As one member of the in-group put it, "generally there were relatively few people who were interested, the ones who did show an interest certainly got anything they wanted, but it was a matter of responding to any request we got. I remember thinking at the time that the thing must have been extraordinarily lonely for Simon [Dow] trying to get the thing off the ground. Our department had the lowest influence of all."

REDUNDANCY AND THE FALSE DAWN, 1972–76

With Cowan and Hunt now gone Dow had to wait until 1974 before he could persuade his director to allow him to recruit another training adviser who would have specialist responsibilities for behavioural science and OD matters. The new recruit, Watkins, came from another part of ICI, and he and Smyth – the training officer responsible for the engineering function in Plastics Division, a man with works OD experience – with Dow jointly took on the mantle for OD in T&PD. But if anything the impact of the 1972 redundancies in Plastics and the worsening business situation was to make organisational change even more difficult to obtain at Welwyn. Even with a new chairman, and at least three new directors who were predisposed to use OD techniques, and certainly were sensitive to the need for significant changes in management culture and practices, the division appeared, as one manager put it, to "freeze":

> By 1971 the effect of perhaps being slightly slow to recognise various kinds of changes external to ICI were beginning to have an impact, we went into a major cutback – redundancies. The ability to change in some ways became harder although fairly major change was wanted. Once we ran into a contracting situation with people, one would always run up against blocks of how you cope with the people concerned with change. I have an overall impression the division tends to rather freeze on things because it is too difficult to set it up in different ways.

After the shock and the reduced activity which resulted from the 1972 redundancies T&PD attempted a period of rebuilding but more based on individual initiatives than any collectively agreed upon and externally sponsored plan. The successful training and OD work begun around the period of WSA continued at three of Plastics Division's works but T&PD staff were little involved in this work. T&PD's conventional training activities for middle managers continued also to receive support, and a new division leadership course got off the ground and with the Group Achievement Course was one of the few activities that T&PD members shared. One of the T&PD staff training officers who was a shrewd observer and actor in the Welwyn informal social and political scene managed for the first time in 1973 to get a group of managers, supervisors, and shop stewards together in a workshop training event. As Dow said, "this would have been unthinkable 2 or 3 years before".

Watkins and Smyth, the focus for OD activities, continued to face problems of lack of acceptance inside and outside T&PD. Both of them were not well received when they first arrived in the T&PD office to start work. Watkins talked of "a lot of testing going on, people were trying to prove they were more subtle than I was". Smyth said, when he arrived in T&PD, "I felt a bit deserted. I did not have a telephone to start with and there did not seem to be an office arranged for me. I felt unwanted." Part of the problem Smyth and Watkins faced would be explained by the history of in-group – out-group split in the department, and, of course, the public knowledge that Dow and his personnel director had decided that if anyone were to survive the 1972 redundancies in T&PD it was to be the OD component of the department. But Smyth and Watkins did have this body of expertise – and perhaps also a set of proclaimed values which the training officers in T&PD felt were quite inappropriate for the Welwyn culture.

Watkins described his values in 1976 in these terms:

> I would see a society which is more caring and which is less based on greed and fear, more based on love. I accept the reality of power and the necessity for it but I think there is a great need for a change of emphasis. I believe that people can have a great deal more creativity within themselves than organisations give them the scope to use; to the individual's and the organisation's detriment. Given those sort of values then I would want to encourage more questioning of assumptions, ways of doing things: more considerations of alternatives, more fun, more excitement.

Smyth answered a question on his values, also in a 1976 interview, by revealing how he thought the training officers in T&PD saw him:

> Apparently I do a lot of talking. I go away and do funny things like meditation. I have learned all about psychoromatics and they say "what is that? It is a way-out thing Norman does." I go to encounter groups. I do re-evaluation counselling and I talk a lot about things which are concerned with the behaviour change individuals can bring about in themselves. It is seen as being rather hairy and unrelated to real life, and I have found that I have had to play that down.

Certainly the training officers did react – perhaps over-react – to what they saw of Smyth's and Watkin's values. One said:

> One of the things that gets in the way is what he calls his value system. I tend to get the feeling if my value system differs from his then mine is either automatically wrong or inferior, and if other people pick up that same message then I reckon he is going to come across pretty badly. I see his value system where everything concerning people is all important to him, and must take priority over every other consideration, as unrealistic, totally impractical in business.

Given the Welwyn management culture and their own predispositions, neither Watkins nor Smyth found it easy to generate work which they found professionally appealing. Smyth remarked that "I felt tension every time I thought about approaching a client. I did not know what the reactions were likely to be. I felt unsafe really. I felt much safer with just getting on with running courses so that was largely what I concentrated on doing for a year or so." Watkins, as the only member of T&PD who didn't have a functional training "parish" to retreat into, had, of course, to be more active in seeking out clients for OD-related work and this eventually encouraged Smyth to be more initiative-taking, but neither of them found it easy. Watkins stated the obvious painful truth:

> There are taboos which are specific for the OD function. One is: don't be ambitious in an OD sense. It is a low-key, low-status function. I don't think the division is really interested in a really professional approach to OD which is to do a real system diagnosis of the total system, identify what are the significant blockages and really blast through with the power behind you to sort them out. There is a pretty strong status taboo about, for instance, going to the managers meeting which is held from time to time. How one is supposed to do organisation development work when you are denied access to where all the important issues get discussed, I don't know.

In spite of this obviously non-receptive climate for their work Smyth and Watkins persevered and occasionally they did generate project-based OD work with middle management clients in Welwyn departments, but there was little sense of momentum or direction behind this work and even where their clients did report on the OD work as being successful, repeat work or follow-up work was uncommon.

Asked about the contribution of T&PD over the period 1969–76 most managers concentrated their positive remarks on the educational and conventional training side of T&PD work. This meant that to most managers T&PD's impact had been in the area of personal development rather than organisation development. Great scepticism was expressed as to the value of employing specialist OD resources on organisation problems unless they were external consultants from one of the big business consultancy firms. And as for behavioural science, a commonly expressed view by Plastics Division managers in 1976 was that "it was unfortunate that a lot of this stemmed from America. It sounded like the latest American gimmick, and people tend to think that's alright for the Yanks but won't work over here. Again, universities have got a bit of an image to live down. So academics from America are doubly dubious."

Dow's strategy by this time for dealing with T&PD's continuing legitimacy problems was on the one hand to try and de-emphasise what he called "the soft end of the business", i.e. interpersonal related interventions, to coach and counsel and feed information to Smyth and Watkins where he felt this might provide them with an entry, and to try and get as close as he could to some of the new members of the divisional board who appeared initially to be looking to create organisational changes. From about 1972 onwards Dow appears not to have put a great deal of energy into team-building in T&PD, no doubt partly because the in-group–out-group split was well established, but also because most members of the department had by now come to some accommodation with their differences, and largely went their own way with whatever work and sponsors they generated. Dow's tendency to manage by or through individual coaching drew some criticism from T&PD members who argued they at times needed more direction but acknowledged that they might have resisted it had it been offered. The other part of Dow's leadership style of shielding his board-level contacts from group members, and releasing information selectively to individuals, while done for the best of intentions, had the effect of raising group suspicions about his motives, and his actual capacity to help them.

Most of Dow's time was now spent trying both to encourage and facilitate directors and senior managers who wished to create change in culture or organisation, and to quietly plot with a small number of allies and help them develop their own change initiatives. Perhaps the three most important pieces of work Dow was involved with in the period 1973–76 were to finally succeed in getting a consultant working for the Plastics Board, to help set up a divisional mechanism for senior managers to influence the direction of the division, and to help create the educational package Minding Our Own Business (MOOB). All three of these activities were a return to his long term, and by this time seemingly unattainable goal of attempting to create some degree of culture change in Plastics Division.

The Plastics Division board and organisation development

The Plastics Division board in 1974 was composed of a chairman, three deputy chairmen, and nine directors. Of the nine directors, four were functional directors, four were directors and general managers of business areas, and one was Plastics Director ICI Europe. The lack of team working on this board was described earlier in this chapter. The reader will recall that power was heavily concentrated in the Chairman and his three deputies, and that the individual directors largely played representational roles for their function or business area, rather than members of a collegiate board assessing the overall problems of the division and making decisions as appropriate. The historical trend for concentration of power with the chairman and his three deputies ("the top box"), and for detailed reviewing and assessment of directors' and senior managers' activities, was given a further twist by the worsening business situation of the mid-1970s. One senior manager in the division summarised the workings of the board in the mid-1970s in these terms:

> Well the board is undoubtedly very much deferred to in terms of power, and relatively minor things have to go to at least the executive sub-committee of the board for approval. Tightness in the business in the last couple of years has meant that more stuff has been retained by the board for approval than it was even a few years ago – even something as trivial as the number of apprentices we might take on next year. And it is not just the board as a whole, there is a fairly tight group on the board which retains the power to itself, that is the chairman and his three deputies.

As we have seen, Dow's first attempt to influence the attitudes and behaviours of individual board members in 1969 and 1970 through the use of behavioural training experiences had met with a mixture of scepticism, opposition, and deflection. Dow, Hunt, and Cowan had all talked of the pre-1972 board as being "very reactionary", of there being one or two supporters of OD but these one or two being "overwhelmed by one or two people who were right down on OD". With the death in 1972 of the last of the chairmen who had come into the division on its creation in 1945, Millbank saw this as an opportunity to bring in not only a new chairman from another division but also younger men from inside and outside Plastics who might help to dilute the old culture. But unfortunately two of the old directors most resistant to cultural change stayed on into the mid-1970s and continued to be "a drag on innovation" – and certainly innovation spearheaded by OD methods and behavioural science ideas.

One of the two deputy chairmen most resistant to behavioural science ideas emphasised that it was T&PD's attempts to push participative management styles which created board resistance, and once Dow and his group had been "branded as theoretical" or "impractical" almost anything that came from them was likely to be rejected:

> I think they have been thought by some of the managers to be going rather too rapidly towards changes in management style, changes from the rather more oldfashioned, not necessarily authoritarian but classical, traditional management style, towards a fully participative style ... T&PD's association with behavioural science has inhibited the acceptance of some of their views among some of the

older and more traditional managers. There is perhaps a feeling that because of a rather theoretical treatment of relationships, some managers have rejected the probably very sensible practicable, very obvious message which they are also putting across at the same time. Certainly one of our division directors was so opposed to the behavioural science aspects which Simon Dow was putting forward that he almost rejected everything which came from that department, and there might just be a little bit of that in some of the rest of the board, possibly a little bit of that in me.

This was the kind of context that the new chairman and the new directors who followed him came into between 1973 and 1975. Two of these new directors had been early adopters of OD methods in the late 1960s, and both had successfully used internal and external OD consultants to assist with team building, culture change, and organisation design problems. Both were surprised, even dismayed, by what they found on the Plastics board:

I was brought into this division, and I came with this OD background, its values, and it came rather as a shock to me. I had assumed the rest of the company was moving at this pace and it took me many months to discover that people were not even on the same wavelength. OD was not accepted, and in a number of areas was being positively rejected. I began to see that I was in an entirely different culture . . . There was a complete blockage any time you mentioned something like OD, behavioural science; we need to do something about the culture. The hackles went up, the resistance was there, and it was very widespread. Simon Dow let me know about this very early on. I could hardly believe it, I had to learn the hard way that he was absolutely right. It was looked on as some new-fangled thing – behavioural science – that knocked the stuffing out of people, it removed control from authority, it weakened structural authority, all sorts of things you dare not let in.

The other director was equally emphatic about the reactions of the Plastics board to OD and behavioural science, and he realised that if he was to survive he had to disassociate himself from OD methods and behavioural science language:

OD was not understood: I don't think many of the other board members had been through the experience I'd been through . . . When I first came down here, all full of behavioural science, I was taken aside and told if I wanted to last, to be listened to, I better drop that. I don't use the jargon now, well not collectively, maybe with one or two people.

Undismayed by what he knew of the history, and with what he saw as some potential supporters coming onto the board, in mid-1974 Dow saw an opportunity to introduce a distinguished British social scientist, Sam Roberts, into Plastics Division. The opportunity arose because the central OD man, Stewart Dudley, invited Sam Roberts to spend a week in London and different divisions had time with him. Dow takes up the story – "It was quite difficult to get this division to respond . . . we have learned a bit and a certain amount of deviousness was used by my boss and myself to get people. We couldn't get any directors. It was up to head of department level – there were about eight or nine of us."

This group of eight or nine met in London for a day with Roberts, each arriving with a flip chart describing the problems of Plastics Division. Dow remarked "the incredible thing was the similarity of the independently arrived at conclusions . . . it really got people turned on, you could see they felt very deeply about it." Encouraged by this cathartic experience, Dow took his notes from the day to his personnel director "who approached the chairman and said this was something pretty serious . . . and we then employed Roberts as a consultant to the chairman".

Before going on to describe what Roberts did alongside the Plastics board it may be useful to summarise a few of the key points made by the nine managers at the London workshop, and Roberts's initial reactions to the managers' diagnosis. There is a remarkable similarity between these managers' accounts of the division's problems and the message rejected in Cowan's 1972 report on the Organisation Problems of Plastics Division. The problems were classified in four areas: company philosophy, motivation and morale, manpower problems, and organisational difficulties. The division was said to be not aware of, and responding to, changes in its social environment, not to be recognising that a growing proportion of its monthly staff were becoming increasingly alienated from the company, and that the recent 20% drop in monthly staff was having a significant effect on the division's age distribution and promotion prospects. Crowning these issues, however, was "the busyness of seniors", "everyone wanted to be consulted"; matrix "was leading to interference, to confused messages, to dissonance, and to unclarity as to *who* is managing. Management levels were failing to cohere and communicate: individual middle managers thought they were correctly diagnosing the situation, but the top managers had no time to listen, so did not hear." Apparently "organisational pressures were preventing top management from stopping to listen to the warning signals that are likely to undermine their strategies for the business. Somehow a 'uniting for change' mechanism must be developed."

Roberts' view was that it was the duty of senior management to represent these views upwards, however unpalatable, and they might have to persevere over a long period of time until the validity of their message became undeniable. In the meantime what was required at Welwyn was a process of "de-bureaucratisation", a loosening of control from the top in order to transform Plastics Division into a "learning system", and the management group below the board required to form an assembly or assemblies in order to "help create their own future".

One of the senior directors favourably disposed to OD takes up the story of Roberts's activities after the London managers' workshop:

I don't think the chairman knew very much about that first meeting [in London] but the outcome of that meeting was certainly fed to him, and Roberts was introduced to the chairman, and the chairman was, I think, quite interested in what Roberts might be able to do and listened to him . . . my own view of the managers' meeting was that it was very valuable because it began to loosen things up a bit, but at that stage I was still a bit naive about the resistance. Roberts gave a number of cautions that there was anger around and frustrations and that we had a problem in this division because something or other wasn't getting unleashed. Then we did have some quite useful sessions where each member of the board had a session with Roberts, and then Roberts had a feedback with us all, and with the chairman. We had one very good session which looked as if it was going to make some progress. Then there was another session where I do not know what went wrong but he just did not come across well at all and there was a rejection, a very powerful rejection from one or two of the then deputy chairmen.

Dow explained that in the preliminaries to the final meeting with the board, Roberts and the chairman had requested each of the directors to prepare individual papers on "culture and organisation – more emotional things rather than the mechanistic things". In order to prepare the papers the directors had meetings with their senior managers, some of these "were extraordinary – one was scheduled to go from 2 to 4 and went on until 10 p.m without a break". These papers were to have been discussed at a board meeting for a whole afternoon with Roberts present. Again Dow supplies the detail:

The meeting was absolutely disastrous. The morning business spread into the afternoon and in the end there was 20 minutes for Roberts to give feedback which he'd prepared for an hour or two. He didn't acquit himself well and 2 of the deputy chairmen became antagonistic and became a focus of strong opposition. They persuaded the chairman we shouldn't go on. Roberts came back once, but really he's been quietly dropped.

Even though Roberts built up his data about the division first from a senior management group representing many of the interest groups in the division, and then from individual board members many of whom concurred with the levels below them about what some of the problems of the division were, he eventually ran into a brick wall created as much as anything else by two of the deputy chairmen, and with the acquiescence of the chairman. One of these deputy chairmen had this to say about Roberts's intervention:

To be only fair I had a remarkable lack of sympathy with Roberts actually. In the one interview I had with him I am afraid we were at loggerheads the whole time. I didn't know what he was about and he didn't know what I was about. I thought his perception of what was going on was utterly wrong, particularly his perception of the relationship between the board and management . . . It seemed to me he was listening to all of the criticisms and documenting them very carefully and without paying any attention to the occasions when people thought this bit of structure or this bit of organisation was all right. I think he did have a meeting with the board. It didn't seem to me that we got a great deal out of that. You maybe are getting a rather extreme view from me – but the other deputy chairman was just as critical – even more so than myself. This was not only, I hasten to say, because Roberts was fairly critical of the way the deputy chairmen behaved. He was critical but I don't think his criticisms were too well based on that specific occasion.

With hindsight this was probably Welwyn's last chance to change its internal structure and management culture to meet the exactitudes of its rapidly changing business environment. In Roberts' terms, to create a self-learning and self-adaptive system to provide a clearer set of policies and management processes to help meet and better manage the environment that was fast encroaching on them and closing down their business options. As we have already noted, Plastics Division did not actually seriously contemplate radical changing business environment. In Roberts's terms, to create a self-learning and self-adaptive system to provide a clearer set of policies and management and Petrochemicals Divisions fell off the cliff in April 1980.

Dow, seemingly never dispirited, tried to introduce another well-known British academic into the division in 1975 but this was equally disastrous. A meeting was arranged over dinner at Digswell Lodge between one of the two deputy chairmen who had seen Roberts off, and this new British academic. Dow takes up the story:

> It was a hot day and Frank [the academic] turned up not wearing any socks. Oh dear! So a stereotype built up about external people. I'm not quite sure why the deputy chairman took such a dislike to Frank but he clearly did. He was extremely rude to him. I suspect it was partly because it was a recommendation from my boss and myself – rather than from a trusted person.

Dow's final two interventions in Plastics Division

In spite of the promise and then the failure of the Roberts's intervention, Dow in a 1976 interview described the period 1975–76 as "OD in the bloodstream". By this he meant "this was the first year in which I thought things were happening of their own accord – with management taking their own initiatives. They didn't talk about OD, but they acted." The source of the action in, for example, the engineering function was the movement out of traditional managers and a new divisional engineering director, and a new engineering manager. More generally the pressure for change was coming from Millbank, faced with poor financial results in 1975 and a renewed desire to improve ICI's productivity levels in comparison with their European and North American competitors. So if there was change in the air in 1975 and 1976 it was not because of a belated recognition of the value of OD objectives and methods, it was because of line management pressure. The question was, would Dow and T&PD be used any more than they had been in the past?

In fact what happened was that a new deputy chairman tried to use the 1975 productivity drive to start more general processes of change in the division, facilitated, if not spearheaded, by Dow in a new role as staff resources adviser. Initially this seemed to be on, and Dow moved out of his role as manager of T&PD to become division staff resources adviser. Unfortunately board level opposition meant the deputy chairman had to back off his intended use of Dow and other internal and external OD resources and, as Dow put it, "I'm not sure that I'm in as strong a position now as I was before. I fear I may not be." Not long after this – in fact in 1977 – Dow was promoted out of Plastics Division to another part of ICI. But while Dow was changing roles in the division over the period 1975–76 he managed to encourage a trio of informal supporters; himself, a personnel manager, and Reilly, the new management services department manager, to engineer two significant interventions in the division. One of these, involving off-site conferences for the division's managers, was partially successful, at least for a time, and the other, the MOOB educational package, was an undoubted success inside and outside of ICI.

But the deputy chairman's words take us back to the 1975 productivity initiative and his hopes to use OD help:

> I was made deputy chairman in 1975 when we were down into another trough and I was given as one of my prime areas to cover productivity. I thought: well at least I can ensure we handle this in the right way to keep the team motivated. The other deputy chairmen were utterly opposed to this and they came out really. It was the first time I really realised where the power source of the opposition determined to stop Simon in his tracks was. I probed a bit further. It was this thing he was doing which was seen as undermining authority – it was going to weaken authority at the top. So fears were around, it wasn't put into words but I could see what was going on . . . I wanted Simon to work with me as redeployment manager. Simon was quite excited about the opportunity because I could level with him what I wanted to do. At this point I tabled with my colleagues and got the shock of my life. I wanted new consultants in OD and teams working and then the battle broke out between myself and the other deputy chairmen. I had to back right up because I could not get the chairman to overrule the others. I really retreated and said O.K. we will define the job in a much more acceptable way to my colleagues.

After that the deputy chairman had to conclude that "an OD man at the senior level for this division is not quite justified – but I do want managers who are sympathetic to its use and realise its value." Not long after Dow left Plastics this deputy chairman was also promoted out of Plastics to a very senior-level appointment elsewhere in ICI. The Plastics Division management culture was to perpetuate itself come what may.

One of the resisting deputy chairmen had this to say as a final epitaph on T&PD in the Dow era:

> I regard OD and organisation change as very much a major part of the terms of reference of the board. I think initiatives ought to come both from the board and the deputy chairmen, it also ought to come from the sharp end of the business, the works, the selling organisation, and R&D. It will be nice if it also came from the management services department but that's a service department – a ways and means department rather than a department which initiates thoughts . . . If we are coming up to any organisational change in the division I personally would not have thought of Simon's department as the prime mover. I don't think T&PD was or should have been particularly concerned with OD. I am interested that you have obviously got a fixture in your mind that if you were looking for an OD unit in this division, it is that department that matches it, I don't see it that way at all . . . Simon has had a very good influence on the education, training, further

development of middle management in this division. Where I differ from him has been when he does in fact seem to broaden out beyond the individual into questions of structure and change.

Line management, and in particular very senior line management, were to initiate discussions of structure and change, and implement those changes through their own methods and processes. Dow's role was to concern himself with questions of personal development and training of middle managers – anything else was just a non-starter.

With any possibility of Dow or other members of T&PD working with the Plastics board now virtually ruled out, Dow set his store with another long-term ambition, to try and link T&PD, Personnel Department, and Management Services Department to help facilitate what he still felt was a bottled-up management desire for change in the division. There had of course, been difficult relations between T&PD and the Plastics personnel function ever since T&PD was formed in 1969. The use of "personnel" in the title training and personnel development department had, of course, caused "great confusion" with the personnel function, and management services were running training courses for the division and doing organisation studies before T&PD was born. Going back to 1970 there had been "a running problem with Personnel Department, sort of: we don't understand what you're doing (i.e. T&PD are doing) and it doesn't seem to have any real value and, frankly, the important things are the things we're doing . . . so you carry on but it's not of any great interest to us." Never accepting these prickly relations, and recognising the obvious overlaps between T&PD, personnel, and management services, Dow had in 1971 tried to conduct joint workshops with the other two departments to assist the process of identifying complementary activities and common needs for professional leadership, but these had failed to produce the kind of integration at the departmental level he had looked for. Personnel Department continued to insist management development was "in their area", that the T&PD training officers had "too much spare time" and how were we to know what results were to come from a department "so generously staffed?" Management services, although careful not to be seen to be "tarred with T&PD's long-haired and unworldly image" did co-operate with T&PD successfully with the Group Achievement Course.

While relations at a departmental level between the three overlapping departments were often distant and indifferent, Dow always had a good personal relationship with the personnel manager responsible for manpower planning, and when in 1974 those two were joined at Welwyn by Reilly the three began to meet informally and share information, problems, and hopes for change. These informal meetings coincided in 1975 with the deputy chairman's productivity change initiative and the deputy chairman sponsored a series of three conferences, each chaired by a different director, and with the process organised by Dow and his two compatriots. Dow and his two colleagues "felt well rewarded by our efforts in designing the conferences and the preparation of papers for it . . . and in a culture often quick to criticise, there was hardly any criticism" from the senior managers who attended. Again there was a cathartic experience for a management group who felt over-inspected, and over-controlled by the levels above them, and were desperately looking for ways out of the gathering problems of the business environment. But again while there was great consensus and commitment about what the problems of the division were – no action followed. The deputy chairman recalled that "we got a very positive constructive feedback with messages loud and clear to the board. Problems followed because the management were almost expecting overnight the board to suddenly change its style of behaviour." Dow and his colleagues acknowledged that while the conferences "had proved a valuable means of establishing a better understanding of division business strategy . . . they also called for a change in management style leading to trust between board and managers, and an elimination of detailed monitoring." These changes were too much for the board to take on in the short term, especially from an assembly of their subordinates. Dow put the fate of the conferences into stark perspective: "the greatest failure was in the planning of how to get the conference [ideas] into the rest of the power system".

Dow's final intervention at Plastics, and probably the one he would regard as his most successful, also came out of informal meetings between himself, Reilly, and the personnel manager. In the context of the 25% inflation in Britain in 1975 "we felt that there really was a dangerous lack of understanding of basic economics amongst trade unionists and even some managers; for example, a MORI survey recently showed that 54% of people in the sample thought that profits went to directors". The trio felt there was a contribution they could make not just in Plastics division but in ICI more generally, and perhaps in industry beyond, to develop a learning package which would help both shop floor and managers better understand the language of business and accountancy and connect it to their own factory or office situation.

Realising from past experience the Plastics board were unlikely to finance a training package on business realities training, the trio persuaded an ex-works manager who, although shortly to retire, was still influential, to join them in helping to develop the package which became known as Minding Our Own Business, or MOOB. After 3 months the ex-works manager proposed the package in its embryonic form to the works managers' committee. One of the works managers then agreed to help pilot the package in his works. There a shrewd training officer helped prepare the handouts, overheads and video films to make them acceptable to shop stewards. With the pilot deemed acceptable the production director acknowledged "this is just what we want" and the other works managers took their cue from this. With interest in MOOB solid in the production areas, other divisions interested, and a main board director regularly publicly calling for business realities training, and even a quote from a senior shop steward to be used – "the more we understand the business the more we'll understand one another" – the Plastics board eventually were shown MOOB and nearly all approved. Eventually most other divisions of ICI bought MOOB, and they and other organisations developed and modified Plastics' 11 video films, handouts, and slides. The package was eventually licensed to Training Films International for marketing.

As Dow said, eventually 25–30% of Plastics Division employees experienced MOOB, "still the biggest education intervention we had". But MOOB only got off the ground because it was steered around the Plastics board until it was a demonstrable success. No chances were taken this time. One of the design trio later remarked that "we were later accused by a director of spending £*x* thousands without any consultation with the board; meanwhile the outside world was saying this is marvellous."

But the time was now 1977, Dow had had his success in Plastics Division and was looking forward to a promotion elsewhere in the company. He must have felt some relief to be leaving Welwyn after so many years' toil in such an unreceptive context. Mike Reilly, the management services manager, was given responsibility for OD and it was left to him to watch both the rate of change increase at Welwyn and the T&PD variant of OD finally slip out of sight and out of mind.

THE DEMISE OF ORGANISATION DEVELOPMENT IN PLASTICS DIVISION

Given the history of lack of legitimacy of OD in Plastics Division, and the continuing problems of credibility its individual practitioners had, the reader may by now be wondering why and how it managed to survive so long. But survive it did and for 4 more years after Dow left Plastics Division in 1977.

Initially when Dow moved over in November 1975, to become Staff Resources Adviser, T&PD continued as a separate training function with its own manager – a man with a long period of experience in personnel work. His early mission had been to give more direction to the conventional training side of the department and generally to give the function a more businesslike appearance. He was plainly uncertain, however, how to assist Smyth and Watkins with their OD work:

> There is some concern about what everybody always describes as the behavioural end of the business and how effective it is. . . . Smyth and Watkins have great difficulty in making any significant entries into the division – they are not naturally called upon for interventions. If the division wants some fairly straight training activity to be done they would think of us, but they would not think of us if they wanted something done in support of OD. Whereas they might pop into management services, initially perhaps in a routine way if they wanted a study done . . . I do believe we are in a situation of seeking work in the OD field; this is a nonsense to me, either there is a natural demand for it or we don't do it.

Both Smyth and Watkins later acknowledged the veracity of their new manager's statement of the obvious. Smyth in particular freely admitted the "low acceptability" of his attempts to operate as a change agent – "OD was not accepted or understood by managers in this division; one could pick out the managers on the fingers of one hand who understood". Watkins, whose deeply held values about caring were well represented in his work, felt there was some acceptance "for work I was doing, and for myself in a role people couldn't define – it was more me being personally helpful in meetings, and as a person to talk to." But there must have been an element of wishful thinking in this and Watkins was deeply hurt by redundancy in 1981.

Dow's successor as a manager of T&PD did not have to wrestle with his problem for too long, for when in 1979 the division acquired a new chairman and a robust new personnel director, one of the first actions he took was to disband T&PD as a separate department and place it as a section within the personnel department.

Mike Reilly, the manager of management services, meanwhile had taken over in 1977 as "OD focus for the division". He defined his role in terms of OD as "acting on behalf of the company and division as a focus for the group of individuals – irrespective of departmental location – whose activities are mainly concerned with aiding the processes of change within the division." Encouraged first of all by Watkins, Reilly tried to pull together the OD resources in the division initially into what was called a "sensing group", and then what became known as the "OD core group". These groups of eight or nine individuals from management services, training, and personnel met periodically, sometimes with external consultant help, sometimes in consort with specialist OD groups from other firms, and every 3 or 4 months inside the division to discuss strategy, objectives and tactics – and to offer one another mutual support. But in the context of the history of attitudes to OD in the division, and the new sense of urgency and action by senior line managers "to get the fixed costs down" and "sort out the business" – the OD core group was left largely to talk to itself. As Smyth said "when the individuals left the group, they came up against the same barriers – the lack of power, the many people in high places who didn't value time being spent on development work".

For a time Reilly was optimistic there might be a role for OD methods and some of his core group. This was especially after three members of the board, and then on a separate occasion, three members of the OD core group, attended the company management of change seminars. The idea of these seminars was that with both senior managers and middle-level managers or specialists now using the same language to think about change processes they might form into "critical masses" to facilitate change. But the critical mass for change in Plastics, and indeed by this time in much of ICI, was the line management system, and the OD core group was not part of attempts to create change.

Reilly later commented that "I didn't spend enough time doing a selling job [for OD] with the board in general. That was a mistake." But Reilly was in a dilemma, he knew that the board were hunting fixed costs and all service functions were vulnerable – "I was a bit scared of making the OD function too visible – I was reluctant to make too many overt moves." Ultimately the board must have felt that "OD planning for change would slow things down and actually cause less people to go than ruthless management would. There were two strands in that, first a genuine belief in autocracy and secondly a more subtle thing. People were doing things they didn't like doing and felt they didn't want to be reminded. They didn't want a group reminding them of this. I don't think that was a valid perception of what we actually could have done. We could have more positively harnessed energy and purpose."

Reilly did have his successes in using external consultants, particularly in the strategy planning area, but he "could never persuade my boss (a director) to spread this. He felt if it was put up to the board it would be turned down, therefore better to leave it." The problem, Reilly insisted, was that it was "very counter-cultural to be seen to be using management techniques. There's something in Plastics about being a successful businessman which makes you not want to reveal that this is just a mechanism, and not just a brilliant piece of entrepreneurial thinking".

A problem for the Plastics board in 1979 and 1980 was, of course, that they were not producing the financial results expected of successful businessmen. One result of this was the merger of Petrochemicals and Plastics Division in 1981 and the large-scale redundancies in both divisions during 1980, 1981, and 1982. The joint division was still making a loss of around £70m after only two quarters of the financial year ending December 1982. But by mid-1981 the training function, and nearly all of the individuals who would have considered themselves as internal OD resources, had now left ICI employment. As one senior director put it "We were unable to use those resources. It isn't the culture or behaviour of this division to understand or comprehend organisation. Welwyn is divorced from the production plants and the sites where organisation and people are very important. Here they are all pragmatists – what prices can you get in the market, and individualists – not managers in the true sense of the word. People at Welwyn don't manage large groups of people, they work things out on an individual-to-individual basis. Therefore there is a feeling that "well what are those guys going to do for me? How much more profit am I going to get out of this guy?"

Ironically perhaps OD resources were thrust upon Welwyn in 1981 as a result of main board intervention. A well-known American external consultant, Tom Bainton, and Tom James the former head of Petrochemicals Division OD unit, were drafted into Welwyn to assist with the process of merging Petrochemicals and Plastics Divisions. Their activities will be described in Chapter 10 of this book when we examine Millbank's attempts to bring major structural change to ICI over the period 1977–83.

But before moving on to consider the ICI corporate changes of the late 1970s and early 1980s, there is the Mond Division experience of OD to examine. Mond Division started the 1970s with a management organisation and culture as divided as that to be found in Plastics Division of the same period, but the consistent top-level support for developmental activities in Mond from 1973 onwards meant that eventually, in Mond, OD methods and concepts were linked to some of the critical business, management, and organisational problems of the late 1970s. How and why this happened is the subject-matter of the following chapter.

9 The Top-Down Strategy for Creating Change: Mond Division

Until the merger of Petrochemicals and Plastics Divisions in 1981, Mond Division was the largest of the ICI divisions. In 1980 Mond represented 15–20% of ICI's interests in the UK in terms of capital assets, sales, and number of employees. As well as being large Mond had two other claims to prominence within the ICI group. One was its roots not only in the foundation of ICI in 1926, but before that to Brunner, Mond Ltd and the United Alkali Company. In addition, for most of the 1970s Mond had been second only to Agricultural Division in terms of the size and stability of its profits to the ICI Group. Mond was big, successful, confident and had a concept of self-worth founded not only in its latter-day business results, but also in its place in the history and development of ICI.

The 1980 economic recession badly affected Mond's profitability in the alkali and chlorine and derivatives product areas, and the fall from grace accelerated into 1981 and 1982. Only now (in 1983) is there some evidence of an improving level of business performance in parts of Mond, and this improvement could not have appeared on "the bottom line" without the £40m per annum savings in fixed costs derived from organisation and manpower changes made between 1979 and 1983. The structural changes made between 1979 and 1983 have affected the overall shape of Mond and have permeated to every level and most units. For example, the board of Mond has been reduced to a chairman and four directors, from an early 1979 situation of a chairman, two deputy chairmen, and nine directors. The senior management group of the division in 1979 was 270; by the Summer of 1983 this was down to 160, with the clear policy objective that 125 posts was the senior staff population required to run the business. Looking at the division as a whole, total employees were 15,684 in 1979 and by May 1983 this was down to 10,385 with 9000 as the policy objective by the end of 1984. Of the 5299 employee reduction made between 1979 and May 1983, around 1250 of the 5299 was a product of the transfer of Mond weekly and monthly staff onto the payroll of other ICI divisions. Nevertheless, these are dramatic changes combined as they have been with the reduction in the number of business areas, the appointment of a single general manager responsible for the total aspects of each business, the merging of a number of production works to form larger manufacturing sites, and the merging of some headquarters functional departments.

These changes in manpower and organisation were driven by a chairman and board of Mond who had been uplifted by the business pressures of the day. But in this case it was not just a question of a combination of the business imperative galvanising business purpose and political will to create necessary change, the other part of the jigsaw present in the Mond situation was the guiding influence of an intellectually coherent and well-communicated framework for thinking about the content of the changes, and the fairly broad development in the division of the process capability to make the top-down vision of the future shape of the division a reality rather than just a hope. The evolution of the above framework for change, hereafter referred to as the Mond Management Model, and the political will and process skill to make it happen, can be explained as a result both of the business imperatives of the day, and a long-term process led by a number of senior board members of Mond – with consultancy help, to first open up, and then clarify, the purpose and total business development of Mond in the changing social, economic, and political environment of the 1970s and 1980s.

The unique and eventually critical feature of the Mond OD work, as compared with the other divisions described in this book, was that for a variety of changing motives, and in different ways, it was led always by a small but powerful group on the board. This continuing top-level political support, persistence in using an American external consultant alongside a few internal development resources, and a long-term strategy which explicitly said start at the top and work down, not only helped to link developmental resources in and outside the line to business concerns, but eventually diffused developmental thinking and skills, far enough down into the Mond system to quickly and effectively respond to the business crisis of 1980. The fact that in Mond eventually developmental thinking and action were harnessed effectively, from the board's point of view, to the core business problem of survival does not mean that process was characterised by rational strategic intent, linearity, tidiness, and control. In fact, even with a certain level of top political support, the process of engaging OD to business matters in Mond was faltering, meandering, and haphazard. Some of the reasons for the faltering and meandering character of OD's engagement with Mond relate not just to the inevitable inexperience of those who sought to apply developmental thinking and action in the division, but also to certain core features of the business, organisation, and management culture of the division, which shaped the starting point and context within which developmental thinking had to make a start. It is to those important features of the business history and development, organisation, and management culture of Mond which I now turn.

BUSINESS HISTORY, ORGANISATION, AND MANAGEMENT CULTURE

The origins and development of the Mond Businesses

Mond Division is named after Ludwig Mond, who, in 1873, together with John Brunner, set up the first UK soda ash plant using a technical process developed by the Solvay brothers at Couillet in Belgium. One business and cultural stream running through the development of the compendium of business units eventually created and named in 1964 as Mond Division is the Brunner, Mond company which has manufactured and sold soda ash to the glass and detergent industries from a base in mid-Cheshire in north-west England, since the days of Queen Victoria. It was largely the drive of Sir Alfred Mond, Ludwig's son, and Sir Harry McGowan of Nobel Industries which led in 1926 to Brunner, Mond and Nobel Industries essentially taking over the two weaker companies, the United Alkali Company and the British Dyestuffs Corporation to form ICI. The truth of the takeover, as Reader (1975:3) asserts, was made brutally clear by the composition of the original board of ICI. Sir Alfred Mond was Chairman, McGowan was President, and all six other full-time directors came in equal numbers, from Nobels and Brunner, Mond. The other partners had to be content with part-time representatives.

What had been the Brunner, Mond business interests pre-1926, became known in ICI first as the Alkali Group, and then from 1944, the Alkali Division.

The second business stream flowing into Mond are the business descendants and developments from the United Alkali Company Limited. Predating the technical process for manufacturing soda ash developed by Solvay had been the Leblanc process. In the third quarter of the nineteenth century a sizeable chemical industry had developed around the Leblanc process producing not just sodium sulphate and hydrochloric acid, but also soda ash and eventually chlorine. It was the environmental devastation caused by the Leblanc manufacturers, which was so bad at Widnes even in those days as to stimulate litigation, which partly encouraged Ludwig Mond to bring the relatively cleaner Solvay process into England. By the 1880s the Leblanc manufacturers had all but conceded the UK manufacture of soda ash to Brunner, Mond, and by judicious use of recovery processes and other technical developments had expanded their product range to include soda crystals, caustic soda, and more crucially, chlorine. In 1881 the separate manufacturers in the Leblanc industry formed themselves into the United Alkali Company and tried to fight back in the soda ash business by setting up a new ammonia soda plant at Fleetwood in Lancashire; but in the period up to the creation of ICI the return on capital employed and profits of Brunner, Mond were far in excess of the United Alkali Company (Dick, 1973).

In his useful book *A Hundred Years of Alkali in Cheshire* Dick (1973:30) argues that the "ill-feeling between Brunner, Mond and the United Alkali company which existed over the years, encouraged, it must be said, by Brunner, Mond's scornful and suspicious attitude towards the United Alkali Company persisted in later generations and was slow to die." The persistence Dick is referring to, of course, is the tension which continued after the formation of ICI. What had been the United Alkali interests in chlorine, chlorine derivatives, and soda ash became first the United Alkali Group, and then the General Chemicals Division of ICI. The overlap in business interest between Alkali Division and General Chemicals Division was clarified early on in ICI's history by the transfer of electrolytic chlorine and caustic soda manufacture from the Brunner, Mond Group in ICI to the United Alkali Group in exchange for the ammonia soda plant at Fleetwood. This left Alkali Division with complete control over ICI's soda ash business and a monopoly of soda ash manufacture in the UK, but meant that General Chemicals Division consolidated their hold of the more rapidly expanding and developable businesses associated with chlorine and its derivatives.

Alkali Division's gentlemen with a taste for chemistry opened up the possibility of diversification from soda ash when at the Winnington Research Department in 1933 they discovered a "waxy solid found in reaction tube" which became generally known as the plastic polythene, but which was sold by ICI under the trade name "Alkathene", to celebrate its discovery in Alkali Division. Alkali Division's inherited prestige from Brunner, Mond was now consolidated by this important discovery, and by 1939 soda ash manufacture in mid-Cheshire was now complemented by the full-scale production of poly-thene. Even after the creation of Plastics Division, Alkali Division was able to ensure they remained responsible for the production, fundamental research, pricing, and licensing agreements associated with polythene's development. A 1943 agreement merely gave Plastics Division responsibility for sales, technical service and development of "Alkathene". Just after the 1939–45 war and into the early 1950s Alkali Division's standing in the ICI Group probably peaked. Reader (1975:309) is able to show that not only did a larger proportion of the younger men coming onto the ICI Board post-1940 have scientific and tech-nical backgrounds rather than commercial skill and experience, but a disproportionate number of the new main board directors came from the Alkali Division board at Winnington.

By 1952 Reader (1975:499) indicates the joint activities of the linked businesses then separately organised as Alkali, General Chemicals, Lime, and Salt Divisions employed assets of £89m and produced external sales of £50m with a trading profit of £9.23m. Billingham Division, the biggest single division in 1952, employed capital of £65.5m, had external sales of £60m, and generated a trading profit of £8m. A further indicator of the relative size, prestige, and business development of the UK divisions was the capital expenditure over the period 1937–52. In that period Alkali Division was third behind Dyestuffs and Billingham, and with £21m as a total for the period, only £1m ahead of General Chemicals. Lime Division and Salt without heavy capital requirements, being more concerned with extraction rather than manufacturing, spent respectively only £2.2m and £1.6m over the whole period 1937–52.

As we have seen elsewhere in this book the 1950s witnessed a surge of research, and process and product development activity, in ICI's Fibres, Plastics, and Heavy Organic Chemicals business areas. General Chemicals also continued to grow, partly because of demand for caustic soda, chlorine, and solvents from UK manufacturing industry, but also because of product linkages with other ICI divisions.

Meanwhile Alkali Division received the first of a series of blows to its identity and pride when in 1957 the main board of ICI decided to transfer complete responsibility for polythene and all the people working on it from Alkali to Plastics Division. Dick (1973) reports that the main board decision to remove polythene from Alkali was received at Winnington with "bitterness and distress". Worse was to come. By 1959 it was clear that neither Lime nor Salt

Divisions were likely to be able to grow or diversify to a level which would justify the fixed costs of separate status, and in 1960, Lime Division, and in 1961 Salt Division, were merged with the Alkali Division. Alkali Division knew now that the process which had started in 1957 could only end in one outcome. In 1963 the announcement was made by the main board that Alkali Division and General Chemicals Division were, from 1 January 1964, to be merged in a single unit, to be known as Mond Division.

In business and technical terms what had been happening throughout the 1950s was a soaring increase for General Chemicals Division's chlorine for products such as PVC and chlorinated solvents, and for products which required chlorine as an intermediary in their production such as ethylene glycol and propylene oxide. However, co-produced with chlorine through the electrolysis of brine was caustic soda at a level and a cost structure with which the lime-soda caustic made at Winnington could not compete. As a result General Chemicals Division took over increasing proportions of ICI's caustic soda production, and Alkali Division was left again to major in soda ash. Given the continuing business overlap between the two divisions, their reliance on similar raw materials and energy sources, the geographical closeness of the headquarters of the two units, and their associated manufacturing plants – most of which were concentrated in Cheshire and Lancashire, and the fact that the bad business results of 1958 and 1961 meant the ICI main board were hunting overhead – all made the four into one merger a sound business move. How the 1964 merger was handled, and its impact on the developing organisation and management culture in Mond Division, will form the theme of the next section of this chapter. For the present, perhaps a quote from Dick's book (1973:59), himself an ex-Alkali man will reveal something of what was to happen as Alkali was taken over rather than merged with General Chemicals:

> There was a very marked difference between the management styles of General Chemicals and Alkali. The analysis of this would be a complex and delicate task. Perhaps it can be summed up by saying that while over the years the climate at Winnington had tended towards a laissez-faire paternalism, that in General Chemicals Division was more authoritarian.

The newly created Mond Division started with a board of 20 Directors and 20,000 employees. Great energy had been and continued to be absorbed in what was seen to be vitally necessary re-structuring, and for a time in the 1960s "business evolution almost took second place to structural evolution". The headquarters of the new division was the recently built headquarters for the old General Chemicals Division at Runcorn. The division was organised into five product groups. The biggest of these, the Chlor-Alkali Group, was made responsible for the production and sales of all soda ash products, as well as of chlorine and electrolytic caustic soda. The second product group concerned themselves with chlorine derivatives such as chlorinated solvents and mono-mers, and chlorinated compounds for the plastics industry. The third product group looked after the fluorinated products which eventually developed into the valuable general chemicals product range used as refrigerants, aerosol propellants, dry cleaning solvents, anaesthetics, and fire-fighting agents. The final two product groups were the Salt Group and the Lime and Limestone Group. Apart from the merging of the Lime and Salt Product Groups into one group no significant changes occurred in this product group system until 1979.

On the production side the division had, and still has two centres of gravity. The manufacture of soda ash and related products at the mid-Cheshire Works – Winnington, Wallerscote, and Lostock. The other, and numerically larger, focus of manufacture are the production works around Runcorn and Widnes which produce chlorine and chlorine derivatives, and general chemicals. These works are Castner-Kellner, Rocksavage, Weston Point and Widnes Works. In addition to these two major sites, Mond also has production interests at Fleetwood – Hillhouse Works – and until recently had production works on both the Billingham and Wilton sites. Meanwhile rock salt is mined at Britain's only salt mine in Winsford, Cheshire, and limestone is quarried at Buxton in Derbyshire.

During the 1960s Mond joined in the general ICI race to develop and build new plant and processes and to close down or upgrade some of their existing plant. Runcorn in particular was a continuous construction site for much of the 1960s as Mond changed its feedstocks and the nature and scale of their plants in order to improve the output and operating efficiency of plants pouring chemicals into the expanding markets for chlorine, chlorine derivatives, and general chemicals. Plants were also developed at Hillhouse and in the north-east of England, but for reasons we will shortly explore, the assets in mid-Cheshire were relatively speaking neglected. However, for the engineers of the old General Chemicals Division known widely in ICI as the Engineers Division, life at Runcorn was all technological change and development.

ICI do not publish figures for the business performance of their UK divisions – what they have done since 1973 is to publish figures on a worldwide basis for each of their classes of businesses. Mond Division's performance is tied up in the set of figures ICI publish under the label General Chemicals. Taking 1974 as a benchmark, when in fact ICI did extremely well as a group, will allow us to explore something of the relative positioning of the General Chemicals businesses in ICI that year, and to estimate the business structure and performance of Mond early in the 1970s.

General Chemicals contributed just under 15% of group trading profits in 1974, making it the fourth-largest business area in profits terms after Agriculture, Petrochemicals, and Plastics. ICI's sales of General Chemicals in 1974 totalled £465m (including inter-class sales). Of these £322m (69%) were generated by UK investments and the remaining £143m arose from overseas activities centred mainly in Australia and Canada. In 1974 approximately 75% of total group investment in General Chemicals was located in the UK. That 75% really represents Mond Division, which covers the majority of General Chemicals in the UK.

Of UK sales of £322m in 1974, some 50% were to external customers, 25% were exports – mainly soda ash, caustic soda, and high-added-value air

TABLE 26   UK General Chemical sales (£m) estimated, 1974 and 1975

	1974		1975	
Chlor-Alkali Chemicals	140	43%	145	40%
General Chemicals	108	33%	135	37%
Solvents and Monomers	55	17%	65	18%
Lime	12	4%	10	3%
Salt	7	3%	5	2%
	322	100%	360	100%

conditioners and solvents, and the remaining 25% were to other divisions within the ICI group, over half of which went to Plastics Division.

Fielding, Newson-Smith and Co., a City of London stockbroking firm estimated in a 1976 publication on ICI that ICI's general chemical business sales in the UK could be assessed in terms of Mond Division's business areas, as shown in Table 26.

Taken together these figures reveal something of the strengths and weaknesses of Mond's competitive position by the mid-1970s. Its strengths were both product diversity in general and the marketing of products across a range from low value commodity chemicals to high-added-value specialty chemicals. It had modern up-to-date plant located close to controlled raw materials sources in the faster-growing general chemicals and chlorine–chlorine derivative areas. It was the UK's major producer of chlorine and caustic soda, and the sole UK producer of soda ash. It had, however, one major strategic weakness in the early 1970s, and a variety of others which escalated in importance as energy costs, currency changes, and over-capacity in commodity chemicals loomed larger by the end of the 1970s.

Mond's major strategic weakness was and still is its heavy sales and manufacturing weighting in the UK. Even by 1979 , and with a conscious strategic thrust of some years standing by the Mond board towards continental Western European and North American markets, about 70% of Mond's external sales were to UK customers. ICI's attempt in 1978 to buy into North American chlor-alkali and VCM markets by acquiring assets over there at Baton Rouge, Louisiana, quickly turned out to be a poor business decision, and by 1980 their Baton Rouge assets had been sold off to the Formosa Plastics Corporation. However, Mond's concentrated attempt to build up assets and market penetration was in Continental Western Europe. The public view in Mond Division at the moment is that the so-called Tripod Project conceived in the mid-1970s to link Mond with Wilton and a new chemical complex at Wilhelmshaven in West Germany, was strategically right but tactically unfortunate. The Wilhelmshaven facility, part of which is now on stream, will manufacture vinyl chloride and PVC with the chlorine feedstock coming from a plant which ICI acquired from Alusuisse in 1978. With plant occupancy of only around 50–55% the Wilhelmshaven complex, far from being Mond's future, appears in the short and medium term to be an additional drain on its cash flow and profitability.

However, the falling away of growth rates and over-capacities in the Western European commodity chemicals markets, and the consequent squeezing of margins, was not part of the conventional thinking of either the ICI Group or Mond Division as Mond began to peak in terms of business performance in 1976 and 1977. A combination of a weak pound sterling which allowed profitable exporting, the recovery of volumes in soda ash after the 1974/75 dip in output, UK price control legislation which paradoxically allowed regular inflation-based price rises, near-monopoly position in some products and markets which also contributed to healthy margins, all meant that for a time Mond "was minting money". Table 27 shows the sales, trading profit, and ratio of trading profit to sales for ICI's worldwide General Chemical businesses for the period 1973–83.

Mindful again that these are all worldwide rather than just Mond Division figures, it is still possible to interpret trends in Mond's business performance. 1976–79 were good years in terms of profit, with the division actually peaking in terms of trading profit and the ratio of trading profit to sales in 1976 and 1977. Mond was probably making a profit of around £130m in 1976 and 1977; inflation-adjusted at 1982 prices that would represent around £300m. However, as with so many businesses at that time Mond were really making spurious profits. The numbers were going up but all on the back of inflation. Mond was essentially trying to maintain its business position by raising prices. In this era of spurious growth the main board of ICI agreed to go ahead with the Tripod project based on growth rates of 6–8% per annum. Apparently there was a debate as part of ICI's international strategic thrust as to whether to put a chunk of the cash being earned in the ICI Group in the mid-1970s either into North America or Continental Western Europe. The choice was posed in terms of Petrochemicals at Corpus Christi in Texas, *or* General Chemicals at

TABLE 27　ICI General Chemicals worldwide sales, trading profit, and ratio of trading profit to sales, 1973–83 (£m)

	Sales	*Trading profit*	*Ratio of trading profit to sales*
1973	353	58	16.4
1974	465	66	14.2
1975	551	71	12.9
1976	738	136	18.4
1977	858	146	17.0
1978	895	128	14.3
1979	1038	141	13.6
1980	1143	99	8.7
1981	1232	75	6.1
1982	1386	60	4.3
1983	1472	107	7.3

Wilhelmshaven in Germany. The trade-off was that *both* investments were made and ICI is now the owner of still more capital assets it cannot profitably use. As one of the Mond Directors put it to me, "one or two people did see the changes in the environment (the falling away of growth rates) but generally it was beyond man's experience to see that as a possibility at that time".

Table 27 shows the sharp overall decline in ICI's worldwide General Chemical businesses in 1980, 1981, and 1982, but it conceals the extent of Mond's weakening business performance. A senior Mond Director put the business change like this:

> In 1980 we were thumped between the eyes by a combination of general economic recession, overvalued sterling, excessive advances in UK energy costs relative to Continental Western Europe and elsewhere . . . It was a most terrible fall from grace, accentuated by the fact that our strategic investment thrust at Wilhelmshaven, while right from an overall strategic point of view caught the full impact of being barely off the ground when the recession arrived – that added to the problems of profitability and cash flow.

Mond had in fact, budgeted for a divisional profit of £120m in 1980 but Table 27 shows the worldwide realised figure for General Chemicals was only £99m. Mond revised their budget for 1981 for a profit of £40m but it is doubtful if the division did all that much better than break even for 1981 and 1982, and that could not have happened without the "draconian changes" already referred to which had produced £40m annual savings in fixed costs by 1982.

The 1980 economic recession revealed Mond's competitive weaknesses all too clearly. Its business performance was still too tied to the fortunes of the UK economy. As large parts of UK manufacturing industry either fell by the wayside altogether, or in the case, for example, of UK glass manufacturers, lost significant market share to Continental Western European competitors, so the demand for Mond's solvents and soda ash declined. Between 1980 and 1983 Mond lost 30% of their invoicing points in the UK Engineering industry as firms in the "metal bashing" industries went into decline or out of business. The high value of sterling considerably weakened Mond's increasing attempts to get into European markets, and overcapacity in European markets, especially for vinyl chloride, but also for some solvents, meant that margins decreased dramatically. The threat of natural ash from the United States which had been a prospect for the latter part of the 1970s, and had curtailed Mond's capacity to raise prices, now became a reality, and pressure from US imports plus falling UK demand meant that the mid-Cheshire soda ash businesses became unprofitable. On top of all these worsening trends, Mond also had the continuing problem that their production processes were highly energy-intensive, and the prices they had to pay in the UK for electricity were twice the bulk tariffs available to their European competitors.

Many of the above macro-trends were not under Mond's control, and few could be influenced in the short term. The problem of European over-capacity in some commodity chemicals certainly couldn't be solved by unilateral action by one company, although the swop deal made with BP Chemicals in June

1982, helped to reduce the over-capacity problem for vinyl chloride in the UK. Pressure on the EEC about the so-called dumping of natural ash in Europe by the United States led in 1982 to the imposition of anti-dumping duties and the obtaining of undertakings on price levels from importers. This helped to take some of the pressure off Mond's soda ash business, but there was no relief from the Thatcher government on the vexed question of their high-cost energy policy and its impact on Mond's chlorine and soda ash businesses.

Apart from hoping for a reduction in the value of sterling – which eventually came, keeping up the pressure on government to bring UK energy costs down to other European levels, and redoubling their marketing emphasis outside the UK, the Mond board, as I have already indicated, took control of the division's fixed costs, an area which at last became a priority, and where they felt capable of taking effective action. The theme became "make sure you survive by ensuring your relative competitive position is better than your competitors". This new strategic priority became the focal point which finally engaged Mond's developmental resources from the top to the bottom of the division, and produced a new pattern of organisation, and perhaps the emergence of a different organisational culture in Mond.

Organisation and management culture in Mond

When Mond Division was created in 1964, it was not just a question of putting together two sets of businesses, and two organisations; the enforced wedlock between Alkali Division and General Chemicals Division was the linking of two quite different organisational cultures. For the moment I shall dwell on the differences in management culture between Alkali and General Chemicals, but as we shall see the differences in shop floor culture between mid-Cheshire and Merseyside were as distinct as those already reported between Billingham and Wilton.

From the account of the history of the Mond Division businesses in the previous section, it will be clear that the Alkali Division was the direct descendant of the Brunner, Mond Company, and indeed of two of the founders of the British Chemical Industry, John Brunner and Ludwig Mond. As such, Alkali Division inherited the Brunner, Mond tradition under ICI, with all that meant in terms of paternalistic labour policies and the gifted superiority of the Winnington management ethos. Winnington's progressive labour policies and practices and strong sense of community and self-respect brought on it jibes such as the nineteenth-century taunt "White Slaves of Winnington", and the shafts launched more recently towards the management culture as the "Squires of Winnington Hall". Set against that General Chemical could only claim the much weaker business lineage, lower prestige, and indistinct traditions of the United Alkali Company.

The part played by the Winnington Hall Club had an "inestimable effect on the style of management developed by Brunner, Mond and then by the Alkali Division," (Dick, 1973:108). Formed in 1897 "the Hall Club" was both a residence for the bachelor senior managers of Brunner, Mond, and an elegant dining room and social centre where the largely Oxbridge-trained chemists who joined Alkali could mix informally and play bridge, billiards, or croquet. Membership was at the invitation of the directors and was a carefully guarded privilege extended only to the few. Membership was determined by professional background, social qualifications, and standing in the company. Oxbridge-trained chemists were welcomed along with a few lawyers and accountants, but the uncertain status of engineers and commercial men in the first 20 years or so of the twentieth century in Britain meant they were excluded. Even by the time of the Mond merger in 1964 only 600 of the 6900 monthly staff in the new division were members of the Winnington Hall Club. The social homogeneity of the Hall Club, certainly in its pre-1939 days, was based on a combination of technical academic background, Oxbridge training, and public school personal background. In this atmosphere of shared assumptions and mutual trust much reminiscent, as Reader (1975:71) suggests, of an officers' mess or an Oxford college, "the hard cutting edge of professional efficiency was always present but never indelicately exposed". Rank and position in the Alkali hierarchy were accepted as part of the natural order of things but not dwelt upon in the club atmosphere at Winnington, where there was a frank and easy atmosphere between different levels and functions which was quite absent in the rank-conscious, authoritarian, and some have said repressive atmosphere in General Chemicals.

It is worth remembering that the Winnington culture was nourished in an organisation which was in a monopoly situation as far as its main product of soda ash was concerned, and where there was very little change in the technical environment of the division. Soda ash was produced in the 1960s by a manu-facturing process very similar to the process being used in 1926 when ICI was formed. In this controlled business and technical environment the Winnington chemists had the freedom, space, and ability in the 1930s to discover polythene. This, of course, added to Alkali Division's strong sense of identity and self-worth, especially when, as we have already noted, a procession of Alkali directors were promoted onto the main board of ICI between 1940 and 1950. As Dick (1973:112) remarked, "this did not go unobserved by other divisions of ICI, although Winnington did not advertise its merits; it merely was convinced of them".

It was, of course, Alkali's explicit and implicit claims to superiority which grated hardest on their near-neighbours in business and geographical terms, General Chemicals Division. Reflecting on the period in the late 1950s and early 1960s before Mond was created, senior people in Mond Division, then part of General Chemicals, recalled Alkali in these kinds of terms:

> Alkali were living in the shadow of past glories. They had been the strongest original constituent of ICI but in the period up to 1964 they had been living through a period of steady decline, though I doubt if they fully appreciated that fact. They regarded themselves and their business as immortal, and of a very high order.

* * *

Alkali Division were always the gentlemen of ICI. They wined and dined at Winnington Hall Club. They did a little work but normally arranged for others to do work for them ... General Chemicals people referred to Alkali as 9–1 management, start at 9 and finish at 1 ... Works managers used to shoot quail over the lime beds in the afternoon. They would keep their dogs panting under their desks, and then take the dog for a walk around the works. When television arrived some kept them in their office to watch the afternoon horse racing. It was a place of style and panache based on a background of very attractive earning capacity and no hint of failure in even the darkest years. It was full of remarkable people, who did extraordinary things. Eccentrics had to stay because they were afraid to let out the technical secrets of the soda ash process – a quite remarkable place.

A chemical engineer who eventually joined General Chemicals described his interview with Alkali in the early 1960s in these terms:

They didn't know what a chemical engineer was. I was one of the few they interviewed who didn't come from Oxbridge. They tried to find out if I was a chemist or an engineer, and concluded I wasn't either. The whole atmosphere was, are you a gentleman or not? I felt technically I didn't have what they required. The Personnel guy asked me if I would be prepared to help run the scout troop that Alkali sponsored. I said yes. I'm absolutely sure that's why they offered me a job.

Ex-Alkali managers acknowledged "the semi-humorous, semi-envious, cynical views of us from the rest of ICI – arriving at a training course for managers, when it became apparent I was from Alkali the remark was made 'you're from Alkali, should I carry your bags for you'? In the late 1950s Alkali were still very selective in recruitment. They kept numbers in the works as slim as possible, with few levels of management and wide spans of control. In the still relatively homogeneous management culture of Alkali, the pattern of shared values and easy relationships in the division, regenerated by appropriate recruits meant that managers could be given a lot of space, you were given your head, and not closely supervised."

The above laissez-faire culture within the management group was complemented by the Brunner, Mond tradition operating at lower levels in the system. In the works the foremen were key carriers of the tradition, and before the development of shop steward power in the late 1960s the foremen were the critical link between the management culture and the shop floor. The young officer managers needed the cultural knowledge and tactical skills of the foremen non-commissioned officers.

Looked at from either their headquarters in the centre of Liverpool, or their focal point for manufacture at Runcorn–Widnes, it was no wonder General Chemicals were labelled, or assumed the status of, "the cloth cap brigade". General Chemicals had grown rapidly after the 1950s on the back of process and product developments made in the chlorine and chlorine derivatives areas. The emphasis in General Chemicals was on the design and development, and operating efficiency, of new plant to meet rising UK demand for chlorine. The division recruited the best chemical and mechanical engineers it could get, and it quickly acquired the ethos in ICI as the Engineers Division. As one General Chemicals recruit put it:

> General Chemicals was technically very strong. We always attracted first class chemical engineers. There was very little attention to social or organisational development. The belief was that technical factors were the key to everything. There was very little concern with marketing. The products sold themselves either because they were strong technically or because we could make them cheaper than anybody else (in the UK).

Even the General Chemicals managers acknowledged the authoritarian and instrumental management culture in their division:

> It was a tough, no-nonsense, sane, straightforward, whack them harder operation. There was a constant flow of new technology, the scenery was always changing, history doesn't matter too much.

Alkali managers naturally preferred their own laissez-faire, "give him his head approach" to the General Chemicals attitude where:

> Everyone was assumed to be a skiving so and so, therefore you had to screw him down, supervise him closely, otherwise he'll do you down. This attitude and behaviour of close supervision, complex reporting relationships, close monitoring applied from top to the bottom of the management hierarchy in General Chemicals.

These mutual stereotypes were, of course, reinforced by the shotgun marriage which created Mond Division, and the obvious fact that General Chemicals were not merged with, but rather took over, Alkali Division. The take-over was symbolised by the fact that the first chairman of Mond had been Chairman of General Chemicals since 1961, and even more tangibly by the placement of the new headquarters of Mond at the recently created General Chemicals head office at Runcorn Heath. A manager in General Chemicals, later to become a senior member of the Mond board, recalled the takeover of Alkali Division:

> One saw the gradual but steady elimination of the ex Alkali Directors and of the ex Alkali influence. In business terms the manufacture of soda ash has suffered because of market considerations a gradual decline. Its status today in Mond in 1983, is one of four business groups, and by no means one of the biggest. Northwich is now just a couple of operating plants – a dramatic change.

Another senior member of the present Mond board described the differences between Alkali and General Chemicals, and the eventual decline of Alkali in these terms:

> They were two different worlds. If they had a bad egg in Alkali and he was shifted over to General Chemicals it was said at the time of the merger, it would improve

the tone of both Divisions. I found Alkali extremely wedded in the past, they knew everything . . . From a market point of view it was a monopoly and yet the lowest priced soda ash in the world. The thinking was if we make excess profits we'll get caught up by the Labour Government. Cash flow was good but profit was nowhere near what it should have been. Before 1973 we were selling soda ash at £19.50 a ton when the German price was £27 a ton. The customer's perception was that the Alkali part of Mond got no credit for this. "Here is your quota – this is the price, still sticks with the customers . . ." Alkali were under threat by the growth of chlorine demand and by the increase of chlorine–caustic soda relative to the lime-caustic soda at Winnington. The 2 divisions were put together in order to manage the reduction of lime-caustic soda at Winnington. Alkali saw the merger as a terribly traumatic experience. General Chemicals were dominant. If you look at the directors who went between 1964 and 1966 they were from the Alkali side. That period is still referred to "as the night of the long-knives".

If General Chemicals directors very quickly dominated the Mond board, it was technical and production people also from General Chemicals who dominated the works at Runcorn and mid-Cheshire. The General Chemicals people who moved into mid-Cheshire to manage the old soda ash plants were horrified at what they saw:

> This side had seen plants go up and become obsolete in 10 years, the soda ash end was like the British Empire – the sun will never set on soda ash. They were very resistant to change. If you made any suggestions for change you got the response that was tried 50 years ago and didn't work . . . Their willingness to see change, apply standards horrified me – their plants were shambolic.

An ex-Alkali manager noted how there had been "real acrimony at the top of the two merged divisions – tremendous wasted energy, no real effort at integration beyond structural integration".

> They tended to look at our plants in mid-Cheshire as "heaps of scrap iron", no-one worth his salt would want to work in those plants. So no young people in Mond wanted to work in mid-Cheshire, this wasn't the place of the future, so for a time this area was denuded of good people.

Very occasionally a senior production man from mid-Cheshire would be promoted into the Runcorn–Widnes complex. Although managers who went in both directions both had difficulties understanding one another's technology and culture, the attempt on one occasion to introduce Alkali management structures, style, and culture into the Runcorn–Widnes complex proved a major and expensive failure, and further reduced the credibility of the Alkali management system.

Slowly some of the productivity objectives that had been part of merger aims were realised. The Mond board declined in size from 20 in 1964 to 14 in 1968, and total employees declined from 20,044 in 1964 to 17,799 by 1970. What didn't change, however, was the great concern with technology. The chairman of the late 1960s, two of his deputies, and seven or eight of the remaining members of the board were either scientists or engineers. Plant was being designed and commissioned at Runcorn, Hillhouse, and Widnes almost with the fervour and scale of Wilton in the mid-1960s. Mond thought of technology and production as first priorities, and far down the list was the concern for the market.

> Marketing was sales control literally, we told the customer how much he could have and how much he would have to pay for the privilege of having the product. The customer orientation just wasn't there, money was too easy to make.

The division was "stuffed up to the eyebrows with technical people, all of them high quality, and a lot of them generating work for each other". Get yourself down to the works, and then into plant design was the career path for the young graduate who wanted to move fast in a growing business. "Keep the ship going, we want all the production you can make, costs aren't all that important" was the ethos. In the plants the concept of a good manager was very much presenting and dealing with technical problems – "my job was 80–90% technical, people were not a bother – I didn't know what a shop steward was in the late 1960s, he wasn't an important figure in my world".

Alongside this technical ethos, the developing Mond culture also reinforced two of the less attractive features of the old General Chemicals way of life – the concern with hierarchy, and the concern with control. The Chairman of Mond in the late 1960s is said to have been "a believer in management by fear"; even without his personal influence, however, the Mond culture at that time was featured by "bureaucracy attention to detail – everything was systematised".

> Mond was very tightly managed, plant managers couldn't see the plant costs, only section managers could see those. Even section managers couldn't send a letter to divisional headquarters without his works manager counter-signing it – there was great formality. I found it a very repressive environment and so did my seniors. This repressiveness started at the very top.

It was Mond's developed sense of hierarchy and the distancing between levels which this created which was the central force in the way it operated. Talking of the late 1960s and early 1970s a then senior manager summarized the core of the culture by saying:

> Mond is hierarchical, the best thing you can do is profess the faith in front of your betters.

Given the authoritative, some would say authoritarian, and certainly hierarchically conscious management culture at Mond Division in the early 1970s, it would seem the only way developmental resources could be influential in that culture would be if they either engaged with the very top of the organisation, or if indeed the top became itself the pressure point for change. In what follows I shall briefly sketch in the overall pattern of evolution of development work in Mond, before the chapter proceeds to chronicle in more detail the what, the why, and the how of changes in the division over the period from the late 1960s until the early 1980s.

As in other divisions of ICI, OD thinking and methods were brought into Mond with the Millbank-driven change programmes MUPS/WSA and SDP. Like the other divisions there was an attempt in Mond to keep the momentum for change going, post-WSA and SDP, by using a group of Eastbourne-trained "change agents" or internal OD consultants. For reasons to be explored later these change agents in Mond by and large were deemed ineffective helpers by the Mond power system, and the group was quickly allowed to wither away, although one or two individuals continue to this day to work within particular production environments. There was never any real pretence in Mond that third-party helpers using behavioural concepts and methods would have either the personal standing or positional power to operate within a management culture where hierarchical position was undisguisedly the only practicable basis for action.

The vacuum created by the early recognition of the impotence of internal OD resources on their own as a basis for either strategising about or acting in the organisational change area, was initially filled in a sporadic and unco-ordinated fashion by a small number of works managers each in their own way trying to wrestle with a divided and socially not very skillful management team desperately trying to cope with an increasingly questioning and militant set of works shop stewards and employees. One of these works managers, Frank Bay had been involved in the manning studies leading up to MUPS. Bay and Tom Peters had been works managers at Mond's Hillhouse Works near Fleetwood when Hillhouse was more or less successfully used as a MUPS trial site. Bay later went on to become Personnel Director, and Chairman of Mond in the late 1970s. Bay and Peters were followed as works manager at Hillhouse by a shrewd and voluble Welshman, Dylan Jones, who brought the structured problem-solving technique Coverdale into Hillhouse Works and helped to diffuse Coverdale into other parts of the division. Jones eventually succeeded Bay as personnel director when Bay was promoted to deputy chairman. In 1976 Jones was succeeded as personnel director by Nicholas Mann. Mann's role as a persistent counsellor, catalyst, and intellectual and process leader for OD in Mond was critical from 1976 onwards. In addition from about 1973 Mann had used his personnel manager role to assist the division's works managers to coalesce around some key industrial relations problems. Jones in time went on to become one of the two business directors in the five-man Mond board of the early 1980s. The experience, perspective, and continuity at the top by Bay, Jones, and Mann during several periods when developmental thinking and methods were under severe questioning, both on the Mond board and in the senior management, helped to keep OD alive in Mond until it could at last be harnessed to a core business problem for the division.

Around 1972 there was the beginnings of a dawning of awareness amongst a few senior individuals in Mond that the singular pursuit of technological priorities which had successfully carried Mond in business and management terms through the relatively easy commercial and industrial relations environment of the 1960s, was no longer in itself an ethos to help carry Mond through the different business, social, and political environment of the 1970s. Mond needed to learn how to market its goods internationally and reduce its dependence on UK customers, to develop in its managers not only greater commercial acumen but also the confidence and ability to tackle social and organisational problems through methods often alien to those fascinated by and locked into technical problem-solving processes. It also had in the short term to learn how to prevent, and tactically manage some of the industrial relations fires burning with increasing frequency and effect in some of their key plants. All this had to be done, of course, without denuding the division's more traditional and tried skills as designers, commissioners, and operators of large capital-intensive plant.

Amongst the many things getting in the way of picking up some of the above problems was the organisation and culture of the division. Mond was complex both in terms of its range of products, its number and spread of works, and the cultural differences still present between the factory and management cultures of mid-Cheshire and Merseyside. Crucially it was run in a very hierarchical fashion by an executive committee of the Chairman and his three deputy chairmen. As we shall see, the board was confused about its role, purpose, and practical operating style. Like the Plastics Division board of the 1970s, the Mond board for at least half of the 1970s met as a collection of individuals, and worse still related to the rest of the division as a set of individuals. A still divided and increasingly pressurised set of works managers below the board looked in vain for a unified and consistent set of policies from the board to help them deal with the social and political pressures of the day.

The spark who provided a starting platform to begin to understand and tackle some of the above problems was the then deputy chairman of Mond, Tony Woodburn. Woodburn had been a director of Agricultural Division at the time of George Bridge's social innovations at Billingham, had been the technical deputy chairman of Mond, was chairman of Mond from Spring 1973 until Spring 1977, and as we shall see in the following chapter, then joined the ICI main board and continued to use OD methods to help change the structure and style of the ICI Group.

Woodburn had joined George Bridge on one of his fact-finding visits to see OD ideas being applied in a number of big US corporations. They had both been impressed by the work carried out in a number of Procter and Gamble plants by, amongst others, an American OD consultant called Tom Bainton. Woodburn and Bainton struck up a strong work and in time personal relationship, and early in 1973 just before Woodburn became chairman of Mond, Bainton was invited to spend three days in London with Woodburn, Bay, and the other deputy chairman examining the working relationships within the Mond board. This was the starting point for what eventually became an articulated strategy to link first Bainton, and then his partner Bernard Wilson, into a small group on the board to help crystallise board thinking and eventually action, on changing the business focus, organisation, systems, and management processes in Mond. A critical feature of this developmental strategy, and one which of course matched the hierarchical character of the Mond culture, was that change had to start at the top, and proceed from there down. The process of creating, modifying, and implementing this developmental approach was long, faltering, and meandering. Its chances of success were materially enhanced in Mond by continuity of personalities and perspective amongst always a small group on the board who, using different change targets and methods, kept the process alive. The Mond story, of top-down change, is different from the other example of top-down change in this book, Petrochemicals Division, where there was no continuity of developmental thinking at the top once Harvey-Jones had left the division to join the main board.

While Woodburn was trying to use open-systems planning and team-building techniques both to get the Mond board to consider its business, social, and political environment, and work on improving its internal processes, events were stirring down in the division. By 1974 a combination of a politically better-organised local trade union system using their new power with greater impact, a still divided group of "cruiser captain" works managers feeling they were being picked off one by one in industrial disputes, and a feeling amongst the works managers that they were receiving only capricious demands and no practical support from the Mond board, led to open pressure on the board for policy support and a closer working relationship. This pressure was labelled at the time "the works managers revolt".

If Tony Woodburn was the man who led moves to change the character and operation of the Mond board, the individuals who eventually emerged amongst the works managers and in the Personnel Department to encourage greater formal and informal coherence amongst the works managers, and to challenge the board to engage more effectively with senior production people were Sandy Marshall and Nicholas Mann. Marshall's lead position in the newly effective works managers group, his history of encouraging the use of Coverdale and other human relations techniques in Wallerscote and Lostock Works, and his developing association with Bernard Wilson, the American consultant, all contributed to Marshall being encouraged out of a line job in 1975 to become the central internal development resource in Mond.

Marshall, conscious of the importance of hierarchical symbolism in Mond, set himself up in an office in what had been the old Alkali directors corridor at Brunner House. He was also careful to avoid being associated with the division personnel function which, with the notable individual exception of Nicholas Mann, had kept distant from any of the emerging development work in the division so far, or the rump of the Eastbourne-trained change agents who, still being unsure how they could relate to the division, sought unsuccessfully to co-opt Marshall into their group, on what Marshall perceived to be their terms.

Seeing the works manager group apparently increasing in coherence, strength, and influence, the managers of the headquarters departments began to meet with the American consultants. This period, around 1974 and 1975, produced sets of guidelines for what were perceived to be some of the problems of the day, which were variously labelled Industrial Relations Principles, Employee Relations Principles, and then from the managers of headquarters departments, Business Operating Principles.

Of course, not much happened as a result of these principles, partly because the board were still wrestling with questions that not all of them felt were worth asking, such as did the board have a role, and if so what should it be? In the business environment of the mid-1970s when Mond was turning in large profits just by regularly raising prices, only Woodburn, Bay, and Dylan Jones were really committed to thinking through issues about the purpose and governance system of the division. Many of the other directors were becoming increasingly impatient with the "love-ins" and "Pacific English" which were a feature of contact between the two American consultants and the board.

With energy draining away from development work on the board, and a certain cynicism and disillusionment at the levels below the board, partly from the board's inertia, and partly because the wordy principles that were produced delivered very little, Woodburn, Bay, Jones, Mann, the American consultants, and Marshall agreed that the time was ripe to experiment with some developmental projects in the division. Of the three areas chosen to pilot more participative ways of working using the American consultant's problem-solving process called "open systems planning", the most important was the commissioning of a new plant at Lostock Works. The Lostock experiment, leading as it did to virtually joint decision-making between management and shop stewards, was a good deal more risk-taking than anything tried up at Billingham, but in spite of some major issues of learning for the division this project raised and dashed a lot of hopes. Nothing like Lostock has been tried in Mond since the process of working there was abandoned after a 1978 strike.

Picking up the theme of the board's developmental process, this changed in character when Woodburn left the division in 1977. Woodburn, before he left, was careful to hold a workshop at Stratford-upon-Avon to try and draw some of the threads together after four years' work, and to help his successor Frank Bay maintain continuity for the work that had been going on. Bay was, of course by now personally committed to keeping developmental activities going, and he was being supported by a deputy chairman, Dylan Jones, and Mann, but there was still not a satisfactory answer to the sceptics for questions about what is the purpose of this development work, where is it leading us, and why? Mond was still highly profitable, and there was no real pressure for organisational change which would require changes in the strategy, structure, and systems of the whole division. Nevertheless Bay persisted. He had been impatient with the conceptual emphasis given to development work under Woodburn and Bainton's influence and wanted to tie things down more and point to specific areas of progress and action.

One manifestation of Bay's urge to cohere around work done so far, and to signal to the rest of the division that the board was looking to the future, was the publication in August 1977 of the Mond Charter. This four-page document presented the board's thinking on the purpose, aims, and principles of the division – the sort of organisation that the board wants Mond to be. The Mond Charter, and the more detailed board handbook which followed it, may have helped to reaffirm within the board that there was now a semblance of unity of purpose at the top, but both documents left the rest of the division under- whelmed. What can we do with "motherhood statements such as these?"

By 1978 the developmental stream in Mond looked as if it was finally going to meander into the sand. The Lostock experiment was widely regarded as a failure, there had been no follow-up from the Mond Charter, Tom Bainton was no longer working for the division, and Sandy Marshall[1] had retired from his position as the central internal development resource, and left his more junior assistant Geoff Campbell as the solo full-time development man. In amongst consistent cries that, after the mistakes of Lostock, in future change events or processes had to be firmly line management-led, even Bernard Wilson, the one external consultant still working in the division, had to be protected by his now small group of supporters on the board.

But out of the ashes rose the phoenix. First of all tentatively in the guise of a Wilson-inspired management development programme tapping the now accepted view that the division's managers, senior and junior, had to increase their capability as leaders, and then more down-to-earth and pragmatic events on "Leading change within a works" which Sandy Marshall and Campbell ran. Moving into 1979 a change in the top leadership of the division – Bay retired and he was succeeded as chairman by a man of long commercial experience Mark Warwick – coincided with the realisation that Mond was entering a rapidly worsening business scene. In the meantime the personnel director, Nicholas Mann, had been working with a group of senior works and business managers to develop what became known as the Mond management model. This management model, focussing as it did on the structure, systems, and management processes of the division, provided an elegant, practical, and intellectually coherent way of answering what became the strategic question of 1980 – how can we run the division's business activities more effectively at substantially less cost? At last the necessary elements had emerged for strategic change in the organisation and systems of Mond. The business and environ- mental pressure was there, the political will was there, an intellectually sound and practical framework had been developed largely by Mann to solve the critical problem of the day, the only question remaining was had all this investment in developmental thinking and training equipped the division's managers to successfully implement and stabilise the required changes?

ORGANISATION DEVELOPMENT AND THE MOND BOARD, 1970–76

Organisation development in Mond had two starting points at different points in time, and in two different parts of the division. Chronologically the work

---

[1] However Marshall was retained as an active external consultant to the division.

which was stimulated by MUPS/WSA and SDP was the true starting point, but in terms of eventual impact the work which really mattered started some seven years later in 1972 when Tony Woodburn was appointed Deputy Chairman of Mond. Eventually, of course, the MUPS/WSA development work which had started at Hillhouse Works in 1965, and gathered its own and varied momentum in the different works and production sites, met up with the board development work in 1974 at the time of the works managers revolt. But more of the works development stream in the next section of this chapter.

At the time of Tony Woodburn's appointment as chairman of Mond Division in the Spring of 1973 the board was made up of a chairman, three deputy chairmen, and nine directors. Figure 11 shows the board responsibilities at that time, and shows the strong product group organisation at the top of the division. What it does not, of course, reveal is the heavy technical background and predisposition of those carrying out the various roles. The chairman, two of his deputies, and six of the nine directors had all had research, engineering, or production backgrounds. There is, however, no production director, this role being fulfilled either by a deputy chairman or the personnel director – at this time an ex-works manager, as appropriate.

Woodburn's two predecessors in their different ways had left their mark on the division. D. C. Tiger, chairman from 1967 to 1970, was a former chief engineer and had run the technical side of the board as a deputy chairman since the 1964 merger. His style was described by a director "as abrupt and brutal, he had the image of squeezing the last drop of blood out of every stone – in fact I believe that was 90% image and 10% delivery". Tiger, an ex-General Chemicals director, is widely regarded as ensuring General Chemical's particular brand of authoritarianism was quickly stamped onto the Mond management culture. Tiger was succeeded by Rosewall, one of the few ex-Alkali directors to survive the post-1964 "night of the long knives". Rosewall, a commercial man, did three things in his tenure of office between 1970 and 1973. He "drove through some investments, saw the need to humanise the outfit after D. C. Tiger, and saw the need to begin to switch the emphasis in the division from technical to commercial."

The Mond board in 1973 was a board in name only. The division executive committee of the chairman and his three deputies "was the real powerhouse". One of the directors, however, described the deputy chairmen as "jumping on every Company bandwagon going. We felt they were pulling levers connected to nothing – they were big work generators for the levels below them." Another director of the time described the continual monitoring that went on between the executive committee and the individual directors:

> The directors were a loose chorale of people who responded to the top 4. There was immense formality. Each function and product group director responded to the executive committee each month. This meant a ½-day session with each director. One week out of four was taken up with these sessions. That was a quite unnecessary and destructive elaboration because it cramped people's style down the line, and led to people at far too senior levels pulling up roots and looking at them every two minutes.

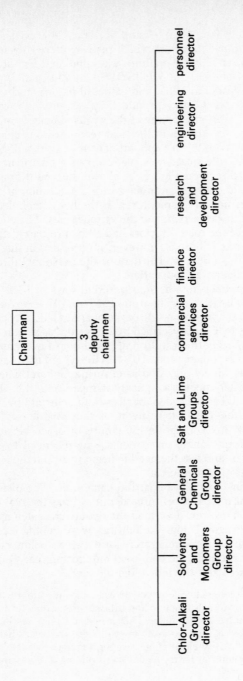

FIGURE 11 Mond Division board: March 1973

The tendency of the executive committee to relate to the directors individually through monitoring and controlling activities, of course, forced those individuals and the levels below them back into their product group or functions and inhibited any kind of unified thinking at the level of the business as a whole. The atmosphere at the top was one of hierarchy and formality. The levels below the board felt distant from individual directors, and considered the deputy chairmen and the chairmen were up in the stratosphere. The thinning out of people after the 1964 merger had taken much longer to produce results at the senior management levels than it had done amongst the directors, so "there was much evidence of duplication of roles, and double banking" below the board.

When the thirteen-man board did actually meet they had real problems trying to find a content for their discussions, and enormous difficulties handling the social process of communicating and decision-making. As another director put it:

> The board did not function as a board, as a group in the early 1970s. It had difficulty even finding an agenda. It had no experience of thinking or functioning in ways peculiar to a board.

The personnel director remarked:

> The only common thing the board had was in personnel issues – industrial relations. Also, you had to accommodate everyone on expenditure proposals, it was a very slow, very cumbersome, very bureaucratic process.

It was these features of the board and senior management culture, the formality, the concern with hierarchy and distancing between levels, the lack of clarity about the board's role and purpose, the emphasis on monitoring and controlling and the games-playing that went with that, but above all the lack of a unifying perspective on what Mond was, and where was it going, that was the starting point for any change during Woodburn's period as chairman.

Tony Woodburn is one of a handful of really senior people in ICI who were far-sighted enough to sense during the early 1970s that changes in ICI's social, business, and political environment might require the company to change a good deal more quickly than it was doing. Furthermore, having sensed the need for change he was prepared to take the risk to use OD concepts and techniques to try and guide the bit of ICI he was responsible for towards a different shape by working in a different way. Although Woodburn had a Ph.D. in chemical engineering, his personal background and career history was not standard ICI. He came from a working-class background – his father was a chargehand. His Ph.D. was from a redbrick university – Birmingham, and he had spent nearly two years in the United States on a Marshall Aid Fellowship after he had joined ICI. This two years was spent partly studying chemical engineering at Northwestern University, and also getting some experience of the working methods of a number of North American corporations.

Upon returning to the UK, Woodburn then followed the more standard ICI path for promising technical graduates of plant management, engineering design, and then a period as a works manager, before being promoted in 1964 to be technical and engineering director of Agricultural Division. He was then involved in the traumas of the technical and social innovations going on at Billingham. George Bridge had persuaded him to go off on an American T-group, and Woodburn said he returned "profoundly influenced". Bridge, the energy behind so much seeding of developmental ideas in ICI in the late 1960s and early 1970s, then encouraged Woodburn to go with him on a trip to the US to see some of the innovative work using participative management methods going on at Procter and Gamble plants. On this trip he met the American OD consultant Tom Bainton, and struck up a work and personal relationship which has carried on to this day.

Encouraged by his promotion to deputy chairman and probably knowing he would be the next chairman of Mond, Woodburn invited Bainton into the division "to improve at least the elementary processes of interpersonal relations in the executive committee, for starters". Two months later, in April 1973, and with the committed support of one of his deputies Frank Bay, and his personnel director, Dylan Jones, Woodburn risked the first team-building event with his full board of 13, and Bainton and his partner Bernard Wilson. As one of the directors later put it, in 1973 "the big thing was moving out from a closed to an open system". In other words trying to encourage the Mond board to analyse the present and future environmental pressures on the division, and consider what kinds of responses Mond should make to those demands. But if this work on environmental scanning was greeted with "very little commitment", worse was to follow when Bainton and Wilson encouraged the individual members of the board to construct personal collages depicting how they felt now, and ideally how they would like to feel. This concern with personal values and then interpersonal processes, was directed towards dealing with one of Mond's problems at that time, "they operated in a fairly mechanical way – there wasn't much thought about what their beliefs in certain areas were". The trouble was this was not the sort of problem the majority of the board either intellectually could recognise as a class of problem or more to the point emotionally would acknowledge as having anything to do with their effectiveness as individuals or in their role as directors.

The majority sceptical view was that they had no enthusiasm for these "love-ins", or "sandals and beads OD". After acknowledging the strong support given to this board OD work by Woodburn, Bay, and Jones another director explained:

But the rest of us were pretty heathen in our approach at that stage and supped with a very long spoon to the whole initiative ... Looking back on it Tony Woodburn was sowing seeds on some pretty barren ground, which took an awful long time to germinate. One of the weaknesses of the early stages was these techniques and approaches were not owned by the board as part of the normal management regime. We would have Board Events with a capital B and a capital E where we as a board would work our way through these processes and then come back and carry on as before. The impact of these techniques on our day-to-day work was minimal at that stage, it gradually increased of course, but it was very,

very patchy . . . The whole theme, and this was put over very faithfully at the beginning, was that this was part of a long-term evolutionary development. The board was merely the first step of a long chain that had to harness the total management – we wouldn't see the pay-off for a long time. But because it was faithfully put over, most of us, including myself at that time, were a long way out from knitted into the process, it made the problem of getting past stage one much more difficult.

But if the sceptics and opponents of OD on the Mond board were intolerant both of the tactics and the starting-point – the concern with their values, processes, and perspective on the business, and then being told that the strategy could only mean no short-term payoff, they were also confused by the indefinitiveness of Woodburn's vision and fearful of the only solution they could pick up from Woodburn's thinking – participation was the answer. Bernard Wilson's recollection that "Woodburn's need was not problem driven, it was more potential driven, improving the potential of something rather than solve a particular problem", of course while probably accurate and laudable as an objective was far too imprecise and uncomfortable for a set of people who had been rewarded throughout their career for being "instrumental" and "mechanical" in their thinking and problem-solving behaviour. The indefinitiveness of what Woodburn's vision represented to others is well caught in the following quote:

Tony Woodburn thought there was something of value to be grasped from this developmental work, but he didn't know what it was or how to go about it. He hoped something would come out, feeling it was the right thing to do.

Like most visions, Woodburns's, while rooted in discontent with the present, was articulated in terms of value statements about a future which was only vaguely sketched in terms of outcomes, and even vaguer in terms of first practical steps to get there. Where Woodburn was precise in terms of his values about participation he created anxiety. He later acknowledged how his approach in Mond was value driven and what difficulties this had created:

I tried to introduce my ideas. I'm in a political sense left of centre. I don't like authoritarianism, and was and still am very much committed to participation as far as the shop floor is concerned, and I mean participation and not just consultation. I believe in the end that is the only way to go. That kind of idealism wasn't well received around Mond at that time.

As I have hinted, during 1974 and 1975 Mond were involved in a whole series of industrial relations disputes, one of Woodburn's directors recalled the difficulties of trying to pursue ideals about participation at that time:

This was a very difficult political period to manage – the growth of union power. It was very difficult to maintain commitment to an ideal when subjected to a lot of difficulties in the industrial relations field.

A works manager at the time recalled even more graphically how he saw Woodburn's ideas about participation and his association with Tom Bainton intruding on Woodburn's relations with the board and the works managers:

> Woodburn was highly conceptual, and he had a high will towards participation. He was not easily engaging in bringing that about, but he was very supportive in giving a lot of space and encouragement. His thinking was very much influenced by Tom Bainton, who he saw as a personal counsellor and consultant . . . Members of the board were hostile because they saw him as politically to the left and they suspected his close friendship with Tom Bainton. They were puzzled by things called afterwards "love-ins" . . . There was general kind of support at the works manager level, but he didn't easily relate to them. He was kind of distant – up there. I visualised a scene at the time. I was a manager standing on a sandy island, waves all round me, sharks in the sea, and a big powerful voice with a megaphone shouting participate, participate. With a shark – and the waves rolling on! It was a dangerous activity . . . and I didn't participate in whatever he was doing, it was participate from my level down.

Woodburn's belief in participation as a way of breaking down barriers between management and the shop floor led to the important Lostock experiment – of which more later. By the time towards the end of 1976 when Woodburn knew he was leaving Mond to join the main board, his board at Mond "was still divided about the value of OD work into the pro group of Woodburn, Bay, Jones, and Mann, a small group who openly said 'this is all rubbish', and a middle group who were basically in sympathy but hadn't come to grips with the thing to appreciate its value." A director recalled that before Woodburn left he had "taken us all – the board and their wives, into Purdah for a weekend workshop at Stratford. We spent 3 days with Bainton and Wilson taking stock of the whole programme. In retrospect that was immensely valuable, it caused most of the middle group to pass through the eye of the needle, and they were positively on board after that."

The Stratford workshop was something of a turning point, if only because it clarified that the new chairman, Frank Bay, was committed both to further work on developing the role of the Mond board in running and developing the division, and in increasing the capacity of senior managers to handle internal and externally generated change. Stratford produced the important practical requirement for a long-term process of evolutionary development – continuity of top support and leadership, and as we shall see through Bay a greater sense of task-focussed urgency. What it is doubtful if it did was to ensure all the middle group of sceptics "passed through the eye of the needle". The director who argued that the middle group was now on board may have just been sensing a general positive surge from his own change of heart. Interestingly, his change of heart was in his own admission associated with a promotion to deputy chairman, and therefore membership of the still powerful executive committee:

> My perspective had changed by that time because I was now a deputy chairman and part of the inner sanctum and therefore more heavily under the influence of the high priests of the (OD) culture.

But even by early 1977 and after 3 or 4 years of effort:

> There was a complete failure at that stage to get OD methods and thinking into the total management system, so that even if board members and one or two senior managers outside the board were converts the mass of the body politic were not, and that was the main reason why the whole message had a very limited impact.

Perhaps also the mass of the body politic were still as confused by the board's inability to cause something to happen as a result of the use of developmental resources. Perhaps also the continuing, indeed by 1976 improving, financial results of Mond meant there was no real felt need for change in structure, systems, and management processes. Perhaps also, as we shall see now, much of the important production areas of the division were too busy in the trenches wrestling with the more tangible problem of how to deal with trade union disputes whilst the board, in the works managers' view, demanded much but supported little.

ORGANISATION DEVELOPMENT IN THE TRENCHES:
THE WORKS AND INDUSTRIAL RELATIONS, 1965–76

Looking back on the birth and evolution of developmental activities in Mond, a key trigger which was used to draw consultants into the division was the worsening character of industrial relations over the period 1969–76. The apparent strength of shop steward power and organisation over that period, apart from assisting weekly staff achieve some of their aspirations, also exposed a number of faults in the pattern of management organisation and behaviour towards weekly staff in general, and employee representatives in particular. The beginnings, by shop stewards, of greater awareness of and confidence in using power, exposed the lack of policy thinking and practice on the Mond board about industrial relations matters, the quite inadequate for the times system of organisation and communication between works managers in the division and the overall quality of man-management skills amongst a set of production and engineering managers who were still defining their priority areas in the workplace as technical rather than people, politics, or organisation. The industrial relations fires which began to burn across Mond's works in the north-west of England in the early 1970s meant that Mond began to acquire the kind of dubious reputation that the other centre of burgeoning technological development in ICI – Wilton – had acquired at the end of the 1960s. The process of diagnosing and tackling these industrial relations problems was a key stream in the development work in the division, which eventually met up with the slow progress of change on the Mond board, when around 1974 and 1975 it became clearer that the issues of management structure, culture, and capability affecting the division's functioning required linked and interdependent changes at and between the board, the business managers, and the works managers of the division. This practical manifestation and recognition of the simple truism that in organisations all things are interdependent, gave greater credibility and force to the open-systems planning techniques being introduced into the division by Bainton and Wilson, and helped those arguing for the strategy of developing the division through a centrally co-ordinated approach based on a clear set of principles and values hammered out initially at the top.

In examining the pattern of workplace relations in Mond, one has to start with the recognition that the shop floor cultures of mid-Cheshire and Runcorn are quite different. Mid-Cheshire, as we have seen, was the home of the Brunner, Mond tradition of industrial relations in ICI with all that meant in terms of paternalistic care stretching from housing, education, recreational amenities, to early trade union recognition, innovations in improving hours of work and working practices, and Works Committees – the forerunners of the ICI Works Councils.

Like Billingham, the mid-Cheshire town of Northwich was really an ICI community, and a community based in a rural area where there had not been a history of industrial development. In this community all were dependent on ICI, not just at work but also at play. The traditions perpetuated from the Brunner, Mond days by the gentlemen chemists at Winnington Hall, by a stable and successful business in a monopoly situation, meant there was the time, the space, and the willingness to develop a sense of community and loyalty to ICI. Grandfathers, fathers, and sons were all glad to find employment in the soda ash plants, and daughters could also take up clerical and secretarial work at Brunner House, the former Alkali Division headquarters.

It was precisely this kind of stable, loyal workplace community which even in the nineteenth century stimulated the taunt already referred to of "the white slaves of Winnington". Of course after the Second World War as state legislation played an increasing part in policies for housing, health, recreation, and industrial relations, so Alkali Division appropriately enough began to withdraw from some of its obligations and felt responsibilities "while remaining prepared to provide support if this were sought" (Dick, 1973:107). A shop steward from mid-Cheshire recalled that the first real change post-1945 he could remember at Northwich was the influx of people from Liverpool in the early 1950s to meet the demand for labour in developing plants. He remarked "this is one of the resentments local people in Northwich have now got against ICI. They brought these outside people in, and now (in 1982) they are cutting back". The outsiders from Liverpool had their roots only about 20 miles from Northwich!

Worse was to come, however, after the 1964 merger with General Chemicals and the influx of a certain number of General Chemicals-trained senior managers into the mid-Cheshire plants. An ex-Alkali Division manager's view of how the creation of Mond influenced work place relations in mid-Cheshire was:

Alkali Division was very patriarchal – it really did look after its people. Father will look after, father will provide, father really cares for us. When the merger occurred with General Chemicals they felt father had left them. He didn't care, he was in Runcorn. Also father's behaviour was really quite different. He was more remote, more critical, he cut off money into the place – there was a run down appearance here . . . People who had grown up in the culture of Merseyside couldn't relate when they came here – there was a feeling of more remoteness amongst the men.

Of course, not long after 1964, MUPS and then WSA were introduced into ICI. One of the major effects of MUPS/WSA, as we have seen in other divisional chapters, was to formalise and strengthen the role of the shop steward. This happened as pressures for collectivism were gathering momentum in the UK generally, and as attitudes were changing to authority and its use. These forces began to come together at mid-Cheshire and elsewhere and to focus around the formal and capricious use of managerial directives. There was plenty of evidence of hierarchy, formality, and authority in mid-Cheshire. A recent managerial recruit into a mid-Cheshire works at that time commented:

> The works manager had his luncheon dining table, with a long list of managers sitting according to length of service and status. He sat there and carved the roast and passed the plates down . . . Supervisors were still to be seen taking off, or touching, their hats to managers and referring to them by title. Even junior managers referred to senior managers by title. People were locked into formal behaviour in a hierarchy, I was shocked by this.

A shop steward interviewed about the character of managerial behaviour in mid-Cheshire confirmed the above picture of an increasingly distant and unilateral management. The range of behaviour varied from every employee getting a Christmas card in his wage packet from the works manager, to technical people coming into the plant and making adjustments and not telling the workers, what or why. It was a matter of "management sending out instructions through supervisors – there was very little consultation. There was a build up of resentment against the management instruction approach – people just said enough of this, and when the 1970 strike came management were completely shocked that this could happen."

If the company town atmosphere around Northwich was very reminiscent of the pre- and early post-war Billingham, Runcorn on a smaller scale had many of the characteristics of Wilton. Runcorn's near neighbour across the River Mersey was, of course, Widnes, one of the birthplaces of much of the UK Chemical Industry. Whereas the population of Widnes had endured the Leblanc industry since the latter half of the nineteenth century, Runcorn as a site for a rapidly developing chemical industry, and a new town, was essentially a product of the late 1950s and early 1960s. The Liverpudlians who flocked into Runcorn new town were more used to a tradition of casual labour based on employment in the docks and the merchant marine, than the stable occupational community atmosphere around Northwich. There was not the same tradition of ICI employment around Runcorn, nor the kind of loyalty to ICI found in mid-Cheshire. The engineers of General Chemicals Division were building new plant almost continuously at Runcorn throughout much of the

1950s and then after the 1964 merger. ICI employees at Runcorn were neither being offered nor were probably seeking, the kind of paternalism being displayed in mid-Cheshire. Instead they were part of almost continual technical change with all that meant in terms of a management ethic preoccupied with technology, repeated demands for adaptability in the workplace, and the ever-present distractions on the site of non-ICI construction labour. One works manager described Runcorn as:

> Being much more volatile [than mid-Cheshire], much more used to quick construction and demolition going on all the time. There was a tradition of clearing off to Fords if they didn't like what was being offered by ICI. "Blow you Jack, I'll look after myself, I'm alright", was a common attitude on the shop floor.

By 1969 turnover at the big ICI Castner Kellner plant at Runcorn "was 30%, and it was a real hotbed of industrial relations problems".

Of course, MUPS/WSA had been introduced into the worsening industrial relations climate at Runcorn and mid-Cheshire, and indeed right across Mond Division. As in other parts of ICI an effect of MUPS/WSA in Mond was to reveal management's lack of preparedness and skill in handling the problem-solving and negotiation processes with shop stewards that were now required of them. The vehicle of WSA itself, and the general increase in collectivism and shop steward power, all demanded man-management skills. In this situation, and again as we have seen to varying degrees in different parts of ICI, some works managers became in effect early adopters of OD methods. In Mond, Frank Bay, Tom Peters and Dylan Jones at Hillhouse Works, and Sandy Marshall at Lostock Works emerged as leaders in drawing developmental resources into the works – they also persisted throughout the 1970s in trying to spread developmental thinking throughout the division.

The existence of MUPS co-ordinators helped to legitimate to some the value of third-party helpers in some of the works, and when the MUPS co-ordinators were no longer needed, the increasing use of behavioural packages such as Coverdale and Blakes Grid, and then the appearance of SDP, encouraged Mond to send two groups of six people to be trained as change agents at Eastbourne 1 and Eastbourne 2.

The use of specialist internal change agents in Mond seemed, with one or two exceptions, a failure right from the start. The first group of six to go to Eastbourne were mostly middle-ranking line managers. This first group of six were so disturbed by what had happened to them at Eastbourne 1, that "the division had to scratch around to find six people prepared to go on Eastbourne 2, and they came up with some junior personnel officers, training officers, and a section manager from management services." When the 12 returned they were dispersed around the division in various works and departments and were told:

> You bring about change. Of course, they replied "oh no we can only counsel and coach". It didn't go anywhere, it was all a bit pathetic.

At the beginning of the 1970s, in a fairly unco-ordinated fashion these change agents, who were, of course, very junior people in Mond's very formal and hierarchy-conscious management culture, ran into the same problems of resistance that even the Chairman and his more prestigious group of external consultants had in trying to introduce the value of process management skills to the Mond board. The change agents' concern with behaviourism, with process skills, was seen as "much too soft". One works manager of the time also felt the change agents were challenging management from a very weak base:

> These so called change agents, they worked hard, one in my works began to use words like I was his client. But he had great difficulty in understanding the complexities of my problems, he tended to be saying things too black and white, dealing with issues out of context. He wasn't sufficiently malleable . . . Also he continually challenged my values, my sense of values. "Authority is malevolent, what right have you to be making decisions over others?" I resented being challenged in this way by someone who hadn't sat in my seat, didn't know the total load that was there. If I'd said to him "take it", he wouldn't have known where he was.

A director who later had to decide what to do with the remnants of this change agent group said:

> These guys, they felt they were right in the forefront. But they were unloved and neglected – they felt extremely vulnerable. Some we had to pull out and push back into the line, some were unacceptable back in the line and they faded away.

In fact one or two of this change agent group did survive the ordeal by fire the Mond management culture must have represented to them, and they are still working in a couple of the works. Only one of the Mond Eastbourne-trained group, Geoff Campbell, survived this period and made the transition to become part of the top-down change strategy which started with Tony Woodburn in 1973.

Given that the Mond management culture couldn't seem to support a more bottom-up change strategy facilitated by specialist change agents who had neither "the right message", the right positional power, or the appropriate experience, the path of development that occurred in the early 1970s was virtually to allow each works manager to do his own thing, in his own environment. One of the only clear patterns that emerged out of this do-your-own-thing approach[2] in the face of industrial relations adversity, was the use of the Coverdale problem-solving technique. Coverdale was probably felt to be effective by works managers in Mond for the same reason it took off at Wilton – it was a comfortable, structured way of thinking about people expressed within the discipline of solving problems. It made sense in a culture which was still heavily focussed on technical problem-solving. A works manager in the early 1970s commented:

[2] The early lack of success in using the Eastbourne-trained change agents in Mond, may have been one reason why Mond did not involve itself in Dudley's internal OD network during the remainder of the 1970s. Mond essentially went their own way.

> I went for Coverdale because it had an underlying objective – it was task-related.
> The focus on problem-solving fitted our culture better [than more unstructured
> behavioural science approaches] therefore people learnt from it.

As the 1970s developed a new set of shop stewards emerged at Runcorn and
mid-Cheshire to exploit the base of operation for trade unionists created by
WSA, the new ICI Joint Consultative arrangements, and general support on the
shop floor for collectivism in an economy increasingly beset by inflation.
Individual developmental initiatives were taken by works managers at Hillhouse, Castner-Kellner, and Lostock Works, with varying degrees of management support and impact, but as the number of industrial relations problems
increased so it became apparent that no amount of blanket-throwing in individual works using OD and management development methods, would tackle
problems on the management side which were really being caused by the
general structure, culture, and management processes in the division.

Two events, one in 1973 and the other in 1974, eventually triggered
management action first of all amongst the works managers, and then at the
board. In 1974 "Some co-ordinated action led by key shop stewards in mid-
Cheshire challenged the annual wage negotiation process going on in London
by putting pressure on this part of the company. This had never happened
before – previously all the shop stewards in the works had kept separate, not
loving each other any more than management in the factories loved each other.
They got wiser faster than we did and put on an overtime limitation co-
ordinated through a shop stewards committee."

The effectiveness of this shop steward committee galvanised some of the
more perceptive works managers into action. At that time "works managers in
Mond behaved virtually as if they worked for different companies . . . they were
practically vying with one another while the shop stewards were getting
themselves organised". A works manager using a nautical metaphor explained
that:

> The works managers were cruiser captains. They cruised in their own direction,
> but with the unification of the trade union structure they were being torpedoed,
> and they had to start proceeding in convoy with the destroyer screen of the
> personnel function around them.

But the problem wasn't just that the cruiser captains were divided amongst
themselves, they were also divided from a board which itself was not offering
unified leadership to the division.

> We were separated because of the way we were being managed – the way the
> Product Group Directors operated. They would come round, look at the
> performance of each works, and then compare one with the other.

The Personnel Director of the time explained the problems of lack of unity on
the board:

I had very great difficulty to get the co-operation of the four Product Group Directors. The attitude was do what you like but don't lose us a shift's production – this was a profitable period. The other posture was – why do we have these problems – it means Personnel are not doing their job. It was very difficult to get people to accept what is a totality of business risk-taking.

Of course, the shop stewards knew that management's need for high levels of output considerably increased their power potential, the Mond board's reaction to this appears to have been a "policy of continual appeasement". The appeasement policy, combined as it was with feelings in the works of ill-informed and unreasonable demands from the board, reaped its own harvest:

The management response was one of dislike – frustration in trying to manage in that sort of climate a feeling of being impotent to manage – supervisors commented on not having management back up, of declining standards of management performance.

* * *

A lot of us felt under a lot of pressure with not much help from above. The attitude was we can't manage industrial relations if we don't get support from the bloody directors. Their attitude was output at all costs, and don't tell us your bloody problems with shop stewards, we pay you to sort that out. 'Get on with it, and if you can't sort it out, we'll find someone who can sort it out.'

Eventually a group of four works managers got together and shared a view "that there was a lack of direction in the division".

We didn't know what the board was doing – where are we going? The world is changing around us. What is the policy regarding this or that? We asked. The four of us sat down and wrote what subsequently became known as the Works Managers Charter.

This was, of course, extremely counter-cultural behaviour in Mond, and the activities of the four were described as the 'works managers revolt'. The four met the then Chairman Tony Woodburn, who responded by saying 'Okay, but do the other works managers agree?' Woodburn set up a meeting of the business general managers and the works managers, but not including directors. Sandy Marshall, one of the four, recalled that the message communicated by the group "wasn't welcomed with open arms by the rest, but they couldn't deny there was something there".

Not much tangible in the short run appeared from the works managers revolt, except for a one-page document written by Mann which appeared in April 1974 titled "Desirable Elements of Mond Strategy". This document, a product of further meetings between the works and general managers and the Chairman, talked of "good quality information exchange between the board and senior managers, works managers joining with the board to establish direction and pace in the development of WSA and SDP principles, and each works and department operating harmoniously within an agreed, shared management philosophy, style and sense of direction." No action followed because, as we discussed earlier in this chapter, the board, helped by Bainton and Wilson, were themselves at this time still grappling with questions about their role, identity, and the policy focus for the division. Nevertheless the works managers revolt had reinforced the Chairman's philosophical position that change was necessary in Mond, had given the works managers greater confidence in bridging the "gynormous gap in systems terms between themselves and the board", and had also signalled to the external consultants that there was energy for change amongst some of the works managers.

While much of the above had been going on Bainton and Wilson had been encouraging Mond Personnel Department to visit the scene of some of their use of open systems planning methods in the United States. During 1972 this encouraged the Works Manager of Castner-Kellner works at Runcorn to try an experiment in the cell-room amongst the mechanical maintenance group there "to release fruitful ideas and initiatives from the shop floor, to facilitate their implementation, and to improve the effectiveness of the Group". The idea was for management to link with a work group where there was evidence of internal energy for change and where communications are regularly and naturally established, in order to focus on a "core process", which in this case could have been "the progressive elimination of the need for maintenance measured by increased plant availability etc." Open systems planning would then have progressed the agreed "core process" by the management and maintenance group jointly examining the environment around the core process, and looking to manage the surrounding systems of support and constraint, in order to build commitment for agreed plans for change.

Wilson described the objectives of the Castner-Kellner experiment "as not to reduce manpower at that time, but to improve the maintenance group's motivation to examine how they worked – the way they worked rather than direct attempts to improve productivity". No shop floor reports are available on this experiment. Management reports indicate that the failure to include the trade unions in the experiment, a tactic of course possible in some North American factory experiments using participative methods, eventually brought the experiment's downfall:

> The works manager got a good response from the shop floor, but he hadn't included the trade unions in this activity. They closed in on it and wouldn't tolerate differences in working being developed in the cell-room – differences in output levels and demarcation levels. This was seen by the shop stewards as threatening. It was an ill-conceived experiment, it was incomplete, they left out a very important political group ... The experiment just fizzled out because of trade union opposition and when its works manager patron moved on, and his successor wasn't keen.

Some learning was taken from the Castner-Kellner experiment, and when the much more ambitious Lostock Works development began in 1975, no attempt was made to keep the full-time trade union officers or shop stewards out of the activity.

But returning to the general theme of industrial relations developments in Mond, it took a major industrial relations dispute about weekly staff shift disturbance allowance which started in mid-Cheshire and spread to Merseyside, to really trigger action beyond what was possible from the works managers revolt. Sandy Marshall reports that the Deputy Chairman, Frank Bay, came to him and said:

> We're at some kind of watershed in industrial relations, can you (with a personnel manager) do a study of how other companies when they get this far – when they get into these confrontary states, how did they handle them?

Marshall and his colleague visited half a dozen different firms, including ICI's people at Wilton:

> We came back and said there's too big a gap between the businesses and industrial relations. There's lack of integration between the different operating units – we're fighting each other, not reinforcing each other. There's no central forum where we can learn from each other, and there's no forward policy on how we can improve the quality of industrial relations.

This time with the shift disturbance dispute having lost significant output, and a lot of negative reaction from customers, together with Millbank showing increasing interest in the poor quality of industrial relations in Mond plants in north-west England, substantial action followed quickly. A works managers group was created[3] linking a deputy chairman, all the works managers and relevant personnel people. A further group linking the same Deputy Chairman – Frank Bay, the Personnel Director, all four Product Group Directors, and all the business general managers was created to deal with problems not resolveable at the works manager level. At the time these groups were created in the Summer and Autumn of 1974 there were "36 industrial relations fires burning in the Mond plants in Cheshire". There was now a resolve to try and reassert effective management control through a mixture of involvement and firm directiveness.

The division's historical stance, of avoiding union trouble because of financial costs, was now to be replaced by a short-term strategy of law and order – a simple no work, no pay approach, and then followed up with a strategy of using the American consultants and the newly created internal developmental resources of Marshall and Campbell to "try and provide the skills and knowledge base for managers to begin to involve the shop floor in a different sort of way". In fact, although there was not too strong a realisation of this at the time, these attempts to deal with the industrial relations problems through

[3] There had been a works managers' group in existence for years in Mond but the above events considerably strengthened and made more purposeful works managers' meetings.

works manager–director level contact did help to make some of Woodburn's attempts to influence the board on questions of organisation and management processes that much more tangible. As Nicholas Mann later said:

> Industrial relations was the trigger to try and develop a more unified management, coming through that we realised we wanted a more unified management not just for industrial relations, but also to run the business.

But following the thread of unity at the top around business purpose will take us back to the developmental activities of the Mond board after Woodburn had left in 1977. But before we move on to consider that, there is Woodburn's vision of participation at work to consider and this requires a close look at the important experiment conducted at Lostock Works.

THE LOSTOCK EXPERIMENT AND ITS LEGACY

Before examining the particular characteristics and impact of the Lostock Works experiment, it is important to recall some aspects of the Mond context at the time the experiment began in 1975. A brief look at the context will remind us that we are looking at parallel and interdependent streams of development activity, some occurring at the board level, some as we have just seen being stimulated by highly tangible industrial relations problems, some being prompted by Woodburn's vision of improved relations between the managers and the shop floor, others by experience and conceptual ideas brought into the division by the American consultants Bainton and Wilson, and still others spinning up from individual works managers and production units. In no sense yet was this process either part of some rationally conceived master plan for the division, or indeed supported by anything more than a small subset of people although the subset of supporters of the Mond development work continued to be at and near the top of the division's power system. We are, therefore, discussing a meandering process where a combination of rational intent, inarticulate intervention, imprecise vision, chance, and opportunity were together shaping the unravelling of the Mond developmental stream.

The decision to use the open systems approach to assist the participative design, construction, commissioning and operation of the new cell-room in the Lostock Chlorine Works, was taken when and where it was for a mixture of reasons. The political will to conduct the experiment at Lostock, and the less visible and intensive change projects started at Buxton Works and in part of the division's Research and Development Department, undoubtedly came from Tony Woodburn. Lostock was chosen because the Product Group Director responsible for the chlor-alkali businesses strongly supported an initiative there, because under Sandy Marshall's prompting there had been a history of development work in Lostock Works, and because the American consultants took the view that the high energy and commitment usually generated in new plant start-ups would create a supportive climate for an experiment attempting to link technical, social, and organisational aims.

The timing of the Lostock experiment was no doubt influenced by a desire by Woodburn and his supporters to see something tangible happening after the vague promises of the industrial relations, and employee relations principles had been enunciated and also because another group of Mond people had only just returned from a visit to the United States to see the impact of Bainton and Wilson's work on open systems planning in a number of Procter and Gamble plants. A works manager who had been on this trip remarked that the Procter and Gamble plant had looked like an attractive proposition because it had:

> Low cost production, low levels of supervision, few tiers of management, high skill levels, and people were really motivated by what they were doing.

When the works managers returned from their American trip they gave a presentation to the Mond board; the board's reported reaction to this talk on "autonomous work groups", gives some indication of the highly sceptical views still around at the top of the division just as the Lostock work commenced:

> With the exception of Woodburn, Bay, and Jones there were a lot of doubters on the board. "Get in there and straighten them [the Unions] out, never mind this round-about stuff. It's okay for those Yanks but not over here" was the view. The board, instead of being a generator of support, was still a sponge to effort coming up.

This majority view at the top, of let it happen rather than support it happening, was of course eventually fateful when the Lostock project predictably ran into a number of powerful barriers. A shop steward closely committed to the experiment for much of its duration ultimately said:

> The event was started off by senior management in Mond division. They did not have the strength to see it through, so they must be responsible at the end of the day for the failure.

The overall purpose of the Lostock experiment was to create a commissioning structure and process "to enable people in all parts of the plant and associated functional departments to feel they were part of a complete business system composed of technical, commercial, and social components". Joint management–union groups were created to encourage processes of designing the form of organisation and training which would meet a number of aims about business, jobs, industrial relations, support systems, and environmental care whilst commissioning this £17m new cell-room. Beyond this broad but immediate framework of aims, was the secondary objective, "to enable people to acquire the capability to think and behave in the way needed for the organisation to function effectively in achieving its goals". In other words it was hoped that through the various shared tasks and processes of plant commissioning, the overall capability of individuals and therefore of the system would be raised, and this improvement of capability would become a continuing feature of the plant's functioning.

The commissioning structure and process developed for the Lostock cell-room was quite different from what had gone on before in Mond. The custom was for a project manager to run a commissioning project team of managers with engineering design, construction, and operating plant responsibilities. The usual pattern was for this project team to consult with many groups about technical matters but:

> Management influenced all thinking about the organisation of the new plant. Management would sort out the structure and manpower numbers based on work study and technical considerations – the unions would then be told/persuaded of these structures and numbers and training also designed by management would proceed.
>
> In Lostock the concern with organisation, training and environmental consider-ations were all jointly tackled by management and the unions, and the whole thing was pulled together by a core group – which was also a new concept.

Bainton and Wilson played a crucial lead role in designing in process terms what would happen. A start was made by discussing the idea of a participative process in the Lostock Works Committee. With this agreed a group of 50 people, of whom about 15 were shop stewards, took part in activities designed to develop a shared philosophical base for the project, and generate shared long-term objectives. From this group the Lostock Charter was created. The charter was a statement about the values and direction informing the project as they related to matters of business, community, jobs, support systems, and industrial relations. Following the drafting of the Lostock Charter those involved in the commissioning sought to generate additional support for what they were doing. Members of management and unions went out in pairs into the company and union hierarchies and told them in individual sessions about the charter and invited their comments and ideas for improvement.

Following this an organisation structure was agreed to see the project through with maximum participation by representatives of the work force at all stages. At the heart of the organisation was a core group of monthly and weekly staff responsible for the speed and direction of the whole project.

In addition four task forces were formed. These were groups of people capable of managing the project's main areas of concern – technical, training, organisation, and care of the environment.

Also on hand was a boundary resource group of senior managers and full-time union officials. These were people who:

(a) had a capacity to provide assistance and resources where appropriate;
(b) were able to interpret and influence the constraints under which any decision relevant to the project needed to be taken;
(c) were outside the immediate area of the project but who were affected by or could affect what took place.

Finally, the core group was itself guided by a small facilitating group of four people. These were the assistant works manager at Lostock, Sandy Marshall the ex-works manager at Lostock but now Mond's senior internal development resource, a shop steward, and the internal consultant working full-time in Lostock Works.

These groups went through activities variously described as "vision building", "searching", "testing", "questioning", "principle building", "problem solving", "individual capability building", and "joint decision-making" which because of the intensity and depth of challenging and questioning of conventional solutions to issues of organisation, manning, and training took an inordinate amount of time. As the work progressed enormous energy and commitment was put into it by a number of key managers and shop stewards, and the core group, on the advice of its various task forces, began to take on some fairly revolutionary recommendations as far as the Mond, ICI Group, and trades union systems were concerned. A shop steward recalled that:

> We came up with a common wage structure for monthly and weekly staff and agreement that everybody should know what everyone else was getting in the way of rewards; take the secrecy out. We also wanted to create multi tradesmen on the plant with supervisors from any background supervising people from any background.

Sandy Marshall indicated that:

> We wanted to pay people more on the basis of personal skill levels than job descriptions. The range of work a person could do would be recognised. People could apply to train for additional skills, be tested on those skills, and then paid for them.

As these various revolutionary suggestions were agreed inside the core group and then taken outside, so the Lostock cell-room project began to run into more and more vested interests that neither the enthusiasm nor the intellectual argument of the core group could deal with. Of course, it had been one of the objectives of setting up the boundary resource group to deal with some of the systems implications of the Lostock ideas, but communicating ideas to a boundary resource group was one thing; having a group with the power to deal with the vested interests that moved in on the Lostock plans was another matter altogether. One of the internal development resources commented:

> The boundary resource group never really learnt what its proper purpose was in this activity, and they didn't spend enough time together. They were called an umbrella group; they were meant to stop raindrops falling on Lostock, and to help legitimate what was going on. But it needed to be a more active group. I will change the environment to allow this to go on, rather than just hold an umbrella, should have been their approach, but it was too passive a group. Of course we didn't have enough muscle in the core group to shift the environment either – that's the case.

The real problems started when the Lostock ideas meant not just changing the organisation and the work methods but the payment systems. In no time restraining pressure appeared not only from the Mond Personnel Function, but also Central Personnel Department in Millbank, and the national officers of the relevant unions:

> I remember lack of support from the Personnel people. "You're mad, you're really giving these boys too much space. You're building them up with skills that they'll take us on and beat us with. It's unhealthy, it's way out. This doesn't conform – we're building rods for our backs. You're creating expectations that you'll never be able to deliver on. The fly back from this is really going to be so bad you really won't believe it."

* * *

> I perceived Personnel as rather standing off, a concern not to become tainted with this developmental thought because of their negotiating role ... They saw Lostock as giving away information and decision making authority.

A personnel manager confirmed the above impressions:

> In spite of the environmental scanning, Lostock didn't sufficiently take into account the environment it was in. The expectations raised among key union people were more than the system was going to meet. There was no way the pay system across ICI was going to be modified because of Lostock. Bernard Wilson did not appreciate the sheer institutional barriers to change the British union system presents, the craft–general differences. There was an over-optimistic belief those processes could be worked through.

A shop steward even in 1983 prepared to say the Lostock project "was the right road to go down", admitted both that some of the stewards "kept their scepticism to themselves – they only went along with the exercise", and that the stewards like him who openly supported Lostock were put under pressure by their peers, their membership; and managers elsewhere on the Lostock site:

> The Arthur Scargill type people in the trade union movement were saying ICI is conning you; when ICI have got out of it what they require that'll be it. It's just a device to get their will ... But one of the things that did happen was that we became isolated from our members by spending too much time shut up in the core group ... Really a mistake we made was to try and put a wall around a piece of work. I was acting one way here, and then when I went elsewhere on the site management were expecting me to act in the same way. I couldn't; I had my traditional role to play elsewhere. It influenced me but I couldn't behave the same elsewhere and management found that very hard to live with.

A further boundary problem the Lostock project had was with the engineering commissioning team, who were under the traditional pressures to have the cell-room start up on time and to cost:

The engineering part of the job somehow always managed to stay separate from the project – they just wanted to get the plant built. We were holding back the completion date – frigging about.

The "frigging about" mentioned was, of course, attempts to reach understanding and consensus about what should be done in complex, and as we have seen, contentious issues about organisation, manning, and pay. The problem was finding a marrying of the slow processes to reach consensus on organisational issues with the often speedier day-to-day technical decision-making of the engineers and their commissioning team.

A further problem that emerged some way down the process of commissioning Lostock was that "the middle management, section and plant managers were not supportive of what was going on – they didn't understand it, and no great attempt was made to bring them on board as to why it was being done. Publicly they would say okay, but privately they thought what on earth is this all about?"

Of course, the reality of Lostock which worried local management most was the fact that:

It was almost getting to joint decision-making. There's a spectrum from joint decision making to telling. Lostock got close to joint decision making and that's what worried a lot of people. We went out on a limb.

A shop steward noted the anxiety created at local management level because of loss of authority:

I think local management didn't want it. Plant managers because they saw their position being eroded. The participative arrangements meant that decisions would be made when the plant became operational by a sub group in the plant; or if not totally made by them then certainly fully discussed by them and influenced by them. Supervisors also felt their authority would be compromised by this.

The irony of a set of people using a problem-solving process requiring open systems thinking and mechanisms such as boundary resource group and then running into so many brick walls was not lost on the long-term sceptics of the Lostock project. As one crisply put it:

They were preaching open systems, yet couldn't handle their environment. They seemed to set aside the fact that there was an ICI payments system, raised expectations of people that they would be paid differently, then couldn't deliver, so it was a big let down.

The Lostock chlorine plant was eventually commissioned in April 1978, some eleven months behind the commissioning date envisaged by the Company in March 1976. Not all the delay by any means can be attributed to the complicated organisation and social process chosen for the project. More significant than the delay, however, was the fact that "the reassertion of management authority", and a strike in October 1978 meant that the structure and process of working created with such promise and enthusiasm in 1975 were abandoned.

A manager described the break-up of the Lostock project in this way:

> There were some sub-optimal decisions from the process which eventually management found unacceptable. For example, boilermakers on shift to check that fitters didn't do boilermakers' work. Management eventually took a stand and said the resolution of inter-union patterns isn't what the project is all about, and we really have to take those principles now and as managers put together a proposed organisation. That was part of the background to the 1978 strike, it wasn't the public cause but it was part of the difference between management and union. In effect management had to assert their authority, and the structure broke up. The core group stopped functioning, and eventually disintegrated.

A shop steward explained that there had been difficulties just before the strike because the ICI assessment system was coming up with job grades below what they expected. The real flare-up, however, developed over an overtime ban:

> As part of the annual wage bargaining the mid-Cheshire trade unions were putting in an overtime ban. Pressure was put on us to put the same ban on. We didn't want to do that at that time, because we had enough problems trying to raise the grades of other people. But we had our responsibilities to the trade union exercise, so instead of having an overtime ban, we suggested a planned overtime ban. This meant we would still be available to come in for overtime, all management had to do was phone the men they wanted and pay the necessary money. We explained this to the assistant works manager, production, and he was quite happy. But next day he came back and said we can't agree to this and gave no explanation. Someone outside Lostock Works didn't believe what we were saying, didn't trust us . . . After this the relationships between management and the workers were soured and the management decided the Lostock work would no longer carry on.
>
> There was a strike and the general unions withdrew from consultation for about 12 months.
>
> The aftermath of that is that management in our eyes are determined to manage now [in 1983]. We have very little involvement in decisions. The operation of the Lostock chlorine plant is no different from any other in mid-Cheshire. Also it's forced the trade unions in Lostock Works to go back into a mid-Cheshire role rather than a Lostock role. Now we follow the mid-Cheshire line, and since 1978 we've had 2 or 3 strikes.

Nobody interviewed in this study described the Lostock cell-room project as a success; in fact most people categorised it as a failure, although some would also acknowledge that the learning from Lostock stimulated activity which was of great benefit in the post-1979 business survival era. A senior member of the present Mond board remarked:

At the time it appeared to be reasonably successful but it wasn't. Again it was sowing the seeds in fairly alien fields, and it was perceived as an oddity. It didn't have a critical mass behind it to turn it into the norm, and therefore it didn't have the lasting effect we thought it might have at the time.

Another board member made the essential point:

> It is very, very difficult to change history, to change culture without some physical change around you, preferably a new location. It is difficult to reverse history . . .

In terms of learning for the future the director who made the above point about the structural and cultural impediments in history remarked:

> Lostock was not a solution to the institutions problems, but it was of considerable value as an investment. In OD there is a high element of redundancy, like research in general. You've got to do experiments, learn as you go along, the body of knowledge is increasing all the time.

The particular areas of learning people pointed to to inform their future behaviour were putting better boundaries around change activities so they don't get too ambitious for the surrounding structures and culture, avoiding dependence on external consultants to lead the change process, the recognition of the tremendous peer group pressure put on individuals on the management and the trade union side when they are creating what is perceived to be an exclusive and threatening change, and above all in Lostock the recognition of the necessity of management leadership capability in handling change. I doubt, however, given the kind of outcomes emerging from the Lostock project, and the degree of threat those outcomes posed to powerful interests on both the management and the union side – in and outside Mond Division, if a different kind or more skilled leadership would have made any difference to Lostock. Except perhaps the kinds of leadership which would have steered the project to much more culturally and politically acceptable processes and outcomes than were tried in the Lostock cell-room. As one person closely involved with Lostock said:

> We really said we must not go back and run any projects unless the whole culture and management philosophy of the place could handle change from underneath.

The real lesson from the Lostock project which the system did assimilate, but still could not do anything about, was that in Mond Division really significant change of the kind contemplated at Lostock would have to be a unified top-down management activity. Within 18 months of the dissolution of the Lostock core group, a highly unified power system in Mond was creating very significant change indeed. This led one of the visionaries associated with the Lostock work to argue:

> I look back with sorrow at the brutal way some of those things have been pushed into the background. I worry that there will be a backlash should the power balance shift.

THE BEGINNINGS OF PURPOSE AND UNITY ON THE MOND BOARD, 1977–79

The review earlier in this chapter of the Mond board development work up to early 1977 concluded with a quotation from a senior member of the board indicating little impact on the board and even less impact on "the mass of the body politic". This same board member went on to argue that the basic scepticism remained for much of 1977 and 1978, and was still around when the present Chairman took over in 1979. His quote reveals this scepticism, and also interestingly how much some members of the board hoped for perhaps, and certainly expected a change of direction each time a new chairman came into office. Understandably, Mond directors and senior managers still took their cue from the Chairman:

> I remember when Tony [Woodburn] went people approached me and said Tony's gone now can we forget all that stuff? And then 2 years later when Frank [Bay] went and I took over they said the same thing to me. There's always that about.

Even Tony Woodburn was happy to acknowledge that as he was leaving Mond, his work with the Mond board was only just beginning to have some impact:

> It took me a long time, in fact I'd only just really started to get the whole of my board – about 13 of them on board with all this.

Of course, the state of the business environment in 1977 is the obvious explanation for the absence of "any major real blitz on productivity and organisational improvement". With sales of £858m, profits of £146m and a ratio of trading profit to sales of 17, the General Chemicals Product Sector results for the whole ICI Group in 1977, put them top of the pile. Mond with hindsight was in a false dawn situation, but the business climate in 1977 was one of growth and further success. The division was busily recruiting and gearing itself up for major new capital investments at Wilton and Wilhelmshaven.

In the absence of any business reasons for across-the-board strategic changes, the Mond development work continued to plug away at development work in the works situations where there was the continuing problem of poor industrial relations:

> There was a lot of pain in the industrial relations – social scene, and there was a lot of energy to find better ways of handling that part of our affairs. I hardly had a summer holiday for 3 years because of all the aggravation going on. Frank Bay and others were very exercised about that. The search therefore in the various experiments at Lostock and Buxton was not for business strategic development, but how can we run the people side better?

In spite of the above context for development work on the Mond board, Tony Woodburn was determined not to leave the division without managing some kind of continuity with his successor Frank Bay. The meeting Woodburn organised over a weekend at Stratford in the Autumn of 1976 to review progress so far and help propel the board forward is widely regarded in retrospect as a watershed in the meandering process which so far had characterised attempts to influence the culture and perspective of senior people in Mond.

Strange as it may seem, a clear decision was made at Stratford that indeed the Mond board did have a role alongside the powerful four-man executive committee. Prior to this some directors had wondered, because of the limited agenda of board meetings and the nature of the meetings themselves, if the board was necessary.

Also at Stratford the board formed themselves into seven topic groups and a co-ordinating group, each with a specific task, which were collectively aimed at the development of Mond Division as a total business system, sensitive to trends in its environment, and having an ability to adapt continually in a way that ensured its future prosperity. The seven topic groups were asked to focus on board relationships and processes, Mond's future business scenario, Mond as a corporate entity, Mond's organisation, Mond's environment, Mond's culture, and the development of a document that became known as the Mond Charter. Mann was made responsible for progressing and co-ordinating the work of these seven topic groups.

Frank Bay's reported style as chairman by Mond senior managers and directors is different from Woodburn's. Woodburn is often described as a broad-brush conceptualiser – a climate setter for things to happen, whilst Bay was said to be more results-oriented, impatient/practical, and concerned to cause things to happen. Bay caused the Mond Charter to happen in August 1977. Using headings such as aims of Mond Division, business operating principles, environment, financial, employees, and organisation the Mond Charter was an attempt to present a view "of the sort of organisation the division board wants Mond to be". The process of producing this document may have helped members of the board to clarify and unify values and perspective but it seemed to leave levels below the board mystified about what they could do with a charter. A director whimsically commented:

> I remember saying of the Charter let's get this down on paper – who's going to be Moses and who will be Aaron? It was the 10 commandments. Management were very sceptical – this is another good intent, will the board live by it?

One of the development resources remarked:

> The product they produced had tremendous meaning for some of them, but what they were not very skillful about was actually passing the message onto others. Some directors just sent the charter out with a memo, others had a meeting and people felt what was all that about! Managers' reactions were "it's motherhood", "pie in the sky", "airy fairy", "what do we do with it?" A fair number of the directors, of course, didn't know what they would do with it once they'd got it.

A manager confirmed that the charter was "a bit of a lead balloon – it was published and forgotten about, it wasn't clear what you could do with it, and so not much happened as a result of it".

Not dulled by the no doubt well-concealed scepticism to the Mond Charter, the board, aided now by the single consultant Bernard Wilson, began to focus in on some concepts and processes which they felt would inform a strategy for management and organisation development. However the continuing problem the board faced was what to develop and for what purpose? The Mond Charter, in spite of its breadth of coverage, was still perceived by many board members as:

A strictly behavioural synopsis of management objectives, which had some sympathy with the drive in those times for better industrial relations, participation, and greater social awareness in the community, and therefore very much emphasised that side as compared with the business side.

More energy was put into the board development work in the Autumn of 1977. This time four new topic groups were created, and eventually the four became three as more focussing was directed to the topics of business, organisation, and resources. But the doubts remained, where was the output of all this thinking and concept development? Real pressure was put by some directors to discontinue Wilson's contract, and it was now apparent that management had to reassert its authority in the Lostock experiment. The Spring of 1978 was a period of real doubts about the purpose and impact of development work in Mond Division. In spite of more and more articulate reflection at the board level on the principles, values, and policies that might inform the character and shape of the Mond businesses and their organisation, and their codification in the charter and a board handbook, the board still didn't "know what their thinking about the leadership of change was leading towards". It appeared what was being developed was a more and more sophisticated motor car with a well-thought-out engine, fuel system, and gearbox but not yet having a sufficiently unifying and engaging reason for pushing the gear lever into gear to carry the vehicle towards an agreed point. All this was to dramatically change with the changes in the business environment first recognised in 1979, but before then there was another period of assembly, polishing, and refuelling before the Mond management model left the garage on Runcorn Heath.

BUSINESS CRISIS: HARNESSING THE DEVELOPMENTAL CAPABILITY IN MOND, 1979–83

Although in the writer's view the reasons why the Lostock project got into difficulty were because powerful interests were challenged, one of the interpretations key people in Mond put on the outcome of Lostock was that if such a change project had been led by managers with real leadership capability rather than by external consultants, a rather more successful outcome would have been the result. Whatever the cause or causes of the demise of the Lostock project in early 1978, by the Summer of that year Bernard Wilson had persuaded the key decision-makers on the Mond board "that we were lacking in conscious leadership skills – there was capability, but it wasn't being harnessed properly and therefore we needed:

(a) to consciously recognise that fact;
(b) to develop a means of creating and deploying such leadership capability.

Having raised the need, Wilson then used his undoubted creative talents as a conceptualiser to put together a management development activity called the Leadership Series. The chairman, virtually all the directors, general managers, site managers, and heads of departments (some 40 people) attended the Leadership Series during 1978/79 with Wilson, Marshall and Campbell acting as designers and trainers. This educational activity, the Leadership Series, plus a framework for thinking about effective management processes and structures on a manufacturing site known as the Lostock Management Model, may be considered as two additional pieces in the jigsaw; two other pieces of preparation in readiness for the events of 1979 and beyond.

The Leadership Series is interesting because it develops a view of leadership way beyond leader-subordinate relations behavioural styles, and tries to place leadership processes within an appreciation both of individual knowledge and experience and business strategy and context, and environmental trends. The key variable pinpointed for development is the individual's thinking capacity within the above broad perspective on leadership. The hope is that improvements in individual thinking capability will lead to more effective leader behaviour.

Individuals interviewed in this study, while on the one hand saying that the quality of management thinking in Mond has been raised, find it difficult to explain how and why. A director commented:

> Wilson raises the quality of thinking going on – how he does it I'm not quite sure. Some of his stuff is extremely difficult to comprehend but by designing settings for discussion he raises the plan and the questioning.

A senior member of the Mond board said "my reaction when I went on the Leadership Series was I've never heard such a load of balls in all my life. We all went through that phase." Other people talked of the Leadership Series being "too abstract, there weren't enough back connections", of it "being extremely difficult, hard to understand". Someone else said he recognised the improving of the quality of thinking objective "but what about outcomes, the practical side – I want to see evidence that in practice it helps." A senior manager captured a general view in saying the Leadership Series course:

> Was a very, very intense and mind-stretching week's course full of Pacific English and jargon of the worst possible kind which is very, very difficult to understand. Explaining how thoughts work establishing a conceptual approach to hang-ups

one has in dealing with people. Describing a process for asking the right questions about change.

The difficulties with the Leadership Series raise a general point about the use of gifted outsiders – their management in effect to maximise the chances of their contribution being picked up and used. Nicholas Mann noted that over the years he had chosen to more deliberatively manage and protect Wilson:

> It is partly a question of me spending more time with Wilson, but also focussing him in on areas of work where people could achieve and see beneficial results, and shielding him from other projects and people.

What in fact began to happen after Lostock was that Wilson focussed in more and more on relationships with a very small number of key people on and just below the board. This strategy was complemented by the interpreting, translating, and practical focus supplied by Mann in his work with others on the Mond Management Model, and by Marshall and Campbell using educational events to link the Mond Management Model and Wilson's thinking down into the division. Campbell explains:

> From late 1978 onwards Marshall and I have dedicated ourselves to translating the abstractness and diffuseness of Wilson's approach. We said if we are to get the application of the Wilson ideas we need a different way of doing that than the Leadership Series. But how could we apply them without losing their quality?

In fact what happened was that Marshall and Campbell developed two more concrete and practical educational events. One of these, called "Leading Change within a Works", which started in 1980 and up to the end of 1982, had involved over 600 people from four works. The other, "Leading Business Improvement", draws its audience from monthly staff in marketing, sales, accountancy and from those managing particular products, and has similar change and productivity objectives as the works course. These educational events have had a very important role in linking the purposes and aims of the top management system to the particular contexts and management skills necessary to motivate and give confidence to middle managers attempting to create change.

Circling back in time again to pick up the board development activities, real doubts were emerging in late Spring of 1978 about the value of the board- and works-based development work. These doubts were expressed at board meetings and they forced Nicholas Mann – then the Division Personnel Director, to take up a much more up-front position in drawing together the threads of what had been happening and trying to structure up further agreement on strategy for management and organisation development. Board meetings in April and May 1978 clarified that the Coverdale work would be continued, that Wilson would be launching his Leadership Series, and that "our aims should be that managers understand what the board has been doing and see it as sensible, and that managers do not see this as the latest imposed central initiative". The particular strategy proposed mentioned that there were to be no more experiments or "window shopping", that the developments should "be management-led", and focus on "total business development rather than simply on personnel development".

Shortly after these board deliberations Mann encouraged the Lostock Works management to consider what form of organisation and management processes would have to be created in order to produce an effective manufacturing unit serving a particular business or businesses. Faced with this question the works manager, and the two assistant works managers of Lostock Works assisted by Wilson and Marshall, helped to develop the Lostock Management Model. This model and its development and sharpening under the guidance of a team led by Nicholas Mann to produce the Mond Management Model, was to play a crucial justifying and enabling role in the changes still in the wings but ready to appear in 1980.

Briefly the Lostock Management Model suggested a works could be understood as requiring five discreetly different activities or processes, for each of those processes particular concepts could be developed to guide the performance of those processes. The five processes were:

1. *On-going activities* such as plant operation, cleaning, and maintenance which would normally be carried out by weekly staff.
2. *Improving the on-going activities* concerned with improving the way in which on-going work is done, including managing the variances when this work is to be done. These activities would rarely have a long time horizon and would normally be carried out by supervisors.
3. *Adapting activities* which involve, for example, work of a longer time scale such as introducing new technology or equipment into a works. Plant managers who would do this kind of work should guard against slipping into improving activities.
4. *Business linking activities* concerned with marshalling and adapting resources and services in order to satisfy business demands.
5. *Improved thinking activities* are concerned with broadly understanding environmental trends and business and technical demands and ensuring that the overall capability of the system continually develops to meet those demands. This role would be performed by the works manager.

This way of thinking in terms of activities and guiding concepts for those activities was quickly picked up by Nicholas Mann who asked the question can this be applied to the division as a whole rather than just a works, and if so what does that mean in terms of the future structural configuration of Mond Division? Fortunately that question was posed not only when there was the basis of providing an intellectually coherent and practical answer to it, but more importantly still when the division did at last have a business need to have the question asked and answered. The meandering was over.

Top-down change

Frank Bay's retirement in 1979, and his replacement as chairman of Mond by Mark Warwick, coincided with "a kind of collapse of the business" – although in fact that bad financial results did not show up clearly until 1980. There was a more or less immediate stepwise change in the use of developmental thinking – the vehicle finally snapped into gear. A senior manager reviewed the contributions of Woodburn, Bay, and Warwick to creating change in Mond in these terms:

> The enormous difference from the past was Warwick actually saying "right we're actually going to move towards that". Woodburn generated enthusiasm to get things going, Frank let them continue, but never said "we've got enough data, now here's where we're going to go". Five years ago OD was optional based on an individual managers' predilections. The chairman is now saying here is the direction we're going in, there will be differences in the way to get there from place to place, but these are the Mond principles.

With due modesty, Warwick confirmed his part in the above process:

> The most recent stage since I have been in the Chair have coincided with an abrupt change in the overall business scene and the immediate focus on the business imperative to a degree we hadn't previously; I emphasise not because of any brightness of mine but because the needs were pressing in on us.

The ingredients that created the changes in organisation structures, employee numbers, systems and procedures, and management processes which began in 1980 are as follows. The first ingredient, and necessary one, was the change in the business environment and the clear recognition therefore of the need to run the division's business activities more effectively at substantially less cost. This need was recognised and defined at the top of the division and clearly stated in terms of change objectives which were communicated effectively to levels below the top. The division was therefore under no doubt there was now the political will to rapidly bring about the desired changes. Another critical ingredient was the creation and effective communication of a framework called the Mond Management Model which provided a guiding set of principles to help managers reach change objectives in particular parts of the division. Finally, the economic recession provided a change in the power balance between management and the unions, which afforded managers both the opportunity and confidence to apply any capabilities in leading the management of change processes which they had acquired through experience and training.

A director described how some of the above elements combined to give force and impetus to the desired changes:

> It was obvious in the division what was going to happen with the change in exchange rates. In the end you had to put some figures on it and say we've got to do something dramatic. The prices will be determined externally, what we need to do is reduce costs.

We set and articulated some pretty challenging targets, we'll get the division down to such and such a number – this was the key to survival. The board made this clear to the line.

Charity had to begin at home, we reduced the size of the board and took out all the assistant works managers. It immediately became clear to the weekly staff. "By God this must be pretty serious look what's happening to the managers!" We shared the business situation in general across the division, and in particular businesses – scene setting with employees in broad and particular terms . . . We made it known early retirement terms were available. We asked for manpower--cost options for every site and department. The board put on the pressure and agreed with each unit what the targets were, and it went on and on and on, and we kept on refining the targets . . . The key thing that enabled it was a good deal of very clear top leadership. It was clear thinking in relation to the management model, applied in a fairly dramatic way at board and senior management levels.

A manager in a works environment described how he saw the above process from below the top and looking up:

It happened because of business pressures. Secondly I was convinced, persuaded it was the right thing to do. I didn't used to believe cost reductions were necessary – now I could see the need . . . Employee costs to added value, the graph for 1964–79 shows employee share of the cake gradually going down after 1979 the employee share was rising like mad . . . I remember Frank Bay saying to the Division Committee before he retired – very tentatively. "The numbers are too high, they'll have to come down by 10% perhaps." That was quite a thing for him to say – you could tell . . . By 1980 the data was being put in, plus the conviction of the guy telling me the information, that had a lot to do with persuading me. He was convinced we had too many layers – we were sloppy, and he didn't exclude himself from that . . . Warwick started off by setting arbitrary targets, and actually saying they are arbitrary. There's much more openness about business information by the way, more training about business information, more understanding about the business.

The importance of the changed business context was reaffirmed by a director who noted the change in managers' attitudes even in a year:

When I'd tried this 12 months previously [to make productivity changes] there was no business imperative and they said "he's up to his old intellectual business again" – no commitment. This time it was different – they acted. They came out with a view that we could easily run this business with 600 less people out of 3000. In fact it became 739 less out of 3000.

As I hinted earlier, the developmental stream made three major contributions to the on-going changes being made in Mond. One was through the long process of trying to unify the perspective and actions of the Mond board; secondly, by creating the Mond Management Model, and thirdly by helping to raise the capability and confidence of the Mond managers to effect change.

The Mond Management Model appeared out of a task force led by Nicholas Mann, and comprising a number of senior business and functional managers.

To his credit, one of the first board responsibilities Mann suggested could be combined was his role as Personnel Director. Not without some scepticism at the time, however, Mann stayed on the board for a further 15 months as Director of Organisation Change. One of Mann's board colleagues later said "one of the best decisions we ever made was to appoint a Director of Organisation Change".

Mann included on his task force Felix Hudson, who had been moved into Lostock Works as works manager to reassert management authority when the Lostock cell-room experiment was starting to get out of hand. Subsequently Hudson had combined with his two assistant works managers and external help to produce the now increasingly influential concepts contained in the Lostock Management Model.

Work on the Mond Management Model began in January 1980. Mann's task then was to "develop within management a common, shared understanding and agreement about how to think about upgrading business performance through the more effective functioning of the organisation". The framework developed during 1980 by Mann's task force is seen by many in the division as a coherent mechanism to guide changes in organisation structure, but it in fact deals with the interconnections between structure, systems and procedures, and management processes and is still evolving and being implemented in 1983. It's most tangible and understandable form is in dealing with structure and systems. The diffuseness and abstractness of the way developmental processes are conceived in terms of the quality and orderliness of thought, although in a sense exemplified in the creative structuring of the Mond model, is at a level of theoretical discourse that many in Mond find difficult to relate to.

Central to the idea of the Model is the desire to provide Mond's businesses with the most cost-effective management system necessary to identify, achieve and maintain the most advantageous relative competitive position for Mond. This is to be achieved by much clearer, sharper and more distinctive contributions and roles throughout the organisation – for instance, through the different roles of business units, services and manufacturing sites; though a clear, new definition of levels in the management hierarchy pointing to a maximum of five within the division; wider spans of control; clearer and simpler reporting and communication channels and a much broader concept of business planning.

The critical feature of the Mond Model in change terms has been the role it has played as a concrete mechanism to legitimate, guide, and structure organisational structural and systems change. A specialist manager explained:

> The key thing was a refinement from an intuitive view by the Board we were overmanaged through 2 important intellectual props that gave impetus to it. One was a general sense throughout the management system that we couldn't afford the number of people we had, and that was related to the financial situation we were in – and that was communicated warts and all. And secondly there was this conscious attempt to produce an intellectually acceptable model against which you could reflect your organisation, as opposed to you must cut numbers by 25%, go

and do it . . . It has produced a general model to act as a unifying concept. It shouldn't be used as a totally prescriptive straight jacket, but my goodness doesn't it force your thinking into what you need to have and what you don't need to have.

Table 28 sets out the manpower numbers in Mond Division since its creation in 1964 until May 1983, when the effect of implementing the Mond Management Model and other structural and systems changes was apparent. The Table indicates both around 48% reduction in monthly and weekly staff numbers between 1964 and 1983, and how large a proportion of those manpower changes have taken place in the last 4½ years. During the period 1964–79 the structure and business activities of Mond remained relatively stable. However, during the period 1 January 1980 to 1 January 1983 a number of significant structural changes took place and several of these significantly affected the total numbers employed in the division with the result that comparisons involving the numbers for this period might be misleading. Between January 1980 and January 1983 Mond gained 436 monthly and weekly staff by acquiring Burn Hall Works from Organics Division, and lost 1098 staff because of the transfer of Bain Works to Petrochemicals and Plastics Division, and Cassel Works to Agricultural Division. In that same period Mond also lost 580 monthly staff who were transferred to the newly created ICI Engineering organisation. In total, therefore, between 1 January 1980 and 1 January 1983 Mond had a net loss of 1242 monthly and weekly staff because of structural adjustments within the ICI UK organisation.

TABLE 28 Mond Division manpower numbers, 1964–83 (May)

Year (end)	Monthly staff	Weekly staff	Total
1964	6907	13,137	20,004
1965	6673	12,707	19,380
1966	6598	12,560	19,158
1967	6263	12,026	18,289
1968	6257	11,852	18,109
1969	6223	11,837	18,060
1970	6238	11,561	17,799
1971	5993	11,129	17,122
1972	5690	10,579	16,269
1973	5557	10,445	16,002
1974	5602	10,368	15,970
1975	5757	10,285	16,042
1976	5656	10,247	15,903
1977	5692	10,306	15,998
1978	5793	10,378	16,171
1979	5688	9996	15,684
1980	5504	9632	15,136
1981	4826	8380	13,206
1982	3775	7712	11,487
1983 (May)	3523	6862	10,385

TABLE 29   Mond Division manpower numbers end 1979–83 (May) allowing for ICI UK structural changes

	Monthly staff	Weekly staff	Total
1979	4808	9182	13,990
1980	4527	8529	13,056
1981	4055	7670	11,725
1982	3604	7139	10,743
1983 (May)	3523	6862	10,385

In order to reflect a more accurate picture of the effect of the Mond Division's manpower reduction programme, Table 29 presents the number of employees that the division *would have employed* from year end 1979 to May 1983 if the division's structure and production activities had been as they are now, i.e. including Burn Hall Works but excluding Cassel and Bain Works and the Mond Division Engineering Department. The Table illustrates that the overall numbers reductions that can be attributed to Mond management from end of 1979 to May 1983 are 26%, the percentage drop for monthly staff being 27%, and weekly staff being 25%. Taking into account the ICI UK structural changes, Mond have reduced their senior staff population from 270 on 1 January 1980 to 160 by May 1983. The figure of 160 is expected to drop to 125 by the end of 1984. As reported earlier in this chapter, the Mond board has dropped from the September 1978 position of having a chairman, 2 deputy chairmen, 5 product group directors, and 5 functional directors – a board of 11 in all because 2 of the directors shared a functional and a product group role, to the May 1983 position where there is just a chairman, 2 business directors with 2 business areas each, a technical/personnel director, and a commercial services/finance director – 5 people in all. The expectation is that the present board of 5 can be reduced to 4 in the next year or so.

Below the board, the present situation is that within each business area a single general manager is now responsible for all of that business. In addition a number of production works have been merged to form larger manufacturing sites with a single site manager having overall responsibility, and the role of assistant works manager has all but disappeared. Mergers have also occurred within Mond headquarters functional departments.

Such are the practical outcomes that can be achieved when there is a marriage between environmental pressure, internal business need, political will, an intellectually coherent and practical framework to connect with simply stated and well-communicated change objectives, and of course a change in the power balance between management and management, and management and union, and the managerial skill in creating change to exploit the window for change opening, *and* opened.

Some consequences and implications of the post-1979 Mond changes

By the end of the 1981 financial year one desired consequence of the post-1979 Mond changes was being realised – the division was saving around £40m per annum in fixed costs. In a situation where the Mond board could not reduce the value of sterling, could not on their own persuade the Thatcher Government to reduce bulk tariff electricity prices, could not alter the structure of bulk commodity chemicals prices by taking out sufficient of the European over-capacity, the Mond board took control where they still had control and pulled the fixed cost lever. This £40m was the difference between breaking even and not breaking even in 1981 and 1982.

The skill with which the exit of so many monthly and weekly staff was managed is clearly an important issue in terms of the attitudes of staff that remained and ICI's reputation in Cheshire and beyond. Given that the structural and systems changes in the Mond Management Model were hoping to achieve not just sharper business focus, clearer distinctiveness between reduced management levels, and clearer accountability for managers in enlarged jobs, but also the kind of cultural changes which would mean appropriate behaviours would be in place to enable 30% fewer managers to run the Mond business more effectively – then it was important that the overall change process did not end up as short-term concern with efficiency leading to a medium-term loss of effectiveness.

The extent to which Mond is able to put in place a culture which is reinforcing of the structural and systems changes will take some time to elucidate. Whether also Mond will pay a price in terms of reduced commitment and motivation from those who remain because of the numbers reductions of 1979–83, is a question this study could not begin to answer at this point in time.

Mond like other ICI divisions have had available the large carrot of the ICI voluntary severance arrangements. For someone in their mid-50s with a large number of years service, the severance terms have often meant a lump sum and a pension which could produce an income level after tax not far short of what they were earning on the ICI payroll. For the 50-plus age group it could be said ICI have bought their way around the problem. Below 50 there is a problem as exit then means deferring a pension until normal retirement age. It is not so obviously in the individual's self-interest to leave ICI if he or she is below 50, and notwithstanding no enforced redundancy policies, undoubtedly over a period individuals in the 30 to 50 age group have been pressurised to go. Mond have put a great deal of effort into counselling training and other practical help to assist individuals find alternative employment. In the period 1981–83 67% of senior management staff got alternative employment. The expressed view was that a fairly high proportion of the remaining 33% were in the financially safe 50-plus age group and probably weren't looking for employment anyway.

Putting up a simple losses and gains equation, one potential loss to Mond, given that they are the major employer in an area of very high unemployment, is some slippage on their reputation as a caring employer. There may also be some loss of morale amongst the survivors, a hardening of attitudes, a feeling that "this isn't the sort of company we thought we were joining". Mond undoubtedly have cut down on, but certainly not eliminated, new graduate recruitment. The level of present recruitment may be below the level for the division's longer-term needs, and there's always a risk of a diminution of potential management talent in younger age groups. In 5 or 6 years time Mond may find itself somewhat devoid of talent in the younger age groups.

If the above losses are of the mays and might be's character, what certainly isn't, is the fact that the structure of career opportunity in Mond has substantially changed as a consequence of the post-1979 structural changes. With a board of 4 or 5 instead of a board of 12 or 13, merged departments, and reduced numbers of levels in the structure, as a matter of fact opportunities for vertical mobility are less. Given the calibre of people that have traditionally entered ICI, and the expectations and aspirations that group have, how Mond tactically and ethically handle this career problem will have a substantial impact on the kind of culture in the division, and the levels of motivation and commitment of individual managers.

A related question is the problem of how to equip people with the necessary skills, experience, and perspective to operate from a business-driven rather than a functionally driven structure? As the pendulum swings in Mond from technical–production to business–marketing, it is all too easy to assume both that only those with a marketing background can operate in the newly created business general manager positions, and all too easy for the commercial people who move into those roles to interpret them as "super-selling jobs", when in fact they are key linking jobs integrating market, financial, technical, production, and man-management considerations.

On the gains side, after the traumas of the past few years, there are no shortages of positive evaluations from the Mond Management System. Having managed to reduce the size of the Mond board largely but not completely by natural wastage, there is a clear view there both that "functions are more sharply differentiated" and that "small groups tend to work much better than bigger ones". A senior member of the board felt that there are "sharper management standards all around", and "we're much more disciplined in our use of each other's time".

I have had to be brought up very sharply to realise that in a slimmer structure, there's no good asking for that information, you won't get it, and in any case you don't need it – you shouldn't have asked for it in the first place. There's a learning process for everyone in the system to go through of that sort.

The sharper management standards are leading to "more objective performance measurement than ever before, and if people aren't measuring up they are told much earlier in their career than previously, and at a stage when they can do something about it". Because of the much clearer and better articulated distinction of roles, "people are clearer what they have to do in their work group", there's "less duplication", less of "people sitting on each other's toes", and the "nice to have rather than need to have activities have disappeared, or are disappearing".

Broader claims are also being made that:

> People have a much stronger shared and agreed view of what the system as a whole is trying to do. It's purpose and what their purpose is as part of the whole. All that induces in people a much stronger confidence in terms of what to do, and how to do it. Confidence if I push down this path, it will be compatible with and supported by other folk around me.

I do not have the data to support or contradict the above claim, and indeed it is probably too soon yet to find valid information to verify such an outcome. What is clear is that the ethos of survival which has been the prime source of legitimacy for so much management action since 1979, has quite superseded its predecessor the ethos of growth as the ideology to engage management commitment and action. One wonders if the survival ethos will have a life cycle similar to the growth one, and if so what ideology will replace survival, if and when survival is assured.

One also wonders whether the halting, meandering, some might say inefficient process of connecting developmental thinking and resources to issues of structure, systems, culture, and management processes in Mond, needed to be as meandering as it surely was? But before returning to try and answer that question using experiences from a variety of ICI divisions, there is the equally meandering process of the ICI main board's use of developmental resources to consider. That is where we go next in this book.

10 Strategic Change and Organisation Development at the Centre of Power, 1973–83

The three years from January 1980 until January 1983 saw more changes in organisation and manpower in ICI than had occurred in the previous twenty. This was the revolution after years of inertia.

Having come into the Chairman's seat in April 1978 and dampened any enthusiasm for organisation change by saying "let me hear no more talk and work on organisation, let's get on with the business and make some money", Sir Maurice Hodgson when faced with business pressures promptly pursued organisation change with vigour. The fact that he was succeeded in April 1982 by John Harvey-Jones, was a clear signal both to Harvey-Jones and the rest of ICI that more change was the order of the day.

The reader may recall from Chapter 7, Harvey-Jones's interest in organisation change, and belief in using OD ideas and techniques when he was chairman of Petrochemicals Division in the early 1970s. Harvey-Jones's arrival at Millbank as a main board director in April 1973 brought a man with a different perspective, personal style, and values into the main board; someone capable of asking questions about the role and methods of operation of the main board, the overall structure of the company, and the efficacy of the ICI and Millbank culture to meet the fresh challenges of business, economic, and political change during the 1970s. The fact that Harvey-Jones was able to play this challenging role, and at the same time survive and prosper in the ICI power system, says something both about his own skill as a change agent and a businessman, but also the extent of the business difficulties ICI were in by the time of the 1980 recession. Without those business difficulties it is doubtful whether 1980–83 would have witnessed the degree of organisation change it did, or whether Harvey-Jones would have been elected Chairman of ICI in November 1981.

But what were the changes in organisation and manpower announced and implemented in the first three years of the 1980s, and what were the business pressures which created the climate for that degree of change?

After the expected cyclical high point of 1979, when with the additional help of the favourable European operating conditions caused by the consequences of the Iranian Revolution of 1979, ICI achieved their best trading margins since 1976, in 1980 ICI promptly experienced a sharp decline in profitability. In 1980 trading profits of the ICI group fell by 48% to £332m. The third quarter of 1980 produced the first loss in ICI's history, and by the end of that year four of ICI's business areas, fibres, petrochemicals, organic chemicals, and plastics, were between them showing worldwide losses of £200m. The ratio of trading profit to total sales fell from 11.8 in 1979 to 5.8 in 1980, and worse was to come in 1982. A combination of fundamental problems of overcapacity in the European petrochemicals industry, the impact of a severe UK recession, and currency factors arising from the strength of sterling had removed the mask obscuring ICI's inactivity in the 1970s. ICI began to realise at the heartfelt level what they knew at the intellectual level – they had substantially overinvested for their markets.

Faced with this problem Sir Maurice Hodgson set in motion a rationalisation programme to remove some of the excess production capacity, and stimulated a series of organisation changes to reduce fixed costs. Announcements were made in 1980 to close a polyester fibre plant at Kilroot in Northern Ireland, and a nylon salt plant at Ardeer in Scotland; and Fibres Division again reduced its head office staff and its work force at Pontypool, Doncaster, and Gloucester. Sodium and titanium plants were closed at Wilton in 1981, and then the No. 5 Olefin cracker at Wilton was put into mothballs.

In April 1981 the loss-making Petrochemicals and Plastics divisions were merged under a single board, and their service functions were combined with significant loss of employment amongst management and professional staff. Mond division continued the process it had been pursuing since the late 1970s to simplify its structure, reduce the numbers of levels of management, and reduce numbers.

In 1982 the numbers reductions continued in Fibres, Petrochemicals and Plastics, and Mond Divisions. A deal with BP was announced in June 1982 whereby ICI would increase its stake in the jointly owned Olefine 6 cracker at Wilton, withdraw from LDPE production in the UK, and acquire some of BP's PVC production capacity.

While all this was going on ICI collapsed its divisional engineering organisation into a regional system and severely reduced its cadre of investment engineers, thought about making an equivalent structural change in its research and technical operations, but made do with trimming numbers and refocussing research effort, and made good use of the window for change provided by the recession and high levels of unemployment to generally reduce numbers and improve working practices in its manufacturing and maintenance operations.

The effect of these manpower changes, most of which were achieved through the company's voluntary severance arrangements, was to reduce ICI's UK employees from 89,400 in 1979 to 61,800 in 1983, a reduction of 31.0% over five years. Over the same five-year period the number of ICI employees outside the UK declined from 58,800 to 56,100, a reduction of only 4.6%. By the end of 1984, for the first time ever, there will be more people working for ICI outside the UK than inside the UK.

Most of the changes reported above were either announced or implemented in the final two years of Sir Maurice Hodgson's Chairmanship. When John

Harvey-Jones took over formally as Chairman in April 1982 he at last was able to introduce changes in the role of executive directors and method of operation of the main board which had been discussed prior to Harvey-Jones's arrival on the main board in 1973. Throughout much of the 1970s Harvey-Jones and a small number of his peers on the main board had unsuccessfully attempted to reduce the size of the main board, and refocus the attention of executive directors away from their allegiances to individual functions, ICI products, or ICI territories and the short-term management of the UK assets, and to get the executive directors to concentrate on the strategic planning and direction of the worldwide ICI group. The beginnings of this change in role and style for the executive directors was made in October 1982. While this announcement was made of the executive directors' intentions to distance themselves from the operating units and to think through the strategic direction of the ICI group as a team, the newly designated chief executive officers of the operating units were offered increased delegation of authority, but also a new budgeting and control system from the centre.

Harvey-Jones, however, was still not able to persuade a large enough group of his colleagues that the time was yet ripe to merge Mond Division with Petrochemicals and Plastics Division and create a massive heavy chemicals division which could take operational charge of the great bulk of the UK assets. He was able to announce, however, a change to reduce the company's 'over-managed and overmanned centre'. If the company could operate with a smaller more strategic board then it required a smaller support staff, if it had a smaller support staff then the prestige headquarters at Millbank was too big. ICI thus began to look for a new headquarters building in London, and to persuade those not required in this building to leave the company, or join the declining support groups for the UK operations. The intended move out of Millbank was a signal that the changes in ICI were for real, if they could be carried through and implemented. What was hoped for was not just a change in manpower and structure, but a necessary change in company culture to meet the much harsher business conditions of the 1980s. As one main board director put it:

> I see the Millbank change as being the outward and visible sign of the inward and spiritual grace. That signals to the outside world and the units that we are going to do something very different. It's not quite piddling on the altar, but it's certainly saying there must be a more functional headquarters for the church than Canterbury Cathedral.

The 1980s revolution, if it could be implemented, involved changing people, structures, operating systems, roles, relationships and company culture. Why did all this change have to happen at once? Would this degree of change so destablise ICI as a group that it would imperil its business survival? Would the necessary changes in attitude and behaviour, and people with the necessary capabilities and capacities emerge from the old ICI to make these new roles, structures, and systems work? Or would the old ICI culture smother the fledgling organisation before it got on its feet and achieved a life and momentum of its own? These are crucial questions which the time frame and data base for this book cannot comprehensively answer. Neither is there space in this book to chronicle all the lessons from the implementation of those strategic changes so far.

The role of this chapter is to continue to explore the theme of the contribution of OD resources in creating and implementing change in ICI. The reader may recall that Chapter 4 described and analysed the role that OD resources played in implementing a strategic change those resources had no part in fashioning. Here the focal point for analysis is the attempt made by a relatively small number of OD consultants to try and create the conditions for, and reality of, some of the changes that were implemented in the early 1980s. The difference therefore between this chapter and the other chapters of this book lies in the fact that here we are discussing the role played by specialist resources in creating strategic change alongside the main board and chief executive officers of ICI. The point of intervention is the top power system of the company and the focus of the intervention was often the governance, structure, and operating style of the company.

It will, of course, be impossible to analyse the contribution made by internal and external OD resources at the centre of power without also detailing the more significant impact made by various chairmen and executive directors of ICI in inhibiting and pushing for organisational change. If as Harvey-Jones maintains the story of ICI in the 1970s was "a very fast-changing external scene to which we have reacted too slowly", then the contribution of those executive directors seeking to create change, and the role that OD resources at times played as helpers to that process, will have to be set in the context that created a climate for inertia.

This chapter begins by examining some of the forces for stability and continuity in ICI. While those pressures for continuity were the seeds of much of the company's strength, they were also the seeds for a great deal of the unresponsiveness to change now seen to be characteristic of the 1970s. These crucial parts of the context which often became the objects of change efforts were the size, organisation, and working culture of the main board and the Millbank culture, and the systems and relationships which linked the main board and Millbank to the operating units.

Having established aspects of the context for change, and the way that context was seen by some to be inhibiting the running of the business, the second part of the chapter moves on to analyse the conditions of central OD after the WSA/SDP implementation, and chronicle the use made of OD resources in trying to open up ICI for strategic change in the period 1974–77. Here the focus for change was the role and method of operation of the main board, and the linkages between the main board and the chairmen of the UK divisions and overseas operating units. As I have already implied, this work was only partially successful in producing the desired change.

The next part of the chapter explores OD at the centre in the period 1977–82. Now the initial attempt to create change came through the use of an educational strategy. The OD resources created a series of Management of

Change Workshops which had the effect of providing a common language to think about change management, and helped to prepare the top several hundred senior managers in ICI with some of the skills and knowledge they would require when the 1980 stepwise changes came. The late 1970s also provided an opening for one of the change-minded executive directors to dissolve much of the Europa Division and create structures and processes to encourage all of the UK divisions to directly make their headway into European markets. This became known as the Pan European change. Related to this was a need for reasons of business strategy, market planning, and operating efficiency to begin to prepare the ground for a Heavy Chemicals Group in ICI. The late 1970s also saw the creation of a set of mechanisms variously called the Inter Divisional Policy Group, and the Heavy Chemicals Policy Group which eventually led to the partial creation of a Heavy Chemicals Group when Petrochemicals and Plastics Divisions were merged in 1981.

A contribution was made to all of the above changes by the central OD resources. Often this contribution was limited in time and scope, usually it was low-key, often helping with the design of a crucial meeting and strategising with executive directors about when and how they should make a move to carry forward what became a slow, halting, and frustrating attempt to create change. The remarkable thing about the story is not the dramatic impact made by specialist OD help, for except for one occasion in 1974 no such dramatic impact was possible, but rather the fact that in a company of ICI's size and prestige OD consultants ever got near enough the power system to begin to see the possibility of helping powerful people to create organisational change. The other remarkable feature of the process was that the two internal consultants Stewart Dudley and Tom James, and even more interestingly the American external consultant Ron Mercer, survived in and around changes in the ICI power system to be drawn in and out of the process of organisational change.

The final section of the chapter examines in particular the reasons for the survival and impact of Stewart Dudley and Ron Mercer, and in so doing opens up the broader question of the what and the how of using OD to help stimulate strategic change. An important pattern in the way that OD has been used at the centre of power in ICI is the fact that only two of the executive directors have been associated with its use. A further pattern has been the linkages between those two executive directors and a very small number of internal and external consultants. As one of the key internal consultants put it:

> If I look back on major changes in ICI where there has been some assistance from some kind of change (OD) resource, I might be cynical enough to say major change has been the result of manipulative collusion between an external consultant, an internal consultant, and a power figure.

In what follows, the meaning of manipulative collusion and evidence for any justification in using such a phrase to characterise how OD and executive resources have been connected to change problems, will be discussed. But throughout the narrative, often in the foreground, and nearly always in the background, was the prompting, pushing, and pressure for change from

Harvey-Jones. To create change Harvey-Jones needed the support of his board peers and superiors; he also needed the massive enabling opportunity afforded by a worsening business scene. Against the critical nature of those factors in stimulating change, the role of internal and external OD resources could only be described relatively speaking as modest. On the other hand if Harvey-Jones had not in turn been promoted as an executive director, a deputy chairman, and then Chairman of ICI, it is doubtful if OD resources would have played any part at all in helping to create change in ICI. As Tom James has said – admittedly of his patron:

> Harvey-Jones is the most important OD intervention in the company. He provides a real political umbrella, a proactive base from which to work. He's probably the biggest single intervention in this company in the OD field.

But before discussing in detail the role that OD resources played in trying to create change over the period 1973–83, it is important to examine those parts of the top governance, structure and systems, and management culture of ICI which were felt by those pushing for change to be impeding ICI's overall capacity to manage its quickly changing business, economic, political, and social environment.

THE STRUCTURE, SYSTEMS, AND TOP MANAGEMENT CULTURE OF ICI IN THE 1970s

The top structure of ICI

Encouraged by Harvey-Jones in July 1974 Stewart Dudley, the senior internal OD consultant in ICI, wrote a critical paper reflecting on ICI's top organisation and culture. This paper, "A Look at ICI in 1974", was inadvertently sent to all executive directors in August 1974. The furore caused by Dudley's critical paper seriously endangered Harvey-Jones's credibility on the main board, and nearly caused Dudley to be fired. It also helped to open up discussions about changing the top governance of ICI.

The main board in 1974 comprised 18 people, a chairman, 11 executive directors, 3 of whom had deputy chairman status, and 6 non-executive directors. The main board was serviced by 3 principal officers, a secretary, a treasurer, and a solicitor, each of whom had status equivalent to the general managers of head office departments. Three logics of organisation are explicit in Figure 12: a focus around product, a focus around function, and a focus on geographical area or territory. These foci were the principle determinants for dividing the activities of the main board and executive directors into committees, and for allocating the individual responsibilities of executive directors. The principal committees at that time were:

Appointments Committee
Capital Programme Committee
Personnel Committee

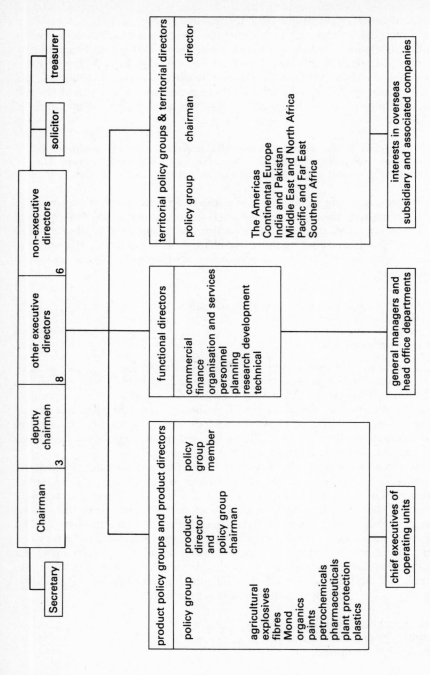

FIGURE 12 ICI Board of Directors: April 1974

Planning Committee
Staff Salaries Committee
Product Policy Groups
Territorial Policy Groups

Apart from being a product director and chairman of a product policy group such as Agricultural, an executive director could also be a policy group member of another policy group such as Plastics, chaired by a colleague executive director; and a functional director, and a territorial director. Each director accordingly held a number of portfolios, the intention being that this would give him a breadth of experience and responsibility which would better equip him to participate in the wide range of topics discussed at board meetings.

The ICI Chairman was not chief executive of the Group, and more significantly he did not in the 1970s behave as such. The Chairman was elected by his fellow board members after a traditional sounding-out process conducted by a senior non-executive director, and possibly also involving the outgoing Chairman. The new Chairman invariably came from the ranks of one of the Deputy Chairmen, and as a contrast to Sir Paul Chambers's eight years in office, the three Chairmen who followed him had either three or four years in office each.

The Chairmen of the late 1960s and 1970s were regarded as, and behaved as, first amongst equals. The Chairman had no singular authority on substantial matters of money or appointments. The Chairman chaired the board, helped substantially to determine its agenda, and allocated portfolios to executive directors. Election to the main board was a board decision, although it varied from chairman to chairman the extent to which the process of appointment was one of the Chairmen sounding out his colleagues and then announcing a name at the board, or whether the process was one of individual soundings leading to a board discussion.

The powers of individual executive directors were also fairly circumscribed. They could sanction capital expenditure in their areas of product or territorial responsibility at a level above the limit set for division chairmen, and of course within the constraints of custom and practice could decide when to take a decision to the board in their area of functional responsibility, but essentially they had to operate within the framework of policy set by the board.

Deputy chairman was a distinct level in the structure. Before 1974 all the policy groups had been chaired by deputy chairmen. By 1974 it was now common practice for the product policy groups to be chaired by executive directors, but all the territorial policy groups bar Southern Africa were still chaired by one of the three deputy chairmen. The deputies were there then not just to deputise for the Chairman, but to act individually almost as managing directors, and collectively as a sounding board, "inner cabinet", or "top box" with the Chairman. The separate managerial level explicit in the deputy chairman role, together with the power and status that went with it, was undoubtedly resented by some of the executive directors in the 1970s.

The executive directors met every Monday morning at the Chairman's weekly meeting. This was a discussion forum rather than a decision-making forum. Decisions were taken by board committees or individual directors, having regard to the Chairman's weekly meeting discussion.

Every two weeks there was a Chairman's conference. This was a body where all executive and non-executive directors would discuss any matter where their collective input would be valuable, prior to its being formally approved as part of ICI policy.

Once a month all executive and non-executive directors would meet as the ICI main board. This was the only body in the governance system which could give top-level decisions and top-level approval to matters within the ICI Group. The main board's principal reserve powers were in the financial and personnel areas.

Of the eight board committees listed on page 381, and discounting the important but specialist role of the appointments and personnel committees, the most pervasively significant committees in the ICI system were the Product and Territorial Policy Groups, and the Planning Committee.

The Planning Committee was chaired by a deputy chairman and had as its secretary the General Manager of Planning. The members of the Planning Committee were otherwise all executive directors, and included, of course, the Planning Director. The Planning Committee met quarterly, did some longer-term thinking for the ICI Group and some investigative studies on the growth, ranking, and development of the ICI businesses, but as we shall see, one of the problems of the ICI top management systems at that time was that macro-planning on the shape, size and growth of the ICI group was not explicitly tackled by the main board or their committees. Instead the ICI planning systems were directed to the shorter-term horizons of producing a group capital programme and the financial plan associated with it. In this regard the planners linked with the finance experts in the Treasurers Department at Millbank to essentially become the slave of the Product and Territorial Policy Groups.

The Policy Group's major responsibilities were to set profit and other targets, and approve the plans of UK divisions and the overseas subsidiary and associated companies. The Policy Groups also approved major items of capital expenditure and investment, including diversification and divestment, and generally acted to provide resources, judge, and control the performance of operating units. In strict organisational terms, of course, the ICI main board approved and decided the plans, capital requirements, and divestment behaviour of operating units, but the behaviour within this system was that once a piece of capital expenditure had been through an operating unit's investigative process, had been scrutinised by representatives of Planning and Treasurers Department and most crucially by the relevant policy group and the Capital Programme Committee and then championed on the main board by the appropriate Policy Group Director, it would not normally be thrown out at the main board level.

Moving away specifically from the board and its committees, there is also the important organisational question of the link between the main board and the chairmen and boards of the operating units. Here, apart from individual contact

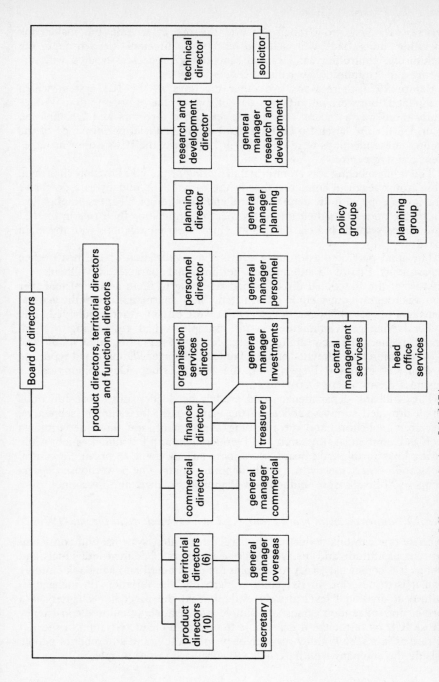

FIGURE 13 ICI Head Office organisation: July 1974

between a policy group chairman and the operating unit, the major link operating units had with selected executive directors was through the monitoring, controlling, and capital sanctioning process associated with the Spring and Autumn policy group meetings.

Before 1977 there were two other meetings in the ICI system which "happened" but were not officially part of the scheme of organisation. Twice-yearly there was a "secret" meeting of executive directors and UK division chairmen for the latter "to be informed" of the financial performance of the group. These meetings were held at Warren House, the ICI's senior management training centre.

The other meeting was an informal gathering of the UK Division chairmen. This group began to come together in the early 1970s initially as a defensive strategy to cope with the central control and direction of UK personnel policy, but by the mid-1970s their interest turned to legitimating their role in the ICI governance system, and clarifying and improving their relations with the main board.

The final part of the top structure is the organisation of the head office departments. Figure 13 summarises the functional character of Millbank.

Most of the functional directors had reporting to them a general manager who was roughly equivalent in status to a division chairman. Each of the general managers ran sizeable departments, which were often further subdivided. The General Manager/Commercial – for example – had responding to him, amongst others, the Central Purchasing, Central Distribution, and Commercial Co-ordination Departments, and the General Manager Planning had reporting to him the Planning Department, the Policy Group Department, and a Business Environment Department.

The Millbank departments could crudely be divided into those functions which provided support services to the main board, for example, secretarys, treasurers, solicitors, and the Planning Department, and those departments such as Commercial, Research and Development and Personnel which, while having links to the main board, were more strictly trying to provide a central focus and service, mostly to the UK operating units. The powerhouse departments in Millbank were undoubtedly Planning, Finance, and Personnel.

The ICI culture, the main board culture, and Millbank culture in the mid-1970s

Because one can talk about specific structures, rules, systems, and consistent patterns of attitude and behaviour across numbers of defined individuals and groups it is somewhat easier to pinpoint the main board and Millbank cultures than it is to describe an ICI culture. Certainly, the variations in managerial culture at divisional level already evident from the preceding chapters is a further note of caution against any simple argument about cultural consistency across ICI. Nevertheless it is possible to present a characterisation of the ICI culture as it is seen both by very senior people in ICI, and a number of people outside the company who have contact with those senior people.

In thinking about ICI in these broad terms in the 1970s it is obviously relevant to note that ICI was very much a British-based and managed multi-national company. There was a reduction from 52% to 43% in the percentage of total Group sales attributed to UK customers between 1963 and 1973, but between 1973 and 1981 that percentage fell only another 4% to 39%. In 1973 66% of ICI's worldwide employees were working in the UK divisions and notwithstanding interests in North America and Western Europe, the main board and Millbank were heavily preoccupied with the UK divisions. ICI was often referred to in the press as Britain's largest manufacturing company, and its prestige offices in London SW1 were within ten minutes' walk of Parliament Whitehall and the main government departments, and the headquarters of the two major political parties. When and if ICI executive directors left the company they often became chairmen of large but lesser UK companies, or played prominent roles in employers organisations such as the Confederation of British Industry. The financial fortunes of ICI were regarded as a barometer for more general upward and downward movements in the stock market, and cer-tainly outside the company there was the view that ICI was a British institu-tion, and had to behave, and be seen to behave, in an appropriately ethical, regulated, and stable fashion. Anthony Sampson's view of ICI in the 1960s as "The Slumbering Giant" was still largely apposite for much of the 1970s.

The tradition in ICI had, of course, been to recruit first-class scientists and engineers and turn them into managers. The requirement from the company's beginning to develop new products and processes and to turn product out in volume into well-regulated markets, meant that technologists and people with production experience were pre-eminent. As one person put it, "things were produced and chaps were told to sell them. You didn't really closely follow the market." The combination of engineering and production bias, and the location in the British national culture were two key determinants of inertia in ICI.

> The line of succession [to top positions] has been 90% technologists of one sort or another, all coming out of the same kinds of schools, playing rugby together at the same kinds of places, and having the same kinds of orientations to life . . . the marketing free-swinging business man or the very innovative science type, as distinct from the good scientific analyst – the free-swingers and entrepreneurs have been in a minority in this company in strategic positions. Put that in the British culture and you get a reinforcement for the inertia, because the British culture is not an entrepreneurial culture, it is an inventing culture.

Many of the people interviewed talked of ICI as a traditional, a conservative organisation, images of the "great ship ploughing through waters and not needing to change"; of well-tried and stable systems, layers of management hierarchy, bureaucratic stops derived from compartmentalisation, and at the centre a heavily functional or disciplinary organisation. ICI was also described as an intellectual culture and while this had its pluses "one of the minuses was people tend to over-intellectualise. We have wonderful seminars about almost everything". A further consistent theme was the difficulty of innovating.

There's a sense of continuity in this place which is old, traditional. It's a hard place to innovate. Change has to be evolutionary rather than revolutionary. The revolutionary is tolerated but seen as a bad boy.

A main board director's summary view of the ICI culture picked up many of the above points:

If you have an organisation which has been by and large successful, it's 50 years old, it's hierarchical, it's almost totally inbred, it advances layer by layer, rank by rank, it has to be very, very conservative. And unless it falls off a cliff as it did in 1980, then people feel just as they would in a plant control room on a Friday afternoon, "keep your hands in your pockets, don't touch anything, it's Friday, the plant's running well isn't it?"

If conservatism was a theme often mentioned to describe the ICI culture, then consensus decision-making was the key theme in discussions of the main board culture of the 1970s. ICI twice had dynamic, autocratic Chairmen, once before, during, and after the Second World War in the persona of Lord McGowan, and then again between 1960 and 1968 with Sir Paul Chambers. Reader (1975) describes how the ICI main board effectively curbed McGowan's executive powers as Managing Director in the late 1930s, but allowed him to continue as Chairman with his autocratic inclinations trimmed by a series of committees. Sir Paul Chambers grew in power while he was Chairman to the point where he was effectively able to make appointments to the board, and so his personal strategy for ICI became the strategy ICI behaved. Chambers's maxim of growth, caught in the catch-phrase he is supposed to have recited to division chairmen, "Give me a good profitable project, and I will get you the money" eventually led to ICI's cash crisis of 1966, the rise of planning as an activity in the company, and Chambers' exit from ICI 2 years earlier than planned in 1968. The tenure of the next four Chairmen did not in any case exceed 4 years, and all behaved as first amongst equals, thus reaffirming a consensual style of board decision-making.

Without doubt the 1970s pattern of giving each Chairman a 3–4 year term acted as a break on change. One executive director remarked:

If you have a Chairman who has a 3-year stint in office, the first year he's not going to lash about him too much because he wants to establish himself. The second year is a year when he can lash about, but the third year he's already saying. "I don't want to prejudice the position of my successor", and guys on the board are not wanting to take big risks because there's always one or two competing to be the next Chairman. So if you analyse the thing you find that you only have one year in three – rather like elephants – when you can mate and make it happen.

Division chairman who became executive directors in the 1970s talked of entry onto the main board as "a numbing experience after being a chief executive"; another said "it was the nearest thing to Devil's Island I'd known, boredom not brutality . . . Ritual dancing time and time again, failure to take the decision, walking away from decisions. Continual frustration through the consensus board where 1 or 2 strong and opinionated voices could stop the whole thing stone dead." Overlaid on top of this was the two-tier system of having a Chairman and three or four deputy chairmen acting as an inner cabinet in relation to the remaining executive directors.

> We had a two-tier system of a Chairman and three deputy chairmen, which wasn't clear, and I felt that well you can't be let out on your own yet, and your instinct was to go on and continue doing a division chairman's job, but this just drives the layer below you potty.

This tendency for executive directors to continue to try and act as super operators alongside the operating units caused frustration and defensiveness with the chief executives of those units. But more importantly the policy groups system and ICI's top-level obsession with capital expenditure and cash management meant that the board became more and more involved with monitoring the operating units and capital expenditure decision-making, and less and less with the strategic direction of the ICI Group. One executive director summed up the problem in these terms:

> There were two obsessions, one the obsession with fixed capital, and the other – and by obsession I mean the thing the mind is always on, the other was a fear of running into another cash crisis like the one in 1966. There was an enormous cultural force pressing people's minds onto fixed capital and cash management. Anything very quickly boiled back again to the capital programme and what are we going to do in 6 months hence. And when you'd had that capital expenditure, the 6 months after that. The key constraint was how much money would it be prudent to spend in the ensuing 12 months. This was something the Treasurers Department and Planning Department worked on quite closely, with the Finance Director putting in rules of prudence and the Treasurers and Planning Departments using that to make recommendations on the total size of the fixed capital programme.

In this atmosphere the planning department worked on the annual cycles of finance and capital and helped create mechanisms such as the business ranking system and strategic business sectors to allow the board to distinguish between the operating units more or less deserving of additional capital. Capital in a world full of technologists and powerful production people became "a virility symbol" and division chairmen and policy group directors measured one another in their success in acquiring fixed assets. Enormous "sectoral pressure" was put on the board by policy group directors pressing for their territorial or product area. Given the consensus style of the board this led to a lot of "I'll support you in this proposal if you support me in that one". An executive director explained how the drive for board consensus managed to ally itself with the sectoral pressure coming onto the board from the policy group system and the policy group directors:

Those that got to the top in the divisions and came onto the main board were very clear that fracturing in a division was highly undesirable. They were equally strong-minded people who were not going to be done down. So you had to have a situation where strong-minded people wouldn't be done down and be no fracturing, and this produces a tremendously strong force for consensus. Not because people tremendously want consensus but because anything else is unthinkable.

This "smoothing rather than problem-solving culture" eventually led to some inadequate selection of capital and left around an undue capital burden in some very embarrassing places. More significantly perhaps, the obsessions of capital and cash meant that "the concept of explicit longer-term strategies in which individual capital expenditures were steps, really was absent".

The Millbank culture was of course dominated by two features. The Chairmen and executive directors on the 6th floor and the general managers or their equivalents – the 9 barons – with their functional or disciplinary departments. One executive director thought "the whole Millbank thing to be wrong":

It gives a feeling of comfort, of immutability, permanence, lack of change, hierarchical organisation ... If I appear in the cafeteria for a pie and a pint it's almost as if space man has appeared ... On the 6th floor every door is shut. There's the affectation that no-one had their name on the door, you could find people wandering around this bloody floor for hours trying to find somebody!

Another executive director was less concerned with the atmosphere of hierarchy and status in Millbank as with the feelings of lack of identity and purpose in the head office compared with a division:

There's no identity in this building in the way there is identity in a division from its production operations and its desire to make money out of its products. There is a highly functional organisation in this building, with not much interpenetration between those functions. There isn't the policy, the objectives, the singleness of purpose you have in a division.

Given the functional organisation at Millbank it was natural that people should acquire much of their consistent identity from the floor they were on and the pattern of work that came from their expertise in their function. Millbank with all its highly intelligent functional experts epitomised the intellectual side of ICI's culture. A departmental head in Millbank described what the norms were in the 1970s in these terms:

Be a good chap – say some interesting things in an intellectual way which are stimulating and challenging, but don't expect anything will happen as a result of them. You will get a name for being a bright boy with all sorts of good ideas. But don't push things too far.

The final part of that quote indicates what the central taboo was:

Don't rock the boat, don't dig too deep, we're pretty well all right thank you, we know most of it. You can dig too deep, too fast. This boat has stood the test of time.

An executive director summarised how the intellectual atmosphere in Millbank, the concern for stability, and the smoothing risk-aversive culture at board level, and amongst the general managers, all contributed to influence the pattern of decision-making at the centre:

> The whole physical environment was structured to dealing in a very hygienic way a splendid paper, a limited discussion, perhaps not an entirely open discussion, leading to a decision. There are many topics where perhaps one wants to talk to people for longer, and in more depth.

These then were some of the critical features of the structure and operation of the ICI top governance system in the 1970s. The short tenure, non chief executive chairmen, the two-tier main board, and executive directors with portfolios allocated by product, territory, and function. The consensus style of decision-making on the main board. The cultural obsession with cash management and capital expenditure. The games-playing between the operating units and the main board, and between the policy group directors over the annual capital expenditure allocation process. The power of the policy groups and the influence of the planning and treasurers departments, and the limited time the main board spent formulating macro-plans and strategies on the shape, size, and growth of the group. The compartmentalised and intellectual culture of Millbank. An expectation that with continuing financial success, but not necessarily brilliant financial results, the great ship would continue to plough its way through the waters. The question was could this smoothing rather than problem-solving culture be convinced that issues of organisation and culture could influence business effectiveness, and if that could be accepted at an · intellectual level, was it possible for the ICI collegial board system to radically change itself?

THE CONDITION AND USE OF ORGANISATION DEVELOPMENT, 1973–77

The two lowest points in the fortunes of OD at the centre during the 1970s were 1972–74, and 1978 to late 1979. If there was a high point that was from 1975 to 1977. These three time periods correspond with parts of the tenure in office of three different Chairmen of ICI. Sir Jack Callard was Chairman from April 1971 until March 1975, Sir Rowland Wright from April 1975 until March 1978, and Sir Maurice Hodgson from April 1978 until March 1982. Each of the Chairmen took a different view of the necessity of change in the structure and top governance of ICI during their respective periods, and as we shall see each thereby behaved differently toward OD.

In November 1972 Sir Jack Callard had the Board Organisation Committee reconstituted. The last occasion this committee had met was ten years before when the McKinsey study of ICI's structure was in progress. The terms of reference of the 1972 organisation committee were:

> To examine the organisation of the board and their method of working and the top management structure of the Group to consider the organisation that would be appropriate having regard to the changes that are expected to take place in the Group's business over the next decade; and to make recommendations.

The committee of a deputy chairman and three executive directors, took evidence from executive and non-executive directors, division chairmen, the heads of some overseas companies, and general managers. Their initial report which contained much criticism of ICI's top structure and the culture surrounding its operation was itself critically received when presented to a meeting of executive directors in July 1973. The revised report dated November 1973 was still revolutionary in character, recommending as it did a more international organisation, greater time to be spent by the executive directors on strategic thinking and worldwide issues, a smaller board, the end of deputy chairmen as a distinct level on the structure, and wider involvement of division chairmen in matters that affected them. At the November meeting the Organisation Committee's report "sank at the first shot", or as another executive director put it the Organisation Committee "presented the parcel to the board, the latter then unwrapped it, and threw the parcel out of the window". Both executive directors blamed the failure of this change attempt on individual directors' fears of this degree of radical change, and the inadequate process adopted by the Committee:

> It had done just about everything you could have done to get it wrong. It had taken massive amounts of evidence and so aroused massive expectations. It had barely reported back to its colleagues, and it had not really carried its Chairman with it . . . also it doesn't take a genius to see that a hell of a lot of executive directors would have been out of a job if this change had gone through. So again the working through had not been done.

*   *   *

> There was little lobbying, persuasion, or involvement of other people by the Organisation Committee.

Someone close to events at that time also pointed out the poor process plan of the Committee, and the fact that with the financial results as good as they were in 1973, there was no desire to rock the boat that fundamentally.

> In that sense the process was wrong – it was a misdiagnosis of the power structure in the board and the readiness for fundamental change. They [the Organisation Committee] were really talking about a culture change. People could give lip service to bits of it, but when it was put back in terms of prove this is better than what we have, why upset the company? There was no external crisis, no business problems, so it was theory against theory.

The above events revealed that Sir Jack Callard and some of his board were not prepared in 1973 to contemplate radical organisational change. With the board split on the issue of change, a compromise emerged which left the top governance of ICI even more complex than it had been before 1972. Now the executive directors "in addition to all the other bloody jobs we already had, we would each take a worldwide product responsibility, and the product area would be enhanced above the territorial areas . . . end of message". Worse still "we had released expectations around the patch of the most lavish scale . . . So when this mouse was produced the main board lost credibility massively." It was in the context of the immediate history of the Board Organisation Committee's failure, that in 1974 John Harvey-Jones and Stewart Dudley began to think through an alternative process for influencing change amongst the top structure of ICI.

The precarious state of OD after WSA and SDP

Reference was made at the end of Chapter 4 to the precarious state OD as an activity was in, once by 1972, the major central change programmes of WSA and SDP had been implemented. WSA and SDP had projected a vision of a future dimension to the company which many managers at Millbank and in the divisions did not share. Talk about more open systems, shared responsibility, more participative management styles, job enrichment, and other fashionable phrases of the late 1960s had been difficult for managers to handle. Those managers felt concerned about losing control of matters for which they felt accountable, and were in no way sure that their bosses were sharing responsibility for any experimental changes made. The fact also that WSA and SDP had been pushed so zealously and determinedly from the centre, and MUPS/WSA had created so much local industrial relations strife, meant that there was widespread scepticism of such "threatening irrelevancies".

OD as the tool used to implement WSA and SDP was guilty by association. By 1972 OD had acquired two negative aspects to its image. The first was it was seen as a manipulative tool for the ICI power system, and particularly for the personnel function. The second was its close association with behaviourism and psychology, and its consequent over-clinical image. Faced with the bad financial results of 1970, 1971, and 1972 there was an emerging "revulsion to behavioural training . . . there was a feeling that that's not what it's all about – what about productivity, and the business, and getting the job done, was the call".

Stewart Dudley recalled that the behavioural training of the late 1960s and early 1970s "had produced increased awareness and understanding, but not organisational change. We knew that. The harder you pushed on that the harder people saw the psychological couch stuff, and if you went down that route the likelihood of political rejection was high."

With Tom Evans now working for another company, and the two other members of the central OD group assigned to other duties, by late 1972 Dudley was the sole survivor of the central OD resources. He had no intention of setting himself up for political rejection, although there was every danger that OD as an activity might disappear altogether. Dudley kept his head down for a time, or as he put it "discarded a semi-confronting position opposite management to a smoothing style ... we were thinking all our work will be wiped out, we'll all go down the hill, it will all be forgotten." Apart from keeping a low profile, Dudley did a number of other things to stabilise his position. He continued to try and maintain his distance and independence from George Bridge and the Central Personnel Department, carried on working in the divisions on workshop and team-building activities with works managers, and in the light of the harsher business climate "realised we have to pick up problems managers were worried about – make ourselves relevant to managers".

Dudley was not invited to take any part in the Board Organisation Committee's work of 1972 and 1973. Quite a considerable amount of staff work came out of the Organisation Committee but it was all handled by a senior consultant from the company Management Services Department who specialised in organisational analysis work, but had not been tarred with the OD brush.

Given the inertia in the ICI system, and in the absence at that time of any hunt to reduce numbers, Dudley would probably have carried on as the central focus for company OD for a number of years. He was saved from this fate as a passive central expert by the arrival on the main board in April 1973 of John Harvey-Jones.

Harvey-Jones is a good example of an individual who exemplifies the institutionalisation of OD. He was first introduced to OD while working in a division. George Bridge introduced him to Ron Mercer and helped persuade him to go on an American T-group. Harvey-Jones increasingly adopted behavioural science first in trying to get MUPS/WSA in at the difficult Wilton site and then in redesigning the structure of his division. He set up the Petrochemicals Division OD unit and used Ron Mercer as an external consultant. There is no doubt Harvey-Jones was an OD convert although he was careful to maintain some distance from the more extreme psychological or behavioural aspects of OD which were likely to arouse most emotional opposition. He was careful too that his presentation of self stressed his successful business image.

Harvey-Jones's arrival on the main board meant that in terms of a sponsor for OD, George Bridge was replaced – and at a higher level – even before Bridge left ICI in 1974. Meanwhile Ron Mercer had slowly been building up his network and credibility throughout the ICI organisation. By 1973 Mercer had worked for varying periods of time with the boards of Agricultural, Petrochemicals, Plant Protection and Organics Divisions. He had also had regular contact with the general managers of Personnel and Research and Development, and had limited contact with Rowland, later Sir Rowland Wright who in the early 1970s was the main board director responsible for personnel matters. A close observer of the OD scene at that time described how Dudley and Mercer worked together to maintain both their positions. Eventually in 1974 the availability of the Dudley–Mercer knowledge and skills, and Harvey-Jones's sponsorship and desire for change produced an opening:

> After Agricultural Division I observed Mercer moving along the system like a puppet with Stewart as the puppeteer. Trying here, trying there, being accepted here. I don't think he was ever rejected, but he was accepted to different degrees. I think I saw him, and indeed Stewart, having at least an implicit aim of getting at the top, not to the top, and I suppose it was 1974–75 when they made a break through at board level.

OPENING UP ICI TO STRATEGIC CHANGE: THE 1974–77 ATTEMPTS

Before Harvey-Jones formally became an executive director in April 1973, he was asked to join the Board Organisation Committee which had been set up in November 1972. The failure of that Committee to influence the board did not deter him from seeking what he felt were appropriate top level organisation changes. Interviewed for the first time in this study in 1976, Harvey-Jones described his change philosophy on entering the board in these terms:

> In my view, the ways in which we have tried to change our organisation in the past have been wrong – because the approach has been to wait until some bit is evidently hurting and then to move in on that bit . . . It then takes quite a while for that change to become effective. If as is usually the case, you are trying to change attitudes you are in for a 4 or 5 year haul – you're too bloody late, you are dealing with the symptoms of the last war . . . so I see my role, since I became Organisation Director, as being to stop trying to frig around with bits of the company and really concentrate on getting some major changes in the board . . . I believe we need to:
>
> (a) try and read the environment about 5 years ahead, and
> (b) try to aim our objectives 5 years ahead and only then to start intervening organisationally.
>
> In the meantime you have to make some interventions . . . but you have to make sure that these changes will be reinforcing to the big changes you are trying to aim for . . . so the main initiative has been and still is to try and make the board change.

But tactically how was he to achieve that objective? Clearly with the Board Organisation Committee of 1973 now stone dead, he realised he would have to wait until the encumbent Chairman retired, seek in the meantime to plan to influence the incoming Chairman, and to use his board responsibility as Organisation and Services Director "to legitimately roam all over the place . . . in a fairly structured way in order to get some of the real dissatisfactions of ordinary guys with the performance of the board – recognised". Harvey-Jones was in a dilemma from the beginning whether it would be politic to publicly use OD help, and yet he could see from his experience on the Board Organisation Committee that some "process help" would be necessary to move the board forward. Somehow or other Harvey-Jones had in the context of his board colleagues' resentment about force feeding of T-groups, and the "long-haired kooks" behavioural image of OD, to "avoid picking up total responsibility for OD – because this would remove my legitimacy as a director", but at the same time "call on the mud-on-the-boots, operating guy type of OD help that Stewart Dudley and Tom James might offer". The way Harvey-Jones handled this was to try and use OD help quietly, and selectively, and that meant Dudley, James, or Mercer, and as he put it counter that by "never missing a chance to make the point that I'm basically an operator".

In fact, during late 1973 and on into 1974 Harvey-Jones encouraged a number of things to happen, some of which were conventional moves to create change, and others were decidedly counter-cultural. He set up a room on the director's floor at Millbank where "anybody could put up a chart to bring the bad news to the attention of the board without having to stand up and say boo! . . . I got a number of studies done of views of where the board was going . . . and I started a real effort to try and get the staff in Millbank to operate better and again put pressure on the board".

Away from Millbank, Harvey-Jones rescued Tom James from the fast-declining Petrochemicals Division OD unit and placed him into ICI's Central Management Services (CMS) Department in order to develop in CMS "a greater sensitivity to change". More significantly perhaps in terms of the long-term structural development of ICI, Harvey-Jones was able to use his role as Board Liaison Director for Petrochemicals Division to set up the Petrochemicals Product Directors Advisory Committee. This was the first mechanism to pull together all the chairmen of divisions connected with Petrochemicals, and the first tangible move on the chess board towards creating a heavy chemicals business organisation in the UK.

While all of the above moves were being made, Harvey-Jones and Stewart Dudley began to meet on a three-weekly basis, first of all to share views about the organisational problems ICI had at that time, and then "to prepare a strategy for opening up a discussion with the main board" about those problems. The essence of their strategy was not to try and influence the outgoing chairman Sir Jack Callard, who was due to go in March 1975, but to try and influence the next Chairman, who they expected to be Rowland Wright. Dudley wrote a paper called "A look at ICI in 1974", and this was to be used as the vehicle to draw the board into a serious discussion about organisation matters. Dudley takes up the story:

We understood Rowland Wright's appointment would be announced round about 26 September 1974. Our plan was to influence a group of directors by going to them individually with the "ICI in 1974" note, rewriting it if they didn't agree with it, but slowly building up a note that was acceptable to a critical mass of directors on an individual level. We then planned to give that note to Rowland Wright immediately after his appointment, but before he formally became Chairman in April 1975. We wanted to try and capture him in the period between knowing he was going to be Chairman, but not actually taking the job, in that pause period. Then we hoped he would pick up and validate the things that were being said to him.

Dudley's handwritten notes of 1974 outlining the above strategy vouch for the accuracy of the interview account. The detail of those handwritten notes, including which director was to be approached first, and who was to be approached next, and by when, indicates the kind of OD help offered in the highly personal and political environment in and around the main board. What was to happen next threw all their rationally conceived plans to the wind, and as a result opened up the ICI main board a good deal more quickly than Harvey-Jones and Dudley had in mind. The following events nicely characterise the role that chance, opportunism, and environmental preparedness can play in hastening processes of change.

The secretarial error

Part of the above plan had been for Dudley to send copies of "A Look at ICI in 1974" to Harvey-Jones, in order that Harvey-Jones could distribute them to each of his board colleagues as and when he felt appropriate. Dudley takes up the story:

> These copies were sent to Harvey-Jones's secretary on a Friday morning when he was away from the office, and as I was going on a fortnight's leave. So there was no chance for the secretary, who I believed had been briefed by John about what was happening, and actually hadn't been, to check with me about what was going on. It so happened that there was a Monday morning director's meeting with an agenda item "Review Company Progress". Harvey-Jones's secretary thought the "ICI in 1974" note was suitable for that item and so she circulated it to every member of the board including the Chairman.

Harvey-Jones's report of what happened next "was that this produced the most fantastic explosion – absolutely marvellous. The Chairman sent for me white with rage, lost his temper, and commanded that I withdrew it, and demanded I fire Stewart. I said 'no way, poor devil. I've asked him to do this. If you don't like it fire me.' That was a real breakthrough in its own way but it hadn't been designed. It meant we were able to get Ron Mercer to the Chairman, it also meant we were able to raise the pain level on the board so that when Rowland Wright became Chairman he did his trips around the Company to talk to people at various levels, and this again increased the pain level and began to open up the possibility of change."

Evidence that Sir Jack Callard received Dudley's note with shock and bewilderment can be seen from his memorandum of 6 August 1974 to Harvey-Jones. "Much of what is said in it is contrary to the impression I have gained travelling at home and abroad amongst the ICI Organisation . . . Are you, or whoever, trying to tell me that my 39 years has been totally wasted? Are you seeking to destroy my faith? Or are you making a bid for a new era launched by enlightened men?"

Harvey-Jones tried to explain the error to his colleagues and recover as many of the papers as possible. On 6 August he wrote to Dudley, who was by this time holidaying, "you beastly horrible old Dudley! This is the best I can do to recover the dropped clanger. Please think quickly what I do now besides shoot myself."

When Sir Jack Callard returned from vacation he was still sceptical of the information and views supplied by Harvey-Jones and Dudley but remarked was there not an outsider who occasionally saw individual board members, and would he not be a more reliable source of data about the company? This conjecture opened up the first opportunity for Ron Mercer to talk directly with the Chairman. Mercer was very nervous going into the meeting feeling that "because of the way the meeting, and I had been set up, it was going to have an impact. I felt pleased that an outside resource was being used to get this information to the Chairman. That was an important step for the organisation. I felt unhappy about what it was going to be like, and felt I might be seeing the last of ICI."

Mercer described the information he gave to Sir Jack as "very painful", "very hurtful". But "although it was hurtful his immediate response was to say this needs to be shared with my colleagues, and he asked me to write a note which he distributed to the board".

Mercer's note of September 1974 contained many of the same points as the "ICI in 1974" paper but given the immediate history was written a good deal more diplomatically. After noting that his remarks about "issues and improvement opportunities in organisation climate and communications", should be read in the context of an organisation whose general "health" is perhaps as good as any organisation in the world, Mercer went on to make the following kinds of observations:

1. Communications between main board and divisions

There were difficulties in this linkage partly because the main board did not make clear priorities, goals, and plans; partly because the board did not think through issues informally and collectively, and therefore tended to communicate different messages from the centre; and partly because division chairmen were not clear where their responsibilities for a business ended and the main board product director began.

2. Company Chairman: Division Chairmen

There was a tendency for division leadership to play down its role as part of company management, and to increase its identification as division leadership. This meant that the spirit of main board intentions was not being communicated below the top division management.

3. The lost battalions

This was a reference to unrest and moves towards collectivism on the part of junior management staff. This was partly due to compensation problems – an established annual bonus for staff at this level had recently been consolidated into a salary increment for one year – and partly due to the fact that junior management in other ways felt "unappreciated, undervalued, helpless to influence their fate".

Mercer used his note to suggest a number of mechanisms to help alleviate some of the above difficulties, and also indicated ICI as a group could benefit from organisational mechanisms and skill development in handling negative information and conflict management generally.

Mercer remarked when he met the board as a group "There were various degrees of belief and disbelief, but this helped to motivate what Rowland Wright was going to do when he took over." The minutes of the meeting ended, however, on a none too optimistic note:

> An improvement in the general area covered by the discussion was most likely to be achieved by a fairly low-profile approach from the top, aiming at gradual rather than sudden or dramatic change.

There had been some movement, at least in legitimising changes in organisation and top management behaviour as a topic for board discussion, even also in opening the way for Mercer to work with the board in the future, but would any action follow this opening up?

The follow-up: some success but continuing inertia

Through the various prepared statements and informal face-to-face contact the message that Harvey-Jones and Dudley had been trying to get through to the board was that there needed to be some reform of the top structure and governance systems of ICI to cope with the increasingly complex business, economic, and political environment the company was facing in the 1970s. ICI had had a tendency to respond slowly to environmental change and when it did the response was to create further internal complexity to try and match the environmental complexity; the result was a further reduction in the organisation's capacity to adapt to change.

The early 1970s had seen a more confident use of grass-roots trade union power. The miners' strike of February 1974 produced an election also in February 1974, and the fall of the Heath Conservative government. The miners were awarded a 25% wage increase by the incoming Labour government who promptly abandoned the Stage 3 incomes policy, and abolished the Pay Board. Inflation started to take off with a vengeance, fuelled not only by large rises in world commodity prices, and particularly oil, but also by large wage increases. The average percentage increase in retail prices from 1973 to 1974 was 16.6%, and the equivalent figure for 1974 to 1975 was 24.3%. Meanwhile the percentage change in wage rates (manual workers all industries) from 1973 to 1974 was 19.8%, and from 1974 to 1975 it was a staggering 29.5%. In amongst these industrial and economic changes the 1970s also saw the increasing growth of white-collar unionisation, and through the Bullock Committee, the beginnings of an attempt to create a national pattern of industrial democracy.

The above environmental trends placed an added burden on the practice of personnel matters in ICI, and increasingly drew the main board into handling UK personnel matters. One consequence of this was the creation in 1973 of the Board Personnel Committee. The existence of the Board Personnel Committee, and in George Bridge a general manager of personnel who believed in providing strong leadership and influence added to the post/WSA/SDP stereotype of personnel as a powerful centrist function which drove policy on to the company. When in 1973 and 1974 ICI attracted a lot of unfavourable publicity in the UK press over their refusal to grant negotiating rights to white-collar unions, and then they compounded those difficulties amongst the "lost battalions" by consolidating a white-collar bonus scheme into salary arrangements, anxiety increased in the divisions both about the activities of Central Personnel Department and the separation of personnel matters from business priorities and concerns.

Out of these increasing concerns about the formulation and implementation of personnel policy two responses began to emerge in the company. One was a move from the Company Personnel Director to meet regularly with the Divisional Personnel Directors as a group. This in turn encouraged a system of regular meetings between senior personnel staff from Millbank's Central Personnel Department, and the Divisional Personnel Managers.

Rather more worrying, however, in terms of the operation of the top governance system of the company, was the formation of an informal meeting of division chairmen, explicitly in its earliest days as a defensive manoeuvre against centrally created personnel policies and practices. This meeting of division chairmen had no position in the scheme of organisation, and was not recognised by the main board.

During 1974 and 1975 the division chairmen, at that time led by the Chairman of Mond, Tony Woodburn, began to examine their role and effectiveness in parallel and initially separate from the stirrings about role and effectiveness carried on by the main board. The division chairmen also utilised OD help; this time Tom James was called on to play the role of process planner, counsellor, and process helper during a series of meetings where that group examined their purpose and impact.

In diagnosing the quality of their existing meetings, the division chairmen noted they were often short term and reactive in the negative sense. They vented frustrations but no considered action emerged. They wanted to be helpful and influential in the company but were beginning to be seen by Millbank as a threatening combine, "a shop stewards committee", who would attempt to resist change which came particularly from the functional directors and general managers. They accepted the ultimate authority of the board but wished for "interpenetration" with the board "so that decisions to change and thereby improve the Company had our commitment".

The above developments amongst the division chairmen no doubt added to the pressure for change amongst the main board stimulated by Harvey-Jones, Mercer, and Dudley, and now given fresh impetus with the impending elevation of Rowland Wright to Chairman. A month before he formally became

Chairman Wright agreed to take the board away for two days for an informal meeting to discuss the top structure and operation of the Group. This was a risky venture for any new Chairman, quite counter-cultural at that time, and Wright was understandably anxious that "it would be very easy for the board to split". Dudley takes up the story:

> Rowland was very concerned about the meeting and used Mercer to produce a process plan for the meeting in which they agreed some syndicate work on various items, and an initial process plan.

Dudley also became involved and produced a document called "February 19–20 Meeting: A Guess", which was "basically aimed at giving the Chairman a feel for what might happen based on some knowledge of group working, leading to what might be the identification of areas of further work, and suggesting how that might be handled". The outcome of this meeting was the setting up of three sub-groups involving all the executive directors and chaired by a deputy chairman, each to work on a different aspect of organisation change. A process was set in train whereby each group was asked to feed back their thinking into the Chairman's weekly meeting so as to keep their colleagues on board. By mid-1975 in Dudley's words:

> We then had a situation where the division chairmen were beginning to stir, and wanting to take the bit between their teeth, and they had Tom James working as a consultant to them. The board was also stirring, Rowland was leading them towards a meeting with the division chairmen which would have led to a top-down initiative. We now had the possibility of a clash between a bottom-up, and a top-down initiative. The need was to bring them together.

In this period Rowland Wright created what became known as the Board Resource Group, an informal grouping of Harvey-Jones and another executive director, plus Mercer and Dudley. The function this group performed was to test out and plan in detail meetings of the main board and meetings of the main board and the division chairmen, and "to provide personal support to the Chairman when he is faced with the personal risk of validating new behaviour and actions". After much careful planning, space was eventually created at one of the quarterly meetings when the executive directors reported on the state of the business to the division chairmen, for both parties to have an extended and informal discussion about the relationship between them. In Wright's summing up of the meeting he began by saying "meeting in this way was of itself significant . . . it should be seen as a start to the process of reviewing, clarifying and, where appropriate, modifying the ways in which directors and division chairmen interact on each other". Wright noted that the directors would continue to spend time reviewing their own methods of working . . . but no organisational change would, however, be introduced without full consultation with division chairmen. He further noted that the division chairmen's meeting had an important consultative/advisory role, particularly in regard to UK corporate matters, and that there was a greater need for directors to clarify and better communicate corporate objectives. Interestingly he ended by indicating that the success of division chairmen and executive directors in working together depended not only on organisation but also on attitudes, and he had been encouraged and impressed by the way in which attitudes had developed during the course of the debate and discussion.

Important as the above meeting of executive directors and division chairmen was, it was not for another 16 months, until January 1977, that its successor, the Chairman's Group Conference, became institutionalised into the ICI system of top-level governance. Indeed for the first time ever in January 1977 the executive directors met together with the division chairmen, the chief executives of the major overseas subsidiaries, and the general managers to discuss at length matters of substance about the policy, aims, and organisation of the Group. The creation of the mechanism of the Chairman's Group Conference was one of the key steps forward in the organisation change area over the period 1974–77.

The first Chairman's Group Conference was held early in 1977 because of the output appearing from a series of executive director task groups during 1976. These task groups had agonised throughout 1976 about the by now familiar issues of the board:

- not spending sufficient time discussing key strategic issues such as the long-term business strategy and shape of the group;
- not being able to have deep, objective discussions on key subjects, and then come to crisp decisions;
- not being able to handle conflicts which came out of the product, territory, function matrix;
- spending too much time managing, not enough time directing;
- and spending too much time on UK affairs to the detriment of ICI's interests as an international operation

These issues, although never aired more comprehensively and openly than in 1976, were not resolved. Again they were left on the table. What did come out of this period of work, however, was a clear statement of the ICI Group's objectives. These were tested out at the January 1977 Chairman's Group Conference, and formally adopted by the main board in March 1977. This in itself was a step forward, but would action now follow on productivity improvement in the UK, the implementation of international strategies for major businesses, and lead to the thrust of new investment towards the markets of Western Europe, including the UK, and North America? Would these statements about a greater requirement for strategic thrust and central direction be turned into action? Would the cultural problems be attacked? Those aspects of management style which impaired ICI's performance – resistance to change, excessive consultation, insular modes of thought and behaviour, and over-concern with the immediate problem, at the expense of the longer term, these were all recognised again but would and could they be picked up and dealt with? For all the effort, the right combination of political will and environmental pressures had not yet assembled themselves in 1977, and the changes which had appeared by then could still be described as cosmetic and not yet fundamental.

By 1977 the composition of the main board was beginning to change. As Mercer put it "people were coming onto the board, who were, or came to be known as 'for change'". The "young turks" were by no means uniform in their perspective or priorities for change. One stream of new thinking emphasised the importance of marketing and commercial skills alongside worldwide business strategies, as against the technical skills and preoccupations of older generations of ICI management. Another stream of new thinking personified by Harvey-Jones and Woodburn recognised the importance of international commercial acumen, saw that changes in the commercial sphere would also require a rethinking of the organisation, the systems, and the culture of ICI, and gave some place to OD thinking and methods as the way of pushing those changes forward. But for those wishing for change the pace was still too slow. One of the OD consultants remarked:

> Rowland Wright was a very fine help-it-happen person but not a make-it-happen person. Therefore he created an environment in which all sorts of ideas could fly. He also created an environment where communication was open ... But the board objectives of 1977 again created big expectations of the centre, and board committees fussed about all over the place but there wasn't much change. There was a net plus under Sir Rowland Wright but nothing like a clear progression forward.

A similar message, or progress report on change, up to 1978 was communicated by Harvey-Jones and Woodburn. Tony Woodburn described Sir Rowland Wright's role as "permissive and encouraging, but it was you do it and I'll allow you, it wasn't a leadership role". Harvey-Jones's was that Rowland was a believer in evolutionary change, and he found OD methods useful in that respect, so I was allowed to continue to operate ... I got hugged to death, you know, "what a splendid idea", but at the end of the day with great skill emasculated the major changes ... Out of all those board studies at that time something moved a bit but the trouble is you couldn't move the ICI system by moving a bit.

STRATEGIC CHANGE AND THE CONDITION AND USE OF ORGANISATION DEVELOPMENT, 1978–83

The development of OD by 1978

The above account of the role played by the executive directors Harvey-Jones and Woodburn, and the three OD consultants, Dudley, Mercer and James in trying to create structural and stylistic changes in the upper reaches of ICI, is not, of course, a complete picture of the evolution of central OD in ICI up until 1978. Before moving on to consider what happened to OD in the post-1978 period it is important to reveal something of the wider set of activities carried out by the central OD resources in the period 1974–78, the strategy used to manage and project OD out into the divisions, and the attitudes and quality of sponsorship available to OD by 1978.

In terms of personalities the central OD resources in the mid-1970s were a loosely composed group of three internal consultants, and the external consultant Ron Mercer. The three internals were Stewart Dudley based in the Central Personnel Department in Millbank, Tom James based in ICI's Central Management Services Department in Wilmslow, Cheshire, and Rory McBride who was recruited from Organics Division to work with Dudley in late 1974. In addition in 1973 a head office OD group was created with their patch being largely the Millbank departments.

By the mid-1970s Stewart Dudley had created for himself the role of professional leader for OD people throughout ICI. After WSA and SDP he began to consolidate the survivors from the group of internal consultants who had been trained at the Eastbourne events into an informal company network of OD resources. This network would meet three times a year to share experiences, talk strategy, and present and listen to new ideas. As one person put it, Stewart Dudley was "Dean of Faculty of the ICI OD network, he represented the most experienced and professional guy in the trade". There is no doubt that Stewart Dudley represented and projected the skills and knowledge of OD throughout most of ICI during the 1970s. He helped to build the OD network, linked on an ad hoc basis with OD resources based in the divisions, worked as a consultant at the works manager and division board level in a number of divisions, ran company-wide workshops on themes relevant to managers and internal consultants, and as we have seen helped to draw external consultants into the company to work where he saw opportunities and openings. He also was part of the set of resources Harvey-Jones drew on to plan and influence changes in the top governance of ICI. As one of the external consultants clearly stated:

> The moving force behind the development of OD in ICI is Stewart Dudley . . . The story of the growth of OD in ICI is the story of his personal growth, in large part . . . Stewart's just a real good guy at seeing opportunities, at putting people in touch with resources, at doing work himself as an external consultant, at knowing when to put on a training programme, at having the right blend between confrontation and not offending people . . . It would be difficult to explain what has happened if he wasn't around.

If Dudley's presence in Millbank was important as a source of continuity for OD, of equal and if not greater importance was Ron Mercer's continuing linkage into the main board. Throughout most of the 1970s and as I write now in 1983, Ron Mercer comes over from the United States five times a year, for 4 days on each visit to link into and influence the concerns and actions of the top people in the company. His activities in the 1970s were various. Sometimes acting as a counsellor to individual directors, working as a process consultant in the design and implementation of directors' off-site meetings, acting as a communications conduit in the often highly personalised and political world around the main board, and providing ideas and experiences from the academic world and from other firms' experience, to help solve particular problems. Mercer summed up his role and contribution in these terms:

> I visualise myself as a family doctor. It's not something you could bring in a replacement tomorrow. It's a relatively unique role. I'm a living data collection and feedback mechanism, helping to look at symptoms and what to do about them.

John Harvey-Jones took the view that "without Ron Mercer ICI wouldn't have got interested in OD at all. I think he has particular skills which are very precise and which are very attractive to the ICI mentality." Harvey-Jones went on to emphasise the reinforcing and legitimating effect of Mercer's continuing access to top people in ICI:

> Of course the other thing is that he moves easily in the corridors of power, and its been known for a long time that he has moved in the corridors of power. So he's respectable. Any division board is secure in the knowledge that Ron pads along here . . . He's made the whole thing respectable, his knowledge of the ICI ethos, the ICI background has again been useful because he's been able to place things into an ICI perspective.

Dudley and Mercer were an effective team. Mercer could operate at a level in the ICI power system, and on problems it would have been impossible for an internal consultant to work on. Mercer's presence at the top provided some level of spin-off for the continuing use of OD people in other parts of the company. Dudley carefully managed Mercer's continuing presence in the company. Prior to one of Mercer's visits, Dudley would prepare a list of directors and general managers for Mercer to see. This meant both that Mercer had a set of clients waiting for him when he arrived and that "I'm not all billed to one person, so it's not a big deal financially for any one director or department". Dudley's colleague Rory McBride argued that Dudley's skill in managing the external consultant Mercer was important:

> Something Stewart Dudley has done which I haven't seen done anywhere else – managing an external consultant. My hypothesis would be that Dudley keeps Mercer in the system not any main board figure. It means that Mercer hasn't had to run around and perform all the time in the way that a lot of these external consultants have to perform some act of great genius in order that the Chairman will invite them back again.

In effect Dudley and Mercer helped to set up some of the conditions for their mutual survival. Tom James, perceptive as ever, noted:

> They have helped each other. I suddenly realise Stewart probably would not have survived without Mercer, and Mercer would certainly not have survived without Stewart. But had not Mercer been there he would have been invented. Like Stewart would have survived because of somebody else.

Rory McBride, not being part of the Dudley–Mercer duo, did not achieve their level of acceptability in the system. McBride took over from Dudley the stimulation and servicing of the OD network, ran central workshops on the themes of organisation structure, productivity, and conflict management, had a certain number of clients out in the divisions, and wrote many a think-piece paper to try and influence policy. But he had neither Mercer's top connections, nor Dudley's informal leadership position of OD, and Dudley's work management background, and therefore McBride had a more difficult time sustaining his credibility. McBride also ran into a problem finding and keeping a patron on the main board:

> If I have a patron, it's Hogarth. The trouble is that means I can't relate too well to some others on the board who are competing with him for the Chairman's job. But then you have to put your money on one horse and hope!

McBride was unlucky his horse lost, and a lot of his political capital went with his patron's defeat. Tom James, however, picked a winner in Harvey-Jones. With the demise of the Petrochemicals Division OD unit on Harvey-Jones's departure for the main board, James was steered by Harvey-Jones into a managerial role in the Central Management Services Department, and then involved by Harvey-Jones in a whole series of important change processes right up to and including the Petrochemicals and Plastics Division merger in 1981. James had had a work study and management services background, and had grafted onto those structured modes of problem-solving an appreciation and skill in using OD ideas and processes. His rather more planned and orderly approach to work meant that Harvey-Jones was generally predisposed to use James rather than Dudley:

> I find Tom a much easier man to work with than Stewart because Tom can work his way through a plan. You can agree an objective with Tom, and Tom will then produce for you an intelligible plan both in process and also in impact terms which you can then see applying to the business. It's very difficult to get that degree of clarity out of Stewart.

If the above account of the evolution of the central OD resources seems like a catalogue of the activities and credibility of a number of personalities, that indeed was what OD amounted to by the mid to late 1970s. There were the few individuals who for highly specific and personal reasons had a personal ticket to practise their trade; the rest had fallen by the wayside. OD both at the centre and in the divisions was probably at its lowest ebb ever in late 1977 and 1978. A close observer of the OD scene interviewed in 1980 had this to say about the state of OD in the late 1970s:

> There isn't an OD function, it is an informal association of people interested in creating change. Their main need now [in 1980] is some support, encouragement and stimulation, and a feeling that they are not being plowed into the ground. 18

months ago a lot of OD people around the company were getting disheartened. They could take the view that this was something the Company wasn't interested in at all, it was something of a lost cause.

Of course for much of the 1970s OD didn't have a cause, at least not in the sense of the values of individual worth, participative styles of management, and behavioural skills emphasising team work, openness and trust that had been characteristic of the late 1960s and 1970s. There had been no attempt to resurrect a central initiative to replace WSA/SDP, and the view taken by Dudley and James was that "organisational change should occur as a result of an external trigger being appreciated and something being done rather than as a result of philosophical debate".

Dudley and James' statement about the absence of philosophical debate was, of course, not quite accurate. One of the reasons for the limited progress of the Harvey-Jones initiatives to change the top governance of ICI in the period 1974–77 was that in the absence of an external trigger of sufficiently dramatic proportions it became a tussle between a progressive philosophy and an older pattern, and the latter had no difficulty in prevailing. But there was a difference in the mid and late 1970s in the way the central OD resources related to and represented new ideas about organisation and behaviour. Compared with the WSA/SDP period the OD resources were no longer the standard-bearers for the new world. Behaviourism was no longer being propagated through ideas about management style and team-building as an end in itself, but was now clearly being justified as a mechanism to meet business objectives. But even the behavioural concepts were taking a back seat, and Dudley and the others were more likely to describe themselves as "change resources", or as "resources for strategy and planning at the centre" rather than as OD specialists. When they could Dudley, Mercer, and James were now openly colluding with the power figures in ICI who wanted fundamental structural and cultural change. Dudley summarised his stance in these terms:

> We only join the early adopters of ideas we don't try and initiate them from new. We try and link with management, the power system to pick up and build on. We see our role as stimulating thinking without losing the move into action, if we can manage that.

This retreat from proclaiming the values of the "behavioural sixties" and colluding with parts of the power system to create change was in Dudley's eyes also associated with a very low-key approach to selling the activity of OD in the company. Dudley avoided the term or implication that in any sense he was managing a function, which might have required him at various times to publicly defend that function, define for it a set of objectives, and assess the extent to which those objectives had been achieved. Dudley persisted with the model of organisation that implied "holding a network together of people in the divisions and abroad, based on competence". Dudley's implicit acceptance of the position of Dean of Faculty of the OD network, and his avoidance of the position as manager of the function or activity, together with his idiosyncratic style of behaviour, may have contributed both to his personal survival and therefore the continuing presence of a high-level change resource, at the centre, but caused no small confusion and agonising for those around him.

John Harvey-Jones, and another director, David Heaton, to whom Dudley reported, tried for a good deal of the 1970s to encourage Stewart to prioritise his objectives, and in various other ways "to actually organise himself into a specific role".

> It's neither Stewart's wish nor style to do that. So he acts as a free spirit, a very useful free spirit and ICI can afford him, and thank God we can . . . About 3 years ago [in 1977] David and I tried to get Stewart to produce an OD plan but Stewart is not organised in that sort of way . . . We have failed to get an agreed target with him . . . Stewart symbolises the best and the worst of OD in a way he symbolises all the skills, and yet he symbolises an impatience to me that with all that degree of skill the results are so much less than the need.

Others also described Dudley's mode of working as "planned opportunism", and argued had they had the kind of personal credibility Dudley had they would have "tried to get the whole service [of OD] used more strategically . . . I was left to develop my own strategy in my own patch – there was a real absence of a company strategy, to create space for OD to operate." Another OD resource in the Company noted that Stewart "manages well the linking of OD activities he personally observes, but he doesn't have total knowledge of what's going on, and is influenced largely by his own judgment of who is competent and who isn't". Dudley was also accused by some of his peers in the Company of not using his access to the power system to help the junior OD man more:

> But Stewart has not a bad argument about that which is – the people who need help with their credibility are not the people I want to help. Let them get on with it.

Dudley's retort to the query why had OD not been functionalised or formalised more was that it had "gone back to my personal beliefs, back to me as a person, it wouldn't have been right for OD, and it would have reduced my space, my freedom of action. I would have been tied into doing things I didn't want to do, like managing, justifying OD in reports, listing clients and activities. This wouldn't have been good for OD."

Basically, however, as Dudley remarked with no false modesty, "I never, ever as a person admitted that I might not survive in this company, or OD not survive. This was a supreme confidence in my own ability to manage myself, to keep OD going."

By 1978 a number of trends began to come together to influence the need for management of change skills, the acceptability of OD as an activity, and the personal ticket to practise possessed by Dudley, Mercer, and James. As the business and financial pressures increased on ICI, so the gentle arm-twisting that had come from the centre to improve productivity "6% through volume increase and 4% by employee reductions" was replaced by demands for firm action. Meanwhile "the policy and the posture was for line managers to be the change agents", and ICI:

> Tried hard to have behavioural skills absorbed by line management, and applied by them, as opposed to a need for a clearly identified group of external consultants, be they truly external to the company or external to the unit or division concerned. Obviously that is an incomplete process but you can now identify some managers who have high skills in those areas usually through having worked alongside internal or external consultants through a major change process.

As the Company reward system clearly began to act on evidence of line management success in creating change as a key criterion for promotion, so change management skills and the level of change activity increased. This trend brought out into the open and made explicit feelings latent amongst senior personnel people that "I've always had a concept you didn't want your OD resources in specialist people more than you had to. I've always felt OD specialists were valuable, valuable to some people but vulnerable to others. And I've seen too many people come unstuck, have short lives in the Company, because they got too way out . . . now our problem is to build OD knowledge and experience into people doing line jobs." How this knowledge and skill about the management of change was passed on to managers we will explain in a moment. For the present analysis of the condition of central OD in 1978, the other key factor to note is the appearance in April 1978 of Sir Maurice Hodgson as Chairman of ICI.

Given the worsening business scene in 1978 there was no surprise when that year ICI appointed as its Chairman a man with a reputation as a hard-headed financial businessman. Sir Maurice Hodgson's early interjection, and the exact words he used, vary from source to source, but effectively, "I don't want to hear about organisation, all this Company ever does is talk and work on organisation, let's get on with the business and make some money", achieved what it was meant to do, dampen philosophical discussions about change in organisation in ICI. In retrospect, of course, there were great changes in manpower and organisation made under Hodgson's leadership. These changes were justified on the pragmatic and business grounds that Hodgson demanded. One of the executive directors characterised Sir Maurice's approach in these words:

> The only thing that would convince Maurice about making an organisation change would be – "and we can save 2000 people and £200m, and empty that office block and close that site". Maurice would go for it then, that's intellectually justified, we'll do it. But if you started talking changing organisation to improve the efficiency of decision making, he'd say we're off with those behavioural chaps – a load of rubbish.

Sir Maurice thereby changed the climate for using OD resources in and around the board, and both Mercer even, and Dudley found themselves relatively speaking out in the cold. Significantly, in April 1978 as Sir Maurice became Chairman, so Harvey-Jones was promoted to be one of ICI's three deputy chairmen. With this appointment there was now the possibility of Harvey-Jones getting the Chairmanship next time around. This fact, together with a move by Sir Maurice to eliminate the organisation portfolio as one of the functional directorships,[1] meant that John Harvey-Jones drew back from his previous tendency to sponsor organisation changes through the use of OD consultants, and although "he remained a supporter of OD he was much less proactive as a connection". One of the senior internal consultants coolly remarked:

> When Harvey-Jones became a deputy chairman he dropped out . . . This was a recognition by John that he was an ambitious man and therefore he had to watch his rear, his influence base, his political position in order to work for Chairman. He suddenly realised he had a chance. I regretted him dropping out – you mustn't have any taint of the odd-ball.

Harvey-Jones's overt withdrawal from public sponsorship of OD resources did not mean, however, that organisation change was no less a possibility. The worsening business results of ICI in the context of a deep economic recession, plus further changes in the composition of the main board in favour of those looking for change, all helped to create the conditions for first the formulation and then the implementation of strategic change. As we shall see, apart from process help in workshops leading to some of the changes in European organisation, and a major role in the educational task of putting together a series of management of change workshops, the company OD resources largely sat on the sidelines watching as the executive directors and Chairman of ICI put together some fundamental changes in manpower, organisation, and then culture. With these changes designed and decided upon, one or two internal and external OD consultants were called in, almost as an afterthought to help with their implementation. Was this to be another rerun of WSA/SDP, with corporate change designed by a small group at the centre – but this time with more far-reaching structural and manpower changes, and then the OD resources that still remained or were deemed to be still credible, being asked to work with divisional management to construct the operational detail of the changes and try to make them happen?

The economic and business environment and strategic change

> Basically it took so long [to create the required strategic change] because the company appeared to be doing relatively well, and the company appeared to be doing relatively well because it was relatively efficient in a country the exchange rate of which was being set by the inefficient . . . The people there [in ICI] were not change minded, but basically there wasn't enough dissatisfaction with our performance.

[1] Harvey-Jones had held this portfolio since 1973, and it had provided a lot of the legitimacy for his activities to create organisation change.

The above quotation by an ICI main board director in 1982 reveals the extent to which he believes environmental pressure was a cause of change in ICI. Certainly one difference between the period between 1972 and 1977 we have just been discussing, and the period between 1978 and 1983 we are just about to discuss, was that pressures in the environment in the earlier period were now to become dramatically worse. As those environmental pressures increased so the internal forces for change in ICI led by Harvey-Jones and others joined with what became a more responsive internal climate, and a whole series of changes followed. Not that those changes in any sense automatically followed the environmental pressure, for, as we shall see, there were still forces of inertia blocking some of the structural and cultural changes being recommended by the change group on the ICI board.

But what were some of the business, economic, and political pressures facing ICI in 1978, and how did those pressures accelerate to produce the bad business results of 1980–82?

ICI was undoubtedly weakened in the 1970s by its dependence on the United Kingdom. Although it had been a strategic objective of ICI from the 1960s to place capital and increase sales in Western Europe, and do likewise in North America in the 1970s, even by 1978 ICI was still very much a UK company. In 1978, for example, over half of group sales and three-quarters of trading profit originated in the UK. The company was headquartered in the UK, it was in 1978 the largest privately owned industrial company in the UK, and it was thus politically important, and in 1978 61% of ICI's total employees were UK-based. The bulk of ICI's assets and employees were therefore based in an economy which was not growing at the rate of, for example, Germany and the United States, but also where by 1980 and 1981 the UK customer base of ICI started to decline dramatically.

In addition the 1970s also saw the beginnings of the end of the major thrust of chemicals substitution for natural products such as wood and paper, and with this the premium of chemical growth over general growth rates was reduced. In the period 1963–72 the ratio of growth in the UK of chemical industry production to general manufacturing production was 2.1 : 1.00; by 1970–75 this had increased to 5.0 : 1.00; and then there was a significant decline in the period 1975–79, to 1.1 : 1.00. Along with many other European chemical companies it took ICI a long time to realise that their industry was fast maturing, and that certainly in the bulk petrochemicals and plastics areas, there was little growth left at all. ICI's capital sanctioning and policy group system turned out some very strange investment decisions in the mid-1970s, so that by 1978 it was clearly evident that ICI's recent investment behaviour and future plans were out of balance with their current and forecast profitability. In 1978 and 1979 ICI had to draw substantially on its liquid resources to meet its planned capital expenditure, and from 1980 onwards capital expenditure was cut dramatically compared with the levels of 1977–79.

With the development of over-capacity in the European fibres, petro-chemicals, and plastics industries, and the worsening financial position of those divisions in ICI, it began to become clear in ICI that the "Group had not only to continue to change its territorial shape, and to begin to make greater levels of profitability and market penetration into Europe and North America, but also that it had to change its product profile". By 1980 a prime objective of ICI was to stop the flow of cash into its heavy chemicals sector at the previous high rates, and first to attempt to increase the profitability of that sector, and then, when that failed, to withdraw under-utilised manufacturing capacity in that sector.

The arrival of the Conservative government on the scene in 1979, pursuing as it did strict monetarist economic policies, meant high interest rates, a recession in industrial production, and mounting unemployment. The further fall in ICI's UK customer base, and worse still the sharply rising value of sterling against the dollar and the Deutschmark, meant cheaper chemical imports from Continental Western Europe and North America, and a trend for UK chemical prices to move out of line with those in Continental Europe.

Another worsening economic indicator for ICI in the 1970s was the high rate of inflation in the UK. In the 1960s the annual rate of inflation in the UK had varied between 1 and 5%, in the 1970s the annual average rate of inflation was 13% – considerably higher than ICI's European and North American competitors. One measure of the effect of ICI's UK base was the impact of high inflation on its annual profits. From the peak of 1974 to the peak of 1979, ICI's historically based pretax profits rose 44% to £560m. However, on a CCA basis adjusted for inflation, ICI's profits have fallen from £415m in 1974 to £366m in 1979 (Kidder, Peabody & Co., 1981). This is the real effect of being based in a country with an inflationary environment.

On top of all the above difficulties there was also the continuing feeling in ICI that "our productivity failed to match that of our major competitors and the extent to which we could now rely on growth to help improve productivity must be in doubt". One internal estimate of ICI's group overheads in 1978 was that they could be as high as £700m.

Faced with this gathering storm the talk in ICI in 1978 was of the "vital importance of reducing costs", "of reducing Group overheads", "of reducing numbers employed beyond the contribution of 2 divisions" (Fibres and Organics). Other measures to improve profitability besides reducing numbers were also discussed. These included performing better in the market place, upgrading the quality of the customer base, and providing better technical service. Other actions considered included reducing the number of layers of management and accepting changes in corporate philosophy which would eliminate or reduce the need for so many checks and counter-checks. Paradoxically, however, all of the above 1978 statements of required change had to be set against Sir Maurice Hodgson's summary of the same 1978 Chairman's Group Conference; where he noted:

Completion of the recent studies on organisation, also initiated by the Chairman [the outgoing Sir Rowland Wright] meant that a period of relative organisational stability now lay ahead.

By 1980, however, the ICI executive directors were acting:

1. To foster reorganisation which will reduce the number of operating units.
2. To work to reduce the number of significant layers in the management hierarchy.
3. To simplify the activities at head office by concentrating on the essential staff support for the board.
4. To encourage operating units to streamline their organisations and simplify their operations, using lower manpower numbers particularly in monthly staff, and weekly staff support services areas.
5. To work to reduce the number of UK sites.

All this was to be done "whilst maintaining the humane values and personnel policies of the company".

The question and theme was "how can ICI develop a more positive and direct management style and become a slimmer, more effective company?" By 1980 the revolution was about to take place.

The management of change seminars

As we have already discussed, the arrival of Sir Maurice Hodgson as Chairman in April 1978, the promotion of Harvey-Jones to deputy chairman, and the existence of a company personnel director "who doesn't buy OD as a conceptual thing", significantly changed the climate for using OD resources in and around the main board. Ironically as the need for change increased, and senior executives became more and more involved in creating change, so the central and divisional OD resources found themselves more and more in the background. In this situation, and again using Ron Mercer's conceptual thinking and credibility as an individual with various board members, one or two members of Group Personnel Department[2] linked with Mercer to design some management of change seminars. The General Manager of Personnel who claimed responsibility for this initiative (there were two GM's of Personnel at that time), argued that "what I was able to do opposite the board on macro-organisational change was less than we needed to do . . . so I developed the idea of these change seminars as a way of keeping momentum going".

The General Manager of Personnel saw three objectives for these seminars:

> My No. 1 objective was to try and spread around the ownership of OD events at board level now that Harvey-Jones was less proactive as a board connection . . .
> The second thing I wanted was to get a much greater understanding of the technology [of change management], and a common language between members of the board, division chairmen, and their boards. It seemed to me if we could get the top 150 people in the UK understanding what technology there was for managing change, and to use a common jargon, we would have a very much better chance of handling some of the things we had to do.
> The third objective was that from these there would be action programmes that would give opportunities for OD resources to be supported and helped.

[2] The name was changed from Central to Group Personnel Department in 1978.

Starting in April 1978 with a mixture of main board directors, and division chairmen and directors, the change workshops eventually involved several hundred of ICI's most senior managers. Ron Mercer ran the early workshops, and then he delegated their development and operation to a team of internal consultants which included Dudley and James. The participants had to come with at least one other colleague from their part of ICI, and most importantly bring a change problem that they both owned, and had a legitimate authority to intervene on. The 2½ days of workshop activity interspersed short inputs of concepts, ideas, and techniques about the management of change with focussed and practical work on the real change problem participants brought with them.

Nobody interviewed in this study substantially doubted the value of these workshops, although "some participants went back with the reservations about head shrinkers, and the usual stuff". An executive director commented that "they have given more skill, they have given more appreciation down the line, and they have given appreciation to some members of the board who never operated in that way before". Crucially perhaps the workshops helped to signal and clarify what change management was as an activity, to provide a common language for problem-solving about change, and in so doing helped to stimulate a culture for change, at the point in time when environmental pressures demanded real action and outcomes, and the capability to produce those outcomes.

Changing the European business organisation

Like many UK companies, ICI did not become seriously involved in Continental Europe until the early 1960s. Since the 1960s ICI has constructed physical plant in Europe, established selling groups (national selling companies) in each individual market, and encouraged joint ventures with local manufacturers to exploit particular technological or marketing opportunities. Table 30 shows how sales to Continental Western Europe (CWE) have increased steadily as a proportion of total Group sales, although it is noticeable that between 1974 and 1979 the percentage increase was only from 19.1% to 19.6%.

Although sales to Europe have developed both from local production and by exporting from the UK, the profitability of ICI's European production has

TABLE 30   Percentage contribution to ICI group sales: by territory

	1966	1970	1974	1979
UK	50.1	47.1	40.6	41.6
CWE	10.8	15.4	19.1	19.6
North America	} 15.4	11.5	16.2	16.0
Central and South America		2.8		
Australasia	12.3	} 22.9	24.1	22.8
Rest of world	11.4			

remained low. For example in 1974, a particularly good year for the European petrochemical industry, ICI earned an operating profit of £51m in Continental Europe on sales of £450m, but in the subsequent four years operations in the area incurred losses of £15m, £7m, and £2m respectively. The pattern of ICI's development into Europe, majoring as it did in fibres and plastics, the problems of weak prices and over-capacity in the European petrochemicals industry, and sterling fluctuations, all contributed to a business situation of rapid expansion in sales but depression in profits. Although ICI rationalised its fibres operations in Europe in the late 1970s, a decision was taken in 1977 to construct a major chemical complex at Wilhelmshaven in West Germany to manufacture vinyl chloride, and PVC. The collapse of the European petrochemicals and commodity chemicals market in 1980, showed that the Wilhelmshaven project was too large, and certainly too soon.

Given the less than auspicious ICI business performance in Continental Western Europe, it was inevitable that the pattern of ICI's organisation in Western Europe would attract the attention of the board organisation study groups of 1976 and 1977. Although in 1977 some improvement had been made in the relationship between the main board as a group and division chairmen as a group by the creation of the first Chairman's Group Conference, the relatively isolated way the board organisation study groups began to work created new strains between the centre and the divisions and operating companies. A report of division chairmen and general managers' views of the board in 1977 revealed concern that they were being exhorted to behave with responsibility on problems of productivity and capital rationing, "but on a matter of vital impact on the Company, such as its organisation, we are not even wanted". One of the executive directors of that time voiced this description of board processes of working:

> The thing that struck me about the processes they were using was that this was in no way a participative activity. They would occasionally ask some division chairman to do some analysis and report back to them, but they were not saying to the existing organisation, join us in setting a direction for organisation development. There was no question of agreeing objectives and principles for the organisation.

As far as European organisation was concerned what was beginning to emerge in senior reaches of ICI by 1977 was a feeling that the existing scheme of organisation was not sharp enough in accountability terms to meet the business and competitive pressures developing on the continent. Early in the 1970s ICI had tried to spearhead its way into Europe by setting up a Europa Division with its headquarters at Everburg in Belgium. This division was given a mixed role – to manage ICI's interests in its European subsidiary and associated companies, to look after the business interests of ICI's 16 national selling companies, broadly to manage ICI's relations with the EEC and individual national governments, to act as a corporate identity for ICI in Europe, to stimulate further product and investment development into Europe by the UK divisions, and to share in some cases profit accountability in Continental Western Europe with some of the UK divisions' products.

By 1977 the uneven pattern of development of the UK divisions into Europe, the fact that Europa shared profit accountability into Europe with Plastics, Fibres, and Paints Divisions, but Pharmaceuticals and Plant Protection Divisions had sole profit accountability responsibility, began to make ICI believe that third-order organisations such as Europa Division were leading to over-complexity, lack of business sharpness, and therefore inefficiency. There was no great surprise, therefore, when at the 1978 Chairman's Group Conference the executive directors proposed to the division chairmen and chief executive officers that with effect from 1 April 1978 the sharing of profit accountability with Europa Division would cease. Henceforth the UK divisions were to have sole profit-accountability for the whole of their businesses throughout Western Europe. This was thereafter referred to as Pan-European responsibility. With this arrangement it was also proposed that Europa Division would continue to carry out its "services" activities, such as being responsible for the national selling companies, and maintaining links with the EEC Commission.

The Board were clearly concerned about this move; in particular there was a concern that the Pan-European change might create the impression ICI was pulling out of Europe instead of the reverse. This led to a move to consider placing the headquarters of at least one UK division in Europe. Since Plastics Division had the most assets on the ground in Europe the view was that Plastics should move its headquarters from Welwyn Garden City to Continental Europe. The above proposals were greeted with some dismay by the chairmen of Europa and Plastics Divisions, and with no small disquiet by some of the other division chairmen. It was in this situation that Tony Woodburn the executive director now with the combined role as plastics product director and territorial director for Continental Western Europe was given the opportunity to review the European business organisation situation.

Using Tom Bainton, the external consultant he had known since his Mond days, and Stewart Dudley, the first thing Woodburn did was to get all the division chairmen together and try and achieve some measure of agreement of business aims and business organisation for a Pan-European ICI "so that the aims and solutions have the depth of personal understanding and commitment necessary to make any change happen in fact, not just in words". As Woodburn later put it, "I said to the chairmen – "Look fellows we [the board] are about to drop a bomb on you – would you like to get involved in designing the bomb?" Both Harvey-Jones and Woodburn were by this time becoming increasingly sceptical of the possibility of creating change in ICI, but as Woodburn remarked "occasionally one would see the opportunity to put the ball into space and run after it". The Woodburn, Bainton, and Dudley meetings with the division chairmen in 1978 became such an opportunity to put the ball into space, for not only did the above group agree on action on the Pan-European question, they also set in train the further development of strategy and marketing linkages between the heartland divisions (Mond, Petrochemicals, and Plastics), and reviewed the relations between the UK divisions, Europa Division, and the national selling companies.

What happened was that at the first Woodburn, division chairmen's meeting, Woodburn's successor as chairman of Mond Division had said "are you working the right problem first? Before you decide what to do with Plastics in Europe, should we not decide what we are going to do with the whole divisional organisation – clearly the divisional organisation is now obsolete." Having announced at the 1978 Chairman's Group Conference there would be no changes of divisional boundaries and no divisional mergers to close down speculative thought in those areas, the board now found themselves not for the first time faced with pressures from below for fundamental change. Harvey-Jones and Woodburn took their opportunity.

The Heavy Chemicals Divisions and the Petrochemicals and Plastics Division Merger

Two concrete decisions came out of Woodburn's 1978 work on European organisation. One was the view that ICI could achieve their business objective of a larger share of the European market by requiring all divisions to operate on a Pan-European basis from 1 August 1978. The second decision was the agreement that ICI Europa jointly with Mond, Plastics, and Petrochemicals Divisions would direct the expansion and penetration of their businesses in the Pan-European market by developing integrated marketing and selling plans in that territory. The latter decision to pull together some of the strategic and marketing thinking of ICI's Heavy Chemicals Divisions was a continuation of pressure to link business perspective and action which Harvey-Jones had been pushing since he created a quasi-formal grouping called the Petrochemical Product Directors Advisory Group as far back as July 1973.

By 1978 it was becoming clearer that "the divisional boundaries were primarily bureaucratic in nature, that they inappropriately separated technologies from one another, more importantly they separated marketing activities from one another. Equally inappropriately because they were UK based – as a whole they created a sort of Anglo-centric attitude which was not felt to be particularly helpful to European market penetration in increasingly competitive times." Tony Woodburn's recollection of events in 1978 was that out of the work on Pan-European organisation "came a realisation that we were over-fragmented, we didn't really use our total competitive strength. It was that thought that led John Harvey-Jones and I to seize our opportunity in the board, and to say there ought to be some way of putting the heavy divisions together."

Amongst the many problems in the way of pulling Mond, Petrochemicals, and Plastics together two were critical. The first was the fact that the executive directors still had their portfolios divided by product, function, and territory, so that not only were there conflicts and ambiguities in handling that matrix, but also each product director was placed in an advocacy position for the product area or division he was responsible for. Furthermore, the Policy Group System overlaid on top of the Product and Territorial Directorships added to the fragmentation and sub-optimal decision-making, particularly around capital investment decision-making, but also around issues of product and market development. The Policy Group System was not only leading to endless paper-chasing and gamesmanship between individual directors and operating units, it was also leading, as one executive director put it, to:

> Horse and cart investment decisions. It was a case of you build a cracker to make ethylene – why are you doing that? Oh! because there's a demand for ethylene. Where's the demand for ethylene. Oh! that's down the road in PVC and polyethylene. Meanwhile if you asked Plastics Division why they were building this new polyethylene plant, one of the answers you'd get was because we want to use up some of the ethylene on Petrochemicals Division's brand new cracker.

Harvey-Jones and Woodburn realised it was too late for financial, market and technological integration to occur at board level, and given the structure and mode of operation of the board, it wouldn't occur there – so it had to occur further back in the operating divisions. Politically speaking there was still no majority on the board in 1978 to contemplate merging divisions, so Harvey-Jones and Woodburn had to go back and invent some intermediary and parallel systems of operation which would tap energy at division chairmen level for more integrated strategic thinking, and in so doing move another piece on the chess board in the direction they wanted, while they waited for the appropriate conditions to push for the bigger change.

As I mentioned a moment ago, Harvey-Jones's first attempt to bring together the strategic thinking of Petrochemicals, Plastics, Mond, and Europa had been in July 1973 when he used his board position as petrochemicals product director to create the Petrochemicals Product Directors Advisory Group. This was an informal grouping of himself, the four division chairmen, the general manager of planning, and the relevant policy group secretary which had no place in the official scheme of organisation, but which used working parties to examine energy policy, European strategy, and the development of thinking about the Wilhelmshaven project.

The above advisory group carried on until the end of 1976 and was then replaced by a much stronger executive grouping called the Inter-Divisional Policy Group (IDPG). The IDPG was made up of a deputy chairman, the executive directors with product director responsibility for Mond, Petrochemicals, and Plastics, and Harvey-Jones as territorial director for Continental Western Europe. By 1978 Harvey-Jones was a deputy chairman and took over as chairman of the IDPG, and shared this role with chairman of the Continental Western Europe territorial policy group. He had as his product directors on the IDPG, Woodburn as the product director of Plastics, the Mond and Petrochemicals product directors, and Woodburn was also territorial director for Continental Western Europe.

With both Harvey-Jones and Woodburn linked into the IDPG and the Continental Western Europe policy group, the right personalities for change now had the right mixture of board portfolios to begin to link not only the three heavy chemicals divisions together, but to do that linking in the context of business thinking across Continental Western Europe.

Politically Harvey-Jones and Woodburn saw the way to keep any momentum for change going was to use the IDPG mechanism, and to try and connect to that any energy for change coming up from the division chairmen. In August 1978 Harvey-Jones chaired a meeting of the IDPG, plus the chairmen of the three big UK heavy chemicals divisions, the chairman of Europa Division, and the head of policy groups department. The external OD consultant Bainton, and Harvey-Jones's favoured internal consultant Tom James helped to design the process for the meeting, and were present themselves. The Marlow meeting had two principal agenda items:

1. The role, mission, and method of working which the IDPG intended to pursue.
2. The operational structure for the Pan-European region appropriate for effectively carrying out the policies decided on.

The Marlow meeting achieved a number of important steps forward. Firstly, its purpose and role was clarified, and legitimated with the main board. The purpose of the IDPG was firmly "to ensure that the strategies for the group's heavy chemical and polymer businesses are created and integrated on a world-wide basis". Within that purpose its role was to "create conditions and structures which will encourage, stimulate, and help the operating units to discharge the above responsibilities". Harvey-Jones and Woodburn now had a vehicle to legitimately pull together the strategies of three divisions which had previously been the responsibility of three separate product directors, and they had some licence to continue to work on creating new structures in that area.

Further steps were made symbolically to tie together the three UK divisions, when in January 1979 the IDPG's name was changed to the Heavy Chemicals Policy Group (HCPG). Also in January 1979 the financial results for the three heavy chemicals businesses were for the first time presented to the board in total. In February 1979 a Pan-European steering group was created. This was a group of the four division chairmen (Mond, Plastics, Petrochemicals plus Europa) – put together to promote the integration of those businesses in Europe.

The events described above reveal how a combination of executive will, the creation and use of mechanisms such as the IDPG, and the HCPG, plus drawing on the involvement of the division chairmen helped to push events forward in 1978 and early 1979. This slow, additive process of water dripping on a stone might have continued in this way had not the business and political environment changed in 1979, and had it not become clearer that worse was to come in 1980 and beyond.

Harvey-Jones called a follow-up meeting of the HCPG at Streatley in September 1979. The shared view at this meeting was that the business environment had changed dramatically as a result of:

1. the Iranian Revolution which had produced an oil shortage and resultant jump in prices;
2. the strengthening of sterling and associated UK monetary policy;
3. the acceleration of inflation;
4. high and predicted higher unemployment.

The result for ICI was slower growth, increased competition (both in the UK and overseas), a 15% relative increase in UK employment costs, inadequate profitability, and a shortage of cash for capital expenditure. The conclusion of the Streatley meeting was that "in this more hostile environment increased profit could arise only from better decisions in a simplified organisation progressively slimming down towards a much lower cost base".

In spite of the worsening business scene in 1979 the ICI main board rejected for the first time the Harvey-Jones–Woodburn proposition to merge Mond, Petrochemicals, and Plastics Divisions. Woodburn later acknowledged that the three executive directors openly pushing for a merger may have made a tactical error in 1979 of "pushing too far", and getting rejected. After the Streatley meeting Harvey-Jones thus found himself with a worsening business scene, more head of steam from the HCPG and the relevant division chairmen, but faced with a clear statement from the board that there should be no attempt to merge the three divisions in one step, and that the unified direction of the three divisions by a single individual at below board level would not be acceptable.

What Harvey-Jones and Woodburn were able to achieve in the immediate aftermath of Streatley was legitimation for the existence of an interactive business area called the heavy chemicals business area, and agreement that the division chairmen would have a maximum of 3 months to prepare proposals for "a wider, potentially all embracing, integration of the functional activities of the three divisions". Harvey-Jones was by now mightily frustrated at the pace of change and wrote to his executive director colleagues:

> While I believe that the above represents about the best we can hope to achieve, acting within the constraints that my colleagues have so far set on our activities, and working in the traditional ICI manner ... I have to make clear that I do not believe the response is likely to be adequate in terms of the time it is likely to take us to start taking effective action ... I understand, however, the fears and concerns of my colleagues in this area and am prepared to continue making such progress as we can along the lines outlined above. It may well be that, if time was on our side, this would produce the best long-term solutions. I do not, however, believe we have the time to allow this more protracted approach and would be grateful to hear the views of my colleagues.

ICI were not, of course, just sitting on their hands at this time. Within the constraints set by the divisional boundaries, vigorous attempts were being made to close works, reduce maintenance costs, and slim down managerial levels and numbers. With the clear sign that the recent massive period of capital expenditure was over, ICI had the problem of what they were going to do with the large investment engineering resources they had in each of the large capital spending divisions. Early in 1980 moves were set in train to move from a divisional to a regional engineering organisation and save large amounts in salaried employee costs.

On the question of divisional mergers some progress was made politically by the retiral of executive directors, and the inescapable fact of the collapse of demand, prices, and margins in the European Petrochemicals and Plastics markets. When in April 1980 both the Petrochemicals and Mond product directors retired this allowed Woodburn to take over board responsibility for the Plastics and the Petrochemicals product areas. As Woodburn later put it:

> For the first time in ICI's history Petrochemicals and Plastics were the responsibility of one man on the board. I couldn't have arguments with myself about transfer pricing. Within months I was reporting horrendous losses from the whole Petrochemicals–Plastics system.

Implicitly and privately (to the board) at this point in mid-1980 a very much more operational and executive group than the heavy chemicals policy group was created called the heavy chemicals executive. This group, chaired by Harvey-Jones, and with Woodburn and the Mond product director, began the detailed task of preparing the operational plans for how to make any merger happen. When in late 1980, in the midst of ICI's first losses in their history, the board made the decision in favour of a merger the option chosen was the more conservative one of a two rather than a three division merger. One of the three executive directors pushing for a three into one change remarked "it was an absolutely typical compromise trade-off, with the three of us pushing for a three division merger, and being told no you can only have two".

The reasons why the bulk of the board rejected a three divisional merger in 1979, again in 1980, and again even when Harvey-Jones had become chairman of ICI in 1982, were a mixture of business-related, organisation-related, and political. The view of the detractors was that while Petrochemicals and Plastics were well integrated technology and business-wise, Mond was less so. Also why make yet another organisation change by adding a still profitable Mond to a very unprofitable Petrochemicals and Plastics, when the newly formed division was virtually fighting for its business survival? Crucially perhaps against the three into one merger was the argument that politically "our colleagues couldn't handle it. To them it meant vast numbers of people and assets in one unit. It meant an accretion of power to one or two individuals on the board, and a very powerful division chairman. They couldn't handle anyone in the boardroom with that sort of weight around, and particularly as Harvey-Jones was emerging as a very rank outsider for the Chairmanship."

However, the Petrochemicals and Plastics Division merger went ahead as from April 1981. The story of the implementation of that merger is an interesting one but beyond the confines of this book. It is relevant to the continuing story of OD in ICI to note that both Bainton and James were drafted by Harvey-Jones and Woodburn to help with the process of managing the Petrochemicals and Plastics merger. The fact that the new chairman of the

Petrochemicals and Plastics Division was told to have Bainton and James is indicative of the continuing belief by Harvey-Jones and Woodburn of the value of OD resources, but also indicative of the long years of lack of penetration of the value of OD skills amongst the boards of the old Petrochemicals and Plastics Divisions. Bainton had a considerable impact in influencing the character, structure, and systems of the merged division by working with the new chairman and his board. Evidence of his continuing credibility came when he was invited in 1982 to help with the further changes necessary on the huge manufacturing site at Wilton.

With some level of change now accepted in the structure of the UK divisions, Harvey-Jones and Woodburn, and their supporters, now turned to Harvey-Jones's long held ambition to try and change the role and mode of operation of the ICI main board. Would they be successful this time?

The role, size, and method of working of the main board

> Given the collegial board system in ICI the question is: can a democratic society change itself radically? I'm increasingly uncertain about that ... If the rate of evolution is not fast enough to cope with the external environment I just don't know where we'll be ... ICI is not that evidently unsuccessful to make that change evidently necessary.

The above quotation from an interview with John Harvey-Jones in 1977 indicates both Harvey-Jones's continuing desire for change in the mode of operation of the main board, and his justifiable scepticism that the board studies encouraged in 1976 and 1977 by Sir Rowland Wright would run into the sand as completely as had the 1973 board organisation committee's recommendations. In fact, of course, small changes did accrue from both the 1973 and 1977 attempts to change the role of the board. In 1977, for example, in view of continuing criticisms of the lack of sharpness of decision-making coming out of the board's existing meetings and committees, the decision was taken to add an executive committee to these meetings. The executive committee was a meeting of the executive directors only, and allowed those directors to make decisions on matters of substance without waiting for the once-a-month meeting of the full ICI main board.

As we have already noted the appointment in 1978 of Sir Maurice Hodgson as ICI Chairman, Harvey-Jones's elevation to deputy chairman, and the end of the board portfolio of organisation director all took the steam out of any attempts to radically change the ICI top governance system. However, by late 1979 and 1980 the fast-declining business fortunes of ICI were creating a better climate for change, and Harvey-Jones used the March 1980 Chairman's Group Conference "to open Pandora's box". One of the syndicate groups asked to report at the conference repeated the by now familiar diagnosis of the problems at the top. The board were invited by the conference to review their mode of operation in the light of unease about some aspects of ICI's management style, and the capacity of existing ways of operating the top structure to meet the challenges of the 1980s. It was suggested to the board that a smaller, more cohesive board concentrating more on the development and implementation of strategy might be a model to work towards, and that the extant problem of implementing board decisions might be helped by the appointment of a "director of change" on the board.

Although at the time Sir Maurice Hodgson's summary and review of the conference debate "very greatly dampened the head of steam we'd got", Hodgson followed up the suggestions of the conference that the board should again consider its role, size, and method of working. During the summer of 1980 Sir Maurice interviewed all of the executive directors individually, and met the non-executive directors in small groups to see if there were areas of agreement for change. Hodgson's data revealed that the recent pattern of having 3- or 4-year Chairmanships was not good, and that in future the Chairman should hold office ideally for 5 years. On the size of the board, then 17 including the chairman, the consensus view was that there is no longer any support for the argument that a smaller board is desirable *per se* on the grounds that an arbitrary reduction in size would force desirable behavioural change and make us more effective. The directors also took a no-change position on another previously controversial point – the existence of deputy chairmen. On the more discursive question of the role of the board, again there was the strongly expressed view that the board spent too much time managing the on-going business in the UK and Europe and too little identifying major changes they should be driving for in terms of the group's international shape and priorities.

Sir Maurice concluded his review of the views of his colleagues by stating there was little pressure for revolutionary changes in the role, size, or functioning of the board, but that the major problems ICI were facing in 1980 indicated that the board's operation needed to be improved.

At this point in late 1980 with Sir Maurice beginning the soundings to find his successor, and with all three of the deputy chairmen being candidates, the ICI top governance system "went into a state of baulk". Sir Maurice would presumably not want to make any changes which would constrain the style of the new Chairman, and in an election atmosphere none of the three candidates would surely wish to over-expose themselves by pushing for radical change which affected the position of the electorate. The pattern was broken in November 1981 when with mixed amazement and delight John Harvey-Jones, got the job as Chairman of ICI.

A main board director not normally associated with the "for change caucus" on the board during the 1970s had this to say about why Harvey-Jones got the Chairman's job:

> The events of the last 3 years have shown that ICI's old way of doing things, and old approach to a number of questions haven't served it terribly well. Whether it would have been possible to have done things differently, had clearer foresight, and taken better avoiding action I think is exceedingly debatable. But with hindsight the way we had done things hadn't served one terribly well – there could

be no argument about that. Therefore there was a realisation that things needed to be different, and the man to my knowledge for the last 8 years in Millbank who has said most persistently and consistently, and without too much regard for how the message was received – there are a lot of things we ought to be doing differently – was John. Change was needed, the obvious change agent was given the job.

Harvey-Jones wasted no time in trying to clarify, share, and reach agreement with his Board colleagues about the principles underlying his vision of the future organisation and style of ICI. In December 1981 he circulated a discussion paper on the shape of ICI and the shape of the ICI board in 1984. Within a week of him formally taking over in April 1982, he set up an informal meeting of his executive team to discuss the mission, role, and method of operation of the board. Ron Mercer had a role in the process planning of this meeting, and in addition was invited to attend the meeting itself. From this meeting and subsequent discussions the following objectives and principles emerged:

1. The Chairman of ICI henceforth should be given a greater degree of personal responsibility for the group. This meant in effect that the Chairman was to be the group's chief executive officer, although the harshness of individuality implied in that title was clothed slightly by describing the Chairman as the company's principal executive officer.
2. The board would comprise a smaller executive team, operating as a team, and supported by a leaner, and more effective head office, concentrating on the strategic direction of the group.
3. There would be an increase in the freedom of chief executives of businesses and territories to run their businesses in accordance with agreed strategies and plans, coupled with greater accountability.
4. There would be greater recognition of the differences between businesses and territories and their problems, opportunities, and aspirations.
5. The style of the group would need to change in order that there was built into the group a self-perpetuating dynamic for change to cope with the uncertainties and opportunities of the future.

Most of the above principles, and certainly those requiring firmer and more strategic leadership from a smaller board operating more as a team, had been part of the changes recommended as far back as the board organisation study of 1973. At last these principles were now part of the official ICI view of the future. But there is a world of a difference between formulating a vision and making it happen, and the task of the top leadership of ICI in 1983 has become how to translate the vision of a more strategic, flexible, tolerant, accountable ICI into a set of structures and systems, together with the appropriate patterns of behaviour, which will make those structures and systems happen in practice. Having at long last got his way as a formulator of strategic change, Harvey-Jones's major task in the 5 years he has as Chairman will be in implementing strategic change. In this task of implementing change, it is doubtful if the few remaining specialist OD resources in the company will have a role to play any more substantial than the limited one they were able to play in helping to formulate strategic change.

THE CONTRIBUTION OF ORGANISATION DEVELOPMENT RESOURCES AND METHODS TO STRATEGIC CHANGE IN ICI

As I write in the Summer of 1983 some real progress has been made by ICI in producing strategic changes in organisation and systems, if not yet in culture and behaviour. Effectively ICI now has a Chairman who is a chief executive. The executive team is now composed of a Chairman and seven executive directors, a net loss of three deputy chairmen and one executive director since April 1974. This smaller group intend to work less as a set of individuals divided by functional, territorial, and product loyalties, and more as an executive team providing leadership on the overall strategic direction of the ICI Group. Some of the functional directorships have been discontinued. Although individual executive directors will be designated as business or territorial directors and will be expected to give guidance and in some cases direction to the chief executives of operating units, those executive directors will not act as advocates for the businesses or territories whose direction they guide.

With the end of the time-consuming games-playing of the policy group system, and the elevation of the board to considering the portfolio management of the group, it is hoped chief executives of operating units will have greater freedoms within a more considered strategic framework. The activities and performance of the operating units will now be assessed by means of a new budgeting and control system.

Now that the board[3] intends to focus on the strategic direction of an international ICI group, they hope correspondingly to distance themselves from the previous concern with the UK divisions and assets. With the merger of Petrochemicals and Plastics Division, the first stage of creating a Pan-Europeanised Heavy Chemicals Group has been made. If and when Mond Division is added to the new merged division there is the basis of an organisation to represent ICI's interests in the UK and Europe. Service functions such as engineering, puchasing, distribution and personnel could then be rationalised further, and the umbilical cord tying the group personnel department to the ICI board could then be broken. The personnel department of a heavy chemicals business area could then look after the UK personnel scene. The above process of setting up organisations to satisfy business areas rather than historical divisions might be extended to the creation of a "light brigade" to go alongside the "heavy (chemicals) brigade". The light brigade might comprise the existing Paints, Plant Protection, and Pharmaceuticals Divisions – but action in this area is not contemplated in the short term.

The process of first regionalising, and then centralising, the company's engineering function continues. Manufacturing sites and individual works have been closed, assets have been swopped with competitors, other assets have been

---

[3] By the Summer of 1983 the ICI main board was composed of a Chairman, 7 executive directors and 6 non-executive directors.

divested. Managerial levels and numbers have declined significantly in the period 1979–83, and pressure continues to cut weekly staff numbers – particularly in maintenance areas. ICI's UK employees dropped from 89,400 in 1979 to 61,800 in 1983, a fall of 31%.

In amongst the reshaping explicit in the above structural changes, ICI hope to increase the proportion of their earnings deriving from products with wider margins, and from territories where the customer base is secure and capable of expansion. Both through acquisition and by developing a more flexible, positive, and entrepreneurial management style, ICI hope to regenerate the company during the likely difficult economic, business, and political conditions of the 1980s.

Although not all of the above-mentioned changes have materialised yet, sufficient of them have to characterise the period 1980–83 as an era of strategic change in ICI's history. One might ask if so many of these changes had been contemplated as long ago as 1973, why did they take so long to materialise? Part of the answer to that question lies in the discussion earlier in this chapter of the general ICI culture, and the culture and mode of operation of the main board. The succession of short-tenure Chairmen, the *primus inter pares* Chairmen, the formal consensual style of decision-making on the board, the hierarchical and layered structure, the risk-aversive institutional character of ICI, and its place in British society. Real change only came when the above culture was threatened by a punishing change in the business and economic environment; only then did ICI become sufficiently dissatisfied with its performance to act. But if the environment was critical as a trigger for change, the narrative in this chapter has also emphasised the role played by a number of key individuals in trying to challenge and break down the old culture, open up and free channels of communication to see uncomfortable sorts of data, and then slowly put in place ideas and mechanisms, together with a sense of direction and a gathering political will which could spell out and accept strategic change. The process of influence used by Harvey-Jones, Woodburn and the other directors interested in change required persistence, patience, the capacity to see where they wanted to be but to make small additive moves in the desired direction, and "to kick the ball into space" as soon as an opening appeared. One of the OD consultants described the process in terms of:

Building up support on a 1 to 1 basis, trying things out, using and making opportunities to test the water, observing how people are shifting, pushing, and then backing off.

Woodburn's view was that:

You have to wait – it is politics of course. There's no way you can drive the thing like you can in a division when you are a chief executive. You have to learn and develop even more skills of persuasion in designing in quite considerable detail how you are going to influence people, and get the support and power.

Harvey-Jones's picture of the process implied frustration, and the necessity for persistence:

> I conceived of the process as just going on and on and on, continuously trying to make small movement.

Undoubtedly the Petrochemicals Product Directors Advisory Group, the Inter-Divisional Policy Group, and the Heavy Chemicals Policy Group were important step-by-step moves towards the 1981 divisional merger. Those mechanisms legitimated cross-divisional senior contact, and thereby provided commitment-building mechanisms for change which crossed the boundaries between divisions, and between the divisions and the main board. But as Harvey-Jones said:

> They were only limited responses to a perceived need, they were a way of putting Petrochemicals, Plastics, and Mond Divisions together without doing so. I actually believe we would have done a bloody sight better if in 1975 we'd put Petrochemicals and Plastics together.

Harvey-Jones and Woodburn constantly had to make compromises, run things in parallel with existing systems when they would have preferred their own and eliminated others. But gradually with a number of additive steps in place, changes in the composition of the main board, "the crumbling lustre of the UK asset base", and a breakdown in the credibility of the policy group system, the level of dissatisfaction increased at senior levels, and the early 1980 recession provided a window for change in ICI.

Strategic change in ICI occurred when it did in the early 1980s as a result of a mixture of business and economic pressure, and the belated influence of a relatively small number of change-minded directors. There had been a history of dissatisfaction with the top governance, structure, operating systems, and culture of ICI, but for most of the 1970s there was not enough senior level dissatisfaction with the business performance of the company to warrant the massive personal and organisational disruption implied by the necessary changes.

As we have seen, there were individuals in senior positions dissatisfied with the status quo, but their energies were totally absorbed not only in their normal directorial responsibilities of handling the present-day demands of the system, but also in trying to mobilise dissatisfaction with some of the worst consequences of those structures and systems. While those individuals were absorbed raising doubts about current ways of doing things, their imprecise vision of a better kind of ICI often appeared too theoretical, too impractical, to their sceptics. It was an uneven persuasion process of new concepts and new theories of the future against the tried and sure methods of the present. In this struggle of new theory against old theory, the protagonists for change often found it difficult to articulate the first practical steps towards their concept of a better future for ICI. Stacked up against the imprecise vision of a better way of directing ICI, and what appeared to be unjustified and vague first-action steps, were the massive forces of inertia in the ICI structures, systems, and political processes.

In the absence for so long of a clear business rationale for change, and the political will that might have come from that rationale, what was undoubtedly crucial in the long-term process of creating change was the continuity in office and persistence of those executive directors pushing for change. The group for change which eventually emerged, recognised through experience which started for some with the failure of the 1973 board organisation committee, that they were engaged in a political and strategic process, and that consideration of the process of reaching their end point was as crucial if not more crucial than the practical specification of what that end was. It would be inaccurate to suggest that in the long process of trying to generate commitment for change, that those for change had a rationally conceived and articulate process plan to influence the relevant parts of the ICI governance system. In so far as any process plan existed, certainly in the mid-1970s that plan had fairly limited and pragmatic objectives, and the initial steps were not seen as part of a longer-term management process.

Discussing the series of attempts to create change in the 1970s, Ron Mercer acknowledged that one of the pieces of learning for him had been that:

> The strategy of building in – of finding the win – wins on the way to the ultimate win was not followed as clearly as it might have been. If one has a total strategic plan to get from here to there the first step was never treated as an end step. When it began to happen, it happened. The Pan-European meetings, the Heavy Chemicals Policy Group, those were some of the steps that began to say hey that moves it, and that moves it. It was only when they dealt with identifiable components of the problem and set up specific commitment getting mechanisms, and management, and transition management mechanisms that they moved. Those build on one another, and then you move to something else.

But if the momentum for change increased as the overall change problem was divided into politically manageable bits, and then progressed by setting up mechanisms such as the Heavy Chemicals Policy Group and the Heavy Chemicals Executive, which performed the duel function of legitimating change and connecting those changes into existing ICI structures and systems, the problem at the early stage of the change process was how to develop a concern or belief in top circles of ICI that something is not as it should be. Without doubt the internal OD resource Dudley, and the external consultant Mercer, had an important part to play in assisting Harvey-Jones to bring the bad news to the senior reaches of ICI and in so doing try and raise the level of dissatisfaction and concern with certain aspects of the status quo. Dudley's early paper "A Look at ICI in 1974", which was inadvertently sent to the ICI main board before it could be written in a more diplomatic fashion, although rejected as not ringing true with the conventional views of the time, did by chance speed up the process of getting a wider set of data about ICI's functioning to the main board.

The process of opening up ICI started by Dudley's paper, and Harvey-Jones's leadership, propelled Mercer out into the open with a diagnosis of ICI's problems that the Chairman of the day found very painful but insisted on sharing with his colleagues. The next chairman, Sir Rowland Wright encouraged a climate where information about ICI's structure, culture, and systems could more freely pass around the main board, and between the main board and the division chairmen. Encouraged by Harvey-Jones, Mercer, and Dudley he also set up a number of board working parties and the Chairman's Group Conference, both of which had the effect of moving the change process from the stage of development of concern that all was not well, to the beginnings of an acknowledgement and understanding of some of the particular problems of change.

However, the phase of concrete planning and acting to make changes happen, required changes in the personal composition of the main board that came in the late 1970s, the irrefutable pressure of a worsening business scene, and consistent, persistent, and more adroit and selective pressure from the change group on the main board. Given the track record, ability, and highly personalised and political atmosphere that surrounded the upper reaches of a company such as ICI, there is no doubt that personal views and individual position played their part in the change process. For those looking for change, new people were sought for their support, backing off was necessary when opposition from key people was strong. Opportunities created by retirals were seized to combine portfolios and use new linkages between parts of the system previously divided, to kick the ball into space and release options deadlocked by internal political pressures. Risks were taken in challenging existing norms, there was the necessary persistence of water dripping on stone, and then ultimately being prepared to mobilise support for action, and act, when the business crisis came.

Strategic change in ICI has occurred throughout much of its history in an episodic pattern. The periods of high levels of change activity have tended to occur around every decade, and are associated with the second low point of the 4.5-year business cycle. Thus there were concentrations of organisation and manpower changes involving the reshaping and relabelling of divisional boundaries during and immediately after the business downturns of 1961, 1971, and 1981. Metaphorically these were the revolutionary episodes which were followed by considerable periods of incremental adjustment. Given the different stage of development the chemical industry had reached by 1980, and the much more severe business and economic pressure of the early 1980s, ICI pulled five levers of change in 1980–81 compared with the more modest revolution of 1971. It is in the context of this episodic and environmentally driven change response, where in each case the formulation of the strategic changes was in the hands of a small group of very senior executives, that the role of OD resources and methods have to be understood.

The use of OD resources and methods to create strategic change in ICI has always been, and still is, a minority preoccupation on and just below the main board of ICI. It is abundantly clear that without Harvey-Jones and Woodburn's support and protection neither Dudley, Mercer, James, nor Bainton would have survived long enough to have any impact on senior reaches of the company. Those who sponsored OD at the highest levels are prepared to admit that their support was partially a question of individual belief, that OD's use in ICI "has been incredibly patchy, and in particular its use at the main board has been very inadequate".

> I think you've got to recognise that for any businessman to really espouse OD is in the first case an act of faith unless you have actually used it in a number of real life situations and found it helps you to solve problems which you would have been unable to solve by other more direct approaches.

Harvey-Jones acknowledged that he'd always had OD advice on the sort of change programmes he'd been trying to initiate through the board, "but these have always been from a subordinate position."

> The attitude of the Chairman of the time has varied from malevolence to good natured "well if he wants to play around with that sort of thing let him" ... Believing in it and wanting to use it is an individual thing. OD requires a particular style of boss. If you are unself-confident, a bit uptight, like to keep things to yourself, and you're leading something, you may still be an effective leader, but you'll never use OD.

One of the consequences of this highly personalised, patchy, and necessarily cautious sponsorship of OD methods and people at the top was that the in-house consultants Dudley and James always lacked credibility with the majority of the main board, and Harvey-Jones and Woodburn could only use them as consultants to them "on specific delegated tasks". There was never any question of either the internal or external consultants working openly or continuously on tasks given priority and substance by a critical mass of the main board. Even Mercer, who had the advantage of the external role and therefore was not part of the internal ICI career and political system, and yet had the credibility that came from a long period of association and testing inside ICI, tended to work on an individual-to-individual basis with members of the main board. Perhaps it would have been impossible to work on a group basis with a set of very senior people on predetermined and prioritised tasks, if they themselves were not yet working on a team basis to produce a clearly articulated framework of purpose and policy.

But if the OD resources were not tied into a set of tasks derived from a pattern of development decided by the main board, why did they survive throughout the 1970s and early 1980s, and what sort of impact on company policy, structure, systems, and behaviour did they have?

Stewart Dudley retired from ICI in November 1982, at for ICI the comparatively advanced age of 57. Tom James did likewise in June 1983. They are quite different personalities and survived in a developmental role in ICI for such a long period for different reasons. One crucial thing about their background which did influence their fate in the ICI system, where they had an advantage over so many of the others who went into an OD role in the company, was that they had both acquired some status in the ICI system prior to taking on developmental work. Dudley had been a works manager in Mond Division, and James had been head of a large management services department in HOC/ Petrochemicals Division. As we have seen, Dudley was able to use his credibility as an ex works manager both to help set up the works management training programmes which helped to rescue MUPS/WSA, and to link with works-based clients in the low point for OD work after the implementation of WSA and SDP. James meanwhile was early on in ICI able to graft OD skills and knowledge onto the more structured problem-solving skills and reputation he had acquired from working in work study and management services. James also had the advantage of a good working relationship with John Harvey-Jones.

Asked how and why Dudley and Mercer had survived Harvey-Jones replied:

> Bluntly I suppose they have had protectors . . . I suppose I would be a protector of both of them. But I haven't had to actually intervene and say "keep your filthy mits off" . . . But you can't really tell if protection is overtly necessary because in a company like ICI the fact that somebody at the top who is perceived to have some power is known to be in favour with somebody is in fact protection.

As we have seen, Dudley survived the post-WSA/SDP period to become "Dean of Faculty" of the ICI OD network, partly because of his well-recognised knowledge, skill, and experience in using OD concepts and techniques, partly because he distanced himself from George Bridge and the more traditional members of the central personnel department, and ultimately because he was the last and most senior central OD resource. To have removed Dudley would have taken out the focal point for internal OD work in the company. This would publicly have said to the rest of ICI, OD as a body of knowledge and skills is no longer relevant to ICI. Given that Mercer, Dudley, and James were fast trying to move the image of OD away from its more clinical and behavioural extreme to connect more with issues of strategy, business, and organisation, no-one in ICI was able that decisively in the mid-1970s to pull the carpet away from OD.

Dudley's strategy of organising OD on a company-wide basis as an "informal network based on competence", avoided any connotation that he was in any sense managing a function which would require publicly stated objectives and accountabilities. Without the need to articulate certain strategies or tasks as priority areas for OD work, Dudley retained control of the development of OD in the company in a way that gave him maximum room for personal freedom to grasp opportunities as and when they presented themselves. Some of his superiors and peers eventually were to criticise Dudley for what they would describe as the "laissez-faire", "expediency", and "opportunistic" manner in which he interpreted his central role. When by 1980 the topic of Dudley's successor was being openly discussed in ICI in the context of massive internal change, a widely held view was that:

Dudley's successor should manage, not co-ordinate, actually manage the creation of appropriate levels of new OD resources in the company, and manage the interface between the needs of board members for OD support on the one hand, and the supply of these services from the inside or the outside of the company on the other.

Someone was actually appointed in 1980 as Dudley's successor but he retired after about a year because of ill-health. When Dudley himself retired at the end of 1982, he was replaced by the former personnel director and director of change of Mond Division, Nicholas Mann – of which more later.

Earlier in this chapter it was argued that while Mercer's professionalism and skill earned him the unique access he had to individuals on the ICI main board covering the period of four Chairmen, a factor in both his and Dudley's survival was their mutual dependence on one another. Dudley needed Mercer to keep OD methods and ideas alive on the main board, and to counsel and support the change group on the board, and Mercer needed Dudley to manage his continuing access into the diaries of the top group of executives in ICI.

In terms of activities Mercer was capable of being an individual counsellor, an information transmitter, a problem diagnostician, an advisor on the process planning of key meetings and change interventions, a process observer of meetings, a provider of expert inputs from the academic world, and anonymously from other large firms, and a high level trainer. He explicitly saw himself as an outside, and clearly trusted doctor, in a doctor–patient relationship where help could be provided under the controlled and safe conditions of a role-to-role, rather than a person-to-person, relationship. His approach was:

> A low key kind of consulting, not very flashy, so it's not very painful to the client . . . my style is to honour or support what and where people are, and to watch out for getting sucked into distortions. I'm in the perspective business. If I went in and passed on all the terrible things going on in the universe I would be out of business. I am constantly trying to empower people, use my influence, brains, outsideness to help them to work towards using their own potential, and to unblock where that's not happening.

Another central tenet of Mercer's approach was to keep his level of visibility in the ICI system low:

> In this kind of consulting there's an inverse relationship between the effectiveness of an intervention and who knows about it. So if your needs for money, rewards, fame grow out of feedback about your performance, or grow out of visibility, you better get the hell out of this racket.

Mercer's approach in relating to the top people in ICI was very much on an individual-to-individual basis. He refused to attend board meetings,[4] arguing

---

[4] Mercer may not have been invited to attend the full meetings of the ICI main board. He has attended various meetings of the executive team which is a group including the Chairman and executive directors.

"that the degree to which the consultant provides value-added is overshadowed significantly by the over-potency of the consultant at the meeting". A close observer of Mercer's consulting style noted that only Mercer and Dudley had a copy of Mercer's programme of contacts on his visits to ICI so that "no-one else could see who Mercer was seeing and get at them beforehand". Mercer's approach to the executive directors closely mirrored the one-to-one style they preferred for relating to one another. As one of the executive directors put it:

> Ron helps by dropping round and cross-pollinating, doing good by stealth.

While individual executive directors remarked "that without Ron Mercer ICI wouldn't have got interested in OD at all", there was the same sense of questioning about Mercer as about Dudley – with all that skill could their contribution not have been tied down and managed more? Could Mercer not have related to the ICI main board, not through a set of individual relationships, and doing good by stealth, but through a set of agreed business-related tasks?

> Now if you're going to employ a resource like Mercer, I would like to have hoped that the Chairman would say to him "look Ron, this is where I am trying to move the board, this is where I see my problems". Now what do you think you can do to help this? And at a minimum you ought to use him as a sounding board – "Hey, we're a bit worried here" – it's not sort of pulled together. Nobody pulls all that lot together and says "right what comes out of all that?"

Asked what learning about the organisation and use of OD resources Mercer had taken from his ICI experience he commented along lines very similar to the above executive director:

> If I was starting over I would build a network of three or four outside consultants, managed from the inside and I would require linkage between inside and outside consultants. I would have periodic, at least twice a year, meetings of the system sharing experiences, developing strategies. I would manage the process quite differently, and have recommended they manage the process quite differently than the laissez-faire motive and the expediency motive . . . It wouldn't therefore just be creating an OD network for technical and clinical stuff, but around OD strategy and its relation to the business.

If the above points about personal background and experience, bases of credibility, personal working style, and strategy and organisation for doing OD work, indicate some of the reasons why Dudley, James, and Mercer were able to survive and continue to work at senior levels in ICI when as far as the main board was concerned between them they never had more than two or three active political sponsors; what can be said about the impact of OD methods and resources in the period 1973–82?

One way of thinking about the development of an organisation over time is to regard change as a natural process combining elements of external pressure and internal management action. In this process four stages may be discernible.[5]

[5] This four-stage process has been developed by Steward Dudley.

They are:

1. *The development of concern* by a subset of people in the organisation that, possibly as a result of environmental change, the present stage of the organisation no longer is compatible with its operating environment.
2. *The acknowledgement and understanding of the problem* the organisation now faces, including an analysis of the causes of the difficulties, and alternative ways of tackling those difficulties.
3. *Planning and acting* to create specific changes in the light of the above diagnostic and objective-setting work.
4. *Stabilising the changes* made by detailed and careful implementation plans which include how the organisation's reward, information, and power systems reinforce the intended direction of change.

Thinking back to the pattern of events described earlier in this chapter, it is clear that for much of the 1970s those that were pushing for change in ICI essentially were locked into a process which encapsulated the first and second of the above two stages.[6] For reasons already described, the planning and action stage had to wait until the business crisis of 1980–82, and the stabilisation process will stretch on into the mid and late 1980s. No doubt the stabilisation processes necessary to absorb the changes of 1980–82 will themselves be overtaken by further environmental change, and if the cultural changes intended in the early 1980s revolution work – more assertive and entrepreneurial management action.

In assessing the impact, if any, of OD methods and resources in the above long-term process of change two overriding points should be made. Firstly, as we have seen, Harvey-Jones was and is the biggest single intervention in ICI in the OD field. Secondly, aside from questions of impact, what is unique about the ICI experience of OD in the United Kingdom is that internal and external OD resources have been involved at all in processes of strategic change where the targets for change have included the role, size, and mode of operation of the main board, the senior operating structures and systems of the ICI group, the relationships between the main board and the chief executives of operating units, the merging of divisional organisations, and the attempt to change the management culture of senior levels of the company.

On the question of impact, in broad terms specialist OD resources have been involved in stages 1, 2 and 4 of the above processes, but have been largely excluded from the planning and acting stage. Throughout most of the 1970s the role that Dudley, Mercer, and James played was to help Harvey-Jones and others to raise the level of concern and dissatisfaction with the status quo in ICI, and to help create flows of information, meetings, organisation mechanisms, and processes whereby a critical mass of senior people in ICI then began to acknowledge that questions of organisation, systems, and management

[6] In Chapter 11, page 473, an initial stage of problem sensing is added to the above four-stage process. It is clear that those pushing for change in ICI were much concerned with signalling and legitimating certain problems as worthy of top-level discussion and decision.

culture and processes were legitimately connectable to issues of business environment, strategy, and business survival. Dudley's paper "A Look at ICI in 1974", Mercer's "bad news" meeting in 1974 with the outgoing chairman Sir Jack Callard, Mercer's access to the main board, and Sir Rowland Wright's decision to pick up the bad news and set up sensing meetings to draw on views throughout the company can all be seen as part of the development of concern stage. The work done in the mid-1970s to draw the division chairmen together as a more effective advisory group to the main board, the creation of the important mechanism of the Chairman's Group Conference which altered the character of head office – field relationships both continued the process of opening ICI up to the possibility of further changes. The process planning work which went into the board task forces on organisation of the period 1976–77, the process support work on the Pan-European changes of 1978, and the important climate-building and skill-development objectives of the management of change workshops all contributed to the acknowledgement and understanding stage.

However, looking back over this period one is struck by the slowness, the meanderings, the massive inefficiency of this process of change. One of the consultants commented:

> The most frustrating experience has been the amount of time and energy it has taken over many years to get the board to function anything like optimally in its decision-making. Another has been the inability of the board to change almost anything – the slowness of things. Another one has been the lack of capacity of Millbank to act as an entity, to make it as active as a division, to try and clean it up.

Only the business crisis of 1980 was able to short-circuit this meandering and often deadlocked process. When action was finally deemed necessary the working up of the plans and the action itself were in the hands of a small group of very senior executives. Depending which group of senior executives were involved in which change would condition whether OD methods were deemed relevant or not. Discussing the formulation stage of the Petrochemicals and Plastics Division merger, Harvey-Jones said:

> On the Petrochemicals and Plastics thing we've been working on it for over a year with a group of three division chairmen and three main board directors. I would say we've done that entirely on an OD basis but we have not in fact used an OD resource . . . I do believe I'm capable of organising a process plan for myself now.

Asked what his view of an "OD basis" was, Harvey-Jones replied:

> By an OD way I mean we had meeting after meeting outside this building with flip charts, letting it all hang out, hacking about how was the best way of organising it, and what we were trying to achieve, until we got a real head of steam and commitment amongst the six of us, even though the three division chairmen knew that inevitably at least one of them, perhaps two, wouldn't make it.

The above change episode reveals two features about the impact of OD methods by 1980. One is, of course, the fact of some degree of institutionalisation of OD problem-solving processes on the main board of ICI. Unfortunately, even by 1983 that institutionalisation is probably still only confined to Harvey-Jones and Woodburn, the two executive directors of the 1970s who had already been converted to such methods. The bulk of the main board as individuals still remain neutral, to sceptical, to opposed to what are often described as "time-consuming" or "long-haired" processes. The problem still remains for OD that its diffusion is still highly dependent on a patchily spread cast of individuals.

The Petrochemicals and Plastics merger also illustrates the more general point that when it came to the crunch the planning and action about strategic change was perhaps inevitably a senior executive-conceived and designed activity, with the task of stabilising such changes left amongst others to the specialist OD resources. As one internal OD resource commented with some feeling:

> OD has been more involved in picking up the pieces after the revolution, and not in the shock troops for forming the strategy of change. The personnel department deals with the human driftwood, and the OD people get involved in training others to accommodate to the new situation, to understand what's been done to you – you have no part in formulating what's being done.

This feeling that OD could only be used, had only been used to try and influence the climate for strategic change, and then to assist processes of accommodation and stabilisation after the change, led one external consultant to conclude "that efforts in OD are basically cosmetic, health maintaining and not health inducing". One of his internal OD consultant colleagues had a similar way of reviewing the limited cultural impact of OD at the highest levels in ICI when he concluded:

> I think in circumstances which are not panic circumstances we have marginally improved our ability to relax, and think more effectively about problems. But in panic situations, about panic situations, we've probably learnt nothing.

Continuity or change?

Stewart Dudley retired from ICI on 30 November 1982; he was followed 6 months later by Tom James. Ron Mercer is creeping towards his mid-60s and the question of any successor to him is being asked in terms of what are ICI's continuing needs at the highest levels for external consultancy help on matters of strategy, organisation, and change?

Nicholas Mann, supported by his successes in Mond Division, but suspecting that his job wouldn't exist and he woudln't have been in it had Harvey-Jones not been ICI Chairman, is now faced with the task of creating a role and a power base for himself as the central OD resource for the ICI group. Given the rate of change in ICI in 1983, there is no shortage of work to do in implementing and stabilising present changes, never mind thinking of organisation and employee development for the rest of the 1980s. At present Mann has taken on the operational management role as project manager of the move from Millbank to the new, but as yet undefined, London headquarters. This managerial task is clearly bringing him into regular contact with senior people on a matter of signal importance to the ICI group. His stance is already different from his predecessors, but these are early days yet. Given the history, will he find there is a job for him to do, and will he be able to fashion the circumstances to allow himself to do it? Certainly the lessons of ICI's history indicate it will be a number of years before the impact of this new role could become apparent in the ICI group.

11 Processes of Strategic Change: Some Patterns

The research reported in this book has afforded an unusual opportunity to descriptively examine, in a comparative mode, long-term processes of continuity and changing. The time has come now to reveal some of the patterns in these descriptive accounts of changing, first of all in this chapter by focussing on five of the reported cases of strategic organisational change, and then in Chapter 12 by comparing and contrasting the different pathways of development, impact, and fate of specialist OD resources in the four largest divisions and the corporate headquarters of ICI.

The initial purpose of this chapter is to move away from the empirical detail of the ICI cases of change, to summarise elements of the literature on strategic change, and thus to clarify the conceptual starting point for identifying some of the patterns in the processes of strategic change in ICI.

Following the approach taken by Pettigrew (1977) and Mintzberg (1978) strategic changes are viewed as streams of activity involving at various times the differential attention of individuals and groups, which occur mainly but not solely as a consequence of environmental change, and which can lead to alterations in the product market focus, structure, technology, and culture of the host organisation. Strategic is just a description of magnitude of change in, for example, structure and organisational culture, recognising the second-order effects, or multiple consequences of any such changes.

Although single strategic decisions have been referred to in the previous case study chapters, and it is recognised that changes of note can follow from any one strategic decision, it should be clear that the analytical approach favoured in this research has not been to treat the single decision as the unit of analysis. Strategic decision-making and change are here regarded as continuous processes. Understanding strategic changes as continuous processes, with no clear beginning or end, allows for the analysis of both discrete and identifiable decision events, the pathways to and outcomes of those events – what may be called the front stage of decision-making; and indeed the back stage of decision-making, the processes by which novel ideas for change gain currency and legitimacy in the organisation, or are otherwise suppressed and immobilised and never reach a form where they can be openly debated, decided, and acted upon.

Strategic change processes are best understood in context. Drawing on Mintzberg's (1978) useful distinction between intended and realised strategy, strategy is operationally taken to mean that which is realised in practice through consistency in a stream of actions and decisions over time. Part of the context is the location of strategy in time. Yesterday's strategies will provide some of the pathways to and inputs for today's strategies; and today's strategies will have a concept of the future built into them. The consequences of the implementation of today's strategies will provide part of the context for tomorrow's strategies. But time is but a segment of the context. Context also includes the social, economic, political, and business environment of the firm and changes thereof, and various features of the internal context of the firm, the structures and systems, leadership arrangements and processes, the culture or cultures of the organisation, and the systems and dynamics of control and power in the organisation, all of which mediate what is seen and acted upon in the way of environmental change. As we have seen, the genesis of strategic change is often to be found in the advocacy by a small number of people of a performance gap arising from some perception of an incipient or actual environmental change and the internal structure and organisational culture of the firm. But differential perception by various parties inside the organisation of a changing context which is only being partially understood and acted upon can provide not only the tensions and enabling conditions for new strategies to evolve, but also the dynamic conservatism (Schon, 1971) to sustain in place the existing definitions of what the organisation's core issues are, and how they are to be continued to be tackled through customary views of strategic content and process. Therefore the real problem of strategic change is anchoring new concepts of reality, new issues for attention, new ideas for debate and resolution, and mobilising concern, energy, and enthusiasm often in an additive and evolutionary fashion to ensure these early illegitimate thoughts gain powerful support and eventually result in contextually appropriate action.

The starting point for this analysis of strategic change is the notion that formulating the content of any new strategy inevitably entails managing its context and process. Thus theoretically sound and practically useful research on strategic change should involve the continuous interplay between ideas about the context of change, the process of change, and the content of change, together with skill in regulating the relations between the three. Posed in this way the development of strategic change in the firm is seen as a long-term conditioning and influence process designed to establish the dominating legitimacy of a different pattern of relation between strategic content, context, and process. However, in examining a large enterprise such as ICI over a 20-plus year period continuity is a good deal easier to see than change. What is apparent is the continuity of existing dominating ideas in the firm, of existing frameworks of thought with their associated structures, systems and power relations all being used to interpret changes in external and internal context and continue the existing patterns of thought and action about strategy. Such continuity of strategic content is a function, as Huff (1982) has suggested, of the dominating frames of thought which develop as firms experience and appreciate the business and economic conditions of certain industry sectors. The continuity may also be interpreted as Selznick (1957), Child (1972), Normann (1977), Miles (1982), and Boswell (1983) have indicated, as a product of the values and assumptions of the powerful groups who control firms over an era, and in consequence of the deep-seated political and cultural roots of strategy.

But the ICI data also reveal periodic patterns of challenge, and eventually change, from the existing order of things. Of insubordinate minorities, often in very senior line positions sensing environmental change and organisational inertia, developing a widening caucus of concern around new problem areas for the firm, using cognitive and analytical skill to fashion new rationalities and ideas to compete in the strategy formulation process, and seizing on the opportunities provided by environmental change to put together new marriages of strategic content and context. The rise of these new rationalities and strategic frames may be seen as long courtships, in which novel and opportunistic processes are used to find mutuality between strategic content and context; in which instant marriages occur between strategic content, context, and process as contexts rapidly change, and existing solutions now acquire legitimacy for newly acknowledged problems in the new context. As we shall see, critical to the success of these long processes of courtship between strategic content and context are the interest, attention, and persistence of the would-be innovators and their supporters. Once established, the new marriages between strategic content and context often lead to rapid changes initially in organisational structure, people, and systems, followed by greater clarity in strategic articulation and direction, long periods of stabilisation and adjustment as the structural, systems and possibly cultural messages of the revolution are implemented and then more widely understood, and then another slow dissolution of the existing marriage between content, context, and process as circumstances and contexts, people, problems and available solutions change, and new courtships begin. In this way patterns of strategic change at the level of the firm may be understood in terms of long periods of continuity, learning, and incremental adjustment interspersed with hiatuses or revolutions featuring abnormally high levels of change activity.

In the review in Chaper 1 of the literature on strategic change and organisational change and development, attention was drawn to the various currently available process theories of choice and change. Necessarily brief reflections were offered on process theories using the language of rationality, bounded rationality, garbage can, incrementalism, and politics. Some attempt was made to highlight the analytical power of each of these approaches as separate spectacles looking at the same organism, but overlaps between these process theories were identified, and space was taken to indicate how so-called political and cultural analyses of process may be profitably combined and refined. Without rehearsing the arguments of Chapter 1 comprehensively here, it is important in further setting the scene for identifying some of the patterns in the ICI data on strategic change to remind the reader of some of the key findings and conclusions about process approaches to choice and change made earlier in this book.

During the 1970s progress has been made by authors such as Bower (1970), Allison (1971), Pettigrew (1973), March and Olsen (1976), Mintzberg (1978), and Quinn (1980) to rescue the linked literature on strategic decision-making and change from its prevailing concern with rational analytical schemes of intentional process and outcome, and to begin to see strategic decision-making and change in a variety of process modes. The kinds of process theories of choice and change proposed by the above authors in the main tend to use the rational deductive view of problem-solving propounded by the neoclassical theory of the firm, and its equivalents in the strategy literature (Andrews, 1971; King and Cleland, 1978), as a whipping boy. As applied to the formulation of strategy the rational approach describes and prescribes techniques for identifying current strategy, analysing environments, resources and gaps, revealing and assessing strategic alternatives, and choosing and implementing carefully analysed and well-thought-through outcomes. Depending on the author, explicitly or implicitly, the firm speaks with a unitary voice, can be composed of omnipotent, even heroic general managers or chief executives, looking at known and consistent preferences and assessing them with voluminous and presumably apposite information, which can be organised into clear input–output relationships. Thus the early preoccupation in the strategy literature (Ansoff,[1] 1965; Andrews, 1971) with the analytical content of strategy, with limited views of context, an avowedly rational picture of business problem-solving, and no developed theory of strategic change essentially takes as given what the incremental, political, and garbage can views of process seek to explain. Igor Ansoff's more recent writing (1979) is much more sensitive to political and cultural views of strategic change.

In the strategy literature we have the empirical studies, in particular of Bower (1970), Mintzberg *et al.* (1976, 1978), and Quinn (1980) to thank for challenging the rational–analytical views of strategy formulation and change. Now strategy was to be treated not as an output but as a process. With the counterbalance of the above empirical process studies, strategy formulation was now accepted as a multi-level organisational activity, and not just the province of a few, or even a single general manager. Outcomes of decisions were not just a product of rational or boundedly rational debates, but were also shaped by the interests and commitments of individuals and groups, the forces of bureaucratic momentum, gross changes in the environment, and the manipulation of the structural context around decisions. With the view that strategy development was a continuous process, strategies could now be thought of as reconstructions after the fact, rather than just rationally intended plans. The linear view of process explicit in "strategy formulation is followed by strategy implementation" was questioned, and with increasing interest in enduring characteristics of structural and strategic context (Bower, 1970; Burgelman, 1983), Chandler's (1962) dictum that structure followed strategy was modified by evidence indicating why and how strategy change could follow structural change (Galbraith and Nathanson, 1978).

However, the empirical study of strategic change with the greatest overlap from an interpretative and empirical view with this study of ICI is Quinn's (1980) book, and its derivative (Quinn, 1982), suggesting that strategic change can be understood as a process displaying patterns of logical incrementalism. Quinn (1980:56) conceives strategic change as a joint analytical and political process in which executives are described as, and recommended, "to proceed flexibly and experimentally from broad concepts to specific commitments, making the latter concrete as late as possible. Strategic change is thus seen to emerge as a cautious, step-by-step evolutionary process, where executives muddle through with a purpose." While recognising that the empirical variant of incrementalism which he describes can include some element of formal analysis, Quinn (1982) is clear that large firms do not make strategic changes through the rational–analytic schemes often described in the literature on corporate planning.

It is indeed Quinn's recognition of the process, as well as the cognitive limits on the management of strategic change, where his writing is particularly valuable descriptively and prescriptively. These process limits, the concern with the timing and sequencing of action and events in order to build awareness, comfort levels, and consensus for strategic change are easily recognisable in the cases of strategic change reported in this book. But if the continuous, evolving, political, consensus-building view of the process of strategic change espoused by Quinn (1980, 1982) fits well with elements of these data on ICI, the corollary of that view of process, that strategies emerge in a continuous incremental and thereby additive fashion, is contradicted both by Mintzberg's (1978) findings that strategic changes occur in spurts, each followed by a period of continuity, by Boswell's (1983) useful empirical observations on phases of policy concentration in three steel companies, and as we shall shortly further emphasise, the periods of revolutionary strategic change in ICI interspersed with eras of learning and incremental adjustment.

Of the various process theories of choice and change mentioned in Chapter 1, the one developed the fullest, and seen to have the greatest potential value in explaining continuity and strategic change, is the one which combines a political and cultural analysis of organisational life (Pettigrew, 1973, 1977, 1979; Pfeffer, 1981; Peters and Waterman, 1982). The interest in culture directs attention to sources of coherence and consistency in organisational life, to the dominating ideas or ideologies which provide the systems of meaning and interpretation which filter in and filter out environmental and intra-organisational signals. The recognition that organisational culture can shape and not merely reflect organisational power relationships directs attention both to the ground rules which structure the character of the political process inside the firm, and the assumptions and interests which powerful groups shield and lesser groups may only with fortitude challenge. The acts and processes associated with politics as the management of meaning represent conceptually the overlap between a concern with the political and cultural analyses of organisations. A central concept linking political and cultural analyses particularly germane to the understanding of continuity and change is legitimacy. The management of meaning refers to a process of symbol construction and value use designed to create legitimacy for one's ideas, actions, and demands, and to delegitimise the demands of one's opponents. Key concepts for analysing these processes of legitimisation and delegitimisation are symbolism, language, ideology, and myth (Pettigrew, 1976, 1979).

As Hardy (1983) and Astley and Rosen (1983) indicate, the important feature of this cultural treatment of organisational politics is that it helps to provide a framework to examine not just front-stage decision-making and power, but also back-stage decision-making and therefore control. The front-stage view of decision-making and power closely resembles Lukes's (1974) one-dimensional and two-dimensional views of power, while the interest in deeper processes of control conforms to Lukes's third dimension of power. As Hardy (1983) has succinctly put it, a concern with both power and control as explanations of strategic choice and change processes, would in effect correspond to two uses of power. Power used to defeat competition in a choice or change process, and power used to prevent competition in a choice or change process. In both of these processes there would be an explanatory role for unobtrusive systems of power derived from the generation and manipulation of symbols, language, belief and ideology – from culture creation; and from the more public face of power expressed through the possession, control, and tactical use of overt sources of power such as position, rewards or sanctions, or expertise.

There are two further essential points to derive from the above way of thinking about process. The first is that structures, cultures, and strategies are not just being treated here as neutral, functional constructs connectable to some system need such as efficiency or adaptability; those constructs are viewed as capable of serving to protect the interest of dominant groups. This means that not only can the existing bias of the structures and cultures of an organisation in general terms protect dominant groups by reducing the chances of challenge, but features of intra-organisational context and socioeconomic context can be mobilised by dominant or aspiring groups in order to legitimise existing definitions of the core strategic conerns, to help justify new priorities, and to delegitimise other novel and threatening definitions of the organisation's situation. These points are as pertinent to understanding processes of choice and change as they are to achieving practical outcomes in strategic change. As Normann (1977:161) has so aptly put it "the only way to bring about lasting change and to foster an ability to deal with new situations is by influencing the conditions that determine the interpretation of situations and the regulation of ideas".

The above political and cultural view of process gives a central place to the processes through which strategies and changes are legitimised and delegitimised. The content of strategic change is thus ultimately a product of a legitimisation process shaped by political/cultural considerations, though often expressed in rational/analytical terms. This recognition that intervening in an organisation to create strategic change is likely to be a challenge to the dominating ideology, culture, and systems of meaning and interpretation, as well as the structures, priorities, and power relationships of the organisation, makes it clearer why and how the processes of sensing, justifying, creating, and stabilising strategic change can be so tortuous and long.

The preceding discussion of some of the currently available theories of choice and change will have alerted the reader to the virtues of trying to understand strategic change in terms of patterns of revolution and evolution, of long processes of logical incrementalism, and of the role that organisational culture and politics in the firm can play in creating the conditions for and dynamics of continuity and change. Before launching into a closer examination of some of the patterns in the five ICI cases of strategic change, the recognition of the potential value of the revolution–evolution, incremental, and politi-cal–cultural approaches to the process analysis of change reaffirms one of the other starting points of this book. Beware of the singular theory of process, or indeed of social and organisational change. Look for continuity and change, patterns and idiosyncrasies, the actions of individuals and groups at various organisational levels, and processes of structuring. Give history and social processes the chance to reveal their untidiness. To understand strategic change, examine the juxtaposition of the rational/analytical and the political, the quest for efficiency, growth, power and business survival, the role of exceptional men and of extreme circumstances, the vicariousness of chance, the enabling and constraining forces of the environment, the way organisational culture shapes people's interpretations of environmental forces, and explore some of the conditions in which mixtures of these occur.

With the scene now partially set, the remainder of this chapter is divided into three sections. The first section takes a broad look at the overall pattern of continuity and change in ICI over the period from the late 1950s until 1983, and assesses the evidence for so-called revolutionary and incremental periods of organisation development. This is followed by a section which picks up and examines the similarities and differences between the processes of creating strategic change in five different parts of ICI. These are the corporate strategic change process over the period 1972–83, the changes in the governance, structure, manpower, and culture of Mond Division in the period 1973–83, the period of social innovation in Agricultural Division whilst George Bridge was personnel director between 1962 and 1967, and the changes in the top structure of Petrochemicals Division made between 1970 and 1973. From the perspective of 1983 the first two of the above cases show clear evidence of strategic change after long periods of persistent though at times unfocussed advocacy. The Agricultural Division and Petrochemicals Division cases with the benefit of greater historical perspective show to varying degrees evidence of change and then regression from change after key individuals had been removed from those divisions, and the fifth case, Plastics Division between 1969 and 1979, demonstrates the absence of strategic change. The final section of the chapter, managerial activities in strategic change, distills some of the practical messages about the management of strategic change evident from the ICI experience.

THE OVERALL PATTERN OF CHANGE: REVOLUTION AND INCREMENTAL ADJUSTMENT

One of the many analytical difficulties of trying to understand processes of social and organisation change is the problem of over-availability of metaphors and images associated with the various theories of change. The choice varies on a spectrum between evolution and development, life cycle and phase, continuity and flow, contradiction, revolution, intrusion, and crisis, with the problem of choice exacerbated by the implicit world view and model of man contained in these various sub-theories and metaphors.

An advantage of the otherwise factious and complicated situation in sociological theory where structural functionalists, neo-evolutionists, symbolic interactionists, power and conflict theorists, and Marxist and Neo-Marxist all propound different theories of societal change, is that the debates which have ensued have teased out into the open some of the implicit analytical assumptions and ideological posturing contained in those approaches, see Nisbet (1969) and Eisenstadt (1978) for critical reviews of the alternative theories of social change. In organisation theory, however, even with the appearance of useful books such as Burrell and Morgan (1979), interest in theorising about organisational change and the implicit assumptions of those theories is a good deal more rudimentary, and biological metaphors such as life cycle are used in a largely uncritical fashion (Kimberly and Miles, 1980).

In the literature on the evolutionary development of the firm, (Chandler, 1962; Wrigley, 1970; Scott, 1973; and Greiner, 1972) there has been a tendency to present normative and historically consistent views of corporate development stages. Thus depending on the author three or four growth steps are postulated, each with its own strategy and structure. If there is natural scepticism about the analytical value of seeing the firm move naturally and inevitably through a set of stages, what is the view of the process of moving from stage to stage in those evolutionary models? Leontiades (1980) collects together the Chandlerian and Greiner models of corporate development and labels their view of process as providing a metamorphosis view of change. Evolutionary movement occurs from stage to stage but not through a continuous process, but a series of interrupted stages. The trigger or triggers necessary to move the firm from one stage to another come from environmental disturbances of sufficient magnitude and impact that the firm must now react and change its strategy and structure to cope with the new set of pressing circumstances.

As I have implied, there are a number of problems with this attempt to explain organisational change. One has to be doubtful about the simple determinism of stages, about implied notions of progressive linear development to higher levels of growth or greater "maturity" and the reification explicit in statements about the firm behaving, rather than individuals or groups producing an effect which could be labelled as the firm behaving. However a potentially valuable feature of such metamorphosis models of change is the explanatory role played by environmental disturbance in creating change.

Recent theoretical and empirical work on strategic change by Mintzberg (1978), Mintzberg and Waters (1982), Miller and Friesen (1980), and Miller (1982), has extended this thinking about environmental disturbances to produce some interesting ideas and empirical evidence about identifiable revolutionary and evolutionary periods as firms change. Using retrospective analyses of the step-wise escalation of the Vietnam War and patterns of strategic change in Volkswagen, Mintzberg (1978) is able to identify two key patterns. One was the tendency of a strategy to have a life cycle from conception to decay and death, and secondly a tendency for strategies to change not in a continuous incremental fashion but rather for change – even incremental change – "to take place in spurts, each followed by a period of continuity" (Mintzberg, 1978:943). Miller (1982) distinguishes between quantum, revolutionary, and evolutionary changes. Quantum changes occur when many elements of the organisation change is a major or minor way within a brief interval. Revolutionary changes imply quantum changes "radically transforming many elements of structure, while change is incremental or evolutionary when it is piecemeal and gradual, i.e. when only a few elements change either in a minor or a major way" (Miller, 1982:133). Using Kuhn's (1970) idea of scientific development, Miller (1982) then goes on to argue that organisations have tradition-bound periods punctuated by non-cumulative revolutionary breaks. Organisational changes, it is argued, tend to come in packages. In fact Miller and Friesen (1982) also contend from their data that high-performing firms are more likely to make quick, decisive, and dramatic changes rather than rely on slow incremental adjustments which leave the organisation from a strategy and a structure point of view in a continuing state of disharmony with their business environment.

The Mintzberg (1978), Miller (1982) and Miller and Friesen (1982) work usefully identify both the ebb and flow of individual strategic concentrations in the firm and also the existence of periods of revolutionary and evolutionary change; what these authors do less precisely is to develop a process theory which links together the periods of high levels of change activity and low levels of change activity and thus begins to explain the timing and relative intensity of those periods. An approach, again relying at least partially on a crisis theory of change which does have more to say about precrisis, crisis, and stabilisation, and thus the linkages between revolutionary and evolutionary periods is that offered by Jonsson and Lundin (1977), Starbuck, Greve and Hedberg (1978), and Brunsson (1982). By introducing more explicitly into their analysis the importance of organisation ideologies and standard operating procedures both as inhibitors and, in the case of changing ideologies, precipitors of change, these authors offer a more satisfactory way of explaining revolutions and evolutions, and the links between high levels of change activity and lower levels of change activity in organisations. Brunsson (1982) in an elegantly written paper argues that organisations periodically jump from one predominant ideology to another, and that radical changes have to be preceded by and initiated by ideological shifts. To the question, but how are ideologies changed, Brunsson (1982) answers: as a result of a combination of externally driven crises, shifts in leadership, and the properties of ideologies themselves. The most stable ideologies are those which are vague and widely applicable, sharper more definite and particular ideologies are easier to question and eventually debunk in the face of a changing reality. Crucially Brunsson (1982) also argues that the periods when ideological shifts are in process, i.e. when the dominant ideology has not yet been debunked and when any aspiring new ideology still lacks a critical mass of support, are poor contexts for action. This is because ideological inconsistencies increase uncertainty and make it difficult to marshal the strong commitments and high levels of motivation and energy which are necessary to create radical organisational changes. Thus, he argues, an ideological shift has to be completed before radical action in the change sphere can begin.

As we shall see the overall pattern in the ICI data on strategic change indicates further confirmation both of the waxing and waning of particular strategies in the firm, and for changes to tend to occur in radical packages interspersed with longish periods of both absorbing the impact of revolutionary action, and then coming to terms with the fact that further changes are eventually necessary. Crucial to the timing of such radical actions are real and constructed crises (Pettigrew, 1983; In Press), changes in leadership and power, and the transformation of organisational ideologies.

An examination of the corporate development of ICI over the period from the late 1950s until 1984 reveals three periods of high levels of change activity. Two of these three periods, the ones between 1960 and 1964 and between 1980 and 1984, could be sensibly labelled as revolutionary periods in that they featured ideological, structural, and business strategy change, whilst the third period, between 1970 and 1972, was a period of substantial if lesser change when further structural change was made and elements of the ideological and business strategy changes made ten years earlier were accelerated or de-emphasised. The periods in between these packages of changes were occasions for implementing and stabilising changes, and most notably between 1973 and 1980, eras of organisational learning when ideological justification was prepared for the revolutionary break between 1980 and 1983.

Each of these periods of high levels of change activity were associated with world economic recessions, with their associated effects on world chemical

TABLE 31 ICI record of sales, profits, and ratio of trading profit to sales in peak and trough years, 1958–82 (£m)

	Sales	Profits	Ratio trading profit to sales
1958	463	51	11.0
1960	558	93	16.6
1961	550	65	11.8
1964	720	113	15.7
1966	885	99	11.2
1969	1355	190	14.0
1971	1524	130	8.5
1974	2955	461	15.6
1975	3129	325	10.4
1979	5368	634	11.8
1980	5715	332	5.8
1981	6581	425	6.4
1982	7358	366	5.0

production, markets, and prices and in turn on ICI's relative level of business performance. Table 31 shows the peaks and troughs in ICI's profits and ratio of trading profit to sales over the period 1958 to 1982.

Since 1958 there have been 5 years of peak profits followed by downturns of varying severity with each cycle lasting from 4 to 5 years. The improvement from trough to peak has been 82% (1958–60), 74% (1961–64), 92% (1966–69), 255% (1971–74), and 95% (1975–79). The period from 1980 to 1983 evidenced a step-wise change in macro-economic trends, a sustained recession, a dramatic downturn in ICI's profitability, and as we saw in Chapter 10 major structural, manpower, ideological, and business strategy change.

The two periods of revolutionary change between 1960 and 1964 and 1980 and 1984 were preceded by and further reaffirmed ideological shifts, were associated with, in the first occasion the 1958 and 1961 economic and business downturns and on the second occasion the 1980–83 recession. They were also occasions when new business leadership was supplied by men who had not spent their whole career in ICI. In 1960 Paul Chambers (later Sir Paul Chambers), a former senior civil servant and the first non-technical man for some years, was appointed Chairman. He began to emphasise financial and commerical management skills in a management culture heavily preoccupied with science and technology. And in November 1981 the announcement was made that an ex Naval intelligence officer, John Harvey-Jones, was to be Chairman of ICI. His ideological contribution is emerging as a lessening of bureaucracy and centralisation in ICI, sharper business accountabilities, and a greater emphasis on entrepreneurial skills and continuous change into the 1980s.

Both revolutionary change periods witnessed organisational structural and business strategy changes, with the structural changes occurring in a cumulative way over a relatively short period of time, and the business strategy changes emerging and being implemented rather more slowly after the ideological and structural changes had been justified, and then introduced.

Looking for a moment at the business and economic context of ICI prior to the 1960–64 changes, the situation was of a slow build-up of environmental changes. The world economies were picking themselves up after the Second World War, and aided by the productive stimulus of the Korean War and general rises in consumer expectations and expenditure, the UK economy was featured by full employment, minimal inflation, and for a time acceptable relative levels of economic growth. Although the world chemical industry was just about to enter its great period of growth and capital investment based on the rise of the organic chemical sector with relatively cheap oil feedstocks and burgeoning demand for plastics and artificial fibres, the end of the protective cartels and a lot of new entrants into the industry produced a more international, and a more competitive industry. However, as Roeber (1975:33) argues, the break-up of the old cartels did not change old attitudes in ICI. For a time the demand for ICI's products appeared to exceed their capacity to supply that demand. Sales control departments allocated product rather than sold it. In the absence of financial or market pressures those functions and skills had no reason to develop in ICI, and in an era of "profitless prosperity" there was little inducement in ICI to break new ground in technical, market, managerial, or labour productivity matters.

However, as a number of elements in the ICI business environment began to change together so the pressures became more tangible. New technical areas opened up in the industry. Some of the older strengths of the company were under threat because of technical obsolescence or declining industries which had provided traditional markets. Full employment, growing unionisation and changing attitudes in the workforce meant relatively high manning levels and made ICI's personnel policies begin to look less progressive and less effective.

The trigger for change in ICI came in 1958 when a US-led recession unmasked the general excess of demand over supply in organic chemicals. Faced with a substantial drop in home markets in 1958, the big US chemical firms began hunting for customers in Continental Western Europe and the UK. Chemicals were "dumped" in Europe, the overcapacity led to falling prices and reduced margins particularly in plastics and artificial fibres. When the events of 1958 were repeated in the economic recession of 1961 ICI had started to come to terms with more competitive and international markets, and their own relative competitive position, and began to act.

The first obvious changes were structural, with the objective in some cases to reduce fixed costs *per se*, in others to introduce more up-to-date technology which could allow structural and manning changes, and on other occasions to release faster-growing business areas from old divisional organisations in order to allow the newer areas greater attention and scope for growth. Thus in 1958 the creation of Heavy Organic Chemicals Ltd meant that Billingham Division lost its Heavy Organic Chemicals interests and one-third of its staff and two works. In 1960 Lime Division was absorbed into Alkali Division, and then in 1961 Alkali also acquired the old Salt Division. In 1963 much bigger business refocussing and cost savings became possible with the announcement that in 1964 Alkali and General Chemicals Divisions would merge and become a single operating unit called Mond Division. In 1961, with ICI continuing to hunt overhead in hard times, the Wilton Council was summarily abolished and the new HOC Division was reluctantly given the task of running the rapidly expanding Wilton manufacturing site. In addition, between 1958 and 1965 the number of weekly staff at Billingham declined substantially as a result of a change in feedstock from coal-coke to oil.

Parallel to and post the above structural changes came a number of changes in strategy which were manifestations of the new ideological concern in ICI with international competitiveness. In a situation of US intrusiveness in European markets, the creation of the EEC, falling chemical prices, reduced margins, and increases in wage and salary costs, ICI began to cohere around four strategic changes which it was hoped would improve their international competitive position. These changes were:

1. *Technological* – the emphasis in the capital programme changed in 1960 from expenditure designed to increase existing capacity by comparatively low cost

modifications to existing plant, to expenditure on the construction of new, larger, more efficient plant. With this change the size of capital authorisation and expenditure increased dramatically from expenditure levels of £32m in 1959, to £67m in 1963, and the peak for the 1960s of £197m in 1966. Much of this capital spending was designed to increase the relative size and importance of organic chemicals in ICI, not just in HOC Division but also in the downstream activites of Plastics and Fibres Divisions.

2. *Labour productivity* – stimulated by his return in 1960 to the ICI main board from presiding over Canadian Industries Ltd, ICI's new deputy chairman, P. C. Allen, encouraged a range of studies comparing ICI's labour productivity with their American and German competitors. The concern that eventually developed from these studies focussed the main board's attention on labour productivity, led to the main board approving the 1964 Rutherford Panel recommendations, and hence MUPS and WSA.

3. *Market Focus* – in 1960 ICI began the long and in 1984 still incomplete process of moving their sales and capital away from the old markets and manufacturing sites of the UK and the British Empire towards first of all Continental Western Europe, and then belatedly into the United States.

4. *Management culture and organisation* – although Sir Paul Chambers encouraged an era of technological expenditure in ICI which eventually led to the cash crisis of 1966, £110m of additional loan stock debt, and the rise of planning as a discipline in the company, his period in office is also associated with an attempt to sharpen the technologically predisposed management culture of ICI with market and financial considerations. This change process was symbolised in 1962 by the organisation studies carried out by the main board organisation committee and the McKinsey consultancy firm, and by the decisions taken with various degrees of earnestness in 1964 to implement product/functional matrix organisations in several of the ICI divisions in place of the old functional organisations.

Throughout the 1960s ICI struggled to implement these four elements of strategic change against the backcloth of a UK economy which was now evidently growing slower than its European and North American counterparts, where inflation rates were higher, and where an industry predisposition for counter-cyclical investment as an ongoing strategy produced periodic feasts and famines when over-capacity led to falling prices, reduced margins, and barely acceptable levels of profitability. Vivian, Gray & Co. (1980) have noted that in the 11 years from 1960 to 1971, years of excellent growth for the chemical industry, ICI managed to increase real pre-tax profits by only 2.5% per annum compound. Perhaps because of continuing pressure on margins and the clear requirement for product to be available in quantity in the feast times, ICI majored on the technological and labour productivity components of their 1960s strategies. They were, of course, drawn more into these strategies by the major problems of building new plant and introducing MUPS/WSA described earlier in this book.

Of the other two strategies, major progress was made in the 1960s in getting into European markets, but little substantial impact was made in North America. In July 1960, ICI had created a European Council to study the desirability of large-scale manufacture within the EEC markets. The construction of physical plant and establishment of selling groups in each individual market, plus the creation of a Europa Division to co-ordinate and facilitate the entry of UK divisions into European markets, all had an impact on the proportion of ICI sales going to Continental Western Europe. The percentage of ICI Group Sales going to Continental Western European customers thus increased from 11% (£66m) in 1963 to 17% (£364m) in 1973.

Although shaken by the economic downturn of 1966, difficulties in utilising new plant, falling profitability, and a cash crisis, ICI was too busy implementing what they already had on board to take on further substantial change at that time. However, by the 1971 recession WSA had been substantially implemented and the troubled new plants were now pouring out product, but unfortunately into difficult economic and market conditions. A slowing down of the growth of world industrial production and trade in 1970 and 1971, a drop in the growth of world chemical production from under 4% in 1971, compared with 5% in 1970, and 8½% per annum in the decade up to 1970, plus a rise in European chemical output of 8% and 5% in 1970 and 1971, led to worldwide excess capacity for many chemical products. In the UK, industrial production increased by only 1% in 1970 and 1971, as compared with the 3% per annum increases of the 1960s. All this meant a very limited expansion of sales volume for ICI in 1970 and 1971, and prices could not be pushed up to cover inflationary costs emanating partially from UK economic conditions. The result was that 1971 was the third year running in which the ICI group was subjected to much higher costs for raw materials, wages, and salaries not matched by proportionate increases in selling prices. The management response to these accumulating environmental pressures was another package of structural and manpower changes.

Early in 1971 declining profitability in ICI's explosives, fibres and dyestuffs business areas and the weak business performance of the Heavy Organic Chemicals and Plastics Divisions produced reorganisation and redundancy. Nobel Division, which had operated the explosive assets of ICI, lost its separate status as a division. Dyestuffs Division combined with parts of Nobel Division to become Organics Division, and Heavy Organic Chemicals Division reluctantly added to their burdens by absorbing fibres intermediates from ICI Fibres Ltd, but were given a glossier identity by being renamed Petrochemicals Division. The near financial disaster in Agricultural Division of 1969 had stimulated a series of plant closures and the shutdown of the anhydrite mine so that their employees dropped from 13,009 to 10,376 between year end 1970 and year end 1972. Not even Plastics Division could ignore these pressures and in 1972 the axeman came and reduced monthly staff by around 20%. 1969 was in fact the peak year for ICI's total UK employees, but the 9% drop which occurred between 1969 and 1973 was not earnestly followed up until the crisis conditions of 1980 produced even more vigorous structural and manpower change.

The other notable element of the early 1970s package of changes was that ICI at last acted on their stated policy of entering the United States by acquiring Atlas Chemical Company in 1971.

As we have seen in Chapter 10 of this book the corporate direction of ICI between 1972 and 1978 was characterised by heavy capital expenditure in strategic business sectors and territories informed by ICI's consensual style of main board decision-making and the influence of powerful planning and policy groups system. These investment decisions left ICI's Petrochemicals, Plastics, and General Chemicals interests in the UK, USA, and Europe substantially over-capitalised for the market conditions prevalent by the late 1970s and early 1980s. The outcome of a long process of developing concern about a mismatch between ICI's business strategy, organisation, and top governance and culture and their business and economic environment, were the revolutionary changes in company ideology, structure, and strategy which finally came with the severe economic and chemicals recession of the early 1980s. Beginning with the substantial cuts in Fibres assets and manpower, and moving through a continuing series of philosophical debates about company objectives, priorities and style, there emerged a package of strategic changes between 1979 and 1983 as revolutionary if not more revolutionary than anything attempted since the last period of substantial awakening in the first years of the 1960s.

By 1979 a new and more integrated business organisation and strategy had emerged for penetrating European markets. Fibres and Organics Divisions lost more assets and people. Assets in the two biggest loss-making divisions, Petrochemicals and Plastics, were closed, and then the two divisions were merged in 1981 under a single, smaller board. By 1982 Mond Division were taking out £40m of fixed costs per annum by reducing the number of levels of management and cutting employees by around 30% in three years. ICI's UK employees fell by 31%, from 89,400 to 61,800 between December 1979 and December 1983 as a result of the above structural changes, and additional changes in the service functions to the various UK division, and cuts in headquarters staff. With the arrival of John Harvey-Jones as Chairman in March 1982, the ideological, top governance, and stylistic changes he and others had been championing for some years became manifest in changes in the role, style, and mode of operation of the main board and the decision to move out of Millbank. Through all this the business strategy changes which are becoming tangible are behaviour designed to reduce the proportion of ICI's total sales emanating form the low-growth heavy chemicals sector, marshalling resources to buy further assets in specialty chemicals with high margins such as pharmaceuticals, agro-chemicals, and chemicals used in electronics, and the continuing talk of a big US acquisition to acquire a dominating role in the specialty end of the US chemical industry.

Having established the theme in ICI's recent corporate development of packages of changes occurring around every decade, with a revolutionary break involving sequential changes in company ideology, structure, and business strategy occurring every 20 years in association with environmental crisis and changes in leadership composition and style, the next task of this chapter is to probe into the processes of emergence and implementation of five strategic changes in ICI's recent history to see if there are any patterns in those processes.

SOME PATTERNS IN PROCESSES OF STRATEGIC CHANGE

Care has been taken throughout this book to emphasise that strategic change processes are best understood as contextually located continuous processes with no clear beginning or end. The previous section of this chapter, focussing as it did on a 25-year period of ICI's development, allowed an analysis to reveal periodic eras of high levels of change activity precipitated by, but not solely explained by, economic and business-related environmental disturbance. Clearly a potential danger of an analysis which might infer too simple a relation between economic and business crisis and organisational change is that the firm may thus end up being seen just "bobbing on the economic waves, as so many corks on the economic bathtub" (Boswell, 1983:15). It should be clear that no such brand of simple economic determinism is intended here. Behind the periodic strategic reorientations in ICI are not just economic and business events, but also processes of managerial perception, choice, and action influenced by and influencing perceptions of the operating environment of the firm, and its structure, culture and systems of power and control. Any adequate framework for examining strategic change must include not only objective changes in economic and business forces, but the role of executive leadership and managerial action in intervening in the existing concepts of corporate strategy in the firm, and using and changing the structures, cultures, and political processes in the firm to draw attention to performance gaps resulting from environmental change, and lead the organisation to sense and create a different pattern of alignment between its internal character, strategy, and structure and its emerging concepts of its operating environment. As was emphasised earlier in this chapter the real problem of strategic change is ultimately one of managerial process and action; of signalling new areas for concern and anchoring those signals in issues for attention and decision, of mobilising energy and enthusiasm in an additive fashion to ensure that new problem areas found and defined eventually gain sufficient legitimacy and power to result in contextually appropriate action.

The role of this section of the chapter is to take a more detailed look at any evident patterns in the processes of managerial action in five cases of strategic change described in earlier chapters. To put a spotlight on the *how* of creating strategic change without losing sight either of the what and why of change, or of the intra-organisational and environmental contexts through which those processes flowed. Of these five cases one deals with corporate-level strategic change, and the other four involve strategic changes attempted by divisional level managerial action confined to divisional problems, but to varying degrees influenced by some of the corporate preoccupations of the day. All are strategic changes in so far as they largely but by no means exclusively involved the top decision-makers of each organisation wrestling with consequential changes in one or more elements of business strategy, structure, culture, and manpower levels or employment practices.

The case of corporate-level strategic change, over the period 1973–83 will be used both to emphasise how antecedent factors eventually shape the character and content of changes made at the revolutionary point when the changes are delivered – in this case of course the delivery started in 1979 and 1980 – and also to pinpoint key patterns of managerial behaviour which helped to produce such outcomes. The other four cases will then be examined for the presence or otherwise of such patterns of management action, and for the impact of strategic context and process on the content of strategic changes which eventually emerged.

The cases do involve processes of change suggesting different outcomes. The corporate level change of 1972–83 and the Mond changes in top governance, organisation structure and manpower, examined over the period 1973–83 brought clear changes, but changes which are still being implemented. These two cases, therefore, are still very much in process and the effect of those changes, including any regression from them, is a question for future analysts of ICI's corporate development. This point about the analytical importance of the time frame for assessing change processes and outcomes is borne out by a look at two further cases. The change in top structure and culture of Petrochemicals Division over the period 1970–73, and the period of social innovation in Agricultural Division whilst George Bridge was Personnel Director from 1962 to 1967 to varying degrees indicate how strong change leaders can make changes happen, but with their succession, how those change processes and outcomes do not necessarily stick. All of the cases indicate the importance in managerial terms of strong, persistent, and continuing leadership to create strategic change. The Petrochemicals and Agricultural Division cases illustrate the regression and/or changes of direction which can occur when continuity of leadership is broken. The final case, Plastics Division, illustrates the absence of strategic change over the time period under examination, and thus invites analysis of what features of the context and process of management produced a different outcome in that division as compared with the other parts of ICI covered in this book.

The starting point for this analysis of the *how* of strategic change is the notion that finding and clarifying the content of any strategic change crucially entails managing its context and process. Therefore the focus for the descriptive and prescriptive understanding of managerial action in strategic change entails the interplay between ideas about the context of change, the content of change, and the process of change, together with skill in regulating the relations between the three. The recognition that creating strategic change is in essence a long-term conditioning, educating, and influence process designed to establish the dominating legitimacy of a different pattern of relation between strategic context and content suggests that the theoretical and practical starting point for managerial analysis and action should be the pre-existing pattern between strategic context and content in the firm. The examination of that context will reveal most tangibly and forcefully the sources of continuity existing in any large organisation but also any performance gaps resulting from misfits between the content of existing strategies and management processes and the outer and inner context of the firm, and thus areas of apparent or realisable tension which can be developed and magnified in order to stimulate energy and enthusiasm for change. The beginnings of any descriptive process analysis of change must therefore reside in an analysis of context and continuity. Context and continuity shape the starting point in which change processes emerge, falter, and proceed.

Strategic context is being treated here in two senses. Firstly, outer context refers to the economic, political, and business environment of the firm and the way changes in those factors help shape the market and competitive position of the firm relative to others operating in similar markets or industries. And secondly, inner context refers to the business stategy, structure, cultural, and political context which help shape the management processes through which ideas for strategic change proceed. The previous section of this chapter which connected outer context factors such as gross changes in business and economic environment to ICI's changing competitive position and hence to revolutionary patterns of organisational change will have reminded us that context is being treated here not just as a source of constraint but also a source of opportunity for managerial action in the change sphere. Indeed as we shall shortly indicate, a crucial part of managerial action in creating strategic change rests not only on the skill in mobilising changes in business and economic trends to achieve desired practical effects, but also actions taken to amplify or use pre-existing changes in the structural, cultural, and political context of firm – or even direct attempts to change those features of inner context by leaders of strategic change ideas, in order to help provide the conditions and processes to legitimate the content of strategic changes.

But although it is recognised that natural changes in context and deliberate interventions to change context can be built upon to encourage change processes, it is also evident from these five cases that variability in the contextual starting point for change, and indeed differential difficulty in changing the context through managerial action whilst the change process evolved, materially affected the capacities of managerial action to influence and create the desired strategic change. But why are some organisational contexts more receptive and others more inhibiting of strategic change? Partly it seems from these cases from the absence of certain factors. In the first place the absence of sufficient business and economic pressure, and in consequence the lack of sufficient negative energy for change that comes from dissatisfaction with the status quo. And secondly the absence of the positive energy and tension for change which can be created by the vitality, imagination, visionary ideas, and persistence of a leader championing a particular strategic change, or even the necessity for increasing the organisation's overall capacity for continuous change.

But these cases indicate that variability in context is not just a question of the absence of environmental disturbance and leadership skill in orchestrating a new marriage between strategic context and content. Strategic change is also a question of the way management processes in integrative and segmentalist organisational structures and cultures are in turn broadly facilitative of, and inhibitive of, the processes of vision-building, problem-identifying and acknowledging, information-sharing, attention-directing, problem-solving, and commitment-building which seem to be necessary to create change. Kanter (1983) has recently argued that the endemic problem-solving processes she found in integrative structures and cultures were broadly supportive of change processes whilst segmentalist structures and cultures were generally inadequate contexts for certain kinds of change processes to materialise.

As she admits Kanter's (1983:396) useful distinction between integrative and segmentalist structures and cultures and the managerial problem-solving processes associated with those structures and cultures, is a development of the now familiar dichotomy of organic and mechanistic organisations propounded in Burns and Stalker (1961). Integrative structures and cultures, Kanter argues, provide three of the enabling conditions for innovation: a diffuse climate of encouragement for change and thus the motive or desire for change; managerial processes which aid power circulation and power access and thus empowerment for change; and a variety of integrative mechanisms and team-building devices which encourage the fluidity of boundaries vertically and horizontally in the organisation which allow both the circulation of new ideas and participative arenas for those ideas to be shaped, supported and carried through to action plans.

Segmentalism, on the other hand, encourages a style of thinking and problem-solving which is anti-change, and thus the motivation to solve problems declines in segmented systems. Segmented cultures and structures are finely divided by levels and functions, so that one-on-one relationships prevail, clear status and power gaps compartmentalise ideas and problems, and information is a secret rather than a circulating commodity. This leads to a situation where innovation and change are difficult to handle. "Change threatens to disturb the neat array of segments . . . as soon as a problem is identified, it is surrounded and isolated . . . those operating segmentally are letting the past – the existing structure – dominate the future" (Kanter, 1983:29).

Having stretched her data into these two polar categories, Kanter is careful to argue both that segmentalism as a style of organising is appropriate for activities of high certainty where routine, habitual action is efficient and desirable, and that segmentalist tendencies may protect the successful organisation against unnecessary change, ensuring that it will repeat what it already "knows" (Kanter, 1983:31). Kanter also argues that where change did occur in segmentalist systems the evident pattern was for it to come from either mandates from the top, formal tests or change projects and experiments initiated at the top, by bringing in outsiders who could operate with greater degrees of freedom than people inside the system, or as a result of "holes in the system", unplanned change opportunities.

Without taking on board all of Kanter's explicit value biases towards entre-preneurial spirit and co-operative modes of problem-solving as prerequisites for change processes she prefers, there are some similarities between her broad findings and the conduct of strategic change in these five cases in ICI. Indeed critical to all the cases where change occurred was the necessity for managerial action to change predominantly segmentalist structures and cultures in ICI towards her integrative ideal, to encourage the rather different processes of managerial problem-solving which were necessary to champion novel and substantial ideas for change through the system. In Plastics Division, on the other hand, where changes in the operating environment and competitive position of the division from 1967 onwards might have warranted strategic change, the particular brand of segmentalism that had stabilised there meant the division was poorly equipped from a context and managerial process point of view to change itself. In Plastics Division the combination of a tradition of effortless growth and secure if unspectacular business success, a division structurally little disturbed by corporate realignments, run from the top by a stable management group, there developed a segmentalist structure and culture which restricted awareness and perception of environmental change and inhibited the development of integrative management problem-solving proces-ses which might have seen and taken opportunities for strategic change.

So if both characteristics of the outer context and features of the inner context of the firm can shape the starting point for continuity and change, how does change actually occur – through what sort of process?

These five ICI cases certainly corroborate Quinn's (1982) findings that they do not occur according to the rational–analytical schemes touted in the planning literature. There is little evidence in the ICI data of change occurring as a result of a rational linear process of calculatedly forming a strategy and then sequentially proceeding to implement it through controlled and programmatic planning. Forming and implementing strategic changes is not a steady, undisturbed progression from one routine to another, but rather a slow and incomplete process of breaking down old marriages between strategic context and content, and in an additive, intuitive, and occasionally opportunistic fashion building up a climate of acceptance for change.

In Chapter 10 a simple four-stage model was used to suggest key parts of this process: phases of developing concern with the status quo, then getting acknowledgement and understanding of the problems that needed tackling and why, a planning and acting phase, and then a period of stabilisation. These phases, of course, do not occur over similar time periods, neither do they necessarily follow the sequence indicated. Concerns raised and problems acknowledged get blocked, the context changes, new concerns appear and the process accelerates through to action, using solutions made available by previous debates.

If there is no mechanical pattern of phases in these ICI cases of change one pattern that is evident is the role of leadership in initiating strategic change. George Bridge in Agricultural Division, John Harvey-Jones in the Petrochemi-cals Division structure change and the corporate change process of the 1970s and early 1980s, Tony Woodburn in Mond Division, all started change processes by sensing, and at first imprecisely articulating, concerns about mismatches or performance gaps between aspects of their organisation and what they saw as a changing environment. In this process of leadership, as Schon (1983) reminds us finding, drawing attention to, and helping to define a problem a critical mass will accept as important, is as important as solving the problem found. But this important early activity of problem-finding, of developing concern about the continuance of the status quo, was also linked to another leadership activity designed to raise the level of tension in the organisation – the presentation of usually an imprecise vision of where the organisation ought to be moving towards in the future.

The change process was also influenced in four of the cases by attempts made to alter the structural and cultural context in which strategy changes were being articulated. These context changes included using new ideological posturing to challenge traditional ways of thinking and acting, setting up management development programmes such as the Management of Change Workshops to focus attention on the need for new management capabilities and skills, and creating permanent and temporary changes in administrative mechanisms and working groups to build energy and commitment around particular problems and their solution. As I have already said the above activities were rarely part of some grand process design. Instead opportunities were taken as they presented themselves to break any emerging global vision of a better future into manageable bits; of finding small steps on the way to larger breaks; of using any political momentum created by a number of complementary moves to bind a critical mass of powerful people around a set of principles which eventually would allow a series of pieces in the jigsaw to be moved simultaneously.

The above processes required understanding and skill in intervening in the organisation's structure, culture, and political processes. As Selznick (1957:70) has argued, "a wise leader faces up to the character of his organisation, although he may do so only as a prelude to designing a strategy that will alter it". This kind of process management also necessitated patience and perseverance; waiting for people to retire to exploit any policy vacuum so created; introducing known sympathisers as replacements for known sceptics or opponents; using succession occasions to combine portfolios and responsibilities and integrate thought and action in an otherwise previously factious and deadlocked area of change; backing off and waiting, or moving the pressure point for change into another area when continuing downright opposition might have endangered the success of the whole change exercise.

Having broadly established some of the features of outer context, and integrative or segmentalist organisational contexts which may inhibit or facilitate change, and then indicated what kinds of activities in managing processes of change may create strategic reorientations, I wish now to move on and illustrate how those features of strategic context and process influenced the particular content areas of change in the five cases.

The five cases of strategic change

Of the five cases of strategic change reported in this book, the corporate change process described in Chapter 10 and the Mond change process outlined in Chapter 9 provide the fullest treatment of how the interactive effects of a changing context and management thinking and action led to strategic change. There are clear similarities in the starting context and management processes in these two cases. Of course regarding strategic decision-making and change as continuous processes means that breaking into the process to note a beginning is something of an arbitrary act, but since in both cases new leadership in change process terms was initiated when John Harvey-Jones became a member of the main board in 1973, and when Tony Woodburn became chairman of Mond in 1973, that year is a sensible empirical point to cut into both processes.

Both Harvey-Jones and Woodburn began their search for change in management structures and cultures with many segmentalist features. The ICI main board at that time featured a succession of short-tenure, non-chief executive Chairmen, a two-tier board with a top box of the Chairmen and his three deputies, and a series of executive directors who were compartmentalised by portfolios allocated by product, territory, and function. The board was being driven by the twin obsessions with cash management and capital expenditure, and little time was being devoted to the potentially unifying activity of developing thought about the overall size and shape of the ICI group in which individual capital expenditure decisions were being made. In the smoothing–consensus style of decision-making in and around the main board, there was much evidence of games-playing between the board, the policy group directors, and the operating units over the annual capital expenditure allocation process. The main board were surrounded by the compartmentalised functional structure, and intellectual culture of Millbank where the central taboo was "don't rock the boat, don't dig too deep, too fast. This boat has stood the test of time."

The Mond top organisation and management culture in 1973 was equally segmentalist, in fact the Mond board at that time was a board in name only. The powerhouse of the division was the executive committee of the chairman and his three deputies. The directors were a loose chorale of individuals who responded to the top four in an atmosphere of formality and hierarchy. The tendency of the executive committee to relate to the directors individually through monitoring and controlling activities, forced those directors and the levels below them back into their product groups and functions. The level below the board felt distant from individual directors, and considered the deputy chairmen and the chairmen were up in the stratosphere. These features of segmentalism at Mond meant there was an absence of unified thinking at the level of the business as a whole as evident as that on the main board.

Finding fellow-travellers to rock the boat in structures and cultures as clearly segmentalist as those in Mond and on the main board was clearly not going to be an easy task. The task was made that much more difficult because in 1973 both ICI as a group and Mond in particular were just about to enter a period of what with hindsight turned out to be a more limited period of business success than was apparent at the time. Not only was there no readily apparent performance gap to build on to help justify change but had a gap in principle been there to exploit, it is doubtful if the pattern of management process in either situation could have adequately sensed the problem and put together a unifying and actionable solution to meet the challenge. The intuitive understanding by Woodburn and Harvey-Jones of the inadequacies of the management problem solving processes around them, plus for Harvey-Jones the stark failure of the 1972 and 1973 board organisation committee, for what he and others attributed to process planning and political reasons, meant that if they were to make the impact they felt appropriate in business and environmental strategic change then one of their starting points for change had to be the management processes they were part of. But where and how were they to start, because business-environmental change of a substantial kind could not be justified by the business performance of the day, and changing the structures and cultures which were nourishing the prevailing management process was not yet legitimate as an area of board discussion, never mind a lever to be pulled to create strategic change which would have a demonstrable impact on business performance.

As I have already indicated, the process of change that developed from those contexts, and in various ways required action to move those contexts from segmentalist towards a more integrative set of characteristics, is best thought of as a long-term conditioning, educating, and influence process of marrying an emerging view of the content of strategic change with changing perceptions of the context of change. A process which may, as Pettigrew (1973) and Narayanan and Fahey (1982) have argued have a phase where demands for change emerge (gestation processes in Narayanan and Fahey's terms) involving vision-building, issue-sponsoring, problem-identifying, and attention-directing, all of which attempt both to raise the development of concern that things are not as they should be, and also eventually lead to some acknowledgement and understanding of issues that can be labelled as problems worthy of legitimate concern. These initial phases of education and influence are of course highly interdependent with the activities of resolving dilemmas and problems now on the front stage of decision-making; of breaking global problems and imprecisely articulated visions into manageable and therefore politically actionable bits; of using deviants and heretics to think the unthinkable, and say the unsayable; of mobilising a changing outer and inner context to question traditional ideologies; of using novel permanent and temporary administrative and managerial mechanisms to expose information and problems previously compartmentalised by traditional structural and political arrangements, and then build on this more integrative exposure of ideas and people to create the political will, the necessary commitment to solutions which may have been around a good deal longer than the problems they can now be legitimately connected to.

The gestation process of strategic change in Mond and on the main board are both associated with the sensing and articulation of vague discontents and imprecise global visions of individuals who adopted leadership positions for change. Both were initially hamstrung by the lack of felt need for change by their colleagues, by the highly segmented management process around them, and by in Woodburn's case perhaps rather more than Harvey-Jones, the counter-reactions and implicit control tactics of their colleagues. The fact that Woodburn's initial approach appeared to be potential-driven and not problem-driven, improving the potential of the Mond board rather than solving a particular problem, was too uncomfortable and imprecise for a set of people rewarded up to then in their career for instrumental and mechanical problem-solving behaviour. When this potential-driven rationale for change was linked in the minds of part of the board with "love-ins" and "sandals and beads OD" further uncertainty ensued. Faced with this uncertainty about the outcomes of such interventions, comfort was restored for some by labelling and stereotyping Woodburn as a "left winger", and as "all for participation", in a management–union context characterised by open disputes which hardly seemed compatible with Woodburn's ideals.

Harvey-Jones's learning from the process failures of the 1972–73 board organisation committee, and from the difficulties George Bridge had stimulated by championing T-groups, meant he was stylistically more cautious in change initiation, more careful in his own words never to let others lose sight of his "operator" capabilities. Nevertheless if stylistic differences are discernible between Woodburn and Harvey-Jones, the common feature of their approach was the recognition they were both initiating long-term processes, using both change methods and change objectives which had themselves to be legitimated as part of this process of change. Harvey-Jones's approach was to try and get some major changes in the role, size, and style of operation of the main board as a vehicle to improve the company's ways of managing strategic change, and to move from the existing situation where in his view ICI waited for some bit of the company to be evidently hurting and then move in on that bit to:

(a) try and read the environment about 5 years ahead, and
(b) try and aim our objectives 5 years ahead and only then to start intervening organisationally.

In the meantime he said "you have to make some interventions . . . but you have to make sure that these changes will be reinforcing to the big changes you are trying to aim for . . . so the main initiative has been and still is to try and make the board change."

Harvey-Jones's early activities were designed to improve the flow of disconfirming information to the main board about its and the ICI group's role and processes, by setting up study teams, using internal and external consultants, and sponsoring people into departments such as management services where they could have indirect effects on people's perspectives about problems. It would have been very much more difficult for him to be associated with such activities, and indeed to legitimate concern about organisation and management issues had he not had the legitimacy to roam all over the place that came from his functional responsibilities as organisation and services director. This requirement to use the existing structure to change the existing structure and processes should not go unnoticed.

Both Woodburn and Harvey-Jones made use of OD consultants. Being chairman, and after ensuring sufficient support of his deputies, Woodburn was able to directly employ Bainton and Wilson, the two American consultants, to use open-systems planning and team-building techniques with his board. Harvey-Jones had neither the positional power nor informal political position on the main board in 1973 to attempt such direct methods. The plan he and Dudley concocted after the board organisation committee failure was to wait for the outgoing Chairman's retirement and in the meantime to raise their diagnosis of company problems individual by individual in the hope of presenting a unifying position paper to the Chairman-elect before he took office. The secretarial error which fortuitously but prematurely released Dudley's paper "ICI in 1974" simultaneously to all the main board further speeded up the process of releasing disconfirming information, and nicely illustrates the role of chance and opportunism, alongside foresight and intent, in change processes.

The furore created by the above incident did nothing for Dudley's credibility in the short run, but it did allow Mercer the external OD consultant access for the first time to an ICI Chairman, and continuing but intermittent impact on the processes of top-level change right through until the 1980s. The above process was built upon by further activities designed to open up debate at the top of ICI. The new Chairman in 1975 was persuaded to break tradition and take the main board away for a 2-day meeting to discuss the structure and operation of the Group. This led to the setting up of three board task forces to consider different aspects of strategic change in the group, and an agreed process of reporting back to their colleagues.

Further common features of the Mond and corporate change processes of the 1970s was that those pushing for change in both situations were able to build and capitalise on the stirrings of other groups for change and access to decision-making processes, use environmental disturbances which temporarily caught management attention, and help create integrating mechanisms to manufacture consent for bits of the emerging change problem to be picked out and implemented. Thus in Mond the IR problems of the mid-1970s forced not only eventually a change in strategy for dealing with the unions, but also first a unifying of perspective amongst the previously divided cruiser captain works managers, then a problem which forced dialogue between the works managers as a group and the board as a group, and eventually at least a start in terms of developing a set of unifying principles to manage the division through the IR and business operating principles and the Mond Charter. The IR fires also triggered Sandy Marshall's move from being a works manager to becoming the division's senior internal development resource, and he was to play a significant role after that both as a linking mechanism between the board and levels below the board, but also a trainer helping to improve the change management capabilities of middle and senior managers in the division.

The upward pressure coming to the main board was of course from the division chairmen. The board development resource group sanctioned by Sir Rowland Wright encouraged process help to be made available to the, at that time, organisationally illicit division chairmen's meeting, and to a company Chairman who was breaking some of the traditions of the main board's mode of operation, and first got the Division Chairman's meeting legitimated and regulated, and then in 1977 created the crucial integrating administrative mechanism of the (Company) Chairman's Group Conference. Beyond the stage now of developing concern for change, this annual Chairman's Group Conference meeting became a crucial structural mechanism for the main board, chief executives of overseas subsidiaries, chairmen of the UK divisions, and the UK general managers to jointly share information and get common acknowledgement and understanding of problems and priorities. At the stage of planning and acting to create strategic change in the late 1970s the Chairman's Group Conference was also an important mechanism for the main board to test, refine, and legitimate action; and thus a key political mechanism to unify ideological change, and bring back bits of the change problem which were ready for action to ensure the commitment of key segments of the Company.

The length of time it took in both situations to move beyond the phase of philosophical debate, of developing concern that all was not well and acknowledging and understanding some of the problems that eventually caught a critical mass of management attention, towards the phase of concrete planning and action for change illustrates the difficulty of shifting an organisation the size of ICI. Stacked up against the imprecise vision of a better way of directing ICI, and what appeared to be unjustified and vague first-action steps, were the massive forces of inertia in the ICI structures, systems, and political processes. These forces of inertia were broken in Mond and on the ICI main board by a number of interrelated factors.

The continuity and persistence of change advocacy in both situations was critical. The problems couldn't go away, even if they couldn't be resolved, for as long as there was some continuity of change advocacy to wait it out, wear opponents down, appeal to new ideas and changing contexts, create teams to invite sceptics in, and orchestrate any signs of progress.

The change of personalities and style on boards can critically affect the balance of power for and against new ideas and particular changes. The arrival of more internationally commercially minded men onto the main board of ICI towards the latter end of the 1970s changed the balance of ideological preoccupation from technology towards ideas about international market competitiveness. Even if those individuals didn't necessarily line up immediately behind the changes in structure and style being advocated by Harvey-Jones, their ideas helped further discredit and muddy the waters of the dominant ideology of the day – the preoccupation with cash management and capital expenditure. In Mond the change over from Woodburn to Bay as chairman, and the appointment of Nicholas Mann as Division Personnel Director with the continuing presence in the "for change group" of Dylan

Jones, all helped to make the development stream there more task-oriented and focussed.

However, the momentum for change in Mond and in the main board accelerated when by 1978 it was more apparent to senior managers in parts of ICI other than Fibres Division that a punishing change in the business and economic environment was more of a reality than a prospect. Only then did ICI become sufficiently dissatisfied with its performance to act. The global problem being discussed started to appear and be discussed as pieces of the jigsaw under pressure. Tackling the problem of European business organisation through task groups containing executive directors and division chairmen brought the realisation amongst the subset of people involved that "we were over-fragmented, we didn't really use our total competitive strength". Harvey-Jones and Woodburn then seized their opportunity to pick up another piece of the jigsaw, putting some of the UK heavy chemicals divisions together. Again a slow, additive use of integrating mechanisms such as the Petrochemicals Product Directors Advisory Group, the Inter-Divisional Policy Group, the Heavy Chemicals Policy Group, and at the point of action the Heavy Chemicals Executive, all helped to build commitment and legitimacy for change across divisions, between executive directors and divisions, and ultimately on the main board. Without detracting from the display of managerial skill in Mond, perhaps an inevitable difference between the action phases of the Mond changes and the corporate changes of 1980–83 was that the more limited scale of the management task in the divisional case made it easier to articulate an overall guiding set of principles – the Mond Management Model, to help justify and detail the particular changes made. The sheer size of the corporate problems being tackled at that time, the necessity on logistical and political grounds to divide the problem into manageable bits so that change was proceeding in amongst at least some relative areas of stability, and as personnel moves released politically deadlocked areas, meant there was no overarching and modestly detailed framework guiding the corporate changes. The fact that the framework, and in some cases the detailed systems and structures, were being invented after the announcement of changes had been made, will significantly affect the implementation and stabilisation of those changes into the mid-1980s and beyond. It was this realisation that led one of the OD consultants involved in the corporate change processes to query how much had been learnt by senior people in ICI over the previous ten years:

> I think in circumstances which are not panic circumstances we have marginally improved our ability to relax, and think more effectively about problems. But in panic situations, about panic situations, we've probably learnt nothing.

So in spite of the anticipatory and enabling processes which occurred at the corporate level and in Mond Division between 1973 and 1979, enabling processes which produced a degree of ideological change, alterations in structure and context towards more integrative management processes, and indeed some additive changes in the content of strategic change, it took dramatic change in business context to unify management action around now starkly clear change objectives.

The Mond and corporate change processes both illustrate well the development of concern, acknowledgement and understanding, and planning and action phases of strategic change processes but cannot at this juncture reveal much about the stabilisation of change, although the comments just made about the presence in Mond of a coherent framework or philosophy for change in the form of the Mond management model, and the absence of an equivalent framework in the corporate change, suggests a more comprehensive and effective stabilisation process in Mond than in the ICI corporate sphere. The next two change processes – the attempt to change the management culture of Agricultural Division between 1962 and 1967, and the attempt to change the top structure and management culture of Heavy Organic Chamicals/ Petrochemicals Division between 1970 and 1973 – again show the fragmented, evolutionary, opportunistic, and political character of top-level change processes, but also illustrate well the difficulties of trying to create changes in top management culture in the short run, and the kinds of regression that can occur in strategic change when there is little thought and action devoted to stabilising change processes.

In Chapter 5 a detailed description was offered of George Bridge's attempt to change the overall management culture of Agricultural Division in amongst the major technological revolution going on in the 1960s and the broader social innovation implied in attempts to implement MUPS. Likewise Chapter 7 provided a comprehensive account of the attempts made by John Harvey-Jones to use the vehicle of a divisional organisation development unit around a more limited objective of changing the top structure of Petrochemicals Division from a purely functional to a matrix form, and also in a less focussed way to impact on the less explicit and tangible objective of influencing a predominantly hierarchical and authoritarian management culture in the direction of "relaxing its attitudes and behavioural processes". No attempt can be made here to repeat those narrative accounts; rather the focus will be on drawing out some of the broad similarities and differences between the Agricultural and Petrochemicals (PCD) change processes, and between those two processes and the Mond and corporate change processes already discussed.

One similarity between the Agricultural and PCD change processes is that both occurred after, and were precipitated at least partially by, disturbances in the outer context of the two divisions. Billingham Division (the pre-1963 name for Agricultural Division) found itself in 1959 in a loss-making situation poorly placed to compete in its traditional markets. It had an out-moded technology and was being priced out of international markets by the high feedstock costs of its coal-coke fed processes of manufacturing ammonia for fertiliser. With 17,000 employees it was overmanned, and its functional structure was inappropriate for handling technical and market change. Its board and set of senior managers had been in post for many years, were interpreting their role in a hierarchical and formal manner, and there was evidence of increasing industrial relations problems. The sense of crisis which developed around these interrelated business and organisational elements led firstly to managerial action to change the technology. In fact the technological change which replaced coal-coke as the feedstock with oil which occurred between 1959 and 1964, was quickly followed between 1965 and 1970 by the construction of large new single-stream ammonia plants, and then a further change in feedstock from oil to natural gas. These changes meant plant closures and significant manpower reductions.

On the organisation structure front, Billingham Division had lost all of its Organic Cehmicals assets to the newly created HOC Ltd in 1958, had been required to change its name to Agricultural Division in 1963, and had also been stimulated by corporate pressure to move from a functional to a matrix structure in 1963. Millbank interest in the effectiveness or otherwise of the management of Agricultural Division also led to a new chairman, and four new directors of Agricultural Division being appointed from outside the division's existing management group around the period 1962–63. One of those five new board members was the new Personnel Director, George Bridge.

The above pattern of change in outer and inner context was also evident prior to the PCD structural changes of 1972, although to nowhere near the same extent. The HOC board had been galvanised into action by the main board's interest in implementing MUPS/WSA on the conflict-ridden Wilton site, by their own very poor business results during 1970 and 1971, by the realignment of divisional boundaries which affected them in 1971, and by John Harvey-Jones's appointment as division chairman in July 1970.

If the context of both divisions had been destabilised by the above events, another force for change was the visionary leadership provided by George Bridge and John Harvey-Jones. Bridge entered Billingham in 1962 with a Millbank reputation "as the most revolutionary, impossible person" and promptly tried to live up to that reputation by trying to dent and break up the hierarchy at Billingham. Bridge's diagnosis of what was wrong with the Billingham management culture (described on page 143) was a good deal more explicit than his vision of what he hoped to replace it with. Bridge's search for a more clearly articulated way of connecting his concerns at Billingham to a legitimising framework which would help pinpoint the content of desired changes took him to the United States. There in amongst a host of behavioural scientists he found the mechanism of change he thought appropriate – the behavioural sciences, and a particular behavioural scientist, Douglas McGregor, who provided him with a language and a philosophy to help structure his problem of culture change.

Having clarified his problem, moving Billingham from a directive theory X culture to a participative theory Y culture, in a faltering, untidy, opportunistic but persistent fashion he introduced Billingham to the behavioural sciences. Directors and senior managers went off on T-groups, prominent American behavioural scientists were invited into Billingham to give lectures, conduct field experiments, and run novel training programmes, and with Douglas

McGregor's death, Ron Mercer began to work with the Agricultural Board as a consultant.

Bridge also tried to facilitate the above process by changing the structural and policy context within which personnel work was carried out in the division. He developed a more interactive process for generating personnel policy in the division, and decentralised personnel work from staff and labour departments in the divisional headquarters, down into the individual works and departments. By creating new personnel officers who he hoped would interpret their role in a more proactive problem-solving rather than reactive fashion, he hoped to start change processes at the middle of the organisation, works by works, and department by department.

Of course whilst Bridge and his right-hand man Tom Evans were making the above interventions into the Billingham management system, Bridge was also a leading figure in orchestrating the development of the company change programme MUPS. The launching of MUPS in 1965 was used by Bridge and Evans to continue the pressure for change at Billingham, and for a time the Bridge–Evans realisation that success of MUPS was predicated on the need to change managerial attitudes and behaviour as much, if not more than, those of the work force, meant there was a wider and more compelling contextual reason for pushing for a change in the Billingham management culture than the one he had started with in 1962.

Bridge and Evans continued the additive pressure for change in Agricultural Division right up until they left in 1967 and 1968. Various complementary activities were allowed to start at different levels in the structure. The onset of a new system for management and supervisory training, the Sandsend community joint management and union events, the activities of the Teesside Industrial Mission, a newly developed system for shop steward training, the workshop activities for managers on group process skills, and the early joint union–management workshops in Products Works all helped to seed developmental ideas into the division, draw out early adopter managers who were predisposed to alter the old ways of doing things, and break some of the old barriers in the management and union system about contact between management and employee representatives outside more formal industrial relations procedures.

Even though Bridge and Evans tried to broaden the width of their bow wave for change through the above seeding and climate-building activities, and undoubtedly some of the seeds did germinate after they had gone, in Bridge's absence from 1968 onwards there was never the same board level energy or pressure for a social innovation to complement the technical one that business pressures made an imperative. Bridge's forcing and pushing style made things happen but pushed resistance underground. With Bridge gone his methods and imprecise objectives could be openly criticised and his successor as personnel director was not allowed the same degrees of freedom by the Agricultural Division board. A new division chairman in 1968 meant the exit of Ron Mercer as a board consultant, and only the appearance of Noel Ripley with a more bottom-up rather than top-down change strategy helped support some of the change activities Bridge had started, and begin to germinate others. Any continuity and stabilisation of change process possible in Agricultural Division was left to Noel Ripley and his voluntary association – The Swallow Group, described in Chapter 6.

A similar process of a powerful change leader, searching for the appropriate change content in a destabilised business and organisational context, finding at the second attempt that changing structure was an acceptable change area, but this time failing to institutionalise an on-going change process, was also evident in Petrochemicals Division between 1970 and 1973. In PCD John Harvey-Jones was able to create a change from functional to matrix structure, one of his change objectives in his 1970 paper on "long-term organisational aims", but was not able either to change the management culture at PCD in the direction he felt appropriate, or to institutionalise the PCD Organisation Development Unit (the ODU) as a vehicle to bring continuity of change process in the division. Within 6 months of Harvey-Jones's departure to the main board, the ODU had been wound up, all talk of cultural or management style change had virtually evaporated in the top echelons of the division, and the PCD board returned to their 1960s preoccupation with the acquisition of, with hindsight, what turned out to be some highly questionable capital assets. As a participant in the PCD management culture of the time so crisply put it:

> They [the PCD managers] weren't in the business of innovation . . . Their notion was minimum disturbance and maximum production. That was heavily ingrained and where you were having fun on new investment that was a deeply technical matter . . . straight down the line was the PCD culture. After WSA and SDP, they simply blew off the froth – organisation development – and got on with the straight drinking.

The problem in PCD then was not just outside the structural area to stabilise a change started by John Harvey-Jones by, for example, developing successors who would have perpetuated tension in the system for change in culture and management process, but also there was evidently so little ideological change under even Harvey-Jones's leadership. Given Harvey-Jones's short tenure in office as division chairman, his desire to force change through quickly in an area of cultural acceptability (organisation structure) little effort was devoted to legitimating ideological change as a content area of strategic change, never mind unifying the PCD power system to acknowledge that ideological change could impact on business focus and performance, and then get them to act appropriately in that sphere. No such ideological change occurred in PCD, of course, until after the business traumas of 1980 and 1981, and until the main board implemented the merger of Petrochemicals and Plastics Division in April 1981.

Plastics division, 1967–79

Chapter 8 amply described the series of attempts made by Simon Dow and the small group of change-minded internal OD resources, sometimes with the not too persistent help of a few line managers and the occasional director, to change the management culture and core management processes of Plastics Division to help deal with the changing business, economic and political environment which faced ICI's Plastics interests from about 1967 onwards. The failure of those attempts is clear enough for apart from a period in 1972 when "the axeman cometh", no substantial changes in business strategy, organisation structure, management culture or management systems and processes occurred until the business traumas of late 1979 left the then Plastics board and indeed the main board of ICI no choice but to impose revolutionary strategic change on ICI's Plastics businesses. The pertinent question to ask is why did Plastics Division not appear to have the capacities and capabilities to change itself?

The answer to that question, as was hinted earlier in this chapter, has to do with a mixture of features of context and management which were present to varying degrees over different time periods in the four other cases of strategic change, but were absent in the Plastics Division situation. The missing factors in Plastics were the absence of the kind of business–environmental disturbances which attracted main board and divisional board attention and action in Agricultural Division and HOC/PCD Divisions; the absence of the kind of top-level visible championing of structural, cultural, and business change that was evident in the activities of John Harvey-Jones, Tony Woodburn and his successors at Mond, and George Bridge. However, what was present in Plastics Division to a degree arguably in excess of anything seen in PCD and Mond was a stable segmentalist management structure and culture which in the absence of gross business disturbance and a visionary interested in revolutionary change, proved to be a setting quite impervious to strategic change.

The reader will recall from Chapter 8 some of the features of Plastics Division's history and development which distinguished it in terms of the extent and the stability of its segmentalist management structure and culture. In the heady days of growth for the plastics industry in the 1950s and early 1960s, Plastics Division had settled for a divisional ideology of "growth forever, profits forever", although the profits were never that spectacular even in the years at the top of the 4.5-year business cycle. The division was run by the same small group of ex-Alkali Division people who had joined Plastics when the division was created just after the Second World War. By the end of the 1960s the Plastics board had the highest average age in the company, and it was not until the death of their chairman in 1972 that Millbank was able to bring in as chairman a man who had not been socialised amongst the research chemists who had traditionally dominated the Plastics management culture.

The stability of growth in sales volume, and continuing if unspectacular profits, the stability of senior management personnel, after polypropylene (in

1962–65), the remarkable lack of change in the division's products and technical processes, and the way Plastics was not affected by any of ICI's occasional redrawing of business areas and boundaries, all added up to a remarkably constant environment in which developed a highly segmented management structure and culture.

The change in 1964 from a functional to a matrix organisation form encouraged the development of a more market and product focus in the division to counteract the power of the functions, and in particular the research and technical areas but in the absence of a team concept of board working, the division was fragmented from a management point of view in virtually every dimension possible. There was a clear distancing between the chairman and his three deputies (the top box) and the rest of the directors. Until a new chairman arrived in 1973 the Plastics Division board did not even have a formally instituted set of monthly board meetings and executive committees. If there was little evidence of integrative thinking and planning on the board, there was plenty of evidence of what directors described as fragmentation; of role-bound behaviour, and directors being in watertight categories. The hierarchical distancing between the "top box" and the directors and the fractionation between the directors was carried on down the line. Managers below the board talked of the board being "a difficult culture to penetrate", "a lot of things are played very close to the chest". "They're a bit closed – I personally see it as a weakness because they haven't resolved their own internal differences." Again this lack of integrative thinking and action at the top, exacerbated any natural tendencies in a matrix for functions and products to divide. The 1972 management redundancies, rather than opening up the above management culture, seemed to freeze it rather than relax it. A consequence was that many of the core business issues of the 1970s, the heightening international competition, the sensing and responding to falling real growth rates for bulk plastics, what to do with maturing products, and how and when to develop new specialty products, were not faced up to. Instead, as one director put it, the board remained "10 individuals doing their own thing". A board spending too much time "feeding data to the centre [Millbank] and reacting to situations". Or as another director described the essentially defensive rather than change minded and initiating attitude of the board he was part of:

We are details men – so we'll never be caught out by Millbank.

The new directors brought onto the Plastics board from 1972 onwards either did not appear to see the need for strategic change, or could not see where support could be generated for the first practical steps forward, or if they came with a predisposition and with experience in using behavioural science or OD methods were explicitly dissuaded from using such ideas and methods by some of their more senior colleagues.

In the face of such a well-established, stable, and segmentalist management culture, and in the absence of top-down and powerful change leadership to change itself, one saw a succession of plainly impotent attempts at culture change led by Dow and his associates. Only with business crisis came business strategy, structural, and cultural change, and regrettably only at that point did the senior managers of the division start to fundamentally appreciate the necessity of some level of capability in the division for managing organisational and business change.

MANAGERIAL TASKS IN CREATING STRATEGIC CHANGE

A comprehensive managerial strategy of change requires a more thorough understanding of change in organisations, not a theory of how to introduce any arbitrary change, but a theory of how to direct somewhat the conventional ways in which an organisation responds to its environment, experiences, and antici- pations. (March, 1981:575).

In the above quotation, and in a subsequent paper on change and reorganis- ation in government, March and Olsen (1983) make the essentially simple and elegant point that any practical theory of change has to be based on contextually based knowledge and action about the factors and processes which create and sustain continuity as well as change. March and Olsen come to this conclusion on the basis of their empirical observation that while incremental and less visible changes in government not linked to a major reorganisation often succeed, comprehensive reorganisation tends to consolidate opposition and thus fail. In this view, leadership in change management requires skill in timing small interventions so that the force of natural organisational processes amplifies those interventions. This recognition that major reforms seem to require commitment, patience, perseverance, and repetition fits well with part of the descriptive findings of this study on creating strategic changes. Since business strategies are likely to be rooted both in the idea systems which are institutionalised in an industry sector at any point in time, and are represented in the values, structures and systems of powerful groups who control the firms in any sector, changing business strategies has to involve a process of ideological and political change which eventually releases a new concept of strategy which is ideologically acceptable within a newly appreciated context.

But how is this done, indeed prescriptively how can it be done? Is it possible to describe and codify the tasks and skills appropriate for such a contextually sensitive activity as managing strategic change without reducing the change process to a mechanical and over-determined set of phases or stages, and the activities of changing to a set of platitudinous generalities? Quinn (1980, 1982), with his discussion of logical incrementalism, has offered one prescriptive view of strategic change. Quinn describes and prescribes a process of strategic change which is jointly analytical and political and where executives are recommended to proceed flexibly and experimentally from broad concepts to specific commitments. A cautious step-by-step activity of building awareness of the need for change, legitimising new viewpoints and challenging old assump- tions, making tactical shifts and finding partial solutions, overcoming and neutralising opposition whilst building political support around particular ideas, and then formalising commitment for action. Muddling through with a purpose, as he puts its.

Kanter (1983), on the other hand, sees a prototypical innovation having three waves of activity occurring in sequence or as successful iterations. Firstly information is acquired, sorted, and exchanged to shape the definition of a problem which may become the focus for change. Then coalitions are built, teams created, and individuals encouraged to buy in or sign on for the change in question. Finally there is a mobilisation and completion phase in which the boundaries and momentum for the change are maintained, opposition and interference is dealt with and the change proceeds through periods of secondary and subsequent redesigns until particular pieces of the change are implementable. Kanter (1983) sees champions for change ideas holding together and managing the above three-stage process. Using what she calls power skills to persuade others to invest information, resources, and support in new initiatives; team skills to share information, resolve differences, and generate enthusiasm and commitment to particular solutions; and change architect skills to design and construct micro-changes which are eventually connectable to macro-changes or strategic orientations.

Both of these prescriptive views of change put their fingers on important aspects of the practice of change, but both also under-emphasise or ignore other elements of the management task. Quinn's (1980) view captures well the additive, evolving, nature of the task but tends to underplay the role of environmental disturbance, and the contribution that changing features of intra-organisational context can play in creating a new pattern of learning, thought, and action as change proceeds. Kanter, on the other hand, clearly emphasises the power skills required to create change. How innovators have to compete in a knowledge market – a market-place for ideas; an economic market – where resources are required; and a political market for support and legitimacy. Her discussion of segmented and integrated contexts critically pinpoints how some contexts are more receptive and enabling of change than others, and indicates how the career of a change idea might crucially depend not just on power skills as such, but on skill in changing a context towards more integrative features whilst the change idea is being championed. But neither Kanter nor Quinn deal with the key management tasks of stabilising a change once changes have taken place or are taking place.

An approach to the practice of change management which is complementary both with the views of Kanter and Quinn and with the empirical findings of this study is that propounded by Johnston (1975). Johnston's argument is predicated on three assumptions. The first of these is that some evolution is occurring in a natural way in most organisations. Secondly that this natural evolution is in response to external pressures and is therefore retrospective and remedial, rather than preventative. And thirdly that any such change process absorbs a great deal of energy in the firm because it may require power redistribution, role changes, the abandonment of past practices and old ideologies, and restructuring. Johnston, building on these assumptions, makes an assertion highly compatible with the findings of this study that development or change processes are often dependent on a few people, reactive to the external world, and can peter out or be reversed. A way to try and prevent such regression or reversals is to conceptually understand the evolution of natural processes of change in organisations and to help establish an organisation process of change with the necessary internal skills, actions, and systems to maintain development in the direction sought. Prescriptively this means in the broadest sense that the first step in the change process should be to improve and build on any natural processes of change by tackling questions such as how can existing processes be speeded up, the conditions that determine people's interpretations of situations be altered, contexts mobilised to achieve practical effects, along the way to move the organisation perhaps additively, in a different strategic direction? Thus any adequate approach to managing change must be based on the principle of understanding the context, of knowing what you are dealing with, and of choosing as a starting point some area of movement that can be built upon. Of identifying something which is happening which has a significant group of early adopters linked to it, and where more than likely the energy for strategic change is based on the recognition of environmental pressure and an early sensing of a gap between the organisation's present and its desired future relationship with its business – competitive, and social, political, and economic environment.

For all its oversimplifications, including the tendency to assume both discrete and exclusive categories and linear sequential development, Johnston's (1975) four stages in the natural process of change do usefully capture broad elements of the descriptive processes of change elaborated in this book, and allow one to make sensible prescriptive statements about necessary management tasks at each of the four stages. The reader may recall the four stages are:

– the development of concern;
– the acknowledgement and understanding of the problem;
– planning and acting;
– stabilising change.

In fact the data from this study, particularly about the contribution of visionary leaders and early adopters in change processes, indicates the importance of an initial *problem-sensing stage* which may predate a stage of development of concern. In the sphere of strategic change signalling problems as worthy of attention and getting those problems a legitimate feature of corporate discussion and decision-making, is itself a time-consuming and politically very sensitive process. One of the contributions made by Lord Beeching and George Bridge in the 1960s, and by Harvey-Jones and Woodburn throughout the 1970s was to sense and flag key problems worthy of management attention. From a political process point of view it is critical not to rush prematurely from problem-sensing to planning and action in the change sphere. Actions recommended about problems which themselves are not yet accepted as legitimate topics of debate invariably produce the rejection of the change idea. The essence of the political learning process implied in this view of change is that individual sensing of problems must be complemented with activities which encourage some level of shared problem-sensing, spreading of development of concern about the emerging problem, and eventually broadly based understanding of the problem, if novel ideas for change are not to be imperilled at birth.

The development of concern stage assumes the presence of a small group of early-adopters, or even as we have seen from four of the five cases of change in this book the presence of a single visionary change leader, sensing and imprecisely articulating a performance gap between the organisation's present condition and some feature or features of its operating environment. The key management task here is to more broadly educate the organisation by building on the perspective, information, and contacts of the early-adopters. In effect to recognise the group doing this early sensing, to broaden the group by helping to connect them to peers, bosses, and subordinates with similar views, and to prepare more of a critical mass of people to help influence key power figures. This educational process may also involve getting unusual meetings going which cross existing organisational and departmental boundaries and help spread information and views and integrate such data around particular issues or problems. Key line managers or consultants may also be able to set up meetings where power figures receive and test data, or personally counsel individuals to act on the emerging views of the problem in parts of the organisation where at that point in time it is legitimate to do so. As we have seen from these studies of ICI, it can be valuable at this stage in the change process for deviants, even heretics, to think the unthinkable, and say the unsayable, and for key line managers to be persuaded to help break traditional patterns of thought by setting up unconventional meetings where the process of discussing the previously undiscussable can begin.

In the next stage, the process of trying to get acknowledgement and understanding of problems and issues which are emerging, the key management of change task is to help the early adopters and key power figures maintain and develop any structured dialogue about the problem, and avoid a tendency either to escape from the problem by for example projecting it onto others, or a precipitous and ill-considered rush into action before the present situation has been carefully diagnosed, change objectives clarified and agreed, and a process plan to move from the present to the desired future developed. This stage is not only critical in terms of perpetuating any ideological change now in process, but also is important in rational–analytical terms by exposing alternative diagnoses of the problem, exploring causes, and generating alternative solutions with reflections on their implications and the development of criteria for choosing a solution.

The data from the Mond change process and the corporate change process suggest that the above two stages of problem-finding, educating, and climate and tension-building for change are long processes with many iterations, blocks, deadends, and unpredictable areas of movement. Persistence and patience in championing change seems to be necessary to initiate and perpetuate this process of conditioning and influence, and deliberative attempts to alter the structural and cultural context of decision-making, and capitalise on environmental disturbances, seem necessary to break out from mere acknowledgement and understanding of problems into a stage of executive planning and action. We have seen that because radical changes require strong commitments and high motivations, they also presuppose the existence of ideological reorientations, and therefore the unequivocal availability of a new ideology which precisely and enthusiastically endorses the changes. Ideological reorientations can occur through the above processes of climate-building and education but major ideological change also requires other deliberate management action: efforts made to influence patterns of socialisation by changing career paths and reward systems; visibly using the newly promoted as role models to additively signal behaviour required in the new culture; using retiral situation to combine portfolios and responsibilities previously divided, and to release energy along sub-parts of the change problem previously deadlocked by individual power figures and sectional interests. Ideological reorientation may also be facilitated by breaking the global problem into actionable bits which reinforce one another, and by creating temporary or permanent task forces, co-ordination committees and business teams which resolve conflicts and imbue enthusiasms and commitment for action around pieces of the change.

Johnston's (1975) otherwise helpful prescriptive view of change management tends both to underemphasise management action to change and thereby restructure the context in which change processes develop and the extent to which effective action in managing strategic change is dependent on mobilising environmental disturbances and crises in order to achieve practical effects. Gross changes in the environment of the firm can be orchestrated and capitalised upon to create opportunities for organisational learning, to destabilise power structures, and connect previously unrelated solutions around now more precisely stated and more enthusiastically supported organisational ideologies. But if crises provide ideological closure and therefore justification for action, it is evident that some organisations are more likely to be able to capitalise on the "window for change" provided by environmental disturbances than others. Here of course what has or has not happened in the pre-crisis circumstances may crucially affect the quality of planning and action taken to implement strategic changes. Paradoxically the delays and incremental movements in the development of concern and acknowledgement and understanding of problems stages, may have not only sensitised a wider set of people to the incipient problems, and enabled debates to occur around a variety of solutions, but also helped to draw out and test new leaders, possibly with the capabilities to manage the new circumstances, and if not with the opportunity to use temporary structures and administrative mechanisms to prepare the ground for new patterns of organisation. As we have seen in two of the five cases of strategic change reported in this book, management training and development experiences can be used in the pre-crisis situation to develop a common language for thinking about change management, and to increase the capability and capacities of managers to carry through operational change management tasks delegated to them by senior executives.

The planning and acting tasks in change management have been well codified and described in the concepts and techniques reported in Beckhard and Harris (1977) and Beer (1980). In the planning of change the most important tasks are; defining the present condition of the organisation in relation to its changing environment; clarifying the desired future state for the organisation in relation to its changing environment; building commitment around particular change objectives, and appointing transition managers to move parts of the organisation from the present through the transition state, to the change objective by the means of detailed and contextually sensitive action plans. As the Mond Division experience reported in this book indicates, this operational process of change management is greatly facilitated by unity of philosophy and purpose amongst the senior executives leading the change process. In the case of Mond Division this has meant giving clear, simple messages and maintaining those consistently and without dilution within a broad philosophy – which justifies and conceptually holds together a series of change initiatives.

If the top leadership role at the action stage in change management is to put tension into the organisation by providing a clearly articulated rationale for change and some consistently stated change objectives, the operating management responsibility is to plan and organise the use of this tension to generate movement. Here agreeing the targets of change and the form and timing of their publication is important. The publication process is really a contracting–negotiation exercise which takes into account the different positions of individual units, deals with possible differences in interpretation of the leadership message, and manages apparent conflicts in the implications of the messages. There is clearly a monitoring task to ensure progress, and a support task to ensure that problems inhibiting progress are dealt with creatively and ethically, and that operating managers are provided with a "political umbrella" for the risks they have to take.

A key to success in these kinds of change activities is the effective management of the links between the senior group leading the change and the operating managers carrying through the details of implementing particular changes. Even in crisis-driven circumstances the operating management role is likely to involve detail and grinding on over time, and is very dependent upon the leadership role being consistently maintained. If someone in an operating management role is close to acceptance of hard targets in his sphere of negotiated influence, his work could be undermined and even destroyed by a weakening of the leadership position.

As we have seen in this book strategic change is not just a question of justification and initial action, of making things happen, it is also a question of making things which happen stick. Here is the additional management task of stabilising changes of making sure that reward systems, information flows, and power and authority distributions support the newly emerging state. Since changes are often initiated by or otherwise associated with key figures, and changes often remain as long as those key figures remain, a critical part of the stabilisation process has to do with the development and choice of successors who will want to maintain the new situation, and more idealistically perhaps who will maintain and then initiate changes themselves when external pressure on the organisation makes further change appropriate.

12   The Use, Impact, and Fate of Specialist Change Resources

The purpose of this chapter is to compare and contrast the natural history of development and impact of the various groups of internal and external OD consultants who worked in the corporate headquarters and Agricultural, Petrochemicals, Plastics, and Mond Divisions of ICI. Simply stated there is the requirement to explain why by 1983, through different pathways of development, and after varying life histories and effects, two of these divisional OD groups had ceased to exist while the head office OD activities and the other divisional OD activities continued in 1983, if not in anything like the same size and form as they had emerged in the different business, social, and organisational context of the late 1960s and early 1970s.

In asking questions about the fate of these OD consultants, and indeed their contribution if any to creating organisation change in ICI, it is important to place such questioning in the context of the findings reported in Chapter 11 about the pattern, timing, and processes of creating strategic change in ICI over the period 1960–83. The role of internal and external specialists in creating change has to be considered alongside a pattern of evolution in ICI where over a 20–30-year period continuity is a good deal easier to see than change; and where strategic change when it does occur tends to occur in packages linked to major changes in the business and economic environment of the company, and to related changes in the power system and ideology of the top decision-makers in the company. But if there is this evidence of periods of high levels of change activity led by very senior executives when major structural and strategic reorientations occur, the periods in between such reorientations are occasions when the new structures and strategies are implemented and stabilised, and indeed when another generation of leaders begin to champion a new ideology and strategy which they consider more appropriately matches their sense of where the company is in relation to a changing social, economic, and political environment. As we have seen, the process of breaking down the old dominating ideas system in the firm, even when such a process is being led by a small but not yet critical mass of senior executives, is a long, faltering process requiring persistence and patience, and much skill in using and changing features of the inner and outer context of the organisation to justify the new marriage between strategic content and context.

The fact that it is so obviously difficult even for very senior executives to build commitment and energy for radical changes of ideology, structure, and strategy, and that the final planning and acting stages of such change processes often require the enabling and unifying force provided by business crises, indicates something of the context in which specialist OD resources begin their attempt to fashion a role for themselves in processes of creating organisational change. Whatever brand of initial idealism, special techniques and language, or hard-learnt political realism the OD consultant brings with him or her, the starting point for impact must be the context they enter and the needs of the corporate or divisional power systems which ultimately dictate the OD consultant's acceptability, legitimacy, and impact.

Thus in ICI organisation development as an activity began out of a need by senior executives in the company to help justify, and more crucially implement, the centrally driven MUPS/WSA productivity bargain which was being resisted by management and trade unionists in many of the divisions. MUPS/WSA and then the ill-fated SDP were the main initial vehicles for corporate and divisional OD in ICI. In Agricultural Division in the early to mid-1970s the business need for new plant to be commissioned more effectively than the division had managed in the 1960s, and for an industrial relations climate to be created which would allow uninterrupted production from big, new, cost-effective plant, meant that for a time the joint problem-solving techniques of the local third-party OD consultants were an appropriate match and means for some of the local senior works managers' pressing problems. Similarly in Mond Division, as the IR fires exposed the poor system of organisation and communication between the Mond works managers, and the lack of unified thinking on the Mond board about personnel and other policy matters, so developmental energy was put into creating unity of purpose and perspective amongst the Mond board and the works managers in the division, and ultimately between the board and the senior management group below them. Likewise in Petrochemicals Division (PCD) between 1972 and 1973, pressure by the division chairman created the legitimacy and the space for part of the OD unit to help design a change in the top structure and governance of the division. Without the division chairman the PCD OD unit would not have been created and could not have facilitated the structural change they did. However, as we noted, having relied on such an exclusive source of political sponsorship, once the chairman departed the division, so the OD unit was comprehensively tidied away. Meanwhile in Plastics Division where the then board did not perceive the need for strategic, structural, and cultural change until the business crisis of the late 1970s was practically upon them, the OD resources tried unavailingly both to stimulate organisational change and to create some legitimacy for themselves as interventionists in the organisational life of the division.

Although from a pragmatic point of view the key question to ask of these internal and external OD resources is what impact did they have in their particular context, a related question which the longitudinal character of this research can ask, and try and answer, is why and how did some of these groups of specialist advisors survive over a long enough time period and in a form where they might have increased their chances of impact? Studies of the natural history of development of communes by Kanter (1972), of social movements reported by, for example, Zald and McCarthy (1979) and Freeman (1983) and of innovating groups inside formal organisations by Pettigrew (1973, 1975a), all indicate the precariousness of groups whose purpose is to change some feature of their present or emerging context. As Sarason (1972) has argued, those who seek to create new settings in established contexts are likely by definition to claim to have, or be perceived to have, superior missions and ideas which inevitably compete with pre-existing ideas and values. The challenges posed by self-professed or environmentally attributed change agents, thus attract the politics of disrepute and the withdrawal of bureaucratic support, resources, and legitimacy. The decline and demise which follows is represented amongst the would-be innovators in the replacement of early optimism by pessimism, by polarisation rather than commitment and cohesion, and by a desire to hang on and exist and survive even if that entails accommodation with the local context to a degree where the original pioneering change objectives slip into the background.

A group of OD specialists, like other advisors such as operational researchers, systems analysts, and corporate planners, can represent the anti-routine aspect of organisational functioning and be seen as an insubordinate minority. A group advocating change from a specialist, advisory base is likely to be abnormal rather than normal, illegitimate rather than legitimate, marginal rather than central, and powerless rather than powerful. Its activities and resource base have to be justified, its members have to generate credibility in particular and varying contexts, and success, failure, and survival can be a question of the vagaries of the last project or activity. This is the position from which an OD group concerned with change ordinarily begins its struggle for impact.

Given the interest in this study in the analysis of social process, Sarason's (1972) finding that what he calls the "before the beginnings phase" can be fateful for the survival of a new setting, and Freeman's (1975) data suggesting that birth processes of new groups can be an important determinant of subsequent evolution, this study examines the antecedent conditions which led to the emergence of the various ICI OD groups, and the form and nature of the birth processes of those groups. Why, when, and how did the groups emerge, and what role did contextual and precipitating factors play in their genesis? What were the backgrounds, aspirations, and values of the early group members? Was there any attempt to build commitment and cohesion around a distinctive set of group values, priorities, and techniques? Did these OD groups to different degrees go through an early pioneering phase when they wrapped themselves around their task with unreflective enthusiasm? Did the OD groups take on some of the characteristic values and behaviours of innovative sub-systems: high involvement and commitment to the task, and the unit's goals, high energy given to the solution of a novel problem or set of problems, a strong sense of group identity and spirit leading to extensive in-group social contact in and out of the workplace, the development of group rituals often as a way of socialising new members, and unconventional styles of dress and language? Were such processes encouraged or inhibited by the early leaders of such groups? If the leaders concentrated their energies early on in what Gusfield

(1957) has described as the mobilisation functions of leadership – the concern with building and reaffirming goals, values, and commitment inside the group, did the tendencies towards exclusiveness which such group building would create, lead to tension and counterpressure from groups in its environment? Was there any evidence for the early flush of enthusiasm characteristic of innovating groups in a pioneering mode, being followed by periodic or sustained phases of collective self-doubt when the change group perhaps begins to overperceive and overreact to threats in its environment, turns in on itself and breaks up into cliques and factions, some of whom challenge the values, objectives, and style of the group leader? Given these features of the internal and external evolution of the OD group, did each group have a strategy and tactics for managing its internal dynamics and external boundaries in such a way that the needs of internal commitment and cohesion did not compromise actions taken to generate and sustain legitimacy in a changing context?

The above questioning naturally draws attention to the what, why, and how an innovating group acquires its resources, generates its sense of group identity and cohesion, chooses its activities, exercises influence, secures its boundary, and builds the network of relationships which help to sustain its information sources and political base. However, these features of internal and external evolution are likely to be influenced not only by antecedent conditions, birth processes, and the continuing sense in which a group's tactics and actions help to create their own consequences and implications, but also by the structural form adopted by the group, and by the initial and changing features of the inner and outer context in which the various OD groups had to make their way in the world.

Research on the different structural forms adopted by social movement organisations (Gerlach and Hine, 1970; Gamson, 1975; Gerlach, 1983) indicates that different structural forms have varying consequences for social movement strategies, fate, and impact. Thus Gamson (1975) argues from his sample of social movements that centralised, hierarchical movements with well-developed divisions of labour may be efficient for achieving short-range change goals in which the survival of the movement is not the dominating concern. Gerlach and Hine (1970) and Gerlach (1983), as a counterpoint to the above centralised and bureaucratic view of structure, identify what they label as segmentary, polycephalous, and reticulate structures in some social movement organisations. By this they mean movements so structured that they are made up of a variety of groups or cells, led not by a central command but by decentralised cell leaders, all linked together into a network or reticulate structure, and bound together by travelling evangelists or spokesmen, overlapping participation, joint activities, and the sharing of common objectives and opposition. Rather than being inefficient Gerlach (1983) uses his case study data to indicate that such decentralised network structures may be highly effective and adaptive in innovating and producing social change and in helping social movements to survive in the face of attempts at opposition and social control. The network structure has the advantages of resistance to suppression, together with increasing possibilities for multipenetration and adaptive variation as each cell or part of the network does its own thing in a way appropriate for reaching its change objectives in the particular context or contexts in which it operates.

The fact of variation in structural form across the different ICI OD groups along a spectrum of a distinct and hierarchically led functional unit on the organisation chart, through a temporary task force, to a group of like-minded individuals forming a voluntary association and then an extended network in their division, to the attempt to create and maintain a wider ICI OD network across most of the UK divisions, offers some scope for suggesting how variability in structural form may have influenced the strategies and pathways of development of each group.

Although the focal level of analysis here is clearly the group, no satisfactory analysis of each OD group's emergence, development, and fate would be complete without reference to the immediate and more distant context within which each OD group had to make its way. In discussing factors which inhibited or facilitated attempts by executives to create strategic change, the point was made that variations at any point in time or through time, either in what was described as features of inner or outer context of company or division, could signally influence the timing and extent of particular changes. Equally well, the argument was made that part of the executive skill in generating energy and commitment for strategic change rested on the executive's ability to understand, come to terms with, and then alter, features of their inner context such as the divisional structure and culture, and to mobilise changes in outer context such as economic trends and business competitive position to help justify and unify action in the change sphere. The same logic applies to attempts by specialist resources to create change, indeed because advisory groups by definition are clearly weaker than executives in structural and strategic terms, then antecedent conditions and auspicious and inauspicious features of present and emerging context may play an even greater role in explaining the fate and impact of specialist attempts to make change happen.

The more immediate context surrounding each OD group is referred to as the *inner context*. Here variability in context is examined for auspicious and inauspicious antecedent conditions and settings in which each group was born, and for the evolution and selective impact of that context both in the constraining and enabling senses, as each group itself developed through time. Particular features of the inner context of each group examined are company and divisional organisational cultures (Pettigrew, 1979) stability and change in norms, power distributions, and recurring conflicts (Pettigrew, 1973, 1975), the social control and other attitudes and behaviours directed towards each group by key figures and interest groups in their environment, and the relationship between these factors and the organisational impact and survival of the OD groups.

But as we saw in examining the determinants of strategic change, contexts of a receptive or non-receptive kind to change are also influenced by features of the *outer-context* level of analysis. Outer-context refers to the business performance and competitive position of ICI as a whole, and to each division under study throughout the period 1960–83, and to corporate and divisional policy in the manpower and personnel spheres over the past two decades. Also included here are the broad social, economic, and political trends in UK society throughout the past 25 years, in so far as they affected the business fortunes and general personnel policies of ICI, and as they impacted on the emergence and changing use made of OD consultants, their techniques, knowledge, and skills.

The overriding assumption behind this analysis of the emergence, evolution, fate, and impact of ICI OD groups is that the pattern of each group's development is a result of a complex interplay of contextual factors and factors related to the internal structure, strategies, leadership, and activities of each group. The interplay between these external and internal factors is of course best understood as a continuous process evolving through time. In terms of the balance or weight of explanation of external or internal factors as contributors to the development, survival, and impact of innovating groups, the predisposition is to treat aspects of the inner and outer context together with specific antecedent conditions (the external factors) as the necessary conditions which provide the boundaries of opportunity and constraint within which the sufficient conditions of the strategic capabilities and action of the innovating group can be differentially expressed.

But having divided the world into necessary conditions – factors external to the innovating group, and sufficient conditions – factors internal to the group, it is recognised that at the level of understanding and action, a key part of the process influencing an OD group's fate rests on their perception of features of inner and outer context, together with the skill with which they act on that understanding in the light of changing features of context through time. An advisory group interested in creating change must itself attempt to fashion a social context in which it can survive and prosper. Such attempts to legitimate specialist group actions and objectives by, for example, linking the content and process of specific changes to issues and concerns given special credence by changes in power distributions and/or economic and business trends, conceptually represents the link between the group level of analysis and the inner and outer context levels of analysis. Context is then being treated neither just as descriptive background, nor as a source of opportunity and constraint for change, but as something which must be accessible and understood by the innovating group, and ultimately mobilised to achieve practical effects.

This chapter is divided into four sections. Immediately following this introduction the reader is briefly reminded of the natural history of development and fate of the OD resources in Group Personnel Department in Millbank, and in Agricultural, Petrochemicals, Plastics, and Mond Division. There then follow two sections, the first of which explores variability in the context, antecedent conditions, and birth processes of the various OD groups, and this is followed by a section examining the role of leadership, group-building, and strategies of boundary management and legitimisation in influencing the character of development and fate of the different OD groups. The chapter ends by pinpointing some of the practical implications of the ICI OD experience in using internal and external OD consultants for others seeking to harness specialist skills to help create processes of organisational change.

VARIATION IN THE NATURAL HISTORY OF DEVELOPMENT AND IMPACT OF
ORGANISATION DEVELOPMENT RESOURCES IN ICI

Although in one way or another the creation of all five sets of OD resources reported in this study was linked to the corporate-driven change programmes of the late 1960s and early 1970s given the acronyms MUPS/WSA and SDP, and none of these groups exist now in 1983 in a size or form comparable with how they were in the early 1970s, all five sets of OD resources had quite different processes of development, experienced to degrees a different fate, and had varying impacts on the settings with which they engaged.

The corporate OD resources

As was described in Chapters 4 and 10, ICI's corporate interest first of all in the behavioural sciences and then as it had become to be known by late 1960s as organisation development, was linked to the package of strategic changes formulated in the early 1960s to try and improve the company's competitive position. Part of the company's solution to the competitiveness problem was defined in terms of improvements in manpower productivity, and given the national political and economic context of the day, the most appropriate vehicle for attempts at productivity change was the productivity bargain. OD performed two critical functions in and around ICI's particular form of productivity bargain MUPS/WSA. Initially the concepts and language of the behavioural sciences and OD, helped to provide some of the justificatory language and values to launch the more expansive social and change objectives of MUPS/ WSA. But crucially OD really took off at the corporate level as it became more and more apparent in 1967 and 1968 that in MUPS ICI had a strategy for change without the corporate or divisional capability to implement it. Faced with widespread management and trade union resistance in the divisions to what was perceived as a centrally imposed change, George Bridge and Tom Evans were brought down from Billingham to Millbank to rescue and revitalise the ailing MUPS and transform it, from the trade union point of view, into the more acceptable WSA.

In 1968 George Bridge created the development and applications groups of Tom Evans, Stewart Dudley and two more junior people to create a corporate focus for bringing the behavioural sciences into the company, and to help deal with resistance to MUPS/WSA. With the direct political sponsorship of Bridge, and indirectly the support of those members of the ICI main board advocating MUPS/WSA, the four-man central OD group wrapped themselves around the clear and legitimate task of helping divisional management accommodate to the new management style and problem-solving skills now necessary to engage with shop stewards to effectively implement MUPS/WSA.

In terms of internal development and evolution it is important to note that the central OD group was never more than a shifting, informal group of the senior and more ideologically and professionally committed pair of Evans and Dudley, and a less committed and more junior pair of helpers. Between 1968 and 1971 these four ran a series of behavioural workshops for the 500 or so key production managers in ICI, acted as a link for the many external OD consultants brought into ICI at that time, began the process of training and creating a network of some 50 divisional internal OD constultants, and then helped to devise and implement the company-wide staff development programme which involved more than 40,000 middle managers.

This was the zenith of central OD activity on this sort of broad scale. By the end of 1971 with WSA and SDP substantially implemented, and the ICI line management system exhausted by the efforts in absorbing WSA, cynical towards the purposes of SDP, and now engaged in various divisional manpower reductions exercises, the opponents and doubters of OD came out into the open. OD was not only guilty by association because of its links with WSA and SDP, but it had acquired two other negative aspects to its image. The first was that it was seen as a manipulative tool for the ICI power system, and particularly that part of the power system which needed it and used it most – the personnel function. Secondly OD's close association with psychology, its overclinical image, and threatening messages about shared responsibility and participative management, were difficult for managers to handle, especially when those managers were in no way sure that their own superiors were sharing responsibility for any experimental changes that were made.

With the above changes in context and in attitudes to the vehicle of OD, the perceived management need for and legitimacy of OD declined, and during 1972 the central OD resources were rather suddenly reduced in size and influence. Without the focus provided by the unhappy mother vehicles of WSA and SDP, central OD's sole survivor Stewart Dudley had to work his way around the economic blizzard and short-term expediency management of 1972 to find an independent role for OD. There was no pretence of a central OD group throughout the 1970s. The story of the development of corporate OD after 1972 is the continuing access to the main board of the external OD consultant Ron Mercer, the highly selective sponsoring of Dudley and James by two executive directors, Harvey-Jones and Woodburn, the very non-directive almost laissez-faire management and support of the Company OD network by Dudley and McBride, and the clear change of strategy by Dudley, Mercer, and McBride to play down the behaviourist image of OD of the 1960s, and project OD as a process resource to help selected power figures on questions of strategy, planning, and change at the centre of power. As we described in Chapter 10, Dudley, Mercer, and James did play a continuing role throughout the 1970s in assisting Harvey-Jones and Woodburn influence the climate for strategic change at the corporate level, and eventually aid the processes of accommodation and stabilisation of change, but in no sense could it be said they were part of the direct process of planning and action to create change. Dudley and James survived until their retirement in 1982 and 1983 respectively.

Significantly a high-level central OD resource was retained when Nicholas Mann was appointed to succeed Dudley.

Agricultural Division OD resources

Of the ICI divisions studied in this research, apart from Mond Division, Agricultural Division is alone in still using OD resources in 1983, although in Agricultural Division little visibility or publicity is given to the term organisation development in the early 1980s. The Agricultural Division OD story is an important case because at Billingham the OD group had in earlier times a not inconsiderable impact on problems of industrial relations, the processes of designing and commissioning new plant, and the operating management of large chemical plants. The Agricultural Division OD resources also had some success, and certainly much more so than the groups in Petrochemicals and Plastics Divisions, in institutionalising the precepts, techniques, and problem-solving approach of OD amongst selected key managers, and at times, powerful shop stewards until by the mid to late 1970s an increasingly risk-aversive works management culture withdrew from contact with an increasingly tired group of internal consultants whose third-party methods and joint management–union problem-solving approaches seemed increasingly out of touch with the line management concerns and business priorities of the day.

If the corporate OD resources had been propelled into existence by the powerfully sponsored but ultimately singularly dangerous requirement to help implement a centrally imposed change programme, no such specific need faced the OD group constituted in 1969 at Billingham by Noel Ripley, the newly employed young American internal OD consultant. Ripley entered a context which had been opened up by a combination of 10 years of almost continuous technological change, by the dangerously poor levels of business performance of the late 1950s and late 1960s, and of course by the immediate antecedent of George Bridge's era of social innovation at Billingham. Bridge's initiatives towards opening the social system of Agricultural Division to change left behind a legacy of a number of personnel officers and trainers wishing to know more about OD, a seedbed of line managers who became some of the early clients of Ripley and his group, together with confusion and misunderstanding about what the behavioural sciences and OD might offer, and real resentment amongst some line managers about being force-fed behavioural science ideas on Bridge's ever pushing spoon.

Ripley arrived at Billingham into a highly decentralised personnel function. This was critical because it meant that even if Ripley had desired it, there was no question of setting up a central OD unit in the personnel function. Instead Ripley began with a change strategy the opposite to that chosen by Bridge. Change processes had now to be mutual and collaborative and not imposed. There were to be no more change projects or programmes, changes would emerge slowly and organically, step by step from a base provided by where managers felt their problems to be, and where they wanted to start.

The early internal evolution of OD resources in Agricultural Division was dominated by three factors. First of all the clarity of Ripley's leadership in propagating an organic change strategy and a coherent set of values to inform the direction of OD in the division. Secondly Ripley's skill in drawing together a set of personnel officers and trainers into the network or voluntary association of like-minded individuals which was the OD group, and thirdly Ripley's use of the Swallow group meetings to build his network of third-party helpers into a committed and cohesive group with the skills and sense of support to assist them take the risks of offering line managers help through unconventional means.

With the base supplied and created by Bridge's opening up of the Billingham management culture, Ripley's leadership and OD skills, and the informal association of the Swallow group, the OD resources began to establish a network of clients in the middle to upper reaches of the project and engineering, and production parts of the division. A watershed for the OD group was provided by their heavy involvement with the commissioning of the Methanol 2 project. It was critical to the division that this major new plant was successfully commissioned, and the effective use of OD resources in producing a success helped the legitimacy of OD in the division.

Set against these early successes it is important to note that the OD group's network of clients did not extend outside production, nor did the group become much involved with board members. After 2 or 3 years of functioning the OD group began to attract some doubts and hostility from personnel officers who felt themselves excluded from the club-like atmosphere of the Swallow group, and from senior industrial relations and line managers who were suspicious both of the neutral third-party role adopted by the OD group, and what they perceived to be threatening, almost anti-system or revolutionary statements coming from some members of the Swallow group.

Although by 1972 Ripley was still the informal leader of the OD group, for some time a personnel manager, Paul Miles, had been formally asked to manage the division's OD resources. The period when the early intensity of the Swallow group meetings began to wane, was associated both with greater confidence by individual group members in working with clients, and also the diffusion of OD methods and skills into the joint management–union problem-solving work in Ammonia Works, and the open-systems planning work in Engineering Works. Effectively this was a demonstration of Ripley's organic strategy. From the base supplied by the Swallow group and their clients, an extended OD network had now been built out into two of the major works in the division.

However, in 1974 after an unsuccessful attempt to establish OD clients on the division board and in some of the division's headquarters departments, Ripley returned to the United States. In 1976 Miles also left the division. By then the internal OD consultants were becoming tired and disillusioned, as they found the market for their services disappearing, and as their organic strategy looked more and more in need of self-renewal and different leadership. OD survived into the 1980s in Agricultural Division because of three factors. First of all the external OD consultant Larsen continued to be used by the division's senior management and board. Secondly the assistant personnel manager, Moores, who now had responsibility for developmental activities in the personnel function, chose to forget about the neutral third-party role and connect OD help into the division through the legitimate channel of his functional interest in career and manpower matters; and finally because both Larsen and Moores sought to coalesce OD skills around the critical management concern of the early 1980s, structural and cultural change and manpower reductions. OD survived by a refocussing of its content and style to match the management priorities of a new business and organisational context. OD was still just about in business in 1983, and one reason why it was, was that the term OD was never used to describe the work that Larsen, Moores, and their small team did.

The Petrochemicals Division OD unit

The Petrochemicals Division (PCD) OD unit was born in mid-1970 and was disbanded at the end of 1973. In this 3½-year period part of the OD unit worked closely with the chairman of PCD, John Harvey-Jones, in formulating and implementing a major structural change. When their powerful sponsor was promoted out of the division, his successor quickly tidied the OD unit away. It could be argued that the OD unit was effective in the limited role it had as a top management task force, but left little behind to improve the capacity of PCD to manage change on an ongoing basis.

The PCD OD unit's only advantage at birth was its sponsorship by John Harvey-Jones. Although the Wilton manufacturing site had been the recipient of some management and social change as a consequence of WSA and the Coverdale programme, the HOC/PCD board and senior management had been little affected by the "behavioural sixties", and certainly their preoccupation with the continual growth and technical development of the division in the context of a fairly volatile profitability record, had not been interrupted by any attempt at social architecture of the kind that Bridge had been encouraging in Agricultural Division.

Unlike the Agricultural Division OD group which had evolved slowly from the voluntary association of the Swallow group into an extended network of OD resources that linked into the middle and senior levels of production management, the PCD OD resources made an instant appearance as a high-level three-man task force of Heath, Parker, and James, which then constituted itself as a distinct unit in the structure when it acquired Ward, Brown and the other former members of the OD projects section of the recently disbanded Divisional Management Services Department. From the beginning there were differences of view and confusions about what the OD unit's role should be. John Harvey-Jones, in May 1970 still a deputy chairman of HOC Division saw the OD unit contributing to some of his longer-term organisational aims of relaxing the attitudes and behavioural processes of the division. Concern amongst his senior colleagues that the OD unit might pitch the division too forcefully into culture change, meant that Harvey-Jones had to take the senior and respected Heath and Parker and create a trio which would confine themselves to an investigation and recommendations about the division's structure. This was an inauspicious beginning for a task force trio and a resource group of Ward and his colleagues who had to find coherence and identity in a demonstrably non-receptive context.

The internal life of the OD unit was from the beginning characterised by a split between "the right wing" and more respectable trio who had a clear task and a high level sponsor, and "the left wing" or behavioural group who once they had implemented the never popular or acceptable SDP, had to find a task and negotiate sponsorship where they could. Heath, the manager of the OD unit, resisted any attempt at team- or group-building of the variety that Ripley had orchestrated at Billingham for the Swallow group; he and Parker clearly believed they were part of a temporary task force and kept their distance from what certainly Heath regarded as the behavioural excesses and exclusive value position of the "left wing".

The task force trio's first attempt to recommend an organisational change was overtaken by the structural changes of 1971 which added bits of other divisions to HOC and reconstituted HOC Division as Petrochemicals Division. Parker and Heath left the OD unit in 1971 and early 1972, and with the bulk of SDP work now over the "left wing" of the unit was reduced in size. James's accession as manager of the OD unit coincided with Harvey-Jones's renewed interest in a structural change for PCD. James worked closely on the second organisation study with PCD directors, and the external OD consultant Ron Mercer, so that this time a firm recommendation went to the board to change the top structure which was politically acceptable.

Meanwhile the "left wing" struggled to find clients and credibility in the headquarters departments. They had some successes in following up interest generated by SDP in the R&D and Engineering departments, but these were the two least powerful functions in the division and the scattered work they did there was neither sustainable in those departments nor exportable into the more prestigious marketing, technical, or production functions.

Before Harvey-Jones was promoted out of the division in April 1973, most of the behavioural wing of the OD unit had either left the OD unit or the company. With the organisation study completed and the structural change implemented, James left for another part of ICI. The task force's task now complete, and with the new chairman's energies firmly focussed on further capital development and growth for PCD, there was no need for an OD resource, and in November 1973 the recommendation was made to wind up what was left of the OD unit.

The Plastics Division OD resources

The Plastics Division OD resources survived for about 10 years in a division which was at times both hostile and indifferent not only to the OD group and their particular view of the requirements for change in the division, but also the concept of, and need to change, the business, organisation, and culture of the division. From this weak base the OD group, perhaps from choice and perhaps from force of circumstance, formed themselves into a fractionated, exclusive group whose specialist role and contribution was easy for others to question and at times denigrate. In this context, whether it was from top management indifference or inattentiveness or not, perhaps the Plastics Division OD resource's greatest success was their own survival for so long.

Paradoxically, of the divisions analysed in this book, Plastics Division had the greatest need for business, organisational, and management culture change, but because it had the greatest need, it had ill-developed capacities and capabilities to see that need, never mind perceive the need and act on it. The fact of birth into such an inauspicious context, combined with the low-key and low-level antecedents and origins of the Plastics Division OD resources was fateful for the continuing development, legitimacy, penetration, and impact of OD in this division.

OD crystallised in Plastics Division around the interest of an assistant personnel manager, Paul Miles, and the divisional education officer, Simon Dow. When in 1969 Miles was promoted up to Agricultural Division, Dow was allowed to recruit a young British social science Ph.D., David Cowan, and an ex-member of the sales/marketing function David Hunt, to form the rump of his OD resources. Dow had the name of his education department changed to Training and Personnel Development Department, T&PD, and he, Hunt, and Cowan quickly were labelled and assumed the role of the OD in-group in a mixed department of apprentice and secretarial trainers, and management and supervisory training officers. The split in T&PD between the pro- and anti-OD factions was a continuing drain on the department's energy and credibility throughout its life, and prevented any real attempt at group-building and coherence in the face of an already unreceptive environment.

Given that as they started Dow, Cowan, and Hunt had neither skill, experience, nor training in OD, and they had no experienced internal consultant like Ripley, or external consultant such as Mercer to lead them or help build a climate to support their work, their early efforts were directed to training themselves and providing fairly conventional training activities for the division's middle managers. Dow sensed early on that he would make little progress until he dented the technocratic, rationalistic, and reactive senior management culture at the Welwyn headquarters departments and on the Plastics board, but his attempts in 1970 and 1971 to influence the top managers in the division by encouraging them to go on T-groups and other behavioural training events, by and large was a failure.

The 1972 redundancies cut Dow's department by over 50%, but he was able to retain all of his in-group, much to the chagrin of the survivors of the out-group. As Dow began to tire of attempts to pull the T&PD department together, he concentrated more and more on relating to his staff through individual counselling relationships and allowed a pattern of working to develop whereby individuals got on with their own thing. The replacement in 1973 of

Hunt and Cowan by two other OD resources neither cured the in-group–out-group split in the department or substantially influenced the legitimacy of OD in the division.

Not even the arrival of a new chairman and three or four new directors during the period 1972–74 had much impact on the division's receptivity to change. Some of these new directors were previous users of OD methods and consultants, but open and powerful opposition from at least two senior members of the Plastics board meant that if they were to retain their credibility on the board they had to forgo appeals to cultural change, and certainly abandon the use of OD techniques and language. In spite of the unavailability of these potential senior allies, Dow persisted in his attempts to influence the culture and management processes in the division. Two further attempts were made to bring prominent external consultants into the division but they were eventually rejected by senior figures on the Plastics board.

Eventually Dow left Plastics Division but not before he and two colleagues had developed the highly successful training package Minding Our Own Business (MOOB). In the worsening business conditions of the mid to late 1970s many divisions of ICI and indeed other UK firms bought MOOB as a package to try and educate their employees about what they saw as the financial and business realities of the day. Needless to say Dow and his colleagues got little credit from the Plastics board for developing MOOB. The OD resources in T&PD staggered on into 1980, co-ordinated now by the head of the Management Services Department, but in the sharp dose of redundancies made during 1980 after the very bad financial results of that year, virtually all of the OD resources in the division, and all of the management trainers, were made surplus to requirements.

The Mond Division OD resources

As we saw in Chapter 9, the organisational locus, use, and eventual impact of OD resources in Mond Division was quite different from the three other divisions reported in this study. The unique and significant feature of the Mond OD work was that for a variety of changing motives it was launched and led not by a group of internal or external specialists, but by a small but powerful group on the Mond board. Starting in 1973 with the lead given by the then new division chairman Tony Woodburn, a lead which crucially was sustained by his two successors, and materially assisted by the personnel directors Dylan Jones and Nicholas Mann; and the continuing use of an external consultant and a very small group of internal consultants, the political focus for OD was around a long-term strategy which said "start at the top and work down". However, even with this continuity of political support at the top of the division's power structure, the process of engaging OD thinking and expertise to the business and organisational problems of the division was faltering, meandering, and haphazard. Nevertheless this long period of learning and preparation eventually bore fruit when in the business crisis of 1979–83 there was a clear, practical, and profound connection of OD thinking and action to the strategic problems of the day.

Before Woodburn began his top-level initiative in 1973 to influence the style and purpose of the Mond board, and increase individual director's awareness of changing features of the division's business, social, and political environment, there had been two lower-level developmental initiatives in Mond. The first connecting point for OD in the division had been the stimulant provided by MUPS/WSA in the production areas. The opportunity MUPS/WSA allowed to bring behavioural packages such as Coverdale into the division, gave early encouragement to more socially and politically aware works managers such as Bay, Jones, and Marshall to try and move an excessively technocratic set of production managers to consider engaging with an increasingly militant work force in a less distant and hierarchical manner. In a situation where in the early 1970s there were no clear personnel policies coming from the Mond board, and where the "cruiser captain" works managers were used to high degrees of autonomy about means if not always about ends, this early developmental work was idiosyncratic and unco-ordinated. It was only the increasingly visible, and from a business point of view, punishing industrial relations fires of the 1972–75 period which forced the hand of the Mond board and the Mond works managers and helped to develop more effective management processes between the works managers, and between the board and their senior production people. The IR fires thus acted as a trigger for Woodburn's attempts to unify the Mond board, and to encourage the then deputy chairman Frank Bay to ask the works manager Sandy Marshall to take up a full-time role as a divisional development resource. This was an important step in its own right at the time, for it meant that OD now had legitimate activists with political standing on the board and at senior management levels, but in the longer term it was even more important, for Marshall and his junior colleague Campbell linking with the external consultant Wilson played a key role in increasing the capability and confidence of senior and middle managers to diagnose and manage processes of change.

Aside from the important seeding of developmental thinking which had gone on in the production areas during and after the implementation of WSA, the other OD initiative taken prior to Woodburn's chairmanship was the failed attempt to train and launch internal change agents into the division. Mond sent a group of fairly junior line managers to the Eastbourne 1 workshop organised by Evans and Dudley to train a cadre of ICI change agents. Given the feedback from this first group of trainees, Mond found it difficult to scratch together a group of personnel and trainers to attend Eastbourne 2. All the interview reports comment how difficult these change agents found it to make any impact on the hierarchical and segmented Mond management culture. The change agents were seen to challenge management values and competences, and their behaviourist ideas and process skills were quickly dubbed "sandals and beads OD". Although a few of these change agents settled down to contribute in individual works, the majority were "unloved and neglected". There was never any pretence in the upper reaches of Mond that in the context of that hierarchical management culture, a bottom-up change strategy facilitated by specialist change agents who had neither the right message nor the right positional power, could be effective. Starting at the top and working down was the only politically feasible change process for the Mond context, as indeed it was in Plastics Division, but the difference between Mond and Plastics was there was continuity of leadership in change management in Mond that was never available in Plastics Division.

Another key input into the Mond development activities was provided by the American external OD consultants Bainton and Wilson. They provided many of the early ideas and process mechanisms, together with the support and encouragement for Woodburn to try to break some of patterns and traditions in the division, and create a more unified board with a sharper awareness of the pressures building on the division from a changing environment. As often is the case with consultants, Bainton's position in the division was dependent on his relationship with Woodburn and when Woodburn was promoted onto the main board, Bainton faded away. However, increasingly carefully managed and at times protected by Nicholas Mann, Wilson carried on working with the Mond board acting as an innovative conceptualiser, pragmatic helper, and high-level trainer up to and beyond the 1979–83 strategic changes.

It should not be under-emphasised the extent to which the stream of developmental activities in Mond was held together in the pre-1979 crisis situation by Nicholas Mann, and then released in the crisis situation through Mann's significant role in creating and articulating the Mond Management Model. This model provided an intellectually coherent set of principles and concepts, and indeed a pragmatic content for the structural and manpower changes made during 1979–83. With the window for change provided by the post-1979 crisis, thanks to the developmental stream of by then 6 years duration, Mond was well placed to act in the change sphere. There had been considerable progress in unifying the perspective and actions of the Mond board, the Mond Management Model provided a coherent content and rationale for change, and real strides had been made in helping to raise the capability and confidence of senior and middle managers to effect significant organisational, cultural, and manpower changes. Here was OD put to effective use in the interests of the top management of the division – precisely what the aspiration had been as long ago as 1973.

CONTEXTS, ANTECEDENTS, AND BIRTH PROCESSES OF ORGANISATION DEVELOPMENT IN ICI

Earlier in this chapter the point was made that primacy of explanation of the growth, decline, and impact of innovating groups such as OD specialists lies in exogenous factors in their environment, rather than the internal developments and strategies of those groups as such. This, of course, is not to argue that the leadership, strategic capabilities and actions of such groups are not connectable to discussions about their fate, but merely that aspects of the inner and outer context surrounding any embryonic group, together with immediate antecedents of the group's birth, and the character of the birth processes themselves, shape the very existence and direction of development possible for any innovating group. Balancing strategic explanations against environmental explanations of the fate of social movement organisations Freeman (1979:167) argues that "what is clear is that whatever strategy a group desires, it must be developed within certain confines. The group can do no more than its resources and its environment permit, and if these are inadequate to meet the dictates of its ideology it is usually doomed to inefficacy". Freeman's (1979) emphasis on environmental determinism is clearly harder than the more action-oriented theoretical approach adopted by this author, for in her sensible attempt to stipulate the confining characteristics of environment, she underemphasises both the opposite possibility of receptive contexts to innovating groups, and the differential ability of innovators to understand and act on changing features of inner and outer context as part of their strategy for creating a social context in which survival chances and impact may be increased. But put in broader terms the point should not be lost that "the social soil into which an individual attempts to plant and nurture the seeds of change is undoubtedly fateful for what will grow" (Sarason *et al.*, 1977:186).

However, as we saw in Chapter 1, one of the problems with the literature on organisation change is that it has rather more to say about processes of change, often in terms of general principles about diagnosis, feedback, and evaluation and so on, than it has about the context of change. This is a major pragmatic difficulty in thinking and acting about change for, as we saw in our discussions of strategic change in Chapter 11, changes often occur when there is some degree of matching between choice of change process and change content, for a particular context. A further problem with developing and implementing change processes is that they take place in unique or nearly unique contexts; and while it may be sensible to argue that it is the context or perceptions of the context which ought to govern the choice of change content and process mechanisms, it is difficult to discuss context in anything other than a very general or in a case-specific way.

One might have assumed that in a large organisation like ICI, with a distinctive company culture and at least in the personnel and manpower areas a long history of clear attempts to formulate and implement consistent policies and practices, that the four divisions in this study would have provided similar contexts for the emergence and development of OD resources. However, the accounts of the business history and development, and management and shop floor cultures of those divisions indicate not only clear differences in context between divisions at any point in time, and within divisions over time, but also differences in response patterns to changes emanating from the ICI corporate centre. At the time in the late 1960s and early 1970s when OD resources were emerging in the various ICI divisions one relevant part of the context was the framework of personnel policy and practice explicit in WSA and SDP. Our historical chapters showed that responses to MUPS/WSA and SDP varied both across divisions, and between different works and departments in divisions. However our historical chapters also demonstrated that in the late 1960s the divisions were in different competitive positions in their product-markets, were experiencing and had experienced different levels of volatility or stability in their profitability, were facing different rates of technological change, varied in the age and stability of the management group who controlled the division, and in Kanter's (1983) terms had more or less segmented or integrative structures and cultures. As a consequence of mixtures of these factors the power systems of each division perceived they had different issues, grievances, and concerns to deal with, to varying degrees had change-minded executive leadership prepared to pick up and grapple with those issues, and to varying degrees the boards and senior management of the divisions offered support, opposition, and indifference to the creation of specialist OD resources. Even without the variability in the birth processes and immediate historical and idiosyncratic antecedents of each OD group, it is evident that some OD groups were born into more repressive and inauspicious contexts than others.

Of the four divisions in this study the Agricultural OD resources seem to have been born into the most receptive context while the Plastics OD resources faced the most repressive environment. Simply put the Agricultural Division context was more receptive to innovation using OD techniques and methods because of the mixture of stability and change going on amongst elements of the Billingham context, because of the antecedents of OD prior to 1969; and as we shall argue in the next section of this chapter, the sound fit between the structure and strategy chosen for OD at its birth. In terms of change potential the important thing about Billingham in the 1960s was that not only was it being challenged by new outside directors and its weakening competitive position into making technological and productivity changes, but that key features of the Billingham structure, culture, and political system remained stable enough in amongst the changes that did occur to absorb those changes and the methods and processes of change associated with OD activities.

A brief comparison of the contextual differences between Agricultural Division and HOC/PCD will reveal both some of the stable features of Billingham management culture which may have helped change, and features of the HOC/PCD context which were not conducive to the use of specialist change resources in general and the OD variant of those in particular. Agricultural Division at Billingham had a much longer history than HOC/PCD, had developed a brand of paternalistic management in much more of a company town atmosphere than was evident at Wilton, and had developed a more stable and integrated management culture than existed in HOC/PCD. The stability of the Agricultural Division structure after the 1963 change from functional to a matrix structure, plus the network system of relations amongst a reasonably stable group of senior and middle managers, and the undisputed and continuing power of the production function in the division created a social system which responded to the competitive and technological pressures of the day, and was able at some level to engage with OD when it came.

HOC/PCD, on the other hand, was a much younger organisation with less tradition in its mode of operations and in relations between various groups of people in the division. It was not subjected to any single major commercial threat during the 1960s and early 1970s, although its profit levels were highly volatile. Its major problem during the 1960s appeared to be how best to co-ordinate the various growing elements of its activity. There was not the same clarity of power distribution in HOC/PCD as there was in Agricultural Division. In HOC/PCD around 1970 power appeared to be contested between the technical, production, and marketing functions, and there was much more talk of inter-functional conflict in HOC/PCD than was mentioned in relation to Agricultural Division. The HOC/PCD management culture was also described as being more achievement-oriented and aggressive than Agricultural Division, perhaps because of the rapid growth of HOC during the 1960s and the reinforcing effect of continual influxes of bright new technologists who found at that time easy scope for job satisfaction and promotion. If technological arrogance, the desire for technical perfection and the inconceivability of saying "I don't know" were other hallmarks of the HOC/PCD management culture, a manifestation of those features of the culture crucial to the eventual response to the OD unit was that managers were expected to be self-sufficient in solving their own problems. On top of any additional fragmentation that may have resulted from this atomistic view of managerial problem-solving, HOC/PCD was in a state of almost continual flux not just because of the repeated injections of new capital, but because of regular structural change. There was a strong belief in HOC/PCD which was reflected in behaviours, that the best way to make change in the organisation was by re-design, re-appointment, and re-grouping. The original minimally acceptable purpose of the HOC/PCD OD unit was, of course, to be concerned with structural change, and more than 50% of the original members were victims of the recent demise of the large divisional Management Services Department.

Thus unlike Agricultural Division, which had been opened up by massive technological innovation and a severe commercial threat, HOC/PCD had experienced no commercial trauma and witnessed the mere addition of capital rather than the total revamping of existing technology. A further difference in context in these two divisions relevant to the question of receptivity to OD approaches to change was that, unlike Billingham, the expanding, rapidly changing HOC/PCD without historically based, stable networks of relations between managers, was relatively poorly placed in integrative terms to absorb the ideas of the OD unit or tolerate the perceived riskiness of its objectives and methods.

Moving away just from differences of receiving context for OD between Agricultural Division and HOC/PCD, another important issue was the different immediate antecedent conditions which created rather varying pre-beginnings for OD in the two divisions. Led by George Bridge and Tom Evans, enabled by MUPS, and supported by some of the stable elements in the Agricultural Division management culture mentioned above, Billingham experimented in a fairly radical way with behavioural science ideas and OD methods in the 6- or 7-year period before Noel Ripley came to give real conceptual, value, and organisation focus to OD activities. Directors went off on T-groups, managers and shop stewards were exposed to unconventional training methods, a series of well-known American behavioural science consultants were trawled through the division, and a more active and developmentally minded concept of personnel was encouraged in a newly decentralised personnel function. Compared with all this activity, the climate setting for OD amongst the HOC/PCD board and senior and middle managers in all the major departments other than production was almost non-existent. The weaknesses in the management processes and organisation on the Wilton site exposed by the effective for a time resistance to MUPS/WSA, gave rise to a major management development activity in which £250,000 was spent on the package OD programme, Coverdale, but the effects of this were not really felt on the HOC/PCD board or the headquarters departments such as Technical, Marketing, R&D, or Engineering. Worse still for the yet-to-be-born HOC/PCD OD resources than the absence of any seeding or climate setting for OD, was the fact that the rump of the left or behavioural wing of the OD unit was acquiring a negative image whilst still in the Management Services Department, because of their association with the unpopular SDP, and their own style of zealously advocating and putting across SDP. Compared with this Bridge's efforts were creating a set of interested individuals who Ripley would recruit into and create the Swallow Group, and a number of awakening managers who would become the first clients and early adopters of OD concepts and methods. In addition after the Bridge bow wave, Ripley's step-by-step, client-centred, organic approach to change was to have its supporters if only because of its contrast with Bridge's powerful and pushing style. Alongside all this the HOC/PCD OD resources had the single political sponsorship and ideas of John Harvey-Jones as the motive force behind their birth, and even at the creation of the task force Harvey-Jones was being persuaded by his more cautious and conservative peers to ensure that the wild behavioural men were supervised and contained by Heath and Parker.

The central OD resources came directly out of the ICI policy context which created MUPS/WSA and SDP; this was their opportunity and their problem. Like the PCD OD unit they were too tied to one or two activities, and were linked at birth too exclusively and threateningly from the viewpoint of some of their potential clients in senior and middle management, to the needs of the top power system. In this sense, although the central OD unit did play an important role in helping to implement MUPS/WSA and SDP, and the HOC/PCD OD unit were instrumental in creating a top-level structural change, neither group was able to recover from the particularities of their antecedents, or their structural location and rationale at birth.

The context and antecedents of OD in Plastics Division were substantially more unreceptive than in any of the other divisions in this study; indeed it is surprising that OD was ever allowed a toe-hold in the division. Paradoxically the toe-hold that was created was a result of the very same cautious, segmented, management culture that created management processes so inimical to the sensing and making of strategic change. Faced in the late 1960s with Millbank pressure to devote resource to management training and development Simon

Dow did what was minimally necessary to get at that stage non-threatening things to happen within the Plastics segmented culture and political system. He persuaded his functional boss the personnel director that a rather conventional divisional education department should be turned into a department with at least a sub-set of people with OD skills. OD thus began in Plastics Division in association with a low status activity – education and training, and with no more understanding and legitimacy than was available from Dow and his functional boss. In most situations this would have been a recipe for difficulty, in the confines of the Plastics inner and outer context, as far as OD was concerned, it was a hopeless start and a lost cause.

The reader will recall Plastics Division had most of the elements of a classic segmented management structure and culture. Plastics Division was a compartmentalised and hierarchical world where the chairman and his deputies related to their directors on a one-to-one basis; where in consequence there was little board policy-making and planning, and where the upper reaches of the division were divided by function and business area; and where there was as big a gap between the senior managers and the directors as there was between the directors and "the top box" of the chairman and his deputies. Businesswise the 1950s and 1960s had been an era of scientific-led growth with easy if not large profits. Other core features of the Plastics management culture were the great stability and continuity in the top management of the division right up until 1972, the relative isolation of Plastics from many of the structural and business area changes of ICI, the geographical separation of the Plastics production sites from one another and from the divisional headquarters at Welwyn, and the attitudes and behaviour of the management culture with the emphasis on hierarchy, deference, scientific rationality, and non-risk-taking. In this situation, in spite of the first signs of commercial difficulty evident in the 1967 recession, there was no top management perception of commercial threat, nor any internal pressure for destabilising the divisional social system from a social architect such as Bridge or Harvey-Jones. The context and antecedents of OD in Plastics meant that the social soil in which the OD seed was thrown was particularly inauspicious for germination, for as Kanter (1983:62) argues under segmentalist conditions change is a threat. Where segmentalism has prevailed, security comes in the form of control, and loss of control is the supreme threat. For many of the Plastics board the activities of Dow, Hunt, and Cowan were a topic of indifference or doubt, but for two or three senior members of the Plastics board OD began to signal a fear of loss of control and this meant Dow had the additional problem of dealing with downright opposition as well as death through indifference. The fate of OD in Plastics Division was all but sealed before it had a chance to project itself out into the division.

This section has outlined why and how differences in context, antecedent conditions, and birth processes can provide the boundaries and therefore necessary conditions for the development, survival and impact of innovating groups. Given the boundaries of operation set by these factors, in what follows we examine how the different structures, strategies, and tactics of mobilisation attempted by each group influenced their ability to generate legitimacy for their objectives, methods, values, and activities. How did the groups develop in relation to the inner and outer contexts in which they emerged? To what extent did the immediate pre-history of the divisions propel them forward or block their progress? Here the concept of legitimacy is the nearest we come to a dependent variable in this research. We look on it as a central outcome of the interactions under analysis but do not view it as a dependent variable in the strict sense because the interest in process analysis requires that the implications of legitimacy at one time be traced forward into subsequent periods and events. Legitimacy is important and problematic for innovating groups because they face the dilemma of finding an appropriate middle ground. Towards one extreme, total illegitimacy will lead to rejection or, at best, minimal functioning in any culturally significant areas of the organisation. At the other extreme, total legitimacy means the group has little, if anything to offer in terms of a vision or process to facilitate change.

THE STRUCTURE, INTERNAL DEVELOPMENT, STRATEGY, AND LEGITIMACY OF THE ORGANISATION DEVELOPMENT GROUPS

Although an OD group cannot choose the context and antecedent conditions in which it is born, and may rarely be able to choose the timing, rationale, and location of its birth, it may in principle be able to influence a number of other factors which, interacting with the initial conditions, help to direct the pattern of its development and fate. These other factors include the choice of group members, the way and extent to which the group builds identity and commitment around a set of values, concepts, and activities, how it resolves conflict, exercises leadership, and structurally organises itself. In terms of the group's external evolution what is obviously critical is the locus and nature of the group's work, how it connects to existing organisational networks or builds its own, how it generates sponsorship and defends its boundaries, how it exercises influence and broadly nurtures and maintains its legitimacy in its particular context.

In focussing in on these different elements of a group's internal and external evolution it may also be possible to discern certain patterns or phases of group development when particular problems of leadership, cohesion or conflict, and boundary management and legitimacy occur. Thus Pettigrew (1975a) has developed a phase model of the evolution of innovating groups and departments which describes and analyses conception, pioneering, and self-doubt phases, and suggests how the choice of adaptive and maladaptive responses to managing the uncertainties of collective self-doubt can crucially influence the demise, absorption, consolidation and renewal of a specialist unit. Furthermore, although there is little evidence in these studies of OD groups, of those groups putting together elaborate and intendedly rational strategies to shape their fate, there is some evidence of groups drifting towards elements of what may be described as exclusive and inclusive stances in relation to their environment. The suggestion developed in this section is that the choice between different elements of these exclusive and inclusive stances constitute general pragmatic dilemmas faced by many innovating groups seeking to change their world while they try to live within it.

In looking at the content and consequences of strategic choices for innovating groups, it should not be forgotten that any such choices have to be made within the context and confines of some of the prior conditions already mentioned. Equally well, of course, we are talking about a continuous process where the factors influencing development and demise are cumulative. Finally it is analytically important to appreciate that the ground moves as the figure evolves and develops. Innovating groups are influenced not just by prior conditions and their strategic choices, but by changing fashions of concern and discontent, by what Downs (1972) describes as the attention cycles of issues, resulting from changes in this case of business, political, and organisational context.

Of the five accounts of the natural history of development of OD in this book, the Mond division experience is strikingly different from the others in so far as the harnessing and use of OD there was so much more clearly a senior executive and external consultant-led activity than it was an internal specialist activity. In looking at the other four groups the Plastics Division experience obviously stands out because of the unreceptiveness of its environment and the continuing inability of the group to generate enough acceptability to make any impact on its context. The central OD group was of course allowed and encouraged to fade away with the end of WSA and SDP, and the story of strategic choice for central OD after 1972 is really a story of a set of individuals grappling with questions of sponsorship, image, credibility, choice of activity, and impact. In terms of general questions about the evolution and impact of specialist innovating groups, the points of similarity and especially difference between the Agricultural division and HOC/PCD division experiences are probably the most instructive, for here we see evidence of impact in change terms by both groups arising from quite different choices in terms of structure, strategy, leadership, and internal team-building and commitment.

We have already noted that although Agricultural and HOC/PCD Divisions are two divisions of the same company located in the same part of the same country, in 1970 they were of similar size, and part of the same broad industrial grouping, the context and antecedent conditions for OD in those two divisions was quite different. It is also important before dwelling on some of the important differences between the two OD groups in those divisions to note some of their similarities. The groups were created within a year of each other, and geographically worked within a mile of one another. They were always small units of six to ten members. The term "OD" was used in reference to them and they were influenced more or less directly by American writing and practice in this area, and both groups were involved, to some extent, in team-building activities with clients. Both groups saw themselves and were perceived to be somewhat distinctive in relation to their own contexts, and thus acquired some of the opprobrium of distinctiveness. Further, there was a similar sort of conflict within each group on a behavioural versus business dimension, and the formal leader of each group to differing extents was seen as representing the business – structural – task end of that dimension.

However, given the straightforward facts that these were small OD groups in large business organisations, the differences between them are quite striking. In terms of conception and structure the HOC/PCD group made an instant appearance under Harvey-Jones's sponsorship, and was organised initially as a high-level three-man task force and then when it incorporated Ward's behavioural sub-section from the moribund Management Services Department, it formed into a distinct and visible structured unit on the organisation chart, with, from the business point of view, the credible leadership of Heath as its manager. Both wings of the HOC/PCD unit had clear, and from a wider divisional point of view, imposed tasks to complete. The task force trio were asked with varying degrees of commitment by the HOC/PCD board to examine the division's structure and recommend changes, and Ward's behavioural wing had the externally imposed change programme of SDP to implement. The combination of the OD unit's distinct structural visibility and their evidently clear task remit led them from a consulting point of view into an expert or directive stance, where from the behavioural wing rather more so than the task force trio they were not responding to an internally created demand for change, and certainly in the main were not working with volunteer clients. As one of the HOC/PCD board members put it, in 1970 although there was little clarity and agreement on the board as to what OD was and what it might do, it was recognised by some board members that the OD unit was to be used as a rather crude instrument of high-level change – "to hit the donkey [of HOC/PCD division] in between the eyes with a brick".

It seems because of their greater business experience and credibility and closer contact with directors that the task force trio were clearer from the beginning that the OD unit was just to be a temporary arm of top management. Heath and James in particular knew of HOC/PCD's predisposition to make changes through redesign, structural change, and reappointment, and they understood they were liable to have the rug pulled out from under them at a moment's notice. This, of course, had just happened to James with the break-up of his Management Services Department. Sure enough with the ICI business area changes which affected PCD in 1971 Parker was reassigned to other duties, and then early in 1972 Heath was asked to head a new central resource department offering specialist help in the business-relevant area of strategic planning. Thus although Heath and Parker were committed to the initial task remit supplied by the division chairman, they were not committed either to the OD unit as a continuing vehicle for divisional change, or indeed to OD as a specialist body of technique, concepts, and values. Politically this was undoubtedly an appropriate position given the PCD context and history.

Meanwhile Ward, Brown and their behavioural wing were searching for a different understanding both of change processes in the division, and for a continuing role of specialist OD help in those change processes. But the more junior status of the behavioural wing, with their backgrounds in the relatively politically weak R&D and Engineering departments, the way their zealous pursuit of MBO and SDP, together with their proclaimed OD values, challenged some of the established norms of the culture, all contributed to their isolation and the confinement of their work after SDP to sporadic team-building interventions in R&D and Engineering. Long before the behavioural wing's legitimacy became really precarious in late 1972 they tried to persuade Heath, Parker, and James to put energy into planning and developing the OD unit's external strategy and internal commitment and cohesion; but Heath in particular was explicitly against too much discussion of interpersonal issues, values, and team-building. The result was that the OD unit's meetings largely concentrated on business matters about tasks and roles, and in consequence the OD unit never had a sufficient sense of internal identity and commitment, or more crucially a pragmatic rationale for the continuance of OD which they could take out to meet an ever more unreceptive context. In consequence the behavioural wing's preparation for their demise while James was actively and this time successfully working on the structural redesign of the division, was a period of internal reflection and collective self-doubt. This, of course, hastened the by then inevitabilities of their fate, and James's reassignment with the successful completion of his task.

The above analysis of the PCD OD unit has demonstrated how and why the organisation, and initial membership and sponsorship of an innovating unit, can be critical in moulding that unit's strategy for dealing with aspects of its internal and external environment. The PCD example also illustrates how, in the case of the task force trio, a penetrating understanding of the rules of the game in making changes in the division was helpful both in thinking and acting on their present task and the future development of the OD unit, and in a sense avoiding the label of OD specialist being put on them; and at the same time controlling the activities of the behavioural specialists in the unit. The PCD OD unit's experience also illustrates Freeman's (1979:185) general point about the political circumstances of aspiring change groups. "Finding leverage points within the political system generally requires some intimate knowledge of its workings and so is an alternative available only to those not totally alienated from it." This problem of the lack of political perceptivity and access of the behavioural wing of the OD unit was of course a problem shared by the Plastics OD specialist resources, and a feature of the development of innovating groups we shall return to when discussing the dilemmas of exclusivity and inclusivity.

It should be clear, from the above analysis of the PCD OD unit, that the choice of the high-level but essentially task force form of organisation, together with the relatively safe content area of structural change, fitted well the traditions and culture of that division. The price of that approach to change in that context was some change in divisional structure but no change in divisional culture towards Harvey-Jones's long-term aim of "loosening the attitudes and behavioural processes of the division". Such a cultural change would clearly have required a top-down, long-term change process of the kind that went on in Mond division, and PCD did not have either the continuity in senior executive change leadership or continuity of high-level external consultant support that was available in Mond. The other price of the PCD OD unit structure and strategy, although few of the managers in the division at that time would regard this is a price of much note, was that there was no institutionalisation of OD knowledge and skills in the division. It was probably not until the business traumas of 1980 and the merger in 1981 with, from a change process point of view, the equally ill-prepared Plastics Division, that line management capabilities in change management really acquired strong legitimacy in either of the two merged divisions.

Different as the organisation and strategy of using OD resources in Agricultural Division was to the experience in HOC/PCD, it can also be argued that the choice of structure and approach in Agricultural division was initially at least as it had been in PCD well suited to the structure and culture of Billingham. However, a crucial difference between the two divisions was that the leadership, organisation, and rationale for OD in Agricultural Division was such as to connect OD there more penetratingly to the key business concerns of the day (industrial relations and plant commissioning), and in the medium term to diffuse and institutionalise OD concepts and approaches more widely into Billingham than occurred in PCD division.

In Agricultural Division Ripley's leadership, and the decentralised nature of the personnel department where he was located, meant there was no attempt to create a formally structured OD unit visible on the organisation chart, nor any attempt, unlike those made in the Bridge era or in PCD, to launch particular change projects or programmes on the division. As we have described elsewhere in this book, Ripley's view about organisation was to slowly build up a network of OD resources, to encourage those resources to practise the role of third-party neutral facilitators or process consultants, and to engage OD to the division through an organic strategy of building out additively from the problems line managers were sensing as worthy of attention.

Since Ripley's views about the organisation and strategy of OD resources were so important in determing what happened at Billingham in the late 1960s and early 1970s, it is important to know something about his background, experience, and style as inputs into understanding how he stimulated the internal and external evolution of OD in the division. Although recruited by the personnel director as a full-time internal consultant rather than a part-time external consultant, Ripley as a 30-year-old American with a Ph.D. in OD and 3 or 4 years' experience in the United States as an internal consultant, was very much an outsider to the Billingham culture. In fact for a time Ripley's true outsider status enabled him to sharply see both important aspects of the workings of the Billingham culture and attitudes to the Bridge strategy for introducing OD. This sharp understanding helped Ripley to legitimate his own concept of OD, whilst personally challenging aspects of the Billingham culture in face-to-face contact with managers through his neutral role as a third party. Ripley more so than any of the other divisional OD practitioners at this time, perhaps because of his greater education and experience, seems to have been able to combine a penetrating understanding of the culture where he worked with an intellectually coherent and articulate set of concepts about creating change from a specialist base. This coherence of style and conceptual substance was very similar to the leadership of a network of change resources in a community context described in Sarason *et al.* (1977). In both cases leadership in the realm of ideas and values was critical both to the process of binding the change resources into a network, and to the process of providing a legitimate rationale to connect the service offered to the needs of whatever clients could be found.

Given that (unlike the PCD OD unit) Ripley had neither a ready-made department nor a ready-made set of tasks and a predetermined group of clients, Ripley had to work to create all three. The process of working at developing a network and some clients created some of the cumulative events and conditions which helped to at least partially institutionalise OD into the division. But what was Ripley's network and how did he build it? The starting point both for Ripley's network of OD resources and his earliest clients was the set of people who had been intrigued, even enthused by the Bridge era of social innovation. Ripley's task was to find these people and allow them to find him and to develop them into a voluntary association. Building on the existing work and interest of the personnel officers in R&D and Projects and Engineering department, and the trainers who had been invigorated by the early management–union workshops in Products Works, Ripley before long gathered together a group of 6–10 like minds – people who were personally interested in OD approaches and in Ripley's ideas.

Crucial to the creation of this network were the group building processes of the Swallow meetings. The procedures of these meetings were very influenced by T-groups. Task issues were discussed but much time was given over to conversation and exercises which surfaced personal issues, values, and assumptions about what they were or might do. The offsite location of these meetings in a local hotel, the allocation of up to 2 days at a time and the personal orientation all contributed to the development of a shared identity that was recognisably different from the organisation as a whole. Partly because of the Swallow Group meetings, commitment was said to be "massive", "very high", "very strong", "real" in the early days. But it was a commitment to each other and to certain values, it was not collective in the sense of commitment "to walking out the door with an agreed agenda". The kinds of values and beliefs which the group engendered were strong and distinctive. They seemed to centre around "concern for people, with a strict resistance to organisational values". Another Swallow Group member went even further: "it was almost anarchistic – certainly different values from the divisional norm". The notion that the group was distinctive is reinforced by the fact that myths, for example, about nudity in Ripley's early T-groups and memories of other unusual activities were alive in the division some 6 or 7 years after those early pioneering days.

Writers on the natural history of social movements and communes such as Scott and Lyman (1970), Kanter (1972), and Wilson (1973) have discussed the importance of ritualistic meetings such as the Swallow meetings for creating and reaffirming the common creed. Scott and Lyman (1970:133), in their analysis of student revolutionary groups of the late 1960s also discuss the functional importance of solidarity for change-minded groups in so far as they avert the sense of isolation, impotence, meaninglessness, and sense of self-estrangement easily felt by individuals going against the grain.

If a crucial difference between the internal evolution of the PCD and Agricultural Division OD groups was that the former was a structured unit of specialists, and the latter a highly committed voluntary association or network with contacts in a variety of works and departments, how did the Agricultural Division OD network engage with its environment? This after all, as Sarason *et al.* (1977) remind us, is the critical question determining the legitimacy and impact of a set of people purporting to be interested in change. "Agreement on values and goals [in a network] is not always easy to obtain, but that is far less difficult than to sustain agreement in the course of action, which has a way of tearing apart the fabric of agreement and exposing the fragility of that fabric to the climate of action" (Sarason *et al.*, 1977:26).

Ripley's strategy of building his OD network amongst people who had dual affiliations, to the Swallow Group and the particular department or works where they formally had the position as personnel officer, personnel manager, or trainer, meant that from the beginning OD had natural links into potential client groups through individuals with varying levels of credibility in those contexts. But critical to the early success of OD in Agricultural Division was the fact that Ripley's organic change strategy was both a contrast to Bridge's bow wave of directive change and a contrast that was acceptable for that context. Organic change processes of additively building out from a base are most likely to work in contexts where stable, identifiable networks of potential clients already exist (Aiken and Alford, 1970; Curtis and Zurcher, 1973). We have already indicated that the middle and senior management levels at Billingham were featured by a relatively homogeneous and stable management group. However, although this management group was relatively homogeneous in its identity of interest around production, engineering, and science and technology, there was another tradition at Billingham, of works developing their own identity and culture. Ripley's strategy of encouraging change to develop around issues managers felt important, and at a pace and in a form they desired, fitted the established pattern on the Billingham site for management teams in individual works to find their own means of reaching whatever division objectives were important. Furthermore Ripley's strategy of seeking out, and focussing on managers' problems meant there was some chance of identifying content areas of change where managers might be persuaded to make a start, even with the as yet for many managers culturally unacceptable methods and processes of OD. There was thus some association and identity between Ripley's change strategy and the context and content of changes that began to emerge.

Before long the OD group found its early adopter clients mainly from individuals "opened up" by the Bridge era, and began to work around the culturally central issues of industrial relations and then plant commissioning within the dominant production function, and mostly at the level of works manager and below. It is important to note that there was only one attempt to work directly at the board level, by Ripley in 1973 and 1974, and that was unsuccessful. But the by then extended OD group did have a series of "friends in court" in the form of successive personnel directors, who were prepared to hold up some kind of political umbrella. There were, in addition, some doubters on the board, who group members felt were hostile or at least questioning. However, unlike the situation with the PCD OD unit, doubters and opponents of OD in the Agricultural Division were always at one remove from the OD work itself, which had to be evaluated largely from the viewpoint of production managers.

The Agricultural Division OD group's posture with respect to evaluation was a logical extension of their client-centred organic approach to change. They argued that they should not be evaluated in terms of some vague criteria about the group as a whole, but rather in terms of specific clients' views of their contributions to particular works or projects. In addition since the managers and union leaders who were their clients tended to stay in the organisation, satisfied clients provided repeat business.

What was attempted in Agricultural Division was the marriage of essentially new and non-legitimate methods with existing business problems. That these problems were defined by clients, not the consultants nor by board remit, is very important. Over the period 1969–75 some legitimacy was achieved for OD methods at least within the production function. This conclusion is based on the continuing requests for OD help, the diffusion of OD methods into a variety of works, and the initiatives taken by line managers in particular in the Ammonia and Engineering Works and in the commissioning of Methanol 2 and Ammonia 4. But this conclusion must not be overstated. It does not mean that the whole organisation accepted OD, nor indeed that the divisional board did. In what follows we shall examine how even with some elements of both an exclusive and inclusive stance, the social control tactics of the Agricultural Division OD group's detractors, the problem of sustaining and renewing the network, and perhaps critically changes in the divisional context, all cumulatively contributed to weakening the OD group's base of legitimacy, and creating the condition of collective self-doubt amongst the OD resources still practising their trade by 1975 and 1976.

THE DILEMMA OF EXCLUSIVITY AND INCLUSIVITY FOR INNOVATING GROUPS

To change the World one must live with it (Wilson, 1973:167)

In his discussion of how new bureaus come into being within the existing framework of government bureaucracy, Downs (1967:5) argues that "a bureau starts as the result of aggressive agitation and action by a small group of zealots who have a specific idea they want to put into practice on a large scale". However, no matter how much the psychological climate of a new group of innovators focusses energy and activity on the realisation of the new idea in some future state, the requirements for group survival and task achievement necessitate that the group understands and intervenes effectively in the context of the heavy hand of the past, and the dynamics of the present. The innovating group thus has the difficulty of looking three ways at the same time, to its past, present, and the future, and in so doing of facing up to a dilemma faced by all change groups of applying new values and ideas whilst living with the world as it is rather than the world that might yet be. Stated in its most passive mode a feature of this dilemma of how to change the world whilst living with it, is the requirement of groups to adapt to their context whilst maintaining the cutting edge of their own distinctiveness and membership commitment, and in so doing avoiding the impotence which may result from co-optation.

A significant factor in the survival and flourishing of any system, whether it be a total organisation, or a subunit of specialists within a firm, is how that system relates to its immediate and more distant environment. Boundary management refers to the system of exchanges a function, activity, or a role has with its environment. These exchanges include how the activity:

– acquires its inputs (resources) and disposes of its outputs (services);
– exercises influence;
– builds relationships and activates its image;
– protects its integrity, territory, and technological core from environmental pressure and threat;
– co-ordinates activities with other units, roles or organisations.

While boundary management is an important consideration for any system it is particularly crucial for advisory/service activities within organisations because advisory units by definition do not command line authority, neither can they assume their advice will be listened to, or their services needed. In this situation the legitimacy of the activity, and the credibility of individual practitioners, has to be developed and maintained over time if the activity is to flourish. The development of the resources which form the power base for carrying out the advisory activity, together with the strategy and particular unit adopts about how legitimate or illegitimate it chooses to appear to different parts of its environment represent two of several areas of choice and action involved in this key activity of boundary management.

However, research by Pettigrew (1975a) on groups of operational research, organisation development, and general management consultants, and further research on trainers reported in Pettigrew *et al.* (1982), indicates the task-oriented and politically limited perspective evident amongst groups of internal specialists means that often such groups do not develop explicit strategies for managing their internal and external environment, at least in the conception and pioneering phases of the groups' evolution. Only when the certainty of the original pioneering task nears completion, and uncertainties about future tasks and political sponsorship for the group become starkly evident, do groups of innovators sit down, often by then in an atmosphere of collective self-doubt, and begin to try and put together a home and foreign policy. But although groups of innovators do not necessarily always have coherent intended strategies, they clearly do display attitudes and values and act on their environment in such a way that an implicit stance is taken, or is perceived by their supports, doubters, or opponents to be taken.

This section examines various aspects of boundary management by innovating groups by developing the idea that change-minded groups may relate to their environment through patterns of attitude and behaviour labelled as exclusive or inclusive. In recent social science thinking the polar types exclusive and inclusive have been used by authors such as Olson (1965), Zald and Ash (1966), and Curtis and Zurcher (1974) to analyse the internal characteristics and dynamics, and patterns of external relationship adopted by interest groups and social movements seeking survival and impact in their various context. Although she does not use the dichotomy of exclusive and inclusive, Kanter (1972) in her discussion of the survival of nineteenth and twentieth-century communes, focusses in on what she describes as the twin pulls in the social life of communes, of expressing values and implementing practical concerns, and mentions some further associated dilemmas which derive from living with those twin pulls. Drawing on and developing the above authors' work it is possible to break down the exclusive and inclusive polar types into the dimensions shown in Figure 14, which can be related with profit to features of the natural history of innovating groups in organisation.

Exclusive Stance	*Inclusive Stance*
Little Permeability of Boundary	Highly Permeable Boundary
Culturally Dissimilar	Culturally Similar
Specific Values	Diffuse Values
Unilateral Exchanges with Environment	Mutual Exchanges with Environmer
Limited Network and Linkages	Well-developed Network and Linkaç
Limited Range of Transactions with Environment	Broad Range of Transactions with Environment

FIGURE 14   Dimensions of exclusive and inclusive stances

Broadly the innovating group behaving the exclusive stance, either as a product of deliberate intent or cumulative circumstance, or both, is offering a distinctively sharp and culturally deviant presentation of self to its environment. Its message for change has been nourished in a group possibly with high levels of commitment and cohesion around fairly specific values and goals, and these goals are wrapped up in fairly singular and unilateral attempts to push their values and where possible particular changes on their environment. Groups of innovators behaving the exclusive stance are likely therefore to contain at least a proportion of Downs's (1967) zealots, with their sacred policies, implacable energy, their refusal to be impartial, and their willingness to criticise openly the status quo. While zealots may be functional for organisations operating in rapidly changing environments, because they help to generate and focus the enormous amounts of energy necessary to overcome bureaucratic inertia, zealots operating from an advisory position may have to sacrifice their own impact and survival, for the short-term comfort and certainty of expressing their own values. As we shall see, the OD zealots in ICI tended to attract the attention of powerful critics, and were controlled by stigmatising and labelling in the terms of Cohen's (1980) "folk devils".

The inclusive stance, on the other hand, is the behavioural representation of the aphorism that to change the world one must live with it. Here is the attempt literally to change the world by inclusion in it, to understand and where appropriate identify with local cultures, and to use such cultural identification to cultivate the access and information which will reveal the pragmatic starting point or points for change. Although innovators adopting such a stance may have their own values, goals, and technologies, these are proclaimed less visibly, and are made available much more flexibly and opportunistically than is suggested with those innovators adopting an exclusive stance.

These two ideal typical stances can be broken down into the six dimensions listed in Figure 14. Thus an innovating group adopting an exclusive stance is likely to have a relatively impermeable boundary, while the inclusive stance implies a much more open boundary and thereby greater opportunities to give and receive information, gather resources, evaluate and alter services, and possibly recruit different kinds of personnel. The second dimension refers to the structural and cultural similarity between an innovating group and its environment, and in the case of an exclusive group suggests significant differences in language, rituals, problem-solving style, and mode of organisation between that exclusive group and its host environment. Specificity and diffuseness of values captures the extent to which the change group has a highly developed sense of commitment to specific values informing decisions and actions, or in the case of the inclusive stance the adoption of value indeterminism with all that offers in flexibility of action to meet changing inner and outer contexts. Groups pushing out from a base of cultural distinctiveness and value determinism in the language of consultant–client relationships are likely to be behaving in a directive or consultant-rather than client-centred manner. There is therefore a heavy element of unilaterism in the relationship between the innovator and those who he seeks to influence. The final two dimensions refer in turn to the extent to which the innovators build up multiple linkages and networks of relationship in their environment, and the extent to which the change groups cross the boundary with single or multiple tasks and services.

The major proposition implied by the exclusive and inclusive ideal types is the expected high degree of association, or in the statistical sense intercorrelation between the six dimensions at either end of the polar types. But in addition the adoption of exclusive and inclusive stances points to certain critical dilemmas in organising and acting to create change. The major of these dilemmas is that actions taken to build commitment, coherence, and identity in an innovating group by having an impermeable boundary, adopting specific values, and being culturally dissimilar, tend to have the consequential effect of cutting such a group off from its environment; while on the other hand features of the inclusive stance may tend to displace a change group's values and goals, and dissipate the group's sense of distinctiveness in relation to its environment, and homogeneity in relationship to itself. Any move through time by a change group from the exclusive to a more inclusive stance may in effect be a move from the sacred to the profane, from high principle to pragmatism, or from change agentry to absorption and co-optation.

An examination of the natural history of development and stance of the PCD OD unit – and particularly the behavioural wing of that unit; the OD "in-group" in the Plastics Division Training and Personnel Development Department; and the Millbank-based corporate OD unit over the period 1969–72, reveals a clear pattern of exclusivity in all three groups. This pattern of exclusivity arose and developed in all three cases as a result partly of the confines around each group resulting from the antecedent conditions and receiving culture they were born into, but also from the value positions and actions taken by the group members as they struggled for legitimacy in their contexts, and as they attempted to face up to the control strategies adopted by their doubters and opponents.

Thus the behavioural wing of the PCD OD unit initially had the centrally imposed task of SDP to work on as their sole transaction. If they had any political sponsorship it was all wrapped up in the person of Harvey-Jones. Their post-SDP tasks were largely confined to helping James with his second organisation study and doing team-building and role clarification work in the politically weak R&D and Engineering functions. Furthermore, the limits imposed by their uncertain legitimacy and the way this represented itself in their limited tasks and network, were exacerbated by the group's presentation of self as having distinct and superior values, and through their proclamation of these values in a distinctive language and problem-solving style for thinking about learning and change which emphasised their cultural dissimilarity from the predominant management culture of PCD at that time. Worse still was the fact that as part of the price for setting up the PCD OD unit, Harvey-Jones had had to accept Heath and Parker as early senior members of the OD unit, and probably sensibly from their point of view, Heath and Parker as representatives of the division establishment distanced themselves from the behavioural science ideas and methods being pushed with zeal by Ward and his colleagues. The result was that the change group at PCD was always weakened by being divided within itself, and OD methods never gained complete legitimacy within the OD unit, never mind outside it.

A similar pattern of external and internal causes created the exclusivity evident in the Plastics Division and central OD units. The central OD resources of the late 1960s and early 1970s were from a task point of view almost exclusively concerned with WSA and SDP, were overdependent on George Bridge for political sponsorship and legitimacy, were too easily associated with the policy objectives and power needs of the central personnel department, and of course over-identified with behavioural and psychological frames of reference and solutions, and values which appeared to cherish individual growth and development to the detriment of business needs and purposes.

These brief illustrative points will have made it clear that exclusivity is partially a product of the control strategies of groups questioning or hostile to change groups. If a change group can be confined in terms of the permeability of its boundary, the extent of its political linkages, and required to specialise in narrow tasks with finite time limits for implementation, then to all intents and purposes the group can be allowed in the absence of support, new tasks, or replacement personnel, merely to wither away on the vine. In PCD, Plastics, and in the central OD unit this process of withering on the vine was facilitated by the additional sense and reality of entrapment which followed from the visible way those groups proclaimed their cultural differences, and the additional control behaviour that visibility and perceived deviancy attracted.

In HOC/PCD Division, Ward's OD section in the management services department was already being perceived and treated as a deviant group before the creation of the OD unit. Ward and Brown described their group as being "enthused" and "highly committed" to the behavioural sciences, and of considering themselves as heavy users of jargon "because we thought we were the bee's knees". Ward's group's values about "openness", "data not opinion", "boundaries not being sacrosanct" and their emphasis on "people values and growth potential" at work clashed with the hierarchical, technically arrogant tone of the HOC/PCD culture and quickly attracted them the labels "head-shrinkers and trick cyclists", and a feeling "we weren't very identified with the business". The Plastics division OD group of the early 1970s also got themselves trapped "peddling values, humanistic psychology and the like", and pushing some of the fashionable phrases and solutions of the day such as "theory Y", "participation", "co-operation and delegation". Worse still, even in the 1975–77 period when the ICI management system was identifying more and more with pragmatic, economic values, two of the internal OD consultants were still proclaiming values emphasising laudable notions such as "caring", "creativity", individual growth and freedom, and "fun and excitement" within organisational life. One of the trainer critics of OD in the mid-1970s remarked that "one of the things that gets in the way [of OD having an impact] is what he calls his value system . . . I see his value system where everything concerning people is all important to him, and must take priority over every other consideration, as unrealistic, totally impractical in business."

In the literature on the sociology of deviance (Downes and Rock, 1979; Cohen, 1980; Downes and Rock, 1982) there are ample theoretical frameworks available to analyse processes of social control by groups threatened or otherwise disturbed by deviant sub-groups. For the present purposes of examining some of the consequences for innovating groups of adopting an exclusive stance in their environment, Cohen's (1980) interesting book *Folk Devils and Moral Panics* is particularly apposite. Using a detailed case study of the Mods and Rockers phenomenon in Britain over the 1960s Cohen (1980) analyses the general processes which generate folk devils and the moral panics which sustain them. Moral panics are defined as episodes when a person or a group emerges to become recognised as a threat to societal values and interests, and is presented in stylised and stereotypical fashion by the mass media. Such stereotyped groups thus acquire the role of folk devils – "visible reminders of what we should not be" (Cohen, 1980:9).

Although it would be to exaggerate to argue that the phenomenon of OD in ICI created any sustained moral panic, without doubt the occasions when OD people visibly confronted or were perceived to confront some of the core values of their host culture in a situation where of course they were structurally and strategically weak, they did attract the exaggerated stereotypes which escalated local feeling and allowed opponents of OD to decry OD methods as deviant, and OD people as folk devils. Thus in PCD, when it looked at one stage as if Ward and Brown's emphasis on self-direction and autonomy for managers might actually tap real energy and support from those dissatisfied with "a very mechanistic bureaucratic organisation", the director responsible for OD began to fear loss of control from a bottom-up change process. He was saying "I don't like what's happening. I feel we're losing control." Similarly in Plastics Division some members of the board in the mid-1970s considered "behavioural science – that knocked the stuffing out of people, it removed control from authority, it weakened structural authority". According to a deputy chairman of Plastics Division in the mid-1970s, it was the perception of key people on the board that OD was or could undermine authority – weaken authority at the top, that meant Simon Dow "had to be stopped in his tracks". One of the board members opposed to OD in Plastics Division admitted that concern about OD's attempts to move the division from an "old-fashioned, not necessarily authoritarian but classical, traditional management style, towards a fully participative style . . . meant that he and a senior colleague were so opposed to the behavioural science aspects that Simon Dow was putting forward that almost everything put forward by Dow's department was rejected". Similar attempts by the Mond division change agents of the early 1970s to question and challenge managerial values and practices around authority, of course led to the characterisations of OD "as being too soft" and "sandals and beads OD", which prepared the ground for those change agents to be ignored and allowed to wither away.

The PCD, Plastics, and central OD group cases well illustrate some of the factors external and internal to innovating groups which create the pattern of exclusivity which can made a change group so vulnerable. The Agricultural Division OD case is an interesting contrast to these three cases in so far as there was a clear mix of exclusive and inclusive elements in the early stance of that group, and an explicit attempt to move the group's strategic positioning more unequivocally over to the inclusive stance after a period of contextual change had invalidated many of the precepts guiding the group at an earlier phase in its existence. In combining an appropriate, for that context, mix of exclusive and inclusive at an early phase in its development, it may be argued that the Agricultural Division OD resources were able to offer from a content point of view a distinctively different message about change whilst retaining the linkages necessary to provide the access, the information, and the leverage to reach the people and the problems in the division where an impact could be made.

The ideas and values about change brought to Billingham by Ripley and then nourished and activated by the intensity of the Swallow group meetings, ensured that the Agricultural OD group had specific and distinctive values which were culturally dissimilar from the Billingham management culture. Indeed there was a greater coherence and commitment to values and change approach in the Swallow group than in any of the other ICI OD groups, and yet those elements of exclusivity were combined with an organic and mutual style of relating to their environment which allowed and encouraged a relatively permeable group boundary, well-developed linkages in the key production area around a variety of transactions relevant to the two key management problems of the day.

The Agricultural Division OD group did attract hostility from some division directors because some members of the group were perceived to be "anti-system", even "revolutionary", but this labelling was contained to some extent by a number of features. Firstly the directors were one stage removed from the actual OD work, and the OD group's middle and senior manager clients protected and supported them from folk devil epitaphs. Secondly, the fact that the OD group all had dual affiliations, to the Swallow group and their more conventional divisional roles as a trainer or a personnel man allowed them to balance out their identities and associations. Crucially, the fact that the OD group had two leaders: one Ripley acting as a creator, interpreter, and protector of their values, and Miles acting as a political umbrella and link with the management and personnel system, meant the group didn't become too exclusive and detached from other viewpoints, values, and concerns in the division.

However, after the success of the Methanol work, and with both senior line managers and senior industrial relations managers in the division seeking to launch their own initiatives to improve IR on the Billingham site, the Swallow group came increasingly under pressure. The Swallow group's interest in the individual before the organisation became increasingly portrayed as "anti-system and revolutionary", their desire to keep all doors open with as many groups as possible by casting themselves in a neutral third-party role – and the unorthodox links with shop stewards this led to, plus a feeling amongst some personnel people that they were excluded from their inner sanctum of the Swallow group – all produced a desire to contain the group. Miles responded to these control strategies by refocussing the Swallow group away from their own internal workings and values to trying to develop a more explicit political strategy for the group under these new conditions, and of course this helped to stimulate the extended OD group with its cells in Ammonia and Engineering Works. But a combination of the loss of Ripley, the difficulties of renewing the old network and organic approach to change, the tiredness of the old Swallow group members after several years in very stressful roles, and crucially the more risk-aversive and cash-rich era of the mid-1970s all exposed the lack of ideas and purpose in the OD group. It wasn't until the era of real productivity change in the late 1970s that Moores was able to use the legitimacy of his personnel role, and the external consultant Larsen's acceptability with the divisional board and senior management, to mobilise the changes of business context around a series of developmental activities in the manpower, training, and careers areas, that OD emerged again, but of course, by then the work Moores and Larsen did was not, could not, be described as OD. The content, style, and language of OD had to move on to survive in the new context.

In summary this section on features of the internal development and boundary management of innovating groups has emphasised some of the tensions and dilemmas of managing the survival and impact of such groups through time. The most general dilemma for an innovating group is how to change the world whilst living with it; how to be exclusive or different enough to retain a vision or process to facilitate change but not so different that the group creates a moral panic, acquires the stereotype of folk devils and is controlled by overt attempts to limit contacts, tasks, and resources, or more subtly is ignored and allowed to slowly disappear. Part of the dilemma of how to live with a community whilst changing it is caught up in the stylistic problem of how visible or invisible the group is, and whether it is able to manage the timing and extent of its visibility. Groups propelled out into the open by working exclusively for the top management, and/or being associated just with formal top-down change programmes, or being seduced by their own inner momentum into proclaiming their superior values, can find themselves trapped and vulnerable when their political sponsor moves on, the change programme is implemented or otherwise recedes from public attention, and when a changing context makes their self-consciously proclaimed values manifestly irrelevant for the changed times.

This requirement to maintain flexibility of values and activities in order to live in a changing context conflicts with some of the virtues of specialisation. Sarason (1972:121) has commented that "in the short run specialization appears to have productive consequences in terms of new knowledge and practice, but in the long run it seems to render the individual, or field, or agency increasingly unable to assimilate and adapt to changes in surrounding social events and processes". There is always the danger that professionalism and specialisation transform unfamiliar problems into familiar ones at the price of relevance, and for this reason few if any innovating groups can justify an indefinite future.

THE ICI USE OF ORGANISATION DEVELOPMENT: SOME LESSONS

One of the major lessons of the ICI experience in using the knowledge and skills of internal and external OD specialists to help create change, must be the pessimistic one of "don't expect too much"; and certainly in the context of strategic change without a business crisis, "don't expect too much too soon". If the evidence of this book has substantiated how difficult it is for chief executives and senior and middle line managers to justify and implement strategic and operational changes, then what chance have specialists with their fragile political position and often illegitimate message and methods to create change? And yet with every decade new groups of specialists appear with a new set of techniques, new values, still greater promises and in some cases the latest brand of polished presentation. Some come and some go. With the arrival of computers came the programmers and systems analysts, the logic of organisational form and process would now be moulded by the changing possibilities offered by computer technology, and earlier bands of organisational settlers, such as work study officers and organisation and methods officers retreated to their camp fires to consider their fate. We have seen in this book how the arrival of OD specialists provoked much camp fire chat not only amongst executives, but also in personnel and training departments, once the sole guardians of human resource management. But we have also chronicled the fading away of a generation of OD specialists in ICI who arrived on the scene in the context of the optimistic social and economic values of the 1960s, and for the most part did not survive the harsher and more pragmatic economic and political context of the late 1970s and early 1980s.

Of course much of the early misguided optimism for OD came not from the expectations of ICI executives but from the almost social movement quality of writing and thinking about OD values and techniques in the 1960s, and early 1970s. These early texts and articles (Bennis, 1969; Beckhard, 1969; Solomon, 1971) with their grand statements about the possibilities of planned organisation-wide change, informed by humanistic values emphasising individual dignity, participative and open processes of decision-making and change, and honest and authentic relationships between people at all levels in organisational life, for a time seemed to gel with the optimistic and questioning times of the 1960s. Certainly the above kinds of assumptions about the possibilities and values of OD had been well internalised by the American consultants who trained most of the ICI internal OD specialists. The result was that the ICI specialists were socialised at events like the Eastbourne 1 and 2 training programmes in techniques and values which in the context of the economic difficulties ICI was facing in 1970 and 1971 already seemed to jar with their working contexts. One of the American external consultants who worked closely with the ICI internal specialists commented in this way about how they were socialised:

> Essentially Eastbourne and other such training events for OD consultants were much too oriented around the humanistic ethos which tended to make people think that almost any problem could be solved by developing co-operation. In that I think they confused ends and means. Because if your end is to develop co-operation and participation, your means may often be to be initiating, and structuring, and confronting, and plan-full and a lot of stuff that people didn't learn in this consultant training.

But if lessons could be drawn about the kinds of ethos in which the ICI OD people were trained, a more telling lesson from those early days was the kind of people who were recruited or volunteered to be internal ICI OD specialists. As one participant in the ICI OD work put it:

> They usually took staff who could be spared. So they took people who, in terms of the norms of the organisation, were kind of weak, personally goal-less, not very courageous, not very successful. Then when you take that material and teach people to be more receptive, better listeners, more democratic, you are strengthening what was already a disadvantage . . . So I'm personally convinced that one of the biggest lessons from the ICI experience is that if you want an OD effort to be successful you start with high energy, rather successful line managers and try to teach them behavioural skills.

From a selection point of view it is clear that many of the ICI internal OD consultants were hampered by the fact that they were perceived to be middle managers that could be spared, or were junior managers or specialists "who couldn't require anybody to take any combination of us". The internal consultants that survived for any length of time to have an impact were people like Dudley, James, and Marshall who were fairly senior line managers before they became internal OD resources, and had the advantage of being scarce and therefore for a time pivotal exemplars of OD in their chosen working environment. Other survivors included people such as Moores in Agricultural Division who used the legitimacy of his personnel role to generate the information, the political access, and the credibility to carry on using OD methods, and was shrewd enough to change his methods and areas of work to fit the changing business and political context where he had to work. The most solid evidence for ICI's doubts about the value of using internal specialists as "change agents", was the clear statement of policy that had emerged by the last few years of the 1970s that in the foreseeable future line managers were to be the vanguard of attempts to create the significant changes in organisation that eventually came with the recession of the early 1980s. By then most of the internal specialist OD resources in ICI were either disappearing or had disappeared, and an important role played by the few credible specialists that remained was to help train and develop senior line managers for the managers' task of initiating or implementing the manpower, structural, and then strategy changes of the period 1979–83. This, of course, is suggestive of a pattern of retaining a very small number of internal OD specialists who act as professional centres of excellence, drawing new ideas and techniques, and in some cases external consultants into the organisation around problems being flagged by the line management system; and where relevant help to develop the line management system, without the zealous attempts to create the ambitious, planned, and across-the-board changes which were a feature of OD in ICI in the days of WSA and SDP.

A view has been expressed to me about the ICI OD experience, without too much of a self-justificatory tone that OD is like any other developmental activity, you spend a lot in the hope that there will be pragmatic returns but there must be a high wastage rate of resource. A corollary of this position is that ICI had to go through their early strategy and experience of training a lot of internal specialists and sending them out to "do OD", in order to reach the level of appreciation they were at by the late 1970s that if OD was to be harnessed at all as a means to change, it could only be in response to a perceived need by the owners of a problem, and then the leader of the change had to be the relevant member of the line management system. There is clearly some sense in that pragmatic view of the reality of how organisations learn, but nevertheless one wonders if there are other lessons to be appreciated about how the way some of the OD groups were set up and managed contributed to their effectiveness and ineffectiveness.

We have seen in this study that the broad receiving context, immediate antecedent conditions, and birth processes of an OD group can crucially set the bounds or provide opportunities for that group's subsequent activities and fate. Groups which were born with minimal consultation into settings where there was little perceived need amongst the key power figures for organisational change, never mind understanding, of the potential utility of OD resources, and as in Plastics where these difficulties were compounded by the inexperience and lack of training of the early specialists, hardly had the chance to begin to create an impact. In other divisions such as Agricultural Division where there had been an opening up of the social system prior to Ripley's arrival, where climate-building for organisational and cultural change had seeded the division with at least a smattering of potential line manager clients and minimally experienced potential OD specialists, and where the early leader of the group had a coherent conceptual rationale for OD which was appropriate for that context, then there was some scope for connecting specialist OD resources to management-defined local problems. Creating a new group of internal specialists, whether they be OD consultants, corporate planners, or operational researchers, is a change like any other change and as such requires not only forethought about the appropriateness of those skills for that context, but also climate-building and support-generation to link the new resources into the existing system. By and large the rush to set up the ICI OD resources as means to rescue the centrally imposed MUPS/WSA, and fashion and implement the equally centrally imposed SDP, meant that not only were those groups trapped by the unpopularity of their initial task of serving the ICI personnel system, but little constructive thought was given to other key issues which can be crucial to the impact of new groups of specialists.

Setting up an internal specialist or consultancy group is a form of innovative planning and as such requires at least some moderate amount of diagnostic activity at the point of conception and birth. But in ICI fundamental questions about identifying client needs, predicting a mix or range of potential clients, the distinctive competence of the OD unit and its relationship to the choice of how the OD resources would be structured and located, the type of leadership appropriate, and issues of work style and selection of the right mix of staff tended to receive only passing attention in the haste to set up the new resources and get on with or find the first series of tasks.

Equally well, once the OD resources had been set up, it wasn't until their initial tasks were near completion and/or their initial political sponsorship had disappeared or had otherwise changed their attention, that some of the groups began to think positively about a continuing strategy to maintain sufficient legitimacy for them to operate effectively as change resources in their particular context. As our discussion of exclusivity emphasised, innovating groups must actively manage their various boundaries and support base to have an impact in their context. In broad terms this requires continuous sensitivity to the past, present, and future context of the group's work; to continuously raising the capacity of the group through training and development and personnel changes; to repeated attempts to alter the nature and possibly range of tasks and services the group provides; and through developing the range and quality of networks of linkage and support which will translate group objectives into reality.

In terms of alternative ways of structuring and organising specialist resources, the ICI data have revealed some of the strengths and weaknesses of the network approach versus the formally structured unit approach. The PCD OD unit, with its identifiable structured status, credible business leader, close links with at least part of the PCD power system, and clear task, did in fact eventually achieve the task for which it was set up, but at the price of the group's demise. In addition there was practically no institutionalisation of OD skills and knowledge in that division. The more organic modus operandi and network approach to organisation adopted by the Agricultural OD group did achieve a measure of both task impact and institutionalisation of OD knowledge and skills into the Billingham culture. The success, for a time, of the Agricultural Division OD resources did seem to be the result of a variety of factors: the fact that the Billingham management culture was based on a relatively stable network of managers who had already been introduced to OD methods; the coherent and strong value and conceptual leadership given by Ripley, both in providing a rationale for OD in the division, and in building a resounding team spirit amongst the early network members. However, there are dangers and difficulties with the continuing and non-reflective use of the network approach to organising specialist resources. Networks require regeneration with new leadership and new personnel. Networks can also become cosy retreats where groups of specialists who have lost their sense of purpose just sit around and talk to each other about former triumphs and the latest concepts and techniques. In this sense, and especially in hard times, a specialist network can become a deliberately low-visibility way of concealing a service rather than projecting a service. Although by no means impossible, it is very much more difficult to conceal a unit or a function which is likely to have a manager required to publicly state objectives and accountabilities. Dudley was eventually criticised in ICI for adopting a too laissez-faire attitude to running the ICI companywide OD network. In effect Dudley was blamed for co-ordinating the network rather than managing it; for adopting an "expediency" or "opportunistic" approach rather than actively using and developing the network to build an OD strategy which actively linked the network to key business problems through the main board and the divisional boards.

But if one of the lessons of the ICI organisation change and development experience is the unreality, the persistent difficulties of grand attempts to plan change, then there must be caution against overemphasising too elaborate attempts by specialist groups to plan and strategise about their linkages and impact on their environment. After all in each of the divisions and locations where this study looked at the use and impact of internal OD resources, only a comparatively small number of individuals both survived in and had an impact on their surroundings from an internal specialist role, and that impact was often dependent on the continuing active support and sponsorship of a relatively small number of clients. As one of the few really senior ICI OD supporters put it, "using OD is in the first case an act of faith . . . believing in it and wanting to use it is an individual thing". If support is that idiosyncratic and individual, then perhaps the only viable form of strategising to develop OD has to be from whatever islands of support continue to project themselves out of the sea.

Turning to examine the lessons that may be drawn from ICI's use of external OD consultants, here again one finds the importance of individual differences, of certain consultants seeming to fit certain contexts, and in effect specialising as helpers for particular clients. Thus Larsen, the American external OD consultant, has been working almost continuously first with senior production people, then more generally with the senior management group outside and inside production, and latterly with the Agricultural Division board over the period from the early 1970s until the present day. Wilson, another American OD consultant, has linked with a selected group of senior managers and the board of Mond division, also for a period of 10 years or more. It is noteworthy that neither of these two consultants has particularly sought to, been encouraged to, or in fact has ended up providing consultancy services to any other part of ICI, even though those two consultants must be considered at some level or other to have been effective in those two divisions, and other divisions of ICI to varying degrees, and at differing times have been users of external OD assistance.

There seem to be a variety of reasons both why certain external consultants appear to fit and survive in certain contexts, and why their impact becomes localised. Early consultant acceptability seems to be as much to do with the personal chemistry of relationships between the consultant and a powerful client, as it has to do with the appropriateness of the consultant's service for that business at that time. The continuing survival and impact of the consultant may be due to the protection afforded by the initial client, the skill with which the external consultant infiltrates the organisation's cultural and political systems, and thereby generates the information and support necessary to alter his product to meet any changing top management views of the problems that require attention. Although as McLean *et al.* (1982) document one of the advantages an external consultant may have over an internal one, is that the external can act as an outside conceptual stimulant, a provider of alternative views; by not being part of the local career and political systems may be able to act as a sounding board and counsellor; in order for externals to survive they also sometimes have to "go native" and demonstrate identification and loyalty and commitment to local problems, and even local people. This identification with key local people and problems often means they can end up as personal gurus or medicine men for power figures, and or are associated with particular conceptual models and techniques for solving certain problems. Given the inevitable competitiveness which has existed between ICI divisions, and one of its consequences the "best if invented here syndrome", it can mean that it is difficult both to export external consultants' ideas and include them personally into other business locations. Finding a way of managing the impact and use of external consultants so they can modify and export ideas throughout the company is a continuing problem for ICI.

Mercer's position as a continuing high-level external OD consultant to the ICI top power system was discussed and reviewed at the end of Chapter 10. Unlike the other external consultants ICI have used Mercer did work with several ICI divisions, and of course has worked for the ICI main board over the period of four Company Chairmen. This is, I suspect, a very unusual occurrence with high-level consultancy where it is common for a consultant's star to wane with the change of top leadership. Mercer stayed in the ICI system because of the positive support in particular of two executive directors, Harvey-Jones and Woodburn, who were championing a number of change ideas; because of Dudley's shrewd management of Mercer's access to individual directors and general managers, and because Mercer's low-key, "doing good by stealth" style of consultancy fitted the highly personal and political environment around the main board.

Dudley's management of Mercer, and indeed Nicholas Mann's management in Mond Division of the external consultant Wilson, indicate a number of lessons for effectively using external help. One lesson is to use externals so they enhance, not compete with, the credibility of internal development resources. Externals also literally require management, not just in the narrow contractual sense, but in directing them to people and problems where their expertise is most likely to be used; by shielding and protecting them from short-term critics; by in the early stages introducing them to key aspects of the local political and cultural systems; and where possible to use their contacts and credibility to legitimise whatever more circumscribed interventions internal OD resources may be considering.

One further and critical aspect of the management of external consultants seems to be the simple to espouse but not always easy to achieve objective of ensuring the external does not usurp management. Examples have been quoted in the case study chapters of line management withdrawing emotional and practical support from change projects and processes once it was felt that the leadership of the change process had moved from the hands of the management to the hands of the consultant. But this is another reflection of one of the themes about creating change mentioned in this and previous chapters of this book. In the absence of crisis/survival circumstances, visible change projects or programmes made all the more visible by upfront consultant presence tend to incur resistance. Lower visibility processes of changing, using consultants to provide complementary processes and ideas to additively build on natural movements in the system, are more likely to combine the appropriate balance between continuity and change to move the organisation slowly in a different direction.

References

Aharoni, Y. (1966) *The Foreign Investment Decision Process*. Cambridge: Harvard University Press.

Aiken, M., and Alford, A. (1970) Community Structure and Innovation: The Case for Urban Renewal. *American Sociological Review* 35: 650–652.

Alderfer, C. P. (1976) Change Processes in Organizations. In M. D. Dunnette (ed.), *Handbook of Industrial and Organisational Psychology*. Chicago, Illinois: Rand McNally.

Alderfer, C. P. (1977) Organization Development. In M. R. Rosenzweig and L. W. Porter (eds), *Annual Review of Psychology* 28: 197–223.

Alderfer, C. P., and Brown, L. D. (1975) *Learning from Changing: Organizational Diagnosis and Development*. Beverly Hills, California: Sage.

Aldrich, H. E. (1979) *Organizations and Environments*. Englewood Cliffs, New Jersey: Prentice Hall.

Allison, G. A. (1971) *Essence of Decision: Explaining the Cuban Missile Crisis*. Boston: Little Brown.

Althusser, L. (1969) *For Marx*. London: Allen Lane, The Penguin Press.

Andrews, K. (1971) *The Concept of Corporate Strategy*. Homewood, Illinois: Irwin.

Ansoff, H. I. (1965) *Corporate Strategy*. New York: McGraw Hill.

Ansoff, H. I. (1979) *Strategic Management*. London: Macmillan.

Argyris, C. (1970) *Intervention Theory and Method: A Behavioral Science View*. Reading, Massachusetts: Addison-Wesley.

Astley, W. G., and Rosen, M. (1983) Organizations: A Politico-Symbolic Dialectic. Unpublished paper, The Wharton School, University of Pennsylvania.

Back, K. W. (1972) *Beyond Words: The Story of Sensitivity Training and the Encounter Movements*. New York: Russell Sage.

Beckhard, R. (1969) *Organization Development: Strategies and Models*. Reading, Massachusettes: Addison Wesley.

Beckhard, R., and Harris, R. (1977) *Organization Transitions: Managing Complex Change*. Reading, Massachusetts: Addison Wesley.

Beer, M. (1976) The Technology of Organization Development. In M. D. Dunnette (ed.), *Handbook of Industrial and Organizational Psychology*. Chicago, Illinois: Rand McNally.

Beer, M. (1980) *Organization Change and Development: A Systems View*. Santa Monica, California: Goodyear.

Bennis, W. G. (1969) *Organization Development: Its Nature, Origins, and Prospects*. Reading, Massachusetts: Addison Wesley.

Bennis, W. G., Benne, K. D. and Chin, R. (1961) *The Planning of Change*. New York: Rinehart and Winston.

Benson, J. K. (1977a) Innovation and Crisis in Organizational Analysis. *Sociological Quarterly* 18: 3–16.

Benson, J. K. (1977b) Organizations: A Dialectical View. *Administrative Science Quarterly* 22: 1–21.

Berlin, I. (1974) Historical Inevitability. In P. Gardiner (ed.), *The Philosophy of History*. Oxford: Oxford University Press.

Beynon, H. (1975) *Working For Ford*. Wakefield: E. P. Publishing.

Blackler, F. and Brown, C. A. (1980) *Whatever Happened to Shell's New Philosophy of Management?* London: Gower Press.

Blake, R. R., and Mouton, J. S. (1964) *The Managerial Grid*. Houston, Texas: Gulf Publishing.

Blake, R. R., and Mouton, J. S. (1968) *Corporate Excellence Through Grid Organization Development: A Systems Approach*. Houston, Texas: Gulf Publishing.

Blake, R. R., and Mouton, J. S. (1976) *Consultation*. Reading, Massachusetts: Addison Wesley.

Blench, E. A. (1958) The Billingham Enterprise: A Short History of the Billingham Division of Imperial Chemical Industries Ltd from 1920–1957. *Chemistry and Industry* July–August: 926–968.

Blume, M. E. (1980) The Financial Markets. In R. E. Caves and L. B. Krause (eds.) *Britain's Economic Performance*. Washington, DC: The Brookings Institute.

Boswell, J. S. (1983) *Business Policies in the Making*. London: Allen and Unwin.

Boulding, K. E. (1972) *A Primer on Social Dynamics: History as Dialectics and Development*. New York: Free Press.

Bower, J. L. (1970) *Managing the Resource Allocation Process*. Cambridge, Massachusetts: Harvard University Press.

Bowers, D. G., (1973) OD Techniques and their Results in 23 Organizations: The Michigan ICL Study. *Journal of Applied Behavioral Science* 9: 21–43.

Bowers, D. G., Franklin, J. S., and Pecorella, P. A. (1975) Matching Problems, Precursors, and Interventions in OD: A Systemic Approach. *Journal of Applied Behavioral Science* 11: 391–410.

Braybrooke, D., and Lindblom, C. E. (1963) *A Strategy of Decision*. New York: Free Press.

Brunsson, N. (1982) The Irrationality of Action and Action Rationality: Decisions, Ideologies and Organisational Action. *Journal of Management Studies* 19(1): 29–44.

Bukharin, N. (1965) *Historical Materialism: A System of Sociology*. New York: Russell and Russell.

Burawoy, M. (1978) Contemporary Currents in Marxist Theory. *The American Sociologist* 13: 50–64.

Burawoy, M. (1979) *Manufacturing Consent*. Chicago: University of Chicago Press.

Burgelman, R. A. (1983) A Model of the Interaction of Strategic Behaviour, Corporate Context, and the Concept of Strategy. *Academy of Management Review* 8(1): 61–70.

Burns, T., and Stalker, G. M. (1961) *The Management of Innovation*. London: Tavistock.

Burrell, G., and Morgan, G. (1979) *Sociological Paradigms and Organisational Analysis*. London: Heinemann.

Campbell, J. P., and Dunnette, M. D. (1968) Effectiveness of T-Group Experiences in Managerial Training and Development. *Psychological Bulletin* 70(2): 73–108.

Cassirer, E. (1953) *An Essay on Man*. Garden City, New Jersey: Anchor Books.

Caves, R. E. (1980) Productivity Differences among Industries. In R. E. Caves and L. B. Krause (eds), *Britain's Economic Performance*. Washington, DC: The Brookings Institution.

Chandler, A. J. (1962) *Strategy and Structure: Chapters in the History of the American Industrial Enterprise*. Cambridge, Massachusetts: MIT Press.

Child, J. (1972) Organizational Structure, Environment and Performance: The Role of Strategic Choice. *Sociology* 6: 2–22.

522 References

Clegg, S., and Dunkerley, D. (1977) *Critical Issues in Organisations*. London: Routledge and Kegan Paul.

Clegg, S., and Dunkerley, D. (1980) *Organisation, Class, and Control*. London: Routledge and Kegan Paul.

⋓ Cohen, M. D., March, J. G., and Olsen, J. P. (1972) A Garbage Can Model of Organizational Choice *Administrative Science Quarterly* **17**: 1–25.

Cohen, S. (1980) *Folk Devils and Moral Panics: The Creation of the Mods and Rockers*. Oxford: Martin Robertson.

Cotgrove, S., Dunham, J., and Vamplew, C. (1971) *The Nylon Spinners*. London: Allen and Unwin.

⋓ Crozier, M., and Friedberg, E. (1980) *Actors and Systems: The Politics of Collective Action*. Chicago: University of Chicago Press.

Curtis, R. L., and Zurcher, L. A. (1973) Stable Resources of Protest Movements: The Multiorganizational Field. *Social Forces* **52**: 53–61.

Curtis, R. L., and Zurcher, L. A. (1974) Social Movements: An Analytical Exploration of Organizational Forms. *Social Problems* **21**(3): 356–370.

⋓ Cyert, R. L. and March, J. G. (1963) *A Behavioral Theory of the Firm*. Englewood Cliffs, New Jersey: Prentice Hall.

Davis, D. S. (1982) Chemical Industry in its Historical Context. In D. H. Sharp and T. F. West (eds), *The Chemical Industry*. Chichester: Ellis Horwood Ltd.

Davis, O. A., Dempster, A. H., Wildavsky, A. (1966) A Theory of the Budgeting Process. *American Political Science Review* **60**: 529–547.

⋓ Deal, T. E. and Kennedy, A. A. (1982) *Corporate Cultures: The Rites and Rituals of Corporate Life*. Reading, Massachusetts: Addison Wesley.

Dick, W. F. L. (1973) *A Hundred Years of Alkali in Cheshire*. Runcorn, Cheshire: Imperial Chemical Industries Mond Division Publication.

Downes, D., and Rock, P. (eds) (1979) *Deviant Interpretations: Problems in Criminological Theory*. Oxford: Martin Robertson.

Downes, D., and Rock, P. (1982) *Understanding Deviance: A Guide to the Sociology of Crime and Rule Breaking*. Oxford: Clarendon Press.

Downs, A. (1967) *Inside Bureaucracy*. Boston: Little Brown.

Downs, A. (1972) Up and Down with Ecology – the "issue-attention cycle". *The Public Interest* **28**: 38–50.

Duncan, R. (1973) Multiple Decision Making Structures in Adapting to Environmental Uncertainty: The Impact on Organizational Effectiveness. *Human Relations* **26**: 273–292.

Duncan, W. B. (1982) Lessons from Past, Challenge, and Opportunity. In D. H. Sharp and T. F. West (eds), *The Chemical Industry*. Chichester: Ellis Horwood Ltd.

Eisenstadt, S. M. (1978) *Revolution and the Transformation of Societies*. New York: Free Press.

Elden, M. (1978) Three Generations of Work Democracy in Norway: Beyond Classical Socio-Technical Systems Analysis. In C. L. Cooper and E. Mumford (eds), *The Quality of Working Life in Western and Eastern Europe*. London: Associated Business Press.

⋓ Esland, G., and Salaman (eds) (1980) *The Politics of Work and Occupations*. Milton Keynes: Open University Press.

Evan, W. M. (1972) An Organization Set Model of Interorganisational Relations In M. F. Tuite, M. Radnor, and R. K. Chisholm (eds), *Interorganizational Decision-making*. Chicago: Aldine Publishing.

Franklin, J. L. (1976) Characteristics of Successful and Unsuccessful Organization Development. *Journal of Applied Behavioral Science* **12**(4): 471–492.

Freeman, J. (1975) *The Politics of Women's Liberation*. New York: McKay.

Freeman, J. (1979) Resource Mobilisation and Strategy: A Model for Analysing Social Movement Organization Actions. In M. N. Zald and J. D. McCarthy (eds), *The Dynamics of Social Movements*. Cambridge, Massachusetts: Winthrop.

Freeman, J. (ed.) (1983) *Social Movements of the Sixties and Seventies*. London: Longman.

ᴎ French, W. L., and Bell, C. H. (1973) *Organization Development: Behavioral Science Interventions for Organization Improvement*. Englewood Cliffs; New Jersey: Prentice Hall.

Friedlander, F. (1976) Organization Development Reaches Adolescence: An Explanation of its Underlying Values. *Journal of Applied Behavioral Science* 12(1): 7–21.

Friedlander, F., and Brown, L. D. (1974) Organization Development. In *Annual Review of Psychology* 25: 313–341.

ᴜ Galbraith, J. R., and Nathanson, D. A. (1978) *Strategy Implementation: The Role of Structure and Process*. St Paul: West Publishing.

Gamson, W. A. (1975) *Strategy of Social Protest*. Homewood, Illinois: Dorsey.

Gamson, W. A. (1980) Understanding the Careers of Challenging Groups: A Commentary on Goldstone. *American Journal of Sociology* 85(5): 1043–1060.

ᴜ Geertz, C. (1973) *The Interpretation of Cultures*. New York: Basic Books.

Gellner, E. (1973) *Cause and Meaning in the Social Sciences*. London: Routledge and Kegan Paul.

General and Municipal Workers' Union (1977) *UK Chemicals: The Way Forward*. Esher, Surrey: GMWU Document.

General, Municipal, Boilermakers & Allied Trade Unions (1983) *The British Chemical Industries – Rationalisation Without Recovery: The 1983 Chemical Industries Review*. Esher, Surrey. GMBATU Document.

Gerlach, L. P. (1983) Movements of Revolutionary Change: Some Structural Characteristics. In J. Freeman (ed.), *Social Movements of the Sixties and Seventies*. London: Longman.

Gerlach, L. P., and Hine, V. H. (1970) *People, Power and Change: Movements of Social Transformation*. New York: Bobbs-Merrill.

Giddens, A. (1979) *Central Problems in Social Theory*. London: Macmillan.

Goldstone, J. A. (1980) The Weakness of Organization: A New Look at Gamson's The Strategy of Social Protest. *American Journal of Sociology* 85(5): 1017–1042.

Goodman, P. S. (1979) *Assessing Organizational Change: The Rushton Quality of Work Experiment*. New York: Wiley-Interscience.

ᴜ Greiner, L. E. (1967) Patterns of Organization Change. *Harvard Business Review* May–June: 119–128.

ᴜ Greiner, L. E. (1972) Evolution and Revolution as Organizations Grow. *Harvard Business Reviews* 50(4): 37–46.

Greiner, L. A. (1977) Reflections on OD American Style. In C. L. Cooper (ed.), *Organisation Development in the UK and USA: A Joint Evaluation*. London: Macmillan.

Grunewald, H. (1982) European Chemical Industry in the Eighties. In D. H. Sharp and T. F. West (eds), *The Chemical Industry*. Chichester: Ellis Horwood Ltd.

Gusfield, J. (1957) The Problem of Generations in an Organization Structure. *Social Forces* 35: 323–30.

Guttentag, M. and Struening, E. L. (1975) *Handbook of Evaluation Research*. Beverly Hills, California: Sage.

Hage, J., and Aiken, M. (1970) *Social Change in Complex Organizations*. New York: Random House.

Hardy, C. (1983) The Contribution of Political Science to Organisational Behaviour. Unpublished paper, Faculty of Management, McGill University.

Herzberg, F. L. (1966) *Work and the Nature of Man.* Cleveland, Illinois: World Publishing.

Herzberg, F. L., Mausner, B., Snyderman, B. (1959) *The Motivation to Work.* New York: Wiley.

Hill, P. (1976) *Towards a New Philosophy of Management: The Company Development of Shell UK Ltd.* Epping, Essex: Gower Press.

Horner, J. (1974) *Studies in Industrial Democracy.* London: Gollancz.

House, J. W., and Fullerton, B. (1960) *Teesside at Mid-Century: An Industrial and Economic Survey.* London: Macmillan.

House, R. J. (1967) T-Group Education and Leadership Effectiveness: A Review of the Empirical Literature and a Critical Evaluation. *Personnel Psychology* 20: 1–32.

House, R. J., and Wigdor, L. (1967) Herzberg's Dual-Factor Theory of Job Satisfaction and Motivation: A Review of the Evidence and a Criticism. *Personnel Psychology* 20: 369–389.

Huff, A. S. (1982) Industry Influences on Strategy Reformulation. *Strategic Management Journal* 3: 119–131.

Johnston, A. V. (1975) Revolution by Involvement. *Accountancy Age* 7(36) 17 September: 11.

Jonsson, S. A., and Lundin, R. A. (1977) Myths and Wishful Thinking as Management Tools. In P. C. Nystrom and W. H. Starbuck (eds), *Prescriptive Models of Organizations* Amsterdam: North Holland.

Kahn, R. L. (1974) Organization Development: Some Problems and Proposals. *Journal of Applied Behavioral Science* 10(4): 485–502.

Kanter, R. M. (1972) *Commitment and Community: Communes and Utopias in Sociological Perspective.* Cambridge, Massachusetts: Harvard University Press.

Kanter, R. M. (1983) *The Change Masters: Innovation for Productivity in the American Corporation.* New York: Simon and Schuster.

Katz, D., and Kahn, R. L. (1966) *The Social Psychology of Organizations.* New York: Wiley.

Kervasdoue, J., and Kimberly, J. R. (1979) Are Organisations Culture Free? In G. England *et al.* (eds), *Organizational Functioning in a Cross-Cultural Perspective.* Kent State University Press.

Kidder, Peabody & Co. (1981) *Imperial Chemical Industries Ltd.* London: Research Department Report.

Kimberly, J. R. (1980) Initiation, Innovation, and Institutionalisation in the Creation Process. In J. R. Kimberly and R. H. Miles (eds), *The Organizational Life Cycle: Issues in the Creation, Transformation, and Decline of Organizations.* San Francisco: Jossey Bass.

Kimberly, J. R. (1981) Managerial Innovation. In P. C. Nystrom and W. H. Starbuck (eds), *Handbook of Organisational Design.* Vol. 1, New York: Oxford University Press.

Kimberly, J. R., and Nielsen, W. R. (1975) Organization Development and Change in Organization Performance. *Administrative Science Quarterly* 20: 191–206.

Kimberly, J. R., and Miles, R. H. (eds) (1980) *The Organizational Life Cycle: Issues in the Creation, Transformation, and Decline of Organizations.* San Francisco: Jossey Bass.

King, D. C., Sherwood, J. J., and Manning, M. R. (1978) OD's Research Base: How to Expand and Utilize it. In W. W. Burke (ed.), *The Cutting Edge: Current Theory and Practice in Organization Development.* La Jolla, California: University Associates.

King, W. R., and Cleland, D. T. (1978) *Strategic Planning and Policy.* New York: Van Nostrand.

Klein, L. (1976) *A Social Scientist in Industry.* Epping, Essex: Gower Press.

Knight, K. E. (1967) A Descriptive Model of the Intra-firm Innovation Process. *Journal of Business* **40**(4): 478–496.

Kochan, T. A., and Dyer, L. (1976) A Model of Organizational Change in the Context of Union–Management Relations. *Journal of Applied Behavioral Science* **12**: 59–78.

Kuhn, T. S. (1970) *The Structure of Scientific Revolutions.* 2nd edn. Chicago: University of Chicago Press.

Lawrence, P. R., and Lorsch, J. W. (1967) *Organization and Environment.* Boston: Graduate School of Business Administration, Harvard University.

Lawrence, P. R., and Lorsch, J. W. (1969) *Developing Organizations: Diagnosis and Action.* Reading, Massachusetts: Addison Wesley.

Lazonick, W. (1983) The Dynamics of Industrial Development: A Research Agenda for Contemplating Britain's Economic Future. Paper prepared for the ESRC Competitiveness Workshop, 18–19 November 1983.

Leontiades, M. (1980) *Strategies for Diversification and Change.* Boston: Little Brown.

Lewicki, R. (1977) Team Building in the Small Business Community: The Success and Failure of OD. In P. H. Mirvis and D. N. Berg (eds), *Failures in Organization Development and Change: Cases and Essays for Learning.* New York: Wiley-Interscience.

Likert, R. (1961) *New Patterns of Management.* New York: McGraw-Hill.

Lindblom, C. E. (1959) The Science of Muddling Through. *Public Administration Review* **19**: 91–99.

Lippitt, R., Watson, J., and Westley, B. (1958) *The Dynamics of Planned Change.* New York: Harcourt, Brace, Jovanovich.

Lukes, S. (1974) *Power: A Radical View.* London: Macmillan.

McGregor, D. (1960) *The Human Side of Enterprise.* New York: McGraw-Hill.

McKersie, R. B., and Hunter, L. C. (1973) *Pay, Productivity and Collective Bargaining.* London: Macmillan.

McLean, A., Sims, D., Mangham, I., and Tuffield, D. (1982) *Organisation Development in Transition: Evidence of an Evolving Profession.* Chichester: Wiley.

Mangham, I. E. (1979) *The Politics of Organisational Change.* London: Associated Business Press.

March, J. G. (1981) Footnotes to Organizational Change. *Administrative Science Quarterly* **26**(4): 563–577.

March, J. G., and Simon, H. A., (1958) *Organizations.* New York: Wiley.

March, J. G., and Olsen, J. P. (1976) *Ambiguity and Choice in Organizations.* Bergen: Universitetsforlaget.

March, J. G., and Olsen, J. P. (1983) Organising Political Life: What Administrative Reorganisation Tells us About Governing. *American Political Science Review* **77**(2): 281–296.

Marrow, A. J. (1969) *The Practical Theorist: The Life and Work of Kurt Lewin.* New York: Basic Books.

Martins, H. (1974) Time and Theory in Sociology. In J. Rex (ed.), *Approaches to Sociology.* London: Routledge and Kegan Paul.

Miles, R. H. (1982) *Coffin Nails and Corporate Strategies.* Englewood Cliffs, New Jersey: Prentice Hall.

Miller, D. (1976) Strategy Making in Context: Ten Empirical Archetypes. Unpublished Doctoral Dissertation: McGill University, Faculty of Management.

Miller, D. (1982) Evolution and Revolution: A Quantum View of Structural Change in Organisations. *Journal of Management Studies* **19**(2): 131–151.

Miller, D., and Friesen, P. (1980) Momentum and Revolution in Organisational Adaptation. *Academy of Management Journal* **23**: 591–614.

526 References

Miller, D., and Friesen, P. (1982) Structural Change and Performance: Quantum v's Piecemeal-Incremental Approaches. *Academy of Management Journal* 25(4): 867–892.

Miller, E. J. (1977) Organizational Development and Industrial Democracy. In C. L. Cooper (ed.), *Organizational Development in the UK and USA A Joint Evaluation.* London: Macmillan.

Mintzberg, H. (1978) Patterns in Strategy Formation. *Management Science* 24(9): 934–948.

Mintzberg, H., Raisinghani, D., Theoret, A. (1976) The Structure of Unstructured Decision Processes. *Administrative Science Quarterly* 21: 246–275.

Mintzberg, H., and Waters, J. (1982) Tracking Strategy in an Entrepreneurial Firm. *Academy of Management Journal* 25(3): 465–499.

Mirvis, P. H., and Berg, D. N. (eds) (1977) *Failures in Organization Development and Change: Cases and Essays for Learning.* New York: Wiley-Interscience.

Mohrman, S., Mohrman, A., Cooke, R., and Duncan, R. (1977) A Survey Feedback and Problem Solving Intervention in a School District: "We'll take the Survey but you can keep the Feedback." In P. H. Mirvis and D. N. Berg (eds), New York: Wiley-Interscience.

Mumford, W., and Pettigrew, A. M. (1975) *Implementing Strategic Decisions.* London: Longman.

Narayanan, V. K., and Fahey, L. (1982) The Micro-Politics of Strategy Formulation. *Academy of Management Review* 7(1): 25–34.

Negandhi, A. R. (ed.) (1975) *Interorganisation Theory.* Kent, Ohio: Kent State University Press.

Nichols, J. K., and Crawford, P. J. (1983) *Managing Chemicals in the 1980's.* Paris: OECD.

Nichols, T., and Beynon, H. (1977) *Living With Capitalism.* London: Routledge and Kegan Paul.

Nisbet, R. A. (1969) *Social Change and History: Aspects of the Western Theory of Development.* London: Oxford University Press.

Nord, W. R. (1974) The Failure of Current Applied Behavioral Science – A Marxian Perspective. *Journal of Applied Behavioral Science* 10(4): 557–578.

Normann, R. (1977) *Management for Growth.* London: Wiley.

O'Connor, J. (1973) *The Fiscal Crisis of the State.* New York: St Martin's Press.

Olson, M. (1965) *The Logic of Collective Action.* Cambridge, Massachusetts: Harvard University Press.

Organisation for Economic Co-operation and Development (1980) *The Chemical Industry.* Paris: OECD.

Paul, W. J. and Robertson, K. B. (1971) *Job Enrichment and Employee Motivation.* Epping, Essex: Gower.

Pavitt, K. (ed.) (1980) *Technical Innovation and British Economic Performance.* London: Macmillan.

Peters, T. J., and Waterman, R. H. (1982) *In Search of Excellence: Lessons from America's Best-Run Companies.* New York: Harper and Row.

Pettigrew, A. M. (1972) Information Control as a Power Resource. *Sociology* 6: 187–204.

Pettigrew, A. M. (1973) *The Politics of Organisational Decision Making.* London: Tavistock.

Pettigrew, A. M. (1975a) Strategic Aspects of the Management of Specialist Activity. *Personnel Review* 4: 5–13.

Pettigrew, A. M. (1975b) Towards a Political Theory of Organisational Intervention. *Human Relations* 28(3): 191–208.

Pettigrew, A. M. (1976) The Creation of Organisational Cultures. Paper presented to the joint EIASM-Dansk Management Center Research Seminar on *Entrepreneurs and the Process of Institution Building.* Copenhagen, 18–20 May 1976. Available from the School of Industrial and Business Studies, University of Warwick, England.

Pettigrew, A. M. (1977) Strategy Formulation as a Political Process. *International Studies of Management and Organization* 7(2): 78–87.

Pettigrew, A. M. (1979) On Studying Organizational Cultures. *Administrative Science Quarterly* 24(4): 570–581.

Pettigrew, A. M. (1980) The Politics of Organisational Change. In Niels B. Anderson (ed.), *The Human Side of Information Processing.* Amsterdam: North Holland.

Pettigrew, A. M. (1983a) Patterns of Managerial Response as Organisations Move from Rich to Poor Environments. *Educational Management Administration* 2: 104–114.

Pettigrew, A. M. (1983b) Contextualist Research: A Natural Way to Link Theory and Practice. Paper presented to conference *Conducting Research with Theory and Practice in Mind.* Center for Effective Organizations, University of Southern California Los Angeles. 3–4 November 1983.

Pettigrew, A. M. (In Press) Culture and Politics in Strategic Decision Making and Change. In J. M. Pennings (ed.), *Strategic Decision Making in Complex Organizations.* San Francisco: Jossey-Bass.

Pettigrew, A. M., and Reason, P. R. (1979) Alternative Interpretations of the Training Officer Role: A Research Study in the Chemical Industry. Research report, Staines: *Chemical and Allied Products Industrial Training Board.*

Pettigrew, A. M., Jones, G. R., Reason, P. R. (1982) *Training and Development Roles in Their Organisational Setting.* Sheffield: Manpower Services Commission.

Pfeffer, J. (1981) *Power in Organizations.* Marshfield, Massachusetts: Pitman.

Pfeffer, J. (1982) *Organizations and Organization Theory.* Marshfield, Massachusetts: Pitman.

Pfeffer, J. and Salancik, G. R. (1978) *The External Control of Organizations: A Resource Dependence Perspective* New York: Harper and Row.

Pollard, S. (1982) *The Wasting of the British Economy: British Economic Policy 1945 to the Present.* London: Croom Helm.

Porras, J. I. and Berg, P. O. (1978) Evaluation Methodology in Organization Development: An Analysis and Critique. *Journal of Applied Bahavioral Science* 14: 151–173.

Porter, M. (1980) *Competitive Strategy.* New York: Free Press.

Quinn, J. B. (1980) *Strategies for Change: Logical Incrementalism.* Homewood, Illinois: Irwin.

Quinn, J. B. (1982) Managing Strategies Incrementally. *Omega* 10(6): 613–627.

Qvale, T. U. (1976) A Norwegian Strategy for Democratisation of Industry. *Human Relations* 29(5): 453–469.

Ranson, S., Hinings, C. R., and Greenwood, R. (1980) The Structuring of Organizational Structures. *Administrative Science Quarterly* 25(1): 1–18.

Reader, W. J. (1975) *Imperial Chemical Industries: A History Vol. II.* Oxford: Oxford University Press.

Reddin, W. J. (1967) The 3-D Management Style Theory. *Training and Development Journal* 8–17 April.

Reddin, W. J. (1970) *Managerial Effectiveness.* New York: McGraw Hill.

Reuben, B. G. and Burstall, M. L. (1973) *The Chemical Economy: A Guide to the Technology and Economics of the Chemical Industry.* London: Longman.

Roberts, C. and Wedderburn, D. E. (1973) ICI and the Unions: The Place of Job

Enrichment in the Weekly Staff Agreement. Unpublished report for the TUC Social Sciences Working Party: Imperial College, London University.

Roberts, K. H., Hulin, C. L., and Rousseau, R. (1978) *Developing an Interdisciplinary Science of Organizations.* San Francisco: Jossey-Bass.

Roeber, J. (1975) *Social Change at Work: The ICI Weekly Staff Agreement.* London: Duckworth.

Rogers, C. R. (1942) *Counselling and Psychotherapy: Newer Concepts in Practice.* Boston: Houghton Mifflin.

Rogers, E. M., and Shoemaker, F. F. (1971) *Communication of Innovations: A Cross-Cultural Approach.* New York: The Free Press.

Rush, H. M. (1973) *Organization Development: A Reconaissance.* New York: The Conference Board.

Salaman, G. (1979) *Work Organisations: Resistance and Control.* London: Longman.

Sarason, S. M. (1972) *The Creation of Settings and the Future Societies.* San Francisco: Jossey-Bass.

Sarason, S. M., Carroll, C. F., Maton, K., Cohen, S., and Lorentz, E. (1977) *Human Services and Resource Networks.* San Francisco: Jossey-Bass.

Schon, D. A. (1971) *Beyond the Stable State.* London: Temple Smith.

Schon, D. A. (1983) *The Reflective Practitioner: How Professionals Think in Action.* London: Temple Smith.

Scott, B. R. (1973) The Industrial State: Old Myths and New Realities. *Harvard Business Review* March–April: 133–148.

Scott, L. and Lyman, S. (1970) *The Revolt of the Students.* Columbus, Ohio: Charles Merrill.

Selznick, P. (1957) *Leadership in Administration: A Sociological Interpretation.* New York: Harper and Row.

Shapero, A. (1975) *Entrepreneurship and Regional Developments.* Cincinnati, Ohio: Proceedings of the International Symposium on Entrepreneurship and Enterprise Development.

Sharp, D. H., and West, T. F. (eds) (1982) *The Chemical Industry.* Chichester: Ellis Horwood Ltd.

Shepard, H. A. (1967) Innovation-Resisting and Innovation-Producing Organizations. *Journal of Business* **40**(4): 470–477.

Silverman, D. (1970) *The Theory of Organisations.* London: Heineman.

Simon, H. A. (1957) A Behavioral Model of Rational Choice. In H. A. Simon (ed.), *Models of Man.* New York: Wiley.

Solomon, L. N. (1971) Humanism and the Training of Applied Behavioral Scientists. *Journal of Applied Behavioral Science* **7**(5): 531–547.

Starbuck, W. H., Greve, A., Hedberg, B. L. T. (1978) Responding to Crises. *Journal of Business Administration* **9**(2): 111–137.

Steele, F. (1975) *Consulting for Organizational Change.* Amherst: University of Massachusetts Press.

Stephenson, T. E. (1975) Organisation Development: A Critique. *Journal of Management Studies* **12**: 249–265.

Strauss, G. (1976) Organization Development. In R. Dubin (ed.) *Handbook of Work, Organization, and Society.* Chicago: Rand McNally.

Summerfield, M. (1969) Introducing SDP in HOC Division of ICI *Unpublished research report:* Leeds University, Department of Management Studies.

Tannenbaum, R., and Davis, S. A. (1969) Values, Man, and Organisations. *Industrial Management Review* **10**: 67–86.

Taylor, L. K. (1972) *Not for Bread Alone: An Appreciation of Job Enrichment*. London: Business Books.

United Nations (1981) *World Industry in 1980*. New York: United Nations.

Vaill, P. B. (1971) *The Practice of Organization Development*. New York: American Management Association.

Van de Ven, A. H. (1979) Book Review of Howard E. Aldrich, Organizations and Environments. *Administrative Science Quarterly* **24**: 320–326.

Vivian, Gray and Co. (1980) *Imperial Chemical Industries: At the Opening of a New Decade*. London: Vivian, Gray and Co. Investment Research.

Wallerstein, I. (1974) *The Modern World-System: Capitalist Agriculture and the Origins of the European World-Economy in the Sixteenth Century*. New York: Academic Press.

Walton, R. E. (1975) The Diffusion of New Work Structures: Explaining Why Success Didn't Take. *Organizational Dynamics* Winter: 3–22.

Walton, R. E. (1978) Teaching on Old Dog Food New Tricks. *Wharton Magazine* Winter: 38–47.

Weick, K. E. (1976) Educational Organisations as Loosely Coupled Systems. *Administrative Science Quarterly* **21**: 1–19.

Warmington, A., Lupton, T., and Gribbin, C. (1977) *Organizational Behaviour and Performance: An Open Systems Approach to Change*. London: Macmillan.

Wassenberg, A. (1977) The Powerlessness of Organization Theory. In S. Clegg and D. Dunkerley (eds), *Critical Issues in Organizations*. London: Routledge and Kegan Paul.

Weinstein, D. (1979) *Bureaucratic Opposition: Challenging Abuses at the Workplace*. New York: Pergamon.

Weisbord, M. R. (1974) The Gap between OD Practice and Theory and Publication. *Journal of Applied Behavioral Science* **10**(4): 476–484.

White, L. (1949) *The Science of Culture*. New York: Grove Press.

White, S., and Mitchell, T. (1976) Organization Development: A Review of Research Content and Research Design. *Academy of Management Review* **1**(2): 57–74.

Wiener, M. (1981) *English Culture and the Decline of the Industrial Spirit, 1850–1980*. Cambridge: Cambridge University Press.

Willmott, H. (1984) Studying Managerial Work: A Critique and a Proposal. Paper presented to the *Annual Conference of the British Sociological Association*. Bradford, April 1984.

Wilson, J. (1973) *Introduction to Social Movements*. New York: Basic Books.

Wittcoff, H. A., and Reuben, B. G. (1980) *Industrial Organic Chemicals in Perspective Part One: Raw Materials and Manufacture*. New York: Wiley-Interscience.

Wrigley, L. (1970) Divisional Autonomy and Diversification. Unpublished DBA Dissertation: Harvard Business School.

Zald, M. N., and Ash, R. (1966) Social Movement Organizations: Growth, Decay and Change. *Social Forces* **44**: 327–341.

Zald, M. N., and McCarthy, J. D. (eds) (1979) *The Dynamics of Social Movements: Resource Mobilisation, Social Control and Tactics*. Cambridge, Massachusetts: Winthrop.

Zaltman, G., Duncan, R., and Holbek, J. (1973) *Innovations and Organizations*. New York: Wiley-Interscience.

Author Index

Subject Index

Note: This index also contains the names of ICI personnel and external consultants.